THE ROUGH GUIDE TO

VENICE & THE VENETO

ROUGH GUIDES

written and re...
Jonathan ...

Contents

BARDOLINO VINEYARD, VERONA

Introduction to

Venice & the Veneto

Venice has been depicted and described so often that on arriving in the city you might have the slightly anticlimactic feeling that everything looks exactly as expected. The Canal Grande's water-lapped palaces are indeed as picturesque as the coffee-table books made them out to be, Piazza San Marco is as perfect as a film set, and the panorama from the Palazzo Ducale is more or less as Canaletto painted it. Any sense of familiarity quickly fades, however, as you start to look around: seeing a stack of furniture being hoisted from a barge up to a top-floor window, or someone fishing knee-deep in the lagoon a hundred metres from dry land, you understand that life here is not like life anywhere else. And the more closely you look, the more fascinating Venice becomes.

Founded fifteen hundred years ago on a cluster of mudflats in the centre of the lagoon, Venice rose to become Europe's main trading post between the West and the East, and at its height controlled an empire that spread north to the Dolomites and over the sea as far as Cyprus. As its wealth increased and its population grew, the fabric of the city grew ever more dense. Cohabiting with the ocean, Venice has a closer relationship to nature than most cities, but at the same time it's one of the most artificial places on earth – there's hardly any undeveloped space on the hundred or so islets that compose

ADDRESSES IN VENICE

Within each **sestiere** the buildings are numbered in a sequence that makes it possible for houses facing each other to have numbers separated by hundreds. This is because, in essence, the numbering system tends to follow walls rather than streets: thus if a small alleyway intersects with a major one the numbering on the major alley may continue round the corner and down the minor alleyway before turning around to flow back towards the main drag. Venetian **addresses** are conventionally written as the street name followed by the *sestiere* followed by the number – eg Calle Vallaresso, San Marco 1312. Sometimes, though, the *sestiere* is placed before the street, and sometimes the street is omitted altogether, which makes the place impossible to find unless you're in the know.

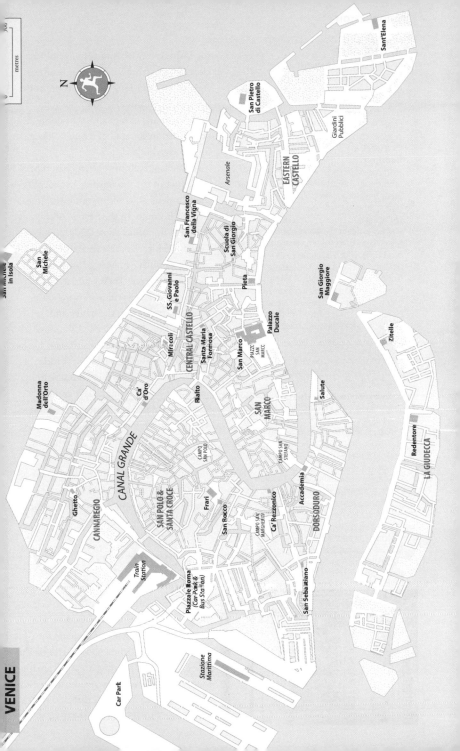

ACQUE ALTE

Floods – **acque alte** – have been an element of the Venetian winter for hundreds of years, but since the middle of the twentieth century there's been a relentless increase in their frequency (see page 342). It's now very rare indeed, between November and late February, for a week to pass without a significant **flooding**.

An *acqua alta* begins with water seeping up through the pavement of the Piazza and other low-lying areas. Soon after, wavelets start spilling over the quayside in front of the Palazzo Ducale. If you hear **sirens** wailing it means that there's about four hours to go before the peak of a significant *acqua alta*, which is defined as a flood that rises in excess of 110cm above the mean lagoon level at the Salute. A single siren tone, repeated, signifies a minor *acqua alta*; floods of greater seriousness are signalled by repeated rising patterns of two, three or four notes – four notes means they're expecting 140cm or more, enough to make many areas impassable.

But the city is well geared to dealing with the nuisance. Shopkeepers insert steel shutters into their doorways, while walkways of **duckboards** (*passerelle*) are constructed along the major thoroughfares and between the chief vaporetto stops and dry land. In extreme instances – such as in November 2012, when the Piazza was under 1.5 metres of water – the *passerelle* can get washed away, but usually the city keeps functioning, and even on the severest days there are many parts that remain above the waves.

If the waters get unruly, invest in a pair of the plastic overshoe boots made by **Goldon** (ⓦgoldon.it), you can buy these for €10–12 a pair from street vendors, souvenir shops and other outlets in the *acqua alta* season.

the historic centre. And very few of its closely-knit streets and squares bear no sign of the city's long lineage. Even in the most insignificant alleyway you might find fragments of a medieval building embedded in the wall of a house, like a fossil lodged in a cliff face.

The melancholic air of Venice is in part a product of the discrepancy between the grandeur of its history and what the city has become. In the heyday of the Venetian Republic, some 200,000 people lived in Venice – nearly four times its present population. Merchants from Germany, Greece, Turkey and a host of other countries maintained warehouses here; transactions in the banks and bazaars of the **Rialto** dictated the value of commodities all over the continent; in the dockyards of the **Arsenale** the workforce was so vast that a warship could be built and fitted out in a single day; and the **Piazza San Marco** was perpetually thronged with people here to set up business deals or report to the Republic's government. Nowadays it's no longer a living metropolis but rather the embodiment of a fabulous past, dependent for its survival largely on the people who come to marvel at its relics.

Where to go

The historic centre of Venice is made up of 118 tiny islands, most of which began life as a micro-community, each with a parish church or two and a square for public meetings. Some 435 bridges tie the islands together, forming an amalgamation that's divided into six large administrative districts known as *sestieri*, three on each side of the Canal Grande. The *sestiere* of **San Marco** is the hub of Venice and the zone in which the most visited sights are clustered. On the east it's bordered by **Castello**, and on the north by **Cannaregio**. On the other bank the largest of the *sestieri* is **Dorsoduro**, which stretches from the tip of the Canal Grande, south of the Accademia gallery, to the docks in the west. **Santa Croce**, named after a now demolished church, more or less follows the curve of the Canal Grande from Piazzale Roma to a point just short of the Rialto, where it joins the most commercially active of the districts on this bank – **San Polo**.

The monuments which draw by far the largest crowds are the **Basilica di San Marco** – the mausoleum of the city's patron saint – and the **Palazzo Ducale** – once the home of the doge and the governing councils. Certainly these are the most imposing structures in the city: the first a mosaic-clad emblem of Venice's Byzantine origins, the second perhaps the finest of all secular Gothic buildings. Every parish rewards exploration, though – a roll-call of the churches worth visiting would feature more than fifty names. In addition, two of the distinctively Venetian institutions known as the *scuole* retain some of the outstanding examples of Italian Renaissance art: the **Scuola Grande di San Rocco**, with its dozens of pictures by Tintoretto, and the **Scuola di San Giorgio degli Schiavoni**, decorated with a gorgeous sequence by Carpaccio.

Although many of the city's treasures remain in the buildings for which they were created, a sizeable number have been removed to one or other of Venice's **museums**,

ANTICHE CARAMPANE, VENICE

FACT FILE
- Attracting one in five of all visitors to the country, the Veneto is the **most popular** of all Italy's regions, and Venice – the **region's capital** – its single most popular city.
- The Veneto is **mountainous** in the north, where the Dolomites extend towards the Austrian border, and flat in the more extensive southern part of the region, where the River Po forms the boundary with Emilia-Romagna. This **fertile plain** is one of Italy's major agricultural zones.
- A fraction under five million **people** live in the Veneto, which is divided into seven **provinces**, centred on Venice, Belluno, Padova, Rovigo, Treviso, Verona and Vicenza. The historic core of Venice is now home to fewer than 55,000 people.
- **Engineering** is the most important manufacturing sector of the Veneto economy, but there are also numerous other large-scale industries here: eighty percent of Italian eyewear and seventy percent of Italian sports shoes are made in the Veneto, and local firms such as Benetton and Diesel are mainstays of the Italian clothing industry.

or to museums elsewhere. (Napoleon in particular helped himself to vast amounts of Venetian art, some of which is now in the Louvre.) The one that should not be missed is the recently expanded **Accademia**, a peerless assembly of Venetian painting; other prominent collections include the museum of eighteenth-century art in the **Ca' Rezzonico** and the **Museo Correr**, the civic museum of Venice – but again, a comprehensive list would fill a page. Equally indispensable for a full understanding of Venice's way of life and development are expeditions to the **northern and southern islands** of the lagoon, especially Torcello.

Taking its name – as does Venice itself – from the pre-Roman people known as the Veneti, the present-day region of the **Veneto** essentially covers the area that became the core of the Republic's mainland empire. Everywhere in the Veneto you'll find the imprint of Venetian rule, but each of the cities of **Verona**, **Padua**, **Vicenza** and **Treviso** has a very distinct character, and none of them suffers from Venice's dependence on tourism. Smaller towns such as **Ásolo**, **Bassano** and **Conegliano** may not have sights as spectacular as the first three of that quartet, but they are well worth an excursion from Venice.

When to go

Venice's tourist season is very nearly an all-year affair. **Peak season** is from **Easter** to **early October**, when hotel rooms are virtually impossible to come by at short notice; if possible, try to avoid July and August, when the crowds are at their fullest, the climate can be oppressive, and many restaurants and bars take their annual break. The other two popular spells are **Carnevale** (leading up to Lent) and the weeks on each side of **Christmas**; again, hotels tend to be heavily booked, especially for Carnevale.

For the ideal combination of comparative peace and pleasant climate, the two or three weeks **immediately preceding Easter** are perhaps the best time of year. Climatically, the months at the end of the high season are erratic: some **November and December** days are so clear that the Dolomites seem to start on the edge of the mainland, but others bring torrential rain or fog so dense you can't see across the Canal

VENETIAN NAMES AND DIALECT

As you'd expect, Venice has a particular array of names for the features of its very particular cityscape. A canal is called a **rio**, and an alleyway that cuts through a building is a **sottoportico** or **sottoportego**. A street in Venice is generally a **calle**, but a major thoroughfare might be a **ruga** or a **salizzada** (or **salizada**), a small street may be a **ramo**, a street alongside a body of water is a **fondamenta** (or a **riva** if it's really big), and a street formed by filling in a canal is customarily a **rio terrà** (or *terà*). A square is usually a **campo** (there's only one Piazza), but it might be a **campiello** if it's tiny, a **piscina** if it was formed by filling in a place where boats used to turn, or a **corte** if it's courtyard-sized.

Among the chief characteristics of the Venetian vernacular are its tendencies to slur or drop consonants and to swallow vowels. For example, the name Giuseppe here becomes Isepo, Luigi becomes Alvise, Giuliano becomes Zulian, Benedetto becomes Beneto, Eustachio becomes Stae, Biagio becomes Biasio (or Blasio), Agostino shrinks to Stin, and Giovanni is Zuan or Zan. Venetian tends to use single consonants where Italian uses doubles – thus Madona, not Madonna; *parochia*, not *parrocchia*; Castelo, not Castello. You'll see *dose* instead of *doge*, *crose* instead of *croce*, *do* for *due*, *nove* instead of *nuove*, *fontego* for *fondaco*, *sestier* for *sestiere*, *and vecio* for *vecchio*. You'll also notice the letter "x" sometimes replacing "z" (as in *venexiana*), and that the final vowel is habitually lopped off Venetian surnames, as in Giustinian, Loredan and Vendramin, to cite just three of the most conspicuous instances.

Grande. However, the desertion of the streets in winter is magical, and the sight of the Piazza under floodwater unforgettable. This **acqua alta**, as Venice's seasonal flooding is called, is common between October and March, and you should anticipate a few inconvenient days in the course of a winter visit.

CARNIVAL MASKS

Itineraries

Believe it or not, even in summer there are parts of central Venice that aren't madly overcrowded – follow our first itinerary for a day of calm contemplation. And as a respite from pounding the pavements, you could take a day to explore the outer reaches of the lagoon. All entries have a page reference to take you straight into the Guide, where you can find out more.

A QUIET DAY

❶ **San Francesco della Vigna** Start the day at this tranquil Franciscan church. See page 152

❷ **San Pietro di Castello** Stroll out to Venice's former cathedral, beyond the Arsenale. See page 161

❸ **Sant'Elena** Buy picnic supplies on Via Garibaldi and eat your lunch on the Sant'Elena waterfront. See page 162

❹ **San Sebastiano** Take a boat across town to Paolo Veronese's church. See page 89

❺ **San Nicolò dei Mendicoli** It's a short stroll to the ancient and tranquil church of San Nicolò. See page 90

❻ **Madonna dell'Orto** From the Záttere take a boat up to Tintoretto's parish church. See page 126

❼ **The Ghetto** Explore the world's first Ghetto, a zone now surrounded by excellent bars and restaurants. See page 124

OUT ON THE WATER

❶ **Torcello** First thing, voyage out to far-flung Torcello, where the story of Venice began. See page 184

❷ **Burano** Take an hour to stroll around Torcello's neighbouring island. See page 182

❸ **Murano** The boat back to Venice calls at the glassmaking island of Murano; stop for lunch at *Busa alla Torre*. See page 179

❹ **San Michele** Next stop, head to this serene cemetery island. See page 177

❺ **La Giudecca** From San Michele the #4.1/4.2 will take you right round the city to the island of Giudecca. See page 192

❻ **San Giorgio Maggiore** It's a one-stop hop to the spectacular church of San Giorgio. See page 189

❼ **Záttere** Catch the #2 to the Záttere, then ramble up to the San Barnaba district for a drink and a meal. See page 87

20

things not to miss

To see only the top-rank sights of Venice and the Veneto you have to spend a lot of time here – but if time is tight, the following tally of the region's highlights should help you to get the most out of your visit. Coloured numbers refer to chapters in the Guide section.

1 BASILICA DI SAN MARCO
See page 39
This mosaic-encrusted Basilica is the most lavish cathedral in Europe.

2 SCUOLA DI SAN GIORGIO DEGLI SCHIAVONI
See page 153
Carpaccio's beguiling pictures, such as this one of St Jerome in his study, make this tiny building one of Venice's essential sights.

3 RIALTO MARKET
See page 98
In business for around a thousand years, the Rialto market is still buzzing – and it's one of the few parts of the city where locals outnumber the tourists.

4 SAN GIORGIO MAGGIORE
See page 189
The pristine church of San Giorgio is a dazzling building – and a climb to the top of its campanile gives you the best view of the city.

5 REGATA STORICA
See page 230
A spectacular procession along the Canal Grande marks the start of Venice's historic regatta.

9

10

11 PADUA
See page 244
The Veneto's liveliest city, thanks largely to its famous university.

12 SANTI GIOVANNI E PAOLO
See page 137
The huge church of Santi Giovanni e Paolo is the doges' mausoleum.

13 VERONA
See page 273
The magnificent city of Verona is an obvious day-trip from Venice.

14 PALAZZO DUCALE
See page 50
Home to the doge and seat of the government and law courts, the Palazzo Ducale was the hub of the Venetian Republic.

15 SAN SEBASTIANO
See page 89
Though it's packed with pictures by Paolo Veronese, this is one of the city's neglected gems.

16

17

18

19

20

SANTA MARIA DELLA SALUTE

Basics

Getting there

Marco Polo, on the edge of the lagoon, is the main airport for Venice (see page 22), but some smaller airlines make use of Treviso, 30km to the north of Venice (see page 23); the airport at Verona, 120km west of Venice, is another possibility, as there are regular trains between the two cities. Flights are most expensive between June and August; fares drop a little during the "shoulder" seasons – September to October and April to May – and you'll get the best prices during the low season, November to March (excluding Christmas, Carnevale and New Year, when seats are at a premium). Note also that it is generally more expensive to fly at weekends.

Flights from the UK and Ireland

Direct flights take around two hours **from London**. EasyJet (W easyjet.com) fly two or three times daily from Gatwick to Venice Marco Polo, and once or twice daily to Verona (high season only), while its chief rival, Ryanair (W ryanair.com), has one or two flights each day from London-Stansted to Treviso, and less frequent services to Treviso from Bristol, East Midlands, Manchester, Edinburgh and Leeds-Bradford. In addition, high-season flights to Marco Polo are offered by Jet2 (W jet2.com), who fly there from Edinburgh, Manchester, Birmingham and Leeds-Bradford, in addition to weekly flights to Verona from Belfast, Edinburgh, Birmingham, London Stansted and Leeds-Bradford. Tui (previously Thomson Airways; W tui.co.uk) operate summer services from Gatwick and Manchester. Of the "full-service" airlines, British Airways (W ba.com) operate direct flights from Gatwick and Heathrow (2–3 daily) throughout the year; BA also have less frequent flights to Marco Polo from London's City Airport, as well as flying twice daily from Gatwick to Verona. Alitalia's (W alitalia.com) flights from Heathrow involve a stop at Rome.

If you book well in advance, it's possible to find a return ticket to Treviso for under £100 in low season, rising to more than £200 in high season. For flights to Marco Polo, you'll pay in the region of £120–160 in low season, and more like £200–300 in high season, depending on your travel date and when you make the booking.

From Dublin, Aer Lingus (W aerlingus.com) flies to Marco Polo up to five times per week, while Ryanair flies three or four times a week to Treviso in high season. In the earliest or latest part of high season

you may pick up a Treviso flight for under €100; at the other end of the scale, a summer return ticket with Aer Lingus will cost €200–300. **From Belfast**, the cheapest option is to fly easyJet to Gatwick and then on to Venice.

Packages

Venice's ludicrous accommodation costs can make a flight-plus-hotel **package** an attractive -proposition, as the preferential hotel rates given to the holiday firms can offset the slightly higher price of the flight. The brochures are dominated by three- and four-star hotels, and there's occasionally a limited choice of one- and two-star rooms as well. You can expect to pay from around £300 per person for two nights for a three-star double room in low season; the same deal in peak season could cost twice as much, or more. At the upper end of the market, packages offering two nights at a top-notch establishment in high season might cost more than £2000 per person.

If you can find a particularly conscientious travel agent, they might contact the package company for you to find out if any of the hotels have rooms cheaper than advertised – something they're more likely to do in the winter months.

Trains from the UK

The most direct rail route from London to Venice is to take the **Eurostar** from London to Paris, then change to the "Thello" sleeper. Alternatively you can take the high-speed TGV from Paris to Milan or Turin, and change there for a train to Venice. Total journey time is 15–18 hours, and a one-way ticket will usually cost in the region of £150–200, though peak prices can be considerably higher, and you might get a lower price in the dead of winter. Bear in mind that in Paris you'll arrive at the Gare du Nord, and will need to get to the Gare de Lyon for the next leg. Booking for these continental routes usually opens three months before the day of travel. Discounts for under-26s are sometimes available and advance booking is essential. If you're planning to include Italy as part of a longer European trip you could invest in an **InterRail pass**; the cheapest pass, valid for five days' travel within fifteen days, costs €269 for travellers aged 26–60, or €208 for under-26s.

Flights from the US and Canada

The only direct service to **Venice from the US** is with Delta (W delta.com), who fly from New York to Marco Polo up to six times a week in summer, and offer connecting flights via Milan or Rome from several other North American cities throughout the year. Between them, British Airways (⦿ba.com), Lufthansa (⦿lufthansa.com), Delta, Northwest/KLM (⦿north-westairlines.us/⦿klm.com) and United (⦿united.com) offer daily flights from all the major US cities via a variety of European hubs. The cheapest **return fares** from New York in low season are around $800 (with stops), rising to about $3000 (non-stop) during the summer.

From Canada, Air Canada (⦿aircanada.com) have direct flights from Montréal to Venice, and various indirect flights from Toronto and Montréal, usually via Frankfurt or New York; low-season fares start at around Can$900, increasing to around Can$2400 in high season. With other carriers and from other Canadian cities you'll have to change planes at a North American airport as well as in Europe.

Flights from Australia and New Zealand

Plenty of airlines fly **from Australia or New Zealand** to Rome and Milan via Asian hubs. Round-trip **fares** from Sydney with the major airlines (Alitalia, ⦿alitalia.com; Qantas, ⦿qantas.com; Emirates, ⦿emirates.com; Japan, Singapore or Malaysian) start at around A$1800 in low season, rising to A$2500–3200 in high season. From New Zealand you can expect to pay from around NZ$2000 in low season to NZ$3000 in high season.

AGENTS AND OPERATORS

Abercrombie & Kent UK ⦿abercrombiekent.co.uk, US ⦿abercrombiekent.com. Classy travel agents with a strong reputation.

Citalia UK ⦿citalia.com. Long-established company offering city-break packages in three- and four-star hotels.

Flight Centre Australia ⦿flightcentre.com.au, NZ ⦿flightcentre.co.nz. Specializes in discount airfares and holiday packages.

North South Travel UK ⦿northsouthtravel.co.uk. Friendly, competitive travel agency, offering discounted fares worldwide. Profits are used to support projects in the developing world, especially the promotion of sustainable tourism.

STA Travel UK ⦿statravel.co.uk, US ⦿statravel.com, Australia ⦿statravel.com.au, NZ ⦿statravel.co.nz. Worldwide specialists in low-cost flights and tours for students and under-26s, though other customers welcome. Also offers student IDs, travel insurance, car rental, rail passes and more.

RAIL CONTACTS

Eurostar ⦿eurostar.com
InterRail ⦿interrail.eu
The Man in Seat 61 ⦿seat61.com. An amazing site, packed with useful tips and info.

Loco2 ⦿loco2.com. A good site for buying tickets from the UK to Italy.
Voyages-SNCF ⦿voyages-sncf.com. Information on international train travel, including tickets and passes.

Arrival and departure

Every year around nine million tourists are funnelled through Venice's Marco Polo airport, with most of the rest coming through Treviso. Arriving by train and coach is painless – but driving into Venice is hellish in summer.

By plane

Marco Polo airport

Most **scheduled** flights and some charters arrive at the recently enlarged **Marco Polo**, a little over 7km north of the *centro storico*, on the edge of the lagoon. The most inexpensive transport to the city centre is provided by the two road-going **bus services** to the terminal at Piazzale Roma: the ATVO (*Azienda Trasporti Veneto Orientale;* ⦿atvo.it) coach, which departs every half-hour and takes around twenty minutes (€8), or the ACTV (*Azienda del Consorzio Trasporti Veneziano;* ⦿actv.it) bus #5, which is equally frequent, usually takes a few minutes longer (it's a local bus service, so it picks up and puts down passengers between the airport and Piazzale Roma), and also costs €8. For €14 you can buy an ACTV bus+boat ticket, which gets you to Piazzale Roma then gives you one vaporetto journey; it's valid for 90min. Note that you can buy an ACTV travel pass at the airport, but you have to pay a supplement if you want to use it for the airport bus (see page 24).

If you'd prefer to approach the city by water, you could take one of the Alilaguna **water-buses** (⦿alilaguna.it), which operate three routes from the airport: the **Blu** line, via Murano, Fondamente Nove, Lido, San Zaccaria, San Marco, Záttere, Giudecca and Terminal Crociere (the docks); the **Arancio** (Orange), via Madonna dell'Orto, Guglie, San Stae, Rialto, Sant'Angelo, Ca' Rezzonico and Santa Maria del Giglio (near San Marco); and the **Rosso** (Red), via Murano to the Lido (April–Oct). The fare is €15 to any stop in central Venice, and €8 to Murano. All services are hourly, and the journey time to San Marco is usually a little over an hour, though at low tides it can take longer. Ticket offices for Alilaguna, ATVO and ACTV buses are in

GETTING AROUND THE VENETO

The administrative region of the **Veneto** extends right to the Austrian border, taking in the portion of the **Dolomites** known as the Cadore. The Dolomites offer some of Italy's most sublime landscapes, but the mountains are quite distinct from Venice's immediate hinterland. This guide concentrates on the mainland sights and towns that can be seen on a day's excursion from Venice, so its northern limit is Belluno.

TRAINS

Trenitalia, the Italian state rail company (W trenitalia.it), runs various categories of train, the fastest being the state-of-the-art *Freccia* trains, which are becoming more numerous by the year. Tickets for these are much more expensive than for other services, partly because you're paying a premium for the speed, and partly because they include a fee for seat reservation; ordinary InterCity (IC) trains also require a seat reservation, but are considerably cheaper than the *Freccia* services. There are no supplements for the other types: **Espresso** (EX), which stop at major towns; **Regionale Veloce** (RV), similar to the Espresso, but with more stops; and **Regionale** (Reg), the slowest services. Alongside the Trenitalia services, there are privately operated high-speed *Italo* trains, but – like the *Freccia* trains – these are of little relevance to exploring the Veneto.

The main towns of the Veneto are well connected by rail. One main line runs from Venice through Treviso and northwards, another through Castelfranco up to Bassano, and a third through Padua, Vicenza and Verona. Frequencies of services are given in the relevant town accounts, but bear in mind that there are occasional gaps in the schedule (often just after the morning rush hour), and that Sunday services are far less frequent.

All train stations have validating machines in the ticket hall and on the platforms, in which passengers have to stamp their ticket before embarking.

BUSES

Buses offer frequent connections between the main towns: they generally cost more or less the same as the equivalent train journey, and in some instances are actually quicker than the trains. For visits to smaller towns, there is sometimes no alternative unless you have a car. Usually the bus station (*autostazione*) is close to the train station, and even when the terminus is elsewhere, many services call at the train station along their route. Tickets have to be bought before getting on board, either from the bus company's office at the station, or from the nearest agent – the name and address is always shown on the timetable at the bus stop. Services are drastically reduced, or nonexistent, on Sundays, and note that lots of departures are linked to school requirements – which sometimes means no services during school holidays.

City buses usually charge a flat fare of around €1.50, and again tickets should be bought before getting on – either from offices at bus terminals and stops, or from *tabacchi* and other shops displaying the company's logo and ticket emblem. Validate your ticket in the machine on the bus as soon as you get on board.

the arrivals hall; in addition to single tickets, you can also get ACTV passes here (see page 24) – a wise -investment for most visitors. ACTV passes are not valid on the Alilaguna service nor on the ATVO bus.

Water-taxi drivers tout for business in and around the arrivals hall. This is the most luxurious means of getting into the city, but it's expensive: you'll pay in the region of €110 to San Marco (see page 25 for more on water-taxis). Ordinary **car-taxis** cost about €50 to Piazzale Roma.

Treviso airport

Treviso, 30km to the north of Venice, is a very small airport used chiefly by **charter** companies and

budget airlines, some of which provide a bus link from the airport into Venice. An ATVO bus service to Venice's Piazzale Roma meets the incoming Ryanair flights; the fare is €12 single and the journey takes 1 hour 10 minutes. In addition, Barzi buses run 10–15 times daily from Treviso airport to Tronchetto (Venice's main car park) – also costing €12, they take just 40 minutes. There's also a regular Busitalia/MOM service direct to Padova (1hr).

Verona airport

Verona's Villafranca (or Valerio Catullo) airport is located just 3km southwest of the city centre. The **Aerobus shuttle** to Verona's main train station departs every twenty minutes for most of the day, and costs €6; trains for Venice are half-hourly, and the journey takes one hour and ten minutes for the fastest services.

By car

People arriving **by car** must leave their vehicle either on the mainland or try for the car parks of Venice itself – either at **Piazzale Roma** or at the adjacent and ever-expanding **Tronchetto**, Europe's largest car park, which is connected to Piazzale Roma by the People Mover shuttle train (€1.50; ACTV travel passes are valid). Neither is a cheap option (around €30 per day, with discounts if you pre-book at Ⓦveneziaunica.it), and in summer the tailbacks can be horrendous. Rates are lower at the Mestre train station car park, which is connected to central Venice by regular trains and ACTV buses.

By train and bus

Arriving by **train, coach or bus**, in most cases you simply get off at the end of the line. The **Piazzale Roma** bus and tram station and **Santa Lucia** train station (not to be confused with Venezia Mestre, the last stop on the mainland) are just a couple of minutes' walk from each other at the top of the Canal Grande, and both are well served by vaporetto services to the core of the city.

City transport

The topography of Venice is uniquely complicated, and at first glance its public transport looks as convoluted as a wiring diagram. But the network is nowhere near as daunting as it first appears: there are clear main routes through the warren of Venice's alleyways, and you'll need to get to grips with only a few of the water-bus routes.

Venice has two interlocking street systems – the canals and the pavements. **Taking a water-bus** is usually the quickest way of getting between far-flung points, but in many cases the speediest way of getting from A to B is **on foot** – you don't have to break sweat, for instance, to cover the distance from the Piazza to the Rialto Bridge quicker than the #1 boat, nor indeed to beat it in a race from the Piazza to the train station, which takes the #1 fifty minutes. And once you've got your general bearings you'll find that navigation is not as daunting as it seems at first: the main thoroughfares in each district are fairly obvious, and signs posted high up on street corners all over central Venice indicate the main routes to San Marco, Ferrovia (train station), Piazzale Roma and Rialto.

Water-bus fares and tickets

The standard fare is an exorbitant €7.50 for a single journey; the ticket is valid for 75 minutes, and for any number of changes of water-bus, as long as you're travelling from point A to point B – it cannot, in other words, be used as a return ticket. There's a €5 ticket for one-stop trips such as a crossing from San Zaccaria to San Giorgio Maggiore, or Zàttere to Giudecca. Should you have more than one piece of large luggage, you're supposed to pay €7.50 per additional item. Children under 4 travel free on all public transport; wheelchair users pay €1.50 for a single ticket, and if the user is accompanied the companion travels for free.

Unless you intend to walk all day, you'll save money by buying some sort of travel card as soon as you arrive. ACTV produces Tourist Travel Cards valid for **24 hours** (€20), **48 hours** (€30), **72 hours** (€40) and **seven days** (€60), which can be used on all ACTV services within Venice. Holders of a Rolling Venice card (see page 28) can get a 72-hour ACTV card for €22. A supplement of €6 per journey is payable if you want to use an ACTV pass for the airport buses.

Tickets are available from most landing stages, shops displaying the ACTV sign and all the tourist offices; travel cards are available from the tourist offices and at Piazzale Roma, the train station, the airport, and at the Ca' d'Oro, Rialto, Accademia, San Marco Vallaresso, San Zaccaria, Arsenale, Zàttere, Fondamente Nove and Tronchetto vaporetto stops. The ticket offices at these larger stops are generally open 8am–9pm daily, whereas smaller ones tend to close between 3 and 5pm. If you can't find anywhere to buy a ticket before you get on board, ask the conductor for one immediately – if you delay, you could be liable for a fine of at least €60. Conductors cannot issue travel passes.

If you're staying a long time, or are a frequent visitor, it could be worth buying a Venezia Unica travel pass – not to be confused with the Venezia Unica Tourist Pass (see page 28) – it costs €50, is valid for five years and entitles you to a hugely reduced fare of €1.50 for a single ticket (valid for 75min), or €14 for 10 tickets, plus cut-price monthly or annual passes. To buy tickets with a Venezia Unica travel pass you charge the card electronically at ACTV ticket booths and machines. It's available, on presentation of your passport, from

WATER-BUS SERVICES

All **water-buses** in central Venice are operated by ACTV (⦿actv.it), and there are two basic types: the **vaporetti**, which are the workhorses used on the Canal Grande (#1 & #2) and other heavily used routes, and the **motoscafi**, which are smaller vessels employed on routes where the volume of traffic isn't as great (notably the two "circular routes" – #4.1/4.2 & #5.1/5.2). This is a run-through of the **routes** that visitors are most likely to find useful. Be warned that so many services call at San Marco, San Zaccaria, Piazzale Roma and the train station that the stops at these points are spread out over a long stretch of waterfront, so you might have to walk past several stops before finding the one you need. Note also that the San Marco stop has two sections, San Marco Vallaresso and San Marco Giardinetti, which are just yards from each other, and that the San Zaccaria stop is almost as close to the Piazza as are the San Marco stops.

#1: The #1 is the slowest of the water-buses, and the one you're likely to use most often. It starts at Piazzale Roma, calls at every stop on the Canal Grande except San Samuele, works its way along the San Marco waterfront to Sant'Elena, then goes over to the Lido. The #1 runs every 20min between 5am and 6.20am, every 10min between 6.20am and 10pm, and every 20min between 10pm and 11.40pm. There's also a #1B service, which runs shuttles between Piazzale Roma and Rialto from 9.30am to 4.30pm, every 12min.

#2: The timetable of the #2 is immensely complicated, but essentially from around 9am to 5pm its clockwise route takes it from San Zaccaria to San Giorgio Maggiore, Giudecca (Zitelle, Redentore and Palanca), Záttere, San Basilio, Sacca Fisola, Tronchetto, Piazzale Roma, the train station, then down the Canal Grande (calling only at Rialto, San Tomà, San Samuele and Accademia) to San Marco Giardinetti; the anticlockwise version calls at the same stops. It runs in both directions every 12min. From around 5–9am, however, the route is truncated with the #2 running back and forth between San Zaccaria and Rialto, via Giudecca, every 20min (it doesn't cover the lower section of the Canal Grande). In summer the #2 is extended out to the Lido, via Giardini.

#4.1/4.2: The circular service, running right round the core of Venice, with a short detour at the northern end to San Michele and Murano. The #4.1 travels anticlockwise, the #4.2 clockwise and both run every 20min from about 6.10am to 7.30pm; before and after that, the #4.1/4.2 together act as a shuttle service between Murano and Fondamente Nove, running every 20min until around 11.20pm.

#5.1/5.2: Similar to the #4.1/4.2, this route also circles Venice, but heads out to the Lido (rather than Murano) at the easternmost end of the loop. The #5.1 runs anticlockwise, the #5.2 clockwise, and both run fast through the Giudecca canal, stopping only at Záttere, San Basilio and Santa Marta between San Zaccaria and Piazzale Roma. Both run every 20min from around 6am to midnight. In the early morning (4.30–6.20am) the #5.1 doesn't do a complete lap of the city – instead it departs every 20min from Fondamente Nove and proceeds via the train station and Záttere to the Lido, where it terminates; from about 11pm to 12.20pm the #5.2 goes no farther than the train station.

#12: For most of the day, from 4.30am until 11.20pm, the #12 runs every half-hour from Fondamente Nove (approximately hourly after 8.40pm), calling first at Murano-Faro before heading on to Mazzorbo, Burano (from where there is a connecting shuttle to Torcello) and Treporti; it runs with the same frequency in the opposite direction.

#N: The main night service (11.30pm–4.30am) is a selective fusion of the #1 and #2 routes, running every 30min from the Lido to San Zaccaria via the Canal Grande, train station, Piazzale Roma, Tronchetto, Záttere and Giudecca – and vice versa. Other night services connect Venice with Murano and Burano, running to and from Fondamente Nove (every hour for Burano; every 30min for Murano) between 11.30pm and 4.15am.

the Venezia Unica ticket points at Piazzale Roma, the Rialto and Tronchetto.

Note that all tickets and travel cards have to be swiped **before each journey** at the meter-like machines which are at every stop. Even if your travel pass is valid you'll still be fined if you haven't swiped it before getting aboard.

Traghetti

There are just four bridges spanning the Canal Grande – the Ponte Calatrava (at Piazzale Roma), Ponte degli Scalzi (at the train station), Ponte di Rialto and Ponte dell'Accademia – so the **traghetti** (gondola ferries) that cross it can be useful time-savers. Costing €2 (€0.70 if you're a resident), they are also the only

KAYAKS IN VENICE

It's possible to rent kayaks and paddleboards for self-propelled exploration of the canals, but the town hall has now banned them completely from the Canal Grande and some other major waterways, and from all canals between 8am and 3pm.

Most Venetians would favour an absolute ban, because kayaking in Venice is a truly stupid idea. For one thing, there are too many boats on Venice's waterways already – congestion was a contributory factor in the accident that killed a tourist at the Rialto vaporetto stop in 2013. Just as importantly, Venice is a city, not a high-culture Center Parc resort, contrary to what some tourists seem to think.

cheap way of getting a ride on a gondola, albeit a stripped-down version, with none of the trimmings and no padded seats: most locals stand rather than sit. There used to be almost thirty gondola traghetti across the Canal Grande, but today there are supposedly seven, only three of which – Santa Sofia–Rialto, San Tomà–Sant'Angelo and Campiello del Traghetto (Santa Maria del Giglio)–Calle Lanza (near the Salute) – are still in anything like regular operation. In theory, they run Mon–Sat 7.30am–8pm, Sun 8.45am–7pm, but in practice their hours are often much shorter, especially in winter, when the last of the three barely exists. The other four routes are still officially listed, but are more or less defunct. They are: Ca' Rezzonico–San Samuele, Riva del Carbon–Fondamenta del Vin, San Marcuola–Fondaco dei Turchi, and Fondamenta Santa Lucia–Fondamenta San Simeon Piccolo.

Gondolas

The **gondola** (see page 58), once Venice's chief form of transport, is now purely an adjunct of the tourist industry. But however much the gondola's image has become tarnished, it is an astonishingly graceful craft, perfectly designed for negotiating the tortuous and shallow waterways: a gondola displaces so little water, and the gondoliers are so skilful, that there's hardly a canal in the city they can't negotiate. Until recently, gondoliers inherited their jobs from their fathers; nowadays the profession is open to anyone who can get through four hundred hours of tough training, which involves acquiring not just the requisite manual skills and a perfect grasp of the city's waterways, but also a deep knowledge of the history of the profession. In 2010 Giorgia Boscolo successfully completed the course, and thus became Venice's first female gondolier. There are more than 420 male gondoliers.

To hire a gondola costs €80 per forty minutes for up to six passengers, rising to €100 between 7pm and 8am; you pay an extra €40 for every additional twenty minutes, or €50 from 7pm to 8am. Further hefty surcharges will be levied should you require

the services of an on-board **accordionist** or **tenor**. (There have been moves to outlaw the singing of the perennial tourist favourite, *O Sole Mio*, on the grounds that performances of this Neapolitan ditty merely reinforce the prejudices of visitors who demand nothing more than a generic "Italian" experience.) Even though the tariff is set by the local authorities, it's been known for gondoliers to extort even higher rates than these – if you do decide to go for a ride, establish the charge before setting off. To minimize the chances of being ripped off by a private individual making a few dozen euros on the side (and there are plenty of those in Venice), take a boat only from one of the following **official gondola stands**: west of the Piazza at Calle Vallaresso, Campo San Moisè or Campo Santa Maria del Giglio; immediately north of the Piazza at Bacino Orseolo; on the Molo, in front of the Palazzo Ducale; outside the *Danieli* hotel on Riva degli Schiavoni; at the train station; at Piazzale Roma; at Campo Santa Sofia, near Ca' d'Oro; at San Tomà, to the east of the Frari; or by the Rialto Bridge on Riva Carbon.

Your gondolier will assume that you'll want to be taken along the Canal Grande or across the Bacino di San Marco, but you'll not be making the best use of the opportunity if you opt for one of these: for one thing, these major waterways look much the same from a vaporetto as from a gondola; and for another, the gondola will tend to get bashed around by the wash from the bigger boats. Better to choose a quarter of the city that has struck you as being particularly alluring, head for the gondola stand that's nearest to it, and ask to be taken there.

Water-taxis

Venice's **water-taxis** are sleek and speedy vehicles that can penetrate most of the city's canals, and can carry up to 10 people. Unfortunately their use is confined to all but the owners of the deepest pockets, for they are possibly the most expensive form of taxi in western Europe, with even a short trip from the train station to Rialto costing around €50. All sorts of surcharges are levied as well: €10 for each extra person if there are more than five people in the party; €5 for each piece of luggage in excess of five items; €20 for a ride between 10pm and 7am. There are five ways of getting a taxi: go to one of the main stands (at Piazzale Roma, the train station, Rialto and San Marco Vallaresso); find one in the process of disgorging its passengers; call one by phone (☎041 522 2303); email at ✉info@motoscafivenezia.it, or book through the website, Ⓦmotoscafivenezia.it. If you phone for one, you'll pay a surcharge, of course. And if your hotel concierge calls a taxi for you, the surcharge could be even worse.

Information

Venice's main tourist office is at Calle dell'Ascensione 71/F, in the corner of the Piazza's arcades (daily 9am–7pm; ☎041 523 0399; Ⓦveneziaunica.it); this is also the main outlet for information on the rest of the Veneto. Another office is located at the station (daily 8am–9pm). Smaller offices are in the airport arrivals area (daily 9am–7pm) and at the multistorey car park at Piazzale Roma (daily 7am–8pm).

For printed information, a useful resource is the English–Italian magazine *Un Ospite di Venezia* (Ⓦunospitedivenezia.it); it gives information on exhibitions, concerts and events, plus extras such as vaporetto timetables, and is free from the reception desks of many four- and five-star hotels. The fullest source of information, though, is *VENews* (€3; Ⓦvenezianews.it), published ten times a year, and sold at newsstands all over the city; it has good coverage of exhibitions, cultural events, bars and restaurants, with a fair amount of text in English as well as Italian.

USEFUL WEBSITES

Ⓦ **churchesofvenice.co.uk** Jeff Cotton's wonderfully detailed website is replete with fascinating facts and stories about the churches of Venice, Verona and Padua.

Ⓦ **govenice.com** A Venice information portal, with loads of links.

Ⓦ **iamnotmakingthisup.net** Erla Zwingle's witty and eye-opening blog on life in Venice.

Ⓦ **veneto.to** The official Veneto tourist office site providing information on places to visit, hotels, weather, festivals and exhibitions.

Ⓦ **veneziablog.blogspot.co.uk** An excellent blog written by Steven Varni, a Venice-dwelling American-Italian.

Ⓦ **veneziaunica.it** This website is the place to go for info on the Venezia Unica passes, and the city's calendar of events.

Ⓦ **venicetravelblog.com** Durant and Cheryl Imboden's website is a good source of up-to-the-minute practical information for visitors to the city.

Museums and monuments

There are two museum cards for the city's civic museums (Ⓦvisitmuve.it). The Musei di Piazza San Marco card costs €20 (€13 for ages 6–14, students under 26, EU citizens over 65 and Rolling Venice Card holders), and gets you into the Palazzo Ducale, Museo Correr, Museo Archeologico and the Biblioteca Marciana; it's valid for three months. The Museum Pass, costing €24/18, covers these four, plus all the other civic museums: Ca' Rezzonico, Casa Goldoni, Palazzo Mocenigo, Museo di Storia Naturale, Ca' Pésaro (the modern art and oriental museums), the Museo del Merletto (Burano) and the Museo del Vetro (Murano). It's valid for six months. Both passes allow one visit to each attraction and are available from any of the participating museums. The sights covered by the Musei di Piazza San Marco card can be visited only with a museum card; at the other places you have the option of paying an entry charge just for that attraction. Accompanied disabled people have free access to all civic museums.

Eighteen churches are part of the ever-expanding **Chorus Pass** scheme (Ⓦchorusvenezia. org), whereby a €12 ticket (€8 for students up to 29, family ticket €24) allows one visit to each of the churches over a one-year period; the individual entrance fee at each of the participating churches is €3. The churches involved are: the Frari; the Gesuati; the Redentore; San Giacomo dell'Orio; San Giobbe; San Giovanni Elemosinario; San Pietro di Castello; San Polo; San Sebastiano; San Stae; Sant'Alvise; Santa Maria dei Miracoli; Santa Maria del Giglio; Santa Maria Formosa; Santo Stefano; San Vidal; San Giacomo di Rialto; San Giuseppe di Castello. The Chorus Pass is available at each of these churches and the tourist offices.

Opening hours are listed throughout the Guide, but bear in mind that the times are prone to sudden alteration, especially in winter, and that many of the

THE VENEZIA UNICA TOURIST PASS & ROLLING VENICE

For tourists who intend to do some intensive sightseeing, the city has a ludicrously complicated scheme called **Venezia Unica** (Ⓦveneziaunica.it), in which you choose a menu of services online (museum passes, water-buses, wi-fi networks, public toilets etc), and are then quoted a price for a ticket that also includes discounts to some other museums and exhibitions. (The collection process is explained on the website.) Note that there are two versions of the Venezia Unica pass: one for tourists, and a "frequent users" pass, which is a travel permit for long-stayers (see page 24). Given that, for example, the three-day version of the Venezia Unica pass costs more than €80 if you want public transport included, and that its period of validity begins when you collect it (whereas ACTV Travel Cards are valid from the moment you first use them), for most visitors it's best just to buy a Travel Card and/or Museum Pass when you arrive in Venice.

For ages 6 to 29, you are eligible for a **Rolling Venice** card, which gives you discounts at certain shops, restaurants, museums and exhibitions (details are given in a leaflet that comes with the card) and entitles you to a 72-hour ACTV travel pass (not valid for the airport bus) for just €22. The Rolling Venice card costs €6 and is available from the tourist offices, on production of a passport.

less-visited churches are often shut because people can't be found to keep them open. Last admission for the major museums is one hour before closing time; for smaller sights, tickets are generally sold up to half an hour before closing. Children under 6 are exempt from entrance charges, while 6–12s are entitled to reductions at nearly all attractions, provided they are accompanied by an adult. Visitors from EU countries who can prove they are aged under 18 are entitled to free admission at the Accademia, Ca' d'Oro, Museo Archeologico and Museo Orientale.

Every year, on dates that differ from year to year, there's a Settimana della Cultura, during which all Italian state museums waive their entrance fees for a week. In addition, state museums are free on the first Sunday of each month (*Domenica al Museo*); this scheme is reviewed annually, so it's not certain to be in operation indefinitely.

The media

Local and national newspapers have a healthy readership, but television plays a more central role in Italian life, despite the poor quality of Italy's numerous local and heavily partisan national channels.

Newspapers

The Veneto's major **newspaper** is *Il Gazzettino* (Ⓦgazzettino.it), which runs national and i-nternational stories on the front pages, with local news farther in; each city has its own edition so the local

coverage in Verona, for example, will differ from coverage in Treviso. Venice's own local paper, *La Nuova* (Ⓦnuovavenezia.it), also sells well in the city, and is a good source of information on events. Of the nationals, the centre-left *La -Repubblica* (Ⓦrepubblica.it) and right-slanted *Corriere della Sera* (Ⓦcorriere.it) are the two most widely read and available. The most avidly read papers of all, however, are the pink *Gazzetta dello Sport* and *Corriere dello Sport*; essential reading for the serious Italian sports fan, they devote as much attention to players' injuries as most papers would give to the resignation of a government minister. News magazines are also widely read in Italy, from the similar *L'Espresso* and *Panorama* to the lighter and celeb-obsessed offerings of *Gente* and *Oggi*.

English and **US newspapers** can be found for around twice the normal price in Venice and the larger towns of the Veneto. Pan-European editions of Britain's *Guardian* and *Financial Times* and the Rome editions of the *International Herald Tribune* and *USA Today* are also usually available on the day of publication.

TV and radio

Italy's three main national **TV** channels are RAI 1, 2 and 3. Silvio Berlusconi's Mediaset runs three additional nationwide channels – Canale 5, Rete 4 and Italia 1 – which are blatantly biased in favour of Berlusconi and his associates. Although the stories of Italian TV's stripping housewives are overplayed, the output is generally unchallenging (and sexist) across the board, with the accent on quiz shows, soaps and American imports. The RAI channels carry less advertising and try to mix the dross with documentaries and news coverage. Numerous local channels concentrate on sport and shopping.

The situation in **radio** is even more anarchic, with FM so crowded that you continually pick up new stations whether you want to or not. There are some good small-scale stations if you search hard enough, but on the whole the RAI stations are the most professional.

Travel essentials

Costs

There is no getting round the fact that Venice is a fantastically **expensive city**: even at the humblest one-star hotel, you'll pay well over €100 for a double room in high season, and the flashiest places charge ten times that amount, and more. A strict diet of coffee and croissant in the mornings, a picnic at lunchtime and pizza in the evening will account for around €30 – and if you go to a proper restaurant you're unlikely to spend less than €40 per person, for three courses plus house wine. Then you have to add the cost of entrance fees and Venice's water-buses. In total, if you want to use the water-buses, see the sights and eat well, you should budget for a daily outlay of at least **€60–70** per person in Venice, **not counting accommodation**.

Note that in almost every restaurant you'll pay a **cover charge** (*coperto*); it's usually €2–3, but in many places in Venice it's now €4–5, and an inexcusable €10 isn't unknown. As well as the *coperto*, **service** (*servizio*) will often be added, generally about ten percent; if it isn't, you should **tip** this amount.

Crime and personal safety

Venice is a very sedate city, and **pickpockets** on crowded vaporetti are the chief menace. On the mainland, the odd bag-snatching is as dangerous as things get in the tourist hotspots of Padua and Verona.

In Italy there are several different branches of the **police**, ostensibly to prevent any single branch seizing power. You're not likely to have much contact with

the Guardia di Finanza, who investigate smuggling, tax evasion and other finance-related felonies. Drivers in the Veneto may well come up against the **Polizia Urbana**, or town police, who are mainly concerned with traffic and parking offences, and also the **Polizia Stradale**, who patrol motorways.

The **Carabinieri** are dressed in military-style uniforms and white shoulder belts (they're part of the army), and deal with general crime, public order and drugs control. The **Polizia Statale**, the other general crime-fighting branch, enjoy a fierce rivalry with the Carabinieri, and are the ones to whom you should **report a theft** at their base, the **Questura** (police station). They'll issue you with a *denuncia*, a form which you'll need for any insurance claims after you get home. The Questura in Venice is at Rampa Santa Chiara 500, on the north side of Piazzale Roma (📞041 271 5511). There's also a small police station on the Piazza, at no. 63.

Electricity

The supply in Italy is 220V, though anything requiring 240V will work. Most plugs are two round pins: UK equipment will need an adaptor, US equipment will need a 220-to-110 transformer as well.

Entry requirements

All EU citizens can enter Italy, and stay as long as they like, simply on production of a valid passport. Citizens of the United States, Canada, Australia and New Zealand need only a valid passport, but are limited to stays of ninety days. When we went to press, the post-Brexit situation was still a matter of guesswork – it's possible that UK citizens will require a visa to visit Italy after Britain leaves the EU – best to check 🌐 gov uk for the latest updates. Legally, you're required to **register** with the police within three days of entering Italy. This will be done for you if you're staying in a hotel (this is why you have to surrender your passport on arrival), but if you're self-catering you should register at the Questura (see above). It used to be the case that nobody bothered too much about this formality, but in recent years the police have begun to be more pedantic with backpacking types in Venice. So if

AVERAGE MONTHLY TEMPERATURES AND RAINFALL

	Jan	Feb	Mar	Apr	May	Jun	Jul	Aug	Sep	Oct	Nov	Dec
Max/min (°C)	6/-1	8/1	12/4	16/8	21/12	25/16	28/18	27/17	24/14	18/9	12/4	7/0
Max/min (°F)	43/30	46/34	54/39	61/46	70/54	77/61	82/64	81/63	75/57	64/48	54/39	45/32
Rainfall (mm)	58	54	57	64	69	76	63	83	66	69	87	54

you think you look like the sort of person a Venetian policeman might deem undesirable, get registered.

ITALIAN EMBASSIES AND CONSULATES ABROAD

Australia Embassy 12 Grey St, Deakin, Canberra, ACT 2600 ☎ 02 6273 3333, ⓦ ambcanberra.esteri.it. Consulates in Melbourne ☎ 03 9867 5744 and Sydney ☎ 02 9392 7900.

Canada Embassy 275 Slater St, Ottawa, ON K1P 5H9 ☎ 613/232 2401, ⓦ ambottawa.esteri.it. Consulates in Montréal ☎ 514 849 8351 and Toronto ☎ 416 977 1566.

Ireland Embassy 63–65 Northumberland Rd, Dublin 4 ☎ 01 660 1744, ⓦ ambdublino.esteri.it.

New Zealand Embassy 34–38 Grant Rd, PO Box 463, Thorndon, Wellington ☎ 04 473 5339, ⓦ ambwellington.esteri.it.

UK Embassy 14 Three King's Yard, London W1Y 2EH ☎ 0207 312 2200, ⓦ amblondra.esteri.it. Consulates in Edinburgh ☎ 0131 226 3695 and Manchester ☎ 0161 236 9024.

US Embassy 3000 Whitehaven St NW, Washington DC 20008 ☎ 202 612 4400, ⓦ ambwashingtondc.esteri.it. Consulates in Chicago, New York, San Francisco and other cities are listed on the website .

EMBASSIES AND CONSULATES IN ITALY

Australia Embassy Via Antonio Bosio 5, 00161 Rome ☎ 06 852 721, ⓦ italy.embassy.gov.au.

Canada Embassy Via Zara 30, 00198 Rome ☎ 06 85444 3937, ⓦ canada.it.

Ireland Embassy Villa Spada, Via Giacomo Medici 1, 00153 Rome ☎ 06 585 2381, ⓦ ambasciata-irlanda.it.

New Zealand Embassy Via Clitunno 44, 00198 Rome ☎ 06 853 7501, ⓦ nzembassy.com/italy.

UK Embassy Via XX Settembre 80a, 00187 Rome ☎ 06 4220 0001, ⓦ ukinitaly.fco.gov.uk. The closest consulate to Venice is in Milan, at Via San Paolo 7 (☎ 02 723 001).

US Embassy Via V Veneto 121, 00187 Rome ☎ 06 46 741, ⓦ italy. usembassy.gov. The nearest US consulate is in Milan, at Via Principe Amedeo 2–10 (☎ 02 290 351), but there's a consular agency at Marco Polo airport (☎ 041 541 5944).

LGBTQ travellers

LGBTQ attitudes in northern Italy are on the whole tolerant, but public displays of affection that extend much beyond hand-holding might raise a few eyebrows, especially in smaller towns. The national gay organization ARCI-Gay (ⓦ arcigay.it) has branches in most big towns. The age of consent in Italy is 18.

Health

If you're arriving in Italy from elsewhere in Europe, North America or Australasia, you don't need any jabs. Citizens of all EU countries are entitled to emergency medical care in Italy under the same terms as Italian nationals. As proof of entitlement, EU travellers have to carry a **European Health Insurance Card (EHIC)**, which is free of charge and valid for five years. It is not clear if UK nationals will be covered by a similar arrangement when Britain leaves the EU – check ⓦ gov.uk for more information. In any case, the EHIC does not cover the full cost of major treatment, and the high medical charges make travel insurance essential. You normally have to pay the full cost of emergency treatment upfront, and claim it back when you get home (minus a small excess); make very sure you hang onto full doctors' reports, signed prescription details and all receipts to back up your claim.

Italy operates a system called *Farmacie di Turno*, which ensures that you are never far from an open pharmacy at any time of day or night. Every one displays the address of the nearest late-opening pharmacy, and there's a full list in *Un Ospite di Venezia* (ⓦ unospitedivenezia.it). Italian **pharmacists** (*farmacie*) are well qualified to give advice on minor ailments and to dispense prescriptions; if you require a **doctor** (*médico*), ask for help in the first instance at your hotel or the tourist office. Follow a similar procedure if you have dental problems. Again, keep all receipts for insurance claims.

In an emergency go to the *Pronto Soccorso* (Casualty/A&E) section of the Ospedale Civile, on Fondamente Nove (by the Ospedale vaporetto stop) or phone ☎ 118 and ask for *ambulanza*.

Insurance

It's always advisable to take out travel **insurance** to cover against illness, injury theft or loss of property will be absolutely essential. Before paying for a new policy, however, check whether you're already covered: some all-risks home insurance policies may cover your possessions when overseas, and many private medical schemes include cover when abroad.

If your existing policies don't cover you, contact a specialist **travel insurance** company. A typical travel policy usually provides health cover, plus cover for the loss of baggage, tickets and – up to a certain limit – cash, as well as cancellation or curtailment of your journey. For medical coverage, ascertain whether benefits will be paid as the treatment proceeds or only after you return home, and whether there is a 24-hour medical emergency number. If you need to make a claim, you should keep receipts for medicines and medical treatment, and in the event you have anything stolen, you must obtain an official police statement.

Internet

Most hotels and many bars in Venice now offer free **internet access**, and even in the depths of the Veneto it's now easy enough to find free wi-fi.

Lost property

If you lose anything on the train or at the station, call ☎ 041 785 531; at the airport call ☎ 041 260 9222; on ACTV water- or land buses call ☎ 041 272 2723; and anywhere in the city itself call ☎ 041 274 8225.

Left luggage

There's a left luggage office at Piazzale Roma (daily 6am–8pm) and beside platform one at the train station (daily 6am–11pm), each costing €6 per item for the first 5hr, then an extra €0.90 per hour until the 12hr mark, and €0.40 per hour thereafter.

Mail

Venice's central post office is at Calle delle Acque 5016, close to San Salvador, (Mon, Tues, Thurs & Fri 8.20am–7pm, Sat 8.20am–12.30pm). The principal branch offices are located at Calle dell'Ascensione 1241 (off the west side of the Piazza; Mon, Tues & Thurs–Fri 8.20am–1.30pm, Sat 8.20am–12.30pm), Calle del Spezier 233 and Calle Priuli 3732 (both Cannaregio; same hours), Zattere 1507 (Dorsoduro; same hours), Campo San Polo 2012 (San Polo; same hours), Via Garibaldi 1641 (Castello; same hours), and Fondamenta Santa Eufemia 430 (Giudecca; same hours). Stamps can also be bought in *tabacchi*, as well as in some gift shops.

Maps

The **maps** in the Guide are adequate for general navigation, but such is the intricacy of Venice's alleyways that absolute accuracy requires a much larger scale. Fuller detail is provided by the Touring Club Italiano (TCI) 1:5000 fold-out map of the city, which is widely on sale in Venice. TCI also publish the best road map of the Veneto.

Money

The Italian currency is the **euro** (€), which is composed of 100 cents. Although it's a good idea to have some cash when you first arrive, **credit and debit cards** can be used either in an ATM (*bancomat*) or over the counter. MasterCard and Visa are accepted in most of Venice's larger stores, hotels and restaurants, but many budget hotels and restaurants won't accept payment by card. Remember that all cash advances on a credit card are treated as loans, with interest accruing daily from the date of withdrawal.

Banks in Venice are concentrated around Campo San Luca and Campo Manin (in the north of the San Marco *sestiere*). Their hours are generally Mon–Fri 8.30am–1.30pm and 2.30–3.30pm. There are clusters of exchange bureaus (*cambios*) near San Marco, the Rialto and the train station. Open late every day of the week, they can be useful in emergencies, but their rates tend to be steep.

Opening hours and holidays

Basic hours for small **shops and businesses** in the Veneto are Monday to Saturday from 8 or 9am to

---

NATIONAL HOLIDAYS

Nearly all fee-charging sights (but not bars and restaurants) will be closed on the following dates:
January 1 New Year's Day
January 6 Epiphany
Easter Monday (variable)
April 25 Liberation Day and St Mark's Day
May 1 Labour Day
June 2 Day of the Republic
August 15 *Ferragosto*; Assumption of the Blessed Virgin Mary
November 1 *Ognissanti*, "All Saints"
December 8 Immaculate Conception of the Blessed Virgin Mary
December 25 Christmas
December 26 St Stephen's Day
In addition, many Venetian shops and businesses close or work shorter hours for the festival of the Salute on November 21 (see page 230).

around 1pm, and from around 3pm to 7 or 8pm, though an increasing number of places (especially in Venice) stay open continuously from around 10am to 7/8pm, with shorter hours on Sunday. Many of Venice's churches now charge admission and have set opening times; others tend to open for Mass in the early morning, around 7 or 8am, and close around noon, then open again at 4 or 5pm, closing at 7pm; more obscure ones will only open for early morning and evening services; some only open on Sunday and on religious holidays; and a few are rarely open at all. Wherever possible, the opening hours of churches are given in the Guide.

It's impossible to generalize about the opening hours of **museums and historic sites** except to say that the largest ones tend to be open every day, most of the others are open six days a week, with Monday and Tuesday the favoured days of closure, and that winter hours are shorter than summer ones; we've given the current opening hours of every museum covered in the Guide.

One problem you'll face is that at any one time many churches and monuments are either completely or partly **closed for restoration**, and it's impossible to predict which buildings will be under wraps in the immediate future – all that can be said with any degree of certainty is that you'll find restorers at work in parts of the Basilica di San Marco and the Palazzo Ducale.

Telephones

Most of Venice's public call boxes accept coins, and all of them take phonecards, which can be bought from *tabacchi* and some other shops (look for the Telecom Italia sticker), as well as from post offices. You're never far from a payphone – every sizeable campo has at least one, and there are phones by most vaporetto stops. **Tariffs** are among the most expensive in Europe; for national calls, the off-peak period runs Monday to Friday from 6.30pm to 8am, then Saturday 1pm until Monday 8am.

To call Italy from abroad dial your **international access code** (00 from the UK, Ireland and New Zealand; 011 from the US and Canada; 0011 from Australia), followed by **39** for Italy, followed by the full Italian number. For direct international calls from Italy, dial the country code, the area code (minus its first 0), and finally the subscriber number. Country codes are as follows: UK 0044; Ireland 00353; US & Canada 001; Australia 0061; New Zealand 0064; South Africa 0027.

To make international **reversed charge** or **collect** calls from Italy (*cárico al destinatario*), dial 170 or 172,

followed by the country code, which will connect you through to an operator in your home country.

Roaming charges for mobile phones have been scrapped in Europe, but it's uncertain where UK users will stand after Brexit; it's a good idea to check the current situation with your provider before you leave.

Time

Italy is on Central European Time (CET): one hour ahead of Britain, six hours ahead of Eastern Standard Time and nine hours ahead of Pacific Standard Time.

Travellers with disabilities

Any city that has more than 400 bridges necessarily presents difficulties for wheelchair users, but the town hall has greatly improved the situation in recent years: key bridges are now fitted with -wheelchair lifts, and an increasing number of bridges have ramps as well as steps. Visit the ⓦ veneziaunica.it website for information on access, including detailed maps of a dozen wheelchair-friendly itineraries (ⓦ veneziaunica.it/en/content/itineraries-without-barriers). It should be said that getting in and out of the water-buses can be hazardous if the water level is low or the canals are choppy, despite the helpfulness of most conductors. At busy times of day **wheelchair** users should avoid the smaller boats – principally the #4.1, #4.2, #5.1 and #5.2 lines – as they have just a small platform around the pilot's cabin, with the main passenger area being below deck level, down steep steps. The captains of these boats, moreover, are not obliged to let wheelchairs on board. The #1 and #2 are accessible and spacious, but at peak hours of the day in high season, they are often packed to capacity. It's also important to note that many Venetian 1- to 3-star hotels and virtually all B&Bs occupy the upper storeys of their addresses, and that staircases often provide the only access. If mobility is at all problematic, check the layout of your accommodation before making a booking.

Travelling with children

It's hard to imagine any child not enjoying Venice, for a few days at least. The experience of travelling around a city by **boat** is a thrill in itself, as is the freedom from road-going traffic. The whole city is a labyrinth, and kids can explore it with no risk of colliding with anything more dangerous than a pedestrian. There are towers to climb, weird carvings and pictures to spot and never-ending activity on the water. In summer you can nip over to the Lido for a paddle and a bout of sandcastling, and as in any Italian city you're only a few minutes away from a delicious ice cream. With younger children, however, you might find that their patience begins to wear thin quite quickly. The stone pavements can be tiring, and Venice has very few green spaces, with just three **playgrounds** of any size, in the Parco Savorgnan (near the train station), in the Giardini Pubblici (over on the eastern edge of the city) and next to the nearby Sant'Elena vaporetto stop. As for Venice's shops, the likeliest to be a hit with the small ones is *Mistero e Magia*, Venice's first and only magic store (see page 238).

Diet might be an issue in seafood-centric Venice – there are a few pizzerias, and some **restaurants** offer kids' favourites such as lasagne and spaghetti Bolognese, but the good ones do not. And if you're going to be pushing a buggy around all day, the endless bridges can become wearying. On the other hand, anyone equipped with a baby is very likely to be warmly received in child-mad Italy, and very few restaurants will treat the small ones as a nuisance. As for **accommodation**, nearly all hotels will put a cot or an extra bed in your room, usually for a surcharge of around ten percent.

San Marco

The *sestiere* of San Marco has been the nucleus of Venice for more than a millennium. In the early ninth century, lagoon settlers decamped from Malamocco to the safer islands of the inner lagoon. The area now known as the Piazza San Marco was where they built the citadel that evolved into the Palazzo Ducale, and it was here that they established their most important church – the Basilica di San Marco. Over the succeeding centuries the Basilica became one of the most ostentatious churches in Christendom, and the Palazzo Ducale grew to accommodate a system of government that endured for longer than any other republic in Europe. Meanwhile, the setting for these two great edifices developed into a public space so grandiose that no other square in the city was thought fit to bear the name "piazza" – all other Venetian squares are campi or campielli.

1

Many of Venice's visitors make a beeline for this spot, spend a few hours here, then depart without staying for even one night. For those who do hang around, San Marco has multitudinous ways of easing the cash from the pockets: the plushest hotels are concentrated in this *sestiere*; the most elegant and exorbitant cafés spill out onto the pavement from the Piazza's arcades; the most extravagantly priced seafood is served in this area's restaurants; and the swankiest shops in Venice line the Piazza and the streets radiating from it.

And yet, small though this *sestiere* is, it harbours some refuges from the crush. Even within the Piazza you can escape the throng, as the **Museo Correr** and the adjoining **archeological museum** are rarely crowded. The Renaissance church of **San Salvador** – only a few minutes' walk from the Piazza – and the Gothic **Santo Stefano** are both magnificent and comparatively neglected buildings, while **San Moisè**, **Santa Maria del Giglio** and the **Scala del Bovolo** rank among the city's most engaging oddities. On the fringes of the *sestiere* you'll find two of Venice's major exhibition spaces: the immense **Palazzo Grassi** and the **Museo Fortuny**, which as well as staging special events also contains a permanent collection of work by the designer Mariano Fortuny.

The Piazza

When the first Palazzo Ducale was built, in the ninth century, the area now occupied by the **Piazza San Marco** was an islet known as Morso. Two churches stood here – San

---

PIAZZA FESTIVITIES

The Piazza's brightest splash of colour comes from the **Carnevale**. Though gangs of masked and wildly costumed revellers turn every quarter of the city into a ten-day open-air party, the action tends to drift towards the Piazza: the festivities commence with the "Flight of the Angel" from the Campanile (see page 60) and the grand finale is a huge Shrove Tuesday ball in the square, with fireworks over the Bacino di San Marco. But the biggest crowd is the one that gathers here on New Year's Eve – some 80,000 people crush themselves into the Piazza for midnight, leaving behind so much debris that the council has to spend in excess of €50,000 on the clear-up.

Mass entertainments used to be far more frequent than they are now, taking over the Piazza on feast days and whenever an excuse could be found. From the twelfth century onwards **pig hunts** and **bullfights** were regular spectacles, but around the beginning of the seventeenth century these blood sports were moved elsewhere, and the Piazza became a venue for performances known as **Labours of Hercules**, in which teams of young men formed human pyramids and towers on platforms that were often a few planks resting on a pair of barrels.

Military victories, ducal elections and visits from heads of state were commonly celebrated with tournaments and pageants: a three-day tournament was held in the Piazza in 1364 after the recapture of Crete, and in 1413 the election of Doge Tommaso Mocenigo was marked by a tournament that was watched by 70,000 people. The **coronation of Doge Ziani** in 1172 was celebrated with a procession with the new head of state scattering coins to the populace; this ritual, adapted from Byzantine custom, was observed by all subsequent doges. Major religious festivals led to lavish celebrations, the most spectacular of which was the **Procession of Corpus Domini**, a performance recorded in a painting by Gentile Bellini in the Accademia.

But no festivities were more extravagant than those of **Ascension Day**, and it was in the wake of Ascension that the Piazza most closely resembled the modern tourist enclave. From the twelfth century until the fall of the Republic, the day itself was marked in Venice by the ceremony of **The Marriage of Venice to the Sea**, a ritual which inaugurated a short season of feasts and sideshows in the Piazza, culminating in a trade fair called the Fiera della Sensa (*sensa* being dialect for Ascension). The Fiera began in 1180, when the city was flooded with pilgrims after Pope Alexander III's proclamation that an indulgence would be granted to anyone who prayed in San Marco during the year. Before long the Fiera became a cornucopia of luxury commodities, and by the last century of the Republic's existence it had grown into a fifteen-day fair that filled the Piazza with temporary wooden shops and arcades.

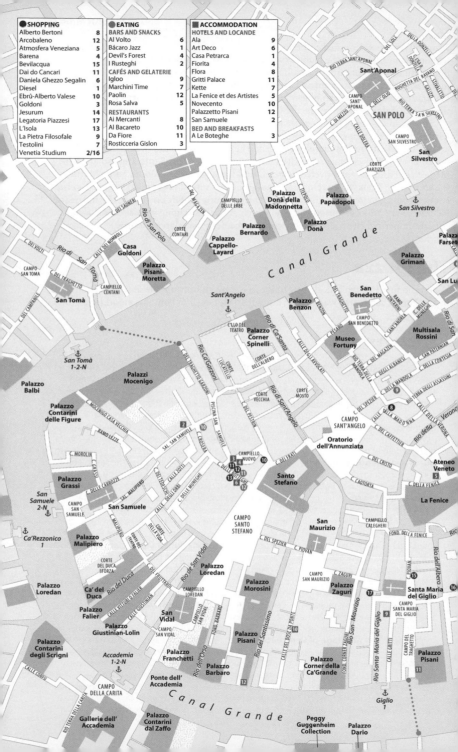

Legend

● SHOPPING

Alberto Bertoni	8
Arcobaleno	12
Atmosfera Veneziana	5
Barena	4
Bevilacqua	15
Dai do Cancari	1
Daniela Ghezzo Segalin	6
Diesel	1
Ebrû-Alberto Valese	10
Goldoni	3
Jesurum	14
Legatoria Piazzesi	17
L'Isola	13
La Pietra Filosofale	9
Testolini	7
Venetia Studium	2/16

■ EATING

BARS AND SNACKS

Al Volto	6
Bácaro Jazz	1
Devil's Forest	4
I Rusteghi	2

CAFÉS AND GELATERIE

Igloo	9
Marchini Time	7
Paolin	12
Rosa Salva	5

RESTAURANTS

Ai Mercanti	8
Al Bacareto	10
Da Fiore	11
Rosticceria Gislon	3

■ ACCOMMODATION

HOTELS AND LOCANDE

Ala	9
Art Deco	6
Casa Petrarca	1
Fiorita	4
Flora	8
Gritti Palace	11
Kette	7
La Fenice et des Artistes	5
Novecento	10
Palazzetto Pisani	12
San Samuele	2

BED AND BREAKFASTS

A Le Boteghe	3

Map labels

Sant'Aponal
SAN POLO
San Silvestro
San Silvestro 1
Palazzo Donà della Madonnetta
Palazzo Papadopoli
Palazzo Bernardo
Palazzo Donà
Palazzo Cappello-Layard
Canal Grande
Palazzo Farset[ti]
Palazzo Grimani
San Lu[ca]
Casa Goldoni
Palazzo Pisani-Moretta
Sant'Angelo 1
Palazzo Benzon
San Benedetto
San Benedetto
CAMPO SAN BENEDETTO
Museo Fortuny
Multisala Rossini
Rio di San...
San Tomà
San Tomà 1-2-N
C.llo del Teatro
Palazzo Corner Spinelli
Palazzo Balbi
Palazzi Mocenigo
Palazzo Contarini delle Figure
CAMPO SANT'ANGELO
Ateneo Veneto
Oratorio dell'Annunziata
Palazzo Grassi
Campiello Nuovo
Santo Stefano
La Fenice
San Samuele 2-N
Ca'Rezzonico 1
CAMPO SAN SAMUELE
San Samuele
CAMPO SANTO STEFANO
San Maurizio
Campiello Calegheri
FOND. DELLA FENICE
Palazzo Malipiero
Ca' del Duca
Palazzo Loredan
Palazzo Morosini
Palazzo Zaguri
Santa Maria del Giglio
Palazzo Falier
San Vidal
Palazzo Giustinian-Lolin
Palazzo Pisani
Palazzo Franchetti
Palazzo Corner della Ca'Grande
Palazzo Pisani
Palazzo Contarini degli Scrigni
Accademia 1-2-N
Palazzo Barbaro
Ponte dell'Accademia
Giglio 1
CAMPO DELLA CARITA
Canal Grande
Gallerie dell'Accademia
Palazzo Contarini dal Zaffo
Peggy Guggenheim Collection
Palazzo Dario

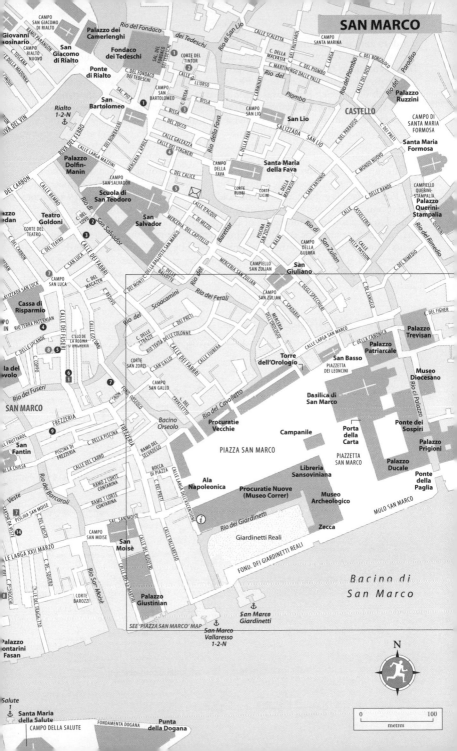

1

Teodoro and San Geminiano – but most of the land was covered by the orchard of the nuns of San Zaccaria. It was in the late twelfth century, under the direction of **Doge Sebastiano Ziani**, that the land was transformed into a public space – the canal connecting the waterways to the north with the Bacino di San Marco was filled in, the canalside San Geminiano was demolished (a plaque close to the Campanile marks where it stood) and a replacement built at the far end. The general shape of the Piazza hasn't changed much since Ziani's scheme, but most of the buildings you see today, excluding the Basilica and the Campanile, date from the great period of urban renewal which began at the end of the fifteenth century and went on for much of the following hundred years.

"The finest drawing room in Europe" was how Napoleon described the Piazza. Less genteel epithets might seem appropriate on an overcrowded summer afternoon, but the Piazza has always been a busy spot, and foreigners have always made up a sizeable proportion of the crowds – if anything, life on the Piazza is less diverse nowadays than it used to be. From the foundation of the city, this area was used by traders (the slave market was here until the end of the ninth century), and as the city grew, so the range of activities taking place on the Piazza multiplied; by the end of the fifteenth century butchers and grocers had established their pitches, moneylenders and notaries had set up kiosks nearby, and makeshift stages for freak shows and masques were regular additions to the scene.

1

CARLO SCARPA

Carlo Scarpa (1906–78), the most celebrated Venetian architect of recent times, is revered by other architects above all for his exquisitely sensuous use of materials, and for the great sensitivity with which he modified the space of pre-existing buildings. One of his finest small-scale creations is the **Olivetti showroom**, at no. 101 on the Piazza, which has recently been restored and is now open to the public (Tues–Sun: April–Oct 11am–6.30pm; Nov–March 11am–4.30pm; €5). Other examples of Scarpa's work in Venice include the Central Pavilion and Venezuela Pavilion in the Biennale grounds, and the Palazzo Querini-Stampalia. His most impressive creations, however, are on the mainland, at the Castelvecchio in Verona, the Canova museum at Possagno and the Tomba Brion at San Vito d'Altivole – all of them covered in this guide.

By the eighteenth century the Piazza might have become a touch more decorous, but it was certainly no quieter. One English visitor characterized the throng as "a mixed multitude of Jews, Turks, and Christians; lawyers, knaves, and pick-pockets; mountebanks, old women, and physicians; women of quality, with masks; strumpets barefaced…a jumble of senators, citizens, gondoliers, and people of every character and condition". Jugglers, puppeteers, sweet-sellers, fortune-tellers and a host of other stallholders seem to have been almost perennial features of the landscape, while Venetian high society passed much of the day in one or other of the Piazza's dozen **coffee shops** – Europe's first *bottega del caffè* opened here in 1683. During the Austrian occupation of 1814–66 the coffee houses were drawn into the social warfare between the city's two hostile camps. Establishments used by the occupying troops were shunned by all patriotic Venetians – *Quadri* became an Austrian coffee house, whereas *Florian* remained Venetian.

The Piazza remains a pivot of social life in Venice. Contrary to first appearances, the tables of *Florian* and *Quadri* – the only eighteenth-century survivors – or at the equally high-toned *Lavena*, the favourite haunt of Richard Wagner, are not exclusively the preserve of tourists. Wander through at midday and there'll be clusters of Venetians taking the air and chatting away their lunch-hour; the evening *passeggiata* often involves a circuit of the Piazza; and even at midnight you'll almost certainly see a few groups rounding off the day with a night-time stroll across the flagstones.

The Basilica di San Marco

Piazza San Marco · Open to tourists Mon–Sat 9.30am–4.45pm, Sun 2–5pm; Loggia del Cavalli also open on Sun morning · Main part of the church is free, but fees totalling €10.50 are charged for certain sections

San Marco is the most exotic of Europe's cathedrals, and it has always provoked strong reactions. To Herman Melville it was beautiful and insubstantial – as though "the Grand Turk had pitched his pavilion here for a summer's day"; Mark Twain adored it for its "entrancing, tranquilizing, soul-satisfying ugliness"; Herbert Spencer found it "a fine sample of barbaric architecture"; and to John Ruskin it was the most gorgeous of holy places, a "treasure-heap…a confusion of delight". The **Basilica di San Marco** is certainly confusing, increasingly so as you come nearer and the details emerge, but some knowledge of the building's background helps bring a little order out of the chaos.

The history of the Basilica

All over Venice you see images of the lion of St Mark holding a book on which is carved the text "Pax tibi, Marce evangelista meus. Hic requiescet corpus tuum" (Peace be with you Mark, my Evangelist. Here shall your body rest). These supposedly were the words with which Mark was greeted by an angel who appeared to him on the night he took shelter in the lagoon on his way back to Rome. This **legend of St Mark's**

1

annunciation seems to have been invented in the thirteenth century, partly as a means of overcoming the discrepancy between the Venetians' notion of their spiritual pedigree – as successors of the Roman Empire, and the first state to be founded as a Christian community – and the inglorious fact that the settlement of the lagoon islands had begun as a scramble to get out of the way of Attila the Hun. It also provided back-dated justification for what had happened in **828**, when a pair of merchants called Buono Tribuno da Malamocco and Rustico da Torcello had **stolen the body of St Mark** from its tomb in Alexandria and, having smuggled the corpse past the Muslim guards by hiding it in a consignment of pork (or so the story goes), brought it back to Venice and presented it to the doge.

As soon as the holy remains arrived in Venice, work began on a shrine to house them; modelled on Constantinople's Church of the Twelve Apostles, it was consecrated in **832**. In 976 a riot provoked by the tyrannous Doge Pietro Candiano IV reduced the

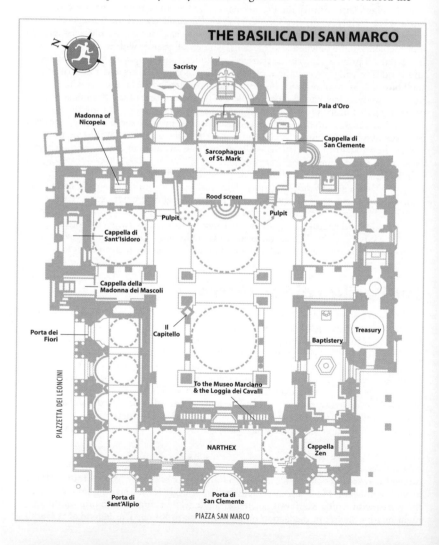

THE BASILICA DI SAN MARCO

Sacristy

Pala d'Oro

Madonna of Nicopeia

Cappella di San Clemente

Sarcophagus of St. Mark

Rood screen

Pulpit   Pulpit

Cappella di Sant'Isidoro

Cappella della Madonna dei Mascoli

Porta dei Fiori

Il Capitello

Treasury

Baptistery

PIAZZETTA DEI LEONCINI

To the Museo Marciano & the Loggia dei Cavalli

NARTHEX

Cappella Zen

Porta di Sant'Alipio

Porta di San Clemente

PIAZZA SAN MARCO

THE PALAZZO PATRIARCALE

The tiny square on the north side of the Basilica is the **Piazzetta Giovanni XXIII**, familiarly known as **dei Leoncini**, after its two eighteenth-century marble lions. Facing San Marco's flank is **San Basso**, a deconsecrated church now used for exhibitions, and at the far end is the **Palazzo Patriarcale**, which was rebuilt in the nineteenth century after it became the home of the Patriarch of Venice, who had previously been based over in San Pietro di Castello. The Palazzo retains the banqueting hall in which the doge used to entertain official guests and, once a year, representatives of the Arsenalotti, the Arsenal workers (it can be seen on a €10 guided tour, every Fri at 3, 4 & 5pm; tickets available at Museo Diocesano); a corridor, now demolished, ran from the hall, through San Marco and into the Palazzo Ducale.

Palazzo Ducale to a pile of ashes and ruined the Basilica too; Candiano was murdered at the church's entrance. A replica was built in its place, to be in turn superseded by a **third church** in 1063–94. It is this third Basilica, embellished in succeeding centuries, that you see now.

The combination of ancient structure and later decorations is what makes San Marco so bewildering, and the picture is made more complicated by the addition of ornaments which were looted from abroad and in several cases have nothing to do with the church. Into both of these categories fall two of the most famous features of the exterior: the porphyry figures of the **Tetrarchs** and the **horses of San Marco**. (To see the real horses you have to go into the church – these are modern replicas.) The reason for the presence of these seemingly profane decorations is simple: the doge was the lieutenant of St Mark, as the pope was the lieutenant of St Peter – therefore anything that glorified Venice was also to the glory of the Evangelist. Every trophy that the doge added to the Basilica was proof of Venice's secular might and so of the spiritual power of St Mark. Conversely, the saint was invoked to sanctify political actions and state rituals – the doge's investiture was consecrated in the church, and military commanders received their commissions at its altar.

As can be imagined, the Venetians' self-image was not conducive to good relations with the Vatican. "They want to appear as Christian before the world," commented Pope Pius II, "but in reality they never think of God and, but for the state, which they regard as a deity, they hold nothing sacred." The Basilica is an emblem of the city's maverick position, for at no time in the existence of the Venetian Republic was San Marco the cathedral of Venice – it was the doge's chapel, and only became the cathedral in 1807, when the French moved the Patriarch of Venice here from San Pietro di Castello.

In effect, the Venetians ran a semi-autonomous branch of the Roman Church: the Patriarch of Venice could convene a synod only with the doge's permission, bishops were nominated by the Senate, priests were appointed by a ballot of the parish and had to be of Venetian birth, and the Inquisition was supervised by the Republic's own, less draconian, doctrinal office. Inevitably, there were direct clashes with the papacy, which sometimes led to serious trouble (see page 129).

The exterior of the Basilica

Shortly after becoming the architectural custodian (*Proto Magister*) of San Marco in 1529, Jacopo Sansovino set about strengthening the building and replacing some of its deteriorating decoration, a procedure that resulted in the removal of around thirty percent of the church's mosaics.

The main facade

On the main facade, the only mosaic to survive this and subsequent restorations is the scene above the **Porta di Sant'Alipio** (far left) – *The Arrival of the Body of St Mark*. Made

1

around 1260, it features the earliest known image of the Basilica. In the lunette below the mosaic are fourteenth-century bas-reliefs of the symbols of the Evangelists; the panels comprising the door's architrave are fifth-century; and the door itself dates from 1300. The next door is from the same period, and the reliefs on the arch are thirteenth-century; the mosaic of *Venice Worshipping St Mark*, however, is an eighteenth-century effort.

The portals

The worst and the best aspects of the facade are to be found above the **central entrance**: the former being the nineteenth-century mosaic of the *Last Judgement*, the latter the

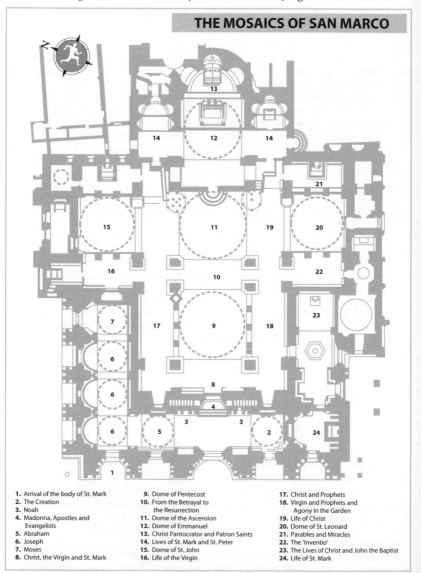

THE MOSAICS OF SAN MARCO

1. Arrival of the body of St. Mark
2. The Creation
3. Noah
4. Madonna, Apostles and Evangelists
5. Abraham
6. Joseph
7. Moses
8. Christ, the Virgin and St. Mark
9. Dome of Pentecost
10. From the Betrayal to the Resurrection
11. Dome of the Ascension
12. Dome of Emmanuel
13. Christ Pantocrator and Patron Saints
14. Lives of St. Mark and St. Peter
15. Dome of St. John
16. Life of the Virgin
17. Christ and Prophets
18. Virgin and Prophets and Agony in the Garden
19. Life of Christ
20. Dome of St. Leonard
21. Parables and Miracles
22. The 'Inventio'
23. The Lives of Christ and John the Baptist
24. Life of St. Mark

Romanesque carvings of the arches. Begun with the innermost arch in the 1220s and completed about a century later, these are among the outstanding sculptural works of their time, but about one visitor in a thousand spares them a glance. The **inner arch** depicts animals, the Earth and the Ocean on its underside, with fighting figures (perhaps intended as the savage antithesis of Venetian civilization) on the outer face; the **middle arch** shows the labours of the months and the signs of the zodiac, with the Virtues and Beatitudes on the outer side; and the **outer arch** depicts the trades of Venice, and Christ and the prophets. The carved panel in the lunette, *The Dream of St Mark*, is also thirteenth-century, but the door – known as the **Porta di San Clemente** – is 700 years older, and is thought to have been a gift from the Byzantine emperor Alexius Comnenus.

The fourth portal follows closely the model of the second; the mosaic of the fifth is similarly an eighteenth-century job, but the marble decoration is a mixture of eleventh- to thirteenth-century carvings, except for the architrave panel of *Christ Blessing*, a remnant of the second Basilica, built after the 976 fire.

The carvings

Of the six marble panels between the entrance arches, only the Roman bas-relief of *Hercules and the Erymanthean Boar* isn't a twelfth- or thirteenth-century piece. The terrace running across the facade above them was the spot from which the doge and his guests watched the festivities in the Piazza; the mosaics on this level all date from the early seventeenth century. The roof-line's encrustation of Gothic pinnacles, kiosks, figures and ornamental motifs was begun in 1385 under the direction of the **Dalle Masegne** family, the leading sculptors in Venice during that period, and was continued through the early part of the following century by various Tuscan and Lombard artists, of whom **Niccolò Lamberti** and his son **Pietro** were the most proficient.

The north facade

In the 1860s and 1870s an extensive and controversial **restoration** of the Basilica was begun, a scheme which was abandoned after an international protest campaign, supported by Ruskin. The **north and south facades**, though, were altered irrevocably by the restorers, who replaced the old polychromatic marble panels with badly fitted sheets of grey stone, creating an effect described by an English stonemason in 1880 as resembling "a dirty lime wash on a white plastered wall".

The **north side** of San Marco, the last to be completed (in the first half of the thirteenth century), is studded with panels from a variety of sources – they include a seventh- or eighth-century relief showing the Apostles as twelve lambs, and a tenth-century piece illustrating Alexander the Great's mythical attempt to reach heaven by harnessing a pair of griffons to his chariot. The entrance on this side, the **Porta dei Fiori**, is thirteenth-century, and most of the sculpture on the upper part is by the **Lambertis**. The tomb of **Daniele Manin** (see page 71) is a bit further on.

The south facade

Jutting out between the **south facade** and the entrance to the Palazzo Ducale is the wall of the treasury, thought by some to be a remnant of the **first palace of the doges** and the chamber in which the body of St Mark was first placed after its arrival in Venice. The screen fragments (*plutei*) set into the walls date from the ninth to the eleventh centuries.

Sometimes the heads of freshly dispatched villains were mounted on the **Pietra del Bando**, the stump of porphyry against the corner of the Basilica; a more benign service was done on the day the Campanile collapsed, when it stopped the avalanche of bricks from hitting the church. Its routine use was as one of the two stones from which the laws of the Republic were proclaimed (the other is at the Rialto). The stone was brought back from Acre in 1258, following Venice's victory over the Genoese there; the two square pillars near to it – Syrian works dating from the fifth century – were filched from

1

Constantinople's church of St Polyeuktos after the Fourth Crusade. High on the Basilica's facade, above the two pillars, a thirteenth-century mosaic of the Madonna is flanked by two lanterns that are kept perpetually lit, in observance of the vow of a mariner who was led to safety across the stormy waters of the lagoon by a light burning on the Piazzetta.

A number of tales centre on the group of porphyry figures set into the angle of the treasury. Thomas Coryat tells a version in which four Albanian brothers plotted against each other for possession of the cargo their ship was carrying, and ended up poisoning each other. But the most popular version turns them into a gang of Saracens who raided the treasury and then contrived to murder each other in a squabble over the spoils – hence they're often nicknamed "The Moors". More properly they're known as the **Tetrarchs**, as in all likelihood they depict Diocletian and the three colleagues with whom he ruled the unravelling Roman Empire – peculiar adornments for a church, bearing in mind Diocletian's notoriety as a persecutor of Christians. What's certain is that, like so much of the Basilica's stonework, they were taken from Constantinople.

The narthex

From the Piazza you pass into a vestibule called the **narthex**, which once, before the partitioning of the baptistery and the Cappella Zen, bracketed the entire west end of the church. The intricately patterned stonework of the narthex **floor** is mostly eleventh- and twelfth-century, and one fragment of it is especially significant: the small white lozenge set into the floor in front of the main entrance is said to mark the spot on which Emperor Frederick Barbarossa knelt before Pope Alexander III on August 23, 1177. Prior to this, the empire and the papacy had been at each other's throats, and this symbolic reconciliation in the portal of San Marco clinched one of Venice's greatest diplomatic triumphs.

The narthex mosaics

Most of the **mosaics** on the domes and arches constitute a series of **Old Testament scenes** which complements the New Testament iconography in the main body of the church. Predominantly thirteenth-century, the mosaics were begun in the dome on the far right, with scenes from Genesis (c.1230 but much restored, as indicated by the inset red lines), and executed in a continuous series right round the narthex. The Genesis dome is followed by: **first arch** – *Noah and the Flood* (note the preferential treatment handed out to the lion); in the **bay in front of the main door** – double tier of niches containing the **oldest mosaics in San Marco**, a group comprising *The Madonna with Apostles and Evangelists* (c.1065); **second arch** – end of *Life of Noah*, and the *Tower of Babel*; **second dome** – *Story of Abraham* and four tondi of *Prophets*; **third arch** – *Sts Alipio and Simon Stylites* and tondo of *Justice*; **third, fourth and fifth domes** – *Story of Joseph*; **sixth dome** – *Story of Moses*.

The narthex tombs

Three doges and one dogaressa have **tombs** in the narthex. That of **Vitale Falier**, the doge who consecrated the Basilica in 1094, two years before his death, is the **oldest funerary monument in Venice** – it's at the base of the first arch. The others are of Felicità, wife of Doge Vitale Michiel I (1101; second arch), Doge Bartolomeo Gradenigo (1342; northwest corner of narthex, beyond third dome) and Doge Marin Morosini (1253; under fourth dome). Two other doges besides these are buried in the narthex, but nobody has a clue where.

The Museo Marciano and Loggia dei Cavalli

Daily 9.45am–4.45pm • €5

On the right of the main door from the narthex into the body of the church (made in 1113–18) is a steep staircase up to the **Museo Marciano** and the **Loggia dei Cavalli**. The

1

Loggia offers a wonderful view of the Piazza, the Gothic carvings of the facade and the ceiling mosaics inside, but the reason most people haul themselves up the steps is to see the famed **horses of San Marco**.

Thieved from the hippodrome of Constantinople in 1204, the horses spent a few years in front of the Arsenale before being installed on the terrace of the Basilica. So close did the association become between them and the people who had stolen them, that the Genoese in 1378 didn't boast that they would tame the lion of St Mark, but rather that they would "bridle those unbridled horses". Made of bronze, they are almost certainly Roman works of the second century, and are the only *quadriga* (group of four horses harnessed to a chariot) to have survived from the classical world. They were cast in two parts, the junction being masked by their collars; medallions used to hang round their necks, but they had gone missing by the time the horses returned to Venice in 1815 after an eighteen-year sojourn on the Champs Élysées. The marks on the horses' skins are not the result of mistreatment – it's thought that the scratches and the partial gilding were added at the time of their creation in order to catch the sun.

The small **Museo Marciano** is a miscellany of mosaic fragments, manuscripts, vestments and so forth from the church. The most interesting exhibits are the wooden cover for the Pala d'Oro, painted in 1345 by **Paolo Veneziano** and his sons, and the cycle of ten tapestries of *The Life of Christ* made around 1420 to designs by **Nicolò di Pietro** – but as likely as not they'll be under lock and key.

The interior of the Basilica

With its undulating floor of patterned marble, its plates of eastern stone on the lower walls, and its 4000 square metres of mosaic covering every other inch of wall and vaulting, the golden **interior** of San Marco achieves a hypnotic effect. There's too much to take in at one go, and the shifting light reveals some parts and hides others as the day progresses, so you should try to call in for at least half an hour at the beginning and end of a couple of days. On most days the electric lights inside the Basilica are turned on for an hour from 11.30am (2pm on Sun) – the lighting isn't as dramatic as full sunlight, but it does make every part of the mosaics visible. Be warned that a system of barriers is used to channel visitors in one direction round the interior of the Basilica, that there is nowhere to sit down inside the church, and that at peak times – which is almost the entire day between May and September – the congestion makes it impossible to stop for a decent look at anything.

The mosaics

The majority of the **mosaics** were in position by the middle of the thirteenth century, but scenes were added right down to the eighteenth century. An adequate guide to them would take volumes: the following account is only a key to the highlights. The mosaics in the nave, transepts and presbytery are dealt with first; the mosaics in the chapels come into the entries on those chapels. The complex shape of the Basilica makes it most convenient to locate the various features by points of the compass, with the high altar marking the east.

West wall and dome

On the **west wall**, **above the door** – *Christ between the Virgin and St Mark* (thirteenth-century, restored). **West dome** – *Pentecost* (early twelfth-century); the paired figures between the windows represent the diverse nations in whose languages the Apostles spread the Word after Pentecost. **Arch between west and central domes** – *Betrayal of Christ, Crucifixion, Marys at the Tomb, Descent into Limbo, Incredulity of Thomas* (all late twelfth-century except the *Marys*, which is a fifteenth-century copy); these are among the most inventive of all the ancient mosaics, both in terms of their richness of colour and their presentation of the intense drama of the events.

1

Central dome

The **central dome**, a dynamic composition of concentric circles, depicts the *Ascension, Virgin with Angels and Apostles, Virtues and Beatitudes, Evangelists, Four Allegories of the Holy Rivers* (late twelfth-century except *St Mark* and *St Matthew*, which are mid-nineteenth-century); the four allegorical figures shown watering the earth are almost certainly a coded reference to the Christian destiny of the city built on water.

East dome and apse

East dome (the *Dome of Emanuel*) – *Religion of Christ Foretold by the Prophets* (early to mid-twelfth-century; tondo of Christ restored c.1500). A *Christ Pantocrator* (1506, based on twelfth-century figure) blesses the congregation from the position in the **apse** traditionally occupied by such figures in Byzantine churches; between the windows below stand the *Four Patron Saints of Venice*, created around 1100 and thus among the earliest works in San Marco. **Arches above north and south singing galleries** (ie linking chancel to side chapels) – *Acts from the Lives of St Peter and St Mark* (early twelfth-century, altered in the nineteenth century); this sequence, mingled with *Scenes from the Life of St Clement*, is continued on the end walls, but is obscured by the organs.

North transept and aisle

North transept: dome – *Acts of St John the Evangelist* (early to mid-twelfth-century); **arch to west of dome** (continued on upper part of adjacent wall) – *Life of the Virgin, Life of the Infant Christ* (late twelfth- to early thirteenth-century); **arch at north end of transept** (above Cappella di Sant'Isidoro) – *Miracles of Christ* (late twelfth- to early thirteenth-century). On **wall of north aisle** – five mosaic tablets of *Christ with the Prophets Hosea, Joel, Micah and Jeremiah* (c.1210–30). This series is continued on the **wall of the south aisle** with figures of *The Virgin, Isaiah, David, Solomon* and *Ezekiel*; above these five is the large and complex *Agony in the Garden* (early thirteenth-century); Mark's Gospel tells us that Christ fell on the ground in the Garden of Gethsemane, Matthew describes him falling on his face, and Luke writes that he simply knelt down – the mosaic thus shows Christ in three different positions. On the wall above and on the arch overhead are *Scenes from the Lives of the Apostles* (late twelfth- to early thirteenth-century).

South transept and aisle

South transept: dome (the *Dome of St Leonard*) – *Sts Nicholas, Clement, Blaise and Leonard* (early thirteenth-century), with *St Dorothea* (thirteenth-century), *St Erasma* (fifteenth-century), *St Euphemia* (fifteenth-century) and *St Thecla* (1512) in the **spandrels**. The formality of the mosaics in the **arch between dome and nave** – *Scenes from the Life of Christ* (early twelfth-century) – makes a striking contrast with the slightly later scenes on the church's central arch; the depiction of Christ's temptation is especially beautiful, showing the protagonists suspended in a field of pure gold. **Arch above Altar of the Sacrament** – *Parables and Miracles of Christ* (late twelfth- or early thirteenth-century); **arch in front of Gothic window** – *Sts Anthony Abbot, Bernardino of Siena, Vincent Ferrer and Paul the Hermit* (1458); **west wall of transept** – the *Rediscovery of the Body of St Mark* (second half of thirteenth-century).

This last picture refers to a miraculous incident known as the *Inventio* (or "Rediscovery"). In 1094 the body of St Mark, having been so well hidden during the rebuilding of the Basilica in 1063 that nobody could find it again, interrupted the service of consecration by breaking through the pillar in which it had been buried. The actual pillar is to your right as you enter the sanctuary, and the very place at which the Evangelist's arm appeared is marked by a marble and mosaic panel.

1

The sanctuary
Same hours as the Basilica • €2.50

Steps lead from the south transept up to the **sanctuary**, via the **Cappella di San Clemente**, where most of the sculpture is by the **Dalle Masegne** family. On the fronts of the singing galleries next to the rood screen are eight **bronze panels** of *Scenes from the Life of St Mark* by **Sansovino** (1537), who also executed the figures of *The Evangelists* on the balustrade of the high altar. The other four figures, *The Doctors of the Church*, are seventeenth-century pieces.

Officially the remains of St Mark lie in the sarcophagus underneath the altar, but it's quite likely that the body was actually destroyed in the fire of 976. The altar **baldachin** is supported by four creamy **alabaster columns** carved with mostly indecipherable scenes from the lives of Christ and His Mother; the date of the columns is a matter of argument – estimates fluctuate between the fifth and the thirteenth centuries.

The Pala d'Oro

Behind the altar, and usually enveloped by a scrum, is the most precious of San Marco's treasures, the astonishing **Pala d'Oro** – the "golden altar screen". Commissioned in 976 in Constantinople, the *Pala* was enlarged, enriched and rearranged by Byzantine goldsmiths in 1105, then by Venetians in 1209 to incorporate some of the less cumbersome loot from the Fourth Crusade, and again (finally) in 1345. The completed screen, teeming with jewels and minuscule figures, holds 83 enamel plaques, 74 enamelled roundels, 38 chiselled figures, 15 rubies, 300 sapphires, 300 emeralds, 400 garnets, 1300 pearls and a couple of hundred other stones.

In the top section the Archangel Michael is surrounded by medallions of saints, with the *Entry into Jerusalem, Crucifixion, Resurrection, Ascension, Pentecost* and *Death of the Virgin* to the sides. Below, *Christ Pantocrator* is enclosed by the four Evangelists, to the side of whom are ranked a host of angels, prophets and saints; these ranks are framed on three sides by scenes from the life of Christ (the horizontal band) and the life of Mark (the vertical bands). The outer frame of the entire *Pala d'Oro* is adorned with small circular enamels, some of which (in the lower part of the frame) represent hunting scenes; most of these enamels survive from the first *Pala* and are thus its oldest components.

Before leaving the sanctuary, take a look at **Sansovino**'s door to the sacristy (invariably shut) – it incorporates portraits of Titian (top left) and Sansovino himself (under Titian's head).

The treasury
Same hours as the Basilica • €3

Tucked into the corner of the south transept is the door of the **treasury**, installed in a thick-walled chamber which is perhaps a vestige of the first Palazzo Ducale. This dazzling warehouse of chalices, icons, reliquaries, candelabra and other ecclesiastical appurtenances is an unsurpassed collection of Byzantine work in silver, gold and semiprecious stones. Particularly splendid are a twelfth-century Byzantine incense burner in the shape of a domed church, and a gilded silver Gospel cover from Aquileia, also made in the twelfth century.

Much of the treasury's stock owes its presence here to the great Constantinople robbery of 1204, and there'd be a lot more of the same on display if the French occupation force of 1797 hadn't given Venice a taste of its own medicine by helping itself to a few cartloads. To be fair to the Venetians, they at least gave the stuff a good home – the French melted down their haul, to produce a yield of 55 gold and silver ingots.

The sanctuary attached to the treasury, in which are stored more than a hundred reliquaries, is hardly ever open to the public.

1

The baptistery

The **baptistery**, off the south aisle (nearly always reserved for prayer), was altered to its present form by **Doge Andrea Dandolo** (d.1354), whose tomb (facing the door) was Ruskin's favourite monumental sculpture in the city. It was Dandolo who ordered the creation of the baptistery **mosaics** of *Scenes from the Lives of Christ and John the Baptist*, works in which the formality of Byzantine art is blended with the anecdotal observation of the Gothic. "The most beautiful symbolic design of the Baptist's death that I know in Italy," wrote Ruskin. The tomb of Dandolo's predecessor, Doge Giovanni Soranzo (d.1328), is on the right as you come in, and **Jacopo Sansovino** – who designed the enormous font – lies beneath a slab at the eastern end. The huge granite block at the altar is said to have been brought back from Tyre in 1126; more imaginatively, it's also claimed as the stone from which Christ delivered the Sermon on the Mount.

The Cappella Zen

In the **Cappella Zen** (nearly always shut, and reserved for prayer when open), adjoining the baptistery, there's an object of similar mythical potency – a bas-relief of the Virgin that is supposed to have been carved from the rock from which Moses struck water. As its rich decoration indicates, the portal from the chapel into the narthex used to be the entrance from the Piazzetta; this doorway was closed in 1504, when work began on the tomb of Cardinal Giambattista Zen, whose estate was left to the city on condition that he was buried within San Marco. The two **mosaic angels** alongside the Virgin on top of the doorway are twelfth-century; the mosaics below are early fourteenth-century and the small statues between them date from the thirteenth. The mosaics on the **vault** show *Scenes from the Life of St Mark* (late thirteenth-century, but restored). The Cappella Zen is sometimes known as the Chapel of the Madonna of the Shoe, taking its name from the gold shoe that adorns the *Virgin and Child* by **Antonio Lombardo** (1506) on the high altar.

The pavement and rood screen

Back in the main body of the Basilica, make sure you give the **pavement** a good look – laid out in the twelfth and thirteenth centuries, it's a constantly intriguing patchwork of abstract shapes and religious symbols. Of the church's other marvels, the next three paragraphs are but a partial list.

The **rood screen** is surmounted by a silver and bronze **cross** (1394) and marble figures of *The Virgin, St Mark and the Apostles* (also 1394) by **Jacobello and Pietro Paolo Dalle Masegne**. The **pulpits** on each side of the screen were assembled in the early fourteenth century from assorted panels, some of them taken from Constantinople; the new doge was presented to the people of Venice from the right-hand one.

The north transept chapels

Venice's most revered religious image is the tenth-century **Icon of the Madonna of Nicopeia**, in the chapel on the east side of the **north transept**; until 1204 it was one of the most revered in Constantinople, where it used to be ceremonially carried at the head of the emperor's army. At the north end of this transept is the **Cappella di Sant'Isidoro**: the mosaics, which have scarcely been touched since their creation in the mid-fourteenth century, depict scenes from the life of the saint, whose remains were grabbed from Chios by Doge Domenico Michiel in 1125. A beautiful mid-fifteenth-century mosaic cycle of *Scenes from the Life of the Virgin*, one of the earliest Renaissance works in Venice, is to be seen in the adjacent **Cappella della Madonna dei Mascoli**, which takes its name from the male confraternity that took it over in the seventeenth century. (The Sant'Isidoro chapel is nearly always closed or reserved for prayer, and you may find the entire north transept roped off to prevent incursions from sightseers.)

1

Il Capitello and the galleries

Against the west face of the end pillar on the north side of the nave stands **Il Capitello**, a tiny chapel fabricated from a variety of rare marbles to house the *Crucifix* on the altar; the painting arrived in Venice the year after the Nicopeia icon (and came from the same source), and in 1290 achieved its exalted status by spouting blood after an assault on it. Finally, the **galleries** merit a perusal from below (visitors are very rarely allowed to walk round them): the parapets facing the aisle consist of reliefs dating from between the sixth and the eleventh centuries, some of them Venetian, some Byzantine. They weren't designed as catwalks, as they now appear: this is what was left when the women's galleries over the aisles were demolished in the late twelfth century to let more light into the building, after some windows had been bricked over to make more surfaces for mosaics. Apart from this, no major structural change has been made to the interior of San Marco since its consecration in 1094.

The Palazzo Ducale

Piazza San Marco • Daily: April–Oct 8.30am–7pm; Nov–March 8.30am–5.30pm • Entrance with Museum Pass or I Musei di Piazza San Marco card • Ⓦ palazzoducale.visitmuve.it

Architecturally, the **Palazzo Ducale** is a unique mixture: the style of its exterior, with its geometrically patterned stonework and continuous tracery walls, can only be called Islamicized Gothic, whereas the courtyards and much of the interior are based on Classical forms – a blending of influences that led Ruskin to declare it "the central building of the world". Unquestionably, it is the finest secular building of its era in Europe, and the central building of Venice. The Palazzo Ducale was far more than the residence of the doge – it was the home of all of Venice's governing councils, its law courts, a sizeable number of its civil servants and even its prisons. All power in the Venetian Republic and its domains was controlled within this one building.

The exterior

Like San Marco, the Palazzo Ducale has been rebuilt many times. The original fortress, founded at the start of the ninth century, was razed by the fire of 976, and fire destroyed much of its replacement in 1106. The third palace was habitable within ten years, and was extended and altered frequently over the next couple of centuries. But it was with the construction of a new hall, parallel to the waterfront, for the Maggior Consiglio, that the Palazzo began to take on its present shape. Work began in 1340, and the hall was inaugurated in 1419; then, three years later, it was decided to knock down the dilapidated remnant of the old Palazzo Ducale and extend the new building along the Piazzetta, adhering to the same style. One feature of the exterior gives away the fact that its apparent unity is the product of two distinct phases of building: if you look at the Piazzetta side, you'll notice that the seventh column is fatter than the rest and has a tondo of *Justice* above it – that's where the two stages meet. (Incidentally, folklore has it that the two reddish columns on the upper arcade on this side were crimsoned by the blood of traitors, whose tortured corpses were hung here for public edification; certainly this is the spot where Filippo Calendario, one of the Palazzo Ducale's architects, was quartered for abetting the conspiracy of Marin Falier (see page 132).

A huge restoration project in the 1870s entailed the replacement or repair of every external column of the palace and the substitution of copies for many of the fourteenth- and fifteenth-century **capitals** of the lower portico. (Many of the originals have been restored, and are on display in the Palazzo's Museo dell'Opera.) In the eyes of John Ruskin, these carvings exemplified the transition from the purity of the Gothic (see the heads of children on the fourth capital from the *Drunkenness of Noah*) to the

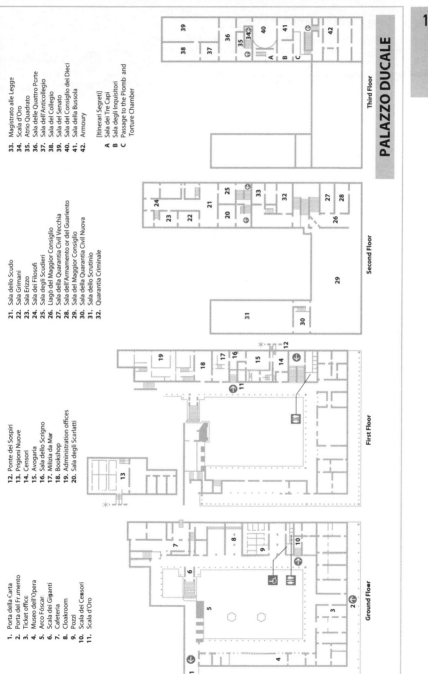

PALAZZO DUCALE

1. Porta della Carta
2. Porta del Frumento
3. Ticket office
4. Museo dell'Opera
5. Arco Foscar
6. Scala dei Giganti
7. Cafeteria
8. Pozzi
9. Scala dei Censori
10. Scala dei Censori
11. Scala d'Oro

12. Ponte dei Sospiri
13. Prigioni Nuove
14. Censori
15. Avogaria
16. Sala dello Scrigno
17. Milizia da Mar
18. Bookshop
19. Administration offices
20. Sala degli Scarlatti

21. Sala dello Scudo
22. Sala Grimani
23. Sala Erizzo
24. Sala dei Filosofi
25. Sala degli Scudieri
26. Liago del Maggior Consiglio
27. Sala della Quarantia Civil Vecchia
28. Sala dell'Armamento o del Guariento
29. Sala del Maggior Consiglio
30. Sala della Quarantia Civil Nuova
31. Sala dello Scrutinio
32. Quarantia Criminale

33. Magistrato alle Legge
34. Scala d'Oro
35. Atrio Quadrato
36. Sala delle Quattro Porte
37. Sala dell'Anticollegio
38. Sala del Collegio
39. Sala del Senato
40. Sala del Consiglio dei Dieci
41. Sala della Bussola
42. Armoury

[Itinerari Segreti]
A Sala dei Tre Capi
B Sala degli Inquisitori
C Passage to the Piomb and Torture Chamber

Ground Floor

First Floor

Second Floor

Third Floor

1

THE GOVERNMENT OF VENICE

Virtually from the beginning, the **government of Venice** was dominated by the merchant class, despite the existence, in the early years, of nominally democratic assemblies in which the general male populace was represented. The principal governing council, the **Maggior Consiglio**, was established in 1172 by Doge Vitale Michiel II, and from the start was in effect a self-electing assembly of the upper class. In 1297 the exclusion of the public was institutionalized by an act known as the **Serrata del Maggior Consiglio** (Locking of the Great Council): any man not belonging to one of the patrician families on the list compiled for the Serrata was ineligible to participate in the running of the city. After a while, this list was succeeded by a register of patrician births and marriages called the **Libro d'Oro**, upon which every patrician's claim to membership of the elite was based.

In times of economic emergency the Maggior Consiglio was "unlocked" and new families were enrolled in the Libro d'Oro in return for huge cash payments: after the plague of 1630, for example, the already dwindling ranks of the patriciate were so severely depleted that between 1647 and 1718 some 127 families were allowed to buy their way in. Nonetheless, by the second decade of the fourteenth century the constitution of Venice had reached a form that was to endure until the coming of Napoleon; its civil and criminal code, defined in the early thirteenth century, was equally resistant to change. Some 98 percent of the population were shut out from active politics. It was the ultimate paternalistic system, in which the city's governors were also its businessmen and chief employers.

What made the political system stable was its web of counterbalancing councils and committees, and its exclusion of any youthful element. Most patricians entered the Maggior Consiglio at 25 (although a group of younger high-fliers was admitted annually) and could not expect a middle-ranking post before 45; from the middle ranks to the top was another long haul – the average age of the doge from 1400 to 1600 was 72. As promotion was dependent upon a network of supporters in the elderly and conservative upper ranks, a situation was created in which, as the diarist Marin Sanudo wrote in the sixteenth century, "Anyone who wishes to dissent must be mad."

However, although Venice's domestic history can seem placid to the point of tedium, backstage politics were as sordid a business as anywhere else. Cabals of the so-called **Case Grandi** (Great Houses) for centuries had a stranglehold on most influential positions, corruption in various guises was endemic, and voting conspiracies were constantly being hatched and thwarted. Even within the Case Grandi there were struggles for influence, the battle lines being drawn between the **Longhi**, the families who claimed descent from the city's founders, and the **Curti**, whose genealogical tables ran a bit short. An outside observer, exposed to the machinations of Venice's rulers, noted "They kill not with blood but with ballots."

THE DOGE

Regarding the **doge**, it's a common misunderstanding that he was a mere figurehead, confined to his palace under a sort of luxurious house arrest. It's true that there were numerous restrictions on his activities – all his letters were read by censors, for example, and he couldn't receive foreign delegations alone – but these were steps taken to reduce the possibility that an ambitious leader might exploit his office, and they didn't always succeed. Whereas his colleagues were elected for terms as brief as a month, the doge was **elected for life** and sat on all the major councils of state, which at the very least made him extremely influential in the formation of policy. The dogeship was the monopoly of old men not solely because of the celebrated Venetian respect for the wisdom of the elderly, but also because a man in his seventies would have fewer opportunities to abuse the unrivalled powers of the dogeship. Thus one can understand why, in 1618, a certain Agostino Nani, at 63 the youngest candidate for the dogeship, feigned a life-threatening decrepitude to enhance his chances of getting the job. A neat summary of the doge's position was made by **Girolamo Priuli** – "It is true that if a doge does anything against the Republic, he won't be tolerated; but in everything else, even in minor matters, he does as he pleases."

vulgar decadence of the Renaissance (compare the fifteenth-century children, second from the Porta della Carta – "capable of becoming nothing but perfumed coxcombs").

Be sure to take a look at the late fourteenth- to early fifteenth-century **corner sculptures**: by the Ponte della Paglia – *Archangel Raphael* and *Drunkenness of Noah*;

Piazzetta corner – *Archangel Michael* and *Adam and Eve*; Basilica corner – *Archangel Gabriel* and *Judgement of Solomon*. Some see these pieces as a cogent sequence, illustrating justice (Solomon) and the counterbalancing qualities of severity (expulsion of Adam and Eve) and compassion (Noah's sons) needed for its administration. The extravagant **balconied window** on the lagoon side is another contribution from the **Dalle Masegne** family (1404); the corresponding window on the Piazzetta facade is a mid-sixteenth-century imitation.

The Porta della Carta

The principal entrance to the Palazzo was the **Porta della Carta**, the name of which derives perhaps from the archives kept nearby, or from the clerks' stalls around it. Commissioned in 1438 by **Doge Francesco Fóscari** from **Bartolomeo and Giovanni Bon**, this is one of the most ornate Gothic works in the city. Many of its carvings used to be painted and gilded, and the lack of colour isn't the only respect in which the Porta della Carta differs nowadays from its original state – the figures of Fóscari and his attendant lion are nineteenth-century replicas. The fifteenth-century pieces were smashed to bits in 1797 by the head of the stonemasons' guild, who offered to do Napoleon a favour by removing from his sight all images of the lion of St Mark. Luckily, his iconoclastic career seems to have ended soon after it began. The solitary remnant of the original is on display inside the Palazzo Ducale.

The passageway into the Palazzo ends under the **Arco Fóscari**, which you can see only after getting your ticket, as tourists are directed into the building through the Porta del Frumento, under the arcades on the lagoon side.

The interior

Several sections of the Palazzo Ducale can be dealt with fairly briskly. The building is clad with paintings by the hectare, but a lot of them are wearying exercises in civic self-aggrandizement (no city in Italy can match Venice for narcissism), and if you take away the paintings, there's not much left to some of the rooms. But it would be perverse not to visit so integral a part of the city, and there are parts you will not want to rush. For this reason a visit needs to be timed carefully. In high season scores of tour groups are being propelled round the place for much of the day, so if you want a stress-free visit, buy your ticket within half an hour of opening, or a couple of hours before closing.

A word of warning: as with San Marco, restoration work is always taking place somewhere in the Palazzo Ducale, and there is rarely any indication before you go in as to how much of the building is under wraps, so prepare to be disappointed – you are almost certain to come across scaffolding and barriers at some point.

The courtyard, Museo dell'Opera and Arco Fóscari

From the ticket office you're directed into the **Museo dell'Opera**, where the originals of more than forty of the capitals from the lower and upper loggias are displayed and explicated. In the last room look out for the stone head of Doge Francesco Fóscari, the only item salvaged from the great sculpture on the Porta della Carta.

On the far side of the courtyard, opposite the entrance, stands the **Arco Fóscari**, which like the Porta della Carta was commissioned from the Bons by Doge Fóscari, but it was finished a few years after his death by **Antonio Rizzo** and **Antonio Bregno**. Rizzo's *Adam* and *Eve* (c.1470), the best of the Arco Fóscari sculptures, have been replaced by copies – the originals, along with the original of Bandini's statue of Francesco Maria I della Rovere (on the courtyard side), are on show inside. In 1483 yet another fire demolished most of the wing in front of you (the east), and led to more work for Rizzo – he designed the enormous staircase called the **Scala dei Giganti**, and much of the new wing. Underneath the lion at the top of the staircase is the spot where the new doge was crowned with the jewel-encrusted cap called the *zogia*; the ungainly figures

1

of *Neptune* and *Mars* were sculpted in 1566 by **Sansovino**. The original statue of St Theodore and his dragon, from the Piazzetta, lurks on the far side of the staircase.

After the 1483 fire reconstruction of the east wing continued under **Pietro Lombardo**, **Spavento** and **Scarpagnino** (who created the **Senators' Courtyard** to the left of the staircase), and finally (c.1600) **Bartolomeo Monopola**, who finished the facade overlooking the Rio di Palazzo and completed the main courtyard by extending the arcades along the other two sides.

The Scala d'Oro and the Doge's Apartments

From ground level the traffic is directed up the Scala dei Censori to the upper arcade and thence up Sansovino's gilded **Scala d'Oro**, the main internal staircase of the Palazzo Ducale, with its stuccoes by Vittoria (c.1558). A subsidiary staircase on the right leads to the **Doge's Apartments**, in which the head of the Republic was obliged to live after his election. All the furniture and much of the decoration have been stripped from this floor, but some of the rooms have ornate ceilings and fireplaces, several of which were installed when the Lombardo family were in charge of rebuilding this part of the palace.

The Sala degli Scarlatti

The first room, the **Sala degli Scarlatti**, is one of the finest. Probably named after the scarlet robes of the officers who attended the corpse of the doge as it lay in state in the adjacent Sala dello Scudo (they wore red rather than funereal black, to signify that the death of an individual doge did not diminish the government), it has a fireplace by **Antonio and Tullio Lombardo**, a bas-relief by **Pietro Lombardo** over the door and a gilded ceiling from 1505. Also displayed here is a heavily restored *Madonna and Child with St John*, by Carpaccio.

The Sala dello Scudo

The **Sala dello Scudo**, the largest room of the apartments, is where the doge would receive those to whom he had granted a private audience. The fire of 1483 reduced to ashes the maps that had been painted on the walls, depicting the extent of Venice's domains and the lands visited by the Polo family. Replacements were soon created and were later augmented; the ones you see now date from 1762, and similarly celebrate the explorations of great Venetians and the wide reach of the city's control.

The Sala Grimani and the rest of the apartments

The **Sala Grimani**, which marks the beginning of the doge's private accommodation, now houses four large paintings of the Lion of St Mark, including the most famous such image, the one by Carpaccio, in which the heraldic lion stands on an imaginary wild island in the lagoon, with the Palazzo Ducale behind him. Next door, the **Sala Erizzo** has another vast fireplace and is decorated with gold and scarlet wall hangings of the sort that would once have adorned many of the building's rooms. Beyond here lies a stucco-laden room from which the doge could enter the patriarchal palace (the door remains but the connecting passageway has gone), which in turn connects with the **Sala dei Filosofi**, a corridor-like extension of the Sala dello Scudo. On one side of this long room a doorway opens onto a staircase; above the door, on the stair side, you'll find **Titian**'s *St Christopher*, a fresco in which the artist conflates the Venice cityscape with the mountains of his native Cadore. On the other side of the corridor, the final sequence of rooms contains a picture showing the mayhem of the annual Ponte dei Pugni brawls (see page 93) and a poor Giovanni Bellini (*Dead Christ*), and culminates with the **Sala dei Scudieri**, the room through which the doge's visitors would have entered his apartments.

The Atrio Quadrato and Sala delle Quattro Porte

The Scala d'Oro continues up to the **secondo piano nobile**, ending in the **Atrio Quadrato**, which has a ceiling painting of *Justice* by Tintoretto. This small anteroom opens into the first of the great public spaces, the **Sala delle Quattro Porte**. Before 1574 this room was the meeting place of the Collegio (see below), but in that year a fire gutted this portion of the building, necessitating a major programme of reorganization and decoration. (Three years later an even worse blaze destroyed the hall of the Maggior Consiglio and other rooms around it – this is why the Palazzo Ducale contains so few paintings that predate the 1570s.) After the repairs the Sala delle Quattro Porte was where ambassadors awaited their summons to address the doge and his councillors. **Tintoretto**'s ceiling frescoes, most of which are allegories of the Veneto cities subservient to the Republic, are in a generally dilapidated condition. The painting opposite the entrance is a reasonably accurate record of the show put on to welcome Henry III of France when he arrived in the city a few weeks before the fire of 1574 – by all accounts the young king never quite got over this week of overwhelming Venetian hospitality. The easel painting at the far end of the room – *Venus Receiving the Homage of Neptune* by **Giambattista Tiepolo** – can be seen at closer range when the itinerary doubles back through here.

The Sala dell'Anticollegio

As regards the quality of its decorations, the next room – the **Sala dell'Anticollegio** (the inner waiting room) – is one of the richest in the Palazzo Ducale. It has looked like this only since the early eighteenth century, though – after the 1574 fire it was decked out with tapestries and gilded leather, a Venetian speciality. Four pictures by **Tintoretto** hang on the door walls: *Vulcan's Forge*, *Mercury and the Graces*, *Bacchus and Ariadne* and *Minerva Dismissing Mars* (all c.1578); it almost goes without saying that these pictures were open to a propagandist reading – eg Ariadne – Venice, Bacchus = the Adriatic. Facing the window wall is **Veronese**'s *Rape of Europa* – "The brightest vision that ever descended upon the soul of a painter," sighed Henry James. The ensemble is completed by Jacopo Bassano's *Jacob's Return to Canaan*, and by Paolo Veronese's badly deteriorated ceiling fresco of *Venice Distributing Honours*.

The Sala del Collegio

Thoroughly humbled by now, the emissaries to Venice were ultimately admitted to the **Sala del Collegio**. Presiding over the Senate and deciding the agenda it would discuss, the full Collegio was the cabinet of Venetian politics, and consisted of the doge, six ducal councillors, the three heads of the judiciary, and sixteen *Savi* (senators with special responsibility for maritime, military and governmental affairs). The **Signoria**, Venice's highest executive body, was the inner council of this inner council, comprising the Collegio minus the *Savi*. In Ruskin's opinion, in no other part of the palace could you "enter so deeply into the heart of Venice" as in the Sala del Collegio – his observation referred not to the mechanics of Venetian power, however, but to the luscious cycle of ceiling paintings by **Veronese**.

Outstanding is *Venice Triumphant*, the central panel above the throne. Veronese also produced the picture on the wall over the throne – *Doge Sebastiano Venier Offering Thanks to Christ for the Victory of Lépanto*, in which, as is often the case in Venetian state-sponsored art, the Son of God is obliged to share top billing. Other doges get similarly immodest treatment in the adjoining paintings: *Doge Alvise Mocenigo Adoring Christ*, *Doge Niccolò du Ponte Invoking the Protection of the Virgin*, *The Mystic Marriage of St Catherine, with Doge Francesco Donato* (all by Tintoretto and his workshop) and, over the door to the Anticollegio, *Doge Andrea Gritti before the Virgin* (Tintoretto).

The Sala del Senato

The room next door – the **Sala del Senato** – was where most major policies, both domestic and foreign, were determined. It was also where the ambassadors of Venice delivered their reports on the countries in which they had served. These *relazioni* were essential to the formation of foreign policy, and a Venetian nobleman did his career prospects no harm by turning in a detailed document; few, however, equalled the conscientiousness of the sixteenth-century ambassador to France whose speech to the Senate kept them in their seats for two whole days. Originally comprising just sixty councillors (who were formally invited to take up office by the doge, hence the alternative name Sala dei Pregadi, from *pregati*, meaning "beseeched"), the Senate grew to contain almost three hundred officials under the doge's chairmanship, holding office for one year and elected by the Maggior Consiglio.

A motley collection of late sixteenth-century artists, Tintoretto and his pupils prominent among them, produced the bombastic decoration of the walls and ceiling. Tintoretto's personal touch is most evident in the picture above the throne: *Descent from the Cross, with Doges Pietro Lando and Marcantonio Trevisan*. For sheer shamelessness, however, nothing can match the centrepiece of the ceiling, Tintoretto's *Venice Exalted Among the Gods*. (On rare occasions the doors to the side of the throne are open – they lead to the doge's chapel and its anteroom; only the marble *Virgin and Child* by Sansovino, in the former, is of interest.)

The Sala del Consiglio dei Dieci

After recrossing the Sala delle Quattro Porte you enter the **Sala del Consiglio dei Dieci**, the room in which all matters relating to state security were discussed. The **Council of Ten** was established in 1310 in response to the revolt of disaffected nobles led by Bajamonte Tiepolo – and the secrecy and speed of its deliberations, and the fact that it allowed no defence counsel, soon made it the most feared of the Republic's institutions. Its members held office for one year and their number was supplemented by the doge and the ducal councillors – which meant, confusingly, that the Ten were never fewer than seventeen.

In the sixteenth century the Ten became even stronger, as an indirect result of the War of the League of Cambrai, when places on the Senate were given to an assortment of social climbers in reward for the loans they'd made for the war effort. The men of the *Case Grandi* (see page 52) retaliated by increasing the power of the bodies they could still control – the Collegio and the Ten. Only in the seventeenth century, when the power of the old families was fatally weakened by the sale of places on the Maggior Consiglio, did the Senate revert to being the nucleus of the Venetian state.

Of the paintings here, the finest are a couple of **Veronese** panels on the ceiling, painted at the age of 25 – *Juno Offering Gifts to Venice* and *Old Man in Oriental Costume with Young Woman*. The central panel is a copy of a Veronese original that was packed off to the Louvre by Napoleon's army and has never made it back.

The Sala della Bussola

The unfortunates who were summoned before the Ten had to await their grilling in the next room, the **Sala della Bussola**; in the wall is a *Bocca di Leone* (Lion's Mouth), one of the boxes into which citizens could drop denunciations for the attention of the Ten and other state bodies. Nobody could be convicted without corroborating evidence, and all anonymous accusations were rejected (or at least were technically illegal), but nonetheless the legend spread throughout Europe that one word to the Ten was tantamount to a death sentence. The door in the corner leads to the office of the Three Heads of the Council of Ten, which in turn leads to the State Inquisitors' room, then on to the torture chamber and finally the prisons – a doleful route that can be followed on the *Itinerari Segreti* (see page 58). As for the decoration, the main ceiling panel is again a copy of a Veronese that was stolen by the French.

The armoury

From the landing, steps lead up to the **armoury**, consisting in part of weapons assembled for the defence of the Palazzo Ducale, and in part of specially commissioned pieces and gifts from foreign rulers. Amid the horrifying but sometimes exquisitely

1

GIVING A DOGE A BAD NAME

Marin Falier remains the most celebrated of Venice's errant leaders, but he is far from being alone in the ranks of the disgraced – by the end of the twelfth century about half the doges had been killed, exiled or run out of office. Nor is he the only eminent Venetian to be posthumously vilified in such a manner: for instance, under the arcade of the Palazzo Ducale there's a plaque perpetuating the dishonour of Girolamo Loredan and Giovanni Contarini, exiled for abandoning a fort to the Turks. In the Venetian Republic, where staunch service to the state was regarded as a duty, the backsliders were the ones singled out for special treatment, and the city is almost devoid of public monuments to its great statesmen.

manufactured metalwork you'll find immense two-handed swords, an ancient twenty-barrelled gun, early sixteenth-century firearms that could also be used as swords, crossbows, maces or axes, and two outstanding pieces of armour: a unique sixteenth-century beaked helmet, and a suit of white armour given to Henry IV of France in 1603 (both in room 2). There's also a bust of Marcantonio Bragadin, whose gruesome demise has kept his name alive (see page 137), and one grotesque piece of non-military hardware – a pronged chastity belt.

The Andito del Maggior Consiglio

The **Scala dei Censori** takes you back to the second floor; here you go along the **Liagò** (or **Andito**) **del Maggior Consiglio** (Lobby of the Great Council), past the **Sala della Quarantia Civil Vecchia**, the seat of the civil court, and the **Sala del Guariento**, the old ammunition store, containing the remnants of a fourteenth-century fresco of *Paradise* by Guariento that used to be in Sala del Maggior Consiglio, where it was covered by Tintoretto's massive image of the same subject. The veranda at the end now houses the sculptures by **Rizzo** and Bandini from the Arco Fóscari; allegedly, the Duke of Mantua offered to buy Rizzo's *Eve* for her weight in gold, but for once the Venetians found it within themselves to resist the lure of huge sums of money.

The Sala del Maggior Consiglio

Now comes the stupendous **Sala del Maggior Consiglio**, the assembly hall of all the Venetian patricians eligible to participate in the running of the city. By the mid-sixteenth century 2500 men were entitled to sit here, but frequently as few as half that number were present. This was the forum of the so-called *giovani*, the younger men on the bottom rung, and it was here that the voice of the populace filtered into the system. Technically, the Maggior Consiglio had little direct impact on government as it voted directly only on administrative legislation, and for much of the time the *giovani* kept fairly quiet in order to stay on the right side of the power-brokers. But if the bosses did something that alienated the majority of the underlings, the Maggior Consiglio was able to make things awkward, because the electoral process for nearly all state officials, including the doge, began here. Its last political act was on May 12, 1797, when it put an end to Venice's independence by voting to accept Napoleon's constitution.

The paintings

The fire of December 1577 destroyed the paintings by Bellini, Titian, Carpaccio, Veronese and others that had lined this room; most of the replacements have the sole merit of covering a lot of space. There are, of course, notable exceptions. The immense *Paradiso*, begun by **Tintoretto** at the age of 77 and completed by his son Domenico, is an amazing feat of pictorial organization and a perfect work for its setting; the cast of five hundred figures is arrayed in the ranks ordained by Dante in Canto XXX of his *Paradiso*. Two of the **ceiling panels** are well worth a crick in the neck – *The Apotheosis of Venice*, a late work by Veronese (large oval above tribune), and *Venice Welcoming the Conquered Nations* by Palma il Giovane (large oval at opposite end).

1

THE ITINERARI SEGRETI

If you want to see the rooms in which the day-to-day administration of Venice took place, take the **Itinerari Segreti del Palazzo Ducale**, a fascinating 75-minute guided tour through the warren of offices and passageways that interlocks with the public rooms of the building. (Six tours daily, in English at 9.55am, 10.45am & 11.35am; €20, or €14 with Museum Card; includes admission to the rest of the Palazzo Ducale. Tickets can be booked up to 48hr in advance through Ⓦ visitmuve.it; for visits on the next or same day go in person to the Palazzo Ducale ticket desk.)

The myriad councils and committees of Venice required a vast civil service, which was staffed by men drawn from the social class immediately below the patriciate – the *cittadini originarii*. (To be accepted into this class of full citizens one had to have lived in Venice for 25 years and never have engaged in manual labour.) Roaming through the shadow-palace in which these functionaries carried out their duties, you begin to understand why, for all the Palazzo Ducale's extravagant show of democratic rectitude, the Venetian Republic aroused in many people the sort of dread a police state inspires.

The tour begins with the chambers of the **Chancellery**, the tiny rooms in which all acts of state were drafted and tabulated, then passes through the eighteenth-century Hall of the Chancellery, lined with cabinets for filing state documents. From here it's onward into the belly of the beast, through the judiciary's suites and into a high-ceilinged den where a rope hangs between two tiny wooden cells – the idea being that their occupants, hearing the screams of the suspended victim, would need no further encouragement to talk. Paintings by Veronese and Tintoretto provide a civilizing gloss in the **Sala dei Tre Capi** – for the Heads of the Council of Ten – and the **Sala degli Inquisitori** – for the officers who investigated charges of treason.

After these, you're led up into the roof to see the timber-lined **Piombi**. By the standards of the day they are not too grim, but the climate up here could be unbearable, and there's a typically Venetian touch of refined malevolence – the doors have a superfluity of locks, just so that the noise of turning keys and slamming bolts would impress upon the inmate the finality of his incarceration. A few were not deterred – you're shown the cell from which Casanova escaped in 1775, with the assistance of a fellow prisoner called Father Balbi. (Displaying typical sang-froid, Casanova made his way to the Scala d'Oro, where the doors were unlocked for him by a guard who mistook him for a civil servant, then stopped on the Piazza for a coffee before heading for the border.) Under the rafters there's a museum of Venetian history that deserves more time than is allotted for it, but you do have time to be stunned by the views from the portholes in the roof. And if you wondered, when you were in the Sala del Maggior Consiglio, how that vast ceiling stays up with no visible means of support, all is revealed near the end.

Tintoretto was commissioned to replace the room's **frieze of portraits** of the first 76 doges (the series continues in the Sala dello Scrutinio), but in the event his son (with assistants) did the work. On the Piazzetta side the sequence is interrupted by a painted black veil, marking the place where **Marin Falier** (see page 132) would have been honoured had he not conspired against the state in 1355 and (as the inscription says) been beheaded for his crime. After two years spent in Venice, Byron wrote that Falier's black veil was for him the city's most memorable image.

The Sala della Quarantia Civil Nuova and Sala dello Scrutinio

The door at the far end (often closed) gives access to the **Sala della Quarantia Civil Nuova**, where civil cases involving Venetian citizens outside the city were heard; it retains some rare examples of Venetian gilt leatherwork (downstairs you'll see another room decorated with it), though nothing really grabs the attention. The adjacent **Sala dello Scrutinio** is where votes by the Maggior Consiglio were counted and certain electoral committees met. The system for **electing the doge** was the most complex of these procedures. In a nutshell: 30 men were selected by lot from the Maggior Consiglio; they reduced themselves by lot to 9 members; these 9 elected 40, who reduced themselves to 12, who elected 25, who reduced themselves to 9, who elected

45, who reduced themselves to 11, who elected 41, who finally elected the doge – 25 votes were needed to win. This rigmarole took a minimum of five days, and in the record-breaking 1615 election the last stage alone went to 104 ballots and lasted 24 days. And what might appear to have been an intricately democratic machinery was in fact extremely undemocratic, because only those with a lot of friends and hangers-on could expect to be nominated to the decisive committees.

Perhaps to ensure that the electoral colleges kept their minds on the job, the decoration of the room is stunningly dreary; among the celebrations of great moments in Venetian military history there is just one decent picture – *The Conquest of Zara*, a late **Tintoretto** painting (first on right). The frieze of the last 42 doges was begun by assistants of Tintoretto and continued by contemporaries of each of the doges.

The Ponte dei Sospiri and the prisons

Sometimes visits are directed down the staircase from the Sala dello Scrutinio, but more often the route backtracks through the Sala del Maggior Consiglio and then goes into the **Quarantia Criminale**, the office of the appeal court. The Scala dei Censori descends from here to the **Ponte dei Sospiri** (Bridge of Sighs) and the **Prigioni Nuove** (New Prisons). The bridge was built in 1600 by Antonio Contino, and takes its popular name from the sighs of the prisoners who shuffled through its corridor. In reality, though, anyone passing this way had been let off pretty lightly, and would soon be at liberty again. Before the construction of these cells in the early seventeenth century, prisoners were kept either in the sweltering **Piombi** (the Leads), under the roof of the Palazzo Ducale, or in the damp, stygian gloom of the **Pozzi** (the Wells) in the bottom two storeys. This new block, which was in use until 1919, was occupied mainly by petty criminals, whose graffiti still adorn the walls.

One room of the Prigioni Nuove contains a miscellaneous display of pottery fragments, zoological debris unearthed in the Piazza and objects relating to the prisons, such as old shoes and toilet-buckets. From here a staircase descends to the prison courtyard, overlooked by the heavily barred windows of the *Pozzi*.

The Censori, Avogaria and Milizia da Mar

You now have to double back, and after recrossing the bridge you pass through the offices of the **Censori**, a two-man institution set up in 1517 to maintain standards of political behaviour at a time when corruption was getting out of hand. After this comes the **Avogaria**, which was occupied by the officers who prepared documents for the courts from the sixteenth century onwards; they also maintained the records of patrician marriages. Marriage certificates were filed in the adjoining **Sala dello Scrigno**, which connects with the office of the **Milizia da Mar**, the functionaries who from 1541 were put in charge of naval recruitment. Beyond this room you reach the bookshop, then the cafeteria and the exit.

The Campanile

Piazza San Marco • Daily: April 1–15 9am–4.45pm; April 16–Oct 8.30am–8.45pm; Nov–March 9.30am–4.45pm • €8

The **Campanile** began life as a combined lighthouse and belltower in the early tenth century, when what's now the Piazzetta was the city's harbour. Modifications were made continually up to 1515, the year in which Bartolomeo Bon the Younger's rebuilding was rounded off with the positioning of a golden angel on the summit. Each of its five bells had a distinct function: the *Marangona*, the largest, tolled the beginning and end of the working day; the *Trottiera* was a signal for members of the Maggior Consiglio to hurry to the council chamber; the *Nona* rang midday; the *Mezza Terza* announced a session of the Senate; and the smallest, the *Renghiera* or *Maleficio*, gave notice of an execution.

1

THE COLLAPSE OF THE CAMPANILE

The Campanile's most dramatic contribution to the history of the city was made on July 14, 1902, the day on which, at 9.52am, the tower succumbed to the weaknesses caused by recent structural changes, and fell down. (At some postcard stalls you can buy faked photos of the very instant of disaster.) The collapse was anticipated and the area cleared, so there were no human casualties; the only life lost was that of a cat named Mélampyge (after Casanova's dog). What's more, the bricks fell so neatly that San Marco was barely scratched and the Libreria lost only its end wall. The town councillors decided that evening that the Campanile should be rebuilt "dov'era e com'era" (where it was and how it was), and a decade later, on St Mark's Day 1912, the new tower was opened, in all but minor details a replica of the original. In recent years cracks again began to appear, prompting a huge restoration project to reinforce the foundations.

The Campanile played another part in the Venetian penal system – wrongdoers ran the risk of being subjected to the *Supplizio della Cheba* (Torture of the Cage), which involved being stuck in a crate which was then hoisted up the south face of the tower; luckier individuals would get away with a few days swinging in the breeze, but in some cases the view from the Campanile was the last thing the sinner ever saw. A more cheerful diversion was provided by the *Volo dell'Anzolo* or *del Turco* (Flight of the Angel or Turk), a stunt performed each year at the end of the Carnevale, in which an intrepid volunteer from the Arsenale would slide on a rope from the top of the Campanile to the first-floor loggia of the Palazzo Ducale, there to present a bouquet to the doge. At the start of the present-day Carnevale, a female angel slithers down a wire to greet a doge impersonator, who awaits her on a specially built stage.

At 99m, the Campanile is the tallest structure in the city, and from the top you can make out virtually every building, but not a single canal – which is almost as surprising as the view of the Dolomites, which on clear days seem to rise in Venice's back yard. Among the many who have marvelled at the panorama were Galileo, who demonstrated his telescope from here; Goethe, who saw the sea for the first time from the summit of the tower; and the Emperor Frederick III, whose climb to the top was achieved with a certain panache – he rode his horse up the internal ramp. The ready access granted to the tourist is a modern privilege: the Venetian state used to permit foreigners to ascend only at high tide, when they would be unable to see the elusive channels through the lagoon, which were crucial to the city's defences.

The Loggetta

Though pulverized when the Campanile collapsed, the **Loggetta** at its base was somehow pieced together again, mainly using material retrieved from the wreckage. **Sansovino**'s design was for a building that would completely enclose the foot of the Campanile, but only one quarter of the plan was executed (in 1537–49). Intended as a meeting place for the city's nobility, it was soon converted into a guardhouse for the *Arsenalotti* (workers from the Arsenale) who patrolled the area when the Maggior Consiglio was sitting, and in the last years of the Republic it served as the room in which the state lottery was drawn. The bronze figures in niches are also by Sansovino (*Pallas, Apollo, Mercury* and *Peace*), as is the terracotta group inside (although the figure of St John is a modern facsimile); the three marble reliefs on the attic are, as ever, allegories of the power and beneficence of the *Serenissima*: *Justice* = Venice, *Jupiter* = Crete, *Venus* = Cyprus.

1

THE BICENTENARY SIEGE AND THE LEGA (NORD)

Being the wealthiest region in Italy, the Veneto is fertile territory for separatist ideologues. It is no coincidence that Umberto Bossi, founder of the virulently xenophobic **Lega Nord**, chose Venice as the place in which to announce the birth of the Republic of Padania, his notional northern Italian nation, whose upright citizens he intended to liberate from the clutches of the unproductive and mafia-ridden south.

In 1997 the rabble-rousing rhetoric of Bossi and his ilk was translated into action, after a fashion. Shortly after midnight on May 9, just three days short of the two-hundredth anniversary of the fall of the Venetian Republic, a camper van and an armour-plated lorry were driven onto the last ferry from Tronchetto to the Lido. Eight men piled out of the vehicles and **hijacked the boat**, forcing the pilot at gunpoint to take them to San Marco. Once the ferry had docked, the gang drove across the Piazzetta, smashed the gates of the Campanile and ascended the tower, having barricaded the entrance with the van. At the summit they unfurled a flag bearing the Lion of St Mark and broadcast a message to the people of Venice, declaring themselves to be the soldiers of the Most Serene Venetian Government. Prepared for a lengthy siege, the guerrillas had brought with them a sub-machine-gun, a bottle of grappa and a few sets of crisply laundered underwear. In the event, they surrendered at 8.30am, after a squad of *carabinieri* scaled the Campanile.

The episode was widely ridiculed, but nobody in Venice doubted that the Campanile siege was indicative of a widespread discontent in the Veneto. In the years that followed, the Lega Nord continued to grow, and in 2010 the Lega's candidate, Luca Zaia, was elected governor of the Veneto, taking sixty percent of the vote. Bossi himself is now a spent force, having resigned the leadership in 2012 amid allegations that the Lega's treasurer had diverted party funds to Bossi's family while laundering money for the 'Ndrangheta, the Calabrian mafia. His party, however, is in the ascendant. Under the leadership of Matteo Salvini, it ditched the 'Nord' from its name and focused its fire on Italy's immigrants and gypsies instead of on the feckless peasants of the south. The strategy proved successful: in June 2018 Salvini became the deputy Prime Minister of Italy, in coalition with the 'anti-establishment' Cinque Stelle (Five Star) party, which shares La Lega's distaste for the EU. La Lega now has widespread support all over the country, but the Veneto remains its stronghold.

The Torre dell'Orologio

Piazza San Marco • Guided tours daily 10am–5pm; tours in English Mon–Wed 10am & 11am, Thurs–Sun 2pm & 3pm • €12 (including admission to Museo Correr, Museo Archeologico and Biblioteca Marciana), or €7 for holders of I Musei di Piazza San Marco card or Museum Pass • Tours must be pre-booked, either on ☎ 848 082 000 or at Ⓦ torreorologio.visitmuve.it

The spectacular **Torre dell'Orologio** (Clock Tower) was built between 1496 and 1506, the central portion being by **Mauro Codussi** and the wings possibly by Pietro Lombardo. A gruesome popular tale relates that the makers of the clock's elaborate mechanism, Gian Paolo and his son Gian Carlo Rainieri, slaved away for three years at their project, only to have their eyes put out so that they couldn't repeat their engineering marvel for any other patrons. In fact the grateful Venetians gave the pair a generous pension and installed Gian Carlo in an apartment in the tower, so that he could keep the timepiece in perfect condition – presumably too dull an outcome for the city's folklorists.

The bell on the tower's roof terrace is struck by two bronze wild men known as "The Moors", because of their dark patina; they were cast in the Arsenale in 1497. If you're in Venice on Epiphany or during Ascension week, you'll witness the clock's star turn – on the hour the Magi, led by an angel, troop out and bow to the figure of the Madonna.

Almost completely replaced in the 1750s, the clock's mechanism has been frequently overhauled since – the digital display to the side of the Madonna was added in 1858 (when it was seen as quite an innovation), and the whole apparatus was dismantled and modernized in a ten-year restoration that finished in 2006. You can now take an hour-long guided tour of the interior, which stops on each of the five floors to explicate the history and the workings of this fantastically complex machine.

The Procuratie

1

To the left of the Torre dell'Orologio stretches the **Procuratie Vecchie**, once the home of the **Procurators of San Marco**, whose responsibilities included the upkeep of San Marco and the administration of the other government-owned properties. Never numbering more than nine, the procurators were second in position only to the doge, who himself was generally drawn from their ranks. With the doge and the Grand Chancellor – the head of the civil service – they shared the distinction of being the only state officials elected for life.

From the time of Doge Ziani, the procurators and their attendant bureaucracies were installed on this side of the Piazza, but the present building was begun around 1500 by **Codussi**, continued after a fire in 1512 by **Bartolomeo Bon the Younger** and completed around 1532 by **Sansovino**. Much of the block earned rents for the city coffers, the upper floors housing some of the choicest apartments in town and the ground floor being leased to shopkeepers and craftsmen.

Within a century or so, the procurators were moved across the Piazza to new premises. Sansovino, who had only recently completed the old offices, proposed a development that involved knocking down a pilgrims' hospice, along with the unsightly shacks around it. The **Procuratie Nuove** were eventually built between 1582 and 1640, first to designs by **Scamozzi**, and then under Longhena's control. Napoleon's stepson Eugène Beauharnais, the Viceroy of Italy, appropriated the quarters for use as a royal palace, and then discovered that the accommodation lacked a ballroom. His solution had the true, gossamer-light Napoleonic touch to it: he demolished Sansovino's church of San Geminiano and used the vacated space to connect the Procuratie Nuove and Vecchie with a wing containing the essential facility. Generally known as the **Ala Napoleonica**, the building is topped by a gallery of Roman emperors – no prizes for guessing whose effigy was meant to fill the gap in the middle.

The Correr and archeological museums

Piazza San Marco • Daily: April–Oct 10am–7pm; Nov–March 10am–5pm • Entrance with Museum Pass or I Musei di Piazza San Marco card • Ⓦ correr.visitmuve.it

Many of the rooms in the Ala Napoleonica and Procuratie Nuove have been occupied since 1923 by the **Museo Correr**, which has grown from the collection bequeathed to the city by Teodoro Correr in 1830 to become the chief civic museum of Venice. In an attempt to siphon tourists into this neglected museum, the authorities have combined the Correr's entry ticket with that for the Palazzo Ducale, and have made the **archeological museum** and Sansovino's library accessible through the Correr. The strategy has had only limited success, for the Correr is generally given the whistle-stop

---

THE PIGEONS OF THE PIAZZA

Until quite recently the Piazza was perpetually swarming with **pigeons**, whose presence was held to be so crucial to the identity of the square that they were fed daily by a council official – though it was also rumoured that the council-sponsored birdseed was laced with **contraceptive**, in an attempt to control the pigeon population. In 2008 it was decided that the droppings of the disease-ridden birds were presenting too great a hazard to the citizens of Venice and the stonework of the Piazza's buildings, and so feeding the birds was **banned**, which quickly led to a sharp reduction in the size of the flocks. You can choose between three improbable stories about the origins of the pigeons: they came here with the refugees from Attila's army; or they're the distant relatives of pigeons released by successive doges during Holy Week, in a ceremony commemorating the return of Noah's dove; or they're the descendants of caged birds given to a doge's wife in an attempt to cheer her up.

1

treatment by sightseers who just want to feel that they've got their money's worth. Nobody could make out that this immense and disparate collection is consistently fascinating, but it incorporates a picture gallery that more than makes up for the duller stretches, and its sections on Venetian society contain some eye-opening exhibits.

Canova and the historical collection

You enter the Correr through the beautiful mirrored ballroom, where the floor is left to Canova's *Orpheus and Eurydice*, created in 1777, when the sculptor was still in his teens. Then comes a sequence of nine recently renovated "Imperial rooms", where the decor largely reflects the taste of the young Elisabeth of Austria, wife of Austrian emperor Franz Joseph, but the rooms also contain a Napoleonic relic, in the form of the bed of Eugène Beauharnais, stepson of Napoleon and briefly Viceroy of Italy. You emerge into a room in which you'll find Canova's faux-modest *Venus Italica* and his figure of *Paris*. Sculpted in gypsum, the latter was in effect Canova's final draft before moving on to the marble: the pins that cover the hero's skin were to enable his assistants to map the coordinates onto the block of marble. Nearby are some of the rough clay models that Canova created as first drafts for his classically poised sculptures – his working methods are fully revealed at his birthplace museum (see page 301). Other pieces by Canova are on show in adjacent rooms, which you pass on your way out, including his *Daedalus and Icarus* (the sculpture that made his name at the age of 21), his reliefs of scenes from the life of Socrates and his design for the tomb of Titian, which became his own monument (see page 113).

After Canova you're into the **historical collection**, some of which will be enlightening only if your Italian is fairly good and you already have a pretty wide knowledge of Venetian history. In the nine-room "Wunderkammer Correr" scores of prints, paintings, books, historical relics, jewels and other objets d'art have been gathered into loosely thematic groupings ("The church", "The glorifiction of the state" etc) in an attempt to impose some sort of order on the Correr's superabundant jumble. The categories might seem a little arbitrary, but there are some beautiful items here, none more impressive than **Jacopo de'Barbari**'s astonishing aerial view of Venice, engraved in 1500. A print of de'Barbari's masterpiece is displayed alongside the original wooden blocks, a dumbfoundingly accurate mirror-image of the city.

The Museo Archeologico

From the lower floor of the Correr you pass directly into the **Museo Archeologico**, the core of which is formed by Greek and Roman sculptures that were bequeathed by members of the Grimani family. Cardinal Domenico Grimani became the first major collector to endow a civic museum when he left his finest specimens to the city in 1523; his nephew Giovanni Grimani, who had inherited the rest of the cardinal's pieces and added to them over the years, left everything to the state in 1587, a donation so substantial that Scamozzi was commissioned to turn the vestibule of Sansovino's library into a public gallery for its display. Augmented by various other gifts over the intervening centuries, the Museo Archeologico is a somewhat scrappy museum, with cases of Roman coins and gems, fragments of sarcophagi and inscriptions, miscellaneous headless statues and bodiless heads interspersed with the odd Bronze Age, Egyptian or Assyrian relic, generally presented in a manner that isn't very inspiring. But some pieces from the Grimani collections are outstanding: look out for an assertive head of Athena from the fourth century BC, a trio of wounded Gallic warriors (Roman copies of Hellenistic originals) and busts of a phalanx of Roman emperors, including Domitian, Vitellius, Hadrian, Trajan, Tiberius, Marcus Aurelius, Septimius Severus and the demented Caracalla.

At the furthest point of the archeological museum a door opens into the hall of Sansovino's library (see page 66).

The Quadreria

The top floor of the Correr is home to the **Quadreria**, which may be no rival for the Accademia's collection but nonetheless sets out clearly the evolution of painting in Venice from the thirteenth century to around 1500.

In the early rooms the outstanding Venetian figure is **Paolo Veneziano**, who in the second half of the fourteenth century began to blend the city's Byzantine pictorial conventions with the more supple styles of Padua, Bologna and other mainland centres. The influence of other artistic schools – especially those of the Low Countries, a region with strong mercantile links to Venice – is a dominant theme in the succeeding rooms, where there are remarkable pieces by **Cosmè Tura** (an angular *Pietà*) and **Antonello da Messina** (a defaced but nonetheless powerful *Pietà*), the latter artist being a conduit through which the compositional techniques of the Tuscan Renaissance came to Venice. The delicate colouring and stillness of Flemish painting are central to the cultural genealogy of the **Bellini** family, to whom the Correr devotes a whole room, featuring a *Crucifixion* that's probably by Jacopo and a few pictures that are definitely by his sons: Gentile's touching portrait of Doge Giovanni Mocenigo, and Giovanni's *Transfiguration, Madonna and Child, Crucifixion* and *Christ Supported by Angels* (the last sporting a fake Dürer monogram, which once fooled the experts).

After the Bellini section you'll pass Alvise Vivarini's portrait of a fine-boned St Anthony of Padua, before coming to the museum's best-known possession, the **Carpaccio** painting once known as *The Courtesans*, but which in fact depicts a couple of late fifteenth-century bourgeois ladies at ease, dressed in a style at which none of their contemporaries would have raised an eyebrow. Originally it illustrated both men and women at leisure, but the top half of the picture – showing young men hunting – was at some point sawn off, and is now owned by the Getty museum. The younger woman's pearl necklace identifies her as a bride, while the plants that flank her – lilies and myrtle – are symbols of purity within marriage. The perilous platform shoes (*ciapine* or *pianelle*), placed beside the balustrade, served a twin function: they kept the silks and satins out of the mud, and they enabled the wearer to circumvent the sumptuary laws, which attempted to limit the volume of expensive materials used in dresses by forbidding trailing hems.

In the room beyond there's another much-reproduced image, the *Portrait of a Young Man in a Red Hat*, once attributed to Carpaccio, now given to an anonymous painter from Ferrara or Bologna. A roomful of fine ivory carvings comes next, then a cubicle of pictures from Venice's community of **Greek artists**, some of whom continued to paint in pre-Renaissance style well into the seventeenth century; this immensely conservative community was the nursery of the painter who later became known as El Greco – there's a picture attributed to him here which you'd walk straight past if it weren't for the label. At room 42 the Quadreria turns into a display of Renaissance ceramics, most of them hideous to modern eyes; beyond it lies the last section on this floor, the library from the Palazzo Manin, which contains **Alessandro Vittoria**'s bust of Tomasso Rangone – his full-length portrait of the same subject is on the facade of the nearby church of San Zulian.

The Museo del Risorgimento

From the Quadreria you're sometimes directed to the **Museo del Risorgimento**, which resumes the history of the city with its fall to Napoleon, and takes it through to the career of Daniele Manin, the anti-Austrian revolt of 1848 and the eventual birth of a united Italy. Although there are some mildly amusing contemporary cartoons on display, and some strange memorabilia (a bottle in the form of Garibaldi's head; portraits of Risorgimento heroes painted on tiny buttons), extensive prior knowledge is again immensely helpful.

The rest of the Correr

Back downstairs, the itinerary passes through a section on Venetian festivals and then a fascinating sequence devoted to Venetian crafts, trades and everyday life, where the

1

frivolous items are what catch the eye, especially a pair of eighteen-inch *ciapine* (as worn by the women in the Carpaccio painting), and an eighteenth-century portable hair-care kit that's the size of a suitcase. After a miscellany of restored stonework, next you'll encounter various exhibits relating to Venetian games and sports, with some remarkable prints of the alarming displays of strength known as the Labours of Hercules.

The Piazzetta and the Molo

For much of the Republic's existence, the **Piazzetta** – the open space between San Marco and the waterfront – was the area where the councillors of Venice would gather to scheme and curry favour. Way back in the earliest days of the city, this patch of land was the garden – or *broglio* – of the San Zaccaria convent: this is the probable source of the English word "imbroglio". But as well as being a sort of open-air clubhouse for the city's movers and shakers, the Piazzetta played a crucial part in the penal system of Venice.

The columns

Those found guilty of serious crime by Venice's courts were often done away with in the privacy of their cells; for public executions the usual site was the pavement between the **two granite columns** on the **Molo**, as this stretch of the waterfront is called. Straightforward hanging or decapitation were the customary techniques, but refinements were available for certain offenders, such as the three traitors who, in 1405, were buried alive here, head down. The last person to be executed here was one Domenico Storti, condemned to death in 1752 for the murder of his brother. Superstitious Venetians avoid passing between the columns.

The columns should have a companion, but the third one fell off the barge on which they were being transported and has remained submerged somewhere off the Piazzetta since around 1170. The columns themselves were purloined from the Levant, whereas the figures perched on top are bizarre hybrids. The statue of **St Theodore** – the patron saint of Venice when it was dependent on Byzantium – is a modern copy; the original, now on show in a corner of one of the Palazzo Ducale's courtyards, was a compilation of a Roman torso, a head of Mithridates the Great (first-century BC) and miscellaneous bits and pieces carved in Venice in the fourteenth century (the dragon included). The **winged lion** on the other column is an ancient 3000-kilo bronze beast that was converted into a Lion of St Mark by jamming a Bible under its paws. When this was done is not clear, but the lion is documented as having been restored in Venice as far back as 1293. Of numerous later repairs the most drastic was in 1815, when its wings, paws, tail and back were recast, to rectify damage done by the French engineers who, in the course of arranging its return from Paris, broke it into twenty pieces. Scientific analysis for its most recent restoration revealed that the lion is composed of a patchwork of ancient metal plates, but its exact provenance remains a mystery – the currently favoured theory is that it was originally part of a Middle Eastern monument made around 300 BC.

The Libreria Sansoviniana

The Piazzetta is framed by two outstanding buildings – the Palazzo Ducale on one side and the **Libreria Sansoviniana** or **Biblioteca Marciana** on the other. **Sansovino**'s contemporaries regarded the Libreria as one of the supreme designs of the era: Palladio remarked that it was "perhaps the richest and most ornate building to be created since the times of ancient Greece and Rome". Venice had an opportunity to establish a state library in the fourteenth century, when Petrarch left his priceless collection to the city, but the beneficiaries somehow mislaid the legacy. In the end, the impetus to build the library came from the bequest of Cardinal Bessarion, who bequeathed his celebrated hoard of classical texts to the Republic in 1468. Bessarion's books and manuscripts were housed in San Marco and then the Palazzo Ducale, but finally it was decided that a special building was needed.

Sansovino got the job, and in 1537 the site was cleared of its hostels, slaughterhouse and bakery, thus turning the Campanile into a freestanding tower. Construction was well advanced when, in December 1545, the project suffered a major setback: frost got into the vaulted ceiling of the main hall and brought it crashing down. Charged with incompetence, Sansovino was thrown into prison, and it took some determined pleading by his cronies – Titian among them – to get him out. Upon being allowed back on the job he belatedly took notice of conventional wisdom, which argued that heavy stone vaults weren't a terrific idea in a place where the land keeps shifting, and stuck a flat ceiling in its place, with a light wooden vault attached, to keep up appearances. The library was finished in 1591, two decades after Sansovino's death.

Entering the library from the archeological museum, you come straight into the **main hall**, one of the most beautiful rooms in the city. Paintings by **Veronese**, **Tintoretto**, **Andrea Schiavone** and others cover the walls and ceiling: five of the *Philosophers* are by Tintoretto, while the pair that flank the entrance door, and three of the ceiling medallions, are by Veronese, whose work in the library earned him a gold chain from the procurators in charge of the project, acting on Titian's recommendation. Special exhibitions of precious items from the library, such as the *Grimani Breviary* of 1500 or Fra' Mauro's 1459 map of the world, are sometimes held here. **Titian**'s *Allegory of Wisdom* occupies the central panel of the ceiling of the **anteroom**, which has been restored to the appearance it had from the end of the sixteenth century, when the Giovanni Grimani collection was first put on show here, until 1812, when Napoleon turned the library into an annexe to the viceroy's palace and shifted its contents over to the Palazzo Ducale. Beyond lies the intended approach to the library, a magnificent staircase encrusted with stuccowork by Vittoria.

The Zecca

Attached to the Libreria, with its main facade to the lagoon, is Sansovino's first major building in Venice, the **Zecca** or Mint. Constructed in stone and iron to make it

---

MONUMENTS AND MAMMON – ADVERTISING ON THE PIAZZA

In 2009 the annual subsidy paid by central government for the **restoration** of Venice's crumbling buildings was cut by more than 25 percent. Shortly before this cut, a law was introduced that allowed the scaffolding on public structures under restoration to carry advertisements, as long as the superintendent (the council official in overall charge of such projects) considered that the adverts did not "detract from the appearance … or public enjoyment of the building". With most of the monuments of the Piazza in need of very expensive work, the consequence was inevitable: the Libreria Sansoviniana and parts of the Palazzo Ducale were soon turned into gigantic **billboards**, before the Correr went the same way. Nobody would argue that these colossal adverts don't detract from the appearance of the Piazza, and the various other buildings on which they have subsequently appeared, but it's impossible not to sympathize with Renata Codello, the Venice superintendent, who said: "I have no choice: last year some of the marble facing of the Palazzo Ducale fell down; this year it was part of the cornice of the Correr museum. Under law I am personally responsible if a tourist is hurt." Venice's financial situation is dire, partly because nearly all the city's special funding for maintenance of the *centro storico* goes directly from Rome into the benighted flood barrier project. So the mega-ads are going to be a feature of the cityscape for the foreseeable future.

1

fireproof (most stonework in Venice is just skin-deep), it was built between 1537 and 1545 on the site occupied by the Mint since the thirteenth century, when it was moved from a factory near the Rialto bridge. Some of the finance for the project was raised on the Venetian colony of Cyprus, by selling the island's slaves their liberty. By the beginning of the fifteenth century the city's prosperity was such that the Venetian gold ducat was in use in every European exchange, and Doge Tommaso Mocenigo could look forward to the day when the city would be "the mistress of all the gold in Christendom". In later years the ducat became known as the *zecchino*, source of the word "sequin". The rooms of the Mint are now part of the library, but are not open to tourists.

The Giardinetti Reali

Beyond the Zecca, and behind a barricade of postcard and toy gondola sellers, is a small public garden – the **Giardinetti Reali** – created by Eugène Beauharnais on the site of the state granaries as part of his improvement scheme for the Procuratie Nuove. Replanted by landscape architect Paolo Pejrone in 2018, it's the nearest place to the centre of the city where you'll find a bench and the shade of a tree, but in summer it's about as peaceful as a school playground. The spruced-up building at the foot of the nearby bridge is the Casino da Caffè, another legacy of the Napoleonic era; currently undergoing restoration, for years it served as the main tourist office.

North of the Piazza

From the Piazza the bulk of the pedestrian traffic flows **north to the Rialto** along the shopping mall of the **Mercerie**, one of the few parts of the city which is almost totally devoid of magic. Apart from the church of **San Giuliano** – one of Venice's lesser eccentricities – only the stately **San Salvador** provides a diversion from the spotlights and price tags until you come to the **Campo San Bartolomeo**.

The Mercerie

The **Mercerie**, the chain of streets that starts under the Torre dell'Orologio and finishes at the Campo San Bartolomeo, is the most direct route between the Rialto and San Marco and thus, as the link between the city's political and commercial centres, was always a prime site for Venice's shopkeepers, a status it retains today. (Each of the five links in the chain is a *merceria*: Merceria dell'Orologio, di San Zulian, del Capitello, di San Salvador and 2 Aprile.) A sixteenth-century account of these streets noted

---

LA VECIA DEL MORTER

Above the Sottoportego del Cappello (it's first left after the Torre) you'll see a stone relief known as **La Vecia del Morter** – the Old Woman of the Mortar. The event it commemorates happened on the night of June 15, 1310, when the occupant of this house, an old woman named Giustina Rossi, looked out of her window and saw a contingent of a rebel army, led by Bajamonte Tiepolo, passing below. Possibly by accident, she knocked a stone mortar from her sill, and the missile landed on the skull of the standard-bearer, killing him outright. Seeing their flag go down, Tiepolo's troops panicked and fled back towards the Rialto. (Scores of other rebels were killed in the Piazza; those ringleaders who survived the carnage were punished with execution or exile – Tiepolo, as a relative of the doge, was let off with banishment, but his house was razed to the ground.) Asked what she would like as her reward for her patriotic intervention, Giustina requested permission to hang the Venetian flag from her window on feast days, and a guarantee that her rent would never be raised; both requests were granted. From then on, until the fall of the Republic, June 15 was celebrated as a public holiday.

"tapestry, brocades and hangings of every design, carpets of all sorts, camlets of every colour and texture, silks of every variety; and so many warehouses full of spices, groceries and drugs, and so much beautiful white wax!" Nowadays it's both slick and tacky: the empire of kitsch has a firm base here, sharing the territory with the likes of Prada, La Perla, Gucci, Furla, Cartier and Benetton (one of the Veneto's most successful companies). The mixture ensnares more window-shoppers than any other part of Venice, and in summer the congestion gets so bad that the police often have to enforce a one-way system.

San Giuliano

Campiello San Zulian • Daily 9am–7pm • Free

The church of **San Giuliano** or San Zulian was rebuilt in the mid-sixteenth century with the generous aid of the physician **Tommaso Rangone**. His munificence and intellectual brilliance (but not his Christian faith) are attested by the Greek and Hebrew inscriptions on the facade and by **Alessandro Vittoria**'s portrait statue above the door, for which Rangone paid almost as much as he paid for the church's stonework. (He originally wished to be commemorated by an effigy on the facade of his parish church, San Geminiano, which used to stand facing the Basilica, but the city's governors vetoed this excessively vainglorious proposal.) Inside, the central panel of the ceiling, *St Julian in Glory* by **Palma il Giovane** and assistants, is one of the better works by this over-prolific artist; over the first altar on the right is a late work by **Veronese** – *Pietà with Sts Roch, Jerome and Mark*; and in the chapel to the left of the chancel there are ceiling stuccoes by **Vittoria**, and three pieces by **Campagna** – terracotta figures of *The Virgin* and *The Magdalen*, and a marble altar panel (all from c.1583).

San Salvador

Campo San Salvador • June–Aug Mon–Sat 9am–noon & 4–7pm, Sun 4–7pm; Sept–May Mon–Sat 9am–noon & 3–7pm, Sun 3–7pm • Free

At its northern end, the Mercerie veers right at the church of **San Salvador** or Salvatore, which was consecrated in 1177 by Pope Alexander III, on the occasion of his reconciliation with Emperor Barbarossa (see page 44). The facade, applied in 1663, is less interesting than the interior, which was begun around 1508 by Spavento and continued by Tullio Lombardo and Sansovino. It's cleverly designed in the form of three domed Greek crosses placed end to end, thus creating the longitudinal layout required by the religious orders while paying homage to the centrally planned churches of Byzantium and, of course, to the Basilica di San Marco. Unfortunately, the original design didn't let enough light into the church; Scamozzi rectified the problem in the 1560s by inserting a lantern into each of San Salvador's domes.

The interior

In the middle of the right-hand wall stands the **tomb of Doge Francesco Venier**, designed by Sansovino, who also sculpted the figures of *Charity* and *Hope*; these were possibly his last sculptures. To the left of it hangs **Titian**'s *Annunciation* (1566), signed *"Fecit, fecit"*, supposedly to emphasize the wonder of his continued creativity in extreme old age; its cumbersome angel is often held to be the responsibility of assistants. A scrap of paper on the rail in front of the picture records the death of the artist on August 25, 1576. The end of the right transept is filled by the **tomb of Caterina Cornaro** (see page 304), one of the saddest figures in Venetian history. Born into one of Venice's pre-eminent families, she became Queen of Cyprus by marriage, and after her husband's death was forced to surrender the strategically crucial island to the doge. On her return to Venice she was led in triumph up the Canal Grande, as though her abdication had been entirely voluntary, and then was presented with possession of the town of Ásolo as a token of the city's gratitude. She died in 1510 and was given a heroine's funeral in the Apostoli church; her body was removed to San Salvador, and this tomb erected, at the end of the century.

1

THE ARMENIAN QUARTER

Very close to San Giuliano lies the heart of the old **Armenian quarter**: take Merceria di San Zulian, which comes into the Campo San Zulian opposite the church, then cross the bridge into Calle Fiubera, and then take the first right – Calle degli Armeni. Under the sottoportego is the door to the best-hidden church in Venice, **Santa Croce degli Armeni**, which was founded as an oratory in 1496 and rebuilt as the community's church in 1688. Nowadays the congregation is so small that the church has just one Mass each month, and the most visible Armenian community is the one on the island of San Lazzaro.

The **altarpiece**, a *Transfiguration* by **Titian** (c.1560), covers a fourteenth-century silver reredos that is exposed to view at Easter. In front of the main altar, a glass disc set into the pavement allows you to see a recently unearthed merchant's tomb, with badly damaged decoration by Titian's brother Francesco, who also painted the doors of the church organ (on the left side of the church) and frescoed a delightful fantasy of bird-filled vegetation high on the walls of the sacristy (the sacristan will let you in, and probably expect a donation). The lustrous *Supper at Emmaus* to the left of the altar is probably from the workshop of Giovanni Bellini, and the third altar of the left aisle (the altar of the sausage-makers' guild) was designed by Vittoria, who sculpted its figures of *St Roch* and *St Sebastian*.

The cloisters of San Salvador, entered from the campo, are sometimes used as an exhibition space.

Scuola di San Teodoro

Overlooking Campo San Salvador is the home of the youngest of the major *scuole*, the **Scuola di San Teodoro**, which was founded in 1530; the facade was designed in 1655 by Sardi, the architect responsible for the front of San Salvatore. It's now become home to yet another fancy-dress orchestra that churns out endless Vivaldi for the tourists. The column in the centre of the campo is a memorial to the 1848–49 revolt against the Austrians, and was placed here on the fiftieth anniversary of the insurrection.

Campo San Bartolomeo and the Fondaco dei Tedeschi

Campo San Bartolomeo (or Bortolomio), terminus of the Mercerie, is at its best in the evening, as this is one of the favoured spots to meet up with friends at the end of the working day. The **church of San Bartolomeo** (Tues, Thurs & Sat 10am–noon) has a landmark campanile, but its interior isn't thrilling: its organ panels, painted by Sebastiano del Piombo, are now housed in the Accademia, and its most famous picture, the altarpiece painted by Dürer at the request of the German merchant Christopher Fugger, long ago migrated to Prague. In the sixteenth century this area would have been swarming with men like Dürer's patron, because the base for the German traders was the **Fondaco dei Tedeschi**, at the far end of the campo. Every foreign trading community in Venice had its fondaco, which was a warehouse-hostel; the word is yet another sign of Venice's close links with the Islamic world, being derived from the Arabic word for an inn, *fonduk*. Formerly the main post office, it's now been expensively converted into a "lifestyle department store", a glitzy bazaar for high-end names such as Gucci, Bottega Veneta, Bulgari and so on. There's a café-restaurant on the ground floor (designed by Philippe Starck), and exhibition spaces plus a panoramic terrace up top. This monument to conspicuous consumption has about as much class as a gargantuan duty-free store, and is a powerful emblem of what tourism has done to Venice. What makes it worse is the extinction of nearby *Coin*, which for seventy years was the city's one real department store; hit by a 500 percent rent increase, it was forced to close in 2018.

Campo San Luca and the Bacino Orseolo

If the crush of San Bartolomeo is too much, you can retire to the nearby **Campo San Luca**, another open-air social centre with a few cafés and bars. Unusually, the church of **San Luca** is not on the campo named after it, but on a campiello some way off, down Salizzada San Luca, then right and then left; it's usually shut, and only has one picture of interest – a Veronese painting that's in a parlous state. From Campo San Luca, Calle Goldoni is a direct route back to the Piazza, via the **Bacino Orseolo** – the city's major gondola depot, and one of the few places where you can admire the streamlining and balance of the boats without being hassled by their owners.

Campo Manin and around

Unusually, the most conspicuous building on **Campo Manin** is a modern one – the **Cassa di Risparmio di Venezia** (designed in the 1960s by Angelo Scattolin and Pier Luigi Nervi), which stands on the spot once occupied by the famous printing press of Aldus Manutius (see page 110). The campo was enlarged in 1871 to make room for the monument to **Daniele Manin**, the lawyer who led the 1848–49 revolt against Austrian occupation; his statue looks towards his house, alongside the left-hand bridge (as you look west). Under Manin's management the provisional government of Venice was run with exemplary efficiency – a legislative assembly was set up, a new currency printed and even a newspaper was circulated. In the course of the Austrian blockade Venice became the first city ever to be bombarded from the air, when explosives attached to balloons were floated over the city. The damage caused by this ploy was not too substantial, but inevitably the resistance was short-lived, and on August 23, 1849, weakened by hunger and disease, the Venetians surrendered. Manin and the other leaders of the uprising died in exile, but his native city honours his reputation not just here but also in the Basilica di San Marco (his tomb is there) and in Calle Larga XXII Marzo, which takes its name from the date on which the uprising started. (Incidentally, the other famous Manin – Lodovico, the feeble last doge – though not an ancestor, was closely associated with Daniele's family: when Daniele's parents converted from Judaism to Catholicism, they took the surname of their sponsor, who was one of Lodovico's brothers.)

Scala del Bovolo

Calle de le Locande 4299 • Daily 10am–6pm • €7 • ⓦ gioiellinascostidivenezia.it

On the wall of the alley on the south side of Campo Manin, a sign directs you to the staircase known as the **Scala del Bovolo**. Added to the Palazzo Contarini around 1500, perhaps to save some space indoors while also making an impression on the neighbours, this flamboyant spiral staircase gets its name from the Venetian word for a

---

PIETRO ARETINO

Somewhere in San Luca church is buried a writer whose name was known across Europe in the mid-sixteenth century – **Pietro Aretino**. Nicknamed "The Scourge of Princes", Aretino milked a hefty income from the rulers of a dozen states, who paid him either in thanks for his flattery or to shut him up. So adept was he at juggling his various sponsors that he managed simultaneously to be on the payroll of Emperor Charles V and Charles's great enemy, King Francis I of France. With Sansovino and Titian (who painted his portrait several times and used him as a model for Pontius Pilate) he formed a clique that made life intolerable for anyone they didn't like – both Lorenzo Lotto and Pordenone suffered at their hands. Aretino's notoriety rested as much on his dubious morals as on his scurrilous poetry and brilliant letters (which were a Venetian bestseller); some idea of the man is given by the story that his death was brought about by his uncontrollable laughter at a filthy story about his own sister. Today there's not even a tombstone left to mark his existence.

1

TRADING PLACES

On the north side of the Piazza you'll find a street called **Frezzeria**. Its name is taken from the arrows – *frecce* – that were made and sold there, and it's just one of the many Venetian streets that bear witness to the traders who once operated in these localities. Roaming round the city, you'll encounter the following businesses, among others:

Barretteri = hatmakers	Pistor = baker
Beccaria = butcher	Remer = oar-maker
Botteri = barrel-makers	Saoneri = soap-makers
Cafettier = coffee shop	Spadaria = sword-maker
Frutariol – greengrocer	Spechieri = mirror-makers
Legnami = carpenters	Spezier = pharmacist
Magazen = pawnbroker	Tagiapiera = stonecutter
Pestrin = milk-seller	Tintor/Tentor = dyer

snail shell. It's an impressive construction, but you might have doubts about paying the fee for the pleasure of the ascent.

The Museo Fortuny

Campiello San Beneto • Mon & Wed–Sun 10am–6pm • Entry charge varies according to what's on – it's usually €10 • ⓦ fortuny.visitmuve.it

The fifteenth-century Palazzo Pésaro degli Orfei, now the **Museo Fortuny**, is hidden away in a tiny campo you'd never accidentally pass – take either of the bridges out of Campo Manin, turn first right, and keep going.

Born in Catalonia, **Mariano Fortuny** (1871–1949) is famous chiefly for the body-clinging silk dresses he created, which were so finely pleated that they could be threaded through a wedding ring, it was claimed. However, Fortuny was also a painter, architect, engraver, photographer, theatre designer and sculptor, and the contents of this rickety and atmospheric palazzo reflect his versatility, with ranks of exotic landscapes, symbolist scenes (several of them derived from Wagner, for whose operas he had a lifelong passion), languorous nudes (including one painted when he was just 17), terracotta portrait busts, photographs, stage machinery and so forth – but none of the sexy frocks. The top floor houses a collection of paintings by Virgilio Guidi (1891–1984), who was born in Rome but spent much of his life in Venice, where he taught at the Accademia. Design and photography exhibitions are held pretty much constantly in the Museo Fortuny, and how much of the building you get to see depends on how extensive the show is – often only a couple of rooms are used. And in high season you'll have to queue, as the palazzo is so fragile that only 75 people are allowed in at a time.

San Benedetto

Campiello San Beneto • Opening hours vary

The church of **San Benedetto** (or San Beneto) – founded in the eleventh century, rebuilt in 1685 – gangs up with Fortuny's house to overwhelm the little square. It has a few good pictures: *St Sebastian* by Strozzi (second altar on right); two paintings of *St Benedict* by Mazzoni (over the doors to the side of the high altar); and *St Francis of Paola* by Giambattista Tiepolo (first altar on left). Finding this church open is a matter of pot luck – late afternoon is normally your best bet.

West of the Piazza

Leaving the Piazza **by the west side**, through the colonnade of the Ala Napoleonica, you enter a zone where the big fashion houses rule the roost, with names such as Prada, Ferragamo, Bulgari, Gucci, Missoni and Vuitton lurking round every corner. For many high-spending tourists, the broad **Calle Larga XXII Marzo**, which begins over the canal from San Moisè, is one of the city's focal points. For a higher proportion of visitors, this part of the city is just **the route to the Accademia** – some pass through with their noses buried in their maps, and hardly break step before they reach the bridge over the Canal Grande. But there are things to see here apart from the latest creations from Milan – the extraordinary Baroque facades of **San Moisè** and **Santa Maria del Giglio**, for instance, or the graceful **Santo Stefano**, which rises at the end of one of the largest and most attractive squares in Venice.

San Moisè

Campo San Moisè • Mon–Sat 9.30am–12.30pm • Free

In naming **San Moisè** after Moses, the early Venetians were following the Byzantine custom of canonizing Old Testament figures, while simultaneously honouring Moisè Venier, who paid for a rebuilding of the church in the tenth century, two centuries after its foundation. Its hideous facade, featuring a species of camel unknown to zoology, was designed in 1668 by Alessandro Tremignon and sculpted largely by **Heinrich Meyring** (aka Enrico or Arrigo Meyring), a follower of Bernini; it was funded by the Fini family, whose portraits occupy the positions in which one might expect to see saints or members of the Holy Family. And if you think this bloated display of fauna, flora and portraiture is in questionable taste, wait till you see the miniature mountain that Tremignon and Meyring created as the main altarpiece, representing *Mount Sinai with Moses Receiving the Tablets*. In the sacristy you'll find a fine example of comparatively restrained proto-Baroque – a bronze altar panel of the *Deposition* by Niccolò and Sebastiano Roccatagliata.

Campo San Fantin

Halfway along Calle Larga XXII Marzo, on the right as you walk from the Piazza, Calle del Sartor da Veste takes you over a canal and into **Campo San Fantin**. The church of **San Fantin**, begun in 1507 by Scarpagnino, is notable for its graceful domed apse, built in 1549–63 to plans by Sansovino. On the far side of the campo is the home of the **Ateneo Veneto**, a cultural institution which organizes some of Venice's more arcane exhibitions. The building was formerly occupied by a confraternity whose main service to the community was to comfort those sentenced to death – hence the name by which it was generally known: the Scuola della Buona Morte. Part of the *scuola's* art collection has been dispersed, but pieces by Veronese and Alessandro Vittoria, among others, are still in the building, inaccessible to hoi polloi.

Teatro la Fenice

Campo San Fantin • Audio-tours daily 9.30am–5/6pm • €10 • Ⓦ teatrolafenice.it

Campo San Fantin is dominated by the **Teatro la Fenice**, Venice's oldest and largest theatre. Meaning "The Phoenix", the name of La Fenice is wholly appropriate to a

---

THE RIDOTTO

Heading west from the Piazza, on the most direct road to the Accademia, you soon pass the **Calle del Ridotto** (on the left), named after the most notorious of Venice's gambling dens, which operated from 1638 to 1774 in the Palazzo Dandolo (no. 1332). Gamblers of all social classes were welcome at the Ridotto's tables – as long as they wore masks – but most of the clients came from the nobility. The consequent damage to the financial resources of the Venetian upper class became so great that the government was finally forced to close the joint. There was, however, no shortage of alternative houses in which to squander the family fortune – in 1797 some 136 gambling establishments were operating in the city.

1

building that is inextricably associated with fire. Built as a replacement for the San Benedetto theatre, which burned to the ground in 1774, **Giannantonio Selva**'s gaunt Neoclassical design was not deemed a great success on its inauguration on December 26, 1792, but nonetheless very little of the exterior was changed when the opera house was rebuilt following a second conflagration in 1836. Rather more extensive changes were made to its interior, a luxuriant, late Empire confection of gilt, plush and stucco which has been fastidiously replicated in the new Fenice, which was built after the catastrophic blaze of 1996, with the addition of a fireproof steel roof and an extra 150 seats squeezed in.

La Fenice saw some major musical events in the twentieth century – Stravinsky's *The Rake's Progress* and Britten's *The Turn of the Screw* were both premiered here, as were works by Prokofiev, Nono (the one great Venetian composer of modern times), Maderna, Sciarrino and Rihm. But the music scene was more exciting in the nineteenth century, when, in addition to staging the premieres of several operas by Rossini, Bellini and Verdi (*Rigoletto* and *La Traviata* both opened here), La Fenice became the focal point for protests against the occupying Austrian army – a favourite trick was to bombard the stage with bouquets in the colours of the Italian tricolour.

The Fenice remains one of Italy's great cultural institutions, but its future is not secure: government funding has been reduced to such an extent that performances have had to be cancelled and fundraising concerts organized. Insolvency is a real possibility.

The audio-guide is packed with information on the building, but unfortunately there's no access to the backstage areas.

Santa Maria del Giglio

Campo Santa Maria del Giglio • Mon–Sat 10.30am–4.30pm • €3, or Chorus Pass • ⓦ chorusvenezia.org

To Venetians the church of **Santa Maria del Giglio** is also known as Santa Maria Zobenigo, an alternative title derived from the name of the Jubanico family, who founded it in the ninth century. You can stare at the front of this church for as long as you like, but you still won't find a single unequivocally Christian image. The main statues are of the five **Barbaro** brothers, who financed the rebuilding of the church in 1678; *Virtue, Honour, Fame* and *Wisdom* hover at a respectful distance; and relief maps at eye level depict the towns that were honoured with the brothers' presence in the course of their military and diplomatic careers. Antonio Barbaro – the central figure and chief benefactor of the church – was not rated by his superiors quite as highly as he was by himself: he was in fact dismissed from Francesco Morosini's fleet for incompetence.

The interior, full to bursting with devotional pictures and sculptures, overcompensates for the impiety of the exterior. In the main body of the church the major works are the *Stations of the Cross* by various eighteenth-century artists and the *Evangelists* by **Tintoretto** behind the altar. The sacristy – packed with reliquaries that house, among other sacred scraps, a lock of St Francis's hair and a fragment of the garb of St Catherine of Siena – has a *Madonna and Child* that's attributed to Rubens. Outside again, the detached one-storey shop right by the church occupies the stump of the campanile, pruned to its present dimensions in 1774.

Campo San Maurizio

The tilting campanile of Santo Stefano looms into view over the vapid and deconsecrated church of **San Maurizio**, a collaboration between Giannantonio Selva and Antonio Diedo, secretary of the Accademia. The inside of the church is used as an exhibition space for Baroque musical instruments from the Artemio Versari (daily 9.30am–6.30pm; free), and the exterior is overshadowed by the fifteenth-century **Palazzo Zaguri**, which has been falling apart since it ceased to function as a school.

BURNING DOWN THE HOUSE: THE 1996 FENICE FIRE

1

Seating just 850 people, the old Fenice had an intimate atmosphere that brought out the best in performers, and its acoustics were superb, thanks largely to the fact that the interior structure was entirely wooden. It was this last characteristic that made the **fire** on the night of January 29, 1996, so disastrous – though the fire brigade was at the site within twenty minutes of the alarm being raised, it was all they could do to prevent the blaze spreading to the surrounding houses. Unable to get right up to the building because the flanking canals had been drained for dredging, the firefighters had to pump water from the Canal Grande and scoop it out of the lagoon by helicopter to contain the damage. La Fenice itself was quickly reduced to its external walls.

A picture taken from a nearby apartment appeared to show that the fire sprang from two different places in the top storey – the only explanation for which would be that the fire was started deliberately. Suspicions of **foul play** were strengthened by the fact that, though by law a caretaker and two firefighters should have been on duty at La Fenice throughout the night, there was just one doorman inside the building to operate its fire extinguishers, and the smoke detectors had been turned off. When investigators realized that the fire could only have spread with such speed if someone had poured inflammable liquids onto the timbers, arson was established as the cause. Inquiries soon focused on the contractors who were at work on a major refurbishment of the opera house at the time. Very quickly a conspiracy theory was in circulation and gaining wide acceptance: the contractors were controlled by organized crime, the argument ran, and their bosses had decided to torch the opera house either to avoid paying the penalties for failing to meet their deadlines, or because they fancied their chances of getting the lucrative contracts to rebuild the theatre.

Eventually **prosecutions** were brought against Enrico Carella – the owner of the subcontractors who had been rewiring La Fenice – and his cousin Massimiliano Marchetti. Both were found guilty, but the judges described them as "surrogates" for other unnamed third parties, the presumption being that Carella's uncle Renato – whose financial dealings looked irregular, to say the least – was the link-man between the mob and the arsonists. Renato Carella's death, soon after his nephew's conviction, left many Venetians convinced that the real instigators of the Fenice fire had escaped punishment. Enrico Carella was sentenced to seven years in prison and Marchetti to six. Released while awaiting an appeal hearing, Carella went on the run, and he remained at liberty until the eleventh anniversary of the fire, when he was tracked down to Mexico, after Interpol had tapped the phones of his mother and friends. As *Corriere della Sera* put it: "He was betrayed in the end by homesickness and his love for his Mamma."

Straight after the disaster it was claimed that the new Fenice would open before the end of 1998, but no sooner had reconstruction begun than it ran into litigation. A Fiat-controlled company originally won the contract on the basis of a plan drawn up by Gae Aulenti, but the firm that came second in the competition for the work promptly objected that Aulenti's scheme failed to meet the specified brief. **Legal action** ensued, and in the end the former runners-up – a German-Italian construction consortium headed by **Aldo Rossi**, one of Europe's greatest modern architects (who was killed in a car crash the year after the fire) – were told they could start building their state-of-the-art replica of La Fenice, a process that was aided by the discovery of the plans that had been used to rebuild the opera house in 1836. Even then, progress was so slow that the replacement builders were themselves dismissed and the work handed over to a Venetian company. Only at the end of 2003 was the new Fenice at last completed.

This district is the antiques centre of Venice, and from time to time the Campo San Maurizio is taken over by an antiques and bric-a-brac fair. The antiques business has a permanent representative on the campo in the form of V. Trois, an outlet for genuine Fortuny fabrics.

In the corner of the campo, at the beginning of Calle del Piovan stands a diminutive building that was once the **Scuola degli Albanesi**; it was established in 1497 and the reliefs on the facade date from shortly after that. In 1504 Carpaccio produced a cycle of *Scenes from the Life of the Virgin* for the *scuola*, and the pictures remained here even

1

after the decline of the Albanian community led to the disbanding of the confraternity in the late eighteenth century. It wasn't until 1808, when the bakers' guild that had moved into the building was itself scrapped, that the series was broken up. The bits that remained in Venice are now in the Correr collection and the Ca' d'Oro.

Stop for a second on the bridge just after the *scuola*, and look down the canal to your right – you'll see that it runs under the east end of Santo Stefano, the only church in Venice to have quite so intimate a relationship with the city's waterways.

Campo Santo Stefano

The church of Santo Stefano closes one end of the next square, **Campo Santo Stefano**. Large enough to hold several clusters of tourists, a few dozen café tables plus a kids' football match or two, the campo is one of the city's sunniest spots, but is at its liveliest in the run-up to Christmas, when a small village of food and crafts stalls is set up here. Bullfights were held here regularly until 1802, when the collapse of a bank of seats killed a number of spectators and provoked a permanent ban on such events.

Nicolò Tommaseo, the scholar and Risorgimento ideologue who was Manin's right-hand man during the 1848 insurrection, is commemorated by the statue in the middle of the campo; the unfortunate positioning of the pile of books (representing Tommaseo's voluminous literary output) has earned the statue the nickname *il Cagalibri* – the Book-shitter.

The most prominent palazzo on the campo itself, the **Palazzo Loredan** (originally fifteenth-century but rebuilt around 1540, with the facade added in 1618), now belongs to the Istituto Veneto di Scienze Lettere e Arte, an organization that also holds large-scale shows in the vast **Palazzo Franchetti**, which flanks the Accademia bridge. Campiello Pisani, which flows into Campo Santo Stefano opposite the Palazzo Loredan, is effectively a forecourt to the gargantuan **Palazzo Pisani**, now the Conservatory of Music. Work began on it in the early seventeenth century, continued for over a century and was at last brought to a halt by the government, who decided that the Pisani, among the city's richest banking families, were getting ideas above their station. Had the Pisani got their way, they wouldn't have stopped building until they reached the Canal Grande.

Santo Stefano

Campo Santo Stefano • Mon–Sat 10.30am–4.30pm • Sacristy €3, or Chorus Pass • ⓦ chorusvenezia.org

Founded in the thirteenth century, rebuilt in the fourteenth and altered again in the first half of the fifteenth, **Santo Stefano** is notable for its Gothic doorway and beautiful **ship's-keel roof**, both of which belong to the last phase of building. The airy and calm interior is one of the most pleasant places in Venice to just sit and think, but it also contains some major works of art. The **tomb of Giacomo Surian**, on the entrance wall, was designed and carved in the final decade of the fifteenth century by Pietro

---

FRANCESCO MOROSINI

Campo Santo Stefano's alternative name, Campo Francesco Morosini, comes from a former inhabitant of the palazzo at no. 2802. The last doge to serve as military commander of the Republic (1688–94), **Francesco Morosini** became a Venetian hero with his victories in the Peloponnese, as is attested by the triumphal arch built in his honour in the Palazzo Ducale's Sala dello Scrutinio, and the exhaustive documentation of his career in the Museo Correr. But to those few non-Venetians to whom his name means anything at all, he's known as the man who lobbed a missile through the roof of the Parthenon, detonating the Turkish gunpowder barrels that had been stored there. He then made matters worse by trying to prise some of the decoration off the half-wrecked temple, shattering great chunks of statuary in the process. Morosini and Venice didn't come back from that campaign empty-handed though – the Arsenale gate is guarded by two of his trophies.

THE PLAGUE PIT OF SANTO STEFANO

Off Calle del Pestrin, near the front door of Santo Stefano, you'll find the raised platform of **Campiello Novo**, otherwise known as **Campiello dei Morti**. Formerly the churchyard of Santo Stefano, it was used as a burial pit during the plague of 1630, and such was the volume of corpses interred here that for health reasons the site remained closed to the public from then until 1838.

Lombardo and his sons. Less easily overlooked is the **tomb of Francesco Morosini**: it's the oversized bronze badge in the centre of the nave. The major **paintings** are in the sacristy: a *St Lawrence* and a *St Nicholas of Bari* by Bartolomeo Vivarini, a trio of late works by Tintoretto – *The Agony in the Garden*, *The Last Supper* and *The Washing of the Disciples' Feet*. The choir of the church (which has superb inlaid choirstalls) is connected to the sacristy by a corridor that houses a small assemblage of sculpture, including items by the Dalle Masegnes and Tullio Lombardo, and Canova's stele for his first patron, Giovanni Falier (1808).

The **cloister** is now out of bounds to visitors, and the frescoes by Pordenone that used to cover much of the cloister walls survive only as a few scraps, today preserved in the Ca' d'Oro. Pordenone was for a while Titian's main rival in the city, and such was his fear of the great man and his cronies that he invariably turned up to work here with daggers and swords hanging from his belt. No assault actually occurred, but there has been plenty of bloodshed within the church precincts – so much, in fact, that the place has had to be reconsecrated half a dozen times.

San Vitale

Campo San Vidal • Mon–Sat 10.30am–4.30pm • €3, or Chorus Pass

At the opposite end of the campo from Santo Stefano stands the deconsecrated church of San Vitale (or Vidal). It's now used for concerts (Vivaldi for 99 percent of the time, but at least they don't play the *Four Seasons* every night), yet it still possesses a fine painting by Carpaccio (*San Vitale and other Saints*, above the high altar), and Piazzetta's *Archangel Raphael and Sts Anthony and Louis* (third altar on the right). If the facade of the church seems familiar, that's because it's a replica of San Giorgio Maggiore's.

Campo Sant'Angelo

A door leads from the cloister of Santo Stefano into the **Campo Sant'Angelo** (or Anzolo), a square almost as capacious as Campo Santo Stefano, but which feels more like a crossroads than a meeting place. It's bounded by some fine buildings, however, including two magnificent fifteenth-century palaces: the **Palazzo Gritti** and, facing it, the **Palazzo Duodo**, home of the composer Cimarosa, who died there in 1801. The minuscule **Oratorio dell'Annunziata** – founded in the tenth century, rebuilt in the twelfth and once the home of the Scuola dei Sotti ("of the Lame") – contains a sixteenth-century crucifix and an *Annunciation* by the omnipresent Palma il Giovane. Nothing remains of Sant'Angelo church, which was the leading player in one of Venice's great architectural cock-ups. By 1445 the tilt of the church's campanile had become so severe that urgent measures were deemed necessary. It was discovered that there was a builder in Bologna who had made such problems his speciality, and he was duly hired. The expert fixed it so the tower stood as straight as a pine tree; the scaffolding was taken down; a banquet was held to honour the engineering genius; next morning, the campanile keeled over. The church was demolished in 1837.

Campo San Samuele

From opposite the entrance to Santo Stefano church, Calle delle Botteghe and Crosera lead up to Salizzada San Samuele, a route that's lined with private galleries, arty shops and a few good places to eat; a left turn along Salizzada San Samuele takes you past the house in which **Paolo Veronese** lived his final years, and on to **Campo San Samuele**. Built in the late twelfth century and not much altered since, the campanile of the church is one of the oldest in the city. The church itself was founded in the previous century but was largely reconstructed in the late seventeenth; apart from some fifteenth-century frescoes by Paduan artists in the apse, the interior is of little interest.

Palazzo Grassi

Campo San Samuele 3231 • €18 combined ticket with Punta della Dogana • ⓦ palazzograssi.it

In 1984 the colossal **Palazzo Grassi** was bought by Fiat and converted into a cultural centre, to designs drawn up by Gae Aulenti, architect of Paris's Musée d'Orsay. Blockbuster overviews of entire cultures and epochs became the Grassi's speciality, but as Fiat's fortunes declined at the start of the new century, the Agnelli family – owners of the company – put the Grassi up for sale. Into the breach stepped the phenomenally wealthy **François Pinault**, chairman of the company that owns, among many other big names, Gucci, Fnac, Le Printemps and Christie's auction house. He is also France's most voracious buyer of modern art, whose ever-expanding collection ranges from Picasso, Miró, Brancusi and Mondrian to contemporaries such as Jeff Koons, Maurizio Cattelan and Marió Merz.

Pinault paid €30 million in 2005 for an eighty percent share in the Grassi (the Venice casino holds the other twenty percent), and commissioned the Japanese architect **Tadao Ando** to restyle the interior in his customary bleached tones. A couple of years later, Pinault also acquired the warehouses of the Dogana di Mare, which has become the main showcase for his vast collection, while the Grassi often stages immense and wide-ranging art shows that usually draw heavily on works owned by Pinault. As if that weren't enough, he then hired Ando to rebuild the **Teatrino Grassi**, the eighteenth-century theatre behind the palazzo; the beautifully austere 225-seater auditorium is used for conferences, lectures, concerts and film shows.

SAN BARNABA CANAL

Dorsoduro

There were not many places among the lagoon's mudbanks where Venice's early settlers could be confident that their dwellings wouldn't sink into the slime, but with Dorsoduro they were on relatively solid ground: the *sestiere*'s name translates as "hard back", and its buildings occupy the largest area of firm silt in the centre of the city. Some of the finest minor domestic architecture in Venice is concentrated here, and in recent years many of the area's best houses have been bought up by wealthy outsiders. The top-bracket colony is, however, pretty well confined to a triangle defined by the Accademia, the Punta della Dogana and the Gesuati. Stroll up to the area around Campo Santa Margherita and the atmosphere is quite different, largely because of the proximity of the main part of the university.

2

The **Gallerie dell'Accademia**, replete with masterpieces from each phase in the history of Venetian painting up to the eighteenth century, is the essential Dorsoduro sight, while the huge church of **Santa Maria della Salute**, the grandest gesture of Venetian Baroque, is architecturally the major religious building of the district. In terms of artistic contents, however, the Salute takes second place to **San Sebastiano**, the parish church of **Paolo Veronese**, whose paintings clad much of its interior. **Giambattista Tiepolo**, the master colourist of a later era, is well represented at the **Scuola Grande dei Carmini**, and for an overall view of Tiepolo's cultural milieu there's the **Ca' Rezzonico**, home of Venice's museum of eighteenth-century art and artefacts. Art of the twentieth century is on show at the **Guggenheim Collection**. More recent work is brilliantly displayed at the **Centro d'Arte Contemporanea Punta della Dogana**, Europe's largest showcase for cutting-edge art.

The Accademia

Campo della Carità • Mon 8.15am–2pm, Tues–Sun 8.15am–7.15pm • €12 • ⓦ gallerieaccademia.it

The **Gallerie dell'Accademia** – one of Europe's finest specialized art collections – began its existence as an annexe to Venice's school of art, the **Accademia di Belle Arti**. A Napoleonic decree of 1807 moved the Accademia to this site and instituted its galleries of Venetian paintings, a stock drawn largely from the city's suppressed churches and convents. Parts of the premises themselves were formerly religious buildings: the church of **Santa Maria della Carità** (rebuilt by Bartolomeo Bon in 1441–52) and the adjoining **Convento dei Canonici Lateranensi** (built by Palladio in 1561 but not completed) were both suppressed in 1807. The third component of the Accademia used to be the **Scuola della Carità**, founded in 1260 and the oldest of the six *Scuole Grande*; the Gothic building dates from 1343, but has an eighteenth-century facade.

The Accademia has recently been expanded to create new ground-floor galleries for some three hundred paintings and sculptures that were previously in storage, a development that has entailed moving the art college to the nearby Casa degli Incurabili. The upper floor now focuses on art up to the seventeenth century, with the lower galleries being devoted mainly to later artists, though there is still some chronological overlap, which presumably won't be the case when the layout is finalised. One-off exhibitions are also held in the new rooms. With San Marco and the Palazzo Ducale, the Accademia completes the triad of obligatory tourist sights in Venice, but admission is restricted to batches of three hundred people at a time, so if you're visiting in high summer and don't want to wait, get there before the doors open.

The fourteenth-century artists

The **first room** is the fifteenth-century former chapterhouse of the *scuola* (with its original gilded ceiling), now filled with pieces by the earliest-known individual Venetian painters. The icon-like Byzantine-influenced figures of **Paolo Veneziano** (first half of the fourteenth century) are succeeded by the Gothic forms of his follower **Lorenzo Veneziano** – look at the swaying stances of his figures and the emphasis on the sinuous lines of the drapery.

Bellini, Carpaccio, Giorgione

Room 2 is given over to large altarpieces from the late fifteenth and early sixteenth centuries, including works by **Giovanni Bellini**, **Cima da Conegliano** and **Vittore Carpaccio**. Carpaccio's strange *Crucifixion and Glorification of the Ten Thousand Martyrs of Mount Ararat* is the most gruesome painting in the room, and the most charming is by him too: *The Presentation of Jesus in the Temple*, with its pretty lute-playing cherub.

There's more from Bellini and Cima da Conegliano in room 3, along with a trio of fine pictures by **Sebastiano del Piombo**. After that comes a room of outstanding small paintings, including a series of *Madonna*s and a *Pietà* by **Giovanni Bellini**, a **Memling** portrait, and a work by the most mysterious of Italian painters, **Giorgione** – his *Portrait of an Old Woman* (c.1509) is a bold and profoundly compassionate image of mortality (the inscription, *Col Tempo*, means "with time").

Titian, Veronese, Tintoretto

2

Rooms 6 to 8 mark the entry of the super-heavyweights of the Venetian High Renaissance. In **room 6**, Jacopo Robusti, alias **Tintoretto**, is represented by several paintings, including a *Creation of the Animals* that features a few species that must have followed the unicorn into extinction, while Paolo Caliari, better known as **Paolo Veronese** (he came to Venice from Verona), is represented by a series of ceiling panels, a genre at which he excelled. In the parallel suite, **rooms 7 to 9**, you'll find the compelling *Young Man in His Study* by **Lorenzo Lotto** (c.1528), a muscular *John the Baptist* and a beguiling *Tobias and the Angel by* **Titian, and work by** Previtali and Savoldo, the pre-eminent high Renaissance artists in Bergamo and Brescia respectively.

Room 6 is in effect the anteroom to the vast **room 10**, one whole wall of which is needed for *Christ in the House of Levi*, painted by **Paolo Veronese** in 1573. Originally called *The Last Supper* – being a replacement for a Titian painting of the same subject that was destroyed by a fire in the refectory of San Zanipolo – this picture brought down on Veronese the wrath of the Inquisition, who objected to the inclusion of "buffoons, drunkards, Germans, dwarfs, and similar indecencies" in the sacred scene. (What really raised their hackles was the German contingent, who were perceived by the Holy Office as the incarnation of the Reformation menace.) Veronese's response was simply to change the title and append an inscription identifying the subject (it's on the balustrade in the lower left portion), emendations that apparently satisfied his critics.

Among the works by **Tintoretto** is the painting that made his reputation: *St Mark Freeing a Slave* (1548), painted for the Scuola Grande di San Marco, and showing St Mark's intervention at the execution of a slave who had defied his master by travelling to the Evangelist's shrine. Comparison with Gentile Bellini's unruffled depictions of miraculous events in rooms 20–21 makes it easy to understand the sensation caused by Tintoretto's whirling, brashly coloured scene. The legend of Venice's patron saint is further elaborated by three other pictures that were also commissioned by the *scuola*: the dreamlike *Translation of the Body of St Mark* (see page 40), *St Mark Saving a Saracen* (both from the 1560s) and *The Dream of St Mark* (1570), which is largely by his son **Domenico**. Tintoretto's love of physical and psychological drama, the energy of his brushstrokes and the sometimes uncomfortable originality of his colours and poses are all displayed in this group. Opposite hangs **Titian**'s highly charged *Pietà* (1576), painted for his own tomb in the Frari; the immediacy of death is expressed in the handling of the paint, here scratched, scraped and dolloped onto the canvas not just with brushes but with the artist's bare hands. It was completed after Titian's death by Palma il Giovane, as the inscription explains.

In **room 11** there's more from **Tintoretto**, including the sumptuous *Madonna dei Camerlenghi* (1566), showing the city's treasurers hobnobbing with the Mother of Our Saviour. Pordenone and Leandro Bassano are also on show here.

At the moment, room 11 also holds some dazzling works by **Giambattista Tiepolo**, but sooner or later these will almost certainly be moved into the new galleries downstairs. The fragments of the ceiling he created for the Scalzi church (1743–44) are all that's left after a bomb went through the roof in 1915; his *St Helena Discovering the Cross* was painted at around the same time, for a convent in Castello; and the long frieze of *The Miracle of the Bronze Serpent* (c.1735) was brought here from a now-defunct church over on La Giudecca and sustained some damage when it was rolled up for storage in the nineteenth century, at a time when the artist was out of fashion

The Vivarinis and Bellinis

The long corridor of **room 12** at the moment marks the beginning of what has always tended to be a rather dull section of the Accademia. When we went to press, these rooms were all being rebuilt, making **room 23** the next stop. Formerly the top part of the Carità church, this huge space contains works mainly from the fifteenth

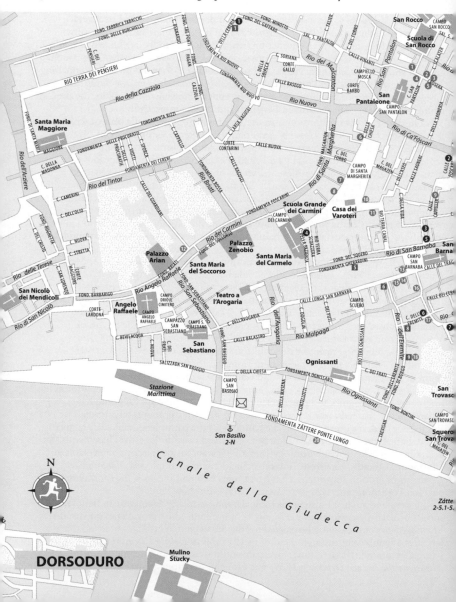

and early sixteenth centuries, the era of two of Venice's most significant artistic dynasties, the **Vivarini** and **Bellini** families. Of the pieces by the Vivarini – **Antonio**, his brother **Bartolomeo** and his son **Alvise** – the most striking is perhaps Alvise's *Madonna and Child with Sts Andrew, John the Baptist, Dominic and Peter*. **Giovanni Bellini** is represented by four workshop-assisted triptychs (painted for this church in the 1460s), and his brother **Gentile** by the intense portrait of *The Blessed Lorenzo Giustinian* (1445). One of the oldest surviving Venetian canvases and Gentile's earliest signed work, it was possibly used as a standard in processions, which would account for its tatty state.

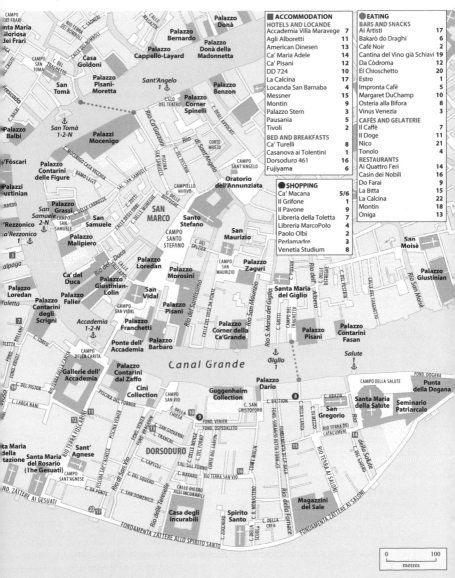

■ ACCOMMODATION	
HOTELS AND LOCANDE	
Accademia Villa Maravege	7
Agli Alboretti	11
American Dinesen	13
Ca' Maria Adele	14
Ca' Pisani	12
DD 724	10
La Calcina	17
Locanda San Barnaba	4
Messner	15
Montin	9
Palazzo Stern	3
Pausania	5
Tivoli	2
BED AND BREAKFASTS	
Ca' Turelli	8
Casanova ai Tolentini	1
Dorsoduro 461	16
Fujiyama	6

● EATING	
BARS AND SNACKS	
Ai Artisti	17
Bakarò do Draghi	6
Café Noir	2
Cantina del Vino già Schiavi	19
Da Còdroma	12
El Chioschetto	20
Estro	1
Impronta Cafè	5
Margaret DuChamp	10
Osteria alla Bifora	8
Vinus Venezia	3
CAFÉS AND GELATERIE	
Il Caffè	7
Il Doge	11
Nico	21
Tonolo	4
RESTAURANTS	
Ai Quattro Feri	14
Casin dei Nobili	16
Do Farai	9
La Bitta	15
La Calcina	22
Montin	18
Oniga	13

● SHOPPING	
Ca' Macana	5/6
Il Grifone	1
Il Pavone	9
Libreria della Toletta	7
Libreria MarcoPolo	4
Paolo Olbi	2
Perlamadre	3
Venetia Studium	8

In the same room you should also find an exquisite *St George* by **Mantegna** (who was married to the sister of Gentile and Giovanni), *St Jerome* **by Piero della Francesca**'s, a batch of paintings by **Hieronymus Bosch and Giorgione**'s gorgeous *Tempest* – the first known painting to have no historical, religious, mythological or factual basis, it seems to have been as perplexing to Giorgione's contemporaries as it is to us.

The Miracles of the Relic of the Cross

There's more from Gentile Bellini over in **room 20**, which is entirely filled by the cycle of *The Miracles of the Relic of the Cross*. The work was produced by various artists between 1494 and 1501, and was commissioned by the Scuola Grande di San Giovanni Evangelista to extol the holy fragment it had held since 1369. Gentile's *Procession in Piazza San Marco* (1496), executed the year the Torre dell'Orologio was started, is perhaps the best-known image of the group; the devotional moment is easily missed – the bare-headed man in a red cloak kneeling as the relic passes him is one Jacopo de' Salis, praying for his son's recovery from a fractured skull. In *The Miracle of the True Cross at the Bridge of San Lorenzo* (1500) Gentile shows Andrea Vendramin, Grand Guardian of the Scuola, retrieving the relic from the spot where it had floated after being knocked into the water during a procession; the fourth figure from the left in the group of donors in the right foreground is alleged to be a self-portrait, and Caterina Cornaro (see page 304) is portrayed on the far left.

A wealth of anecdotal detail adds historical veracity to **Carpaccio**'s *Miracle of the True Cross at the Rialto Bridge* (1494). Set by the Rialto (and showing one of the wooden precursors of the present bridge), its cast of characters includes turbaned Turks and Arabs, Armenian (or Greek) gentlemen in tall, brimmed hats, an African gondolier, a woman beating carpets on an *altana* and a man repairing a roof; the miracle – the cure of a lunatic – is happening on the first floor of the building on the left. **Giovanni Mansueti**'s *Miracle of the Relic in Campo San Lio* (1494) shows what happened at the funeral of a dissolute and impious member of the confraternity: the relic refused to allow itself to be carried into the church for his service. Each window has a woman or child in it, witnessing the shame of the old reprobate.

Carpaccio's St Ursula paintings – and Titian's Presentation

Another remarkable cycle fills **room 21** – **Carpaccio**'s *Story of St Ursula*, painted for the Scuola di Sant'Orsola at San Zanipolo in 1490–94. A superlative exercise in pictorial narrative, the paintings are especially fascinating to the modern viewer as a meticulous record of domestic architecture, costume, the decorative arts and even ship design in Venice at the close of the fifteenth century. The legend is that a British prince named Hereus proposed marriage to Ursula, a Breton princess, who accepted on two conditions: that Hereus convert to Christianity, and that he should wait for three years, during which time he should escort Ursula and her company of 11,000 virgins on a pilgrimage to Rome. The conditions were accepted, and the eventual consequence was that Ursula and her troop were massacred by the Huns near Cologne – as she had been forewarned by an angel in a dream. (Most scholars agree that the legend originated from a ninth-century clerical error: one suggestion is that the abbreviation *XI. M. V.* was misread as meaning "eleven thousand virgins" rather than "eleven martyred virgins".)

After this room, you come to the former *albergo* of the *scuola*; **Titian**'s *Presentation of the Virgin* (1539) occupies the wall over the door, the place for which it was painted – and the triptych by **Antonio Vivarini** and **Giovanni d'Alemagna** (1446) similarly hangs where it always has.

The ground-floor galleries

Nothing in the new ground-floor galleries matches the impact of the upper rooms, but there are some fine pieces here, by artists such as **Canaletto** and **Guardi**, along with **Pietro Longhi**'s quasi-documentary interiors, and a large quantity of sculptures and reliefs by the great Neoclassical sculptor **Antonio Canova**. Also on show are a series of portraits by **Rosalba Carriera**, one of the very few women in the Accademia's collection. Carriera's work established the use of pastel as a medium in its own right, rather than as a preparation for oil paint, and her moving *Self-Portrait*, done at a time when her eyesight was beginning to fail, is a high point of her work.

2

Eastern Dorsoduro

Along the east flank of the Accademia runs the wide Rio Terrà Foscarini, named after **Senator Antonio Foscarini**, victim of the Venetian judicial system's most notorious gaffe (see page 174); he lived at no. 180–181, but the house was radically altered in the nineteenth century. The street cuts down almost as far as the Záttere, but for the direct route to the mouth of the Canal Grande turn left along Calle Nuova a Sant'Agnese, one of the district's main shopping streets.

Campo San Vio

A fine platform from which to watch the traffic on the Canal Grande, **Campo San Vio** opens out onto the water because the houses here were demolished in order to make it easier for the doge and his entourage to disembark for the annual thanksgiving service in the church of Sts Vito and Modesto (contracted to Vio in Venetian); held on the saints' joint feast day, June 15, the service commemorated the defeat of the Bajamonte Tiepolo revolt (see page 68), which occurred on June 15, 1310. The church itself was demolished in 1813; the walls of the chapel that took its place (St George – the city's Anglican church) are encrusted with stone fragments taken from the Tiepolo palazzo, which was destroyed in punishment for their treason.

The Guggenheim Collection

Calle San Cristoforo 701 • Mon & Wed–Sun 10am–6pm • €15 • ⓦ guggenheim-venice.it

In the early years of the twentieth century the leading lights of the Futurist movement came to the quarter-built Palazzo Venier dei Leoni for parties thrown by the dotty Marchesa Casati, who was fond of stunts like setting wild cats and apes loose in the palazzo garden, among plants sprayed lilac for the occasion. **Peggy Guggenheim**, a considerably more discerning and influential patron of the arts, moved in here in 1949; since her death in 1979 the Guggenheim Foundation has looked after the administration of the place and has turned her collection of more than three hundred artworks into the city's second most popular museum, after the Accademia.

Core pieces in this top-quality and beautifully displayed celebration of modernist art include Brancusi's *Bird in Space* and *Maestra*, De Chirico's *Red Tower* and *Nostalgia of the Poet*, Max Ernst's *Robing of the Bride* (Ernst was briefly Guggenheim's husband in the 1940s), some of Joseph Cornell's boxes, sculpture by Laurens and Lipchitz, and works by Malevich and Schwitters; you'll also find work by Picasso, Braque, Chagall, Pollock (whose career owed much to Guggenheim's support), Duchamp, Giacometti, Picabia and Magritte. Marino Marini's *Angel of the Citadel*, out on the terrace, flaunts his erection at the passing canal traffic; more decorous pieces by Giacometti, Moore, Paolozzi and others are planted in the garden, surrounding Peggy Guggenheim's burial place. Not everything on show here is part of Guggenheim's bequest, however. Italian Futurism is represented by 26 works on long-term loan from the Gianni Mattioli

Collection, and in 2012 the museum was augmented by 83 works from the Rudolph and Hannelore Schulhof Collection, an acquisition that has provoked legal action from one of Peggy Guggenheim's grandsons, who – in cahoots with other relatives – is arguing that the Guggenheim Foundation has violated his grandmother's legacy in yielding to "commercial cynicism".

Santa Maria della Salute

Campo della Salute • Daily 9am–noon & 3–5.30pm • Free; sacristy €4

In 1630–31 Venice was devastated by a plague that exterminated nearly 95,000 of the lagoon's population – one person in three. In October 1630 the Senate decreed that a new church would be dedicated to the Virgin Mary if the city were saved, and the result was the **Salute** – *salute* meaning "health" and "salvation" – or **Santa Maria della Salute**, to use its full title.

Resting on a platform of more than 100,000 wooden piles, the Salute took half a century to build; its architect, **Baldassare Longhena**, was only 26 years old when his proposal was accepted. He lived just long enough to see it finished – he died in 1682, one year after completion. Each year on November 21 (the feast of the Presentation of the Virgin) the Signoria processed from San Marco to the Salute for a service of thanksgiving, crossing the Canal Grande on a pontoon bridge laid from Santa Maria del Giglio. The Festa della Madonna della Salute is still a major event in the Venetian calendar, with thousands of people making their way here to pray for, or give thanks for, good health.

The form of the Salute owes much to the plan of Palladio's Redentore – the obvious model for a dramatically sited votive church – and to the repertoire of Marian symbolism. The octagonal shape of the building alludes to the eight-pointed Marian star, for example, while the huge dome (a perilous engineering project in a city of mudbanks) represents Mary's crown and the centralized plan is a conventional symbol of the Virgin's womb. Its decorative details are saturated with coded references: the inscription in the centre of the mosaic floor, "Unde Origo, Inde Salus" (From the Origin came Salvation), refers to the coincidence of Mary's feast day and the legendary date of Venice's foundation – March 25, 421; the Marian rosary is evoked by the encircling roses.

The interior

Less arcane symbolism is at work on the **high altar**, where the Virgin and Child rescue Venice (kneeling woman) from the plague (old woman); in attendance are St Mark and St Lorenzo Giustiniani, first Patriarch of Venice. The Byzantine altarpiece, a little uneasy in this Baroque opulence, was brought to Venice in 1672 by Francesco Morosini (see page 76), never a man to resist the opportunity for a bit of state-sanctioned theft.

The most notable paintings in the Salute are the **Titian** pieces brought from the suppressed church of Santo Spirito in Isola in 1656, and now displayed in the sacristy (€4): an early altarpiece of *St Mark Enthroned with Sts Cosmas, Damian, Sebastian and Roch* (the plague saints), three violent ceiling paintings of *David and Goliath*, *Abraham and Isaac* and *Cain and Abel* (1540s) and eight late tondi of the *Doctors of the Church* (Sts Jerome, Augustine, Gregory and Ambrose) and the *Evangelists*. Tintoretto has included himself in the dramatis personae of his *Marriage at Cana* (1561) – he's the first Apostle on the left. Nearby is a fine *Madonna* by Palma il Vecchio, one of the sixteenth century's more placid souls.

The Pinacoteca Manfrediana

Fondamenta della Dogana alla Salute • Mon–Wed 10am–1pm, Thurs & Fri 3–6pm, Sat 10am–6pm • €6 • ⓦ seminariovenezia.it

Alongside the Salute stands the Seminario Patriarcale, home to the **Pinacoteca Manfrediana**. Recently refurbished after being closed for many years, the core of the collection consists of the sixty-odd pictures collected by Federico Manfredini in the early nineteenth century. There are a few big names here – notably Veronese, Titian, Cima da Conegliano and Filippino Lippi – but it's not a museum to build your day around.

The Punta della Dogana

Fondamenta della Dogana alla Salute • Mon & Wed–Sun 10am–7pm • €18 combined ticket with Palazzo Grassi • ⓦ palazzograssi.it

On the point where the Canal Grande and the Giudecca canal merge stands the huge **Dogana di Mare** (Customs House), another late seventeenth-century building, which was serving as a customs office as recently as the mid-1990s but in 2009 became the **Centro d'Arte Contemporanea Punta della Dogana**. Financed by François Pinault, the co-owner of Palazzo Grassi, the Dogana arts centre – like the Grassi – has been renovated to designs drawn up by the ever-subtle Tadao Ando. The exterior has been restored in a way that gives no indication of the building's new function (the weather vane on top of the Dogana's gold ball is said by most to represent Fortune, though others identify it as Justice), and the shell of the interior has similarly been left unaltered, with massive wooden roof-beams spanning walls of beautiful raw red brick. Within this casing, Ando has inserted walls of pale grey concrete, to create two storeys of elegant exhibition space, centred on a single double-height room. Some three hundred works are usually on show at any one time, and Pinault has invested in many of the really big names of the current art scene, so you can expect to see pieces by the likes of Cindy Sherman, Luc Tuymans, Thomas Schütte and Marlene Dumas, to name but a few. Usually, exhibitions at the Dogana are twinned with equally vast shows at the Grassi.

The Záttere and western Dorsoduro

Known collectively as the **Záttere**, the sequence of waterfront pavements between the Punta della Dogana and the Stazione Maríttima is now a popular place for a stroll or an alfresco meal, but was formerly the place where most of the bulky goods coming into Venice were unloaded onto floating rafts called *záttere*.

The Magazzini del Sale

Fondamenta delle Záttere allo Spirito Santo 266 • Spazio Vedova Mon & Wed–Sun 10.30am–6pm • €8 • ⓦ fondazionevedova.org

A fair quantity of cargo was carted into the state-run and highly lucrative **Magazzini del Sale** (Salt Warehouses), the vast low structure near the Punta della Dogana. In the tenth century the Venetians established a regional monopoly in salt production by destroying the rival town of Comacchio, near the Po delta; some 44,000 tons of salt, most of it made in saltpans near Chioggia, could be stored in this one building, a stockpile that represented at its peak nearly ten percent of the state's income. Part of the complex has been converted by Renzo Piano into a beautiful exhibition space, usually showing a selection of works by the Venetian artist **Emilio Vedova** (1919–2006). Another section is now a boathouse, and other parts are used as exhibition space by the Accademia and the Biennale.

Santa Maria del Rosario (The Gesuati)

Fondamenta delle Záttere ai Gesuati • Mon–Sat 10.30am–4.30pm • €3 or Chorus Pass • ⓦ chorusvenezia.org

There's an appealing mix of architectural exteriors on the eastern reaches of the Záttere: the fifteenth-century facade of **Spirito Santo** church, the **Casa degli Incurabili** (once one of Venice's four main hospitals, now the HQ of the Accademia art college), and the Veneto-Byzantine church of **Sant'Agnese**, begun in the twelfth century but much remodelled since then. However, the first building to stop for is the church of the **Gesuati** or **Santa Maria del Rosario**.

Rebuilt in 1726–43, about half a century after the church was taken over from the order of the Gesuati by the Dominicans, this was the first church designed by **Giorgio Massari**, an architect whose work combines Rococo preciousness with a more robust classicism – here his creation forms a sort of counterpoint to the Redentore, over the water. He often worked with **Giambattista Tiepolo**, who painted the first altarpiece on the right, *The Virgin with Sts Catherine of Siena, Rose and Agnes* (c.1740), and the three magnificent ceiling panels of *Scenes from the Life of St Dominic* (1737–39), which are seen to best effect in the afternoon, when the natural light comes from the same direction as the artificial light in the paintings. The third altar on this side of the church is adorned with a painting of *Sts Vincent Ferrer, Giacinto and Luigi Beltran* by Tiepolo's principal forerunner, Giambattista Piazzetta. Opposite, the first altar has Sebastiano Ricci's *Pius V with Sts Thomas Aquinas and Peter Martyr* (1739), completing the church's array of Rococo propaganda on behalf of the exalted figures of Dominican orthodoxy, followed by a tragically intense *Crucifixion* by Tintoretto (c.1555) on the third altar.

Santa Maria della Visitazione

Fondamenta delle Záttere ai Gesuati • Daily 8am–noon & 3–7pm • Free

Santa Maria della Visitazione has an attractive Lombardesque facade, but the only notable aspect of the interior is its sixteenth-century **ceiling**, with panels painted by Umbrian artists. The lion's-mouth letter box to the right of the facade was for the use of residents with complaints relating to health and sanitation; a complaint posted in 1498 resulted in punishment for the tradesmen who had sold oil that was full of "immonditie e sporchezi" (filth and dirt) – syphilitic patients had been immersed in it as a cure.

GONDOLAS

The earliest mention of a gondola is in a decree of 1094, but the vessel of that period bore little resemblance to today's streamlined thoroughbred. As late as the thirteenth century the gondola was a twelve-oared beast with an iron beak – an adornment that evolved into the saw-toothed projection called the **ferro**, which fronts the modern gondola. (The precise significance of the *ferro's* shape is unclear – tradition has it that the six main prongs symbolize the six *sestieri*, with the backward-facing prong representing La Giudecca.) Over the next two centuries the gondola shrank to something near its present dimensions, developed multicoloured coverings and sprouted the little chair on carved legs that it still carries. The gondola's distinctive oarlock, an elaborately convoluted lump of walnut or cherry wood known as a **forcola**, which permits the long oar to be used in eight different positions, reached something like its present form at this time too.

By the sixteenth century the gondola had become a mode of social ostentation, with gilded prows, fantastically upholstered **felzi** (cabins), cushions of satin and silk and hulls decked out with a profusion of embroidery, carvings and flowers. Sumptuary laws were introduced to quash this aquatic one-upmanship, and though some of them had little effect, one of them changed the gondola's appearance for good – since an edict of 1562 gondolas have been uniformly black, a livery which prompted Shelley to liken them to "moths of which a coffin might have been the chrysalis".

There's been little alteration in the gondola's dimensions and construction since the end of the seventeenth century: the only significant changes have been adjustments of the gondola's asymmetric line to compensate for the weight of the gondolier – a characteristic that's particularly noticeable when you see them out of water. All gondolas are 10.87m long and 1.42m wide at their broadest point, and are assembled from nearly three hundred pieces of seasoned mahogany, elm, oak, lime, walnut, fir, cherry and larch. Plenty of gondolas pass through the boatyards for repair, but each *squero* turns out only about four new gondolas a year.

THE NICOLOTTI AND THE CASTELLANI

Venetian folklore has it that San Trovaso was the only neutral ground between the **Nicolotti and the Castellani**, the two factions into which the working-class citizens of the city were divided: the former, coming from the west and north of the city, were named after the church of San Nicolò dei Mendicoli; the latter, from the *sestieri* of Dorsoduro, San Marco and Castello, took their name from San Pietro di Castello. The rivals celebrated intermarriages and other services here, but are said to have entered and departed by separate doors: the Nicolotti by the door at the traditional "west" end, the Castellani by the door on the "south" side.

2

The squero di San Trovaso

Rio di San Trovaso

Ten thousand **gondolas** operated on the canals of sixteenth-century Venice, when they were the standard form of transport around the city; nowadays the tourist trade is pretty well all that sustains the city's fleet of around five hundred gondolas, which provide steady employment for a few **squeri**, as the gondola yards are called. A display in the Museo Storico Navale takes you through the construction of a gondola, but no abstract demonstration can equal the fascination of a working yard, and the most public one in Venice is the **squero di San Trovaso**, which you'll see when you turn off the Zátter towards San Trovaso church. The San Trovaso *squero* is the oldest one still functioning – established in the seventeenth century, it looks rather like an alpine farmhouse, a reflection of the architecture of the Dolomite villages from which many of Venice's gondola-builders once came. The city's only other gondola *squero* – founded in 1884 by Domenico Tramontin and still run by his descendants – is tucked away on the Rio dell'Avogaria, a short distance west of here, beyond the former Benedictine convent of Ognissanti.

San Trovaso

Campo San Trovaso • Mon–Sat 8–11am & 3–6pm • Free

Don't bother consulting any dictionary of saints for the dedicatee of **San Trovaso** church – the name's a baffling dialect version of Santi Gervasio e Protasio. Since its tenth-century foundation the church has had a chequered history, falling down once, and twice being destroyed by fire; this is the fourth incarnation, built in 1584–1657.

Inside, San Trovaso is spacious and somewhat characterless, but it does boast a pair of fine paintings by **Tintoretto**: *The Temptation of St Anthony* and *The Last Supper*. The former is in the chapel to the left of the high altar, along with *St Crysogonus on Horseback* by Michele Giambono (c.1450), Venice's main practitioner of the International Gothic style; the latter is in the chapel at ninety degrees to the first one. The two large pictures on each side of the choir, *The Adoration of the Magi* and *The Expulsion from the Temple*, were begun by Tintoretto at the very end of his life, but so much of the finished work is by his son and other assistants that they are now attributed to Domenico. Finally, in the chapel next to the south door you'll find a marble altar-front carved with angels; dated around 1470, it's one of the first Renaissance low-reliefs produced in Venice.

San Sebastiano

Campo San Sebastiano • Mon–Sat 10.30am–4.30pm • €3 or Chorus Pass • ⓦ chorusvenezia.org

At the end of the Zátter the barred gates of the Stazione Maríttima deflect you away from the waterfront and towards the church of **San Sebastiano**. The parish church of **Paolo Veronese**, it contains a group of resplendent paintings by him that gives it a place in his career comparable to that of San Rocco in the career of Tintoretto, but the church attracts nothing like the number of visitors that San Rocco gets.

Veronese was still in his twenties when, thanks largely to his contacts with the Verona-born prior of San Samuele, he was asked to paint the ceiling of the **sacristy** with a *Coronation of the Virgin* and the *Four Evangelists* (1555); once that commission had been carried out, he decorated the **nave ceiling** with *Scenes from the Life of St Esther*. His next project, the dome of the chancel, was later destroyed, but the sequence he and his brother Benedetto then painted on the walls of the church and the nuns' choir at the end of the 1550s has survived in pretty good shape. In the following decade he executed the last of the pictures, those on the **organ shutters** and around the **high altar**: on the left, *St Sebastian Leads Sts Mark and Marcellian to Martyrdom*, and on the right *The Second Martyrdom of St Sebastian* (the torture by arrows didn't kill him). Other riches include a late **Titian** of *St Nicholas* (on the left wall of the first chapel on the right), and the early sixteenth-century majolica pavement in the Cappello Lando, to the left of the chancel – in front of which is Veronese's tomb slab.

Angelo Raffaele

Campo de l'Anzolo Rafael • Mon–Sat 8am–noon & 3–5.30pm, Sun 9am–noon • Free

The exterior of the seventeenth-century church of **Angelo Raffaele** (or Anzolo Rafael) is notable only for the two huge war memorials blazoned on the canal facade. Over the doorway, a sixteenth-century relief depicts the angel Raphael with Tobias, whose life is illustrated in the scene on the organ loft inside, which was painted by one or other of the **Guardi** brothers (nobody's sure which). Although small in scale, the free brushwork and imaginative composition make the panels among the most charming examples of Venetian Rococo, a fascinating counterpoint to the grander visions of Giambattista Tiepolo, the Guardis' brother-in-law.

In the campo behind the church is a wellhead built from the bequest of Marco Arian, who died of the Black Death in 1348, an outbreak which he blamed on contaminated water. The **Palazzo Arian**, on the opposite bank of the canal, was built in the second half of that century and is adorned by one of the finest and earliest Gothic windows in Venice – they are the only ones in the city to replicate the distinctive pattern of the Palazzo Ducale's stonework.

San Nicolò dei Mendicoli

Campo San Nicolò • Mon–Sat 10am–noon & 4–6pm, Sun 4–6pm • Free

Although it's located on the edge of the city, the church of **San Nicolò dei Mendicoli** is one of Venice's oldest – said to have been founded in the seventh century, San Nicolò is traditionally predated only by San Giacomo di Rialto. Its long history was reflected in the fact that it gave its name to the **Nicolotti** faction, whose titular head, the so-called *Gastaldo* or the *Doge dei Nicolotti*, was elected by the parishioners and then honoured by a ceremonial greeting from the Republic's doge.

The church has been rebuilt and altered at various times, but in essence its shape is still that of the Veneto-Byzantine structure raised here in the twelfth century, the date of its rugged campanile. The other conspicuous feature of the exterior is the fifteenth-century porch, a type of construction once common in Venice, and often used here as makeshift accommodation for penurious nuns. (The only other example left standing is at San Giacomo di Rialto.) The interior is a miscellany of periods and styles. Parts of the apse and the columns of the nave go back to the twelfth century, but the capitals were replaced in the fourteenth – the penultimate one on the left side bears an inscription dating it January 25, 1366. Above, the darkened gilded woodwork that gives the interior its rather overcast appearance was installed late in the sixteenth century, as were most of the paintings, many of which were painted by Alvise dal Friso and other pupils of Paolo Veronese. Occupying the high altar is a large wooden

statue of St Nicholas, a mid-fifteenth-century piece, possibly from the workshop of Bartolomeo Bon.

The convent and church of **Le Terese**, on the other side of the canal, have been restored as student accommodation and a university auditorium; there's no reason to set foot on the island on which it stands, as it's a zone of docks, new housing developments and warehouses, one of which has been converted into a home for the city's well-reputed University of Architecture.

Campo Santa Margherita and northern Dorsoduro

Campo di Santa Margherita is the social heart of Dorsoduro, and is one of the most appealing squares in the whole city. Piazza San Marco nowadays is overrun with tourists, but Campo di Santa Margherita – the largest square on this side of the Canal Grande – belongs to the Venetians and retains a spirit of authenticity. Ringed by houses that date back as far as the fourteenth century, it's spacious and at the same time modest, taking its tone not from any grandiose architecture (it's one of very few squares with no palazzo), but from its cluster of market stalls and its plethora of bars and cafés, which draw a lot of their custom from the university.

The church that gives the campo its name was closed in 1810, for a while functioned as a cinema and is now a university property; the dragons that feature so prominently in the decorative stonework on and around the church relate to the legend of St Margaret, who emerged unscathed after the dragon that had swallowed her exploded. Isolated at the fish-stall end of the campo stands the **Scuola dei Varotari** (tanners' guild), bearing an eroded relief of the Madonna with members of the *scuola*.

The Scuola Grande dei Carmini

Campo Santa Margherita 2617 • Daily 11am–5pm • €5 • ⓦ scuolagrandecarmini.it

In Campo Santa Margherita's southwest extremity stands the **Scuola Grande dei Carmini**, once the Venetian base of the Carmelite order. Originating in Palestine towards the close of the twelfth century, the Carmelites blossomed during the Counter-Reformation, when they became the shock-troops through whom the cult of the Virgin was disseminated, as a response to the inroads of Protestantism. As happened elsewhere in Europe, the Venetian Carmelites became immensely wealthy, and in the 1660s they called in an architect – probably Longhena – to redesign the property they had acquired. The core of this complex, which in 1767 was raised to the status of a *scuola grande*, is now effectively a showcase for the art of **Giambattista Tiepolo**, who in the 1740s painted the ceiling of the upstairs hall.

The paintings

The central panel, framed by depictions of various virtues in the corners of the ceiling, was restored a few years ago after the cords that suspended it rotted away, causing it to crash from the ceiling. Showing *Simon Stock Receiving the Scapular*, it is not the most immediately comprehensible image in Venetian art. The Carmelite order was in some disarray by the mid-thirteenth century, but it acquired a new edge when the English-born Simon Stock was elected prior general in 1247; under his control, the Carmelites were transformed into a well-organized mendicant order, with houses in the main university cities of Europe – Cambridge, Oxford, Paris and Bologna.

Some time after his death the tradition grew that he had experienced a vision of the Virgin, who presented him with a scapular (two pieces of cloth joined by cords) bearing her image: as the scapular was the badge of the Carmelites, its gift was evidently a sign that Simon should undertake the reform of the order. Tiepolo has translated this crucial episode from the place where it allegedly happened (Cambridge) to his customary floating world of blue skies and spiralling perspectives (a world seen at its most vertiginous in the painting of an angel rescuing a falling mason). The painting was such a hit with Tiepolo's clients that he was instantly granted membership of the *scuola*, a more generous reward than you might think – a papal bull had apparently ordained that all those who wore the scapular would, through the intercession of the Virgin, be released from the pains of Purgatory on the first Saturday after the wearer's decease, "or as soon as possible". This edict was probably a forgery, but the Carmelites believed it, and it would seem that Tiepolo did too.

Santa Maria del Carmelo

Campo dei Carmini • Mon–Sat 2.30–7pm • Free

Santa Maria del Carmelo – usually known simply as the **Carmini**– is identifiable from a long way off, thanks to the statue of the Virgin atop the campanile. A collage of architectural styles, it has a sixteenth-century facade, a Gothic side doorway which preserves several Byzantine fragments and a fourteenth-century basilican interior. A dull series of Baroque paintings illustrating the history of the Carmelite order covers a lot of space inside (the same subject is covered by the gilded carvings of the nave), but the second altar on the right has a fine *Nativity* by Cima da Conegliano (before 1510), and Lorenzo Lotto's *Sts Nicholas of Bari, John the Baptist and Lucy* (1529) – featuring what Bernard Berenson ranked as one of the most beautiful landscapes in all Italian art – hangs on the opposite side of the nave.

Palazzo Zenobio and Santa Maria del Soccorso

The most imposing building on Fondamenta del Soccorso (leading from Campo dei Carmini towards Angelo Raffaele) is the **Palazzo Zenobio**, built in the late seventeenth century when the Zenobio family were among the richest in Venice. It's been an Armenian college since 1850, but visitors are sometimes allowed to see the ballroom: one of the city's richest eighteenth-century interiors, it was painted by Luca Carlevaris, whose trompe l'oeil decor provided a model for the decoration of the slightly later Ca' Rezzonico. In the late sixteenth century a home for prostitutes who wanted to get out of the business was set up at no. 2590 – the chapel of **Santa Maria del Soccorso** – by **Veronica Franco**, a renowned ex-courtesan who was as famous for her poetry and her artistic salon as she was for her sexual allure; both Michel de Montaigne and King Henry III of France were grateful recipients of samples of her literary output.

The parish of San Barnaba

Calle della Pazienza, which flanks the Carmini church, leads to the Rio di San Barnaba, along which a fondamenta runs to the church of San Barnaba. Just before the end of the fondamenta you pass the **Ponte dei Pugni**, the main link between San Barnaba and Santa Margherita, and one of several bridges with this name, which means "Bridge of the Fists". Originally built without parapets, these were the sites of ritual battles between the Castellani and Nicolotti (see page 89). These massed punch-ups took place between September and Christmas (plus special one-offs for the entertainment of visiting dignitaries), and obeyed a well-defined etiquette: the fun would start with a series of one-on-one fights between the star brawlers of each faction (the fours pairs of marble footprints mark the starting places for the solo fighters plus a referee on each side), as a prelude to the main event, which was an almighty scrum for possession of the bridge. Fatalities were commonplace, as the armies slugged it out not just with bare knuckles but with steel-tipped lances made from hardened rushes. Lethal weaponry was outlawed in 1574, after a particularly bloody engagement that was arranged for the visit of Henry III of France, and in 1705 the brawls were finally banned – less dangerous forms of competition, such as regattas, were encouraged instead. Pugilists have now been replaced by tourists taking shots of the photogenic grocery barge that's usually moored at the foot of the bridge.

San Barnaba church

Campo San Barnaba

The huge, damp-ridden **San Barnaba** church, built in 1749, has a trompe l'oeil ceiling painting of *St Barnabas in Glory* by Constantino Cedini, a follower of Tiepolo. Despite recent restoration, the ceiling is being restored again because of moisture damage; while that's going on, the church has been turned over to a touristic exhibition on the "machines of Leonardo". At the time of the church's construction the parish was swarming with so-called *Barnabotti*, impoverished noble families who had moved into this area's cheap lodgings to eke out their meagre incomes. Forbidden as members of the aristocracy to practise a craft or run a shop, some of the *Barnabotti* supported themselves by selling their votes to the mightier families in the Maggior Consiglio, while others resigned themselves to subsistence on a paltry state dole. Visitors to the city often remarked on the incongruous sight of its silk-clad beggars – the nobility of Venice were obliged to wear silk, regardless of their ability to pay for such finery.

San Pantaleone

Campo San Pantalone • Mon–Sat 10am–noon & 1–3pm • Free

A short distance to the north of Campo Santa Margherita rises the raw brick hulk of **San Pantaleone** (or Pantalon), which possesses a picture by **Antonio Vivarini and Giovanni d'Alemagna** (*Coronation of the Virgin*, in the Chapel of the Holy Nail, to the left of the chancel) and **Veronese**'s last painting, *St Pantaleon Healing a Boy* (second chapel on the right). St Pantaleon – a fourth-century martyr whose biography is largely a legend – was credited with medicinal capabilities only slightly less awesome than those of St Rock (San Rocco), and Veronese's scene emphasizes the miraculous nature of his power (he spurns the offered box of potions) and the impotence of non-Christian treatment (symbolized by the limbless figure of Asclepius, the Classical god of medicine).

The church is best known, however, for having the most tumultuous **ceiling painting** in the city: *The Martyrdom and Apotheosis of St Pantaleon*, which kept **Gian Antonio Fumiani** busy from 1680 to 1704. Comprising some sixty canvas panels, some of which actually jut out over the nave, it has a claim to be the largest oil painting in the world. Pantaleon's alleged martyrdom is an extraordinary tale: first he was tortured with fire, whereupon Christ extinguished the flames and healed his burns; then he was plunged into a cauldron of molten lead, which Christ duly cooled; then he was hurled into the sea with a stone around his neck, only for the stone to float; wild animals were set upon him, but departed harmlessly when he blessed them; he was bound to a wheel, but the ropes snapped and the wheel fell apart; the executioner's sword then failed to make an impression on the saint's neck, whereupon the executioner immediately converted to Christianity; and finally, having asked heaven to forgive his persecutors (his name means "all-compassionate"), Pantaleon at last consented to die. When his head came off, the blood that flowed from him was said to be the colour of milk.

Ca' Rezzonico

Fondamenta Rezzonico 3136 • April–Oct Mon & Wed–Sun 10am–6pm; Nov–March 10am–5pm • €10 or Museum Pass • ⓦ carezzonico. visitmuve.it

The eighteenth century, the period of Venice's political senility and moral degeneration, was also the period of its last grand flourish in the visual and decorative arts. The

FASCIST ARCHITECTURE IN VENICE

From Ca' Rezzonico, the quickest route up to the Rialto takes you across the herringbone-patterned pavement of the Campiello dei Squellini, past the entrance to the main university building (Ca' Fóscari) and over the Rio Fóscari. As you cross the Ponte dei Fóscari, look to the right and you'll see the central station of Venice's **fire brigade**, with their red launches moored under the arches. This is one of the few Fascist-era constructions in Venice; two others – the **Palazzo del Cinema** and the former Casinò – are over on the Lido.

2

main showcase for the art of that era, the **Museo del Settecento Veneziano** spreads through most of the enormous **Ca' Rezzonico**, which the city authorities bought in 1934 specifically as a home for the museum. Recently restored, it's a spectacular building, furnished and decorated mostly with genuine eighteenth-century items and fabrics: where originals weren't available, the eighteenth-century ambience has been preserved by using almost indistinguishable modern reproductions. Sumptuary laws in Venice restricted the quantities of silk, brocade and tapestry that could be draped around a house, so legions of painters, stuccoists, cabinet-makers and other such applied artists were employed to fanfare the wealth of their patrons. The work they produced is certainly not to everyone's taste, but even if you find most of the museum's contents frivolous or grotesque, the paintings by the Tiepolo family and Pietro Longhi's affectionate Venetian scenes should justify the entrance fee.

The first floor

A man in constant demand in the early part of the century was the Belluno sculptor-cum-woodcarver **Andrea Brustolon**, much of whose output consisted of wildly elaborate pieces of furniture. A few of his pieces are displayed in the chandeliered ballroom at the top of the entrance staircase, and in the last room on this floor, the Brustolon Room, you'll find a whole lot more of them, including the *Allegory of Strength* console. Featuring Hercules underneath, two river gods holding four vases and a fifth vase held up by three black slaves in chains, this is a creation that makes you marvel at the craftsmanship and wince at the ends to which it was used.

The less fervid imaginations of **Giambattista Tiepolo** and his son **Giandomenico** are introduced in room 2 with the ceiling fresco celebrating Ludovico Rezzonico's marriage into the hugely powerful Savorgnan family in 1758. This was quite a year for the Rezzonico clan, as it also brought the election of Carlo Rezzonico as **Pope Clement XIII**; the son of the man who bought the uncompleted palace and finished its construction, Carlo the pontiff was notorious both for his nepotism (a small painting in this room shows him with his nephews and niece) and for his prudery – he insisted that the Vatican's antique nude statuary be made more modest by the judicious application of fig leaves.

Beyond room 4, with its array of pastels by **Rosalba Carriera**, you come to two other Giambattista Tiepolo ceilings, enlivening the rooms overlooking the Canal Grande on each side of the main portego: an *Allegory of Merit*, and *Nobility and Virtue Triumphing over Perfidy* (which was brought here in the 1930s). Below the latter you'll see some pictures by Giambattista's sons: Giandomenico, and the younger and far less famous Lorenzo. Giambattista's first teacher, Gregorio Lazzarini, is represented by a huge *Death of Orpheus* in room 12, where the ceiling panels (and those of the adjoining Brustolon Room) are by the seventeenth-century artist Francesco Maffei, who painted them for a palazzo over in Cannaregio.

The second floor

In the portego of the second floor hang the only two canal views by **Canaletto** on show in public galleries in Venice. An adjoining suite of rooms contains the museum's most engaging paintings – Giandomenico Tiepolo's sequence of **frescoes from the**

Villa Zianigo near Mestre, the Tiepolo family home. Begun in 1759, the frescoes were completed towards the end of the century, by which time Giandomenico's style was going out of fashion, which may be one reason for the undertone of wistful melancholy in pictures such as *Il Mondo Nuovo* (1791). Showing a crowd turned out in its best attire at a Sunday fair (the *Mondo Nuovo* was a kind of magic lantern show), this picture features a self-portrait – Giandomenico is on the right-hand side, standing behind his father. Another room is devoted to the antics of *Pulcinella*, the ancestor of our Mr Punch, including a marvellous ceiling fresco of Pulcinella on a swing.

There follows a succession of rooms with delightful portraits and depictions of everyday Venetian life by **Francesco Guardi** (including high-society recreation in the parlour of San Zaccaria's convent) and **Pietro Longhi**, whose artless candour more than makes up for his technical shortcomings. Visitors at Carnevale time will recognize several of the festival's components in the Longhi room: the beak-like *volto* masks, for example, and the little doughnuts called *frittelle* or *fritole*. Room 19 boasts a full suite of green and gold lacquer pieces, one of the finest surviving examples of Venetian chinoiserie, and from there you come to the last room, a re-creation of an eighteenth-century bedroom suite, complete with wardrobe and boudoir.

The third floor and the Mestrovich collection

The low-ceilinged rooms of the top floor house the reconstructed **Farmacia ai do San Marchi** (a sequence of wood-panelled rooms heavily stocked with old ceramic jars and glass bottles) and the **Pinacoteca Egidio Martini**, a huge private donation of Venetian art from the fifteenth to the twentieth centuries. Here you'll find a sprinkling of good pieces by Cima da Conegliano, Alvise Vivarini, Palma il Vecchio, Guercino, Sebastiano Ricci and Luca Giordano, but to find them you have to wade through an awful lot of mediocrity – and there cannot be a dafter painting in all of Venice than Pelagio Palagi's *Birth of Venus*, which makes the arrival of the goddess of love look like the grand finale of an aquatic burlesque show. A far smaller private donation – the **Mestrovich** collection – occupies a couple of rooms reached via a staircase off the entrance hall; it contains no masterpieces, but Francesco Guardi's wacky *Madonna* might raise a smile.

CAMPO SAN POLO

San Polo and Santa Croce

The San Polo *sestiere*, which extends from the Rialto market to the Frari area, adjoins the *sestiere* of Santa Croce, a far less sight-heavy district which lies to the north of San Polo and reaches right across to Piazzale Roma. Navigation through this sector of the city is not as baffling as it at first appears. There are two main routes through the district, each following approximately the curve of the Canal Grande – one runs between the Rialto and the Scalzi bridge, the other takes you down towards the Frari and San Rocco, and thence on to the Accademia. Virtually all the essential sights lie on, or just off, one of these two routes, and once you've become familiar with these ways the exploration of the streets and squares between them can be attempted with only a minimal risk of feeling that you'll never see friends and family again.

As far as the day-to-day life of Venice is concerned, the focal points of the district are the sociable open space of **Campo di San Polo** and the **Rialto** area. Once the commercial heart of the Republic and still the home of the main **market**, the Rialto offers a good antidote to cultural overload. Nobody, however, should miss the extraordinary pair of buildings in the southern part of San Polo: the colossal Gothic church of the **Frari**, embellished with three of Venice's finest altarpieces, and the **Scuola Grande di San Rocco**, decorated with an unforgettable cycle of paintings by Tintoretto.

In the northern part of the district, Venice's **modern art**, **oriental and natural history museums** are clustered together on the bank of the Canal Grande. As ever, numerous treasures are also scattered among the minor churches, most notably **San Cassiano** and **San Simeone Profeta**. Lastly, if you're in search of a spot in which to sit for an hour and just watch the world go by, head for the **Campo San Giacomo dell'Orio**, one of Venice's better-kept secrets.

3 The Rialto

Relatively stable building land and a good defensive position drew some of the earliest lagoon settlers to the high bank (*rivo alto*) that was to develop into the **Rialto** district. By 810, when the capital of the lagoon confederation was moved – in the wake of Pepin's invasion – from Malamocco to the more secure islands around here, the inhabited zone had grown well beyond the Rialto itself. While the political centre of the new city was consolidated around San Marco, the Rialto became the commercial area. In the twelfth century Europe's first state bank was opened here, and the financiers of this quarter were to be the heavyweights of the international currency exchanges for the next three hundred years and more. The state departments that oversaw all maritime business were here as well, and in the early sixteenth century the offices of the exchequer were installed in the new **Palazzo dei Camerlenghi**, at the foot of the Rialto bridge. It's telling that, in this quintessentially mercantile city, the Rialto rather than the Piazza San Marco is known as "Il Cuore della Città" – the Heart of the City.

The market

It was through the **markets of the Rialto** that Venice earned its reputation as the bazaar of Europe. Virtually anything could be bought or sold here: fabrics, precious stones, silver plate and gold jewellery, spices and dyes from the Orient. Trading had been going on here for over four hundred years when, in the winter of 1514, a fire destroyed everything in the area except the church. (Most of the wells and canals were frozen solid, so the blaze burned virtually unchecked for a whole day.) The possibility of relocating the business centre was discussed but found little favour, so reconstruction began almost straight away: the **Fabbriche Vecchie** (the arcaded buildings along the Ruga degli Orefici and around the Campo San Giacomo) were finished eight years after the fire, with Sansovino's **Fabbriche Nuove** (running along the Canal Grande from Campo Battisti) following about thirty years later.

Today's Rialto market is much more modest than that of Venice at its peak, but it's still one of the liveliest spots in the city, and one of the few places where it's possible to stand in a crowd and hear nothing but Italian spoken. Nevertheless, the fruit and vegetable traders nowadays can't keep going without the revenue from tourists, who account for some forty percent of their income, and in recent years several stallholders have gone out of business, having found it impossible to turn a profit in the winter months. The future of the fish market, which relies on Venetian customers to a much greater extent, is especially imperilled by the decline in the city's population; the number of stalls has halved in the past few years, to less than ten.

SEX AND THE RIALTO

A sixteenth-century survey showed that there were about 3000 patrician women in Venice, but more than 11,000 **prostitutes and courtesans**, the majority of them based in the Rialto. (Courtesans were self-sufficient and costlier women who usually lived in their own homes or with a small number of similarly upmarket ladies.) Two Venetian **brothels** – the state-run *Casteletto*, which was esteemed for the literary and musical talents of its staff, and the privately operated *Carampane* – were officially sanctioned; both were in the Rialto and had curfews, armed guards and a system for sharing the revenue among the staff. These establishments were founded in the fourteenth century, and efforts were then made to limit prostitution to the Rialto, but by the end of the following century there were brothels all over the city, prompting one writer to remark that "Venice seems to me to have been made a bordello." The *Catalogue of the Chief and Most Renowned Courtesans of Venice*, a directory that told you everything you needed to know (right down to prices), became a perennial bestseller, and if Thomas Coryat's report of 1608 is anything to go by, the courtesans were seen by some as the city's main attraction – "So infinite are the allurements of these amorous Calypsoes that the fame of them hath drawn many to Venice from some of the remotest parts of Christendome."

Coryat, like so many male observers and customers of the city's "Calypsoes", was happy to perpetuate the myth that these women were content in their work. That so many Venetian courtesans were the well-educated offspring of "good" families seemed to indicate that their profession was a matter of free choice. But in a society in which sons were generally the major (and often the sole) beneficiaries of their parents' wills, and fathers were often reluctant to disperse the family fortune by lavishing dowries on their daughters, many young women could expect to be dispatched to a convent as adulthood approached, if no wealthy suitor were on the horizon. It's thus hardly surprising that a large number of **patrician women** should instead choose a way of life that at least offered the prospect of independence. But even the most celebrated of the city's courtesans, **Veronica Franco**, a woman whose beauty and intellectual distinction were praised by princes and writers, was adamant that the cost of selling herself was too great: "to subject one's body and industry to a servitude whose very thought is most frightful … What greater misery? What riches, what comforts, what delights can possibly outweigh all this?"

3

There's a shoal of trinket sellers by the church, gathered to catch the sightseers as they spill off the bridge, and a strong showing of glass junk, handbags and "Venezia" sweatshirts farther on, but the true Rialto market comprises the fruit sellers around the **Campo San Giacomo**, the vegetable stalls and butcher's shops of **Campo Battisti** and the **Pescheria** (fish market) beyond. The Pescheria and most of the larger wholesalers at the Rialto close down for the day at around 1pm, but many of the smaller fruit and vegetable stalls keep normal shop hours. Around the junction of **Ruga degli Orefici** and **Ruga Vecchia San Giovanni** you'll find wonderful cheese kiosks, and the bars and *osterie* of this district are among the best in the city.

San Giacomo di Rialto

Campo San Giacomo • Mon–Sat 10.30am–4.30pm • €3, or Chorus Pass • ⓦ chorusvenezia.org

Venetian folklore asserts that the city was founded at noon on Friday, March 25, 421; from the same legend derives the claim that the church of **San Giacomo di Rialto** (or San Giacometto) was consecrated in that year, and is thus **the oldest church in Venice**. It might actually be the oldest, but all that's known for certain is that it was rebuilt in 1071, about the same time as San Marco's reconstruction.

Parts of the present structure date from this period – the interior's six columns of ancient Greek marble have eleventh-century Veneto-Byzantine capitals – and it seems likely that the reconstruction of the church prompted the establishment of the market here. On the outside of the apse a twelfth-century inscription addresses

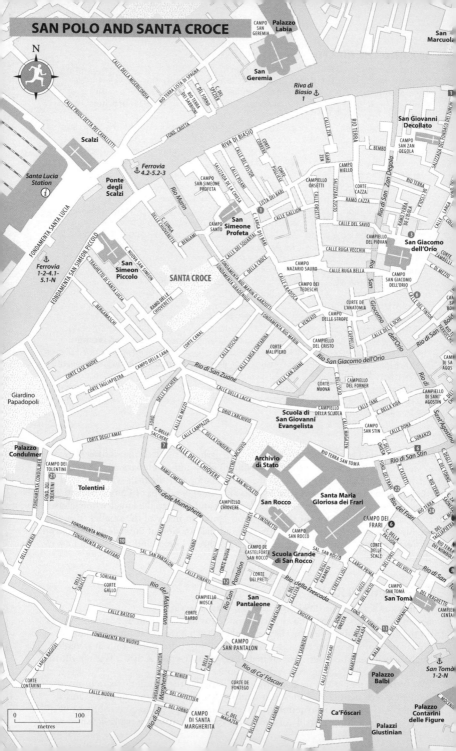

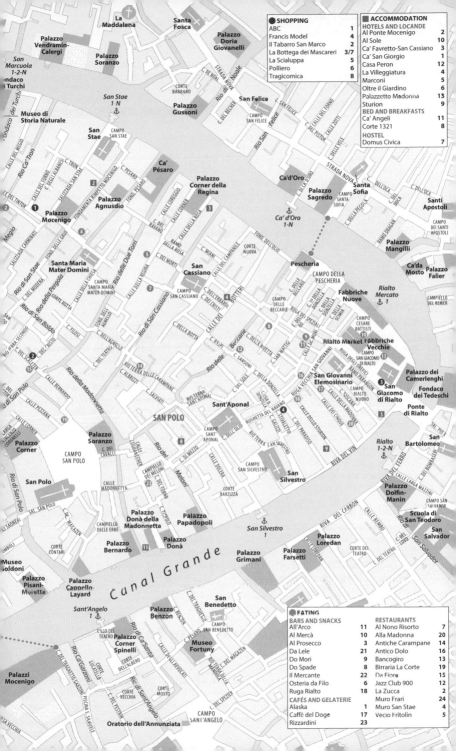

THE GOBBO DI RIALTO

On the opposite side of the campo from San Giacomo crouches a stone figure known as the **Gobbo di Rialto** ("the Rialto hunchback"). It was carved in the sixteenth century and supports a granite platform from which state proclamations were read simultaneously with their announcement from the Pietra del Bando, beside San Marco; it had another role as well – certain wrongdoers were sentenced to run the gauntlet, stark naked, from the Piazza to the Gobbo.

---

the merchants of the Rialto: "Around this temple let the merchant's law be just, his weights true, and his promises faithful." Early Venetian churches often had lean-to porticoes like that of San Giacomo, but this is one of only two examples left in the city (the other being San Nicolò dei Mendicoli). The inaccuracy of the clock above – a fifteenth-century addition, like the portico – has been a standing joke in Venice since the day it was installed.

Like so many of Venice's under-used churches, San Giacometto is used as a concert venue (with Vivaldi featuring heavily); it functions largely as a ticket office, and also houses some musical instruments from the Artemio Versari collection, more of which is on display at San Maurizio.

San Giovanni Elemosinario

Ruga Vecchia San Giovanni • Mon–Sat 10.30am–1.30pm • €3, or Chorus Pass • ⓦ chorusvenezia.org

The Ruga Vecchia – the shopping street leading south from the Rialto market – has one major monument, **San Giovanni Elemosinario**, a church so solidly packed into the surrounding buildings that its fifteenth-century campanile is the only conspicuous indication of its presence. Founded in the eleventh century, it was wrecked in the huge fire of 1514 – only the campanile survived, and after the church was rebuilt in 1527–29 (to designs by Scarpagnino) a bell was rung here every evening, as a signal for all fires to be extinguished for the night. Most of the church's decoration dates from the decades immediately following the rebuild; several pictures by the ubiquitous Palma il Giovane are here, alongside work by Leonardo Corona, but the best are **Titian**'s high altarpiece (*St John the Almsgiver*), and **Pordenone**'s nearby *Sts Catherine, Sebastian and Roch*. The frescoes in the cupola, featuring a gang of very chunky cherubs, are also by Pordenone.

San Silvestro

Campo San Silvestro • Mon–Sat 7.30–11.30am & 4–6pm • Free

If you walk south from the Rialto bridge alongside the Canal Grande you'll be deflected away from water at the back of the church of **San Silvestro**. It's a big but nondescript building, which has one painting of interest: a *Baptism of Christ* by Tintoretto. Across from the church, at no. 1022, is the Palazzo Valier, where Giorgione died in 1510.

West of the Rialto: the route to the Scalzi bridge

Once past the Pescheria, you're into a district which quickly becomes labyrinthine even by Venetian standards. A stroll from the Rialto to the **Scalzi bridge** will satisfy any addict of the picturesque – you cannot walk for more than a couple of minutes without coming across a scene that'll have you reaching for the camera.

San Cassiano

Campo San Cassiano • Tues–Sat 9am–noon & 5–7pm • Free

The thirteenth-century campanile of the barn-like church of **San Cassiano** is the only appealing aspect of the exterior, and the interest of the interior lies mainly with its three paintings by **Tintoretto**: *The Resurrection*, *The Descent into Limbo* and *The Crucifixion* (all 1565–68). The first two have been mauled by restorers, but the third is one of the most startling pictures in all of Venice – centred on the ladder on which the executioners stand, it's painted as though the observer were lying in the grass at the foot of the Cross. The dedicatee of the church is depicted in the Tintoretto *Resurrection* and in a painting that can be seen in a small chapel off the left aisle (reached via the sacristy), where he's shown being stabbed to death by his pupils, after he had refused to conduct a sacrifice to the Roman gods; his demise earned him the status of patron saint of schoolteachers.

Campo San Cassiano was the site of the **first public opera house** in the world – it opened in 1636, at the peak of Monteverdi's career. Long into the following century Venice's opera houses were among the most active in Europe; around five hundred works received their first performances here in the first half of the eighteenth century.

3

Campo Santa Maria Mater Domini

A sign directs you from Campo San Cassiano over the right-hand bridge towards the Ca' Pésaro, passing the back of the Palazzo Corner della Regina. A few metres beyond this palazzo, a diversion down Corte Tiossi from Calle Tiossi brings you to the small **Campo Santa Maria Mater Domini**, which is a perfect Venetian miscellany, untouched by tourism – a thirteenth-century house (the Casa Zane), a few ramshackle Gothic houses, an assortment of stone reliefs of indeterminate age, a fourteenth-century wellhead in the centre, a workaday bar, a couple of shops and a hairdresser's.

Santa Maria Mater Domini

Mon–Sat 10am–noon • Free

Off the end of the campo stands **Santa Maria Mater Domini**, an early sixteenth-century church of disputed authorship – Mauro Codussi and Giovanni Buora are the leading candidates. The rescue of this building is one of Venice in Peril's proudest achievements; now protected by a totally reconstructed roof, the crisp white and grey interior boasts an endearing *Martyrdom of St Christina* by **Vincenzo Catena** (second altar on the right), showing a flight of angels plucking the saint from a carpet-like Lago di Bolsena, into which she had been hurled with a millstone for an anchor. Few works by the elusive Catena have survived, and it is not even certain what he did for a living. He seems to have been a successful spice trader, and thus may have been a businessman who painted for recreation; alternatively, he may have been an artist who subsidized himself through commercial dealings – he is mentioned on the reverse of one of Giorgione's paintings as a "colleague". On the opposite side of the church you'll find yet another of the city's legion of Tintoretto paintings, a *Discovery of the Cross*, painted in the 1560s.

Ca' Pésaro

Calle Pésaro 2076 • ⓦ capesaro.visitmuve.it

The immense **Ca' Pésaro** was bequeathed to the city at the end of the nineteenth century by the Duchessa Felicità Bevilacqua La Masa, an energetic patron of the arts who stipulated in her will that the palazzo should provide studio and exhibition space for impoverished young artists. Although exhibitions were later held at Ca' Pésaro, and the Bevilacqua La Masa foundation still promotes progressive art, the duchessa's plans were never fully realized, and in place of the intended living arts centre the palazzo became home to the city's modern art gallery.

The Galleria Internazionale d'Arte Moderna

Tues–Sun: April–Oct 10am–6pm; Nov–March 10am–5pm • €14 joint ticket with Museo Orientale, or Museum Pass

The name of **The Galleria Internazionale d'Arte Moderna** is slightly misleading. Yes, a few of the non-Italian heavyweights of modern art are here: Klimt, Rodin, Kandinsky, Matisse, Klee, Nolde, Picasso, Ernst and Miró are all present, in small quantities. But in essence this is a selective overview of Italian art in the late nineteenth and twentieth centuries, consisting largely of pieces bought from the Biennale, or acquired from exhibitions held here from 1908 to 1924, when Ca' Pésaro had a reputation for being one of the most daring venues in the country. It's hard to imagine how some of this work could ever have been considered radical: Felice Casorati's once controversial *Young Ladies*, for example, now looks rather coy, and nothing in Ca' Pésaro is likely to make you question the received view that Berlin, Paris and New York were the real hothouses of modernism. But this collection does give space to artists who are often sidelined from the grand narrative – names such as Medardo Rosso or Mario Sironi, for example, both of whom are well represented here, alongside dozens of whom you may never have heard.

Museo Orientale

April–Oct Tues–Sun 10am–6pm; Nov–March Tues–Sun 10am–5pm • €14 joint ticket with Galleria d'Arte Moderna, or Museum Pass

In the top-floor rooms of Ca' Pésaro you'll find the **Museo Orientale**, which is built around a hoard of artefacts amassed by the Conte di Bardi (a Bourbon prince) during a long Far Eastern voyage in the nineteenth century. It's a tightly packed array of porcelain, ceremonial armour, netsuke, musical instruments, clothing, paintings and enough swords, daggers and lances to equip a private army. Many of the pieces are exquisite – look out for an incredibly intricate ivory-and-coral chess set, and a room full of marvellous lacquerwork.

Before leaving Ca' Pésaro you might want to stop for a coffee at the café that's installed at the end of the ground-floor hall (where large-scale artworks are displayed) – its tables offer a superb view of the Canal Grande.

San Stae

Campo San Stae • Mon–Sat 1.45–4.30pm • €3, or Chorus Pass • ⓦ chorusvenezia.org

Continuing along the line of the Canal Grande from the Ca' Pésaro, Calle Pésaro takes you over the Rio della Rioda, and so to the seventeenth-century church of **San Stae**, a contraction of San Eustachio. Its Baroque facade, added around 1710, is enlivened by precarious statues, and the *marmorino* (pulverized marble) surfaces of the interior make San Stae as bright as an operating theatre on a sunny day. In the chancel there's a series of paintings from the beginning of the eighteenth century, the pick of which are *The Martyrdom of St James the Great* by Piazzetta (low on the left), *The Liberation of St Peter* by Sebastiano Ricci (same row) and *The Martyrdom of St Bartholomew* by Giambattista Tiepolo. In the first chapel on the left side there's a bust of Antonio Foscarini (see page 174), wrongly executed for treason, as the inscription explains.

Exhibitions and concerts are often held in San Stae, and exhibitions are also held from time to time in the diminutive building alongside, the early seventeenth-century **Scuola dei Battioro e Tiraoro** (goldsmiths' guild).

Palazzo Mocenigo

Salizzada San Stae 1992 • Tues–Sun: April–Oct 10am–5pm; Nov–March 10am–4pm • €8, or Museum Pass • ⓦ mocenigo.visitmuve.it

Halfway down the *salizzada* flanking San Stae is the early seventeenth-century **Palazzo Mocenigo**, now the home of the Centro Studi di Storia del Tessuto e del Costume (Centre for the Study of the History of Textiles and Clothing). The library and archive

of the study centre occupy part of the building, but a substantial portion of the *piano nobile* is open to the public, and there are few Venetian interiors of this date that have been so meticulously preserved. The main room is decorated with workaday portraits of various Mocenigo men, while the rooms to the side are full of miscellaneous pictures, antique furniture, Murano chandeliers and display cases of dandified clothing and cobweb-fine lacework. The curtains are kept closed to protect the delicate fabrics.

San Giovanni Decollato

Campo San Zan Degolà • Erratic opening hours, but generally Mon–Fri 10am–noon • Free

The deconsecrated church of **San Giovanni Decollato**, known in Venetian as San Zan Degolà (meaning "St John the Beheaded") was established in the opening years of the eleventh century and has retained its basilican layout through several alterations; the columns and capitals of the nave date from the first century of its existence, and parts of its fragmentary frescoes (at the east end) could be of the same age. Some of the paintings are certainly thirteenth-century, and no other church in Venice has frescoes that predate them. The church also boasts one of the city's characteristic ship's-keel ceilings.

Museo di Storia Naturale

Salizzada del Fontego dei Turchi 1730 • Tues–Fri 9am–5pm, Sat & Sun 10am–6pm • €8, or Museum Pass • ⓦ msn.visitmuve.it

In 2012 the **Museo di Storia Naturale**, which occupies the imposing **Fondaco dei Turchi**, at last reopened after many years of restoration, and it re-emerged as a superb museum, using the latest attention-grabbing presentation techniques without dumbing the content down. The opening sequence of rooms takes you through the fossil collection, which has been laid out in such a way as to trace the process of evolution – the fossilized animal tracks set into the floor are a typically imaginative touch. Beyond, there are rooms devoted to locomotion (with separate sections for land, water and air), an extraordinary miscellany of items gathered by Giovanni Miani during his 1859–60 expedition to trace the source of the Nile, a hideous array of African hunting trophies harvested by Giuseppe de Reali and – in the long room overlooking the Canal Grande – a splendid sequence of cabinets illustrating the development of the study of natural history in Venice, with some exquisitely grisly specimens of dissected animals. There's also an excellent reconstruction of a Wunderkammer or Cabinet of Curiosities, a miscellany of zoological, botanical and mineralogical items such as would have been found in the homes of many scholars of the Renaissance and later centuries. It's a huge and fascinating collection, but as you might expect in a museum that gets few foreign tourists, the captions are in Italian only.

San Giacomo dell'Orio

Campo San Giacomo dell'Orio • Mon–Sat 10.30am–4.30pm • €3, or Chorus Pass • ⓦ chorusvenezia.org

Standing in a lovely spacious campo which, despite its size, you could easily miss if you weren't looking for it, the church of **San Giacomo dell'Orio** perhaps takes its enigmatic name from a laurel (*lauro*) that once grew here, or might once have been called San Giacomo dal Rio (St James of the river/canal), or have stood on a *luprio*, the term for a tract of dried swampland.

Founded in the ninth century and rebuilt in 1225 – the approximate date of the campanile – San Giacomo was remodelled on numerous subsequent occasions. Its **ship's-keel roof** dates from the fourteenth century; the massive columns, made stockier by frequent raisings of the pavement, are a couple of hundred years older. Two of the columns – behind the pulpit and in the right transept – were brought to Venice by the fleet returning from the Fourth Crusade; the latter, an extraordinary chunk of *verde*

THE SWEENEY TODD OF VENICE

The **Riva di Biasio**, close to the church of San Simeone Profeta, allows a short walk on the bank of the Canal Grande, with a view across the water to San Geremia. This stretch of paving allegedly takes its name from a butcher named Biasio who was executed between the columns of the Piazzetta after it was discovered that his prime pork cuts were in fact lumps of human flesh.

---

antico, was compared by the ever-excitable Gabriele d'Annunzio to "the fossilized compression of an immense verdant forest". The shape of the main apse betrays its Byzantine origins, but the inlaid marbles were placed there in the sixteenth century. The main altarpiece, *Madonna and Four Saints*, was painted by Lorenzo Lotto in 1546, shortly before he left the city complaining that the Venetians had not treated him fairly; the *Crucifix* that hangs in the air in front of it is attributed to Paolo Veneziano. In the left transept there's an altarpiece by Paolo Veronese, and there's a fine set of pictures from Veronese's workshop on the ceiling of the **new sacristy**: *Faith* and *The Doctors of the Church*. Also in the new sacristy you'll see Francesco Bassano's *Madonna in Glory* and *St John the Baptist Preaching* – Bassano's family provide the Baptist's audience, while the spectator on the far left, in the red hat, is Titian. The **old sacristy** is a showcase for the art of Palma il Giovane, whose cycle in celebration of the Eucharist covers the walls and part of the ceiling. Before you leave, take a look at the very peculiar painting by Gaetano Zompini, above the confessional in the right-hand aisle; it shows the funeral of the Virgin, and the handless man lying on the ground has just attacked the procession – that's why his hands have been miraculously severed, and left glued to the bier.

San Simeone Profeta

Campo San Simeone Grande • Mon–Sat 9am–noon & 5–6.30pm • Free

Originating in the tenth century, the church of **San Simeone Profeta** (or San Simeone Grande) has often been rebuilt – most extensively in the eighteenth century, when the city sanitation experts, anxious about the condition of the plague victims who had been buried under the flagstones in the 1630 epidemic, ordered the relaying of the whole floor. An undistinguished building, it's remarkable for its reclining **effigy of St Simeon** (to the left of the chancel), a luxuriantly bearded, larger than life-size figure, whose half-open mouth disturbingly creates the impression of the moment of death. According to its inscription, it was sculpted in 1317 by **Marco Romano**, but some experts doubt that the sculpture can be that old, as nothing else of that date bears comparison with it. On the left immediately inside the door, there's a run-of-the-mill *Last Supper* by **Tintoretto**.

San Simeone Piccolo

Fondamenta San Simeone Piccolo • Tues–Sat 10am–noon • Crypt €2

Immediately after the Scalzi bridge rises the green dome of the early eighteenth-century **San Simeone Piccolo**, which is the first monument you see when you arrive at the train station. It's a striking sight, but the interior is much less so, except for the extraordinary crypt, a warren of funerary chapels (21 in all, eight of which have been sealed off), covered with damp-damaged wall paintings. The pictures are of no great quality, but some of the images are powerful, and the melancholy atmosphere is augmented by the fact that nobody knows who's buried here, as the church's archives were destroyed during the Napoleonic era. You'll need to find the sacristan to let you in, which might not be possible; some weeks, the church is open only for mass on Sunday morning. Uniquely for Venice, mass at San Simeone Piccolo is conducted in Latin.

From the Rialto to the Frari and San Rocco

South of the Rialto, **Ruga Vecchia San Giovanni** constitutes the first leg of the right bank's nearest equivalent to the Mercerie of San Marco, a reasonably straight chain of alleyways that is interrupted by Campo di San Polo and then resumes with the chic Calle dei Saoneri.

The route to San Polo widens momentarily at **Sant'Aponal** (in full, Apollinare), which is now used as a city archive. Its most interesting feature is on the outside, anyway – *The Crucifixion and Scenes from the Life of Christ* (1294), in the tabernacle over the door. Local legend has it that Pope Alexander III, on the run in 1177 from the troops of Emperor Frederick Barbarossa, found refuge close to Sant'Aponal; over the entrance to the Sottoportego della Madonna (to your left and slightly behind you as you face the church), a plaque records his plight and promises a perpetual plenary indulgence to anyone saying a Pater Noster and Ave Maria on the spot.

Campo San Polo

The largest square in Venice after the Piazza, **Campo San Polo** was once the site of weekly markets and occasional fairs, and was also used as a parade ground and bullfighting arena. Several fine palaces overlook the campo, the most impressive of which is the double **Palazzo Soranzo**, across the square from the church. Built between the late fourteenth and mid-fifteenth centuries, this might seem an exception to the rule that the main palace facade should look onto the water, but in fact a canal used to run across the campo just in front of the Soranzo house. Casanova gained his introduction to the Venetian upper classes through a senator who lived in this palace; he was hired to work as a musician in the house and so impressed the old man that he was adopted as his son.

On the same side of Campo San Polo as the church, but in the opposite corner, is the **Palazzo Corner Mocenigo**, designed around 1550 by Sanmicheli – the main facade is visible from the bridge beyond the church. In 1909 **Frederick Rolfe** (Baron Corvo) became a tenant here, an arrangement that came to an abrupt end the following year when his hosts discovered that the manuscript he was working on – *The Desire and Pursuit of the Whole* – was a vitriolic satire directed at them and their acquaintances. Rolfe was given the alternative of abandoning the libellous novel or moving out; he moved out, contracted pneumonia as a result of sleeping rough and became so ill he was given the last rites – but he managed to pull through, and lived for a further three disreputable years.

A STROLL IN SAN POLO

One of Venice's most seductive backwater townscapes is to be found to the west of Sant'Aponal. Leave Campo Sant'Aponal by Calle Ponte Storto, which leads to the crook-backed Ponte Storto; the gorgeous building on your right, as you cross the water, is the palace where Bianca Cappello was living when she met Pietro Bonaventuri (see page 146). At the foot of the bridge go left onto Fondamenta Banco Salviati, then halfway along the colonnade turn right into Calle Stretta, the narrowest alley in the whole city. Calle Stretta emerges on Campiello Albrizzi, which is dominated by the huge seventeenth-century **Palazzo Albrizzi**. Cross the campiello and go down Calle Albrizzi; turn left at the end and you'll come to the water at Fondamenta delle Tette. Stand on the little bridge here – **Ponte delle Tette** – and to the north you have a terrific view of a ravine of palaces leading towards the Canal Grande, while to the south you'll see the side of the Palazzo Albrizzi, with the foliage of a neighbouring garden spilling over the canal. If you're wondering about the name "delle Tette", it means exactly what you suspect: the bridge marks the edge of the zone within which the Rialto prostitutes were allowed to solicit, and one of their advertising ploys was to air their breasts on the balconies of their houses.

MURDER AT SAN POLO

In 1548 Campo San Polo was the scene of a bloody act of political retribution. On February 26 of that year, Lorenzaccio de'Medici, having fled Florence after murdering the deranged Duke Alessandro, emerged from San Polo church to come face to face with the emissaries of Duke Cosimo I, Alessandro's successor. A contemporary account records that a struggle ensued, at the end of which Lorenzaccio's head was "split in two pieces" and his uncle, Alessandro Soderini, lay dead beside him. The assassins took refuge in the Spanish embassy, but the Venetian government, with customary pragmatism, decided that the internal squabbles of Florence were of no concern to Venice, and let the matter rest.

San Polo church

Mon–Sat 10.30am–4.30pm • €3, or Chorus Pass • ⓦ chorusvenezia.org

Restoration carried out in the early nineteenth century made a thorough mess of the fifteenth-century Gothic of **San Polo church**, which was established as far back as the ninth century. The beautiful main **doorway**, possibly by Bartolomeo Bon, survives from the first church; the detached campanile, built in 1362, has a couple of twelfth-century lions at its base, one of which is playing with a snake, the other with a severed human head.

The rather bleak interior is worth a visit for a superior *Last Supper* by **Tintoretto** (on the left as you enter) and a cycle of the *Stations of the Cross (Via Crucis)* by **Giandomenico Tiepolo** in the Oratory of the Crucifix. This powerful series, painted when the artist was only 20, may persuade you to amend a few preconceptions about the customarily frivolous-seeming Giandomenico, even if some of the scenes do feature some lustrously attired sophisticates who seem to have drifted into the action from the salons of eighteenth-century Venice. A couple of Tiepolo ceiling panels and two other easel paintings supplement the *Via Crucis*; back in the main part of the church, paintings by Giandomenico's father and Veronese are to be found on the second altar opposite the door and in the chapel on the left of the chancel respectively, but neither shows the artist at his best.

Museo Goldoni

Calle dei Nomboli 2794 • Mon, Tues & Thurs–Sun 10am–5pm, Nov–March closes 4pm • €5, or Museum Pass • ⓦ carlogoldoni.visitmuve.it

If you turn right halfway down Calle dei Saoneri as you walk away from San Polo, you're on your way to the Frari; carry on to the end and then turn left, and you'll soon come to the fifteenth-century **Palazzo Centanni**, in Calle dei Nomboli. This was the birthplace of **Carlo Goldoni** (1707–93), who practised law until 1748, by which time he had accumulated some fourteen years' part-time experience in writing pieces for the indigenous *commedia dell'arte*. Like all *commedia* pieces, the scripts written during that period were essentially vehicles for the semi-improvised clowning of the actors impersonating the genre's stock characters – tricky Harlequin, doddering Pantalon, capricious Colombine and so on. Goldoni set about reforming the *commedia* from within, turning it eventually into a medium for sharp political observation – indeed, his arch-rival Carlo Gozzi accused Goldoni of creating an "instrument of social subversion". Despite his enormous success, in 1762 he left Venice to work for the Comédie Italienne in Paris, where he also taught Italian in the court of Louis XVI, and received a royal pension until the outbreak of the Revolution. Goldoni's plays are still the staple of theatrical life in Venice, and there's plenty of material to choose from – allegedly, he once bet a friend that he could produce one play a week for a whole year, and won.

The Goldoni family home now houses the Istituto di Studi Teatrali and the **Museo Goldoni**. Containing a very small collection of first editions, a few portraits of the playwright, some eighteenth-century marionettes, a miniature theatre (similar to the puppet theatre Goldoni's father made for him), and not a lot more, this is the most

3

ALDUS MANUTIUS

Except for the scurrilous hack Pietro Aretino (see page 71) and the altogether more proper Cardinal Bembo (whose high-flown prose spawned an imitative style known as *Bembismo*), Renaissance Venice produced virtually no writers of any importance, and yet it was the greatest printing centre in Italy. By the second half of the sixteenth century there were more than one hundred presses in Venice, and their output was more than three times greater than that of Rome, Florence and Milan combined. The doyen of **Venetian publishers** was **Aldus Manutius** (Aldo Manuzio), creator of italic typeface and publisher of the first pocket editions of the classics, whose workshop stood close to Campo San Polo. Founded in 1490, the Aldine Press employed teams of printers, die-cutters, proofreaders and compositors, but was always on the lookout for casual labour, as the sign over the door made clear – "Whoever you are, Aldus earnestly begs you to state your business in the fewest words possible and be gone, unless, like Hercules to weary Atlas, you would lend a helping hand. There will always be work for you and all who pass this way." Erasmus once did a stint here, when the Aldine workshop was producing an edition of his *Proverbs*.

If you leave Campo San Polo at its northeast corner, walk along Calle Bernardo, cross the canal to Calle del Scaleter and then follow that alley to its end, you'll come to Rio Terrà Seconda, where a plaque at no. 2311 identifies a small Gothic house as the site of the workshop of Manutius. However, documentary evidence makes it clear that the Manutius shop was located "by the Santo Agostino baker". Off Campo San Agostin, which lies at the south end of Rio Terrà Seconda, you'll find a Calle del Pistor ("Baker's Alley"). So in all likelihood it was here rather than at no. 2311 that Manutius was based until the last years of his life, when he moved over the Canal Grande to what is now Campo Manin.

---

undernourished museum in the whole city. The Gothic courtyard is one of Venice's finest, however, and has a beautiful wellhead.

Campo San Tomà

The parish of San Tomà, the base of many of Venice's best silver- and goldsmiths, is focused on **San Tomà** church. For many years a sad, broken-backed structure encased in scaffolding, San Tomà has been gleamingly restored, but is hardly ever open. In the days when the Venetians were known as the sharpest religious relic-hunters around, San Tomà was the city's bumper depository, claiming to possess some 10,000 sacred bits and pieces, and a dozen intact holy corpses.

At the other end of the campo stands the **Scuola dei Calegheri** – the shoemakers' guild, as advertised by the footwear carved into the lintel below the relief by Pietro Lombardo (1478) that shows St Mark healing the cobbler Ananias. The building is now used as a library and exhibition space.

Santa Maria Gloriosa dei Frari

Campo dei Frari • Mon–Sat 9am–6pm, Sun 1–6pm • €3, or Chorus Pass • ⓦ www.basilicadeifrari.it

San Zanipolo and **Santa Maria Gloriosa dei Frari** – customarily abbreviated to the **Frari** – are the twin Gothic giants of Venice: from the campanile of San Marco they can be seen jutting above the rooftops on opposite sides of the Canal Grande, like a pair of destroyers amid a flotilla of yachts. The Franciscans were granted a plot of land here around 1250, not long after the death of their founder, but almost no sooner was the first church completed (in 1338) than work began on a vast replacement – a project which took well over a hundred years. The campanile, the city's tallest after San Marco's, was finished in 1396; in recent years it has been substantially reinforced, having shown worrying signs of instability.

The exterior, a mountain of bare brick, is relieved by just a few pieces of sculpture: on the **west front**, there's a figure of *The Risen Christ* by **Vittoria**, and a *Virgin* and *St Francis* from the workshop of **Bartolomeo Bon**; an impressive early fifteenth-century Tuscan relief of *The Madonna and Child with Angels* is set into the side of the left transept. As is so often the case in Venice, though, the outside of the church is a misleadingly dull prelude to a remarkable interior.

Titian's altarpieces

Entry to the Frari is sometimes through the main door, but more often via the left flank of the church. Whichever way you come in, you'll almost immediately be confronted by Titian's great **Assumption** as you look towards the high altar through the monks' choir. (The choir itself was built in the late fifteenth century, with a marble screen by Bartolomeo Bon and Pietro Lombardo; it's the only one left in Venice that occupies a site in the nave.) A piece of compositional and colouristic bravura for which there was no precedent in Venetian art – for one thing, no previous altarpiece had emphasized the vertical axis over the horizontal – the *Assumption* nevertheless fits its surroundings perfectly. The spiralling motion of the Apostles and the Virgin complements the vertical movement of the surrounding architecture, an integration that is strengthened by the coincidence between the division of the painting's two major groupings and the division of the windows in the chancel. It was instantly recognized as a major work. **Marin Sanudo**, whose *Diaries* are an essential source for historians of the Republic, somehow wrote 58 volumes that contain scarcely a mention of any Venetian artist – yet even he refers to the ceremony on May 19, 1518, at which the picture was unveiled.

The other Titian masterpiece here, the **Madonna di Ca' Pésaro** (on the left wall, between the third and fourth columns), was completed eight years after the *Assumption* and was equally innovative in its displacement of the figure of the Virgin from the centre of the picture. The altarpiece was commissioned by Bishop Jacopo Pésaro, who managed to combine his episcopal duties with a military career; in 1502 he had led a successful naval campaign against the Turks – hence the prisoners being dragged in, behind the kneeling figure of Pésaro himself, to meet the Redeemer and His Mother. Pésaro's tomb (c.1547), with an effigy, is to the right of the picture.

The chapels and chancel

Beyond the Pésaro monument you'll find the **Cappella Emiliani**, which has a fifteenth-century marble altarpiece by followers of Jacobello Dalle Masegne. The **Cappella Corner**, at the end of the left transept, contains a vibrant painting by Bartolomeo Vivarini, *St Mark Enthroned* (1474), and, on the font, a damaged figure of *St John the Baptist* by Sansovino (1554).

St Ambrose and other Saints, the last painting by **Alvise Vivarini**, the nephew of Bartolomeo, stands in the adjoining chapel; it was finished around 1503 by a pupil, Marco Basaiti. A plaque in the floor marks the **grave of Monteverdi**, who for thirty years was the choirmaster of San Marco. The chapel to the left of the chancel contains

---

DOGE FRANCESCO FÓSCARI

Francesco Fóscari occupied the Palazzo Ducale for 34 years, which makes him the longest-serving doge in Venetian history, but the story of his last days could be taken as an exemplar of the dictum that all political careers end in failure. Soon after his election in 1423 he had led Venice into what was to be a long and costly war with Milan, the dominant power in northern Italy. This campaign made him unpopular with many at home, and his reputation was further damaged when, in 1445, his only surviving son, Jacopo, faced trial for bribery and corruption. Jacopo was exiled from the city, and in 1456, after another trial, was imprisoned on Crete, where he died after six months. Doge Fóscari, in poor health for some time, now sank into a depression which his opponents lost no time in exploiting. After several months of pressure, they forced his resignation; a week later, on November 1, 1457, he died. It was reported that when the senators and new doge were told of his death, during Mass in the Basilica, they looked guiltily at each other, "knowing well that it was they who had shortened his life", as a contemporary chronicler wrote.

another striking altarpiece, a *Madonna and Saints* by Bernardino Licinio; one of the finest creations of this Titian-influenced artist, it was probably painted in 1535.

Two monuments illustrating the emergence in Venice of Renaissance sculptural style flank the Titian *Assumption*: on the left the proto-Renaissance **tomb of Doge Niccolò Tron** (1476), by Antonio Rizzo and assistants; on the right, the more archaic and chaotic **tomb of Doge Francesco Fóscari** (see page 111), carved shortly after Fóscari's death in 1457 by **Antonio and Paolo Bregno**.

The wooden statue of *St John the Baptist*, in the next chapel, was commissioned from **Donatello** in 1438 by Florentine merchants in Padua; recent work has restored the luridly naturalistic appearance of what seems to be the sculptor's first work in the Veneto. In the last of the chapels stands a Bartolomeo Vivarini altarpiece, *Madonna and Child with Saints*, painted in 1482.

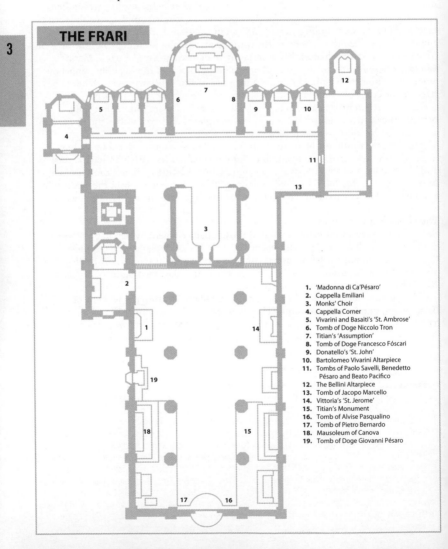

THE FRARI

3

1. 'Madonna di Ca'Pésaro'
2. Cappella Emiliani
3. Monks' Choir
4. Cappella Corner
5. Vivarini and Basaiti's 'St. Ambrose'
6. Tomb of Doge Niccolo Tron
7. Titian's 'Assumption'
8. Tomb of Doge Francesco Fóscari
9. Donatello's 'St. John'
10. Bartolomeo Vivarini Altarpiece
11. Tombs of Paolo Savelli, Benedetto Pésaro and Beato Pacifico
12. The Bellini Altarpiece
13. Tomb of Jacopo Marcello
14. Vittoria's 'St. Jerome'
15. Titian's Monument
16. Tomb of Alvise Pasqualino
17. Tomb of Pietro Bernardo
18. Mausoleum of Canova
19. Tomb of Doge Giovanni Pésaro

The right transept

In the right transept, above the door to the sacristy, most of the space is occupied by three very different tombs. The one on the left is the **tomb of Paolo Savelli** (c.1406), the first equestrian monument in Venice. Next along is **Lorenzo Bregno**'s tomb of another Pésaro – Benedetto, head of the Venetian army, who died in Corfu in 1503. The flamboyant Gothic work on the other side of the door is the terracotta **tomb of Beato Pacifico**, who is traditionally credited with beginning the present church; he was placed here in 1437, nearly a century after his death.

On the west wall of the transept, there's the very odd **tomb of Jacopo Marcello**, supported by small stooping figures (c.1485, probably by Giovanni Buora). High on the wall round the corner is something far less florid but equally strange – a plain black coffin which is said to have been meant for the body of the *condottiere* **Carmagnola**, who, having shown a suspicious reluctance to earn his money against the Milanese (his former employers), was executed after a dodgy treason trial in 1432. Carmagnola's remains are now in Milan, and another tenant occupies the coffin.

3

The sacristy and chapterhouse

Giovanni Bellini's *Madonna and Child with Sts Nicholas of Bari, Peter, Mark and Benedict* was painted in 1488 for the altar of the **sacristy**. It's still there, in its original frame, and alone would justify a long visit to the Frari. Gazing at this picture is like looking into a room that's soaked in a warm dawn light; in the words of Henry James – "it is as solemn as it is gorgeous and as simple as it is deep". While you're here, take a look at the wooden frame carved by **Francesco Pianta** for the clock that hangs beside the sacristy door; it's an astounding piece of work, teeming with symbols of mortality and the passage of time. From the sacristy there's access to the **chapterhouse**, where you'll find the tomb of Doge Francesco Dandolo (c.1340); the painting above it, by **Paolo Veneziano**, contains what is probably the first portrait of a doge ever painted from life.

The monuments in the nave

Facing the Pésaro altarpiece stands one of **Alessandro Vittoria**'s best marble figures – *St Jerome*, for which Titian was reputedly the model. Titian's house-sized **monument**, further along, was built in the mid-nineteenth century on the supposed place of his burial. He died in 1576, in around his ninetieth year, a casualty of the plague; such was the esteem in which Titian was held, he was the only victim to be allowed a church burial in the course of the outbreak, one of the most terrible in the city's history.

The delicate statuettes on the water stoups against the last columns, facing each other across the nave, are *St Anthony of Padua* and *St Agnes*, both by Campagna (1609). The **tomb of Procurator Alvise Pasqualino**, to the left of the door, is attributed to Lorenzo Bregno, whose death in 1523 preceded his client's by five years. Ordering your tomb in advance was not an unusual practice: **Pietro Bernardo** (died 1538), whose tomb (possibly by Tullio Lombardo, who died in 1532) is on the other side of the door, did the same thing – although the finished article was a little more low-key than he had intended. In his will he specified, among other provisions, that his epitaph should be cut in letters that would be legible from 25 paces, and that a monastic choir should sing psalms in front of his tomb on the first Sunday of every month until Judgement Day.

The marble pyramid with the troop of mourners is the **Mausoleum of Canova**, erected in 1827 by pupils of the sculptor, following a design he himself had made for the tombs of Titian and Maria Christina of Austria. Only the artist's heart is entombed here – the rest of the body is interred at his birthplace, Possagno.

Finally, moving along from the Canova monument, you'll be stopped in your tracks by what is surely the most grotesque monument in the city; this is the tomb of yet another Pésaro – **Doge Giovanni Pésaro** (1669). The architecture is usually attributed to Longhena; for the gigantic ragged-trousered Moors and decomposing corpses, a German sculptor called Melchiorre Barthel must take the blame.

> **THE STATE ARCHIVE**
>
> At the fall of the Republic the Franciscan monastery attached to the Frari was taken over for use as the **Archivio di Stato** (State Archive). Its documents, cramming more than three hundred rooms, relate to the Council of Ten, the courts, the embassies, the Arsenale, the *scuole* – to every aspect of Venetian public life – and go back as far as the ninth century. From time to time the archive puts on an exhibition of material dredged from the shelves.

The Scuola Grande di San Rocco

Campo San Rocco • Daily 9.30am–5.30pm • €10 • ⓦ scuolagrandesanrocco.it

Venice may not tell you much about Titian's work that you didn't already know, but in the case of **Tintoretto** the situation is reversed – until you've been to Venice, and in particular the **Scuola Grande di San Rocco**, you haven't really got to grips with him.

"As regards the pictures which it contains, it is one of the three most precious buildings in Italy," wrote Ruskin, and although the claim's open to argument, it's not difficult to understand why he resorted to such hyperbole. (His other votes were for the Sistine Chapel and the Campo Santo at Pisa – the latter was virtually ruined in World War II.) The unremitting concentration and restlessness of Tintoretto's paintings won't inspire unqualified enthusiasm in everyone: Henry James, though an admirer, found the atmosphere of San Rocco "difficult to breathe". But even those who prefer their art at a lower voltage will find this an overwhelming experience.

Brief history of the San Rocco scuola

From its foundation in 1478, the special concern of this particular *scuola* was the relief of the sick – a continuation of the Christian mission of its patron saint, St Roch (Rocco) of Montpellier, who in 1315 left his home town to work among plague victims in Italy, then returned home only to be spurned by his wealthy family and die in prison, aged just 32. The *scuola* had been going for seven years when the body of the saint was brought to Venice from Germany, and the consequent boom in donations was so great that in 1489 it acquired the status of *scuola grande*.

The intervention of St Roch was held to be especially efficacious in cases of bubonic plague, an illness from which he himself had been saved by the ministrations of a divinely inspired dog, which brought him bread and licked his wounds clean. (The churches of Venice are littered with paintings of the saint pointing to a sore on his thigh, usually with a dog in attendance.) When, in 1527, the city was hit by an outbreak of plague, the *scuola*'s revenue rocketed to record levels as gifts poured in from people hoping to secure St Roch's protection against the disease. In 1515 the *scuola*, previously based in a room within the Frari, had commissioned a prestigious new headquarters from **Bartolomeo Bon the Younger**, but for various reasons the work had ground to a halt within a decade; the fattened coffers prompted another phase of building, and from 1527 to 1549 the scheme was taken over by **Scarpagnino**.

When the scaffolding came down in 1560, the end product was somewhat incoherent and lopsided. Not that the members of the *scuola* would have been bothered for long; within a few years the decoration of the interior was under way, and it was this decoration – **Tintoretto**'s cycle of more than fifty major paintings – that secured the confraternity's social standing. An opportunistic little trick won the first contract for Tintoretto. In 1564 the *scuola* held a competition to decide who should paint the inaugural picture for the recently completed building. The subject was to be *The Glorification of St Roch*, and four artists were approached for proposals: Salviati, Zuccari, Veronese and Tintoretto, who had already painted a number of pictures for the neighbouring church of San Rocco. On the day for submissions the first three duly presented their sketches; Tintoretto, though, had painted a finished panel and persuaded a sidekick to rig it up, hidden by a veil, in the very place in which the winning picture was to be installed – the centre of the ceiling in the Sala dell'Albergo. A rope was pulled, the picture revealed and Tintoretto promptly offered the picture as a gift to the *scuola*. Despite his rivals' fury, the crucial first commission was his.

The upper floor

The narrative sequence of the cycle begins with the first picture in the lower room – *The Annunciation*. But to appreciate Tintoretto's development you have to begin in the smaller room on the upper storey – the **Sala dell'Albergo**. This is dominated by the stupendous *Crucifixion* (1565), of which Henry James wrote: "Surely no single picture in the world contains more of human life; there is everything in it." Ruskin was reduced to a state of dumbfounded wonder – his loquacious commentary on the San Rocco cycle concludes with the entry: "I must leave this picture to work its will on the spectator; for it is beyond all analysis, and above all praise." Tintoretto's other works in this room – aside from the contract-winning *Glorification of St Roch* in the middle of the ceiling – are on the entrance wall: *The Way to Calvary*, *Christ Crowned with Thorns* and *Christ before Pilate*.

Tintoretto finished his contribution to the Sala dell'Albergo in 1567. Eight years later, when the scuola decided to proceed with the embellishment of the main upper hall – the **chapterhouse** – he undertook to do the work in return for

3

THE SCUOLE OF VENICE

The Venetian institutions known as the **scuole** seem to have originated in the early thirteenth century, with the formation of the flagellant orders, whose public scourgings were intended to purge the sins of the world. The interaction between these societies of flagellants and the lay brotherhoods established by the city's branches of the mendicant orders (the Franciscans and the Dominicans) gave rise in 1260 to the formation of the confraternity called **Scuola di Santa Maria della Carità**, the first of the so-called **Scuola Grande**. By the middle of the sixteenth century there were five more of these major confraternities – **San Giovanni Evangelista**, **San Marco**, **Santa Maria della Misericordia**, **San Rocco** and **San Teodoro** – plus scores of smaller bodies known as the *Scuole Minore*, of which at one time there were as many as four hundred.

The *Scuole Grande*, drawing much of their membership from the wealthiest professional and mercantile groups, and with rosters of up to six hundred men, received subscriptions that allowed them to fund lavish **architectural and artistic projects**, of which the Scuola Grande di San Rocco is the most spectacular example. The *Scuole Minore*, united by membership of certain guilds (eg goldsmiths at the Scuola dei Battioro e Tiraori, shoemakers at the Scuola dei Calerghi), or by common nationality (as with San Giorgio degli Schiavoni, the Slavs' *scuola*), generally operated from far more modest bases. Yet all *scuole* had the same basic functions – to provide assistance for their members (eg dowries and medical aid), to offer a place of communal worship and to distribute alms and services in emergencies (anything from plague relief to the provision of troops). It was a frequently expressed complaint, however, that the *Scuole Grande* were prone to lose sight of their original aims in their rush to outdo each other.

To an extent, the *scuole* also acted as a kind of political safety valve. The councils of state were the unique preserve of the city's self-designated patrician class, but the *scuole* were administered by traders, doctors, lawyers, artisans and civil servants. Technically they had no real power, but a wealthy private club like the Scuola Grande di San Rocco was capable of being an effective pressure group. Like so many Venetian institutions, the *scuole* came to an end with **Napoleon**, who disbanded them in 1806. Most of their possessions were scattered, and their headquarters were in time put to new uses – the Scuola Grande di San Marco became the city hospital, for example, and the Scuola Grande di Santa Maria della Carità became the galleries of the Accademia. The Scuola di San Giorgio degli Schiavoni and Scuola Grande di San Rocco, however, were revived in the middle of the nineteenth century and continue to function as charitable bodies in the magnificently decorated buildings that they commissioned centuries ago. A third *scuola*, San Giovanni Evangelista, was reinstituted in the twentieth century.

nothing more than his expenses. In the event he was awarded a lifetime annuity, and then commenced the three large panels of the **ceiling**, beginning with *The Miracle of the Bronze Serpent*. With their references to the alleviation of physical suffering, this colossal picture and its companions – *Moses Striking Water from the Rock* and *The Miraculous Fall of Manna* – constitute a coded declaration of the *scuola*'s charitable programme, and the *scuola*'s governors were so satisfied with Tintoretto's conception that he was given the task of completing the decoration of the entire interior. It was a project to which he would give precedence over all his other commissions in the city; thereafter, on every St Roch's day until 1581, Tintoretto presented the *scuola* with three new pictures, a sequence that extended at a slower rate of production until 1588, when he painted the altarpiece of the chapterhouse, with the help of his son, Domenico.

The New Testament scenes around the **walls** are an amazing feat of sustained inventiveness, defying every convention of perspective, lighting, colour and even anatomy. On the **left wall** (as you face the altar) – *The Nativity*, *The Baptism*, *The Resurrection*, *The Agony in the Garden*, *The Last Supper*; on the **right wall** – *The Temptation of Christ*, *The Miracle at the Pool of Bethesda*, *The Ascension*, *The Raising of Lazarus*, *The Miracle of the Loaves and Fishes*; on the **end wall** by the Sala dell'Albergo – *St Roch* and *St Sebastian*; on the **altar** – *The Vision of St Roch*. On easels to the side of the altar are displayed an *Annunciation* by **Titian**, a *Visitation* and a portrait by **Tintoretto** that's often wrongly called a self-portrait, and *Christ Carrying the Cross*, an early Titian (though it's attributed to Giorgione by some) that from about 1510 until 1955 was displayed in the church of San Rocco, where it was revered as a miraculous image. At the other end of the hall, beside the door into the Sala dell'Albergo, you'll usually find *Hagar, Ishmael and an Angel* and *Abraham and an Angel*, both by **Giambattista Tiepolo**; sometimes they are displayed in a small room off the main hall.

The **carvings** underneath the paintings – a gallery of Vices, Virtues and other allegorical figures, plus an amazing trompe l'oeil library – were created in the late seventeenth century by **Francesco Pianta**. Not far from the altar, opposite the stairs, you'll find the allegory of painting: a caricature of the notoriously irascible Tintoretto, with a jarful of brushes.

The lower floor

The **lower hall** – connected to the chapterhouse by a stairway that's lined with pictures recording the plague that struck Venice in the 1630s – was painted between 1583 and 1587, when Tintoretto was in his late sixties. The tempestuous *Annunciation*, with the archangel crashing into the room through Joseph's shambolic workshop, trailing a tornado of cherubim, is followed by *The Adoration of the Magi*, *The Flight into Egypt*, *The Massacre of the Innocents*, *St Mary Magdalen*, *St Mary of Egypt*, *The Circumcision* and *The Assumption*. The landscapes in the *Flight into Egypt* and the meditative depictions of the two saints are among the finest Tintoretto ever painted.

The church of San Rocco

Campo San Rocco • Daily 9.30am–5.30pm • Free

Yet more Tintorettos are to be found in the **church of San Rocco**, built in 1489–1508 to designs by **Bartolomeo Bon the Younger**, but altered extensively in the eighteenth century. On the right wall of the nave you'll find *St Roch Taken to Prison*, and below it *The Pool of Bethesda*; only the latter is definitely by Tintoretto.

Between the altars on the other side are a couple of good pictures by **Pordenone** – *St Christopher* and *St Martin*. Four large paintings by Tintoretto hang in the chancel, often either lost in the gloom or glazed with sunlight; the best (both painted in 1549) are *St Roch Curing the Plague Victims* (lower right) and *St Roch in Prison* (lower left). The two higher pictures are *St Roch in Solitude* and *St Roch Healing the Animals*; the second is a doubtful attribution.

The Scuola Grande di San Giovanni Evangelista

Campiello della Scuola • Tourist visiting hours are posted monthly on Ⓦ scuolasangiovanni.it • €10

Not far from San Rocco, on the opposite side of the Frari, you'll find another of the *Scuole Grande* – the **Scuola Grande di San Giovanni Evangelista**, which was founded in 1261 by one of the many flagellant confraternities that sprang up at that time. Suppressed by Napoleon, it was reborn as the HQ of the Società delle Arti Edificatorie (Society of Building Arts) in the 1850s and was re-established as a charitable foundation in 1929. The *scuola* is heavily used as a conference centre, which is why it has no regular visiting hours.

This institution's finest hour came in 1369, when it was presented with a **relic of the True Cross**, an item that can be seen to this day in the first-floor **Oratorio della Croce**. The miracles effected by the relic were commemorated in the oratory by a series of paintings by Carpaccio, Gentile Bellini and others, now transplanted to the Accademia.

Nowadays the delights of the *scuola* are architectural. The **courtyards** are something of a composite; the mid-fifteenth-century facade of the *scuola* incorporates two mid-fourteenth-century reliefs, and the **screen** of the outer courtyard was built in 1481 by **Pietro Lombardo**. Approached from the train station direction, this screen looks like any old brick wall, but round the other side it reveals itselfto be a wonderfully delicate piece of marble carving. Inside, a grand **double staircase**, built by Codussi in 1498, rises to the main hall and the Oratorio; the ceiling of the hall is covered with rather refined scenes of the Apocalypse, painted by a variety of eighteenth-century artists after Giambattista Tiepolo defaulted on his contract (two of the panels were painted by his son). Around the walls are scenes from the life of St John, most of them by Domenico Tintoretto. As for the neighbouring church of San Giovanni Evangelista, it's one of the select company of religious buildings in Venice that are of no interest whatsoever.

The Tolentini

Campo dei Tolentini • Mon–Sat 8.30am–noon & 4.30–6.30pm, Sun 4.30–6.30pm • Free

Calle della Lacca–Fondamenta Sacchere–Corte Amai is a dullish but uncomplicated route from San Giovanni Evangelista to the portentous church of San Nicolò da Tolentino – alias the **Tolentini**. Venetian home of the Theatine Order, which found refuge in Venice after the Sack of Rome by the army of Charles V in 1527, it was begun in 1590 by Palladio's follower Scamozzi, and finished in 1714 by the addition of a freestanding portico – the first in Venice – designed by Andrea Tirali. Among the scores of seventeenth-century paintings, two stand out. The first is a *St Jerome* by Johann Lys, at the foot of the chancel steps, on the left; it was painted in 1628, just two years before German-born Lys died here of the plague, aged 33. The other is *St Lawrence Giving Alms* by Bernardo Strozzi, round the corner from the Lys painting, to the left. Up the left wall of the chancel swirls the best Baroque monument in Venice: the **monument to Francesco Morosini**, created in 1678 by a Genoese sculptor, Filippo Parodi. That's Francesco Morosini, the Patriarch of Venice, who is on no account to be confused with Francesco Morosini, Doge of Venice (1688–94) – though the latter Morosini did present the Tolentini with the banner of the Turkish general whom he had trounced in the Morea in 1685.

The former convent of the Tolentini is now home to the university's architecture department; the entrance is the work of Carla Scarpa, who also designed the courtyard that lies beyond it. If fatigue is setting in and you need a park bench to flop on, the **Giardino Papadopoli**, formerly one of Venice's biggest private gardens but now owned by the city, is just over the Rio dei Tolentini.

CA'D'ORO

Cannaregio

Within the northernmost section of Venice, Cannaregio, you pass from one urban extreme to another in a matter of minutes, the time it takes to escape the hubbub of the train station and the hustle of the Lista di Spagna – the tawdriest street in Venice – and into the backwaters away from the Canal Grande. There may no longer be any signs of the bamboo clumps that were probably the source of the *sestiere*'s name (*canna* means "reed"), but in all of Venice you won't find as many village-like parishes as you'll see in Cannaregio, and in few parts of the city are you more likely to get away from the tourist crowds.

Imprisoned in the heart of Cannaregio is the **Ghetto**, the first area in the world to bear that name, and one of Venice's most evocative areas. Within a short walk of the Ghetto you'll find **Madonna dell'Orto**, with its astonishing Tintoretto paintings, as well as **Sant'Alvise** and **Palazzo Labia**, the first remarkable for canvases by Giambattista Tiepolo, the second for the same artist's frescoes. The chief museum of Cannaregio is the **Ca' d'Oro**, a gorgeous Canal Grande palace housing a decent collection of paintings and carving. Over in the eastern part of the *sestiere* lie three outstanding churches: the exquisite little church of **Santa Maria dei Miracoli**; the often overlooked **San Giovanni Crisostomo**; and the **Gesuiti**, a Baroque creation which boasts perhaps the weirdest interior in the city.

From the train station to San Giobbe

The area around Venice's train station is one in which nearly every visitor sets foot but very few actually investigate. Nobody could pretend that it's one of the city's enticing spots, but it does repay a saunter. The station building itself is a gracefully functional 1950s effort, but the rail link to the mainland was opened in 1846; within a few years the expansion of traffic had made it necessary to demolish Palladio's church of Santa Lucia, the building from which the station's name is taken.

The Scalzi

Fondamenta dei Scalzi • Daily 8–noon & 4–7pm • Free

Right by the station stands the **Scalzi**, formally **Santa Maria di Nazaretta**. Begun in 1672 for the barefoot ("scalzi") order of Carmelites, it is anything but barefoot itself. Giuseppe Sardi's facade is fairly undemonstrative compared with **Baldassare Longhena**'s opulent interior, where the walls are plated with dark, multicoloured marble and overgrown with Baroque statuary. Ruskin condemned it as "a perfect type of the vulgar abuse of marble in every possible way, by men who had no eye for colour, and no understanding of any merit in a work of art but that which rises from costliness of material".

Before 1915, when an Austrian bomb that was aimed at the train station instead plummeted through the roof of the Scalzi, the church had a splendid **Giambattista Tiepolo** ceiling; a few scraps are preserved in the Accademia, and some wan frescoes by Tiepolo survive in the first chapel on the left and the second on the right. The second chapel on the left is the resting place of **Lodovico Manin** (d.1802), Venice's last doge. The bare inscription set into the floor – "Manini Cineres" (the ashes of Manin) – is a fair reflection of the low esteem in which he was held. His chief rival for the dogeship wailed "A Friulian as doge! The Republic is dead!" when Manin was elected, and although Lodovico can't take the blame for the death of independent Venice, he did display a certain lack of backbone whenever crisis loomed. He meekly surrendered his insignia of office to the French, so that it could be burned on a bonfire in the Piazza, and when later called upon to swear an oath of allegiance to Austria, he fell down in a dead faint.

The Lista di Spagna

Foreign embassies used to be corralled into this area to make life a little easier for the Republic's spies, and the **Lista di Spagna** takes its name from the Spanish embassy which used to be at no. 168. (*Lista* indicates a street leading to an embassy.) It's now completely given over to tourism, with a plethora of shops, restaurants and hotels making most of their money from people who are too tired or lazy to look any further.

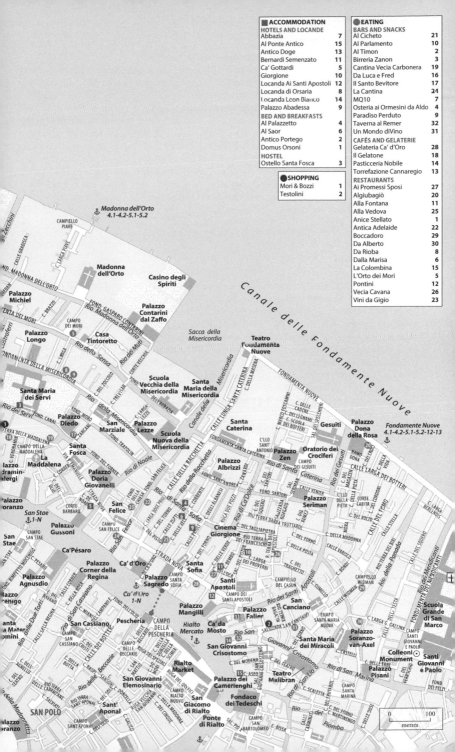

San Geremia e Lucia

Campo San Geremia e Lucia • Mon–Sat 8am–noon & 4–6pm, Sun 9.30am–12.15pm • Free

The Lista di Spagna flows into the campo of the church of **San Geremia e Lucia**, where the travels of **St Lucy** eventually terminated: martyred in Syracuse in 304, she was stolen from Constantinople by Venetian crusaders in 1204, then moved here when the church of Santa Lucia was demolished to make way for the train station. (She was also stolen from this church in 1994, but was soon returned.) She is the patron saint of the blind and those afflicted with ocular ailments, and is usually depicted holding her eyes on a dish. In one version of her legend, Lucy's response to an unwanted suitor who praised her beautiful eyes was to pluck out the offending organs and hand them to him, saying "Now let me live for God"; in another version, she was blinded by her executioner. Her desiccated body, wearing a lustrous silver mask, lies behind the altar, reclining above a donations box that bears the prayer "St Lucy, protect my eyes". Nothing else about the church is of interest, except the twelfth-century **campanile**, one of the oldest in the city.

Palazzo Labia

Campo San Geremia e Lucia

The **Palazzo Labia**, next door to San Geremia e Lucia, was built in 1720–50 for a famously extravagant Catalan family by the name of Lasbias (Labia being the Italianized version), who had bought their way into the *Libro d'Oro* (the register of the nobility) for the obligatory 100,000 ducats in the middle of the previous century. Their taste for conspicuous expenditure was legendary – a party here once finished with a member of the Labia family hurling the gold dinner service from the window into the canal and declaiming the memorable Venetian pun: "L'abbia o non l'abbia, sarò sempre Labia" (Whether I have it or whether I have it not, I will always be a Labia). The impact of the gesture is somewhat lessened by the rumour that fishing nets had been placed in the canal so that the service could be retrieved under cover of darkness.

No cost was spared on decoration either, and no sooner was the interior completed than **Giambattista Tiepolo** was hired to cover the walls of the ballroom with **frescoes** depicting the story of Antony and Cleopatra. (The architectural trompe l'oeil work is by another artist – Gerolamo Mengozzi Colonna.) This is the only sequence of Tiepolo paintings in Venice that is comparable to his narrative masterpieces in such mainland villas as the Villa Valmarana near Vicenza.

Palazzo Labia is owned by RAI, the Italian state broadcasting company, who used to allow visitors inside for a few hours each week, but access has been very limited in recent years. The tourist office will be able to tell you the current situation.

The Canale di Cannaregio

The Palazzo Labia's longest facade overlooks the **Canale di Cannaregio**, the main entrance to Venice before the rail and road links were constructed. If you turn left along its fondamenta rather than going with the flow over the Ponte delle Guglie, you'll be virtually alone by the time you're past the late seventeenth-century **Palazzo Savorgnan**. This was the home of one of Venice's richest families – indeed, so great was the Savorgnans' social clout that the Rezzonico family marked their intermarriage by getting Tiepolo to paint a fresco celebrating the event in the Ca' Rezzonico. Behind the palace lies the **Parco Savorgnan** (daily: April–Sept 8.30am–8.30pm; Oct–March 8.30am–6.30pm), one of Venice's very few green spaces for public use; its main entrance is close to the Guglie bridge.

Beyond the palazzo, swing left at the Ponte dei Tre Archi (Venice's only multiple-span bridge) and you're at the church of San Giobbe (see opposite). If you keep going to the end of the fondamenta you come to the **Macello Pubblico** (municipal slaughterhouse), built by the hygiene-conscious Austrians in 1843 and adorned with ox skulls. It is now used by the university, following many years of discussion; Le Corbusier designed a hospital for the site, but the plan was shelved in the face of local opposition.

On the opposite side of the canal, immediately east of the Ponte dei Tre Archi, stands the **Palazzo Surian**, once the French embassy. **Jean-Jacques Rousseau** lived here in 1743–44 as secretary to an indolent boss: "The French who lived in Venice would never have known that there was a French ambassador resident in the city, had it not been for me," he wrote. His *Confessions* record the political bickerings of his time here, and a number of sexual adventures.

San Giobbe

Campo San Giobbe • Closed for renovation works at time of writing: check Ⓦ chorusvenezia.org for opening hours when it reopens

"So went Satan forth from the presence of the Lord and smote Job with sore boils from the sole of his foot unto his crown," records the Bible. Job's physical sufferings – sanctioned by the Almighty in order to test his faith – greatly endeared him to the Venetians, who were regularly afflicted with malaria, plague and a plethora of water-related diseases, and in the fourteenth century an oratory and hospice dedicated to him were founded on the site of the church of **San Giobbe**. (Like San Moisè, this is an example of Venice's penchant for making saints of Old Testament figures.) In 1428 the complex was taken over by the Observant Franciscans, and in 1443 the order's greatest preacher, Bernardino of Siena, was a guest here, in what turned out to be the last year of his life. Bernardino's canonization followed in 1450, an event quickly commemorated here by the construction of a new church, a Gothic structure commenced by Antonio Gambello.

The interior

The most interesting parts of the building are its exquisitely carved early Renaissance doorway and chancel; begun in 1471, they were the first Venetian projects of **Pietro Lombardo**. The other appealing elements of the interior are the roundels and tiles from the Florentine **della Robbia** workshop, in the Cappella Martini (second chapel on the left); the presence of these Tuscan features is explained by the fact that the chapel was funded by a family of Lucca-born silk weavers. The tomb slab in the centre of the chancel floor is that of **Doge Cristoforo Moro**, the donor of the new building; a satirical leaflet about Moro may have been a source for Shakespeare's *Othello*, even though – as the portrait in the sacristy shows – Moro bore no racial similarity to the Moor of Venice.

San Giobbe's great altarpieces by Bellini and Carpaccio have been removed to the damp-free environment of the Accademia (the original marble frame for the Bellini now encloses a dull *Vision of Job*); in the main part of the church the most notable features are the ludicrous marble beasts that prop up the tomb of the magnificently named **Renato de Voyer de Palmy Signore d'Argeson**, who served as the French ambassador to Venice and died here in 1651. At the end of the nave, beyond Paris Bordone's altarpiece of *Sts Andrew, Peter and Nicholas*, a doorway leads into a room that was once part of the original oratory, which in turn connects with the **sacristy**, where there's a fine triptych by Antonio Vivarini, a fifteenth-century terracotta bust of St Bernardino and a *Marriage of St Catherine* attributed to Andrea Previtali.

4

THE GHETTO ONLINE

A good online source of information on the Ghetto is Ⓦ ghetto.it. For more details on the Jewish community of Venice, past and present, go to Ⓦ jvenice.org.

The Ghetto

The name of the Venetian **Ghetto** – a name bequeathed to all other such enclaves of deprivation – is derived from the Venetian dialect *geto*, foundry, which is what this area was until 1390. The city's **Jewish population** at that time was small and dispersed, and had only just achieved any degree of legal recognition: a decree of 1381 gave them the right to settle in Venice, and permitted them to lend money and to trade in second-hand items. Before the decade's end the Jews of Venice had become subject to legislation which restricted their residency to periods of no more than fifteen consecutive days, and forced them to wear distinguishing badges. Such punitive measures remained their lot for much of the succeeding century.

Brief history: the development of the Ghetto

The creation of the Ghetto was a consequence of the War of the League of Cambrai, when hundreds of Jews fled the mainland in fear of the Imperial army. Gaining safe haven in Venice, many of the terra firma Jews donated funds for the defence of the city, and were rewarded with permanent protection – at a price. In 1516 the **Ghetto Nuovo** became Venice's Jewish quarter, when all the city's Jews were forced to move onto this small island. At night the Ghetto was sealed by gates (marks left by their hinges can still be seen in the Sottoportego Ghetto Nuovo) and guarded by Christian watchmen, whose wages were levied from the Jews. In the daytime their movement wasn't restricted, but they were still obliged to wear distinctively coloured badges or caps. Though barred from certain professions, they were allowed to pursue others: they could, for example, trade in used cloth, practise medicine (doctors were the only people allowed out of the Ghetto at night) and lend money – the Banco Rosso pawnshop, at no. 2911 in the campo, is now a small museum, visitable by appointment (ⓦwww.bancorosso.org).

Changing faith was not a way to escape the shackles, as converts were forbidden "to enter or to practise any activity under any pretext whatsoever in this city … on pain of hanging, imprisonment, whipping or pillory". (This statute is carved in stone a little way down Calle di Ghetto Vecchio.) Yet Venice was one of the few states to tolerate the Jewish religion, and the Ghetto's population was often swelled by refugees from more oppressive societies. Jews expelled from Spain and Portugal in the 1490s came here, as did Jews later displaced from the eastern Mediterranean by the Ottoman Turks.

Parts of the Ghetto look quite different from the rest of Venice, as a result of the overcrowding that remained a problem even after the Jewish population was allowed to spread into the **Ghetto Vecchio** (1541) and the **Ghetto Nuovissimo** (1633), where all accommodation was rented, as in the Ghetto Nuovo – Jews were not allowed to own their accommodation. (The adjectives attached to the three parts of the ghetto can be confusing. The Ghetto Nuovo is *nuovo* – new – because the foundries spread here from the Ghetto Vecchio – the old foundry. The Ghetto Nuovissimo, on the other hand, is "most new" because it was the last part to be settled by the city's Jews.) As buildings in the Ghetto were not allowed to be more than one-third higher than in the rest of Venice, storeys were made as low as possible in order to fit in the maximum number of dwellings; six or seven floors is the norm. The gates of the Ghetto were finally torn down by Napoleon in 1797, but it wasn't until the city's unification with the Kingdom of Italy in 1866 that Jews achieved equal status with their fellow citizens.

THE HOLOCAUST MEMORIAL

In a corner of the Campo del Ghetto Nuovo is a reminder of the ultimate suffering of the Jewish people: a series of reliefs by **Arbit Blatas**, with a poem by André Tranc, commemorating the two hundred Venetian Jews deported to the death camps in 1943 and 1944; the names and ages of all the victims are inscribed on a separate memorial entitled *The Last Train*.

At its peak, in the middle of the seventeenth century, the Ghetto was home to more than five thousand people. Today Venice's Jewish population of around five hundred (which includes a recent influx of young Italians and North Americans belonging to the Lubavitch sect) is spread all over the city, but the Ghetto remains the centre of the community, with a library in Calle Ghetto Vecchio, a school, an old people's home, a kosher restaurant and a baker, and a cultural centre planned to open soon.

The scole and the museum

Museo Ebraico open daily except Sat & Jewish hols: June–Sept 10am–7pm; Oct–May 10am–5.30pm• €8, or €12 with tour of the synagogues

Each wave of Jewish immigrants maintained their own synagogues with their distinctive rites: the **Scola Tedesca** (for German Jews) was founded in 1528, the **Scola al Canton** (probably Jews from Provence) in 1531–32, the **Scola Levantina** (eastern Mediterranean) in 1538, the **Scola Spagnola** (Spanish) at an uncertain date in the later sixteenth century and the **Scola Italiana** in 1575. Funded by particularly prosperous trading communities, the Scola Levantina and the Scola Spagnola are the most lavish of the synagogues (the latter, redesigned by Longhena, greatly influenced the look of the others), and are the only two still used on a daily basis – the Levantina in summer and the Spagnola in winter, as there is only one rabbi.

Depending on the season, either the Scola Levantina or the Scola Spagnola can be viewed, along with the Scola al Canton and the Scola Italiana, in an informative **guided tour** (often in English) that begins at half-past each hour in the **Museo Ebraico**, above the Scola Tedesca on Campo del Ghetto Nuovo. The museum's collection consists mainly of silverware, sacred objects, textiles and furniture.

4

Northern Cannaregio

Land reclamation and the consolidation of the lagoon's mudbanks has been a continuous process in Venice since the time of the first settlers, but the contours of the city have been modified with particular rapidity in the last hundred years or so. As its long, straight canals and right-angled alleyways suggest, much of **northern Cannaregio** has come into existence comparatively recently: the Sacca (inlet) di San Girolamo, for example, was reclaimed in the first half of the twentieth century to provide working-class housing of a higher standard than in much of the rest of the city.

Sant'Alvise

Campo Sant'Alvise • Mon–Sat 10.30am–4.30pm • €3, or Chorus Pass • ⓦ chorusvenezia.org

For all the apparent rationality of the city's layout in this district, the damp-ridden church of **Sant'Alvise** is fairly tricky to get to, standing as it does on an island with no eastward land connection with the rest of the city. Dedicated to St Louis of Toulouse (Alvise being the Venetian version of Louis/Luigi), the church was commissioned in the 1380s by Antonia Venier, daughter of Doge Antonio Venier, after the saint had appeared to her in a vision.

The chancel is dominated by an immense *Road to Calvary* by **Giambattista Tiepolo**, whose slightly earlier *Crowning with Thorns* and *Flagellation* hang on the right-hand wall of the nave. Under the nuns' choir you'll find eight small tempera paintings, familiarly known as "The Baby Carpaccios" since Ruskin assigned them to the painter's precocious childhood; they're not actually by Carpaccio, but were produced around 1470, when he would indeed have been just an infant. The likeliest candidate for their authorship is an unknown pupil of Lazzaro Bastiani, Carpaccio's master. The extraordinary seventeenth-century trompe l'oeil **ceiling** is a collaboration between Antonio Torri (the architectural work) and Paolo Ricchi (the religious scenes).

Campo dei Mori

To get from Sant'Alvise to Madonna dell'Orto you can either take a one-stop vaporetto trip, or cross over the canal to the Fondamenta della Sensa, immediately to the south. One bridge after the early fifteenth-century **Palazzo Michiel** (the French embassy at the time of Henry III's visit), the fondamenta opens out at the **Campo dei Mori**, a square whose name possibly comes from the proximity of the now extinct Fondaco degli Arabi (Arabs' warehouse). There is another explanation: the four thirteenth-century **statues** around the campo are popularly associated with a family of twelfth-century merchants called the Mastelli brothers, who used to live in the palace into which two of the figures are embedded – they hailed from the Morea (the Peloponnese), and hence were known as *Mori*. Aggrieved citizens used to leave denunciations at the feet of "Sior Antonio Rioba" (the statue with the rusty nose), and circulate vindictive verses signed with his name.

Just beyond the campo is the elegant fifteenth-century house where **Tintoretto** lived for the last two decades of his life (1574–94), accompanied by one of his daughters, **Marietta**. Skilled as a painter, and a fine musician and singer too, Marietta was married off to a man who preferred his wife to produce portraits of his colleagues and friends instead of painting more ambitious works. She died aged 34, four years before her father, her career having epitomized the restriction of women's talents to genres compatible with a life of domesticity. None of her paintings is on public show in Venice, though scholars have detected her touch in some of her father's works.

4 Madonna dell'Orto

Campiello Madonna dell'Orto • Mon–Sat 10.30am–4.30pm • €3

Tintoretto, his daughter Marietta and his son Domenico are all buried in **Madonna dell'Orto**, the family's parish church and one of Venice's superlative pieces of ecclesiastical Gothic. The church was founded in the name of St Christopher some time around 1350; ferrymen for the northern islands used to operate from the quays near here, and it's popularly believed that the church received its dedication because Christopher was their patron saint, though there's a stronger connection with the merchants' guild, who funded much of the building and who also regarded Christopher as their patron.

It was popularly renamed after a large stone *Madonna* by **Giovanni de'Santi**, who put it on display in his nearby garden (*orto*), where it supposedly began working miracles; under pressure from the city's ecclesiastical authorities, he sold the statue to this church in 1377, in a deal that was mutually beneficial – the sculptor received a hefty sum of money plus a promise that a Mass would be said for him every day after his death, while the donations attracted by the *Madonna* enabled the monks to finance further building work. The heavily restored figure now sits in the Cappella di San Mauro, which is through the door at the end of the right aisle, next to the chapel containing Tintoretto's tomb; it's set aside for prayer, but access is often allowed if no one's using it.

The main figure on the **facade** is a *St Christopher* by the Florentine **Nicolò di Giovanni**; commissioned by the merchants' guild in the mid-fifteenth century, it became the first major sculptural project in the restoration programmes that began after the 1966 flood. **Bartolomeo Bon the Elder** designed the portal in 1460, shortly before his death. The **campanile**, finished in 1503, is one of the most notable landmarks when approaching Venice from the northern lagoon.

The interior

Restoration work in the 1860s made a mess of the **interior**, ripping up memorial stones from the floor, for instance, and destroying the organ, once described as the best in Europe. Partial reversal of the damage was achieved in the 1930s, when some over-painting was removed from the Greek marble columns, the fresco work and elsewhere, and in 1968–69 the whole building was given a massive overhaul.

An amusing if implausible tale explains the large number of **Tintoretto** paintings here. Having added cuckold's horns to a portrait of a doge that had been rejected by its subject, Tintoretto allegedly took refuge from his furious ex-client in Madonna dell'Orto; the doge then offered to forget the insult if Tintoretto agreed to decorate the church, figuring it would keep him quiet for a few years. Famously rapid even under normal circumstances, the painter finished the job within six months, most of which time must have been spent on the epic images on each side of the choir: *The Last Judgement*, described by Ruskin as the only painting ever to grasp the event "in its Verity … as they may see it who shall not sleep, but be changed"; and *The Making of the Golden Calf*, in which the carriers of the calf have been speculatively identified as portraits of Giorgione, Titian, Veronese and the artist himself (fourth from the left), with Aaron (pointing on the right) identified as Sansovino.

There could hardly be a sharper shift of mood than that from the apocalyptic temper of *The Last Judgement* to the reverential tenderness of *The Presentation of the Virgin*, at the end of the right aisle. It's by a long way the best of the smaller Tintorettos, but most of the others are interesting: *The Vision of the Cross to St Peter* and *The Beheading of St Paul* flank an *Annunciation* by Palma il Giovane in the chancel; four *Virtues* (the central one is ascribed to Sebastiano Ricci) are installed in the vault above; and *St Agnes Reviving Licinius* stands in the fourth chapel on the left. A major figure of the early Venetian Renaissance – **Cima da Conegliano** – is represented by a *St John the Baptist and Other Saints*, on the first altar on the right; a *Madonna and Child* by Cima's great contemporary, Giovanni Bellini, used to occupy the first chapel on the left, but thieves made off with it in 1993. Finally, in the second chapel off the left aisle you'll find a small *Tobias and the Angel* by Titian.

From Madonna dell'Orto to the Scuole della Misericordia

Diagonally opposite Madonna dell'Orto, on the other side of the canal, stands the **Palazzo Mastelli**, former home of the mercantile family of the same name. The facade of the much-altered palazzo is a sort of architectural scrap-album, featuring a Gothic top-floor balcony, thirteenth-century Byzantine fragments set into sixteenth-century work below, a bit of a Roman altar set into a column by the corner, and a quaint little relief of a man leading a laden camel – hence its alternative title, Palazzo del Cammello.

On the canal's north side, at its eastern end, stand the seventeenth-century **Palazzo Minelli Spada** and the sixteenth-century **Palazzo Contarini dal Zaffo**, the latter being one of the many palaces owned by the vast Contarini clan. Numerous though they once were, the last male of the Contarini line died in 1836, thus adding their name to the roll call of patrician dynasties that vanished in the nineteenth century. Already impoverished by loans made to the dying Republic and by the endless round of parties, many of the Venetian aristocracy were bankrupted during the Napoleonic and Austrian occupations, and so, no longer having money for dowries and other related expenses, they simply chose not to marry.

Crossing the canal in front of the Palazzo Contarini dal Zaffo, you quickly come to the fondamenta leading to the defunct **Abbazia della Misericordia** and the **Scuola Vecchia della Misericordia**; neither is particularly lovely, and the latter's proudest adornment – Bartolomeo Bon's relief of the *Madonna della Misericordia* – is exiled in London's Victoria and Albert Museum. The church hit the headlines in the 2015 Biennale, when Christoph Büchel, Iceland's representative, converted it into a mosque (or, as he would have it, an art installation in the form of a mosque), in order to highlight the anomaly that Venice – a city whose economy, art and architecture had strong ties with the Islamic world and is now home to hundreds of Muslims – has no Islamic place of worship. The police quickly closed it down, citing various infractions of legal procedure.

4

> ## THE HOUSE OF THE SPIRITS
> In the garden of the Palazzo Contarini dal Zaffo stands the sixteenth-century house known as the **Casinò degli Spiriti**. (It can be seen from the Fondamente Nuove.) A *casinò* (little house) – a suite set aside for private entertainments – was a feature of many Venetian palaces, and a few were set up in separate pavilions in the grounds. This is one of only two surviving examples of the latter, yet it's best known not for its architectural rarity but for the ghost story that's sometimes said to be the source of its name. A certain noblewoman took her husband's best friend as a lover, and this is where they would meet. At her paramour's sudden death she began to pine away, and shut herself in the *casinò* to die. No sooner had she exhaled her last breath than the ghost of her lover came in, raised her from the bed and, pushing the nursemaid to one side, made off with her. It's likelier, though, that *spiriti* refers to the exalted "spirits" who met here to discuss poetry, philosophy and so forth.

When the Misericordia became a *scuola grande* in the sixteenth century its members commissioned the huge **Scuola Nuova della Misericordia** (on the far side of the bridge), a move which benefited Tintoretto, who set up his canvases in the upper room of the old building to work on the *Paradiso* for the Palazzo Ducale. Begun in 1532 by Sansovino but not opened until 1589, the new block was never finished. Having been used as a sports centre for several years, it's now been beautifully renovated as an auditorium and exhibition space (🌐misericordiadivenezia.it). Its neighbour is the **Palazzo Lezze**, another project by Longhena.

4

Southern and eastern Cannaregio

If you follow the main route east from the station, crossing the Canale di Cannaregio by the Guglie bridge, you come onto the shopping street of **Rio Terrà San Leonardo**. Like the Lista di Spagna, this thoroughfare follows the line of a former canal, filled in during the 1870s by the Austrians as part of a scheme to rationalize movement round the north bend of the Canal Grande. The continuation of the route to the Rialto bridge – the Strada Nova – was by contrast created by simply ploughing a line straight through the houses that used to stand there.

San Marcuola
Campo San Marcuola • Mon–Sat 9.30–11.30am • Free

Rio Terrà Cristo, on the south of Rio Terrà San Leonardo, just before the market stalls of the Campiello del'Anconeta, runs down to Giorgio Massari's church of **San Marcuola**, a name which is perhaps the most baffling of all Venetian diminutives – it's somehow derived from Santi Ermagora e Fortunato. The bare brick ledges and sockets of the exterior, intended for marble cladding but now often crammed with pigeons, are a more diverting sight than the inside, where statues of the church's two patron saints by Gian Maria Morleiter, and an early *Last Supper* by Tintoretto (left wall of the chancel) are the only things to seek out. Those apart, the church's main interest is in a story about one of its priests. He was once foolish enough to announce from the pulpit that he didn't believe in ghosts, and that "where the dead are, there they stay"; that night all the corpses buried in the church rose from their graves, dragged him from his bed and beat him up.

Back on Campiello del'Anconeta, it's worth taking a look inside the supermarket that's now taken occupancy of the neo-Gothic Teatro Italia – it's odd to see fruit and veg on sale in such a lavish interior, but at least the old building is no longer completely neglected, as it had been for a long time.

La Maddalena, Santa Fosca and San Marziale

To the east of the San Marcuola canal the name of the main street changes to Rio Terrà della Maddalena, after the little Neoclassical church of **La Maddalena** (1760), which is set back on its own small campo. Its designer, the unprolific **Tomasso Temanza**, was more noted as a theoretician than as an architect, and his *Lives of the Most Famous Venetian Architects and Sculptors* (modelled on Vasari's *Lives of the Artists*) remains the classic text for those interested in the subject. The church itself is hardly ever open.

If you follow the main drag eastward, the next sight is the nineteenth-century monument of **Paolo Sarpi** that fronts the church of **Santa Fosca** (Tues & Thurs 9.30–11am), an unmemorable building that contains nothing of interest to the casual visitor apart from a Byzantine *Pietà* at the facade end of the north aisle. While you're here, don't miss the **Farmacia Ponci**, on the other side of Strada Nova – the oldest surviving shop interior in Venice, it's a wonderful display of seventeenth-century heavy-duty woodwork in walnut, kitted out with eighteenth-century majolica vases.

The church of **San Marziale**, to the north of Santa Fosca, is open only for Mass (Mon–Sat 4–6pm & Sun 8.30–10am), but it's worth popping in just before the service to see **Sebastiano Ricci**'s ceiling paintings, the works that made his reputation in the city. Also worth a look is the dotty Baroque high altar, depicting St Jerome at lunch with a couple of associates – Faith and Charity. The bridge leading to San Marziale from Campo Santa Fosca is one of the city's Ponti dei Pugni – hence the peculiar marble footprints (see page 93).

San Felice

Campo San Felice • Tues–Sun 9am–noon & 4–7pm • Free

Continuing east from Santa Fosca you're on the **Strada Nova**, a brisk, broad shopping street that's increasingly being colonized by souvenir sellers. The Strada's church of **San**

PAOLO SARPI AND THE EXCOMMUNICATION OF VENICE

Unswerving moral rectitude and intellectual rigour made Servite priest **Fra' Paolo Sarpi** one of the heroes of Venetian history. Author of a magisterial history of the Council of Trent, discoverer of the mechanics of the iris of the eye and a partner in Galileo's optical researches, Sarpi was described by Sir Henry Wotton, the English ambassador to Venice, as "the most deep and general scholar of the world". Sarpi is best known here, however, as the adviser to the Venetian state in its clash with the Vatican at the start of the seventeenth century.

Although Venice's toleration of non-Christians was a cause of recurrent friction with the Vatican, the area of greatest discord was the Republic's insistence on keeping separate the sovereignty of the Church and that of the State: "The Church must obey the State in things temporal and the latter the former in things spiritual, each maintaining its proper rights," to quote Sarpi himself. Matters came to a head when Venice restricted the amount of money that monasteries on the mainland could return to Rome from their rents and commerce, and then imprisoned two priests found guilty in secular courts of secular crimes. Pope Paul V's demand for the return of the priests and the repeal of the monastic legislation was firmly rebuffed, and the upshot was a *papal interdict* in April 1606, forbidding all religious services in Venice. Excommunication for the entire city then followed. In retaliation, Venice booted out the Jesuits and threatened with exile or execution any priests who didn't ignore the interdict – a priest in Padua who insisted that the Holy Spirit had moved him to obey the pope was informed by the Council of Ten that the Holy Spirit had already moved them to hang any who disagreed with them. Sarpi and Doge Leonardo Donà maintained their closely argued defiance of Rome until French mediation brought about a resolution which in fact required no compromises from the Venetians. The moral authority of Rome was diminished forever.

Six months later, Sarpi was walking home past Santa Fosca when he was set upon by three men and left for dead with a dagger in his face. "I recognize the style of the Holy See," the dauntless Sarpi quipped, punning on the word "stiletto". He eventually died of natural causes on January 15, 1623.

Felice, which was founded in the tenth century and rebuilt in the 1530s, is a workaday place of worship rather than a major monument, though it does have a painting by Tintoretto – *St Demetrius with Donor*, on the third altar on the right. One local curiosity: at the far end of the fondamenta going up the east side of the church is the only parapet-less bridge left in the main part of Venice; it leads to someone's front door.

Ca' d'Oro

Calle Ca' d'Oro • Mon 8.15am–2pm, Tues–Sat 8.15am–7.15pm • €6, but more whenever special exhibitions are on; free on first Sun of the month • ⓦ cadoro.org

On the south side of Strada Nova an inconspicuous calle leads down to the **Ca' d'Oro**, or House of Gold, a masterpiece of domestic Gothic architecture and now home to a somewhat patchy art collection, the **Galleria Giorgio Franchetti**. Built for procurator Marino Contarini between 1425 and 1440, the palace takes its name from its Canal Grande **facade**: incorporating parts of the thirteenth-century palace that used to stand here, it was highlighted in gold leaf, ultramarine and vermilion – materials which, as the three most expensive pigments of the day, spectacularly publicized the wealth of its owner. The house's cosmetics have now worn off, but the facade has at least survived unaltered, whereas the rest of the Ca' d'Oro was badly abused by later owners.

After the dancer Maria Taglioni had finished modifying the place, Ruskin lamented that it was "now destroyed by restorations", and today, despite the subsequent structural repairs, the interior of the Ca' d'Oro is no longer recognizable as that of a Gothic building. The staircase in the beautiful **courtyard** is an original feature, though – ripped out by Taglioni, it was reacquired and reconstructed by Franchetti, who likewise put back the wellhead by Bartolomeo Bon (1427). He also imported the mosaic pavement, which is certainly magnificent but not at all authentic – no house would have had a floor like this.

The collection

The gallery's main attraction is the *St Sebastian* painted by **Mantegna** shortly before his death in 1506, now installed in a chapel-like alcove on the first floor. Many of the big names of Venetian art are found on the second floor, but the canvases by Titian and Tintoretto are not among their best, and Pordenone's fragmentary frescoes from Santo Stefano require a considerable feat of imaginative reconstruction, as do the remains of Giorgione's and Titian's work from the exterior of the Fondaco dei Tedeschi. The Ca' d'Oro's collection of sculpture, though far less extensive than the array of paintings, has more outstanding items, notably **Tullio Lombardo**'s beautifully carved *Young Couple*, and superb portrait busts by Bernini and Alessandro Vittoria. Also arresting are a sixteenth-century English alabaster polyptych of *Scenes from the Life of St Catherine* and a case of Renaissance medals that includes fine specimens by **Gentile Bellini** and **Pisanello**.

Santi Apostoli

Campo dei Santi Apostoli • Mon–Sat 7.30–11.30am & 5–7pm • Free

At the eastern end of the Strada Nova, past the negligible little church of Santa Sofia, you come to Campo dei Santi Apostoli, an elbow on the road from the Rialto to the train station, with the church of **Santi Apostoli**, a frequently renovated building last altered substantially in the eighteenth century. The **Cappella Corner**, stuck onto the right side of the hall-like interior, is the most interesting part of the church. It's attributed to Mauro Codussi, and its altarpiece is a beautiful *Communion of St Lucy* by Giambattista Tiepolo (1748). One of the inscriptions in the chapel is to Caterina Cornaro, who was buried here before being moved to San Salvatore; the tomb of

her father Marco (on the right) is probably by Tullio Lombardo, who also carved the plaque of St Sebastian's head in the chapel to the right of the chancel.

San Giovanni Crisostomo

Campo San Giovanni Crisostomo • Mon–Sat 10am–noon & 3.30–6.30pm, Sun 11.30am–6.30pm • Free

Tucked into the southernmost corner of Cannaregio stands **San Giovanni Crisostomo** (John the Golden-Mouthed), named after the famously eloquent archbishop of Constantinople. An intimate church with a compact Greek-cross plan, it was possibly the last project of Mauro Codussi, and was built between 1497 and 1504. It possesses two outstanding altarpieces: in the chapel to the right hangs one of the last works by **Giovanni Bellini**, *Sts Jerome, Christopher and Louis of Toulouse*, painted in 1513 when the artist was in his eighties; and on the high altar, **Sebastiano del Piombo**'s gracefully heavy *St John Chrysostom with Sts John the Baptist, Liberale, Mary Magdalen, Agnes and Catherine*, painted in 1509–11. On the left side is a marble panel of the *Coronation of the Virgin* by Tullio Lombardo, a severe contrast with his more playful creations in the nearby Miracoli.

Calle del Scaletter, virtually opposite the church, leads to a secluded campiello flanked by the partly thirteenth-century **Palazzo Lion-Morosini**, whose external staircase is guarded by a little lion apparently suffering from indigestion; the campiello gives a terrific view of the Canal Grande.

Teatro Malibran and Marco Polo's house

4

Behind **San Giovanni Crisostomo** you'll find the **Teatro Malibran**, which opened in the seventeenth century, was rebuilt in the 1790s, and soon after renamed in honour of the great soprano Maria Malibran (1808–36), who saved the theatre from bankruptcy by giving a fundraising recital here, then donating the fee she had just been paid for singing at the Fenice. Rebuilt again in 1920, the Malibran has emerged from a very protracted restoration to resume its place as the city's major venue for classical music concerts.

PALAZZO FALIER AND CA' DA MOSTO

Two of the oldest houses in Venice are to be found on the small patch between the Rio dei Santi Apostoli and San Giovanni Crisostomo. At the foot of the bridge arching over to Campo Santi Apostoli there's the **Palazzo Falier**, parts of which date back to the second half of the thirteenth century. Traditionally this was the home of the ill-fated **Doge Marin Falier**, a branch of whose family was certainly in possession of the house at the time of his dogeship (1354–55). A man noted for his probity, Falier was greatly offended by the licence routinely allowed to the unruly nobles of Venice; when a lenient punishment was given to a young nobleman who had insulted Falier, his wife and her ladies, he finally went right off the rails and hatched a conspiracy to install himself as the city's benevolent despot – a plot into which he conscripted the overseer of the Arsenale and Filippo Calendario, one of the architects of the Palazzo Ducale. Their plan was discovered and Falier, having admitted the plot, was beheaded on the very spot on which he had earlier been invested as doge; a panel in the Palazzo Ducale perpetuates the memory of his crime (see page 58).

Interlocking with the Falier house is the equally ancient **Ca' da Mosto**, reached through the passage going towards the Canal Grande – though the best view of it is from the deck of a vaporetto. This was the birthplace of **Alvise da Mosto** (1432–88), a Venetian merchant-explorer who threw in his lot with Portugal's Henry the Navigator and went on to discover the Cape Verde Islands. The ruinous state of the building makes it hard to imagine the days when it housed the famous **Albergo del Leon Bianco**; among its guests were J.M.W. Turner, who had himself rowed up and down the Canal Grande while he sketched the city, and two German officers who in 1716 fought a duel in the courtyard and contrived to skewer each other to death.

The Byzantine arches on the facade of the theatre are said to have once been part of the house of **Marco Polo**'s family, who probably lived in the heavily restored palace overlooking the canal at the back of the Malibran, visible from the Ponte Marco Polo.

Polo's tales of his experiences in the empire of Kublai Khan were treated with incredulity when he returned to Venice in 1295, after seventeen years of trading with his father and uncle in the Far East. His habit of talking in terms of superlatives and vast numbers earned him the nickname Il Milione (The Million), the title he gave to the memoir he dictated in 1298 while he was a prisoner of the Genoese. It was the first account of Asian life to appear in the West, and for centuries was the most reliable description available in Europe – and yet on his deathbed Polo was implored by his friends to recant at least some of his tales, for "there are many strange things in that book which are reckoned past all credence". Polo's nickname is preserved by the adjoining **Corte Prima del Milion** and **Corte Seconda del Milion** – the latter is an interesting architectural mix of Veneto-Byzantine and Gothic elements, with a magnificently carved twelfth-century arch.

Santa Maria dei Miracoli

Campiello dei Miracoli • Mon–Sat 10.30am–4.30pm • €3, or Chorus Pass • ⓦ chorusvenezia.org

On the very edge of Cannaregio stands the church which Ruskin paired with the Scuola di San Marco as "the two most refined buildings in Venice" – the jewel-box-like **Santa Maria dei Miracoli**, usually known simply by the last word of its name.

It was built in 1481–89 to house an image of the Madonna that was painted in 1409 and began working miracles seventy years later – it was credited with the revival of a man who'd spent half an hour at the bottom of the Giudecca canal and of a woman left for dead after being stabbed. Financed by gifts left at the painting's nearby shrine, the church was most likely designed by **Pietro Lombardo**; certainly he and his two sons **Tullio** and **Antonio** oversaw the construction, and the three of them executed much of the carving. Richness of effect takes precedence over classical correctness on the **exterior**; pilasters are positioned close together along the sides to create the illusion of longer walls, for example, and Corinthian pilasters are placed below Ionic (in defiance of classical rules) so that the viewer can better appreciate the former's more elaborate detailing. Venetian folklore has it that the materials for the multicoloured marble cladding and inlays, typical of the Lombardi, were the surplus from the decoration of the Basilica di San Marco.

The interior

The marble-lined **interior** contains some of the most intricate decorative sculpture to be seen in Venice. The *Annunciation* and half-length figures of two saints on the balustrade at the altar end are thought to be by Tullio; nobody is sure which members of the family created the rest of the carvings in this part of the church, though it's likely that Antonio was responsible for the children's heads at the base of the chancel arch (which Ruskin hated: "The man who could carve a child's head so perfectly must have been wanting in all human feeling, to cut it off, and tie it by the hair to a vine leaf") and the adjacent siren figures. At the opposite end of the church, the columns below the nuns' choir are covered with extraordinary filigree stonework, featuring tiny birds with legs as thin as cocktail sticks. The miracle-working *Madonna* by Nicolò di Pietro still occupies the altar, while overhead a sequence of fifty saints and prophets, painted in 1528 by Pier Pennacchi, is set into the Miracoli's unusual panelled ceiling.

The Gesuiti

Salizzada dei Spechieri • Mon–Fri 10am–noon & 4–6pm • Free

The major monument in the northeastern corner of Cannaregio is **Santa Maria Assunta**, commonly known simply as the **Gesuiti**. Built for the Jesuits in 1714–29, six decades after the foundation here of their first monastery in Venice, the church was clearly planned to make an impression on a city that was habitually mistrustful of the order's close relationship with the papacy.

The disproportionately huge facade makes quite an impact, but not as much as the **interior**, where the walls are clad in green and white marble carved to resemble swags of damask. The stonework is astonishing, and also very heavy – a factor in the subsidence which is a constant problem with the Gesuiti. Unless you're a devotee of Palma il Giovane (in which case make for the sacristy, where the walls and ceiling are covered with paintings by him), the only painting to seek out is the *Martyrdom of St Lawrence* (first altar on the left), a broodingly intense night-scene painted by **Titian** in 1558.

Oratorio dei Crociferi

Campo di Gesuiti • Thurs–Sun 10am–1pm & 2–5pm • €3 • ⓦ gioiellinascostidivenezia.it

Almost opposite the Gesuiti is the **Oratorio dei Crociferi**, the remnant of a convent complex founded in the twelfth century by the crusading religious order known as the *Crociferi* or The Bearers of the Cross. A part of the complex was given over to a hostel that was originally for pilgrims but by the fifteenth century had become a hospice solely for poor women. (By the late sixteenth century Venice had around one hundred such institutions for the penniless.) In return for free meals and accommodation, these women were required to help in the maintenance of the convent and to pray each morning in the oratory, which in the 1580s was decorated by **Palma il Giovane** with a cycle of *Scenes from the History of the Order of the Crociferi*. Restored in the 1980s, the paintings show Palma's technique at its subtlest, and the richness of the colours is a good advertisement for modern restoration techniques.

Fondamente Nove

The long waterfront to the north of the Gesuiti, the **Fondamente Nove** (or Nuove), is the point at which the vaporetti leave the city for San Michele, Murano and the northern lagoon. On a clear day you can follow their course as far as the distant island of Burano, and see the snowy Dolomite peaks on the horizon. Being relatively new, this waterfront isn't solidly lined with historic buildings like its counterpart in the south of the city, the Záttere. The one house of interest is the **Palazzo Donà delle Rose** on the corner of the Rio dei Gesuiti. Architecturally the palace is an oddity, as the main axis of its interior runs parallel to the water instead of at ninety degrees; the cornerstone was laid in 1610 by **Doge Leonardo Donà** (Paolo Sarpi's boss), who died two years later from apoplexy after an argument with his brother about the house's layout.

CHURCH OF SANTI GIOVANNI E PAOLO

Central Castello

Bordering both San Marco and Cannaregio, and spreading across the city from the vicinity of the Rialto Bridge all the way to the housing estates of Sant'Elena in the east, Castello is so large and unwieldy a district that we've divided it into two sections: this chapter describes the zone that extends from the Cannaregio border to the canal that slices north–south through the *sestiere* from just beyond Santi Giovanni e Paolo to the Pietà; the area to the east of that line, which is dominated by the vast Arsenale complex – is covered in the following chapter.

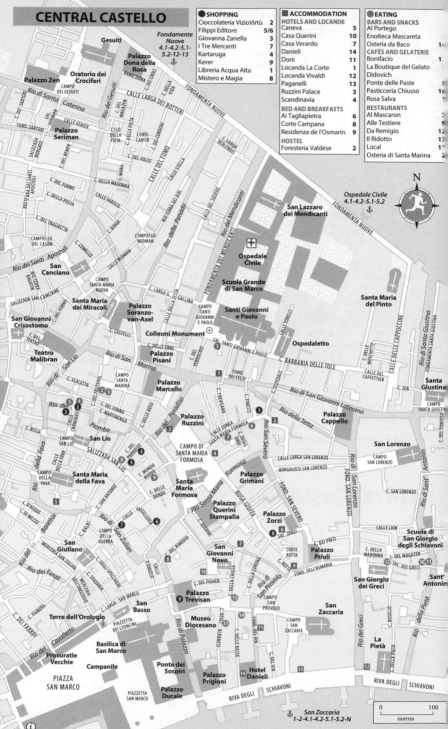

CENTRAL CASTELLO

The points of interest in central Castello are evenly distributed, but in terms of its importance and its geographical location, Castello's central building is the immense Gothic church of Santi Giovanni e Paolo (or Zanipolo), the pantheon of Venice's doges. The museums – the Querini-Stampalia picture collection, the museum at San Giorgio dei Greci and the Museo Diocesano's sacred art collection – lie in the southern part of this area, where the dominant building is the majestic San Zaccaria, a church that has played a significant part in the history of the city, as has nearby Santa Maria Formosa, on the most convivial square in Castello. Busier still is the southern waterfront, the Riva degli Schiavoni, Venice's main promenade.

5

Campo Santi Giovanni e Paolo and around

After the Piazza, the **Campo Santi Giovanni e Paolo** is the richest monumental public space in Venice. Dominated by the huge brick church from which it gets its name, the square is also overlooked by the most beautiful facade of any of the *Scuole Grande* and one of the finest equestrian monuments in the world.

The church of Santi Giovanni e Paolo

Campo Santi Giovanni e Paolo • Mon–Sat 9am–6pm, Sun noon–6pm • €3.50 • ⓦ basilicasantigiovanniepaolo.it

Like the Frari, the massive Gothic brick edifice of **Santi Giovanni e Paolo** – slurred by the Venetian dialect into **San Zanipolo** – was built for one of the mendicant orders which burgeoned in the fourteenth century. Supported largely by charitable donations from the public, the mendicants were less inward-looking than the older orders, basing themselves in large urban settlements and working to relieve the sick and the poor. Reflecting this social mission, their churches contain a vast area for the public congregation, and this requirement for space meant that they were usually built on the edges of city centres. In Venice the various mendicant orders are scattered outside the San Marco *sestiere*: the **Dominicans** here, the Franciscans at the Frari and San Francesco della Vigna, the Carmelites at the Carmini and the Servites at the now disused Santa Maria dei Servi. (The dedicatees of this church, by the way, are not the apostles John and Paul, but a pair of probably fictional saints whose story seems to be derived from that of saints Juventinus and Maximinius, who were martyred during the reign of Julian, in the fourth century.)

The exterior

The first church built on this site was begun in 1246 after **Doge Giacomo Tiepolo** was inspired by a dream to donate the land to the Dominicans – he dreamed that a flock of white doves, each marked on its forehead with the sign of the Cross, had flown over the

---

MARACANTONIO BRAGADIN

To the left of the first altar of the right aisle in San Zanipolo you'll find the **monument to Marcantonio Bragadin**, the central figure in one of the grisliest episodes in Venice's history. The commander of the Venetian garrison at Famagusta during the Turkish siege of 1571, Bragadin marshalled a resistance which lasted eleven months until, with his force reduced from 7000 men to 700, he was obliged to sue for peace. Given guarantees of safety, the Venetian officers entered the enemy camp, whereupon most were dragged away and cut to pieces, while Bragadin himself had his ears cut off in an assault that proved to be a foretaste of days of torture. His eventual execution was appalling – chained to a stake on the public scaffold, he was slowly flayed alive in front of the Pasha. His skin, stuffed with straw, was then mounted on a cow and paraded through the streets, prior to being hung from the bowsprit of the admiral's galley for the return voyage to Constantinople. Later the skin was brought back to Venice and placed in the urn above his monument.

5

swampland where the church now stands, as a celestial voice intoned "I have chosen this place for my ministry." That initial version was soon demolished to make way for this larger building, begun in 1333, though not consecrated until 1430. Tiepolo's simple sarcophagus is outside, on the left of the door, next to that of his son **Doge Lorenzo Tiepolo** (d.1275); both tombs were altered after the Bajamonte Tiepolo revolt of 1310 (see page 66), when the family was no longer allowed to display its old crest and had to devise a replacement. The **doorway**, flanked by Byzantine reliefs, is thought to be by **Bartolomeo Bon**, and is one of the major transitional Gothic-Renaissance works in the city; apart from that, the most arresting architectural feature of the exterior is the complex brickwork of the **apse**. The **Cappella di Sant'Orsola**, between the door to the right transept and the apse, is where the two **Bellini** brothers are buried; it used to house the Scuola di Sant'Orsola, the confraternity which commissioned Carpaccio's *St Ursula* cycle, now installed in the Accademia.

The interior
The simplicity of the cavernous **interior** – approximately 90m long, 38m wide at the transepts, 33m high in the centre – is offset by Zanipolo's profusion of tombs and monuments, including those of some 25 doges.

The Mocenigo tombs
The only part of the entrance wall that isn't given over to the glorification of the Mocenigo family is the monument to the poet Bartolomeo Bragadin, which happened to be there first. It's now engulfed by the **monument to Doge Alvise Mocenigo and his wife** (1577) which wraps itself round the doorway; on the right is Tullio Lombardo's **monument to Doge Giovanni Mocenigo** (d.1485); and on the left is the superb **monument to Doge Pietro Mocenigo** (d.1476), by Pietro Lombardo, with assistance from Tullio and Antonio. Pietro Mocenigo's sarcophagus, supported by warriors representing the three Ages of Man, is embellished with a Latin inscription (*Ex Hostium Manibus* – "From the hands of the enemy") pointing out that the spoils of war paid for his tomb, and a couple of reliefs showing his valorous deeds, including the handing of the keys of Famagusta to the doomed Caterina Cornaro (see page 304).

The south aisle
Giovanni Bellini's painting for the first altar of the south aisle went up in smoke some years ago, but his polyptych of *Sts Vincent Ferrer, Christopher and Sebastian* (on the second altar) has come through the centuries in magnificent fettle, although it has lost the image of God the Father that used to be in the lunette. The oozing effigy reclining below is of Tommaso Caraffini, confessor and biographer of St Catherine of Siena.

The next chapel but one, the **Cappella della Madonna della Pace**, is named after its Byzantine Madonna, brought to Venice in 1349 and attributed with amazing powers. Above the chapel entrance the figures of Doge Bertucci Valier (d.1658), Doge Silvestro Valier (d.1700) and Silvestro's wife, Dogaressa Elizabetta Querini (d.1708), are poised like actors taking a bow.

St Dominic in Glory, the only ceiling panel in Venice by Giambattista Piazzetta, Giambattista Tiepolo's tutor, covers the vault of the neighbouring **Cappella di San Domenico**, alongside which is a tiny shrine dedicated to **St Catherine of Siena**. Born in 1347 as the youngest of 25 children, Catherine manifested early signs of uninhibited piety – wearing hair shirts, sleeping on bare boards and crashing up and down stairs on her knees, saying a Hail Mary on each step. She died in 1380 and her body promptly entered the relic market – much of it is in Rome, but her head is in Siena, one foot is here and other lesser relics are scattered about Italy.

The south transept
San Zanipolo's best paintings are clustered in the **south transept**: a *Coronation of the Virgin* attributed to Cima da Conegliano and Giovanni Martini da Udine, and Lorenzo

Lotto's *St Antonine* (1542). As payment for his work Lotto asked only for his expenses and permission to be buried in the church; presumably the first part of the deal went through all right, but Lotto soon afterwards quit the backbiting of Venice's artistic circles, and eventually died in Loreto, where he was buried. Dominating the end wall of the transept is a superb fifteenth-century **stained-glass window**, which depicts a sacred hierarchy that rises from the four Dominican saints on the lowest row to God the Father at the summit. Thought to be the work of one Giannantonio Licino da Lodi, a Murano craftsman, this is an extremely rare instance of stained glass in Venice, where the instability of the buildings makes ambitious glazing a somewhat hazardous enterprise.

Filling much of the right wall of the second apsidal chapel – the **Cappella della Maddalena** – is a twentieth-century reconstruction of the **monument to Admiral Vettor Pisani**. Pisani's role in the victory over the Genoese at Chioggia in 1380 (see page 200) – a campaign in which he was mortally wounded – is summed up by John Julius Norwich:

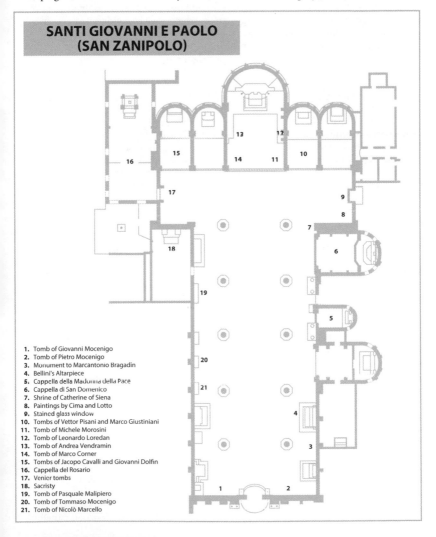

SANTI GIOVANNI E PAOLO (SAN ZANIPOLO)

1. Tomb of Giovanni Mocenigo
2. Tomb of Pietro Mocenigo
3. Monument to Marcantonio Bragadin
4. Bellini's Altarpiece
5. Cappella della Madonna della Pace
6. Cappella di San Domenico
7. Shrine of Catherine of Siena
8. Paintings by Cima and Lotto
9. Stained glass window
10. Tombs of Vettor Pisani and Marco Giustiniani
11. Tomb of Michele Morosini
12. Tomb of Leonardo Loredan
13. Tomb of Andrea Vendramin
14. Tomb of Marco Corner
15. Tombs of Jacopo Cavalli and Giovanni Dolfin
16. Cappella del Rosario
17. Venier tombs
18. Sacristy
19. Tomb of Pasquale Malipiero
20. Tomb of Tommaso Mocenigo
21. Tomb of Nicolò Marcello

5

"It would perhaps be an exaggeration to say that he saved Venice single-handed; the fact remains that she would not have survived without him." The tomb supported by what look like the heads of giant elves is of another sea captain, Marco Giustiniani (d.1346).

The chancel

The **chancel** is one of the high points of funerary art in Venice. **Doge Michele Morosini**, who ruled for four months before dying of plague in 1382, is buried in the tomb at the front on the right, a work which in Ruskin's eyes marked a fault line in European civilization, showing as it does "the exactly intermediate condition of feeling between the pure calmness of early Christianity, and the boastful pomp of the Renaissance faithlessness". The bombastic Renaissance world is represented by the adjacent tombs of **Doge Leonardo Loredan** (d.1521) and **Doge Andrea Vendramin** (d.1478), directly opposite Loredan's, which was moved here in 1818 from the church of the Servi. The sculptor of the Vendramin tomb (probably Tullio Lombardo) carved only the half of the figure that could be seen from below, an act which Ruskin condemned as being of "such utter coldness of feeling as could only consist with an extreme of intellectual and moral degradation". Next to it is the Gothic tomb of **Doge Marco Corner** (d.1368), which was hacked about to make way for its neighbour.

The north transept

Of the **tomb of Jacopo Cavalli** (d.1384), on the right of the final chapel in the north transept, Ruskin scornfully remarked: "I find no especial reason for the images of the Virtues, especially that of Charity, appearing at his tomb, unless it be this: that at the siege of Feltre, in the war against Leopold of Austria, he refused to assault the city because the senate would not grant his soldiers the pillage of the town." As if in response, the Virtues are no longer in place; the frescoes around the tomb are by Titian's nephew, Lorenzo Vecellio. On the left is the tomb of **Doge Giovanni Dolfin** (d.1361), who was being besieged by the Hungarians in Trieste when elected in 1356, and had to charge through enemy lines under cover of darkness in order to take up the post.

The tombs of three members of the **Venier** family adorn the end wall of the transept: the figure of Doge Sebastiano Venier, victor over the Turkish fleet at the Battle of Lépanto, is a twentieth-century creation; the monuments to the left were carved in the early fifteenth century by the Dalle Masegnes – the one above the door is the tomb of Doge Antonio Venier (d.1400), with his wife and daughter, Agnese and Orsola, alongside.

The Cappella del Rosario

The **Cappella del Rosario**, at the end of the north transept, was built in 1582 and dedicated to the victory at Lépanto, which happened on the feast day of the Madonna of the Rosary, October 7, 1571. In 1867 a fire destroyed its paintings by Tintoretto, Palma il Giovane and others, as well as Giovanni Bellini's *Madonna* and Titian's *Martyrdom of St Peter*, San Zanipolo's two most celebrated paintings, which were in here for restoration; arson by anti-Catholics was suspected, but nothing was ever proved. A lengthy twentieth-century restoration made use of surviving fragments and installed other pieces such as **Veronese**'s ceiling panels of *The Annunciation*, *The Assumption* and *The Adoration of the Shepherds*, and another *Adoration* by him, to the left as you enter the chapel.

The north aisle and sacristy

In the **north aisle**, Bartolomeo Vivarini's *Three Saints* (1473), a portion of a dismantled polyptych, is the first thing to grab your eye. Busts of Titian, Palma il Vecchio and Palma il Giovane look down from over the sacristy door, forming the monument which the last of the three designed for himself. The chief draws in the **sacristy** are Alvise Vivarini's luminescent *Christ Carrying the Cross* (1474) and the wood panelling by Andre Brustolon, though there is some historical interest in Andrea Vicentino's painting of Doge Giacomo Tiepolo donating the land for the site of the present church. Most of the other paintings depict scenes from the life of St Dominic or major events in the history of the Dominican order.

After the sacristy the rest of the aisle is stacked with monuments, the first of which is that of **Doge Pasquale Malipiero** (d.1462) – created by **Pietro Lombardo**, it's one of the earliest in Renaissance style in Venice. After the equestrian monument of the *condottiere* **Pompeo Giustiniani** (aka *Braccio di Ferro* – Iron Arm) comes the **tomb of Doge Tommaso Mocenigo** (d.1423) by Pietro di Nicolò Lamberti and Giovanni di Martino, followed by another Pietro Lombardo monument, for **Doge Nicolò Marcello** (d.1474), just before the altar with the copy of Titian's *Martyrdom of St Peter*. Three eminent Venetians of a more recent time – the Risorgimento heroes Attilio and Emilio Bandiera and Domenico Moro – are commemorated alongside; they're also honoured by having a square named after them. On the last altar is a figure of *St Jerome* by Alessandro Vittoria (1576).

The Colleoni monument

The *condottiere* **Bartolomeo Colleoni**, celebrated by the great **equestrian statue** outside Santi Giovanni e Paolo, began his wayward career in Venice's army in 1429, after a spell in the Bay of Naples, and for a while took orders from Gattamelata, who's commemorated in Padua by Donatello's superb monument. In the succeeding years Colleoni defected to Milan, was imprisoned there, escaped, re-enlisted for Venice, fled once again and finally joined the Republic's ranks for good in 1455 whereupon Venice suffered an outbreak of peace which resulted in his being called upon to fight on just one occasion during the last twenty years of his life. Resisting several lucrative offers from France and Rome, he settled into a life of prosperous leisure, and when he died in 1475 he left a legacy of some 700,000 ducats to the Venetian state. But there was a snag to this bequest: the Signoria could have the money only if an equestrian monument to him were erected in the square in front of San Marco – an unthinkable proposition to Venice's rulers, for whom the cult of the Republic took precedence over individual glorification. The problem was circumvented with a fine piece of disingenuousness, by which Colleoni's will was taken to allow the state to claim his money if his statue were raised before the Scuola di San Marco, rather than the Basilica.

Andrea Verrocchio won the commission for the monument in 1481, and difficulties cropped up in this stage of the proceedings, too. Verrocchio was preparing the figure of the horse for casting when he heard that another artist was being approached to sculpt the rider. Insulted, he smashed up his work and returned to Florence in a rage, to be followed by a decree forbidding him on pain of death to return to Venice. Eventually he was invited back, and was working again on the piece when he died in June 1488. The Signoria then hired **Alessandro Leopardi** to finish the work and produce the plinth for it, which he gladly did – even signing his own name on the horse's girth, and taking the self-bestowed title *del Cavallo*. An idealized image of steely masculinity rather than a true portrait (Verrocchio never met Colleoni), the statue made a powerful impact when it was finally unveiled in 1496 – according to Marin Sanudo, all of Venice came to marvel at it. And talking of masculinity, Thomas Coryat noted that Colleoni "had his name from having three stones, for the Italian word Coglione doth signify a testicle".

The Scuola Grande di San Marco

Campo Santi Giovanni e Paolo • Tues–Sat & first Sun of month 9.30am–5.30pm; pharmacy Mon 2–5pm • €5 • Ⓦ scuolagrandesanmarco.it

After its suppression in the early nineteenth century, the **Scuola Grande di San Marco** provided a sumptuous facade and foyer for Venice's hospital for the best part of two hundred years. (With Venice's plummeting population, the hospital – especially the

5

maternity unit – is under perpetual threat of at least partial closure.) The **facade** was started by Pietro Lombardo and Giovanni Buora in 1487, half a century after the *scuola* moved here from its original home over in the Santa Croce *sestiere*, and finished in 1495 by Mauro Codussi. Taken as a whole, the perspectival panels by **Tullio and Antonio Lombardo** might not quite create the intended illusion, but they are nonetheless beguiling.

In 2013, after the restructuring of the hospital and many years of restoration, the main rooms of the *scuola* were opened to the public. The columned *grande andito*, or entrance hall, was designed by Codussi, but was demolished in the nineteenth century; it was later rebuilt, using much of the original material. A Codussi staircase leads up to the huge **Sala Capitolare**, whose spectacular golden ceiling (constructed in the early sixteenth century) hangs over an impressive collection of old medical instruments and books. A cycle of Tintoretto paintings of scenes from the life and afterlife of St Mark used to adorn the walls of the Sala Capitolare; these were removed after the fall of the Republic, and most of them are now in the Accademia and the Brera (in Milan), but the originals of *The Transport of the Body of St Mark* and *St Mark Blesses the Lagoon Islands*, both by Tintoretto and his son Domenico, are still in place. The adjacent **Sala dell'Albergo** was similarly stripped of its pictures by Gentile and Giovanni Bellini, Giovanni Mansueti, Paris Bordone and Palma il Vecchio; amazingly accurate digital reproductions have replaced them.

Next door, the rooms of the disbanded Scuola di Santa Maria della Pace are now home to a collection of specimens of anatomical pathology and a reconstruction of an old pharmacy.

The Ospedaletto

Barbaria delle Tole 6691 • ⓦ gioiellinascostidivenezia.it

Another hospital block is attached to Longhena's church of the **Ospedaletto**, which stands immediately to the east of Zanipolo on Barbaria delle Tole. Known more properly as Santa Maria dei Derelitti, the Ospedaletto was founded in 1528 to provide care for the desperate peasants who were forced by famine to flee the mainland that year. The church itself, with its leering giants' heads and over-ripe decorations, drew Ruskin's wrath – "It is almost worth devoting an hour to the successive examination of five buildings as illustrative of the last degradation of the Renaissance. San Moisè is the most clumsy, Santa Maria Zobenigo the most impious, San Eustachio the most ridiculous, the Ospedaletto the most monstrous, and the head at Santa Maria Formosa the most foul." The much less extravagant interior has a series of eighteenth-century paintings high on the walls above the arches, one of which – *The Sacrifice of Isaac* – is an early **Giambattista Tiepolo** (fourth on the right). The adjoining **music room**, frescoed in the eighteenth century, is still used for concerts. At other times, the only way to see inside the Ospedaletto is by booking a private tour – details are on the website.

Campo Santa Maria Formosa and around

The spacious **Campo di Santa Maria Formosa**, virtually equidistant from the Piazza, San Zanipolo and the Ponte di Rialto, is a major confluence of routes on the east side of the Canal Grande, and one of the most attractive and atmospheric squares in the city. A few fruit and vegetable stalls are pitched here, and occasionally they are joined by sellers of antiquarian bits and pieces. A number of elegant buildings border the square, the most impressive of which is the **Palazzo Ruzzini-Priuli**, now a luxury hotel.

The church of Santa Maria Formosa

Campo Santa Maria Formosa • Mon–Sat 10.30am–4.30pm • €3, or Chorus Pass • ⓦ chorusvenezia.org

Santa Maria Formosa – the only church of this name in all of Italy – was founded in the seventh century by St Magnus, Bishop of Oderzo, who was guided by a dream in which he saw the Madonna *formosa* – a word which most closely translates as "buxomly beautiful". In 943 it gained a place in the ceremonials of Venice when a group of its parishioners rescued some young women who had been abducted from San Pietro di Castello (see page 158); as a reward, the doge thereafter visited the church each year, when he would be presented with a straw hat to keep the rain off and wine to slake his thirst. (The hat given to the last doge can be seen in the Museo Correr.)

Mauro Codussi, who rebuilt the church in 1492, followed quite closely the original Greek-cross layout, both as an evocation of Venice's Byzantine past and as a continuation of the tradition by which Marian churches had a central plan to symbolize the womb. A dome was frequently employed as a reference to Mary's crown; this one was rebuilt in 1922 after an Austrian bomb had destroyed its predecessor in World War I.

There are two **facades**. The one on the west side, close to the canal, was built in 1542 in honour of the military leader Vincenzo Cappello (d.1541); Ruskin, decrying the lack of religious imagery on this facade, identified Santa Maria Formosa as the forerunner of those churches "built to the glory of man, instead of the glory of God". The decoration of the other facade, constructed in 1604, is a bit less presumptuous – at least there's a figure of the Virgin to accompany the three portrait busts of other members of the Cappello clan. Ruskin reserved a special dose of vitriol for the **mask** at the base of the Baroque campanile: "huge, inhuman and monstrous – leering in bestial degradation, too foul to be either pictured or described…in that head is embodied the type of the evil spirit to which Venice was abandoned." Pompeo Molmenti, a great chronicler of Venice's socio-cultural history, insists that the head is both a talisman against the evil eye and a piece of clinical realism, portraying a man with a disorder of the sort that disfigured Joseph Merrick, the so-called Elephant Man.

The interior

The church contains two good paintings. Entering from the west side, the first one you'll see is **Bartolomeo Vivarini**'s triptych of *The Madonna of the Misericordia* (1473), once the church's high altarpiece, but now in a chapel on the right-hand side of the church. It was paid for by the congregation of the church, and some of the figures under the Madonna's cloak are believed to be portraits of the parishioners.

Nearby is **Palma il Vecchio**'s *St Barbara* (1522–24), praised by George Eliot as "an almost unique presentation of a hero-woman, standing in calm preparation for martyrdom, without the slightest air of pietism, yet with the expression of a mind filled with serious conviction". Born in Nicodemia around 300 AD, Barbara infuriated her father by converting to Christianity – he realized she'd become a Christian when she added a third window to her two-windowed bathroom, to symbolize the Trinity. Condemned to death by the Roman magistrate, Barbara was hauled up a mountain by her father and there executed by him. On his way down, he was struck by lightning, a fate which turned Barbara into the patron saint of artillery-men, the terrestrial agents of violent sudden death. This is why Palma's painting stands in the former chapel of the Scuola dei Bombardieri, and shows her treading on a cannon. Her brief was later widened to include all those in danger of sudden death, including miners.

The Pinacoteca Querini-Stampalia

Campo Santa Maria Formosa 5252 • Tues–Sun 10am–6pm • €14 • ⓦ querinistampalia.it

On the south side of Campo Santa Maria Formosa, a graceful little footbridge curves over a narrow canal and into the **Palazzo Querini-Stampalia**. The palace was built in the sixteenth century for a branch of the ancient Querini family, several of whom took refuge on the Greek island of Stampalia after their implication in the Bajamonte Tiepolo plot of

5

1310; when the errant clan was readmitted to Venice, they returned bearing their melodic new double-barrelled name. The last Querini-Stampalia expired in 1868, bequeathing his home and its contents to the city, and the palace now houses one of the city's quirkier collections, the **Pinacoteca Querini-Stampalia**. Although there is a batch of Renaissance pieces – such as Palma il Vecchio's marriage portraits of Francesco Querini and Paola Priuli Querini (for whom the palace was built), and **Giovanni Bellini**'s *Presentation in the Temple* – the general tone of the collection is set by the culture of eighteenth-century Venice, a period to which much of the palace's decor belongs. The winningly inept pieces by **Gabriel Bella** form a comprehensive record of Venetian social life in that century, and the more accomplished genre paintings of **Pietro and Alessandro Longhi**.

Another notable aspect of this museum is that its ground-floor rooms (where contemporary art shows are often held) were brilliantly refashioned in the 1960s by Carlo Scarpa, who also designed the entrance bridge and the garden – an ensemble that constitutes one of Venice's extremely rare examples of first-class modern architecture.

San Lio

Campo San Lio • Mon–Sat 9am–noon • Free

Either of the two bridges on the canalside of Santa Maria Formosa will take you onto the busy Salizzada di San Lio, a direct route to the Rialto. Calle del Paradiso, off to the right as you head towards the Rialto, is a pocket of almost untouched Gothic Venice, overlooked at one end by an early fifteenth-century arch showing the *Madonna della Misericordia*, sheltering two people within her cloak. As indicated by the coats of arms, the arch commemorates the intermarriage of the Fóscari and Mocenigo families; the male figure is thus probably Alvise Mocenigo and the female his bride, Pellegrina Fóscari, whose dowry included no fewer than 26 houses in Calle del Paradiso.

The church of **San Lio** – dedicated in 1054 to Pope Leo IX, an ally of Venice – is notable for its ceiling panel of *The Apotheosis of St Leo* by **Giandomenico Tiepolo**, and for the chapel to the right of the high altar, which was designed by the Lombardi and contains a *Pietà* possibly by Tullio Lombardo; there's also a low-grade late Titian on the first altar on the left.

Santa Maria della Fava

Campo della Fava • Mon–Sat 8.30–11.30am & 4.30–7pm • Free

A diversion south from San Lio down Calle della Fava brings you to the church of **Santa Maria della Fava** or Santa Maria della Consolazione, whose peculiar name derives from a sweet cake called a *fava* (bean), once the All Souls' Day speciality of a local baker and still a seasonal treat in Venice. Canova's tutor Giuseppe Bernardi (known as Torretto) carved the statues in niches along the nave. On the first altar on the right stands Giambattista Tiepolo's early *Education of the Virgin* (1732) in which the open Bible appears to be emitting a substantial cloud of Holy Spirit, with fleshy angels appearing in the mist and Joachim, the father of Mary, apparently warming his hands on the blessed fog. On the other side of the church there's *The Madonna and St Philip Neri*, painted five years earlier by Giambattista Piazzetta, the most influential painter in early eighteenth-century Venice.

Palazzo Grimani

Ramo Grimani 4858 • Tues–Sun 8.15am–7.15pm • €6.50 (more during special exhibitions), free on first Sun of the month • ⓦ palazzogrimani.org

Some of the most impressive palaces in the city stand on the island immediately to the south of Santa Maria Formosa. Turn first left off Ruga Giuffa and you'll be confronted

by the land entrance of the gargantuan sixteenth-century **Palazzo Grimani**, once owned by the branch of the Grimani family whose collection of antiquities became the basis of the Museo Archeologico. The neo-Roman interior, featuring some of the most spectacular residential rooms in the city (the tribune, with its towering skylight, is especially dramatic), has been beautifully restored and furnished, albeit sparsely, with a miscellany of objets d'art. Three small paintings by **Hieronymus Bosch** (*A Vision of the Afterlife*, the *Triptych of the Hermits* and the *St Liberata Triptych*), once owned by Cardinal Domenico Grimani, are sometimes on show here, but it's likelier that they'll be in the Accademia. A remnant of the frescoes that Giorgione painted for the Fondaco dei Tedeschi is always here, and art exhibitions are often held in the palazzo too. For a decent view of the exterior you have to cross the Rio San Severo, which also runs past the Gothic **Palazzo Zorzi-Bon** and Codussi's neighbouring **Palazzo Zorzi**.

San Giovanni in Oleo

Campo San Zaninovo

South of the Querini-Stampalia stands the crumbling church of San Giovanni Nuovo, better known as **San Giovanni in Oleo** (St John in Oil) – the Emperor Domitian is said to have ordered John's execution by immersion in a vat of boiling oil, an ordeal from which the saint emerged unscathed. Now deconsecrated, the church has served as an exhibition space, but its present condition is too perilous for it to be used. Beyond here you come down onto **Campo Santi Filippo e Giacomo**, which tapers west towards the bridge over the Rio di Palazzo, at the back of the Palazzo Ducale.

Sant'Apollonia and the Museo Diocesano

Fondamenta Sant'Apollonia • Tues–Sun 10am–7pm • €5

The early fourteenth-century cloister of **Sant'Apollonia**, which lies beside the Rio di Palazzo, is the only Romanesque cloister in the city. Fragments from the Basilica di San Marco dating back to the ninth century are displayed here, and a miscellany of sculptural pieces from other churches is on show in the adjoining **Museo Diocesano d'Arte Sacra**, where the collection consists chiefly of a range of religious artefacts and paintings gathered from churches that have closed down or entrusted their possessions to the safety of the museum. In addition, freshly restored works from other collections or churches sometimes pass through here, giving the museum an edge of unpredictability. A late fifteenth-century *Crucifix* from San Pietro di Castello is perhaps the most impressive single item, but this is very much one of the city's minor museums.

THE STORY OF BIANCA CAPPELLO

The sixteenth-century **Palazzo Trevisan-Cappello**, which flanks the bridge that crosses the Rio di Palazzo, immediately to the north of Sant'Apollonia, was once the home of **Bianca Cappello**. Born in 1548 to the blue-blooded and colossally wealthy Bartolomeo Cappello and Pellegrina Morosini, she eloped at the age of 15 with Pietro Bonaventuri, a humble bank clerk at the local branch of the Salviati bank, a Florentine institution. In Florence the beautiful Bianca soon caught the eye of the married Francesco de'Medici, Grand Duke of Tuscany, and became his mistress. Within weeks of the death of the Grand Duke's wife in 1578, Francesco and Bianca were married, a union that pleased the Venetians, who saw it as the basis of a political alliance, but appalled many in Florence, who regarded the new bride as little better than a gold-digger. (The hapless Pietro had by this time been murdered, possibly with the connivance of his ex-lover.) On October 17, 1587, at the Villa Medici di Poggio a Caiano, Francesco and Bianca both died. They were probably killed by malaria, but at the time there was a strong suspicion that they had been poisoned by another Medici, probably his younger brother, Ferdinando, who had always detested Bianca and now succeeded Francesco as Grand Duke.

San Zaccaria and the Greek quarter

The principal promenade of Castello is the broad **Riva degli Schiavoni**, which stretches from the edge of the Palazzo Ducale to the canal just before the Arsenale entrance. Throughout the year it's thronged during the day, with an unceasing flow of tourists and passengers hurrying to and from its vaporetto stops, threading through the souvenir stalls and street vendors. The church of the Pietà is the Riva's main monument; a few steps inland you'll find two other fine buildings – **San Zaccaria** and the focal point of the city's **Greek quarter**, San Giorgio dei Greci.

San Zaccaria

Campo San Zaccaria • Mon–Sat 10am–noon & 4–6pm, Sun 4–6pm • Free

Founded in the ninth century as a shrine for the body of Zaccharias, father of John the Baptist (he is encased on the second altar on the right, below the remains of St Athanasius), the church of **San Zaccaria** has a tortuous history. A Romanesque version was raised a century after the foundation; this in turn was overhauled in the 1170s (when the present campanile was constructed); a Gothic church followed in the fourteenth century; and finally in 1444 **Antonio Gambello** embarked on a massive rebuilding project that was concluded some seventy years later by **Mauro Codussi**, who took over the **facade** from the first storey upwards – hence its resemblance to San Michele. The end result is a distinctively Venetian blend of Gothic and Renaissance styles, which looks especially spectacular after its recent cleaning.

The interior

The interior's notable architectural feature is its **ambulatory**; unique in Venice, it might have been built to accommodate the procession of the doges' Easter Sunday visit, a ritual that began back in the twelfth century after the convent had sold to the state the land that was to become the Piazza. Nearly every inch of wall surface is hung with seventeenth- and eighteenth-century paintings, all of them outshone by **Giovanni Bellini**'s majestic *Madonna and Four Saints* (1505), on the second altar on the left. The continuation of the architectural frame (possibly by Pietro Lombardo) into the canvas reveals that the painting hangs in its original spot – although it sojourned briefly in the Louvre, a period in which the top arched segment was removed. Further up the left aisle, by the sacristy door, is the tomb of **Alessandro Vittoria** (d.1608), including a self-portrait bust; he also carved the *St John the Baptist* and *St Zaccharias* for the two holy-water stoups (the latter is a copy – the original has been stolen), and the now faceless *St Zaccharias* on the facade above the door.

The €2 fee payable to enter the **Cappella di Sant'Atanasio** and **Cappella di San Tarasio** (off the right aisle) is well worth it. The former was rebuilt at the end of the sixteenth century, and contains **Tintoretto**'s early *The Birth of St John the Baptist*, some fifteenth-century stalls and a painting by Palma il Vecchio that stood in for the Bellini altarpiece during the years the Bellini was on show in Paris. Although a patch of old mosaic floor has been uncovered here, it's in the San Tarasio chapel that it becomes obvious that these chapels occupy much of the site of the Gothic church that preceded the present one. Three wonderful *anconas* (composite altarpieces) by **Antonio Vivarini and Giovanni d'Alemagna** (all 1443) are the highlight: the one on the left is dedicated to St Sabine, whose tomb is below it; the main altarpiece has recently been restored, a process that has revealed a seven-panelled predella now attributed to Paolo Veneziano, the earliest celebrated Venetian artist (d. c.1358). You can also see frescoes by Andrea del Castagno and Francesco da Faenza in the vault (painted a year before the *anconas*), while the floor has been cut away in places to reveal mosaics from the twelfth-century San Zaccaria, and a fragment that might even date back to the ninth century. Downstairs is the spooky and perpetually waterlogged ninth-century crypt, the burial place of eight early doges.

5

The Riva degli Schiavoni

The name **Riva degli Schiavoni** is a vestige of an ignominious side of the Venetian economy, as *schiavoni* denotes both slaves and the Slavs who in the early days of Venice provided most of the human merchandise. By the early eleventh century Christianity was making extensive inroads among the Slavs, who thus came to be regarded as too civilized for such treatment; in succeeding centuries the slave trade turned to Greece, Russia and Central Asia for its supplies, until the fall of Constantinople in 1453 forced a switch of attention to Africa.

As you'd expect of a locality that commands so magnificent a view, the Riva has long been prime territory for the tourist industry, and today there are hotels strung out along the length of the waterfront, all the way to the Arsenale. George Sand, Charles Dickens, Proust, Wagner and the ever-present Ruskin all checked in at the most prestigious and expensive of these establishments, the **Hotel Danieli.** The beautiful fifteenth-century part of the hotel, formerly the Palazzo Dandolo, was the venue for one of the earliest opera productions, Monteverdi's *Proserpina Rapita*; the *Danieli*'s nondescript extension, built in 1948, was the first transgression of the 1172 ban on stone buildings on this spot (see page 148). Longer-term residents of the Riva include **Petrarch** and his daughter, who lived at no. 4145 in the 1360s, and **Henry James**, who stayed at no. 4161 in 1881, battling against the constant distractions outside to finish *The Portrait of a Lady*.

La Pietà

Riva degli Schiavoni • Tues–Fri 10.15am–noon & 3–5pm, Sat & Sun 10.15am–1pm & 2–5pm • €3

The main eye-catcher on the Riva, rising behind the equestrian monument to King Vittorio Emanuele II, is the white facade of **Santa Maria della Visitazione**, known less cumbersomely as **La Pietà**. **Vivaldi** wrote many of his finest pieces for the orphanage attached to the church, where he worked as violin-master (1704–18) and later as choirmaster (1735–38). So successful did the Pietà become that some unscrupulous parents tried to get their progeny into its ranks by foisting them off as parentless waifs. Founded back in the fourteenth century, the Pietà orphanage is nowadays an organization that cares mainly for infants awaiting adoption, and for socially disadvantaged women with young children.

During Vivaldi's second term at the Pietà **Giorgio Massari** won a competition to rebuild the church, and it's probable that the composer advised him on acoustic

---

MAYHEM ON CAMPO SAN ZACCARIA

Campo San Zaccaria is notorious as the spot where two doges were assassinated: in 864, **Doge Pietro Tradonico** was murdered here as he returned from vespers in the Basilica; and in 1172, **Doge Vitale Michiel II**, having not only blundered in peace negotiations with the Byzantine Empire but also brought the plague back with him from Constantinople, was stabbed to death as he fled for the sanctuary of San Zaccaria. Michiel's assassin fled to his home in Calle delle Rasse, between the Palazzo Ducale and San Zaccaria, and was soon arrested. After his execution his home was demolished (a customary punishment for traitors), and it was later decreed that only wooden buildings should be built in this district – an edict that wasn't contravened until 1948, with the construction of the annexe of the *Danieli* hotel. Though chiefly remembered for his death, Vitale Michiel II also left a permanent signature on his city, in that he was the doge who divided Venice into its six *sestieri*, an administrative innovation designed to facilitate the raising of taxes.

On a lighter note, San Zaccaria also had a reputation for the libidinous behaviour of the nuns in its convent – a state of affairs not so surprising if you bear in mind that many of the women were incarcerated here because their fathers couldn't afford dowries for them. On one occasion officials sent to put a stop to the amorous liaisons at San Zaccaria were pelted with bricks by the residents, but the nuns' behaviour was customarily rather more discreet: Venice's upper classes supplied this convent with several of its novices, and the nuns' parlour became one of the city's most fashionable salons, as recorded by a Guardi painting in Ca' Rezzonico.

5

MUSIC IN VENICE

For hundreds of years the musical life of Venice was dominated by the Basilica di San Marco, where music was performed to celebrate the doge's authority as far back as the thirteenth century. It was with choral music that the city became most closely associated, especially after 1527, when the Flemish composer **Adrian Willaert** became the *maestro di cappella*. By the second half of the sixteenth century, when **Andrea Gabrieli** and then his nephew **Giovanni** were in charge of sacred music at San Marco, a characteristic Venetian form had emerged: *cori spezzati* or polychoral music, in which one group of singers would be placed in each of the organ lofts, with a third group occupying a stage near the main altar. This spectacular and powerful style reached its apogee at the start of the seventeenth century, but was soon displaced by a more streamlined and expressive mode of text-setting, in which greater emphasis was placed on clarity of the text – a style exemplified by **Claudio Monteverdi**, who was made *maestro di cappella* at San Marco in 1613.

Monteverdi's most celebrated choral work, the *Vespers*, was written before he came to Venice. Of the pieces he wrote here, the most significant were perhaps his eighth book of **madrigals** and the **operas** he composed late in his life, of which only two have survived: *Il ritorno d'Ulisse in patria*, performed in 1640 at San Cassiano (which three years earlier had become Venice's first public theatre), and *L'Incoronazione di Poppea*, premiered three years later at Santi Giovanni e Paolo. Monteverdi was one of the pioneers of sung drama, and the numerous theatres of Venice were crucial to the establishment of the new genre, in which the solo voice was the focus of attention and female vocalists (prohibited from singing in church) shared the stage with male performers. In the course of the seventeenth century other celebrated opera houses opened at San Salvador, San Moisè, Sant'Angelo and San Giovanni Crisostomo, the last of which was renowned for the extravagance of its stagings and the lustre of its stars, the greatest of whom was the castrato Carlo Broschi, better known as **Farinelli**.

In addition to San Marco and the theatres, Venice's churches, convents, monasteries, *scuole* and *ospedali* (hostel-orphanages) commissioned a vast amount of new music. Competition among the various *scuole* led to the creation of some impressive ceremonial music, while the four *ospedali* – the Incurabili, Mendicanti, Derelitti (or Ospedaletto) and Pietà – gained a reputation for the virtuosity of their musical pupils. Many of **Antonio Vivaldi**'s more than 450 concertos – including the *Four Seasons* – were written for the girls and young women of the Pietà, though the principal genre of the *ospedali* was the oratorio (a dramatic setting of a religious text). The Pietà, however, didn't have a monopoly on Vivaldi's time when he was in Venice: he also composed operas for the Sant'Angelo and San Moisè theatres, both of which were managed by him.

With the political and economic decline of Venice in the eighteenth century, musical activity went into decline too, though the most famous of all its theatres, **La Fenice**, was founded in 1792, and the Pietà's conservatory survived into the next century, after the other three *ospedali* had gone bankrupt. Several theatres went out of business during the years of occupation by France and Austria, leaving La Fenice as the city's one venue of international significance, a status it has retained to the present. After World War II, Venice had one other claim to musical fame – it was the birthplace and home of one of the greatest modern European composers, **Luigi Nono**.

refinements such as the positioning of the double choir on the entrance wall and the two choir-lofts on the side walls. He may also have suggested adding the vestibule to the front of the church, as insulation against the background noise of the city. Building eventually began in 1745, after Vivaldi's death, and when the interior was completed in 1760 (the facade didn't go on until 1906) it was regarded more as a concert hall than a church. You get some idea of the showiness of eighteenth-century Venice from the fact that whereas this section of the Riva was widened to give a grander approach to the building, Massari's plans to improve the orphanage were shelved owing to lack of funds. The white and gold interior is crowned by a superb ceiling painting of *The Glory of Paradise* by **Giambattista Tiepolo**, who also painted the ceiling panel above the high altar.

5

A concert hall and ticket office is in effect what the Pietà is today: the in-house orchestra plays Vivaldi here two or three times a week, with the *Four Seasons* always on the bill.

The Greek quarter

Venice's **Greek community** became established here in the eleventh century, and burgeoned after the Turkish seizure of Constantinople. This mid-fifteenth-century influx took the Greek population of Venice to around 4000, and provided a resource which was exploited by the city's numerous scholarly publishing houses, and greatly enriched the general culture of Renaissance Venice. Some of the Greek merchants were immensely wealthy too: one of them, murdered in Venice in 1756, left four million ducats to his daughters, a legacy that was said to have made them the richest heiresses in Europe.

San Giorgio dei Greci

Campiello dei Greci • Mon & Wed–Sat 9am–12.30pm & 2.30–4.30pm, Sun 9am–1pm • Free

To the north of the Pietà stands the church of **San Giorgio dei Greci**, easily identifiable from a distance by its lurching campanile. The church was built in 1539–61 to a Sansovino-influenced design by **Sante Lombardo**; the cupola and campanile came later in the century. Inside, the Orthodox architectural elements include a *matroneo* (women's gallery) above the main entrance and an iconostasis (or rood screen) that completely cuts off the high altar. The icons on the screen are a mixture of works by a sixteenth-century Cretan artist called **Michael Damaskinós** and a few Byzantine pieces dating back as far as the twelfth century.

The Museo di Dipinti Sacri Bizantini

Daily 9am–5pm • €4

Permission to found the church was given at the end of the fifteenth century, and a Greek college (the Collegio Flangini) and *scuola* were approved at the same time. The college, redesigned in 1678 by **Longhena**, is now home to the Hellenic Centre for Byzantine and Post-Byzantine Studies, custodian of Venice's Greek archives. Longhena also redesigned the Scuola di San Nicolò dei Greci, to the left of the church, which houses the **Museo di Dipinti Sacri Bizantini**, a collection of predominantly fifteenth- to eighteenth-century icons, many of them by the *Madoneri*, the school of Greek and Cretan artists working in Venice in that period.

San Lorenzo

Campo San Lorenzo

The conspicuously huge church of **San Lorenzo**, to the north of San Giorgio dei Greci, has an illustrious pedigree – it's one of the city's oldest, having been founded in the sixth century at the latest, and its Benedictine convent – established in 854 – grew to be one of the richest in the city. Marco Polo was buried here, but when the church was rebuilt in the sixteenth century his sarcophagus went astray. Damaged during World War I, San Lorenzo is now a barren and hangar-like hulk, and has been undergoing a glacially slow restoration for many years. In return for funding the work, in 2012 the Mexican government was allowed to use San Lorenzo as its national pavilion during the Biennale; the agreement was intended to last a decade, but it's already been rescinded, so San Lorenzo remains almost perpetually shut.

ARSENALE

Eastern Castello

For all that most visitors see of the eastern zone of the sprawling Castello *sestiere*, the city may as well peter out a few metres to the east of a line drawn between San Zaccaria and Santi Giovanni e Paolo, and at first glance the map of the city would seem to justify this neglect. Certainly the sights are thinly spread, and a huge bite is taken out of the area by the pool of the Arsenale, for a long time the largest manufacturing site in Europe, but nowadays little more than a vast relic of the city's heyday as one of the supreme powers in the Mediterranean. Yet the slab of the city immediately to the west of the Arsenale contains places that shouldn't be missed – the Renaissance San Francesco della Vigna, for example, and the Scuola di San Giorgio degli Schiavoni, with its endearing cycle of paintings by Carpaccio.

6

And although the mainly residential area beyond the Arsenale has little to offer in the way of cultural monuments other than the ex-cathedral of **San Pietro di Castello** and the church of **Sant'Elena**, it would be a mistake to leave the easternmost zone unexplored. Except in the summer of odd-numbered years, when the **Biennale** sets up shop in the pavilions behind the **Giardini Pubblici** and elsewhere in the neighbourhood, few visitors stray into this latter area – and there lies one of its principal attractions. The whole length of the waterfront gives spectacular panoramas of the city, with the best coming last: from Sant'Elena you get a view that takes in the Palazzo Ducale, the back of San Giorgio Maggiore and La Giudecca, the tiny islands of La Grazia, San Clemente, Santo Spirito, San Servolo and San Lazzaro degli Armeni, and finally the Lido.

San Francesco della Vigna to the waterfront

The area that lies to the **east of San Zanipolo** is not, at first sight, an attractive district: the church of Santa Maria del Pianto is an abandoned hulk, Santa Giustina is shabby and graffiti-plastered, and round the back of Santa Giustina stand the rusting remains of the gasworks. But it's not all decay and dereliction – carry on for just a minute more and the striking Renaissance facade of San Francesco della Vigna blocks your way.

San Francesco della Vigna
Campo San Francesco • Mon–Sat 8am–12.30pm & 3–6.30pm, Sun 3–6.30pm • Free

The ground occupied by **San Francesco della Vigna** has a hallowed place in the mythology of Venice, as according to tradition it was around here that the angel appeared to St Mark to tell him that the lagoon islands were to be his final resting place. (The angel's words – "Pax tibi" and so forth – remained unchanged on the book held by Venice's symbolic lion until Napoleon substituted the rubric "To the Rights of Men and Citizens" on official proclamations. "At last he's turned the page," remarked an anonymous wit.) Some time after the alleged annunciation the area was cultivated as a vineyard, and when the land was given to the Franciscans in 1253 as a site for a new church, the vines were immortalized in their church's name.

Begun in 1534, to a design by **Sansovino**, the present building was much modified in the course of its construction. **Palladio** was brought in to provide the **facade** (1568–72), and the **interior** was altered by a scholarly monk named **Fra' Francesco Zorzi**, who improved the proportions and enhanced the acoustics and decor.

The interior
Some of Venice's wealthiest clans contributed to the cost of building San Francesco by paying for family chapels: the third on the right belonged to the **Contarini**, and contains memorials to a pair of seventeenth-century Contarini doges; the next is the **Badoer** chapel (with a *Resurrection* attributed to Veronese); and after that comes the chapel of the **Barbaro** family. The Barbaro ancestral device – a red circle on a white field – was granted in the twelfth century after a particularly revolting act by the Admiral Marco Barbaro: in the thick of battle he cut off a Moor's hand and used the bleeding stump to draw a circle on the man's turban, which he then flew as a pennant. Around the corner in the right transept is a large *Madonna and Child Enthroned* by **Antonio da Negroponte** (c.1450), a picture full of meticulously detailed and glowingly colourful birds and plants.

The church's foundation stone was laid by **Doge Andrea Gritti**, whose tomb is on the left wall of the chancel. An intellectually versatile man – he spoke six languages other than Italian and was a close friend of Sansovino – Gritti was also a formidable womanizer, of whom one rival remarked "We cannot make a doge of a man with three bastards in Turkey." After his election he carried on siring children with a variety of women, including a nun named Celestina, but it was his equally Rabelaisian appetite for food that proved his undoing: he died on Christmas Eve after eating too many grilled eels. It's still a traditional Christmas dish in Venice.

Left of the chancel is the **Giustiniani** chapel, lined with marvellous sculpture by the **Lombardo** family and their assistants. Commissioned for the previous church by one of the Badoer family and installed here after the rebuilding, they include a group of *Prophets* by Pietro Lombardo and assistants, and reliefs of the *Evangelists* attributed to Tullio and Antonio Lombardo. A door at the end of the transept leads to a pair of tranquil fifteenth-century cloisters, via the **Cappella Santa**, which has a *Madonna and Child* by Giovanni Bellini and assistants.

Back in the church, the first chapel after the cloister door (another Giustiniani chapel) contains a gorgeous *Sacra Conversazione* painted by **Veronese** in 1562. The predominantly monochromatic decoration of the **Cappella Sagredo**, the next chapel but one, was created in the eighteenth century, and features frescoes of the *Evangelists* and two *Virtues* by Giambattista Tiepolo. On the altarpiece of the adjacent chapel you'll find figures of *St Anthony Abbot, St Sebastian* and *St Roch* by **Alessandro Vittoria**, who also made bronze figures of *St Francis* and *St John the Baptist* on the nearby water stoups. Finally, on the entrance wall, to the left as you leave, there's a fine triptych attributed to Antonio Vivarini.

The Scuola di San Giorgio degli Schiavoni

Calle dei Furlani 3259a • Mon 2.45–6pm, Tues–Sat 9.15am–1pm & 2.45–6pm, Sun 9.15am–1pm • €5

Venice has two brilliant cycles of pictures by **Vittore Carpaccio** – one is in the Accademia, the other is in the **Scuola di San Giorgio degli Schiavoni**, which sits beside a canal to the south of San Francesco.

Venice's relations with the Slavs (*schiavoni*) were not always untroubled – the city's slave markets were originally stocked with captured Slavs, and in later centuries the settlements of the Dalmatian coast were a harassment to Venetian shipping. By the mid-fifteenth century, though, Venice's Slavic inhabitants – many of them sailors and merchants – were sufficiently established for a *scuola* to be set up in order to protect their interests. After several years of meeting in the church of San Giovanni di Malta, the *scuola* built itself a new headquarters on the church's doorstep at the start of the sixteenth century, and summoned Carpaccio to brighten up the first-storey hall. Painted from 1502 to 1508, after the Accademia's *St Ursula* cycle, Carpaccio's pictures were moved downstairs when the building was rearranged in 1551, and the interior has scarcely changed since.

The interior

The cycle illustrates mainly the lives of the Dalmatian patron saints – George, Tryphone and Jerome. As always with Carpaccio, what holds your attention is not so much the main event as the incidental details, and the incidentals in this cycle feature some of the most arresting images in Venetian painting, from the limb-strewn feeding-ground of St George's dragon in the first scene, to the endearing little white dog in the final one. The scenes depicted are: *St George and the Dragon*; *The Triumph of St George*; *St George Baptizing the Gentiles* (George had rescued the princess Selene, daughter of the royal couple being baptized); *The Miracle of St Tryphone* (the dainty little basilisk is a demon exorcized from the daughter of the Roman Emperor Gordianus); *The Agony in the Garden*; *The Calling of Matthew*; *St Jerome Leading the Lion to the Monastery*; *The Funeral of St Jerome*; and *The Vision of St Augustine* (a vision told him of Jerome's death just as he was writing to him).

The *Madonna and Child* altarpiece is by **Benedetto Carpaccio**, Vittore's son, while the panelled upstairs hall is decorated with mundane early seventeenth-century paintings in honour of various brethren of the *scuola*, which is still functioning today.

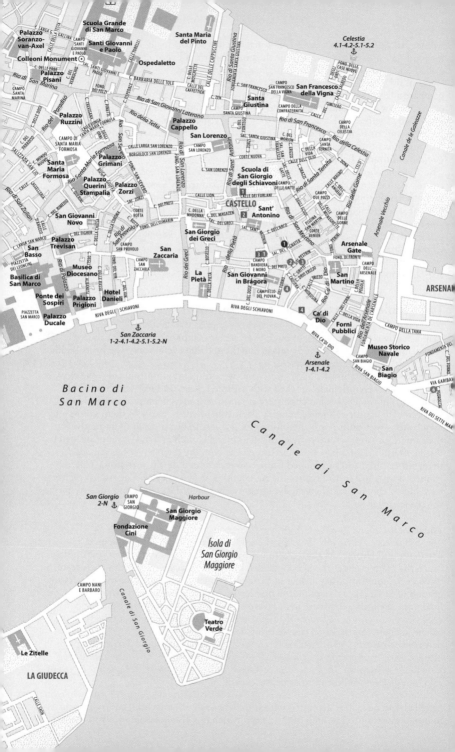

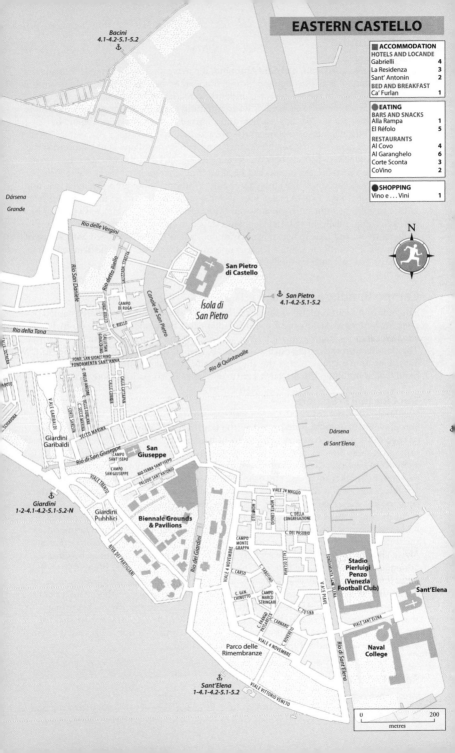

EASTERN CASTELLO

■ **ACCOMMODATION**
HOTELS AND LOCANDE
Gabrielli 4
La Residenza 3
Sant' Antonin 2
BED AND BREAKFAST
Ca' Furlan 1

● **EATING**
BARS AND SNACKS
Alla Rampa 1
El Réfolo 5
RESTAURANTS
Al Covo 4
Al Garanghelo 6
Corte Sconta 3
CoVino 2

● **SHOPPING**
Vino e ... Vini 1

N

Bacini
4.1-4.2-5.1-5.2 ⚓

Dársena
Grande

Rio delle Vergini

Rio delle Riello

Rio San Daniele

CAMPO
DI RUGA

C. RIELLO

CALLE DRIO LA CHIESA

FOND. ZITELLE

CALLE GORNA

Rio della Tana

FOND. SAN GIOACCHINO
FONDAMENTA SANT'ANNA

RAMO STRETA

CALLE LARGA
CALLE CATTAPAN

DELLE ANCORE

C. SECCO MARINA

CORTE SARESIN

SECCO MARINA

V. ALE GARIBALDI

Giardini
Garibaldi

Rio di San Giuseppe

CAMPO
SANT'ISEPO

CAMPO
SAN GIUSEPPE

San Giuseppe

RIO-TERRA SANT'ISEPO

VIALE TRENTO

PALUDO SANT'ANTONIO

Giardini
1-2-4.1-4.2-5.1-5.2-N ⚓

Giardini
Pubblici

**Biennale Grounds
& Pavilions**

RIVA DEI PARTIGIANI

Rio dei Giardini

**San Pietro
di Castello**

San Pietro
4.1-4.2-5.1-5.2 ⚓

Ísola di
San Pietro

Canale de San Pietro

Rio di Quintavalle

Dársena
di Sant'Elena

VIALE 24° MAGGIO

C. MONTELLO

MONTE LONGO

C. DELLA
CONGREGAZIONE

C. DEL PASUBIO

CAMPO
MONTE
GRAPPA

VIALE 4 NOVEMBRE

C. CARSO

C. SABOTINO

CALLE OSLAVIA

CAMPO
MARCO
STRINGARI

C. GEN.
CHINOTTO

C. ZUGNA

V. ALE PIAVE

FONDAMENTA SANT'ELENA

**Stadio
Pierluigi
Penzo
(Venezia
Football Club)**

Sant'Elena

VIALE SANT'ELENA

C. FRANCO
PESCHIERA

C. CARNARO

C. RISORTO

VIALE 4 NOVEMBRE

Parco delle
Rimembranze

Sant'Elena
1-4.1-4.2-5.1-5.2 ⚓

VIALE VITTORIO VENETO

Rio di Sant'Elena

**Naval
College**

0   200
metres

Sant'Antonino

Campo Sant'Antonino

The frequently closed church of **Sant'Antonino**, the next stop south along the fondamenta from San Giorgio, is an unenticing building, founded perhaps as far back as the seventh century but rebuilt in the seventeenth, under the direction of Longhena, whose design for the facade was never completed. It houses nothing of great interest except a *Deposition* by Lazzaro Bastiani (Carpaccio's teacher) and a bust of Procurator Alvise Tiepolo by Alessandro Vittoria, but some good stories are attached to it. The body of a certain St Saba was enshrined here from the twelfth century until 1965, when Pope Paul VI returned the relic to the monastery halfway between Jerusalem and the Dead Sea whence it had been stolen by the Venetians; the monks had been meeting disconsolately every night at their saint's empty sarcophagus. The emblems of Saint Anthony Abbot are a pig and a bell, and this church once kept a sty of belled pigs, which were allowed to roam the parish unfettered until, in 1409, their unruliness so annoyed the locals that their freedom was curtailed by a state edict. And finally, in 1819 an elephant escaped from a visiting menagerie on the Riva degli Schiavoni and took refuge in Sant'Antonino, where it was dispatched with a blast of cannon-fire. Pietro Bonmartini, a Paduan nobleman, commemorated the demise of the poor beast in a pamphlet entitled *The Elephanticide in Venice*.

Campo Bandiera e Moro

Salizzada Sant'Antonin curves down to the quiet **Campo Bandiera e Moro**, named after the Venetians Attilio and Emilio Bandiera and Domenico Moro, who in 1844 were executed for leading an abortive revolt against the Bourbon regime in Calabria. The Bandiera brothers were born at no. 3610, and all three are buried together in Santi Giovanni e Paolo. Across the alley from the Bandiera house stands the campo's handsomest building, the fifteenth-century Palazzo Gritti Badoer, now a hotel.

San Giovanni in Brágora

Campo Bandiera e Moro • Mon–Sat 9–11am & 3.30–5pm, Sun 9.30am–noon • Free

San Giovanni in Brágora is dedicated to the Baptist, and some people think that its strange suffix is a reference to a region from which some relics of the saint were once brought; others link the name to the Greek word for a main public square, *agora*, or to a choice of Venetian dialect words – *brago* plus *gora* (meaning "mud" and "backwater"), or *bragola* ("market square"). The origins of the church itself are equally disputed – folklore insists that this is one of the city's oldest, dating back to the early eighth century, but there's no proof of its existence prior to 1090.

The present structure was begun in 1475, and its best paintings were created within a quarter-century of the rebuilding: a triptych by **Bartolomeo Vivarini**, on the wall between the first and second chapels on the right (1478); a *Resurrection* by **Alvise Vivarini**, to the left of the sacristy door (1498); and two paintings by **Cima da Conegliano** – *Sts Helen and Constantine*, to the right of the sacristy door (1501), and a *Baptism* on the high altar (1494). The remains of St John the Almsgiver, stolen from Alexandria in 1247, lie in the second chapel on the right, though the Venetian church dedicated to him – San Giovanni Elemosinario – is over in the Rialto. Set into an alcove at the west end of the left aisle is the font in which Vivaldi was baptized for the second time, having been given an emergency baptism at home because it seemed unlikely that he would survive more than a few hours.

San Martino

Campo San Martino • Mon–Sat 11am–noon & 5–6.30pm, Sun 10.30am–12.30pm • Free

A group of Paduan refugees are said to have founded a church on the site of the **San Martino** in 593, which would give it one of Venice's longest pedigrees; Sansovino designed the present Greek-cross building in around 1540. The central panel of the ceiling, Jacopo Guarana's *St Martin in Glory*, is framed by perspectival paintings by **Domenico Bruni**. To see it properly you have to lie on your back in the very middle of the church, more or less where most of **Doge Francesco Erizzo** (d.1646) is buried; his heart is in the Basilica di San Marco.

The Ca' di Dio and Forni Pubblici

Follow the fondamenta south from San Martino and then turn right into Calle de la Pegola and you'll emerge on the main waterfront, with the **Ca' di Dio** to your right. Founded in the thirteenth century as a hospice for pilgrims and crusaders, the Ca' di Dio was extended in 1545 by Sansovino; his new wing, with its profusion of chimneys, is visible from the bridge. It's been a retirement home for many years, but now seems fated to become yet another hotel. The building on the other side of Calle de la Pegola, decorated with a second-storey frieze of little stone peaks, is the **Forni Pubblici** (1473), the bakery which supplied the vessels leaving the Arsenale with ship's biscuit, the last stage in the preparations for sailing.

6

The Arsenale

A corruption of the Arabic *darsin'a* (house of industry), the very name of the **Arsenale** is indicative of the strength of Venice's links with the eastern Mediterranean, and the workers of these dockyards and factories were the foundations upon which the city's maritime supremacy rested. Visiting dignitaries were often as astonished by the industriousness of the Arsenale as by the opulence of the Canal Grande. At the beginning of the fourteenth century Dante came to Venice twice (once as ambassador from Ravenna), and was so impressed by what he saw on his first mission that he evoked the sight in a famous passage of the *Inferno*, in which those guilty of selling public offices are tortured in a lake of boiling pitch like the caulkers' vats in the Arsenale.

Brief history of the Arsenale

The development of the Arsenale seems to have commenced in the early years of the twelfth century, when **ship maintenance** became the main industry in this part of the city. Massive expansion was under way by the third decade of the fourteenth century, as the Arsenale established a state monopoly in the construction of **galleys and large merchant vessels**, and by the 1420s it had become the base for some three hundred shipping companies, operating around three thousand vessels of 200 tonnes or more.

At the Arsenale's zenith, around the middle of the sixteenth century, its wet and dry docks, its rope and sail factories, its ordnance depots and gunpowder mills employed a total of 16,000 men – equal to the population of a sizeable town of the time. By then, though, the maritime strength of Venice was past its peak: Vasco da Gama had rounded the Cape of Good Hope in 1497, thus opening a direct sea route to the East; the New World routes were growing; and there was the perpetual threat of the ever stronger Turkish empire. The shrinkage of the Venetian mercantile fleet was drastic – between 1560 and 1600 the volume of shipping registered at the Arsenale was halved. Militarily as well, despite the conspicuous success at Lépanto (1571), Venice was on the wane, and the reconquest of the Morea (Peloponnese) at the end of the seventeenth century was little more than a glorious interlude in a long story of decline. When **Napoleon** took over the city in 1797 he burned down the docks, sank the last *Bucintoro* (the state barge) and confiscated the remnant of the Venetian navy. It was destroyed by Nelson at the Battle of Aboukir.

Under Austrian occupation the Arsenale was reconstructed, and it stayed in continuous operation until the end of 1917 when, having produced a number of ships

6

THE ARSENALE – THE WORLD'S FIRST INDUSTRIAL ZONE

In *The City in History*, Lewis Mumford credits the Venetians with the invention of "a new type of city, based on the differentiation and zoning of urban functions, separated by traffic ways and open spaces", and cites the island of Murano and the Arsenale as Europe's first examples of industrial planning. Of these two, the **Arsenale** most closely resembled a modern factory complex. Construction techniques in the Arsenale were the most sophisticated of their time, and by the fifteenth century the Venetians had perfected a production-line process for equipping their ships, in which the vessels were towed past a succession of windows, to collect ropes, sails, armaments, oars and all their other supplies (ending with barrels of hard biscuits), so that by the time they reached the lagoon the vessels were fully prepared. The productivity of the wharves was legendary: at the height of the conflict with the Turks in the sixteenth century, one warship a day was being added to the Venetian fleet. On the occasion of the visit of Henry III of France in 1574, the Arsenale workers put on a bravura performance – in the time it took the king and his hosts to work their way through a state banquet in the Palazzo Ducale, the *Arsenalotti* assembled a vessel sturdy enough to bear a crew plus a cannon weighing 16,000 pounds.

To an extent, the governors of the city acknowledged their debt to the workers of the Arsenale. They were a privileged group within the Venetian proletariat, acting as watchmen at the Palazzo Ducale whenever the Maggior Consiglio was in session, carrying the doge in triumph round the Piazza after his inauguration and serving as pallbearers at ducal funerals. By the standards of other manual workers they were well paid too, although the 50 ducats that was the typical wage of a master shipwright in the early sixteenth century should be set against the 40,000 ducats spent by Alvise Pisani, one of the most powerful politicians of the period, on the weddings of his five daughters. The *Arsenalotti* were also less docile than most of their fellow artisans, and were responsible for a number of strikes and disturbances. A dramatic protest took place in 1569, when a gang of three hundred *Arsenalotti* armed with axes smashed their way into the hall of the Collegio to present their grievances to the doge in person.

for the Italian navy in World War I, the dockyards were dismantled to prevent them being of use to the enemy forces that seemed likely to invade the lagoon. Since then it has been used by the navy and a marine technology centre, and it's employed as a venue for the **Biennale**.

The Arsenale buildings

There is no public access to the Arsenale except during the Biennale. You can get a look at part of it, however, from the bridge connecting the Campo Arsenale and the Fondamenta dell'Arsenale.

The gate

The main **gateway** to the Arsenale was the first structure in Venice to employ the classical vocabulary of Renaissance architecture – it was built by **Antonio Gambello** in 1460, incorporating, at ground level, Veneto-Byzantine capitals from the twelfth century. You'll notice that the book being held by the Lion of Saint Mark, unlike all the others in the city, is blank, perhaps because the traditional inscription, "Pax tibi…", was thought to be too pacific for this context; the statue above his head, *Santa Justina* by **Campagna**, was put there in 1578.

The **four lions** outside the gateway feature in coffee-table books on Venice almost as frequently as the San Marco horses, and, like the horses, they are stolen goods. Exactly when the two furthest on the right were grabbed isn't known, but they probably came from the Lion Terrace at Delos, and date from around the sixth century BC; the left-hand one of the pair (with the prosthetic head) was positioned here to mark the recapture of Corfu in 1716 – the other was in place slightly earlier.

The larger pair aren't as enigmatic: they were swiped from Piraeus in 1687 by Francesco Morosini, after the reconquest of the Morea. The blurred inscription on the shoulder and side of the lion on the left of the gate (which started life as a Greek fountain) is a piece of runic graffiti, the handiwork of an eleventh-century Norse mercenary serving with the army hired by the Byzantine emperor to suppress a rebellion of his Greek subjects.

The Tana
Within the Arsenale, the two major structures are **Sanmicheli**'s covered dock for the *Bucintoro* (1544–47) and **da Ponte**'s gigantic rope factory, the Corderia or **Tana** (1579). The greater part of the Tana runs along the Rio della Tana; a single 316m-long room (not far off twice the length of the Piazza), it provides an extraordinary exhibition space for the Biennale.

The Museo Storico Navale

Campo San Biagio 2148 • Daily 10am–6pm (Padiglioni delle Navi opens 10.30am) • €10 • At time of writing, the museum was only partially open; it's probable that you'll find major sections closed, and ticket prices accordingly reduced. See ⓦ www.marina.difesa.it for more information

Occupying a vast old granary at the mouth of the Arsenale canal, the **Museo Storico Navale** is a somewhat rambling museum, but it's an essential supplement to a walk round the Arsenale district, and – improbable though it sounds – the beautiful models of Venetian and other craft will justify the entrance fee for most people. It was common practice in the Venetian shipyards to build their boats not from scale drawings but from models, and some of the pieces in the collection are the functional models retrieved from the dockyards after Napoleon's arsonists had done their work.

At ground level there's a room dedicated to Angelo Emo, the last admiral of the Republic, the focal point being Canova's monument to him. A miscellany of armaments occupy much of the rest of the space, with the most remarkable exhibits being a couple of manned torpedoes; a caption by the ticket office, where one of them is displayed, explains how the captain of HMS *Valiant*, which was crippled by one of these weapons, came to recommend a military honour for the Italian lieutenant who had carried out the attack. Among the models on the first floor you'll find an amazing 224-oar fighting galley and the last *Bucintoro*, the state barge; the second floor, where the focus is on more recent naval history, has a display of uniforms, maritime instruments and some cut-away battleships; on the top storey the room devoted to the evolution of the gondola includes Peggy Guggenheim's gondola, while other rooms hold models of Chinese and Korean junks, and a big collection of artless *ex voto* paintings. On a mezzanine floor there's an exhibition on the historic links between Venice and the Swedish navy, with an interesting section on how the Arsenale contributed to the building of Sweden's finest opera house. An incongruous collection of seashells occupies the last room.

A couple of hundred metres along the fondamenta, at the foot of the wooden Arsenale bridge, is a second section of the naval museum, the **Padiglioni delle Navi**, a large collection of craft with Venetian connections.

San Biagio

Campo San Biagio

The church of **San Biagio**, alongside the main museum block, was the Greek community's church before San Giorgio dei Greci, and took on its present municipal-office appearance after an eighteenth-century refit. It's now the naval chapel and is very rarely open, though you can sometimes look through the inner wrought-iron door at the interior, where **Giovanni Ferrari**'s reclining statue of *Admiral Angelo Emo* (1792) is the main point of interest. Tucked behind the church is the bunker known as Palasport (or Palazzetto dello Sport), the city's main indoor sports hall.

Beyond the Arsenale: to Sant'Elena

The Riva San Biagio is the only land route into the districts to the east of the Arsenale, but once over the wide bridge that traverses the Rio della Tana you have to make a choice. By following the waterfront you'll pass the main public gardens of Venice before finally reaching the football stadium and the isolated church of **Sant'Elena**. Opt for the less picturesque Via Garibaldi, and you're on your way to the church of San Pietro di Castello, formerly Venice's cathedral, nowadays a somewhat bereft monument in the midst of boatyards.

6

Via Garibaldi

In 1807 the greater part of the canal connecting the Bacino di San Marco to the broad northeastern inlet of the Canale di San Pietro was covered to form what is now **Via Garibaldi**, the widest street in the city and the busiest part of the eastern district. There's just a couple of spots of cultural or historical significance here. The first house on the right was for a time the home of the navigators **John and Sebastian Cabot**, explorers of Newfoundland (together) and Paraguay (just Sebastian) in the late fifteenth and early sixteenth centuries. The church of **San Francesco di Paola**, opposite the entrance to the tree-lined alley that glories in the name Giardini Garibaldi, has a painting by Giandomenico Tiepolo among the sequence on the cornice (second on the right), illustrating scenes from the life of the eponymous saint.

The island of San Pietro

Originally named **Castello**, after a castle that used to stand here (built by either the Romans or the first "Venetian" settlers), the island of **San Pietro** was one of the very first parts of central Venice to be occupied. By 775 the settlement here had grown sufficiently to be granted the foundation of a bishopric under the authority of the Patriarch of Grado. Within the next half-century Castello joined the immediately surrounding islands to form Rivoalto, the embryonic city of Venice.

THE FESTA DELLE MARIE

One of the major Venetian festivals – the **Festa delle Marie** (Festival of the Marys) – had its origin in an incident that occurred at San Pietro in 943. A multiple marriage in the church was interrupted by a posse of Slav pirates, who carried away the brides and their substantial dowries. Men from the parish of Santa Maria Formosa led the pursuit, and succeeded in retrieving the young women. To celebrate their safe return, every year two girls were chosen from each *sestiere* to be married in a single ceremony at San Pietro, in the presence of the doge. Each bride was renamed Maria for the occasion, and their weddings were followed by an eight-day junket that culminated at Santa Maria Formosa on the Day of the Purification of Mary – the day on which the brides had been kidnapped. However, by the thirteenth century the Festa delle Marie had become something more akin to an open-air beauty pageant than a festival of thanksgiving, so the authorities – determined to reintroduce some religious gravitas – decided that the girls should no longer be paraded through the city: wooden effigies were to be used instead. This reform proved so unpopular that in 1349 a law was passed to prohibit the pelting of the wooden Marys. In 1379 the festival was discontinued, but a fancy-dress re-enactment of the Marys' procession is nowadays a feature of the Carnevale season. At around 2.30pm on the Saturday preceding the official start of Carnevale, the twelve Marys are carried aloft from San Pietro di Castello along Via Garibaldi and the Riva degli Schiavoni to the Piazza, where they are greeted and honoured by a doge impersonator. The event is very much a beauty contest: the twelve young women are obliged to submit to the appraisal of a panel of judges, and the one who is judged to be most attractive is crowned queen of the Carnevale on Shrove Tuesday. And as if that weren't honour enough, the queen – otherwise known as La Maria – plays the part of the angel in the following year's "Flight of the Angel", the opening ceremony of the Carnevale season.

THE VENICE BIENNALE

The **Venice Biennale**, Europe's most glamorous international forum for contemporary art, was first held in 1895 as the city's contribution to the celebrations for the silver wedding anniversary of King Umberto I and Margherita of Savoy. In the early years the exhibits were dominated by standard salon painting, despite the presence of such artists as Ensor, Klimt and Whistler. Since World War II, however, the Biennale has become a self-consciously avant-garde event, a transformation symbolized by the award of the major Biennale prize in 1964 to Robert Rauschenberg, the *enfant terrible* of the American art scene. The French contingent campaigned vigorously against the nomination of this New World upstart, and virtually every Biennale since then has been characterized by the sort of controversy that is now endemic in the publicity-addicted art circuit.

After decades of occurring in even-numbered years, the Biennale shifted back to being held **every odd-numbered year from mid-May to late November**, so that the centenary show could be held in 1995. The main site is by the Giardini Pubblici, with permanent pavilions for about forty countries plus space for a thematic international exhibition. This core part of the Biennale is supplemented by exhibitions in parts of the Arsenale that are otherwise closed to the public, such as the colossal Corderie or Tana (the former rope-factory) and the Artiglierie (gun foundry). In addition, various palaces and other sites throughout the city (such as the salt warehouses on the Zàttere and the Museo Fortuny) are used as national pavilions and as venues for fringe exhibitions, installations and performances. Some of the Biennale pavilions and various other buildings (usually the Corderie) are used in even-numbered years for an independent Biennale for **architecture**, a smaller-scale event which runs from the second week of September to mid-November; this overlaps with a brief music Biennale, and is preceded by a two-week dance Biennale. Information on all of Venice's Biennales is available at ⓦ labiennale.org.

Castello remained the ecclesiastical centre of Venice, but political power was always concentrated in the San Marco district, and the relationship between the Church and the geographically remote rulers of the city was never to be close. In 1451 the first **Patriarch of Venice** was invested at Castello, and succeeding generations of councillors and senators showed no inclination to draw the head of the Venetian Church into the centre of power. San Pietro di Castello remained the cathedral of Venice, emblematically marooned on the periphery of the city, until 1807, when the patriarch was at last permitted to install himself in San Marco – ten years after the Republic had ceased to exist.

San Pietro di Castello

Campo San Pietro • Mon–Sat 10.30am–4.30pm • €3, or Chorus Pass • ⓦ chorusvenezia.org

As with the Arsenale, the history of San Pietro is somewhat more interesting than what you can see. A church was raised here as early as the seventh century, but the present San Pietro di Castello was raised nearly a millennium later, with a facade designed in the mid-sixteenth century by **Palladio**. It wasn't until the end of the century that the facade was built, and the executed project was a feeble version of his original scheme. Similarly, the interior is merely derived from a plan by Palladio, and is the sort of sterile academic exercise that gives classicism a bad name. Nor will the paintings put a skip in your stride: best of the bunch are the altarpiece by Luca Giordano in the Cappella Vendramin (left transept) and *Sts John the Evangelist, Peter and Paul*, a late work by Veronese, above the entrance to the neighbouring Cappello Lando, where you'll find a fifth-century mosaic fragment set into the pavement, and a bust of St Lorenzo Giustiniani, the first Patriarch of Venice. Giustiniani, who died in 1456, lies in the glass case within the elaborate high altar, which, like the Vendramin chapel, was designed by Longhena. The other unusual feature of the church is the so-called **Throne of St Peter** (right aisle), a marble seat made in the thirteenth century from an Arabic funeral-stone incised with texts from the Koran.

The **campanile**, one of the most precarious in the city, was rebuilt by Mauro Codussi in the 1480s, and was the first tower in Venice to be clad in Istrian stone. It's the only stone-clad tower left standing.

The public gardens and the Biennale site

When Napoleon seized Venice he set about confiscating and demolishing churches and convents all over the city. Around eighty churches were razed or deconsecrated by the French, and no fewer than four convents were destroyed to create the **Giardini Pubblici**, which today forms an arc of green space on the eastern edge of the city, with the **Giardini Garibaldi** and **Parco delle Rimembranze**.

Largely obscured by the trees are the rather more extensive grounds belonging to the **Biennale**, a dormant zone outside the exhibition months. Various countries have built permanent pavilions for their Biennale representatives, forming an assortment of work by some of the great names of modern architecture: the Austrian pavilion was built by the Secession architect Josef Hoffmann in the 1930s; the Finnish pavilion was created by Alvar Aalto in the 1950s; the Netherlands pavilion was designed by Gerrit Thomas Rietveld, also in the 1950s; and the Venezuelan pavilion, completed in 1954, is by Carlo Scarpa. By far the biggest building, and the pivot of the whole site, is the one that used to be the Italian pavilion – now renamed the **Palazzo delle Esposizioni**, it's used for international shows. The oldest surviving structure of the Biennale is the Serra dei Giardini, which stands alongside the Giardini Garibaldi; it has become a sort of gardening-centre-café.

San Giuseppe di Castello

Campo San Giuseppe • Mon–Sat 10.30am–4.30pm • €3, or Chorus Pass • ⓦ chorusvenezia.org

If you want to squeeze every last drop from the eastern districts, you could call in at the church of **San Giuseppe di Castello** (or San Isepo), to the north of the Giardini Pubblici – a gateway from the gardens opens onto a street just metres from the church. It houses a vast **monument to Doge Marino Grimani**, designed in 1595 by Vincenzo Scamozzi, with reliefs and figures by Campagna (left side). The main altarpiece, *The Adoration of the Shepherds*, is a late work by **Paolo Veronese**, and was commissioned by Marino Grimani, who appears as his namesake, St Jerome, on the left. Although this church is part of the Chorus scheme, it's often not open at the advertised hours.

Sant'Elena

Campo della Chiesa • Mon–Sat 5–7pm • Free

The island of **Sant'Elena**, the city's eastern limit, was greatly enlarged during the Austrian administration, partly to furnish accommodation and exercise grounds for the occupying troops. Much of the island used to be covered by a meadow, but the strip of park along the waterfront is all that's left of it, houses having been built on the rest. The **church of Sant'Elena** was erected here in the thirteenth century, following the supposed acquisition of the body of St Helena, Constantine's mother. It was rebuilt in 1435 but from 1807 to 1928 it was abandoned, except for a spell as an iron foundry. The spartan Gothic interior has recently been restored, as have the cloister and campanile – the latter so zealously that it now looks like a chimney, which is exactly what it was when the church did service as a factory. The main attraction is the **doorway** to the church, an ensemble created in the 1470s (probably by **Antonio Rizzo**) and incorporating the **monument to Vittore Cappello**, showing him kneeling before St Helena. Cappello was captain-general of the Republic's navy in the 1460s, a period in which the Turks were beginning to loosen Venice's grip on the Aegean; so dejected was he by the signs of decline in the Venetian empire that he was reputed to have gone for five months without once smiling, before dying of a broken heart. Inside the church, a chapel on the right enshrines the alleged remains of Helena, whose body is more generally believed to lie in a tomb in Rome's church of Santa Maria in Aracoeli.

CANAL GRANDE

The Canal Grande

Known to the locals as the Canalazzo, the Canal Grande is Venice's high street, and divides the city in half, with three *sestieri* to the west and three to the east. In addition to the four bridges which traverse the waterway – at Piazzale Roma, the train station, Rialto and Accademia – a number of gondola traghetti provide crossing points at regular intervals, as does the #1 vaporetto, which slaloms from one bank to the other along its entire length. The Canal Grande is almost 4km long and varies in width between 30 and 70m; it is, however, surprisingly shallow, at no point much exceeding 5m. In the fourteenth century an earthquake pulled the plug out and all the water drained away, turning Venice's main thoroughfare into an avenue of slime.

The section that follows is principally a guide to the Canal Grande palaces – the churches and other public buildings that you can see from the vaporetto are covered in the appropriate geographical sections. You'd need an amazing reading speed and a rubber neck to do justice to the Canal Grande in one run, though; even these edited highlights cover around fifty buildings (less than a third of the total). Try to allow for several trips, and don't miss the experience of a nocturnal boat ride.

The Right Bank

Right at the top of the Canal Grande lies the traffic terminus of Piazzale Roma. Orientation is initially difficult here, and it's not until the vaporetto swings round by the train station that it becomes obvious that this is the city's main waterway.

Ponte della Costituzione

The newest feature of central Venice's cityscape links Piazzale Roma to the opposite bank: officially named the **Ponte della Costituzione**, the bridge is known to all Venetians as the **Ponte di Calatrava**, after its designer, the Spanish architect Santiago Calatrava. Modelled on the shape of a gondola's hull, the single span is an elegant 95-metre arc of steel, stone and glass, but the bridge has attracted a lot of criticism.

Ponte degli Scalzi

A short distance downstream, you pass under the **Ponte degli Scalzi**, successor of an iron structure put up by the Austrians in 1858–60; like the one at the Accademia, it was replaced in the early 1930s to give the new steamboats sufficient clearance.

Fondaco dei Turchi

Having passed the green-domed **San Simeone Piccolo**, the end of the elongated campo of **San Simeone Profeta** and a procession of nondescript buildings, you come to the **Fondaco dei Turchi**. A private house from the early thirteenth century until 1621, the building was then turned over to the Turkish traders in the city, who stayed here until 1838. By the 1850s it was in such a state that a campaign for its restoration was started, with Ruskin at the helm; the city undertook the repair, but the result has had few admirers. There's hardly an original brick left in the building, but whatever the shortcomings of the work, the building's towers and long water-level arcade give a reasonably precise picture of what a Veneto-Byzantine palace would have looked like. One of the sarcophagi underneath the portico belongs to the family of the disgraced Marin Falier (see page 132). The Fondaco now contains the natural history museum (see page 106).

CALATRAVA'S TROUBLED BRIDGE

It may look nice from a distance, but Calatrava's **Ponte della Costituzione** is widely regarded in Venice as a disaster. Many locals were never convinced that the Canal Grande needed a new bridge so close to the Scalzi, and the criticism became more vociferous after its long-delayed opening in 2008, when it became known that it had cost at least three times its original budget of four million euros. Then things got worse. For starters, the new bridge was inaccessible to disabled people – so, at great expense, an egg-shaped lift for wheelchair users was stuck on to one side. This alteration took five years, by which time a large number of pedestrians had taken a tumble on the bridge's irregularly spaced steps. There were ten reported injuries in the first twenty days alone.

Palazzo Belloni-Battagia

The crenellated structure next along from the Fondaco is the fifteenth-century **Depositi del Megio** (public granary); its neighbour is a palace by Longhena – the **Palazzo Belloni-Battagia** (1647–63). Longhena's client experienced severe cash-flow problems not long after the house was finished, a consequence of simultaneously building the house and buying his way into the pages of the *Libro d'Oro* (the register of the nobility), and so was obliged to rent the place out rather than live in it himself.

Ca' Pésaro

A short distance down the canal, after the church of **San Stae**, stands a far more impressive Longhena building – the thickly ornamented **Ca' Pésaro**, bristling with diamond-shaped spikes and grotesque heads. Three houses had to be demolished to make room for this palace and its construction lasted half a century – work started in 1652 and finished in 1703, long after Longhena's death. Unusually, the Ca' Pésaro has a stone-clad side; most houses in Venice have plain brick sides, either for reasons of cost, or to make it easier to attach another building to the flank. The Ca' Pésaro is now home to the modern art and oriental museums (see page 104).

Palazzo Corner della Regina

The next large building is the **Palazzo Corner della Regina**, which was built in 1724 on the site of the home of Caterina Cornaro, Queen of Cyprus, from whom the palace takes its name (see page 304); it was formerly the *Monte di Pietà* (municipal pawnshop) and is now owned by the Prada fashion house.

The Rialto buildings

Beyond the Palazzo Corner, there's nothing especially engrossing until you reach the **Rialto markets**, which begin with the neo-Gothic fish market, the **Pescheria**, built in 1907; there's been a fish market here since the fourteenth century. The older buildings that follow it, the **Fabbriche Nuove di Rialto** and (set back from the water) the **Fabbriche Vecchie di Rialto**, are by Sansovino (1552–55) and Scarpagnino (1515–22) respectively.

The large building at the base of the Rialto bridge is the **Palazzo dei Camerlenghi** (c.1525), the former chambers of the Venetian exchequer. Debtors could find themselves in the cells of the building's bottom storey – hence the name Fondamenta delle Prigioni for this part of the canalside. At the foot of the Rialto bridge, on the other side, were the offices of the state finance ministers, in Scarpagnino's **Palazzo dei Dieci Savi**.

Ponte di Rialto

The famous **Ponte di Rialto** superseded a succession of wooden and fragile structures; one of them was destroyed by the army of Bajamonte Tiepolo as it retreated from the Piazza in 1310, and its replacement collapsed in 1444 under the weight of the crowd gathered to watch the wedding procession of the Marquis of Ferrara – one of Carpaccio's *Miracles of the True Cross* (in the Accademia) shows what the next drawbridge looked like. The decision to construct a more reliable bridge was taken in 1524, and over the following sixty years proposals by Michelangelo, Vignola, Sansovino and Palladio were considered and rejected. Eventually the job was awarded to the aptly named **Antonio da Ponte**, whose top-heavy design was described by Edward Gibbon as "a fine bridge, spoilt by two rows of houses upon it". Until 1854, when the first Accademia bridge was built, this was the only point at which the Canal Grande could be crossed on foot.

7

THE CANAL GRANDE

Palazzo Labia

San Marcuola

Palazzo Vendramin Calergi

San Geremia

Riva di Biasio 1

San Marcuola 1-2-N

Palazzo Bello Battagia

Scalzi

Ferrovia 4.2-5.2-3

San Simeone Profeta

Fondaco dei Turchi

Depositi del Megio

Santa Lucia Station

SANTA CROCE

San Giacomo dell'Orio

Ferrovia 1-2-4.1- 5.1-N

San Simeone Piccolo

Piazzale Roma 1-2-3-4.1-4.2- 5.1-5.2-N

Ponte di Calatrava

Santa Maria Gloriosa dei Frari

San Pe

Palazz Cappel Layar

Palazzo Pisani-Moretta

San Tomà

Sant'Ang

Palazzo Balbi

San Tomà 1-2-N

Palazzi Mocenigo

Ca'Fóscari

Palazzo Contarini delle Figure

Palazzi Giustinian

Palazzo Grassi

San Samuele

Ca'Rezzonico

San Samuele 2-N

Ca'Rezzonico 1

Palazzo Malipiero

Ca' del Duca

Sa Vic

Palazzo Loredan dell'Ambasciatore

Palazzo Falier

Palazzo Giustinian-Lolin

Palazzo Franchett

Palazzo Contarini degli Scrigni

Accademia 1-2-N

Ponte dell' Accademia

Palaz Barba

Gallerie dell' Accademia

Palazzo Contarini dal Zaffo

DORSODURO

0   100
metres

Palazzo
Gussoni-Grimani
della Vida

San Stae
1–N

CANNAREGIO

Ca'
Pésaro

Palazzo
Corner della
Regina

Ca'd'Oro
Palazzo
Sagredo

Ca' d'Oro
1–N

Pescheria

Palazzo
Mangilli

Ca'da
Mosto

Fabbriche
Nuove di Rialto

Rialto
Mercato
1

Fabbriche
Vecchie di Rialto

Palazzo dei
Camerlenghi

Fondaco
dei Tedeschi

SAN POLO

Ponte
di Rialto

CASTELLO

San
Silvestro

Rialto
1–3 N

Palazzo
Dolfin-Manin

Palazzo
Donà della
Madonnetta

Palazzo
Papadopoli

San Silvestro
1

Palazzo
Loredan

San
Salvador

Palazzo
Donà

Palazzo
Farsetti

azzo
nardo

C a n a l   G r a n d e

Palazzo
Grimani

Palazzo
Corner
Contarini dei Cavalli

Palazzo
Benzon

azzo
orner
inelli

SAN MARCO

Basilica di
San Marco

Santo
Stefano

La Fenice

S. Zaccaria
1–12–14–20–
4.1–4.2–
5.1–5.2–N

Giardinetti Reali

Santa Maria
del Giglio

Palazzo
Giustinian

Bacino di
San Marco

Palazzo
Corner della
Ca'Grande

Palazzo
Pisani

Palazzo
Contarini-Fasan

San Marco
Giardinetti

San Marco
Vallaresso
1–2–N

N

Giglio
1

Salute
1

Peggy
Guggenheim
Collection

Palazzo
Dario

Palazzo
Salviati

Santa Maria
della Salute

Punta
della Dogana

> **UP ON THE ROOF**
>
> A couple of peculiar features of the Venetian skyline become noticeable on a cruise down the Canal Grande. The bizarre **chimneys** functioned as spark-traps – fire being a constant hazard in a city where the scarcity of land inevitably resulted in a high density of housing. (The history of Venice has been punctuated by terrible blazes – notably at the Rialto, San Marco and, at least four times, the Palazzo Ducale.) The **roof-level platforms** (**altane**) you'll see in places had a variety of uses, such as drying laundry and bleaching hair. For the latter operation, women wore wide-brimmed crownless straw hats, which allowed them to get the sun on their hair while protecting their complexions.

The Papadopoli and Donà palaces

From the Rialto down to the Volta del Canal – as the Canal Grande's sharpest turn is known – the right bank is of more sporadic interest. The **Palazzo Papadopoli** (aka **Palazzo Coccina-Tiepolo**), on the far side of Rio dei Meloni, was built in the 1560s; the Venetian mercantile class rarely wanted adventurous designs for their houses, and the conservative Papadopoli palace, with its emphasis on blank wall spaces broken up with applied decoration, was to prove extremely influential. It's now home to the insanely luxurious *Aman Canal Grande*, the hotel of choice for A-listers such as Mr and Mrs Clooney. The adjacent **Palazzo Donà** and **Palazzo Donà della Madonnetta** (named after the fifteenth-century relief on the facade) date from the twelfth and thirteenth centuries; they have been frequently altered, but some original features survive, notably the main windows.

Palazzo Bernardo and Palazzo Cappello-Layard

The tracery of the mid-fifteenth-century **Palazzo Bernardo** (across the Rio della Madonnetta), among the most beautiful on the Canal Grande, is copied from the loggia of the Palazzo Ducale – you'll find echoes of the pattern all over the city. The sixteenth-century **Palazzo Cappello-Layard**, on the edge of the wide Rio San Polo, was the home of the English ambassador Sir Henry Layard, whose astuteness ensured that the British public profited from the destitution of Venice in the nineteenth century. His collection of nineteen major Venetian paintings, picked up for a song, was left to the National Gallery in London. Another of the National's masterpieces – Veronese's *The Clemency of Alexander* – was bought in 1857 from the **Palazzo Pisani della Moretta** (mid-fifteenth-century), second along on the other side of the rio.

Palazzo Balbi

The cluster of palaces at the Volta constitutes one of the city's architectural glories. The **Palazzo Balbi**, on the near side of the Rio di Ca' Fóscari, is the youngest of the group, a proto-Baroque design executed in the 1580s to plans by Alessandro Vittoria, whose sculpture is to be found in many Venetian churches. Nicolò Balbi is reputed to have been so keen to see his palace finished that he moored a boat alongside the building site so that he could watch the work progressing; he even slept in the boat, and died of a consequent chill. Had Frank Lloyd Wright got his way, the Palazzo Balbi would have acquired a new neighbour in the 1950s, but local opposition, orchestrated from the Balbi palace, scuppered the scheme.

Ca' Fóscari

On the opposite banks of the rio from Palazzo Balbi stands the **Ca' Fóscari** (c.1435), which Ruskin thought "the noblest example in Venice" of late Gothic architecture. The largest private house in Venice at the time of its construction, it was the home of the longest-serving doge, **Doge Francesco Fóscari** (see page 111). When Henry III of France passed through Venice on the way to his coronation in 1574, it was at the Ca' Fóscari that he was lodged. After a gargantuan banquet at the Palazzo Ducale, Henry reeled back here to find his rooms decked out with silks and cloth of gold, and lined with paintings by Bellini, Titian, Veronese and Tintoretto. Venice's university now owns the building.

Palazzi Giustinian

Adjoining Ca' Fóscari are the **Palazzi Giustinian**, a pair of palaces built in the mid-fifteenth century for two brothers who wanted attached but self-contained houses. In the twelfth century the Giustinian family was in danger of dying out, and such was the panic induced in Venice by the thought of losing one of its most illustrious dynasties (it traced its descent from the Emperor Justinian), that papal permission was sought for the young monk who was the one surviving male of the clan to be released from his vows in order to start a family. The pope gave his consent, a bride was found, and twelve Giustinians were propagated; his duty done, the father returned to his monastery, and his wife went off to found a convent on one of the remoter islands of the lagoon. For a while one of the Palazzi Giustinian was **Wagner**'s home. Finding the rooms inimical to the creative process he made a few improvements, such as hanging the walls with red cloth and importing his own bed and grand piano from Zurich. Having made the place comfortable, he settled down, flirted with the idea of suicide, and wrote the second act of *Tristan und Isolde*, inspired in part by a nocturnal gondola ride, as he recorded in his autobiography. At the sight of the moon rising over the city, the composer's gondolier "uttered a cry like a wild creature, a kind of deep groan that rose in crescendo to a prolonged 'Oh' and ended with the simple exclamation 'Venezia!'... The sensations I experienced at that moment did not leave me throughout my sojourn in Venice."

Ca' Rezzonico

A little further on from the Guistinian palaces comes Longhena's colossal **Ca' Rezzonico**. It was begun in 1667 as a commission from the Bon family, but their ambition exceeded their financial resources, and not long after hiring Giorgio Massari to complete the upper part they were obliged to sell the still unfinished palace to the Rezzonico family, who were Genoese bankers. Despite having lashed out 100,000 ducats to buy their way into the *Libro d'Oro* (at a time when 1000 ducats per annum was a comfortable income for a noble), the new owners could afford to keep Massari employed on the completion of the top floor, and then to tack a ballroom and staircase onto the back. Among its subsequent owners was Pen Browning, whose father Robert

---

THE FLOOR PLAN

You'll soon notice that the vast majority of palace facades follow the same pattern, with large windows in the centre and smaller windows placed symmetrically on each side. The earliest palazzi built in Venice – in the so-called Veneto-Byzantine style – tended to have a T shaped plan, with a single large room running parallel to the facade, but in the course of the thirteenth century a new arrangement emerged. On the ground floor was the entrance hall (the **andron** or **androne**), which ran right through the building; this was used as dry dock, and was flanked by storage rooms in homes that doubled as business premises. Above was the mezzanine: the small rooms here were used as offices or, from the sixteenth century onwards, as libraries or living rooms. On the next floor was the **piano nobile**, the main living area, arranged as suites of rooms on each side of a central hall (**portego**), which ran, like the *andron*, from front to back (to maximize the available light), and was used for special gatherings rather than day-to day living. Frequently there was a second *piano nobile* upstairs, generally accommodating relatives of the main family; the attic was used for servants' rooms or storage, and was often the location of the kitchen. This basic plan remained more or less unchanged for five hundred years.

died here in 1889; and both Whistler and Cole Porter stayed here briefly. The Ca' Rezzonico is now home to the Museo del Settecento Veneziano (see page 95).

Palazzo Loredan dell'Ambasciatore and the Contarini palaces

After a couple of canals beyond Ca' Rezzonico, opposite the Ca' del Duca, stands the **Palazzo Loredan dell'Ambasciatore**. Taking its name from the Austrian embassy that used to be here, it was built in the fifteenth century, and is notable mainly for the figures in niches on the facade, which possibly came from the workshop of Antonio Rizzo. On the far side of the next canal, the Rio di San Trovaso, stand the **Palazzo Contarini-Corfu** and the **Palazzo Contarini degli Scrigni**. The "Corfu" bit of the first name derives either from the fact that a Contarini was once a military commander on that island, or from the name of a family that lived in the parish before the Contarini. The two palaces form a single unit; the Scrigni was built in 1609 as an extension to the Corfu, a fifteenth-century Gothic house.

Ponte dell'Accademia

As the larger vaporetti couldn't get under the iron **Ponte dell'Accademia** built by the Austrians in 1854, it was replaced in 1932 by a wooden one – a temporary measure that became permanent with the addition of a reinforcing steel substructure. There's recently been talk of building something that looks a little less ad hoc, but it's very unlikely that anything will happen in the near future.

Palazzo Contarini-Polignac

Yet another Contarini palace stands a few metres past the Accademia bridge – the **Palazzo Contarini-Polignac**. This branch of the Contarini family made itself rich through landholdings around Jaffa, and the dialect version of that place name is the source of the alternative name for the palace: Contarini dal Zaffo. The facade, which was applied to the Gothic building in the late fifteenth century, represents a transitional phase between the highly decorative style associated with the Lombardi and their imitators (see the Palazzo Dario, below) and the classicizing work of Codussi.

Palazzo Venier dei Leoni

The Venier family, another of Venice's great dynasties (they produced three doges, including the commander of the Christian fleet at Lépanto), had their main base just beyond the

---

THE BIG NAMES OF VENICE

More than twenty Venetian palaces bear the **Contarini** name, and at one time there were around thirty. The city has more than a dozen **Morosini** palaces, and a plethora with such names as Loredan, Corner, Donà, Giustinian and Grimani. Intermarriage between big families is one reason for these recurrences – dynastic marriages were often marked by grafting the new relatives' surname onto the house's original name. The other main explanation is that the sons of wealthy patricians, upon receiving their shares of the father's estate, would often set up their own branches of the family in houses in other parts of the city; if they bought a property from another member of the patriciate, the transaction often resulted in a double-barrelled palace name. In some instances, a building's history of ownership can leave it trailing a three-part title, such as the Palazzo Cappello-Trevisan-Miari or the superbly melodious Palazzo Marcello-Pindemonte-Papadopoli. And why stop at three? Near San Stae there's a house that's properly known as Palazzo Boldù-Ghisi-Contarini-Pisani, and if you want to be really pedantic you should refer to the building now occupied by the *Danieli* hotel as the Palazzo Dandolo-Gritti-Bernardo-Mocenigo.

Campo San Vio. In 1759 the Veniers began rebuilding their home, but the **Palazzo Venier dei Leoni**, which would have been the largest palace on the canal, never progressed further than the first storey – hence its alternative name, **Palazzo Nonfinito**. (The "dei Leoni" part of the full name comes from the pet lions that the Veniers kept chained in the courtyard.) Its abandonment was almost certainly due to the ruinous cost, but there's a tradition which says the project was stopped by the objections of the Corner family across the water, who didn't want their sunlight blocked by a house that was bigger than theirs. The stump of the building and the platform on which it is raised (itself an extravagant and novel feature) are occupied by the Guggenheim collection (see page 85).

Palazzo Dario and Palazzo Salviati

The one domestic building of interest between here and the end of the canal is the miniature **Palazzo Dario**, the next building but one after the Palazzo dei Leoni. Compared by Henry James to "a house of cards that hold together by a tenure it would be fatal to touch", the palace was built in the late 1480s not for a patrician family but for a member of the middle ("citizen") class – a chancery secretary named Giovanni Dario, who had distinguished himself on diplomatic missions to the Turkish court. The multicoloured marbles of the facade are characteristic of the work of the Lombardo family, and the design may actually be by the founder of that dynasty, Pietro Lombardo, whereas the huge stone rosettes possibly refer to Islamic motifs that Dario would have seen in Cairo. The inscription on the lowest storey (*Urbis Genio Iohannes Dario*), in which Dario dedicates the house to the "spirit of the city", is a typically Venetian piece of faux-humble civic-mindedness.

7

Several of the Palazzo Dario's occupants have come to a sticky end, giving the place a certain notoriety in Venetian folklore: in 1970, Count Filippo Giordano delle Lanze died here when his skull was smashed by a candlestick wielded by his lover, who fled to London and was himself killed there; the next owner, Kit Lambert, manager of The Who, died three years after moving out, having fallen down a flight of stairs, or been pushed; then came a Venetian businessman named Fabrizio Ferrari, who went bust, after his sister had died in a car crash; ; and in 1993 the industrialist and yachtsman Raul Gardini, who had bought the house in 1985, was found dead in Milan, apparently having shot himself.

Two doors down, the technicolour **Palazzo Salviati** was built in 1924 by the glass-makers of the same name, and vacated by them seventy years later; the most garish building on the canal, its brash decoration is a foretaste of what awaits you in the glass showrooms of Murano.

The Salute and Dogana di Mare

The focal point of the last stretch of the canal is Longhena's masterpiece, **Santa Maria della Salute** (see page 86). It's dealt with in the Dorsoduro chapter, as is the **Dogana di Mare** (Customs House), the Canal Grande's full stop and now home to the Pinault art collection (see page 87).

The Left Bank

Downstream from the train station, the boat passes the church of the **Scalzi** before reaching **San Geremia,** which adjoins the vast **Palazzo Labia**, a palace that was completed c.1750 and is now occupied by RAI, the state TV and radio company. The main facade stretches along the Cannaregio canal, but from the Canal Grande you can see how the side wing wraps itself round the campanile of the neighbouring church – such interlocking is common in Venice, where maximum use has to be made of available space. Its ballroom contains wonderful frescoes by Tiepolo (see page 122).

Palazzo Vendramin-Calergi and Palazzo Soranzo

Not far beyond the unfinished church of **San Marcuola** stands the **Palazzo Vendramin-Calergi**. Now the city casino, it was begun by Mauro Codussi (for the Loredan family) at the very end of the fifteenth century and finished in the first decade of the sixteenth, probably by Tullio Lombardo. This is the first Venetian palace to be influenced by the classically based architectural principles of Leon Battista Alberti, and is frequently singled out as the Canal Grande's masterpiece. The round-arched windows enclosing two similar arches are identifying characteristics of Codussi's designs. In the seventeenth century a new wing was added to the palace, but soon after its completion two sons of the house conspired to murder a member of the Querini-Stampalia family; as the brothers hadn't physically committed the crime themselves, the court had to limit their sentence to exile, but it ordered the demolition of the new block for good measure. The palazzo's most famous subsequent resident was Richard Wagner, who died here in February 1883; the size of the palace can be gauged from the fact that his rented suite of fifteen rooms occupied just a part of the mezzanine level.

The **Palazzo Soranzo**, a bit further along, dates from the same period as the Vendramin-Calergi, and the contrast between the two gives you an idea of the originality of Codussi's design.

Palazzo Gussoni-Grimani della Vida

The **Palazzo Gussoni-Grimani della Vida**, on the near side of the Rio di Noale, was rebuilt to Sanmicheli's designs in the middle of the sixteenth century. From 1614 to 1618 it was occupied by the English consul Sir Henry Wotton, best remembered now for his definition of an ambassador as "an honest man sent to lie abroad for the good of his country" – a remark that earned him the sack from King James I. Wotton spent much of his time in Venice running a sort of import-export business; when he wasn't buying paintings to ship back to England he was arranging for Protestant texts to be brought into Venice, a city he thought ripe for conversion. The Venetians, however, remained content with their idiosyncratic version of Catholicism, as exemplified by Wotton's friend, Paolo Sarpi (see page 129). At the time of Wotton's residence the facade of the palace was covered with frescoes by Tintoretto, but they have long since faded to invisibility.

Ca' d'Oro

Beyond the Palazzo Gussoni-Grimani della Vida, the next palace of interest is the most beguiling on the canal – the **Ca' d'Oro** (see page 130). (*Ca'* is an abbreviation of *casa di stazio*, meaning the main family home.) Incorporating fragments of a thirteenth-century palace that once stood on the site, the Ca' d'Oro was built in the 1420s and 1430s, and acquired its nickname – "The Golden House" – from the gilding that used to accentuate much of its carving.

Palazzo Sagredo

The facade of the **Palazzo Sagredo**, on the near side of the Campo Santa Sofia, is an overlay of different periods, and a good demonstration of the Venetian custom of adapting old buildings to current needs and principles. The tracery of the *piano nobile* is fourteenth-century, and clearly later than the storeys below; the right wing, however, seems to belong to the fifteenth-century.

Ca' da Mosto

On the near corner of the Rio dei Santi Apostoli stands the **Palazzo Mangilli-Valmarana**, built in the eighteenth century for the English consul Joseph Smith, who was one of the chief patrons of Canaletto. More interesting is the **Ca' da Mosto**, close to the rio's opposite bank. The arches of the first floor and the carved panels above them are remnants of a thirteenth-century Veneto-Byzantine building, and are thus among the oldest structures to be seen on the Canal Grande. Alvise da Mosto, discoverer of the Cape Verde Islands, was born here in 1432; by the end of that century the palazzo had become the *Albergo del Lion Bianco*, and from then until the nineteenth century it was one of Venice's most popular hotels.

Fondaco dei Tedeschi

As the canal turns past Ca' da Mosto, the **Ponte di Rialto** comes into view. The huge building before it is the **Fondaco dei Tedeschi**, once headquarters of the city's German merchants. On the ground floor their cargoes were weighed, packaged and stored; the upper storeys contained a refectory and around sixty bedrooms, many of which were rented on an annual basis by the biggest firms. The German traders were the most powerful foreign grouping in the city, and as early as 1228 they were leased a building on this central site. In 1505 the fondaco burned down, and it was rebuilt by Spavento and Scarpagnino; Giorgione and Titian, who had helped the firefighters on the night of the blaze, were then commissioned to paint the exterior walls. The remains of their contribution are now in the Ca' d'Oro. The Fondaco has been renovated several times since the sixteenth century, and is now a shopping mall.

Palazzo Dolfin-Manin

Beyond the Rialto bridge and immediately before the next rio is Sansovino's first palace in Venice, the **Palazzo Dolfin-Manin**. It dates from the late 1530s, a period when other projects by Sansovino – the Libreria, the Zecca and the Loggetta – were transforming the centre of the city. The public passageway (*sottoportego*) running under the facade is a feature common to many Venetian houses. Lodovico Manin, the last doge of Venice, lived here; he had the interior rebuilt, so the facade is the only bit entirely by Sansovino.

Palazzo Loredan and Palazzo Farsetti

The **Palazzo Loredan** and the **Palazzo Farsetti**, standing side by side at the end of the Riva del Carbon, are heavily restored Veneto-Byzantine palaces of the thirteenth century. The former was the home of Elena Corner Piscopia, who in 1678 graduated from Padua University, so becoming the first woman ever to hold a university degree. The two buildings are now occupied by the town hall.

Palazzo Grimani

Work began on the **Palazzo Grimani** (on the near side of the Rio di San Luca) in 1559, to designs by Sanmicheli, but was not completed until 1575, sixteen years after his death. Ruskin, normally no fan of Renaissance architecture, made an exception for this colossal palace, calling it "simple, delicate, and sublime". A Venetian folk tale attributes the scale of the palace to a thwarted passion: it's said that the young man who built it was in love with a woman from the Coccina-Tiepolo palace across the water, but was turned away by her father. The suitor's revenge was to humiliate the father by building a palace which had windows bigger than the main doorway of the Coccina-Tiepolo house. Having served as the city's Court of Appeal for many years, it has now been put up for sale; it's odds-on that it becomes a (yet another) super-luxe hotel.

Palazzo Corner Contarini dei Cavalli, Palazzo Benzon and Palazzo Corner-Spinelli

The **Palazzo Corner Contarini dei Cavalli**, on the other side of the rio from Palazzo Grimani, was built around 1445; the "cavalli" part of the name comes from the horses on the crest of the facade's coat of arms. The pink **Palazzo Benzon**, just before the next canal, was where the most fashionable salon of early nineteenth-century Venice used to meet – regular guests included Byron, Thomas Moore, Ugo Foscolo and Canova. Their hostess, Contessa Querini-Benzon, was celebrated in a song that still occupies a place in the gondoliers' repertoire – *La Biondina in Gondoleta* (The Blonde in a Gondola). The **Palazzo Corner-Spinelli**, on the far side of the Rio di Ca' Santi, is another work by Codussi; it dates from 1490–1510, so preceding his more monumental Palazzo Vendramin-Calergi.

The Mocenigo palaces

Four houses that once all belonged to the Mocenigo family stand side by side on the Volta del Canal: the **Palazzo Mocenigo-Nero**, a late sixteenth-century building; the double **Palazzo Mocenigo**, built in the eighteenth century as an extension to the Nero house; and the **Palazzo Mocenigo Vecchio**, a Gothic palace remodelled in the seventeenth century.

One of the great Venetian scandals centres on the first of the four. In 1621 Lady Arundel, wife of one of King James's most powerful courtiers, became its tenant; before long it was rumoured that the house was being visited by **Antonio Foscarini**, a former ambassador from Venice to England, whose term in London had ended with an abrupt recall and a three-year stay in prison under suspicion of treason. On that occasion Foscarini had finally been cleared, but now there were renewed allegations, and the Council of Ten – believing that Foscarini was passing state secrets to the English – quickly shifted into top gear. Foscarini was arrested, interrogated and, twelve days later, executed. Lady Arundel instantly demanded an audience with the doge, the result of which was a public declaration that she had not been involved in any wrongdoing; and within a few months the Council of Ten had conclusive evidence that Foscarini had been framed. The men who had accused him were put to death, and Foscarini's body was exhumed and given a state funeral.

Byron and his menagerie – a dog, a fox, a wolf and a monkey – lived in the Mocenigo-Nero palace for a couple of years. Much of his time was taken up with a local baker's wife called Margarita Cogni, the most tempestuous of his mistresses – her reaction to being rejected by him was to attack him with a table knife and then, having been shown the door, hurl herself into the Canal Grande. The Palazzo Mocenigo Vecchio is supposed to be haunted by the ghost of the philosopher-alchemist Giordano Bruno, whose betrayal to the Vatican by his former host, Giovanni Mocenigo, led ultimately to his torture and execution in 1600.

The neighbouring building is the early sixteenth-century **Palazzo Contarini delle Figure** – the *figure* are the almost invisible figures above the water entrance. It was begun by Spavento and completed by Scarpagnino, as had previously been the case with the Fondaco dei Tedeschi and the Palazzo Ducale.

Palazzo Grassi

The vast and pristine palace round the Volta is the **Palazzo Grassi**, built in 1748–72 by Massari, who supervised the completion of the Ca' Rezzonico on the right bank opposite. Its first owners were accepted into the ranks of the nobility in return for a hefty contribution to the war effort against the Turks in 1718. Nowadays it's an exhibition centre (see page 78).

Ca' del Duca, Palazzetto Falier and Palazzo Giustinian-Lolin

On the edge of the first canal after the campo of San Samuele stands the **Ca' del Duca**. Commissioned in the mid-fifteenth century from Bartolomeo Bon, it was left unfinished in 1461 when the Corner family sold it to Francesco Sforza, Duke of Milan (from whom it takes its name) – the wedge of rusticated masonry gives some idea of the sort of fortified look the Corners had in mind. In 1514 Titian had a studio here. Across the rio there's the tiny **Palazzetto Falier**, a reworked Gothic house of the fifteenth century, chiefly remarkable for its two roofed terraces. Although they used to be common, very few examples of this feature (called a *liagò*) have survived. Next door is one of Longhena's earliest projects, the **Palazzo Giustinian-Lolin** (1623).

Palazzo Franchetti and the Palazzi Barbaro

At the foot of the Accademia bridge, on the far side, is the huge fifteenth-century **Palazzo Franchetti**; repaired and enlarged at the end of the nineteenth century, it's an imposing building but is often cited as one of the city's most heavy-handed pieces of restoration work. Now owned by the Istituto Veneto di Scienze, Lettere ed Arti, it's an occasional venue for art exhibitions.

On the opposite side of the Rio dell'Orso are the twinned **Palazzi Barbaro**; the house on the left is early fifteenth-century, the other late seventeenth-century. Henry James, Monet, Whistler, Browning and John Singer Sargent were among the luminaries who stayed in the older Barbaro house as guests of the Curtis family in the late nineteenth century. James finished *The Aspern Papers* here, and used it as a setting for *The Wings of a Dove*; so attached was he to the place that when given the opportunity of buying a home in Venice at a very reasonable price, he decided he would rather go on living here as a lodger.

Palazzo Corner della Ca' Grande

Soon after the short fondamenta comes the tiny **Casetta delle Rose**, where Canova once had his studio and D'Annunzio lived during World War I. The Casetta lies in the shadow of one of the Canal Grande's most imposing structures – Sansovino's **Palazzo Corner della Ca' Grande**. The palace that used to stand here was destroyed when a fire that had been lit to dry out a stock of sugar in the attic spread though the whole building, an incident that illustrates the dual commercial-residential function of many Venetian palaces. Sansovino's replacement, commissioned by the nephews of Caterina Cornaro, was built from 1545 onwards, and the rustication of its lower storey – a distinctive aspect of many Roman and Tuscan buildings of the High Renaissance – makes it a prototype for Longhena's Ca' Pésaro and Ca' Rezzonico. Though the Corners were among the wealthiest clans in Venice, the palazzo was partly funded by a large donation from the state coffers. When Caterina Cornaro had died in 1510, the family had not claimed their share of her estate, instead allowing the government to use the money to subsidize the armed forces that were then embroiled in the War of the League of Cambrai. Now the nephews argued that the state owed them some help in funding the construction of a house that would, after all, be an adornment to the city – and the Council of Ten duly authorized the payment of 30,000 ducats.

Palazzo Pisani and Palazzo Contarini-Fasan

The heavily restored fifteenth-century **Palazzo Pisani**, now the *Gritti Palace* hotel (see page 203), looms over the Santa Maria del Giglio landing stage. Squeezed into the line of buildings that follows is the narrow **Palazzo Contarini-Fasan**, a mid-fifteenth-century palace with unique wheel tracery on the balconies.

Palazzo Giustinian

The last major building before the Giardinetti Reali is the fifteenth-century **Palazzo Giustinian**; now the HQ of the Biennale and the tourist board, it was formerly one of the plushest hotels in town, numbering the likes of Verdi, Ruskin and Proust among its guests.

The northern islands

The main islands lying to the north of Venice – San Michele, Murano, Burano and Torcello – used to be good places to visit when the throng of tourists in the main part of Venice became too oppressive. Nowadays the throngs are almost everywhere for most of the year, but a northwards excursion is still a restorative – out here the horizons are distant and the swathes of *barèna* (marshland) give a taste of what conditions were like for Venice's first settlers. A day-trip through this part of the lagoon will reveal the origins of the glass- and lace-work touted in so many of the city's shops, and give you a glimpse of the origins of Venice itself, embodied in Torcello's magnificent cathedral of Santa Maria dell'Assunta.

Those intent on an exhaustive exploration of the lagoon could plan a visit to the islets of San Francesco del Deserto and Lazzaretto Nuovo – the former a Franciscan retreat, the latter a charismatic wasteland.

GETTING TO THE ISLANDS

To get to the northern islands, the main **vaporetto stop** is **Fondamente Nove** (or Nuove), as nearly all the island services start here or call here. For **San Michele and Murano** the circular #4.1 and #4.2 vaporetti both run every 20min from Fondamente Nove, circling Murano before heading back towards Venice; you can hop on elsewhere in the city, of course, but make sure that the boat is going towards the islands, not away from them – the #4.1 follows an anticlockwise route around the city, the #4.2 a clockwise route. Murano can also be reached by the #3, which from around 6.15am to 6.45pm runs to the island from Piazzale Roma and the train station every 30min. For **Murano, Burano and Torcello** the #12 leaves every 30min from Fondamente Nove for most of the day (hourly early in the morning and evenings), calling first at Murano-Faro before heading on to Mazzorbo and Burano, from where it proceeds to Treporti. A shuttle boat (#9) runs between Burano and Torcello every 15min.

San Michele

A church was founded on **San Michele**, the innermost of the northern islands, in the tenth century, and a monastery was established in the thirteenth. Its best-known resident was Fra Mauro (d.1459), whose map of the world – the most accurate of its time – is now a precious possession of the Libreria Sansoviniana. The monastery was suppressed in the early nineteenth century, but in 1829, after a spell as an Austrian

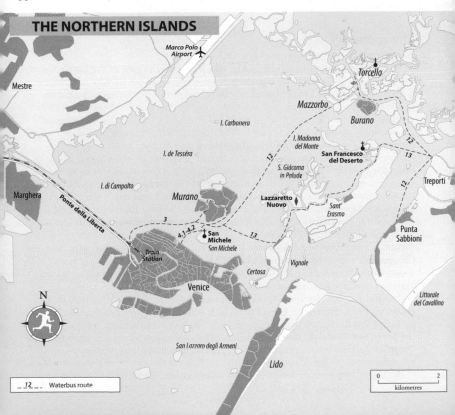

THE NORTHERN ISLANDS

Mestre

Marco Polo Airport

Torcello

Mazzorbo

Burano

I. Carbonera

I. Madonna del Monte

I. de Tesséra

San Francesco del Deserto

S. Giácoma in Paludo

Treporti

I. di Campalto

Murano

Lazzaretto Nuovo

Sant' Erasmo

Marghera

Ponte della Liberta

San Michele

San Michele

Punta Sabbioni

Train Station

Vignole

Certosa

Venice

Littorale del Cavallino

N

San Lazzaro degli Armeni

Lido

_12_ Waterbus route

0 ⸻ 2

kilometres

prison for political offenders, it was handed back to the Franciscans, who look after the church and the cemetery to this day.

San Michele in Isola

Daily: April–Sept 7.30am–6pm; Oct–March 7.30am–4pm • Free

The high brick wall around the island gives way by the landing stage to the elegant white facade of **San Michele in Isola**, designed by **Mauro Codussi** in 1469. With this building Codussi quietly revolutionized the architecture of Venice, advancing the principles of Renaissance design in the city and introducing the use of Istrian stone as a material for facades. Easy to carve yet resistant to water, Istrian stone had long been used for dampcourses, but never before had anyone clad the entire front of a building in it; after the construction of San Michele, most major buildings in Venice were given an Istrian veneer.

Attached on the left, and entered from within the church, is the dainty **Cappella Emiliana**, built around 1530 by **Guglielmo dei Grigi**. Marble inlays and reliefs cover the interior, yet Ruskin was impervious to its charm: "It is more like a German summer-house, or angle-turret, than a chapel, and may be briefly described as a beehive set on a low hexagonal tower, with dashes of stonework about its windows like the flourishes of an idle penman." In front of the main entrance to the church a floor plaque marks the final resting place of **Fra Paolo Sarpi** (d.1623), Venice's principal ideologue during the tussle with the papacy at the start of the seventeenth century (see page 129); buried first in his Servite monastery, Sarpi's remains were removed here when that order was suppressed in 1828.

The cemetery

Daily: April–Sept 7.30am–6pm; Oct–March 7.30am–4pm

There's a small vineyard behind San Michele, but the main part of the island, through the cloisters, is covered by the **cemetery** of Venice, established here by a Napoleonic decree which forbade further burials in the centre of the city. Space is at a premium, and most of the Catholic dead of Venice lie here in cramped conditions for just ten years or so, when their bones are dug up and removed to an ossuary. Protestants are permitted to stay in their sector indefinitely, as each year's new arrivals are never numerous. (There is a separate Jewish cemetery over on the Lido.)

However, even with this grave-rotation system in operation, the island is reaching full capacity, so in 1998 a competition was held for the redevelopment of San Michele. The winning entry, from English architect David Chipperfield, places a sequence of formal courtyards lined with wall tombs on the presently unkempt parts of the island, alongside a new funerary chapel and crematorium. On the eastern side of San Michele two footbridges will connect with a rectangular expanse of reclaimed land, site of a trio of tomb buildings that will overlook two tiers of waterside gardens, which in turn will overlook central Venice. Making much use of Istrian stone and earthenware plasterwork, Chipperfield's cemetery is an austerely beautiful creation – and there's a certain appropriateness to the fact that the twenty-first century's first large-scale addition to the Venetian cityscape is a cross between a necropolis and a philosopher's retreat.

Most tourists head for the dilapidated **Protestant** section (no. XV), where **Ezra Pound's grave** is marked by a small plain slab with his name on it, alongside that of his partner, Olga Rudge. Nobel Laureate Joseph Brodsky is buried here too. Adjoining is the **Greek and Russian Orthodox** area (no. XIV), where you'll find the tomb of **Serge Diaghilev** and the simple gravestones of **Igor and Vera Stravinsky** – Stravinsky was given a funeral service in San Zanipolo, the highest honour the city can bestow. San Michele is also the resting place of another great modern composer, Luigi Nono, who was born in Venice in 1924 and died here in 1990.

Murano

In 1276 the island of **Murano** became a self-governed enclave within the Republic, with its own judiciary, its own administration and a **Libro d'Oro** to register its nobility. By the early sixteenth century Murano had thirty thousand inhabitants, and was a favourite summer retreat for Venice's upper classes, who could lay out gardens here that were far more extensive than those in the cramped city centre. The intellectual life of the island was especially healthy in the seventeenth century, when literature, philosophy and the sciences were discussed in the numerous small **accademie** that flourished here. But the **glass-blowing industry** is what made Murano famous all over Europe, and today the furnaces of Murano constitute Venice's sole surviving manufacturing zone.

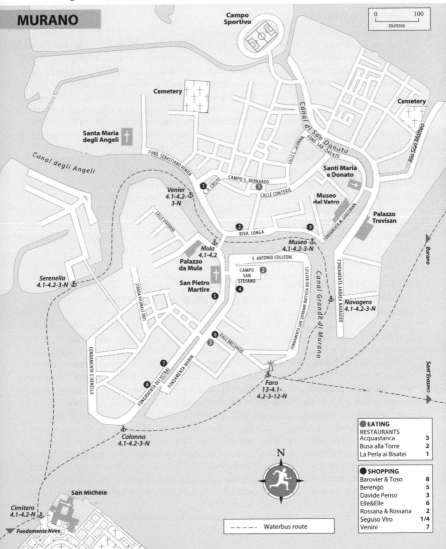

MURANO

● EATING	
RESTAURANTS	
Acquastanca	3
Busa alla Torre	2
La Perla ai Bisatei	1

● SHOPPING	
Barovier & Toso	8
Berengo	5
Davide Penso	3
Elle&Elle	6
Rossana & Rossana	2
Seguso Viro	1/4
Venini	7

The main fondamente of Murano are given over almost entirely to shops selling glasswork, and it's difficult to walk more than a few metres on this island without being invited to step inside a showroom – and once inside, you're likely to be pressured into forking out for some piece of kitsch which may not even have been made here. However, some of the showrooms have furnaces attached, and you shouldn't pass up the chance to see these astoundingly skilful craftsmen in action, even if they're only churning out little glass ponies and other knick-knacks. (The top-quality stuff is produced behind closed doors.) Furthermore, you'll find some very beautiful (and very expensive) items on sale here, and you can see some remarkable work in the Murano glass museum – the island's main sight, alongside the beautiful church of **Santi Maria e Donato**.

San Pietro Martire

Fondamenta dei Vetrai • Mon–Sat 9am–noon & 3–6pm, Sun 3–6pm • Free

From the Colonna vaporetto stop (the first stop for the #4.1/#4.2) you step onto the Fondamenta dei Vetrai, traditionally the core of the glass industry (as the name suggests) and now the principal tourist trap. Towards the far end is the Dominican church of **San Pietro Martire**, one of only two churches still in service on the island (compared with seventeen when the Republic fell in 1797). Begun in 1363 but largely rebuilt after a fire in 1474, it contains a handful of fine paintings, notably **Giovanni Bellini**'s large and elegant **Madonna and Child with St Mark, St Augustine and Doge Barbarigo**. A later altarpiece by Bellini and his workshop – an **Assumption** – should hang nearby; it's been **in restauro** for years, but may return soon. On the opposite side of the church are two pieces by Veronese – **St Agatha in Prison** and **St Jerome in the Desert**.

The Cappella del Sacramento, to the left of the main altar, was originally dedicated to the angels and contains four paintings of personable representatives of the heavenly host. The sacristy, with its modest museum (€2), is worth seeing only for the wood-carving in the vestry, which includes some extraordinary Baroque atlantes depicting historical and mythological characters such as Nero, Socrates, Pythagoras and Pontius Pilate, with the Four Seasons flanking the altar.

The Museo del Vetro

Fondamenta Giustinian 8 • Daily: April–Oct 10am–6pm; Nov–March 10am–5pm • €10, or €12 with Museo del Merletto (Burano), or Museum Pass • ⓦ museovetro.visitmuve.it

Beyond San Pietro, turn right on the far side of the main bridge, the **Ponte Vivarini**, and you'll soon come to the seventeenth-century Palazzo Giustinian. Home of the bishop of Torcello until his diocese was joined to Venice in 1805, the Giustinian now houses the **Museo del Vetro**. Reopened in 2015 after extensive renovation, the museum features pieces dating back to the first century and examples of Murano glass from the fifteenth century onwards, and now has a large ground-floor space for one-off shows. Perhaps the most celebrated single item is the dark blue Barovier marriage cup, dating from around 1460; it's on show in room 2 on the first floor, along with some splendid Renaissance enamelled and painted glass. But every room contains some amazing creations: glass beakers that look as if they are made from veined stone; a chalice with a spiral stem as slender as a strand of spaghetti; sixteenth-century platters that look like discs of scored ice; an eighteenth-century formal garden in miniature; and some stupendously ugly nineteenth-century pieces, such as the life-sized cockerel with individual glass feathers. A separate room is devoted to Murano beads and the techniques of Murano glass-making – look out for the extraordinary **murrine**, the patterned glass made by fusing and stretching differently coloured rods.

Santi Maria e Donato

Calle San Donato • Mon–Sat 9am–noon & 3–7pm, Sun 2–6pm • Free

The finest Murano church, **Santi Maria e Donato**, was founded in the seventh century but rebuilt in the twelfth, and is one of the lagoon's best examples of Veneto-Byzantine architecture – the ornate **rear apse** being particularly beautiful. Originally dedicated to the Virgin, the church was rededicated in 1125 when the relics of St Donatus were brought here from Cephalonia by **Doge Domenico Michiel**, who also picked up the remains of St Isidore and the stone on which Jesus stood to preach to the men of Tyre – both items are now in the Basilica di San Marco. St Donatus allegedly once slew a dragon simply by spitting at it – the four splendid bones hanging behind the altar are supposedly from the vanquished beast.

The glory of the interior is its **mosaic floor**, which was created in the middle of the twelfth century (the date 1141 appears in the nave) and extensively restored and completely relaid in the 1970s. It's a gorgeous weave of abstract patterns and figurative images, such as an eagle carrying off a deer, and two roosters bearing away a fox, slung from a pole (these may be symbols of the triumph of Christianity over paganism). Apart from the arresting twelfth-century **mosaic of the Madonna** in the apse, a variant (without **bambino**) of the contemporaneous mosaic at Torcello, the other features that invite perusal are the fifteenth-century ship's-keel roof, the sixth-century pulpit, the

MURANO GLASS

Because of the risk of fire, Venice's **glass furnaces** were moved to **Murano** from central Venice in 1291, and thenceforth all possible steps were taken to keep the secrets of the trade locked up on the island. Although Muranese workers had by the seventeenth century gained some freedom of movement, for centuries prior to that any glass-maker who left Murano was proclaimed a traitor, and some were even hunted down. Various privileges reduced the temptation to rove – unlike other artisans, the glass-blowers were allowed to wear swords, and from 1376 the offspring of a marriage between a Venetian nobleman and the daughter of a glass-worker were allowed to be entered into the *Libro d'Oro*, unlike the children of other inter-class matches.

A fifteenth-century visitor judged that "in the whole world there are no such craftsmen of glass as here", and the Muranese were masters of every aspect of their craft. They were producing spectacles by the start of the fourteenth century, monopolized the European manufacture of **mirrors** for a long time and in the early seventeenth century became so proficient at making coloured crystal that a decree was issued forbidding the manufacture of false gems out of glass, as many were being passed off as authentic stones. Understatement has rarely been a characteristic of Murano produce: in 1756 Lady Mary Wortley Montagu was wonderstruck by a set of **furniture** made entirely out of glass, and in the twentieth century the less favourably impressed H.V. Morton longed "to see something simple and beautiful". Murano kitsch extends to all price categories, from the mass-produced trinkets sold for a few euros, through to monstrosities such as Peggy Guggenheim's pieces based on figures from the works of Picasso – specially commissioned by her, you can see these on show in the Guggenheim Collection.

The traditional style of Murano glass, typified by the multicoloured floral **chandeliers** sold in showrooms on Murano and round the Piazza, is still very much in demand. However, in recent years there's been turmoil in the glass industry, due to an inundation of cheap Murano-style tableware and ornaments from Asia and eastern Europe. To protect the reputation of the island's craftsmen a Murano "copyright" has been created – it's displayed on all authentic Murano work. And while many Murano factories have been unable to compete with the vendors of low-price ersatz glassware, an increasing number of companies are now following the example of Paolo Venini, the Milanese lawyer and entrepreneur who in the 1920s pulled Murano from the doldrums by commissioning work from designers outside the rarefied world of glass. There are now several innovative glass producers on Murano, but the sharp economic downturn that began in 2008 has hit Murano badly, with the drop in sales to tourists leading to a large reduction in output, and several closures. Dozens of Murano glass companies and retailers have closed down recently, and few of those that remain are in Venetian hands – the long-established firm of Salviati is French-owned, and Venini belongs to the Royal Copenhagen company.

8

Veneto-Byzantine capitals and Lazzaro Bastiani's **Madonna and Child with Saints and Donor** (1484), halfway down the left aisle.

Mazzorbo

After Murano, the next stop for the #12 is at the small island of **Mazzorbo**, a densely populated town a couple of centuries ago, before it became a place of exile for disgraced noblemen, whereupon the undisgraced citizens decamped for homes elsewhere in the lagoon. Nowadays Mazzorbo doesn't amount to much more than a few scattered villas, a lot of grassy space and market gardens, a new housing development and the simple fourteenth-century church of **Santa Caterina**. It does, though, have **Venissa**, one of the best restaurants in the lagoon (see page 220). You can either get off the boat here, and walk round Mazzorbo to the 60m footbridge to Burano (which offers a beautifully framed view of distant Venice), or continue on the boat for one more stop.

Burano

Burano was settled in the seventh century by mainland refugees who named their new home Boreana, perhaps after the **bora**, as the northeasterly winter wind is known. Safely removed from the malarial swamps that did so much to ruin neighbouring Torcello, Burano became a prosperous fishing village, and is still largely a fishing community – you can't walk far along the shores of the island without seeing a fishing boat beached for repair, or nets laid out to dry or be mended, or a jumble of crab boxes. After the peeling plaster and eroded stonework of the other lagoon settlements, the small, brightly painted houses of this island come as something of a surprise. Local tradition says that the colours once enabled each fisherman to identify his house from out at sea, but nowadays the colours are used simply for pleasant effect.

The lives of the women of Burano used to be dominated by the **lace** industry, but the production of handmade lace is now almost extinct, and virtually all of the stuff sold in the shops lining the narrow street leading into the village from the vaporetto stop is made by machine, abroad. Lacemaking used to be a skill that crossed all social boundaries: for noblewomen it was an expression of feminine creativity (by the end of the sixteenth century, lacemaking had become the chief pastime of upper-class Venetian women); for nuns it was an exercise in humility and contemplation; and for the poorest it was simply a source of income. Its production was once geographically diverse, too – **Dogaressa Morosina Morosini** set up a large and successful workshop near Santa Fosca (in Cannaregio) in the late sixteenth century, for instance – but nowadays Burano is the only place where genuine lace is made.

The Scuola del Merletto

Piazza Galuppi • Tues–Sun: April–Oct 10am–6pm; Nov–March 10am–5pm • €5, or €12 with Museo del Vetro (Murano), or Museum Pass • Ⓦ museomerletto.visitmuve.it

> ### BEPI AND GALUPPI
> The boldest exterior decorator on Burano was a resident called **Bepi**, who lived at Via Al Gottolo 339, down the alley opposite the *Galuppi* restaurant in Via **Baldassare Galuppi**, the island's main street; Bepi died in 2002, but his crazy patterns of diamonds, triangles and bars have been preserved. As for Baldassare Galuppi, he was an eighteenth-century Buranese composer, known locally as *Il Buranello*; the main piazza is named after him, and he's further commemorated there with a statue and a plaque at no. 24.

The **Scuola del Merletto** is simply a school rather than a confraternity-cum-guild – unlike all other craftspeople in Venice, the lacemakers had no guild to represent them, perhaps because the workforce was exclusively female. It was opened in 1872, when the indigenous crafting of lace had declined so far that it was left to one woman, Francesca Memo, to transmit the necessary skills to a younger generation of women. Although the **scuola** has not operated as a full-time school since the late 1960s and is now almost moribund, courses are still held here.

Reopened in 2011 after a major restoration, the **scuola**'s museum showcases around 150 examples of Murano lacework in ingenious sliding cabinets, along with paintings and a profusion of other documentation. You might not think that lacework is terribly interesting, but the pieces on show here are astonishing – indescribably intricate, and

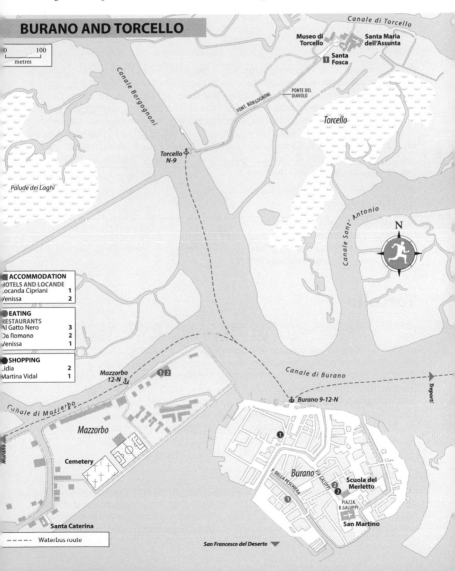

SAN FRANCESCO DEL DESERTO

St Francis ran aground on the little island now known as **San Francesco del Deserto** in 1220, and decided to build a chapel here. Jacopo Michiel, the owner of the island, gave it to the Franciscans soon after the saint's death, and apart from abandoning it for a while in the fifteenth century because of malaria, and being pushed out in the nineteenth century by the military, the Franciscans have been here ever since. The present chapel was built over the original one in the fifteenth century, and was lovingly restored in 1962, uncovering some of the original floor and foundations. Half a dozen friars live here, some in retreat, and a few young men stay for a year before becoming Franciscan novices. With its birdsong, its profusion of plants and its cypress-scented air, the monastery is one of the most tranquil places in the lagoon. If you want to visit, it's a good idea to ring the monastery (☎041 528 6863) to check that it's convenient. To reach San Francesco you have to take a private boat from Burano, costing around €10 per person for the return trip. Visitors are received Tues–Sat 9–11am & 3–5pm, Sun 3–5pm; a donation is requested.

---

delicate as frost. On the ground floor, a film (subtitled in English) and a sequence of illustrative panels serve as an introduction to the main part of the museum, upstairs, where four rooms tell the story of Burano lace from its origins in the sixteenth century to its decline in the age of mass-produced fabrics. The most engrossing, and poignant, display is the live demonstration by master lacemakers – these women, none of them young, are almost certainly the last practitioners of this highly specialized and exacting art. Each lacemaker specializes in one particular type of stitch, so each piece is passed from woman to woman during its construction. Making an average-size lace table centre requires about a month of work.

San Martino

Piazza Galuppi • Daily 8am–noon & 3–7pm • Free

Opposite the lace school rises the drunken campanile of the island's only church, **San Martino**; it has one outstanding picture, a **Crucifixion** by Giambattista Tiepolo, painted in 1725 (on the second altar on the left).

Torcello

"Mother and daughter, you behold them both in their widowhood – Torcello and Venice." So wrote John Ruskin, and it's almost impossible to visit **Torcello** without similarly sensing an atmosphere of bereavement. This outlying island has now come almost full circle. Settled by the very first refugees from the mainland in the fifth century, it became the seat of the bishop of Altinum in 638 and in the following year its cathedral – the oldest building in the lagoon – was founded. By the fourteenth century its population had peaked at around twenty thousand, but Torcello's canals were now silting up and malaria was rife. By the end of the fifteenth century Torcello was largely deserted – even the bishop lived in Murano – and today fewer than a dozen people remain in residence.

Santa Maria dell'Assunta

Piazza di Torcello • Daily: April–Oct 10.30am–5.30pm; Nov–Feb 10am–4.30pm • €5, or €9 joint ticket with campanile

The main reason for a visit to Torcello is to see Venice's first cathedral and the most serene building in the lagoon – the Veneto-Byzantine **Cattedrale di Santa Maria dell'Assunta**. The cathedral has evolved from the church that was founded in the

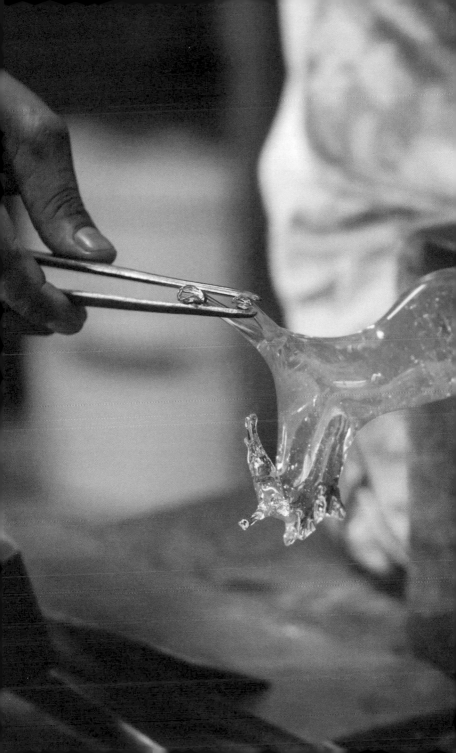

> **THE CHAIR OF ATTILA**
>
> In the square outside Santa Fosca and the cathedral sits the so-called **chair of Attila**, a hefty lump of rock that was perhaps once the throne of Torcello's judges in its earliest days; local folklore has it that if you sit in it, you will be married within a year.

seventh century, of which the crypt and the circular foundations in front of the **facade** have survived. The first major transformation occurred in the 860s, the period to which the **facade and portico** belong (though they were altered in later centuries); most of the structure, however, dates from the first decades of the eleventh century. For the most unusual features of the exterior, go down the right-hand side of the cathedral, where the windows have eleventh-century **stone shutters**. Ruskin described the view from the campanile as "one of the most notable scenes in this wide world", a verdict you can test for yourself, if the campanile isn't undergoing one of its frequent bouts of repair.

The interior

The dominant tones of the cathedral's **interior** come from pink brick, gold-based mosaics and the watery green-grey marble of its columns and panelling, which together cast a cool light on the richly patterned **mosaic floor**, which was laid in the eleventh and twelfth centuries. (Glazed panels in the floor reveal portions of ninth-century mosaic.) On the semi-dome of the apse a stunning twelfth-century **mosaic of the Madonna and Child**, the figures isolated in a vast field of gold, looks down from above a **frieze of the Apostles**, dating from the middle of the previous century. Below the window at the Madonna's feet is a much restored image of **St Heliodorus**, the first bishop of Altinum, whose remains were brought here by the earliest settlers. It makes an interesting comparison with the gold-plated facemask on his sarcophagus below the high altar, another seventh-century vestige. His original Roman sarcophagus is placed to the left of the altar, underneath the **foundation stone** of the cathedral, which was laid in 639, the same year as the fall of Oderzo, the Byzantine provincial capital on the mainland. Named on the stone are the fleeing leaders of that town, both temporal (the **magister militum**) and spiritual (the Exarch), as well as Bishop Mauro of Altinum, the first to transfer his see to Torcello.

Mosaic work from the ninth and eleventh centuries adorns the chapel to the right of the high altar, while the other end of the cathedral is dominated by the tumultuous **mosaic of the Apotheosis of Christ and the Last Judgement**; created in the twelfth century, but renovated in the nineteenth, it features an extraordinary panel in various shades of black and grey, depicting the eternal gloom of hell. Have a good look, too, at the **rood screen**, where paintings of **The Virgin and Apostles** are supported by eleventh-century columns connected by finely carved marble panels.

Santa Fosca

Piazza di Torcello • Daily 10am–4.30pm • Free

Torcello's smaller church, **Santa Fosca**, was built in the eleventh and twelfth centuries for the body of the martyred St Fosca, brought to Torcello from Libya some time before 1011 and now resting under the altar. A dome was planned to cap the martyrium but was never built, perhaps because of the desertion of the Greek builders who alone possessed the secret of constructing a self-supporting dome. Though much restored, the church retains the Greek-cross form and a fine exterior apse; the bare interior, with beautiful marble columns and elegant brick arches, exudes a tranquillity that no number of visitors can quite destroy.

Museo di Torcello

Piazza di Torcello • Tues–Sun: March–Oct 10.30am–5.30pm; Nov–Feb 10am–5pm • €3

The well-laid-out **Museo di Torcello** includes thirteenth-century beaten-gold figures, jewellery, mosaic fragments (including pieces from the cathedral's **Last Judgement**, in which the hands of several artists can be distinguished) and a mishmash of pieces relating to the history of the area.

Lazzaretto Nuovo

Free tours April–Oct Sat & Sun at 9.45am & 4.30pm • ⓦ lazzarettonuovo.com

Once a quarantine encampment, the island of **Lazzaretto Nuovo** now has just one resident, former history teacher Gerolamo Fazzini, who is now the island's guardian; in summer, however, there's an archeology school here, and visitors are welcome. Getting there is simple enough, as the vaporetto #13 to Sant' Erasmo stops at the jetty on request.

In 1468, fear of plague led the Senate to augment the existing plague hospital (now known as Lazzaretto Vecchio) with a dedicated quarantine island, and huge warehouses were erected to store merchandise arriving in Venice from suspect areas, with merchants and sailors quartered alongside. The largest of these warehouses, the **Tezon Grande**, still stands in the centre of the island, and while it's little more than an empty shed, the sixteenth-century graffiti on the far interior wall conjure something of a more cosmopolitan past – picked out in red are lists of cargoes and voyages made to the further corners of the Mediterranean. Much of the island is still encircled by brick fortifications which date from the occupations of Napoleon and the Austrians, when it formed part of Venice's system of defences.

There are plans to make the Lazzaretto Nuovo the joint home, with the Lazzaretto Vecchio, of a new museum devoted to the history of the lagoon, but for now the island has just a small museum of archeological finds. The atmosphere is wonderfully peaceful, though, and the view across the marshes is impressive, with little egrets and herons fishing among the rushes.

8

IL REDENTORE

The southern islands

The section of the lagoon to the south of the city, enclosed by the long islands of the Lido and Pellestrina, has far fewer outcrops of solid land than the northern zone. Once past San Giorgio Maggiore and La Giudecca, and clear of the smaller islands beyond, you could look in the direction of the mainland and think you were out in the open sea – an illusion strengthened by the tankers that move across the lagoon on their way to or from the port of Marghera. But these huge ocean-going vessels are edging along a few narrow deep-water channels that have been dredged out of the silt; the Venetian lagoon is the largest in Italy, yet its average depth is not much more than one metre.

The nearer islands are the more interesting; the Palladian churches of San Giorgio and La Giudecca are among Venice's most significant Renaissance monuments, while the alleyways of the island are full of reminders of the city's manufacturing past. The Venetian tourist industry began with the development of the Lido, which has now been eclipsed by the city itself as a holiday destination, yet still draws thousands of people to its beaches each year, many of them Italians. A visit to the Armenian island, **San Lazzaro degli Armeni**, makes an absorbing afternoon's round trip, and if you've a bit more time to spare you could undertake an expedition to the fishing town of **Chioggia**, at the southern extremity of the lagoon.

San Giorgio Maggiore

May–Sept Mon–Sat 9.30am–6.30pm, Sun 8.30–10.30am & 2.30–6.30pm; Oct–April Mon–Sat 9.30am–dusk, Sun 8.30–10.30am & 2.30pm–dusk • Free, but €6 for campanile

Palladio's church of **San Giorgio Maggiore**, facing the Palazzo Ducale across the Bacino di San Marco, is one of the most prominent and familiar of all Venetian landmarks. It is a startling building, with an impact that's enhanced by its isolation on an island of its own. Ruskin didn't much care for it: "It is impossible to conceive a design more gross, more barbarous, more childish in conception, more servile in plagiarism, more insipid in result, more contemptible under every point of rational regard." Goethe, on the other hand, sick of the Gothic art that was to Ruskin the touchstone of spiritual health, gave thanks to Palladio for purging his mind of medieval clutter.

Designed in 1565 and completed 45 years later, San Giorgio Maggiore was a greatly influential solution to the chief problem of Renaissance church design: how to use classical forms in a structure that, with its high central nave and lower aisles, had no precedent in classical culture. Palladio's answer was to superimpose two temple fronts: the nave being defined by an upper pediment supported by gigantic Composite columns, and the aisles by lower half-pediments resting on Corinthian pilasters. Inside, the relationship between the major Composite order and the minor Corinthian is maintained, so unifying the facade of the church and its interior. The scale of the building and the use of shadow-casting surfaces ensure that the design retains its clarity when viewed from across the water.

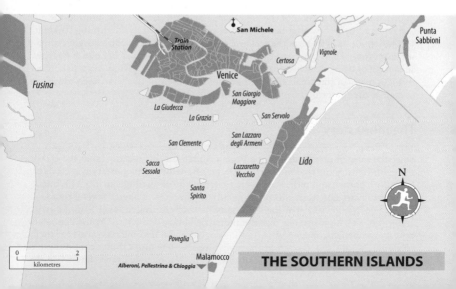

THE SOUTHERN ISLANDS

9

The interior

The Venetians were the first to cover church interiors with white stucco, and the technique is used to dazzling effect in San Giorgio Maggiore – "Of all the colours, none is more proper for churches than white; since the purity of colour, as of the life, is particularly gratifying to God," wrote Palladio. However, the church originally had areas of red plasterwork – the complete whitewashing was carried out in 1650, under the direction of Longhena.

The first altar on the right has an *Adoration of the Shepherds* by **Jacopo Bassano**, which is followed by an alarming *Crucifix* that is sometimes erroneously attributed to Brunelleschi. Most of the other pictures are from the workshop of **Tintoretto**, with two outstanding pictures by the master in the chancel: *The Last Supper*, perhaps the most famous of all Tintoretto's works, and *The Fall of Manna*, one of the few depictions of the event to dwell on the fact that the shower was not a single miraculous deluge but rather a supply that continued for forty years. They were painted as a pair in 1592–94 (the last two years of the artist's life) to illustrate the significance of the Eucharist to the communicants at the altar rail. A *Deposition* of the same date, in the Cappella dei Morti, may well be Tintoretto's last completed painting; like Carpaccio's *St George and the Dragon* (painted several years after the equally gruesome version in the Scuola di San Giorgio degli Schiavoni), it can be seen only on a guided tour, costing €6.

There are few pieces of woodwork in Venice more impressive than the **choirstalls** of San Giorgio Maggiore. Decorated with scenes from the life of St Benedict, they were carved in the late 1590s, as the church was being completed; the bronze figures of *St George* and *St Stephen* on the balustrade were made in the same decade by **Niccolò Roccatagliata**, who also made the florid candlesticks at the entrance to the chancel. Apart from Roccatagliata's pieces, the best sculptures in the church are the *Evangelists* by **Vittoria**, flanking the **tomb of Doge Leonardo Donà**, on the west wall. A close friend of Paolo Sarpi and Galileo, the scholarly Donà was the redoubtable leader of Venice at the time of the Interdict of 1606 (see page 129). The papal nuncio was sent packing by him with the lofty dismissal – "We ignore your excommunication: it is nothing to us. Now think where our resolution would lead, were our example to be followed by others."

The campanile

The door on the left of the choir leads to the **campanile** (€6), via a corridor that houses the original version of the angel that stands on the church's summit; the angel was replaced by a copy after being charred and half-melted by a lightning strike in 1993. Rebuilt in 1791 after the collapse of its predecessor, the San Giorgio campanile surpasses that of San Marco as the best vantage point in Venice, because it has the advantage of being detached from the main part of the city, giving you a panorama that includes many of the canals (all of which are hidden from the San Marco tower) and, of course, the spectacular San Marco campanile itself.

The monastery

Guided tours hourly, daily 10am–5pm; tours in English or French at least 3 times/day – others tours in Italian • €13 • ⓦ cini.it

Since the early ninth century there's been a church on this island, and at the end of the tenth century the lagoon's most important **Benedictine monastery** was established here. Both church and monastery were destroyed by an earthquake in 1223, but were rebuilt straight away, and subsequently renovated and altered several times. Cosimo de' Medici stayed at the monastery in 1433, during his exile from Florence, and it was with his assistance that the monastic library was set up; by the end of the century the Benedictines of San Giorgio Maggiore had become renowned for their erudition. With the upheavals of the early nineteenth century things changed rapidly. In 1806 the Benedictine order was suppressed by Napoleonic decree, and when the

Austrians took over the city they converted the monastery into workshops and offices for their artillery. The decline of the complex continued for another hundred years until, in 1951, it was acquired by Count Vittorio Cini and converted into the home of the **Fondazione Giorgio Cini** (named after Cini's son), a cultural institute that hosts conferences and courses here. Exhibitions are also regularly held at the Fondazione, and the open-air Teatro Verde is occasionally used for plays and concerts.

The restored monastery is one of the architectural wonders of the city. Two adjoining cloisters form the heart of the complex: the **Cloister of the Bay Trees**, planned by Giovanni Buora and built by his son Andrea in the two decades up to 1540; and the **Cloister of the Cypresses**, designed in 1579 by Palladio. Inside, there's a 128m-long **dormitory** by Giovanni Buora (c.1494), a **double staircase** (1641–43) and **library** (1641–53) by Longhena and, approached by an ascent through two anterooms, a magnificent **refectory** by Palladio (1560–62). A dazzlingly accurate reproduction of Veronese's great *Marriage at Cana* fills the end wall of the refectory; the original, stolen by Napoleon's army, is now in the Louvre.

The San Giorgio harbour

The little **harbour** on the other side of the church – flanked by a pair of diminutive lighthouses that were designed in 1813 by a professor of architecture at the Accademia

THE BIG SHIP PROBLEM

If you're in Venice in summer for more than a single day, at some point you'll almost certainly see at least one colossal cruise ship creeping between Giudecca and central Venice, blotting out the buildings on the other side of the water. These oversized vessels are very unpopular in Venice, and not just because they are so hideous: for one thing, there has been no proper assessment of the **environmental damage** they cause (the disturbance of the water lasts for hours after the ships have passed); and for another, the passengers spend little time – and cash – in the city itself.

Unfortunately, Venice's waterways fall under the jurisdiction not of the town hall but of the Venice Port Authority (Autorità Portuale di Venezia), which in the last few years has turned Venice into the **Mediterranean's busiest destination for cruise ships**. A lot of jobs have been created by the ever-expanding APV, both directly and indirectly, and this is at a time when the petrochemical complexes on the mainland have been in decline. And the APV has some powerful allies, not least the company that manages Marco Polo airport, which is used by many of the cruise passengers at the start or end of their trip.

However, attitudes changed somewhat after the *Costa Concordia* ran aground off the Tuscan coast on January 13, 2012, killing 32 people. Francesco Bandarin, of UNESCO, told the Italian government that this accident reinforced "longstanding concern" about the risk that such vessels posed to World Heritage Sites, and to Venice in particular. Perhaps in consequence, in 2014 it was announced that the biggest ships would be banned from the Giudecca canal from 2015. This was widely hailed as good news, but there was a catch: the ban applied only to vessels of more than 95,000 tonnes. To put this in perspective, the *Titanic* was less than half that weight. As a long-term solution, environmentalists have proposed that the cruisers should be removed from the lagoon by building an offshore terminal near the Lido, from where passengers could be shuttled into town on smaller vessels. This idea is opposed by businessman Luigi Brugnaro, who became Venice's mayor in June 2015. He backs the APV's scheme to divert the mega-cruisers to the city docks via the southern lagoon. This would entail redredging the Canale Contorta to accommodate the huge ships – an intervention that critics say will damage the local ecosystem even more than the cruise ships do at the moment.

Cruise ships are getting bigger with every year – the majority of cruisers scheduled to come into operation by 2021 exceed the 95,000 tonne limit. Venice, some argue, cannot afford to lose the custom that these monsters might bring, and everything should be done to lure them into the lagoon. In the words of Sandro Trevisanato, boss of the port's passenger terminal: "Once certain ships are excluded from Venice, they won't come back." Which is exactly what a lot of Venetians are hoping.

9

– was expanded during the second French occupation of 1806–15, when Napoleon decided to accord the island the status of a free port, in emulation of the tariff-free port of Trieste. Nowadays it's used by pleasure craft and by the Cini foundation, and has a café that gives a glorious panorama of the city. Round the corner from the café, exhibitions of modern glass are held in the Cini foundation's **Stanze del Vetro**, and glass-related artworks are often installed in the surrounding area.

La Giudecca

In the earliest records of Venice the chain of islets now called **La Giudecca** was known as Spina Longa, a name clearly derived from its shape. The modern name might refer to the Jews (*Giudei*) who lived here from the late thirteenth century until their removal to the Ghetto, but is most likely to originate with the disruptive noble families who in the ninth century were shoved into this district to keep them out of mischief (*giudicati* means "judged"). Before the Brenta River became the prestigious site for summer abodes, La Giudecca was where the wealthiest aristocrats of early Renaissance Venice built their villas. Michelangelo, self-exiled from Florence in 1529, consoled himself in the gardens of this island, traces of which remain on its south side. The most extensive of La Giudecca's surviving private gardens, the so-called Garden of Eden (at the end of the Rio della Croce), is the biggest in Venice; its name refers not to its paradisal properties but to a certain Mr Eden, the English gardener who planted it.

Giudecca was also the city's **industrial** inner suburb: vaporetti used to be made here; an asphalt factory and a distillery were once neighbours on the western end; and the matting industry, originating in the nineteenth century, kept going until 1950. However, the present-day island is a potent emblem of Venice's loss of economic self-sufficiency in the twentieth century, with abandoned workshops and roofless sheds littering the southern side of the island. Giudecca's last factory closed in the mid-1990s, when timepiece manufacturer Junghans – one of the city's major employers for half a century – called it a day. Tourism, inevitably, has filled the vacuum: the deluxe

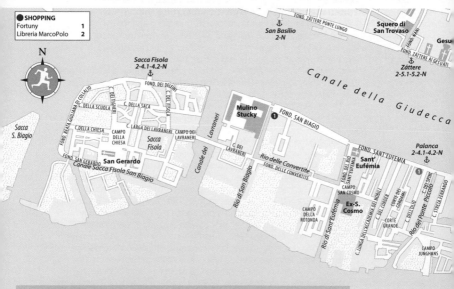

LA GIUDECCA AND SAN GIORGIO MAGGIORE

Cipriani hotel occupies the eastern extremity, while the western edge is dominated by the immense Stucky flour mill, which has become a Hilton.

But in recent years La Giudecca has undergone something of a rejuvenation: a number of housing developments and ancillary social facilities have been built, and under the aegis of the Judecanova consortium a variety of substantial projects is under way: a nautical centre has been constructed within one of the deserted factories, for example, and a residential block for students has risen on the site of the Junghans factory, next door to a beautiful old school building that has been converted into an annexe of the university.

Le Zitelle and the Casa de Maria

The first vaporetto stop after San Giorgio Maggiore is close to the tiny church of the **Zitelle**, which was built in 1582–86 from plans devised some years earlier by Palladio, albeit for a different site. At the moment Le Zitelle is open only for pre-booked visits – details on ⓦgioiellinascostidivenezia.it. The **Casa de Maria**, to the right of the Zitelle, is an inventive reworking of the Venetian Gothic style, built as a studio by the painter Mario de Maria in 1910–13. Its diaper-pattern brickwork, derived from that of the Palazzo Ducale, is the only example of its kind in a Venetian domestic building. The house is now home to the Tre Oci exhibition space, a venue for modern art and photography shows.

Il Redentore

Campo del Santissimo Redentore • Mon–Sat 10.30am–4.30pm • €3, or Chorus Pass • ⓦ chorusvenezia.org

La Giudecca's main monument is the Franciscan church of **Il Redentore**, designed by **Palladio** in 1577. In 1575–76 Venice suffered an outbreak of plague which killed nearly fifty thousand people – virtually a third of the city's population. The Redentore ("Redeemer") was built by the Senate in thanks for Venice's deliverance, and every year until the downfall of the Republic the doge and his senators attended a Mass

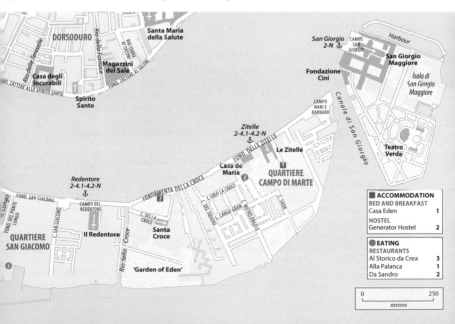

A STROLL THROUGH LA GIUDECCA

For a taste of the economic past and present of La Giudecca, turn down the Fondamenta del Rio di Sant'Eufemia; a circuitous stroll from Campo di San Cosma (where the ex-church of Santi Cosma e Damiano has been converted into a centre for small-scale businesses) to the Rio Ponte Lungo will take you through the core of Giudecca's former manufacturing district. The interior of the island on the other side of the Rio Ponte Lungo is not so densely built up, with a fair amount of open space around the Redentore and the hulk of Santa Croce church. There's even a vineyard behind the Zitelle. Frustratingly, hardly any of La Giudecca's alleyways lead down to the lagoon on the south side; if you want a view across the water in that direction, it's best to take Calle Michelangelo, which comes onto the main fondamenta between the Zitelle and the youth hostel.

here to renew their declaration of gratitude, walking to the church over a pontoon bridge from the Záttere. The Festa del Redentore has remained a major event on the Venetian calendar.

Palladio's commission called for a church to which there would be three distinct components: a choir for the monks to whom the church was entrusted, a tribune around the altar for the dignitaries of the city and a nave with side chapels for the humbler worshippers. The architect's scheme, in which the tribune forms a circular chapel which opens into the nave and blends into the choir through a curved screen of columns, is the most sophisticated of his church projects, as well as the one most directly evolved from the architecture of ancient Rome. Unfortunately, an appreciation of the building's subtleties is difficult, as a rope prevents visitors going beyond the nave.

In the side chapels you'll find a couple of pictures by Francesco Bassano and an *Ascension* by Tintoretto and his assistants, but the best paintings – including a *John the Baptist* by **Jacopo Bassano**, a *Baptism of Christ* by **Paolo Veronese** and *Madonna with Child and Angels* by **Alvise Vivarini** – are in the sacristy, which is rarely opened. The sacristy also has a peculiar array of eighteenth-century wax heads of illustrious Franciscans in various attitudes of agony and ecstasy, displayed in glass cases.

Sant'Eufemia

Fondamenta Sant'Eufemia • Mon–Sat 8.30am–noon & 3–5pm, Sun 3–7pm • Free

Founded in the ninth century and often rebuilt, the church of **Sant'Eufemia** is one of Venice's most engaging stylistic discords, with a late sixteenth-century portico, the nave and aisles still laid out as in the original basilica (with some eleventh-century columns and capitals), and – above the bare brick of the damp-ravaged lower walls – frilly stuccowork and boudoir-like painted decoration. It has one good picture, immediately on your right as you go in: *St Roch and an Angel* (with lunette of *Madonna and Child*), the central panel of a triptych painted in 1480 by Bartolomeo Vivarini.

Mulino Stucky

Beyond Sant'Eufemia, on Fondamenta San Biagio, stands the HQ of the **Fortuny** company, which still makes some of the sumptuous fabrics designed by its founder. Towering over it is the gargantuan neo-Gothic **Mulino Stucky**, which got to look the way it does in 1895–96, after Giovanni Stucky brought in a German architect, Ernst Wullekopf, to expand his flour mill. Planning permission for the brick bastion that Wullekopf came up with was obtained by the simple expedient of threatening to sack all the workers if consent were withheld by the council. By the beginning of the twentieth century Stucky had become one of the richest men in the city, and in 1908 he bought one of the Canal Grande's less discreet houses, the Palazzo Grassi. He didn't enjoy his occupancy for long, though – in 1910 one of his employees murdered him at the train station. With the development of the industrial sector at Marghera after World War I, the Mulino Stucky went into a nose dive, and in 1954 it closed. For decades after that, its future was a perennially contentious issue: there was talk of converting the mill into a sports centre or something else that might be of use to the people of Venice, but instead it's inevitably become a five-star hotel – the *Molino Stucky Hilton*.

Unless you fancy a dip in the municipal swimming pool, there's no point in going past the Stucky; **Sacca Fisola**, the next island along, was created in the last century to make space for the apartment buildings that now occupy much of it.

San Lazzaro degli Armeni

Guided tours daily 3.25pm • €6 • The #20 boat leaves San Zaccaria 15min before the tour starts and returns within 10min of the end

No foreign community has a longer pedigree in Venice than the Armenians. Their position in the economy of the city, primarily as tradesmen and moneylenders, was secure by the end of the thirteenth century, and for around five hundred years they have had their own church within a few yards of the Piazza (see page 70). The Armenians are far less numerous now than formerly, and the most conspicuous sign of their presence is the Armenian island by the Lido, **San Lazzaro degli Armeni**, identifiable from the city by the onion-shaped summit of its campanile.

From the late twelfth century to the beginning of the seventeenth the island was a leper colony (hence *Lazzaro*, Lazarus being the patron saint of lepers), but the land was disused when in 1717 an Armenian monastery was founded here by one Manug di Pietro. Known as **Mekhitar** ("The Consoler"), he had been driven by the Turks from the religious foundation he had established with Venetian aid in the Peloponnese. Within a few years the monks of San Lazzaro earned a wide reputation as scholars and linguists, a reputation that has persisted to the present. And if you're wondering how this monastery escaped suppression by Napoleon, when Venice's other monasteries were closed down, it's allegedly connected with the presence of an indispensable Armenian official in Napoleon's secretariat.

The monastery

Tours are conducted by one of the resident monks, and you can expect him to be trilingual, at least. The tour begins in the turquoise-ceilinged church, in which you'll be given a brief introduction to the culture of Armenia in general and the San Lazzaro Armenians in particular – whereas the Armenian Church is Orthodox, San Lazzaro is an Armenian Catholic foundation, which means it follows the Roman liturgy but is not subject to the authority of the pope. Reflecting the encyclopedic interests of its occupants, the monastery is in places like a whimsically arranged museum; at one end of the old **library**, for example, a mummified Egyptian body is laid out near the sarcophagus in which it was found, while at the other is a teak and ivory throne that once seated the governor of Delhi. The monastery's collection of precious manuscripts and books – the former going back to the fifth century – is another highlight of the visit, occupying a modern rotunda in the heart of the complex.

Elsewhere you'll see antique metalwork, extraordinarily intricate Chinese ivory carvings, pieces of Roman pottery, a gallery of paintings by Armenian painters, a ceiling panel by the young Giambattista Tiepolo and Canova's figure of Napoleon's infant son, which sits in a corner of the book-lined chamber in which Byron studied while lending a hand with the preparation of an Armenian–English dictionary – it took him just six months to acquire a working knowledge of the language, it's said. The tour might also take you into a small museum dedicated to Mekhitar (featuring the scourging chain found on his body after his death), but will certainly end at the monastery's shop. A polyglot press was founded on San Lazzaro in 1789 and an

9

Armenian press is still administered from here, although since 1992 the printing – of everything from books to wine labels – has been done out at Punta Sabbioni. If you're looking for an unusual present to take home, you could buy something here: the old maps and prints of Venice are a bargain.

The Lido

The **Lido** remained an unspoilt strip of land until well into the nineteenth century. Byron used to gallop his horses across the fields of the Lido every day, and as late as 1869 Henry James could describe this island as "a very natural place". Before the century was out, however, it had become the smartest **bathing resort** in Italy, and its prestige lasted for a good while. Until 1960, the grass runway of the Lido's tiny airport was the only point of arrival for tourists flying into the city. Nowadays the beaches are still busy in summer, but the Lido is nothing like as chic as it was when Thomas Mann installed Aschenbach, the central figure of *Death in Venice*, as a guest at the fabulously opulent *Grand Hotel des Bains*. It's indicative of the downturn in the Lido's fortunes that *des Bains* went out of business in 2009, and that the developers who intended to convert it into luxury apartments had to pull the plug on the scheme in 2015; a consortium now plans to reopen the place as a hotel, although the building has deteriorated in the interim and most of its furnishings and fittings have been flogged off.

The hotels along the seafront will charge you a ludicrous fee to rent one of their beach huts for the day, and would like you to believe that you have to pay them for the privilege of merely stepping onto the portion of sand that they overlook. However,

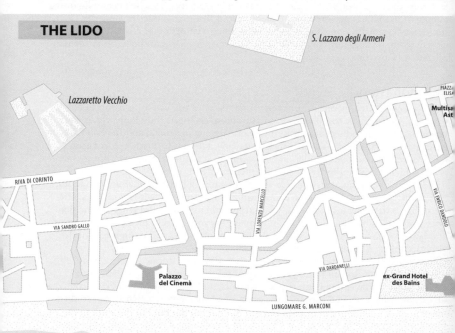

THE LIDO

S. Lazzaro degli Armeni

Lazzaretto Vecchio

PIAZZ
ELISA

Multisa
Ast

RIVA DI CORINTO

VIA LORENZO MARCELLO

VIA ENRICO DANDOLO

VIA SANDRO GALLO

VIA DARDANELLI

Palazzo
del Cinemà

ex-Grand Hotel
des Bains

LUNGOMARE G. MARCONI

during the 2007 film festival actor Rupert Everett was evicted from a prime spot, having spread his towel without opening his wallet, and he duly complained to the authorities, who upheld his claim that the beach should be accessible to all. So you can in theory paddle and sunbathe wherever you like, but if you lack Rupert's chutzpah you may well feel more comfortable on the **public beaches** at the northern and southern ends of the island – but bear in mind that this stretch of the Adriatic isn't one of the cleanest. The northern beach is twenty minutes' walk from the vaporetto stop; the southern one, right by the municipal golf course, necessitates a bus journey, and is consequently less of a crush.

The monuments of the Lido

The green-domed Santa Maria della Vittoria might be the most conspicuous Lido monument on the lagoon side of the island, but at close quarters it's revealed as a thoroughly abject thing. In fact, in the vicinity of the Piazzale one building alone – the **Fortezza di Sant'Andrea** – is of much interest, and you have to admire that from a distance, across the Porto di Lido. The principal defence of the main entrance to the lagoon, the Fortezza was designed by **Sanmicheli**; work began on it in 1543, in the face of some scepticism as to whether the structure would be strong enough to support the Venetian artillery. The doubters were silenced when practically all the cannons in the Arsenale were brought out to the Fortezza and fired simultaneously from its terraces, with no harmful effects except to the eardrums. Never one to overlook a commercial opportunity, Luigi Brugnaro, Venice's mayor, has announced a plan to convert the crumbling fort into a "*grande polo del lusso*" ("a great pole of luxury") – in other words, yet another super-exclusive island resort.

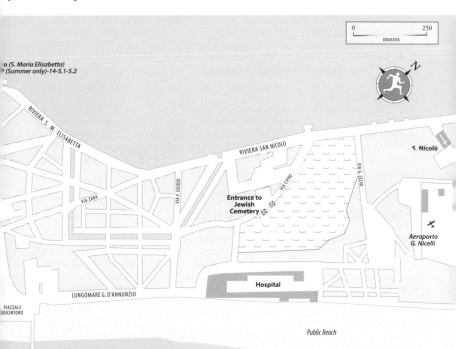

THE SPOSALIZIO

The most operatic of Venice's state ceremonials – the **Marriage of Venice to the Sea** or *Sposalizio* – began as a way of commemorating the exploits of Doge Pietro Orseolo II, who on Ascension Day of the year 1000 set sail to subjugate the pirates of the Dalmatian coast. (Orseolo's standard, by the way, featured possibly the first representation of what was to become the emblem of Venice – the Lion of Saint Mark with its paw on an open book.) According to legend, the ritual reached its definitive form after the Venetians had brought about the reconciliation of Pope Alexander III and Frederick Barbarossa in 1177; the grateful Alexander is supposed to have given the doge the first of the gold rings with which Venice was symbolically married to the Adriatic. It's more likely that the essential components of the ritual – the voyage out to the Porto di Lido in the *Bucintoro* with an escort of garlanded vessels, the dropping of the ring into the brine, "In sign of our true and perpetual dominion" and the disembarkation for Mass at the church of San Nicolò al Lido – were all fixed by the middle of the twelfth century. Nowadays the mayor, patriarch and a gaggle of other VIPs annually enact a sad facsimile of the grand occasion. And in case you're wondering what happened to all those gold rings, a fifteenth-century traveller recorded – "After the ceremony, many strip and dive to the bottom to seek the ring. He who finds it keeps it for his own, and, what's more, lives for that year free from all the burdens to which dwellers in that republic are subject."

The church and Franciscan monastery of **San Nicolò**, from where you get a good view of the Fortezza, were founded in 1044, when there wasn't so much as a brick wall in the area. The doge and his entourage used to visit this church twice a year: on Ascension Day, after the aquatic wedding service, and on the feast day of St Nicholas of Myra (aka Father Christmas), whose body, so the Venetians claimed, had rested here since it was stolen from the Norman port of Bari in 1099. In fact the theft never happened – the Venetian raid on Bari was a classic piece of disinformation, devised to score points off the Normans, and the grand display on the saint's day was a propagandist sham. The present church is notable for its splendid seventeenth-century choirstalls, featuring a multitude of scenes from the life of St Nicholas, and a few scraps of mosaic that have survived from the eleventh-century building.

Jewish cemetery

Via Cipro • Guided tours arranged by the Museo Ebraico; details at ⓦ museoebraico.it

Via Cipro, facing the San Nicolò vaporetto stop, is where you'll find the entrance to Venice's **Jewish cemetery**, which was founded in 1386 and in places has fallen into eloquent decay. Adjoining is a Catholic burial ground, in a corner of which have been stacked the stones from the old Protestant cemetery, ploughed over in the 1930s to make more room for the Lido's tiny airstrip.

From the Lido to Chioggia

There are no major sights between the Lido and Chioggia, unless you count the vast eighteenth-century flood barrier known as the Murazzi. But Chioggia itself is well worth a look, because its distance from the centre of Venice has allowed it to remain authentically itself: whereas the main islands of the northern lagoon have been swamped by tourism, in Chioggia fishing rather than hospitality remains the chief source of revenue.

TRANSPORT TO CHIOGGIA

The quickest way to get from central Venice to **Chioggia** is by land bus from Piazzale Roma, but it's a dispiriting drive and ACTV tourist passes are not valid on this route. Much better to go **via the Lido**, where there are two options: the #11 vaporetto, via Alberoni and Pellestrina, which runs approximately every hour and takes 75min; or by a combination of land bus and boat. The latter option, which takes more or less the same time, involves taking the half-hourly #11 bus from Gran Viale Santa Maria Elisabetta (by the Lido landing stage) down to Alberoni, where it drives onto a ferry for the five-minute hop to Pellestrina; the 10km to the southern tip of Pellestrina are covered by road, and then you switch from the bus to a steamer for the 25-minute crossing to Chioggia. In high season there's also a boat service from San Zaccaria to Chioggia, but it's not operated by ACTV, and it takes about 1hr 40min.

Malamocco

The village of **Malamocco** is the successor of the ancient settlement called Metamauco, which in the eighth century was the capital of the lagoon confederation. In 810 the town was taken by **Pepin**, son of Charlemagne, and there followed one of the crucial battles in Venice's history, when Pepin's fleet, endeavouring to reach the islands of Rivoalto (the forerunner of Venice), became jammed in the mudbanks and was swiftly pounced upon. After the battle the capital was promptly transferred to the safer islands of Rivoalto, and in 1107 the old town was destroyed by a tidal wave. The rebuilt town's most appealing feature – the church's scaled-down replica of the Campanile of San Marco – can be seen without getting off the bus. Incidentally, Malamocco provides one of the bloodier footnotes of Venetian history – the **Canal Orfano**, off the Malamocco shore, was the spot where some of those condemned by the Council of Ten were bound, gagged, weighted and thrown overboard by the executioner. (If you take the vaporetto to San Lazzaro you pass along a section of it.)

Pellestrina

Fishing is the mainstay of life in the village of **Pellestrina**, which is strung out along nearly a third of the 10km of the island that neighbours Malamocco. There's one remarkable old structure here, but you get the best view of it as the boat crosses to Chioggia. This is the **Murazzi**, the colossal walls of Istrian boulders, 4km long and 14m thick at the base, which were constructed at the sides of the Porto di Chioggia to protect Venice from the battering of the sea. The maintenance of the water level in the lagoon has always been a preoccupation of Venetian life: very early in the city's

POVEGLIA

The most ferocious defenders of the lagoon in the war against Pepin came from the small island of **Poveglia**, just off Malamocco. Once populous enough to have a practically independent administration, it suffered greatly in the war against Genoa (see page 319) and went into a steep decline immediately after, becoming little more than a fort and a quarantine station. By the eighteenth century there was so little use for Poveglia's church that its campanile was turned into a lighthouse. For much of the last century it was a hospital island, but since the closure of the hospital in the late 1960s it has been abandoned. Locally Poveglia has a reputation as a haunted place: folklore has it that a number of insane patients were murdered by a doctor at the Poveglia hospital, and it's widely believed that huge numbers of plague victims are buried in its soil.

The Italian government, desperate for cash, has recently been auctioning various pieces of state-owned real estate all over the country. In May 2014 Poveglia **came up for sale**, and was bought for €513,000 by businessman Luigi Brugnaro, who outbid a local collective called Poveglia Per Tutti (Poveglia For All). When Brugnaro – who in June 2015 became the city's mayor – made it clear that he had bought the island to prevent it from being converted into yet another five-star hotel or conference centre, and that he intended to spend €20 million on the restoration of its derelict buildings, it seemed that the locals were going to get what they wanted after all. Then the government stepped in, declaring that Brugnaro's offer was too low to be acceptable. So things are up in the air again. Poveglia Per Tutti has proposed that the island remain in state hands, and be developed for "local use", but nobody is betting against Poveglia's becoming, eventually, a foreign-owned resort of some sort.

9

development, for example, the five gaps in the *lidi* (the Lido–Chioggia sandbars) were reduced to the present three to strengthen the barrier against the Adriatic and to increase the dredging action of the tides through the three remaining *porti*. In time a special state official, the Magistrato alle Acque, was appointed to supervise the management of the lagoon, and the Murazzi were the last major project undertaken by the magistrato's department. Devised as a response to the increased flooding of the early eighteenth century, the Murazzi took 38 years to build, and remained unbreached from 1782 (the year of their completion) until the great flood of November 1966. In recent years the beaches of Pellestrina have been widened and raised to lessen the force of the action of the sea, but the biggest flood-prevention project involves the installation of submersible floodgates at the inlets of the Lido, Malamocco and Chioggia (see page 343).

Chioggia

Founded as a Roman port, **Chioggia** is the second-largest settlement in the lagoon after Venice, and one of Italy's busiest fishing ports. With the exception of a single church, you can see every significant building in an hour's walk up and down the **Corso del Popolo**, the principal street in Chioggia's gridiron layout. (The walk is especially enjoyable on a Thursday, when the weekly market takes over the whole Corso.) The exception is the church of **San Domenico**, which houses Carpaccio's *St Paul*, his last known painting, plus a couple of pictures by Leandro Bassano; you get to it by taking the bridge to the left of the Chioggia landing stage and going straight on.

Along Corso del Popolo

The boat sets you down at the **Piazzetta Vigo**, at the head of the **Corso**, where a pathetic excuse for a lion sits on top of a column – it's known to the condescending Venetians as the Cat of Saint Mark. Only the thirteenth-century campanile of the church of **San Andrea** is likely to catch your eye before the street widens at the **Granaio**, a grain warehouse built in 1322 but spoiled by nineteenth-century restorers; the facade relief of the *Madonna and Child* is by Sansovino. Behind the Granaio is the **fish market**; open for business every morning except Monday, it's quite a spectacle.

In the Piazzetta Venti Settembre, immediately after the town hall, there's the church of the **Santissima Trinità**, radically altered in 1703 by Andrea Tirali and almost perpetually shut – the Oratory, behind the main altar, has an impressive ceiling set with paintings by followers of Tintoretto. **San Giacomo Apostolo**, a bit further on, has a sub-Tiepolo ceiling by local boy Il Chiozzotto, and a much venerated fifteenth-century painting known as the *Madonna della Navicella*. Soon you pass a house once occupied by the

---

THE SIEGE OF CHIOGGIA

Chioggia secured its place in the annals of Venetian history in 1379, when it became the scene of the most serious threat to Venice since Pepin's invasion, as the Genoese, after copious shedding of blood on both sides, took possession of the town. Venice at this time had two outstanding admirals: the first, **Vettor Pisani**, was in prison on a charge of military negligence; the second, **Carlo Zeno**, was somewhere off in the East. So serious was the threat to the city that Pisani was promptly released, and then put in command of the fleet that set out in December – with the doge himself on board – to blockade the enemy. Zeno and his contingent sailed over the horizon on the first day of the new year and there followed months of siege warfare, in the course of which the Venetian navy employed shipboard cannons for the first time. (Casualties from cannonballs were as high on the Venetian side as on the Genoese, and some crews refused to operate these suicidal weapons more than once a day.) In June 1380, with Chioggia in ruins, the enemy surrendered, and from then until the arrival of Napoleon the Venetian lagoon remained impregnable.

family of Rosalba Carriera and later by Goldoni, and then, on the opposite side of the road, the **Tempio di San Martino**, which was built immediately after the war of 1380.

The **Duomo** was the first major commission for **Longhena**, who was called in to design a new church after the previous cathedral was burned down in 1623; the detached fourteenth-century campanile survived the blaze. The chapel to the left of the chancel contains half a dozen good eighteenth-century paintings, including one attributed to Tiepolo; on overcast days they're virtually invisible, a drawback that some might regard as a blessing in view of the subjects depicted – *The Torture of Boiling Oil, The Torture of the Razors, The Beheading of Two Martyrs* and so on.

Buses run from the duomo to **Sottomarina**, Chioggia's down-market answer to Venice's Lido.

The "Hospital Islands"

San Lazzaro is the only minor island of the southern lagoon that's of interest to tourists. The boat out to San Lazzaro calls first at **La Grazia**, successively a pilgrims' hostel, a monastery and a hospital, before being acquired by a business consortium for conversion into a resort-hotel. Next stop is **San Servolo**, once one of the most important Benedictine monasteries in the region (founded in the ninth century), then a psychiatric hospital, then the home of the Council of Europe's School of Craftsmanship and now the base of Venice International University. From time to time the university stages art exhibitions on the island.

San Clemente, to the south of La Grazia, was another hospital island until 1992. After a period as a refuge for Venice's stray cats, it was converted into a super-plush hotel, which went belly-up in the wake of the post-2008 recession; having changed hands, it's now the *San Clemente Palace* resort. A similar conversion has happened on nearby **Sacca Sessola**, an artificial island created in the nineteenth century; once home to a tuberculosis sanatorium, it's been rebranded *Isola delle Rose* (Island of Roses) by the Marriott group.

Until the mid-seventeenth century there was a monastery on **Santo Spirito**, with a church redesigned by Sansovino, but when the order was suppressed most of its treasures, including paintings by Titian, were sent to the Salute church, where they can now be seen.

Lazzaretto Vecchio (south of San Lazzaro) was the site of a pilgrims' hostel from the twelfth century, then took a place in medical history when, in 1423, it became Europe's first permanent isolation hospital for plague victims. A new museum, called the Museo Archeologico della Città e della Laguna di Venezia, is planned for the island, and preliminary work on the project began some time ago. Progress has been hampered, though, by the discovery of mass graves below the building site. The excavation of these graves hit the headlines in 2009, when a skeleton with a brick crammed between its jaws was found in a pit for victims of the plague of 1576. It was once a widespread belief that the plague was spread by vampires, and that vampires, after interment, revived themselves by feeding on neighbouring corpses, a process that could be stopped only by forcing something inedible into their mouths. In the words of Matteo Borrini, an anthropologist from the University of Florence, the brick-eating skeleton of Lazzaretto Vecchio "is the first time that archeology has succeeded in reconstructing the ritual of exorcism of a vampire".

GRITTI PALACE, SAN MARCO

Accommodation

Insatiable demand makes Venice's hotels the most expensive in western Europe, with some one-star places charging in excess of €150 for a double room in high season, and a few super-luxe establishments demanding well upward of €1000. What's more, the high season here is longer than anywhere else in the country – it is officially classified as running from March 15 to November 15 and then from December 21 to January 6, but some places don't recognize the existence of a low season any more. A few hotels, on the other hand, lower their prices in August, as every Italian knows that Venice is hellishly humid and overcrowded at that time, and that many restaurants and bars will be shut for the vacation. There are, though, a few good-value hotels to be found in the city, and an ever-increasing number of bed and breakfast places, as well as a plethora of apartments for rent.

It's never a good idea to turn up in Venice without reserving your accommodation first, and if you intend to stay here at any time during the official high season (or Carnevale) it's wisest to book your place at least six months in advance. Bear in mind, also, that many hotels – especially the smaller ones – require you to stay for a minimum of two or three nights in high season.

HOTELS

Venice has in excess of four hundred **hotels**, ranging from spartan one-star joints to five-star establishments in which a suite will set you back €6000/night in summer, or more. What follows is a rundown of the best choices in all categories. Our guide price indicates the average cost of a standard double room in high season; bear in mind that off-season prices can be considerably lower than this and that prices can fluctuate even in high season, according to demand. Many hotels offer large discounts on rooms booked well in advance, on a non-refundable basis – reductions of twenty-five percent or more are not uncommon. Note also that you pay through the nose for your proximity to the Piazza, so if you want maximum comfort for your money, decide how much you can afford then look for a place outside the San Marco *sestiere* – after all, it's a small city.

In 2000 Italy's laws relating to tourist accommodation were relaxed, which resulted in the opening of several guesthouses called **locande**, and the appearance of a number of private houses offering bed and breakfast. The prefix *locanda* doesn't necessarily indicate an inexpensive place: some upmarket hotels use the label to give their image a more homely finish. The majority of *locande*, however, are small family-run establishments, offering accommodation equivalent to three- or even four-star hotels (24hr room service is just about the only facility they don't provide), but often at considerably lower cost.

SAN MARCO

★ **Ai Do Mori** Calle Larga S. Marzo 658 ☎ 041 528 9293, ⓦ hotelaidomori.com; map p.38. Very friendly, and situated a few paces off the Piazza, this is a top recommendation for budget travellers. The top-floor room has a private terrace looking over the roofs of the Basilica and the Torre dell'Orologio, and is one of the most attractive (and, of course, expensive) one-star rooms in the city. All rooms have their own bathroom. **€160**

Al Gambero Calle dei Fabbri 4687 ☎ 041 522 4384, ⓦ locandaalgambero.com; map p.38. Twenty-six-room three-star hotel in an excellent position a short distance off the north side of the Piazza; many of the rooms overlook a canal that's on the standard gondola route from the Bacino Orseolo. There's a busy (and good) restaurant on the ground floor. **€250**

Ala Campo S. Maria del Giglio 2494 ☎ 041 520 8333, ⓦ hotelala.it; map p.36. The 85-room three-star *Ala* has rooms in both modern and traditional Venetian style, and is situated in a perfect location, on a square that opens out onto the mouth of the Canal Grande. **€180**

Art Deco Calle delle Botteghe 2966 ☎ 041 277 0558, ⓦ locandaartdeco.com; map p.36. This cosy *locanda* has a seventeenth-century palazzo setting, but the interior is strewn with 1930s and '40s objects, and the pristinely white bedrooms have modern wrought-iron furniture. **€210**

★ **Casa Petrarca** Calle delle Schiavini 4386 ☎ 041 520 0430, ⓦ casapetrarca.com; map p.36. A very hospitable one-star, one of the cheapest hotels within a stone's throw of the Piazza – but make sure you book well in advance, as it only has seven rooms. **€180**

Fiorita Campiello Nuovo 3457 ☎ 041 523 4754, ⓦ locandafiorita.com; map p.36. Welcoming *locanda* with just ten rooms, so it's crucial to book well in advance. The rooms here are all en suite and decorated in eighteenth-century style, and many are spacious. **€180**

Flora Calle dei Bergamaschi 2283a ☎ 041 520 5844, ⓦ hotelflora.it; map p.36. This large and ivy-clad three-star has been run by the Romanelli family for three generations. Located close to the Piazza, it has a delightful inner garden. Rooms are beautifully decorated with period pieces, though some are a little cramped. **€250**

★ **Gritti Palace** Campo S. Maria del Giglio 2467 ☎ 041 2961 2222, ⓦ hotelgrittipalacevenice.com; map p.36. Reopened in 2013 after a fifteen-month restoration, the *Gritti Palace* – once the home of Doge Andrea Gritti – now offers every hi-tech facility you'd expect of a super-luxe hotel, but has lost none of its famous old-regime opulence. Each of the 61 rooms and 21 suites is unique, but all are replete with antiques and gorgeous furnishings. Even the lowest prices are astronomical, and rooms with a view of the Canal Grande cost a good bit more, but for a once-in-a-lifetime treat, it's hard to beat the *Gritti*. **€1200**

★ **Kette** Piscina S. Moisè 2053 ☎ 041 520 7766, ⓦ hotelkette.com; map p.36. This five-storey, 63-room four-star is a favourite with the upper-bracket tour companies, mainly on account of its central but quiet location, in an alleyway parallel to Calle Larga XXII Marzo. By Venetian standards, it's very moderately priced, and there are very good offers on the website if you book far enough in advance. **€270**

La Fenice et des Artistes Campiello Fenice 1936 ☎ 041 523 2333, ⓦ fenicehotels.it; map p.36. In business for more than a century, and recently refurbished, this seventy-room four-star has long been a favoured hangout of the opera crowd, performers and audience alike. Each room is individually decorated (some are all muted pastels, others

10

are a riot of gold and scarlet) and there's a small garden for breakfast. **€290**

Monaco and Grand Canal Calle Vallaresso 1332 ☎041 520 0211, ⓦhotelmonaco.it; map p.38. The ground-floor rooms on the waterfront side of this famous four-star hotel (now owned by Benetton) look over to the Salute and are kitted out in full-blown old-world Venetian style, with masses of Murano glass and great swags of brocade. In the annexe – the Palazzo Selvadego – you don't get a view of the water, but the decor is in a lighter nouveau-Mediterranean style, with walls of plain warm colour. **€500**

★ **Novecento** Calle del Dose 2683 ☎041 241 3765, ⓦlocandanovecento.it; map p.36. Beautiful, Baglioni intimate and very welcoming *locanda* with nine individually decorated doubles and luxurious bathrooms. Styling is ethnic/eclectic (furnishings from Morocco, China, Japan and Egypt), and there's a small courtyard for breakfast. **€280**

★ **Orseolo** Corte Zorzi 1083 ☎041 520 4827, ⓦlocandaorseolo.com; map p.38. Three four-room B&Bs are joined to form this superb family-run *locanda* overlooking the Orseolo canal, 50m north of Piazza S. Marco. Most rooms are spacious and light, the breakfasts substantial, and the staff extremely hospitable. Entrance is through a gate in Campo S. Gallo. **€260**

★ **Palazzetto Pisani** Campo Pisani 2814 ☎041 523 2550, ⓦpalazzettopisani.com; map p.36. This super-luxury *relais* – hidden down an alley off Campo Pisani, near Santo Stefano – occupies parts of two adjacent sixteenth-century palazzi (Palazzetto Pisani and Palazzo Benzon Foscolo) that sit beside the Canal Grande very near the Accademia Bridge, and are still owned by descendants of the once mega-rich Pisani family. All of the rooms are fine (many of them overlook the water), and the best of the suites – the Doge's – is out of this world. **€250**

Rosa Salva Calle Fiubera 951 ☎041 241 3323, ⓦrosasalvahotel.it; map p.38. If you're looking for a stylish but not madly expensive hotel right in the heart of the city, you can't do better than the new Rosa Salva hotel. Run by the family who own the city's best-known pasticceria-caffès (there's a branch next door), it has 22 rooms (mostly spacious, by the standards of central Venice) that are furnished and decorated in contemporary style, in which bare wood, leather and soft metallic tones predominate. This zone of San Marco is very busy in high season, but soundproofed windows keep noise to a minimum. **€260**

San Samuele Salizzada S. Samuele 3358 ☎041 522 8045, ⓦhotelsansamuele.com; map p.36. A friendly one-star close to the Palazzo Grassi, with unfussy and individually decorated rooms, some en suite. **€180**

DORSODURO

Accademia Villa Maravege Fondamenta Bollani 1058 ☎041 521 0188, ⓦpensioneaccademia.it; map p.82. Once the Russian embassy, this three-star seventeenth-century villa has a devoted following, not least on account of its garden, which occupies a promontory at the convergence of two canals, with a view of a section of the Canal Grande. **€250**

Agli Alboretti Rio Terrà Foscarini 884 ☎041 523 0058, ⓦaglialboretti.com; map p.82. Friendly and popular family-run three-star, well situated right next to the Accademia. The rooms are plain, but all have a/c and TV, and its high-season prices compare very favourably with those of most others in this category. **€180**

American Dinesen Fondamenta Bragadin 628 ☎041 520 4733, ⓦhotelamerican.com; map p.82. Nicely located, well-refurbished and welcoming three-star, with some rooms overlooking the Rio di San Vio, a couple of minutes' stroll from the Accademia. **€300**

★ **Ca' Maria Adele** Rio Terrà dei Catecumeni 111 ☎041 520 3078, ⓦcamariaadele.it; map p.82. Five of the twelve rooms in this very upmarket *locanda* are so-called "theme rooms", with every item designed to enhance a particular atmosphere – the Sala Noir, for example, is a "voluptuous and hot" creation in cocoa and spice tones. Others include the "Oriental" and the "Moorish" rooms. The non-themed accommodation is less artfully conceived (and a lot less expensive), but spacious and comfortable. The adjacent two-room B&B, *Palazzetto 113*, is similarly sybaritic, and similarly priced. **€350**

★ **Ca' Pisani** Rio Terrà Foscarini 979a ☎041 240 1411, ⓦcapisanihotel.it; map p.82. This glamorous and well-priced 29-room four-star, just a few metres from the Accademia, created quite a stir when it opened in 2000, partly because of its location, on the opposite side of the Canal Grande from its top-echelon peers, but chiefly because of its high-class retro look. Taking its cue from the Art Deco style of the 1930s and '40s, the *Ca' Pisani* makes heavy use of dark wood and chrome, a refreshing break from the Renaissance and Rococo flourishes that tend to prevail in Venice's upmarket establishments. **€300**

DD 724 Ramo da Mula 724 ☎041 277 0262, ⓦthecharminghouse.com; map p.82. In a city awash with nostalgia, the cool high-grade modernist style of this *locanda*, right by the Guggenheim, comes as a welcome change. It has just seven rooms, each of them impeccably cool and luxurious – and not a Murano chandelier in sight. As you'll see on the website, the same team runs a couple of other similarly sleek properties: a palazzo by Santa Maria Formosa, containing four suites; and a single apartment close to *DD 724*. **€370**

★ **La Calcina** Zàttere ai Gesuati 780 ☎041 520 6466, ⓦlacalcina.com; map p.82. Charismatic old three-star hotel in the house where Ruskin wrote much of *The Stones of Venice*. From the more expensive rooms you can gaze across to the Redentore, a church that gave him apoplexy. All rooms have parquet floors (unusual in Venice), and antique wooden furniture. Its restaurant (see page 215) is good too. **€300**

★ **Locanda San Barnaba** Calle del Traghetto 2785 ☎041 241 1233, ⓦlocanda-sanbarnaba.com; map p.82. Exceptionally pleasant and nicely priced *locanda* right by the Ca' Rezzonico. It's worth paying a bit extra for one of the "superior double" rooms, which have eighteenth-century frescoes on the ceilings. €180

Messner Rio Terrà dei Catacumeni 216 ☎041 522 7443, ⓦhotelmessner.com; map p.82. In an excellent, quiet location close to the Salute vaporetto stop, the two-star *Messner* has modern, smart rooms and is run by friendly staff. Some of the rooms are in an annexe round the corner from the smaller but more appealing main building. €220

Montin Fondamenta di Borgo 1147 ☎041 522 7151, ⓦlocandamontin.com; map p.82. The *Montin* is known principally for its upmarket and once-fashionable restaurant; few people realize that it offers some of Venice's best budget accommodation. Only eleven rooms, three of them without private bathroom, all of them plain but perfectly comfortable; the best rooms are spacious and balconied. €170

Palazzo Stern Calle del Traghetto 2792a, Dorsoduro ☎041 277 0869, ⓦpalazzostern.it; map p.82. The *Palazzo Stern* – built in the fifteenth century, then extended in neo-Gothic style in the early twentieth century by the art-collecting Stern family – is one of the Grand Canal's newer hotels, and occupies a prime site, next door to Ca' Rezzonico. A two-year restoration has turned the palace into a sumptuous four-star hotel, with 24 rooms arrayed over four floors. The top-floor standard rooms are nice enough, but are lit by skylights rather than windows, so you may prefer to take a room on the ground floor, or to splash out on a "superior" or "deluxe", overlooking the water. €350

Pausania Fondamenta Gherardini 2824 ☎041 522 2083, ⓦhotelpausania.it; map p.82. This quiet, comfortable and welcoming three-star has a fine location very close to San Barnaba church, just 5min from the Accademia; very good low-season offers – and a nice garden too. €220

Tivoli Crosera S. Pantalon 3838 ☎041 524 2460, ⓦhoteltivoli.it; map p.82. This large and basic two-star, located in the immediate vicinity of the Frari and S. Rocco, often has space when the rest are full. It's also extraordinarily inexpensive. €130

SAN POLO AND SANTA CROCE

★ **Al Ponte Mocenigo** Fondamenta Rimpetto Mocenigo 2063, Santa Croce ☎041 524 4797, ⓦalpontemocenigo.com; map p.100. The relaxed and welcoming *Al Ponte Mocenigo* is one of the best two-stars in the city. Located in a quiet quarter of the Santa Croce *sestiere*, but close to the San Stae vaporetto stop, the main building has just ten rooms, which are focused on a beautiful little courtyard where breakfast is served in good weather. Furnishings and decor are a non-musty version of

the classic eighteenth-century Venetian style, with Murano chandeliers and lots of green, red and gold. The rooms in the adjacent annexe are comfortable too, but it's better to be in the main part. €150

Al Sole Fondamenta Minotto, Santa Croce 136 ☎041 244 0328, ⓦalsolehotels.com; map p.100. Fifty-room three-star hotel in a gorgeous Gothic palazzo near the Frari. The "superior" rooms overlook a quiet canal or the garden, where breakfast is taken in good weather. €200

★ **Ca' Favretto-San Cassiano** Calle della Rosa, Santa Croce 2232 ☎041 524 1768, ⓦsancassiano.it; map p.100. Beautiful 35-room four-star with some rooms looking across the Canal Grande towards the Ca' d'Oro. Has very helpful staff, a nice courtyard garden and a grand entrance hall. It was once the home of the nineteenth-century painter Giacomo Favretto, and is fitted out in the style of the period. Huge off-season discounts. €280

★ **Ca' San Giorgio** Salizada del Fontego dei Turchi 1725, Santa Croce ☎041 275 9177, ⓦcasangiorgio.com; map p.100. Exposed timber beams and walls of raw brick advertise the age of the Gothic palazzo that's occupied by this fine little *locanda*, while the bedrooms are tastefully and very comfortably furnished in quasi-antique style. The gorgeous top-floor suite has its own rooftop terrace. €230

Casa Peron Salizzada S. Pantalon, Santa Croce 84 ☎041 710 021, ⓦalbergo-casa-peron-it; map p.100. A plain, very cheap and congenial one-star in the heart of the university district, very close to San Rocco and the Frari. The rooms are small and clean; most have showers, but few have their own toilet. €130

La Villeggiatura Calle dei Botteri 1569, San Polo ☎041 524 4673, ⓦlavilleggiatura.it; map p.100. This quirky Rialto guesthouse has six individually themed bedrooms, with decor that reflects each room's dedicatee, eg pictures of the four seasons for Vivaldi and *commedia dell'arte* scenes for Goldoni. The Vivaldi is one of two smallish rooms directly under the roof (there's no lift); the other four are more spacious and airy, and the biggest, the Doge, has a nice view of San Cassian church. Excellent breakfast too. It's very popular, so get your reservation in early. €200

Marconi Riva del Vin, San Polo 729 ☎041 522 2068, ⓦhotelmarconi.it; map p.100. Converted from an inn in the 1930s, this three-star hotel is situated just a few metres south of the Rialto Bridge, and offers a view of the Canal Grande from some of its 26 rooms; they vary hugely in price, but most retain some of the charisma of the old building. €260

★ **Oltre Il Giardino**, Fondamenta Contarini 2542, San Polo ☎041 275 0015, ⓦoltreilgiardino-venezia.com; map p.100. This tranquil villa, formerly owned – briefly – by Alma Mahler, has been converted into an immensely stylish six-room hotel; the bedrooms – replete with antiques and works of art – are beautiful and airy, and a gorgeous little garden completes the package. €250

10

10

Palazzetto Madonna Calle Forner S. Elena 2902, San Polo ☎ 041 524 6781, ⓦ palazzettomadonna.com; map p.100. Occupying a beautiful old two-storey palazzo very close to San Tomà, the four-star *Palazzetto Madonna* is one of the best hotels to have opened in Venice in recent years. The decor is imaginative – a vibrant mix of Neoclassic design and bright colour schemes. You might find some of the rooms a little too gaudy (the website has a good gallery of pictures), but there's a high level of comfort throughout, and the management is excellent. Excellent breakfast too. **€370**

Sturion Calle del Sturion, San Polo 679 ☎ 041 523 6243, ⓦ locandasturion.com; map p.100. This immaculate eleven-room three-star has a very long pedigree – the sign of the sturgeon (*sturion*) appears in Carpaccio's *Miracle of the True Cross at the Rialto Bridge* (in the Accademia). It's on a wonderful site overlooking the Canal Grande at the Rialto, and is run by a very welcoming management. Huge discounts in the slack winter weeks. Visitors with mobility difficulties should look elsewhere, however, as the hotel is at the top of three flights of stairs and has no lift. **€230**

CANNAREGIO

★ **Abbazia** Calle Priuli 68 ☎ 041 717 333, ⓦ abbaziahotel.com; map p.120. One of Cannaregio's most restful hotels, the light-filled *Abbazia* occupies a former Carmelite monastery (the monks attached to the Scalzi still live in a building adjoining the hotel), and provides three-star amenities without losing its air of quasi-monastic austerity. Make sure you take in the delightful garden. **€200**

★ **Al Ponte Antico** Calle dell'Aseo 5768 ☎ 041 241 1944, ⓦ alponteantico.com; map p.120. This plush four-star *residenza*, a few metres upstream of the Rialto bridge, is one of the best small hotels in the city. Decorated throughout in eighteenth-century style, with lashings of gold and blue satin in the bedrooms, it has four grades of accommodation – the best rooms, the "Deluxe", have huge windows that open onto the Canal Grande. Exceptionally nice staff, too. **€330**

Antico Doge Sottoportego Falier 5643 ☎ 041 241 1570, ⓦ anticodoge.com; map p.120. Located within a stone's throw of the church of Santi Apostoli, this very comfortable three-star *locanda* occupies part of the palace that once belonged to the disgraced doge Marin Falier. **€260**

Bernardi Semenzato Calle dell'Oca 4366 ☎ 041 522 7257, ⓦ hotelbernardi.com; map p.120. Very inexpensive and rudimentary two-star hidden in a tiny alleyway close to Campo S. Apostoli, with bright and good-sized rooms. There are extra rooms in a pleasant annexe, a couple of streets away. **€110**

Ca' Gottardi Calle Noal 2283 ☎ 041 275 9333, ⓦ cagottardi.com; map p.120. A smart and very welcoming three-star boutique hotel, located just off Strada Nova, the main route through Cannaregio. The prevailing décor is a modern facsimile of eighteenth-century style, and many of the rooms overlook the Rio de Noal, which opens into the Canal Grande opposite Ca' Pesaro. **€250**

Giorgione Calle Larga dei Proverbi 4587 ☎ 041 522 5810, ⓦ hotelgiorgione.com; map p.120. This plush four-star, very close to Santi Apostoli, has a more personal touch than many of the city's upmarket hotels – it has been run by the same family for many generations. Amenities include a quiet garden (with Venice's only open-air saltwater jacuzzi) and a pool table, and some of the 76 well-equipped rooms have a small private terrace. And by four-star standards, its prices are low, especially in low season. **€240**

★ **Locanda Ai Santi Apostoli** Strada Nova 4391a ☎ 041 521 2612, ⓦ locandasantiapostoli.com; map p.120. Occupying the top floor of an ancient palazzo opposite the Rialto market, this ten-room three-star *locanda* has two lovely rooms overlooking the Canal Grande – for which you'll pay as much as €100 more than for the standard doubles. The staff are very helpful, and the location terrific. **€150**

Locanda di Orsaria Calle Priuli dei Cavalletti 103 ☎ 041 715 254, ⓦ locandaorsaria.com; map p.120. Though it's situated close to the train station, this very well-managed eight-room *locanda* is nonetheless perfectly quiet; all rooms are en suite and a/c, and larger than is standard at this end of the price scale. **€200**

★ **Locanda Leon Bianco** Corte Leon Bianco 5629 ☎ 041 523 3572, ⓦ leonbianco.it; map p.120. Friendly and charming three-star in a superb location not far from the Rialto bridge, tucked away beside the decaying Ca' da Mosto. Only eight rooms, but three of them overlook the Canal Grande (for which there's a premium, of course) and most of the others are spacious and tastefully furnished– one room even has a huge fresco copied from a Tiepolo ceiling. **€210**

★ **Palazzo Abadessa** Calle Priuli 4011 ☎ 041 241 3784, ⓦ abadessa.com; map p.120. This gorgeous four-star *residenza d'epoca* is a meticulously restored palazzo behind the church of Santa Sofia; all fifteen of its bedrooms (some of them huge) are nicely furnished with genuine antiques, and there's a lovely secluded garden as well. **€300**

CENTRAL CASTELLO

Caneva Corte Rubbi 5515 ☎ 041 522 8118, ⓦ hotelcaneva.com; map p.136. A peaceful one-star tucked away behind the church of Santa Maria della Fava. Most of the 23 rooms have a/c, a canal view and private bathrooms. **€120**

Casa Querini Campo S. Giovanni Novo 4388 ☎ 041 241 1294, ⓦ locandaquerini.com; map p.136. Friendly *locanda* with six smallish but nicely furnished a/c rooms; it overlooks a tiny campo that's perfectly quiet, even though it's just a few metres from the Piazza. **€250**

★ **Casa Verardo** Calle della Chiesa 4765 ☎041 528 6127, ⊕ casaverardo.it; map p.136. A fine three-star hotel occupying a tastefully refurbished sixteenth-century palazzo between San Marco and Campo Santa Maria Formosa. Twenty-three well-equipped rooms with a breakfast terrace downstairs, a small garden, a sun lounge at the top and another terrace attached to the priciest of the rooms. **€230**

Danieli Riva degli Schiavoni 4196 ☎041 522 6480, ⊕ luxurycollection.com/danieli; map p.136. It may no longer be the most expensive hotel in Venice, but no other place can compete with the glamour of the *Danieli*. Balzac stayed here, as did George Sand, Wagner and Dickens. This magnificent Gothic palazzo affords just about the most sybaritic hotel experience in the *centro storico* – provided you book a room in the old part of the building, not the modern extension. Rooms with a lagoon view are considerably more expensive than standard doubles. **€660**

Doni Calle dei Vin 4656 ☎041 522 4267, ⊕ albergodoni.it; map p.136. Run by the Doni family since the 1940s, this is a plain yet cosy one-star near San Zaccaria, with most of the thirteen rooms overlooking the Rio del Vin or a courtyard. Few of the rooms have a private bathroom, though. **€140**

Locanda La Corte Calle Bressana 6317 ☎041 241 1300, ⊕ locandalacorte.it; map p.136. Located close to SS Giovanni e Paolo, this high-class sixteen-room *locanda* has very welcoming owners and a nice courtyard for breakfast. The best doubles overlook either the courtyard or the canal. **€170**

Locanda Vivaldi Riva degli Schiavoni 4152–3 ☎041 277 0477, ⊕ locandavivaldi.it; map p.136. *Danieli*-style views at a much lower cost, at this stylish, antique-furnished four-star *locanda*, right next door to the Pietà (the *locanda* occupies a portion of a house in which Vivaldi lived). The top-floor breakfast terrace is a treat, and some rooms have whirlpools. **€300**

Paganelli Riva degli Schiavoni 4687 ☎041 522 4324, ⊕ hotelpaganelli.com; map p.136. This three-star is a great place to stay, especially if you get one of the (pricier) rooms on the lagoon side – the ones in the annexe look onto S. Zaccaria, which is a nice enough view, but not really in the same league. Room prices vary a lot at any time of year, and bargain out-of-season rates are available through the website. **€220**

Ruzzini Palace Campo S. Maria Formosa 5866 ☎041 241 0447, ⊕ ruzzinipalace.com; map p.136. One of Venice's newest luxury hotels, the four-star *Ruzzini* occupies a palace that was completed in the early seventeenth century, and the conversion into a 28-room hotel has preserved much of the period character – most notably the frescoes by Gregorio Lazzarini (Tiepolo's teacher) in the gorgeous (and madly expensive) Royal Suite. **€350**

Scandinavia Campo S. Maria Formosa 5240 ☎041 522 3507, ⊕ scandinaviahotel.com; map p.136.

Sizeable, relatively inexpensive and comfortable three-star, decorated mainly in eighteenth-century style (ie lots of Murano glass and floral motifs). Most of the 34 rooms are a decent size, and several of them overlook Campo Santa Maria Formosa, one of the city's liveliest and best-looking squares. **€250**

EASTERN CASTELLO

Gabrielli Riva degli Schiavoni 4110 ☎041 523 1580, ⊕ hotelgabrielli.it; map p.154. The family-run *Gabrielli* has occupied its fourteenth-century palazzo since the 1850s, and is one of the best-value four-stars in town. The rooms aren't as luxurious as at some of its upper-echelon rivals, but 27 of the 103 rooms have *superb* views across the Bacino di San Marco. It also has an attractive little courtyard and a lovely small garden. **€275**

★ **La Residenza** Campo Bandiera e Moro 3608 ☎041 528 5315, ⊕ venicelaresidenza.com; map p.154. This fourteenth-century palazzo is a mid-budget gem, occupying much of one side of a tranquil square just off the main waterfront. The recently refurbished rooms are very spacious (rare at this price) and elegant, and the management extremely *simpatico*. Payment by cash is preferred for short stays. **€200**

Sant'Antonin Fondamenta dei Furlani 3299 ☎041 523 1621, ⊕ hotelsantantonin.com; map p.154. A family residence until quite recently, the tranquil and homely three-star *Sant'Antonin* has good-sized rooms that retain much of the house's old furniture. What really makes this place special, though, is the gorgeous garden, which many of the bedrooms look over; others open onto the front courtyard or onto Rio della Pietà. The location is good, too – it's in a quiet part of the city, but just a ten-minute walk from the Piazza. The full price is quite high, but if you book well ahead you'll find substantial discounts. **€350**

THE NORTHERN ISLANDS

Locanda Cipriani Piazza S. Fosca 29, Torcello ☎041 730 150, ⊕ locandacipriani.com; map p.183. For a dose of rural isolation, you could stay at the tranquil six-roomed inn where Hemingway wrote *Across the River and into the Trees*. Once the day's tourists have gone home, this is just about the quietest spot in the whole lagoon. Rooms are plain but comfortable, and have no TVs to blight the atmosphere. The in-house restaurant is good but not inexpensive. Closed Jan & Feb. **€240**

Venissa Fondamenta S. Caterina 3, Mazzorbo ☎041 52 72 281, ⊕ venissa.it; map p.183. Two stylishly spartan suites and four doubles have been fitted out in the upper floors of Mazzorbo's superbly innovative (and expensive) restaurant (see page 220). They call it the Venissa "wine resort" because the building sits alongside the restaurant's vineyard. Closed Dec–Feb. **€170**

10

10

BED AND BREAKFASTS

As stipulated by the Italian tourism authorities, a **bed and breakfast** establishment is a private dwelling with a minimum of one shared bathroom for guests' exclusive use. As is always the case, however, nomenclature is not straightforward; some larger guesthouses like to call themselves B&Bs, because they think the label gives them a touch of Anglophone chic. The places listed below are all B&Bs as legally defined; guesthouses are included in the hotel listings. There are now hundreds of officially registered B&Bs in Venice, and the number is growing with each year: in 2000, under 100 B&Bs were registered; the number is now in excess of 3000. Some are not terribly attractive, but many of them are excellent, offering characterful accommodation at prices that compare very favourably with hotels. For full listings of Venice's B&Bs, go to ⓦ turismovenezia.it; ⓦ bed-and-breakfast.it is another useful resource, as is ⓦ cross-pollinate.com.

SAN MARCO

A Le Boteghe Calle delle Boteghe 3438 ☎041 523 5366, ⓦ aleboteghe.it; map p.36. Clara and Giordano's three-room, third-floor B&B is a spick-and-span little place, very close to Santo Stefano. Discounts for stays of more than six nights. **€120**

DORSODURO

Ca' Turelli Fondamenta di Borgo 1162 ☎041 523 5094, ⓦ caturelli.it; map p.82. Simple, plain and good-value B&B, a short walk from the Accademia and the Ca' Rezzonico vaporetto stop. If you like soft mattresses, though, this isn't the place for you. **€130**

Casanova ai Tolentini Fondamenta del Gafaro 3515 ☎349 878 2995, ⓦ casanovaaitolentini.com; map p.82. This B&B, located close to Piazzale Roma and the Tolentini church, has one double room, a junior suite and a large suite overlooking a quiet canal. **€135**

Dorsoduro 461 Rio Terà S. Vio 461, Dorsoduro ☎041 528 6172, ⓦ dorsoduro461.com; map p.82. Three en-suite double rooms on the upper floor of the (very hospitable) owner's house, on a peaceful street a short distance from the Guggenheim. Each of the rooms is nicely decorated and furnished, with a few homely antique items to set the tone. Good breakfast too. **€130**

★ **Fujiyama** Calle Lunga S. Barnabà 2727a ☎041 724 1042, ⓦ bedandbreakfast-fujiyama.it; map p.82. Carlo and Wenyu, the owners of this immaculate B&B, are perfect hosts, and have fitted out their rooms in Japanese/Chinese-inflected style. And this is perhaps the only B&B in Venice that serves real tea – there's a nice little tearoom on the ground floor, adjoining the tiny garden. The Shanghai room (the biggest) is the pick of the bunch. **€170**

SAN POLO AND SANTA CROCE

★ **Ca' Angeli** Calle del Traghetto della Madoneta 1434 ☎041 523 2480, ⓦ caangeli.it; map p.100. An outstanding B&B, very close to Campo San Polo. The owners couldn't be more helpful, the doubles are spacious, comfortable and airy, and there's a lovely suite that looks out on the Canal Grande. **€230**

Corte 1321 Campiello Ca' Bernardi 1321 ☎041 522 4923, ⓦ corte1321.com; map p.100. Bright and colourful rooms, in which owners Deborah and Amelia – in tribute to the Venice of Marco Polo – have mixed oriental, Venetian and Persian elements to very good effect. The location, midway between the Rialto and Campo San Polo, is fine as well. **€210**

CANNAREGIO

Al Palazzetto Calle delle Vele 4057 ☎041 275 0897, ⓦ guesthouse.it; map p.120. Well-furnished and sizeable double, triple and quadruple rooms, all of them with private bathroom, in a quiet canalside house, close to the Ca' d'Oro. **€150**

Al Saor Calle Zotti 3904a ☎041 296 0654, ⓦ alsaor.com; map p.120. This isn't luxury accommodation, but the rooms are spacious and clean, all have a private bathroom (some have a kitchen too), the price is unbeatable and the hosts – Francesco and Silvia – are lovely. **€130**

Antico Portego Rio Terrà Farselli 1414a ☎347 495 8326, ⓦ bbanticoportego.com; map p.120. There are two parts to the *Antico Portego*, which is in a nice sixteenth-century palazzo with a double courtyard, on one of Cannaregio's main streets: one part contains a single room and two suites; the other has five roomy doubles, all come with a private bathroom, and all are very comfortable. **€150**

★ **Domus Orsoni** Calle dei Vedei 1045 ☎041 275 9538, ⓦ domusorsoni.it; map p.120. This unusual B&B, located close to the main Cannaregio canal, is attached to the Orsoni factory, which still manufactures glass mosaics. Each of the five smartly spartan rooms is adorned with a large Orsoni mosaic and has a mosaic-tiled bathroom. **€250**

CASTELLO

Ai Tagliapietra Salizada Zorzi 4943, Castello ☎347 323 3166, ⓦ aitagliapietra.com; map p.136. The rooms here are rather plain, but they are perfectly maintained, comfortable, quite spacious and remarkably low-priced. Equidistant from the Piazza, Santa Maria Formosa and San Zaccaria, it couldn't be more conveniently located nor could Lorenzo – the owner – be friendlier. **€100**

Ca' Furlan Corte S. Giovanni di Malta 3257 ☎041 241 0338, ⓦ cafurlan.eu; map p.154. With colour schemes in which lemon, cream and pale gold predominate, and lots of good-quality fabrics in the rooms, this upmarket nouveau-

10

SELF-CATERING APARTMENTS

The often exorbitant cost of hotel rooms in Venice makes **self-catering** an attractive option – for the price of a week in a cramped double room in a two-star hotel you could book yourself a two-bedroomed **apartment** right in the centre of the city. You should be aware, however, that tourist rentals have become a hot topic in Venice, as more and more Venetians are forced out of the city by ever-rising rents, a situation exacerbated by the rise of Airbnb and other such websites – landlords know they can make much more money from a property by renting it to tourists rather than taking long-term local tenants. To make matters worse, many landlords are not registering these holiday apartments as commercial ventures (by some estimates there are around 3000 unregistered properties), thus depriving the city of the revenue that short-let rentals should generate for the public purse. A lot of Venetians want the town hall to follow the lead of Berlin, where restrictions have been placed on Airbnb (a particular bête noire for Venetians) to prevent apartment-owners from renting entire properties solely to tourists.

Airbnb ⓦ airbnb.com. While this is the market leader, quite a few Venetian rentals are of doubtful legality – so if your potential landlord comes up with any dodgy-seeming conditions, walk away.

Cross-Pollinate ⓦ cross-pollinate.com. Around eighty B&Bs and apartments are listed (and reviewed) on this website.

HomeAway ⓦ homeaway.co.uk. This site – which puts you directly in touch with the owners – features hundreds of properties in Venice and the Veneto.

Venetian Apartments ⓦ veniceprestige.com. Specialists in extravagant properties, with a portfolio that includes several Canal Grande *palazzi*.

Venice Apartment ⓦ veniceapartment.com. In business for more than twenty years, this website has around 150 properties on its books.

Venice Apartments ⓦ veniceapartments. org. There are about fifty apartments on this well-structured site.

Views on Venice ⓦ viewsonvenice.com. Well-established company with some eighty high-end apartments, and very good service on the ground.

Rococo B&B is a lot more elegant than most hotels in this price range. **€250**

★ **Corte Campana** Calle del Remedio 4410 ☎ 041 523 3603, ⓦ cortecampana.com; map p.136. A homely and old-fashioned three-room B&B, just 2min walk from the Piazza – Riccardo and Grace, the owners, are extremely welcoming, and the accommodation is amazingly inexpensive, given the location. **€130**

★ **Residenza de l'Osmarin** Calle Rota 4960, Castello ☎ 347 450 1440, ⓦ residenzadelosmarin.com; map p.136. Elisabetta and Rodolfo Maniscalco's lovely canalside B&B – consisting of one double room and three suites – is situated a short distance to the north of San Zaccaria, and

within a few minutes' stroll of the Piazza. The rooms are a decent size, are simply and brightly decorated, and all of them overlook the water. The owners are immensely welcoming, and the breakfast buffet – often featuring Elisabetta's home-made cakes – is unusually good. **€180**

GIUDECCA
Casa Eden Corte Mosto 25 ☎ 041 521 2564, ⓦ casaeden. it; map p. 192. Hidden behind the Zitelle church, the *Casa Eden* is a restful quasi-rustic bolt hole, with three suites on offer: the two-bedroomed Rosa and the single-roomed Tulipano and Gelsomino. Guests have use of the garden, that rarest of Venetian amenities. **€120**

HOSTELS

In addition to big hostel on Giudecca, Venice has a few other hostel-like establishments – most run by religious foundations – offering basic accommodation. Some of the latter are more expensive than hotels and B&Bs; we've listed only the low-cost options.

Domus Civica Calle Campazzo, San Polo 3082 ☎ 041 721 103, ⓦ domuscivica.com; map p.100. This Catholic women's student hostel is open to tourists from mid-June to mid-September. Most rooms are double with running water; showers free; no breakfast; midnight curfew. Very basic, but central and inexpensive. Dorms **€30**

Foresteria Valdese S. Maria Formosa, Castello 5170 ☎ 041 528 6797, ⓦ foresteriavenezia.it; map p.136. Run by Waldensians, this hostel is installed in a wonderful palazzo at the end of Calle Lunga S. Maria Formosa, with flaking frescoes in the rooms and a large communal salon. It has bedrooms ranging from singles to small dormitories that can accommodate up to ten; most of the smaller rooms have a private bathroom. Registration 9am–1pm & 6–8pm. Breakfast is included. Doubles from **€110**, dorms from **€40**

Generator Hostel Fondamenta delle Zitelle, Giudecca 86 ☎ 041 523 8211, ⓦ generatorhostels.com; map p.192. The city's former HI hostel, now thoroughly revamped as one of the *Generator* group of hostels, occupies a superb location looking over the water to San Marco. Rooms are bright, spacious, comfortable and even stylish, ranging from doubles to sixteen-bed mini-dorms (some of them female-only). Prices, however, are rather higher than you'll pay in a bog-standard hostel – double rooms here can cost as much as some three-stars. Breakfast and sheets are included in the price – but remember to add the expense of the boat from central Venice. No curfew. Dorms €44

Ostello Santa Fosca S. Maria dei Servi, Cannaregio 2372 ☎041 715 775, ⓦostellosantafosca.it; map p.120. Student-run hostel in an atmospheric former Servite convent in a quiet part of Cannaregio, with rudimentary bedrooms sleeping two to seven people (some of the larger rooms are female-only), nearly all of them with shared bathrooms. 12.30pm curfew. Dorms from €25

CAMPING

There are some unlovely campsites near the airport – better to head out to the outer edge of the lagoon, to the **Litorale del Cavallino**, which stretches from Punta Sabbioni to Jésolo and has around 60,000 pitches, many quite luxurious; from Punta Sabbioni the #14 vaporetto goes to San Zaccaria via the Lido. Alternatively, you could camp on the mainland at **Fusina**; a *Linea Fusina* water-bus links Fusina to the Záttere in central Venice (ACTV passes are not valid on this route), taking 25min, with an hourly service from 8am until around 10pm (June–Sept), and till around 7.30pm in winter.

Camping Fusina Via Moranzani 93, Fusina ☎041 547 0055, ⓦwww.campingfusina.com. Situated at the mouth of the Brenta River, this is the closest campsite to central Venice. Marketing itself as a "tourist village", it has cabins as well as pitches for tents and camper vans, plus a pizzeria, bar, beer garden, internet café and 24hr laundry. The boat stop for Venice is only 100m from the front gate,

and there's a bus service too. Open all year. Tents €10 plus per person fee €12, cabins /day from €50

Marina di Venezia Via Montello 6, Litorale del Cavallino ☎041 966 146, ⓦmarinadivenezia.it. This big and well-equipped four-star site is a couple of kilometres from the Punta Sabbioni vaporetto stop, on the seaward side of the Litorale del Cavallino, adjoining the beach and the huge AquaMarina waterpark. Has a big range of accommodation, with seven-berth a/c chalets at the top. Open early May to mid-Oct. Tents €32 plus per person fee €13, chalets and bungalows from €150

Miramare Lungomare Dante Alighieri 29, Litorale del Cavallino ☎041 966 150, ⓦcamping-miramare.it. A three-star site, located at the mouth of the lagoon, very near the Punta Sabbioni stop, with bungalows and maxi caravans. Open April–Oct. Tents €20 plus per person fee €9, bungalows from €80

Eating and drinking

There's more than an element of truth to Venice's reputation as a place where mass tourism has produced monotonous menus, cynical service and slapdash standards in the kitchen. Venice has fewer good, moderately priced restaurants than any other major Italian city, it has more really bad restaurants than any other, and in some of the expensive establishments you're paying not for a fine culinary creation but for the experience of dining in an expensive Venetian restaurant. However, things have been getting better in recent years, and in the less overrun parts of Venice there are now several good places where you can get a decent two-course meal, plus house wine, for €35–40 per person – which, in this city, is inexpensive.

And it's possible to eat well in Venice for less. A distinctive aspect of the Venetian social scene is the **bácaro** which in its purest form is a **bar** that offers a range of snacks called **cicheti** (sometimes spelled *ciccheti*); usually costing €2–4 per portion, the array will typically include *polpette* (small beef and garlic meatballs), *carciofini* (artichoke hearts), hard-boiled eggs, anchovies, *polipi* (baby octopus or squid) and sun-dried tomatoes, peppers and courgettes cooked in oil. (The one type of *cicheti* to avoid is the so-called "crab's claw" – it's just a ball of reconstituted fish with a crab's pincer shoved into it.) Many *bácari* also produce one or two more substantial dishes each day, such as risotto or seafood pasta. Many bars of this type are long-established places, but in the last decade or so there's been something of a *bácaro* revival, and you're more likely to find a seating area in these newer establishments.

Excellent food is also served at many of Venice's **osterie** (or *ostarie*), the simplest of which are indistinguishable from larger *bácari*, with just three or four tables, while

---

VENETIAN SPECIALITIES

11

Venetian cuisine bears little trace of the city's past as Europe's trading crossroads, when spices from the East were among the most lucrative commodities sold in the Rialto markets. Nowadays Venetian food is known for its simplicity, with plain pepper and salt as the principal means of vivifying a meal. **Fish and seafood** dominate the menus, much of the former being netted in the Adriatic and the rivers and lakes of the mainland, with the latter coming from the lagoon and open sea. (Don't assume, though, that every restaurant in water-bound Venice cooks only fresh fish and seafood; many places use frozen stuff, so always check the small print of the menu, where, by law, the restaurant has to state if food has come from the freezer. *Surgelato* is the word to look for.) Prawns, squid and octopus are typical Venetian antipasti (usually served with a plain dressing of olive oil and lemon), as are Murano crabs and *sarde in saor* (marinated sardines). Dishes like eel cooked in Marsala wine, *baccalà* (salt cod) and *seppie nere* (cuttlefish cooked in its own ink) are other Venetian staples, but the quintessential dish is the **risotto**, made with rice grown along the Po valley. Apart from the seafood variety (*risotto bianco, risotto di mare* or *risotto dei pescatori*), you'll come across risottos that incorporate some of the great range of vegetables grown in the Veneto (notably spinach, asparagus, pumpkin and peas – *bisi* in the local dialect), and others that draw on such diverse ingredients as snails, tripe, quail and sausages.

Venetian **soups** are as versatile as the risottos, with *brodetto* (mixed fish) and *pasta e fagioli* or *fasioi* (pasta and beans) being the most popular. **Polenta** is a recurrent feature of Venetian meals; made by slowly stirring maize flour into boiling salted water, it's served as an accompaniment to a number of dishes, in particular liver (*fegato*), a special favourite in Venice. In season, the red salad leaf *radicchio* – a Veneto speciality – will feature on most menus. **Pastries and sweets** are also an area of Venetian expertise. In addition to **tiramisù**, (which was invented in the late 1960s, in Treviso, as a mid-morning "pick-me-up" rather than a dessert), look out for the thin oval biscuits called *baicoli*, the ring-shaped cinnamon-flavoured *bussolai* (a speciality of Burano) and *mandolato* – a cross between nougat and toffee, made with almonds. The Austrian occupation has left its mark in the form of the ubiquitous *strudel* and the cream- or jam-filled *krapfen* (doughnuts).

Particular foods are traditional to certain **feast days**. During Carnevale you can buy small doughnuts known as *frittelle*, which come plain, *con frutta* (with fruit), *con crema* (confectioner's cream) or *con zabaglione* (which is made out of egg yolks and Marsala). During Lent there's an even greater emphasis on fish, and also on omelettes (*frittata*), often made with shrimps and wild asparagus; lamb is popular at Easter. On Ascension Day it's customary to have pig's trotter, either plain or stuffed, while for the feast of the Redentore (third Sunday in July) *sarde in saor* or roast duck are in order. Tiny biscuits called *fave* ("beans") fill the *pasticcerie* around All Saints' Day and All Souls' Day (Nov 1 & 2); on the feast of Saint Martin (Nov 11) you get biscuits or heavy quince jelly cut into the shape of the saint on his horse; and on the feast of the Madonna della Salute (Nov 21) it's traditional to have *castradina* (salted smoked mutton). On Christmas Eve many Venetians eat eel, usually grilled, though with variations from island to island; on Christmas Day the traditional dishes are roast turkey, veal, duck or capon.

others have sizeable dining areas. Just to make things supremely confusing, a few *osterie* have no bar at all – some of these are bars that have evolved into restaurants, while others use the name *osteria* to give the establishment an aura of unpretentiousness and good value. And to further blur the division between bars and restaurants, several of Venice's restaurants have a separate bar area on the street side of the dining room. We've classified our bars and restaurants according to which aspect of the business draws most of the customers, but if you're looking for a simple meal in a particular area of the city, be sure to check both sets of listings. In *bácari* and *osterie* with dining areas, full meals are served at the usual lunch and dinner hours, while snacks are served at the bar throughout the day.

As enticing as the city's bars are its cafés and *pasticcerie* (many of which also serve alcohol), where a variety of waistline-threatening delicacies is on offer, and there aren't too many nicer things you can do to your taste buds than hit them with a coneful of home-made Venetian ice cream.

RESTAURANTS

Virtually every budget restaurant in Venice advertises a set-price **menù turistico**, which can be a cheap way of sampling some Venetian specialities, but the quality and quantity won't be up to the mark of an **à la carte** meal, and frequently won't even be acceptable. Value for money tends to increase with the distance from San Marco; plenty of restaurants within a short radius of the Piazza offer menus that seem to be reasonable, but you'll find the food unappetizing and the portions tiny. There are a few notable concentrations of **good restaurants**: the Rialto area; around San Barnabà in Dorsoduro; the zone between San Giovanni in Brágora and the Arsenale; and the area between the Cannaregio canal and Sant'Alvise.

We've supplied the usual opening hours of each restaurant (the vast majority are closed Sun or Mon), but bear in mind that many restaurateurs take their annual holiday in **August**, and that quite a few places close down on unscheduled days in the dead weeks of winter. In most cases, booking a table is advisable in high season, and you should also be aware that Venetians tend to eat early and that restaurateurs routinely close early if trade is slack, so if you're in town at a quiet time, don't turn up later than 8.30pm, unless you're dining at one of the city's more expensive restaurants, which tend to keep longer hours. Italians hardly ever **tip** more than ten percent of the bill; if service charge is included, it's usual to leave an extra five percent or so.

SAN MARCO

★ **Ai Mercanti** Corte Coppo 4346a ☎ 041 523 8269, ⓦ aimercanti.it; map p.36. Reinvented in 2013 as a "Gastrosteria", Ai Mercanti is one of the few places in the San Marco *sestiere* where you'll experience good-quality and creative cooking at prices that you might describe as reasonable – main courses start at around €17. The menu is imaginative (has anywhere else in Venice ever offered a pumpkin and coffee bean risotto?), with more meat than is the norm in this city, and more choices for vegetarians. The

dark wood and golden colour scheme of the dining room is distinctive too. Mon 7–10.30pm, Tues–Sat 12.30–3pm & 7–10.30pm.

Al Bacareto Calle Crosera S. Samuele 3447 ☎ 041 528 9336, ⓦ osteriaalbacareto.it; map p.36. Tucked away on the north side of Santo Stefano, Al Bacareto has been in business here for almost fifty years and remains one of the most genuine places in the San Marco *sestiere*. In recent years it has been getting smarter and more expensive, but it's still fairly good value, with main courses in the €15–20 range – and if you're watching the pennies you can always eat at the bar, where the *cicheti* are outstanding. In summer there are seats outside. Closed most of Aug. Mon–Sat 8am–4.30pm (kitchen open noon–3pm) & 6.30–11pm.

Da Fiore Calle delle Botteghe 3461 ☎ 041 523 5310, ⓦ dafiore.it; map p.36. Established in the mid-1980s, this popular restaurant offers Venetian cuisine in a classy trattoria-style setting. The anteroom is a nice, small bar that offers good *cicheti* plus a small menu of daily specials – you might pay €15 for a fish dish in the bar section, and €25 for the same thing in the restaurant. Mon & Wed–Sun 8.30am–11pm (restaurant noon–3pm & 7–10pm).

Harry's Bar Calle Vallaresso 1323 ☎ 041 528 5777, ⓦ cipriani.com; map p.38. *Harry's Bar* is the most famous of the city's gourmet restaurants (*carpaccio* – raw strips of thin beef – was first created here), though the place's reputation more to do with its exclusivity as with its cuisine: three courses will cost you in excess of €120, and the cocktails and snacks are similarly insane. (The Bellini – a mix of fresh white peach juice and prosecco that's mistakenly thought by many to be a traditional Venetian drink – was invented here too.) *Harry's* was founded in 1931 by Giuseppe Cipriani, who named it after Harry Pickering, a young American who, by way of thanks for a loan that Cipriani had earlier given him to see him through a crisis, loaned Cipriani enough cash to set up his own bar. The Cipriani family continued to run the place until 2013, when, saddled with debts of several million euros, they

PIZZA IN VENICE

Pizza is an obvious standby if you're watching your budget, but it's not a Venetian speciality and most of the city's *pizzerie* are poor, partly because fire regulations make it impossible to use traditional wood-fired ovens. You'll find the best of Venice's *pizzerie* in our restaurant listings. For takeaway pizza slices (*pizza al taglio*) decent choices are the *Antico Forno*, close to the Rialto at Rughetta del Ravano 973 (open daily 11.30am–9.30pm), and *Arte della Pizza*, a short distance north of San Marcuola in Cannaregio, at Calle de l'Aseo 1896 (Tues–Sun 11am–9pm). The pizza slices and pies are also good at *Cip Ciap*, across the canal from the west side of Santa Maria Formosa, at Calle Mondo Nuovo 5799 (9am–9pm; closed Tues).

were forced to cede control to an investment fund. Daily 10.30am–11pm.

Le Bistrot de Venise Calle dei Fabbri 4685 ⓣ041 523 6651, ⓦbistrotdevenise.com; map p.38. This place is done up as a facsimile of a wood-panelled French *bistrot*, but the menu is based on old-style Venetian recipes. It's pricey – main dishes are in the €30–40 range, with set menus for €75 and €110 – but the food is good, as is the atmosphere, as *Le Bistrot de Venise* has become something of an arts centre, with regular music and poetry events from October to May. The bar has a very good wine selection. Bar daily 11am–midnight, restaurant daily noon–3pm & 7pm–midnight.

Osteria-Enoteca San Marco Frezzeria 1610 ⓣ041 528 5242, ⓦosteriasanmarco.it; map p.38. As you'd expect for a place so close to the Piazza, this classy modern *osteria* is far from cheap (expect to pay €25–40 for your main course), but the food is very good and the prices are comparable to those of many inferior places in this area. The wine list is superb as well. Between lunchtime and dinner you can sip wine at the bar. Mon–Sat 12.30–11pm.

Rosticceria Gislon Calle della Bissa 5424a; map p.36. Downstairs the perpetually busy *Rosticeceria Gislon* is a sort of glorified snack bar, serving pizzas, plates of meat and cheese, fried fish and other basic meals. Good if you need to refuel quickly and cheaply, but can't face a pizza. There's a slightly less rudimentary restaurant upstairs, where prices are higher for no great increase in quality. Daily 9am–9.30pm.

DORSODURO

Al Quattro Feri Calle Lunga S. Barnaba 2754a ⓣ041 520 6978; map p.82. A very popular *osteria* just off Campo San Barnaba, with a small menu that changes daily but often consists entirely of fish and seafood; most dishes are priced per 100 gram, so *secondi* will vary according to the size of the fish – expect to pay around €25. Limited seating (some might find the place a bit too cramped), so booking essential at all times. No credit cards. Mon–Sat noon–3pm & 7–10pm.

Casin dei Nobili Calle Lombardo 2765 ⓣ041 241 1841; map p.82. Very popular with both locals and tourists, the *Casin dei Nobili* is a large and dependable trattoria-pizzeria – pizzas are served only in the evenings, and are the best thing they do. The open courtyard is a nice dining area too. It occupies part of a premises that were once notorious as an upper-class gambling-den- bordello – hence the racy logo. Tues–Sun noon–3pm & 6–11pm.

11

Do Farai Calle Cappeller 3278 ⓣ041 277 0369; map p.82. Tucked into an alley close to Ca' Rezzonico, *Do Farai* is a fine and long-established quasi-rustic *osteria*, serving good steaks and other meat dishes, plus excellent seafood and fish – the speciality is a *carpaccio* of sea bass. Main courses are around €20–25. In summer its tables spread out into the neighbouring campo. Mon–Sat noon–2.30pm & 7–10.30pm.

★ **La Bitta** Calle Lunga S. Barnaba 2753a ⓣ041 523 0531; map p.82. Innovative food at a welcoming little *osteria* that's remarkable for featuring hardly anything aquatic. Marcellino runs the kitchen while his wife Debora serves and cajoles the guests, offering expert guidance on the impressive wine and grappa list. Main courses are €20–30. Tiny dining room (and garden), so booking is essential. No credit cards. Mon–Sat 7–10pm.

La Calcina Záttere ai Gesuati 780 ⓣ041 520 6466, ⓦlacalcina.com; map p.82. Stretching onto the waterfront outside the *Calcina* hotel, to which it's attached, this is one of the most pleasant restaurants in Dorsoduro. The service is excellent, the food good (meat and fish dishes from around €20), and the view from the terrace is wonderful. Tues–Sun noon–3pm & 6.30–10pm.

Montin Fondamenta di Borgo 1147 ⓣ041 522 715, ⓦlocandamontin.com; map p.82. One of the most famous restaurants in the city, thanks chiefly to the patronage of artistic luminaries such as Pound, Hemingway and Peggy Guggenheim, *Montin* is undoubtedly a charismatic old place, with its painting-covered walls and vine-covered garden, and many people still rate its kitchen highly. Reckon on paying around €50/head for three courses, excluding wine. Mon & Thurs–Sun 12.30–2.30pm & 7.30–10pm, Tues 7.30–10pm.

Oniga Campo S. Barnaba 2852 ⓣ041 522 4410, ⓦoniga.it; map p.82. One of several mid-range restaurants in the San Barnaba area, this place has received some very good press in Italy, though the food is dependable rather than outstanding. The tone of the place – youthful, friendly and efficient – is appealing, though, and the set lunch, at around €20, is a very good deal; in the evening there's a choice of €30 set meals, including a vegetarian option. Daily noon–3pm & 7–11pm.

SAN POLO AND SANTA CROCE

Al Nono Risorto Sottoportego de Siora Bettina 2338 ☎041 524 1169, ⓦnonorisortovenezia.com; map p.100. Located just off Campo San Cassiano, the "Resurrected Grandad" is a pizzeria-restaurant with a predominantly twenty-something following. It often has live music, and a pleasant wisteria-covered courtyard is a further attraction. No credit cards. Mon,Tues & Thurs–Sun noon–3pm & 6–11pm.

Alla Madonna Calle della Madonna 594 ☎041 522 3824, ⓦristoranteallamadonna.com; map p.100. This roomy and bustling old-style seafood restaurant that's been going strong since the 1950s is now run by the founder's son. Service can be brisk, but this remains one of Venice's most dependable restaurants. Quite good value for money, even if prices have gone up noticeably of late – reckon on around €45/person. Mon, Tues & Thurs–Sun noon–3pm & 7–10pm.

★**Antiche Carampane** Rio Terrà delle Carampane 1911 ☎041 524 0165, ⓦantichecarampane.com; map p.100. If not the most tourist-friendly place in the city (a semi-jokey notice that tells you there's "No lasagne, no pizza, no menu turistico"), the *Carampane* is a thoroughbred high-class Venetian trattoria, serving excellent seafood in a cosy interior – with outside seating in fine weather. The menu is brief and often wholly fish-based, and you'll pay in the region of €70 for three courses. Tues–Sat 12.30–2.30pm & 7.30–11pm.

Antico Dolo Ruga Vecchia S. Giovanni 778 ☎041 522 6546, ⓦanticodolo.it; map p.100. You can pop into this tiny and long-established *osteria* for a few *cicheti* and a glass of Merlot and come away just a few euros poorer; or you can take a table and eat an excellent meal for something in the region of €40. For lunch, the €20 plate of assorted *cicheti* is a tempting offer. Daily noon–10pm.

Bancogiro Campo San Giacometto 122 ☎041 523 2061, ⓦosteriabancogiro.it; map p.100. This very smart *osteria*, in a splendid location in the midst of the Rialto market, was instrumental in making this zone a fashionable one, and though a number of similar operations have opened in the vicinity, none is better than *Bancogiro*. Come here to nurse a glass of fine wine beside the Canal Grande, or nip upstairs to the dining room for a well-prepared meal from the tight and imaginative and not inexpensive menu (around €20–25 for main courses). Tues–Sun 9am–midnight.

Birraria La Corte Campo San Polo 2168 ☎041 275 0570, ⓦbirrarialacorte.it; map p.100. If a pizza is all you want, this large bar-pizzeria-trattoria – occupying a former brewery on the north side of Campo San Polo – will do just fine. The rest of the menu is OK, but the pizzas are the thing – along with the beers, which feature strongly on the drinks list. The outside tables give you a grandstand view of Venice's second-largest square. Daily 10am–midnight (kitchen open noon–2.30pm & 6–10.30pm).

Da Fiore Calle del Scaleter 2002a ☎041 731 308, ⓦdafiore.net; map p.100. Hyper-refined *Da Fiore* is possibly the most famous restaurant in Venice, and is certainly one of the most lauded, both by Italians and foreign foodies. It's also shockingly expensive: the tasting menu is €140/160 (for 6/7 courses) , and you'll be paying €40–50 for your main course à la carte. If you're going to treat yourself here, and there's just two of you, try to get one of the two canalside tables on the tiny terrace. Tues–Sat 12.30–2.30pm & 7–10.30pm.

Jazz Club 900 Campiello del Sansoni 900 ☎041 522 6565; map p.100. Located in a small alleyway a short distance off Ruga Vecchia San Giovanni, the dark-panelled *Novecento* – is a late-opening pizzeria-bar with live jazz every Wednesday from November to March – at other times it's a recorded soundtrack. Tues–Sun 11.30am–4pm & 7pm–2am.

La Zucca Ponte del Megio 1762 ☎041 524 1570, ⓦlazucca.it; map p.100. Long a well-respected restaurant, *La Zucca* was once purely a vegetarian establishment (its name means "pumpkin") but now goes against the Venetian grain by featuring a lot of meat – chicken, lamb, beef – alongside the Eastern-inflected vegetable dishes. The quality remains high, prices are moderate (most mains are under €20) and the oak-slatted dining area is nice. Mon–Sat 12.30–2.30pm & 7–10.30pm.

Muro San Stae Campiello del Spezier 2048–50 ☎041 524 1628; map p.100. *Muro San Stae* offers a good range of pizzas plus an imaginative seafood menu on which main courses cost about €15. The styling is spartan, the service excellent and there is seating outside. *Muro Frari*, at Rio Terrà dei Frari 2604, has the same menu and style. Muro San Stae daily noon–3pm & 6–11pm; Muro Frari daily 11am–1am.

★**Vecio Fritolin** Calle della Regina 2262 ☎041 522 2881, ⓦveciofritolin.it; map p.100. The name translates as "the old frying-place", and one of its signature dishes is a succulent fry-up of estuary fish, but the *Vecio Fritolin* has come a very long way since its time as a purveyor of Venetian fast food – it's esteemed nowadays for its distinctive take on Venetian fishy classics, making imaginative use of seasonal herbs and vegetables. The menu is small but beautifully composed, with three or four main courses on offer, costing upward of €25, and there is often a three-course set menu for around €65, excluding wine. Mon & Thurs–Sun noon–2.30pm, & 7–10.30pm, Wed noon–2.30pm.

CANNAREGIO

★ **Ai Promessi Sposi** Calle dell'Oca 4367 ☎ 041 241 2747; map p.120. Run by former employees of *Alla Vedova*, this moderately priced (mains around €15) and cosy little *osteria* specializes in *baccalà* and other traditional fish recipes. Excellent range of *cicheti* at the bar. Mon 6.30–10.15pm, Tues–Sun 11.30am–2.15pm & 6.30–10.15pm.

Algiubagiò Fondamente Nove 5039 ☎ 041 523 6084, ⊚ algiubagio.net; map p.120. By far the best of several restaurants on the Fondamente Nove, the upmarket *Algiubagiò* has a menu that's notable for featuring a lot of beef as well as the expected fish (all of which is brought daily from the Chioggia market). Most main courses are around €30–35, and there's an unusually imaginative offering of vegetarian dishes (around €18). The high-ceilinged bare-brick dining room (formerly a boathouse) is impressive, and in summer you can eat on the lagoon-side terrace. The front-of-house bar is very good too. Daily 7am–midnight (kitchen open noon–2.30pm & 7–10.30pm).

★ **Alla Fontana** Fondamenta Cannaregio 1102 ☎ 041 715 077; map p.120. Once primarily a bar, *Alla Fontana* has transformed itself into a cosy little trattoria, offering a small menu of classic Venetian maritime dishes, which changes daily according to what the boats have brought in; tables beside the canal are an added attraction in summer. Portions are generous and prices good – you'll pay about €40/person for two courses with house wine. Mon, Tues & Thurs–Sun 7.30–10.30pm (but sometimes closes on Sun in winter).

Alla Vedova Calle del Pistor 3912 ☎ 041 528 5324; map p.120. Located in an alley directly opposite the one leading to the Ca' d'Oro, this long-established little restaurant – formally called the *Ca' d'Oro*, but known to all as *Alla Vedova* – is fronted by a bar offering a mouthwatering selection of *cicheti* and a good range of wines. Meal portions aren't huge, and service isn't always sunny, but it's inexpensive (antipasti and main courses from just €10) and invariably busy, so reservations are always a good idea. No credit cards. Mon–Wed, Fri & Sat 11.30am–2.30pm & 6.30–10.30pm, Sun 6.30–10.30pm.

★ **Anice Stellato** Fondamenta della Sensa 3272 ☎ 041 720 744; ⊚ osterianicestellato.com; map p.120. Located on one of the northernmost Cannaregio canals, this unfussy restaurant is a bit too remote for many tourists, but has become hugely popular in recent years, thanks to the superb quality of its kitchen. It is not inexpensive, however, with starters around €15 and main courses mostly in the €25–30 range. Booking always advisable. Mon 7.15–10pm, Tues–Sat 12.15–2pm & 7.15pm–10pm.

Antica Adelaide Calle Priuli 3728 ☎ 041 523 2629; map p.120. There's been a trattoria on this site for centuries, but in its current incarnation *Antica Adelaide* dates back only as far as 2006. Staffed by a friendly young crew, it's a bright and buzzing *osteria*, with a menu that's full of venerable Venetian recipes, and a nice bar out front. The cooking isn't top-notch but rarely disappoints, and most main courses are under €20. Daily 10am–3.30pm & 5.30pm–1am (kitchen open 12.30–2.30pm & 7.30–10.30pm).

Boccadoro Campiello Widman 5405a ☎ 041 521 1021, ⊚ boccadorovenezia.it; map p.120. This upmarket and very refined *enoteca-osteria* is one of Venice's best, serving extremely good fish and seafood, and some superb pasta courses as well (the pasta is all home-made). The wine list is also very impressive. In fine weather, there's ample seating on the secluded Campiello Widman. Main courses are around €25–30, and without much effort you could run up a bill in excess of €100/person. Daily 12.30–2.30pm & 7.30–9.30pm.

Da Alberto Calle Giacinto Gallina 5401 ☎ 041 523 8153, ⊚ osteriadaalberto.it; map p.120. The decor and menu are simple and traditional (it's nearly all seafood), as befits a place that's been here for almost a century, but *Da Alberto* has a more casual vibe than most Venetian restaurants. Good snacks at the bar; if you want to eat a full meal, it's wise to reserve a table. Main courses around €15. Daily 10.30am–3pm & 6.30–11pm.

Da Rioba Fondamenta della Misericordia 2553 ☎ 041 524 4379, ⊚ darioba.com; map p.120. This smartly austere *osteria* is another top-notch northern Cannaregio eatery; often full to bursting, especially in summer, when tables are set beside the canal, but the management always keeps the atmosphere relaxed. Not cheap, with mains around €25, but the quality is consistently high. Tues–Sun 12.30–2.30pm & 7.30–10.30pm.

★ **Dalla Marisa** Fondamenta S. Giobbe 652b ☎ 041 720 211; map p.120. Duck, tripe, beef and pheasant all feature regularly here – the boss is a butcher's daughter. Usually there's no menu: you just get whatever she's decided to cook that day, which is generally meat, but sometimes fish or seafood. Unpretentious, inexpensive (set lunch for around €20), tiny and very popular, so you'll need to book. One thing to bear in mind: this is one of the very few restaurants in Venice that still feels like a locals' place, and tourists who speak no Italian might not feel entirely comfortable. No credit cards. Mon, Wed & Sun noon–2.15pm, Tues & Thurs–Sat noon–2.15pm & 7.30–8.30pm.

La Colombina Campiello del Pegolotto 1828 ☎ 041 522 2616, ⊚ ristorantelacolombina.eu; map p.120. The petite and very stylish *La Colombina* offers a menu that puts a contemporary spin on Venetian classics – the ingredients may be familiar, but not the presentation. Quality is consistently high; mains are €20–30, and there are two excellent tasting menus (*mare* and *terra*), for €50. The wine list is excellent too, as you might expect from a place that presents itself as a *ristorante-enoteca*. In summer there are seats outside on the tiny and quiet campo. Tues–

11

Sun. 11am–1pm & 5–8pm for drinks; the kitchen is open 12.30–3pm & 7–10pm.

L'Orto dei Mori Campo dei Mori 3386 ☎ 041 524 3677, ⓦ osteriaortodeimori.com; map p.120. As you might expect of a place with a Sicilian boss, the menu at small and cosy L'Orto dei Mori has wider horizons than are the norm in Venice – squid-ink pasta and other Venetians classics are here, but many of the seafood dishes show the influence of other regions. It's not inexpensive, with mains at €25–30, but that's nothing out of the ordinary for Venice. In high season you'll need to book. Mon & Wed–Sun 12.30–3.30pm, 7pm–midnight.

★ **Pontini** Fondamenta Pescheria 1268 ☎ 041 714 123; map p.120. From outside, this looks like any number of ordinary Venetian trattoria-bars, but it's a cut above the average: the staff are extraordinarily welcoming, and the menu consists of plain but high-quality Venetian osteria fare: frittura mista, squid-ink pasta, baccalà and so forth. Portions are generous too, and the prices very good, with mains under €15 and some delicious set meals for less than €30. It's popular with tourists and locals alike, so booking is advisable in high season. Mon–Sat 6.30am–10.30pm.

Vecia Cavana Rio Terà SS. Apostoli 4624 ☎ 041 528 7106, ⓦ marsillifamiglia.it; map p.120. The orange walls and bare-brick arches of this spacious former boathouse (cavana) create an inviting interior, and the menu – a refined and imaginative take on classic Venetian recipes – more than lives up to the setting. The team that's been running this place since 2006 have compiled an excellent wine list too. Main courses at around €25. Daily noon–2.30pm & 7–10.30pm.

★ **Vini da Gigio** Fondamenta S. Felice 3628a ☎ 041 528 5140, ⓦ vinidagigio.com; map p.120. Though this family-run trattoria is firmly on the tourist map, it retains much of its authenticity and is still fairly good value by local standards, with most mains at around €25. It has two short but excellent menus – one for meat dishes, one for fish and seafood – and, as the name suggests, the wine list is a strength. Reservations essential. Wed–Sun noon–2.30pm & 7–10.30pm.

CENTRAL CASTELLO

Al Mascaron Calle Lunga S. Maria Formosa 5225 ☎ 041 522 5995, ⓦ osteriamascaron.it; map p.136. Long-established unpretentious restaurant with an interestingly arty feel, but foreigners can get brusque treatment, which is a shame, as the food is pretty good. Reckon on paying around €20 for your main course. Booking advisable. No credit cards. Mon–Sat noon–3pm & 7–11pm.

★ **Alle Testiere** Calle Mondo Nuovo 5801 ☎ 041 522 7220, ⓦ osterialletestiere.it; map p.136. Very small, expensive (starters around €25, mains €30 – and

you're not allowed to order less than two courses) but very special fish and seafood restaurant in the alley on the other side of the canal from the front of Santa Maria Formosa, with an ever-changing menu and a superb wine selection. Lunch is from noon to 2pm, and in the evening there are sittings at 7pm and 9pm, to handle the demand – booking is essential, always. Tues–Sat noon–3pm & 7–11pm; closed Aug.

Da Remigio Salizzada dei Greci 3416 ☎ 041 523 0089; map p.136. Old-style trattoria, serving straightforwardly excellent fish dishes and homemade gnocchi. The wine list is outstanding too. Be sure to book – the locals (and ever-increasing numbers of tourists) pack this place every night. While many other restaurants have ramped up their prices in recent years, it remains good value– mains are mostly €15–20. Mon 12.30–2.30pm, Wed–Sun 12.30–3pm & 7.30–10pm.

Il Ridotto Campo Santi Filippo e Giacomo 4509 ☎ 041 520 8280, ⓦ ilridotto.com; map p.136. The pale-brick austerity of the dining room tells you that this place is very serious about its food, and this Michelin-starred restaurant indeed has the best kitchen within a short radius of the Piazza. It's also one of the priciest. À la carte, you'll get no change from €100/person, but at lunchtime there's a €35 set menu, giving you three cicheti plus a main course. If expenditure is not an issue, you could go for one of the three excellent tasting menus: five courses for €95, seven courses for €110, or nine for €140. Booking always necessary – it has only nine tables. Mon, Tues & Fri–Sun 12.30–2pm & 7–10.30pm, Thurs 7–10.30pm.

★ **Local** Salizzada dei Greci 3303 ☎ 041 241 1128, ⓦ ristorantelocal.com; map p.136. Run by siblings Luca and Benedetta Fullin, Local offers extremely accomplished and creative cooking, using only local and organic produce (the website allows you to trace the origins of almost every ingredient). The décor of the waterside dining room is cool and airy (the furnishings are all made by local workshops, as are the wine glasses) and the dishes are artfully presented and exquisite. And expensive, of course – à la carte, main dishes are €25–30, and in the evenings there are superb tasting menus for €75 (plus €45 for wine) and €95 (plus €65). Mon & Thurs–Sun noon–2pm & 7–10pm, Wed 7–10pm.

★ **Osteria di Santa Marina** Campo S. Marina 5911 ☎ 041 528 5239, ⓦ osteriadisantamarina.com; map p.136. This has been one of Venice's top restaurants for some time: a very slick and very impressive modern-style operation offering imaginative variants on Venetian maritime standards (eg a vast "gran misto" of raw fish, as a starter – for €40). The wine list is mightily impressive as well. You'll pay around €30 for your main course; there are tasting menus for €60–80. Mon 7.30–10pm, Tues–Sat 12.30–2.30pm & 7.30–10pm.

11

EASTERN CASTELLO

Al Covo Campiello della Pescaria 3968 ☎041 522 3812, ⓦristorantealcovo.com; map p.154. Located in a backwater to the east of Campo Bandiera e Moro, Cesare Benelli's serious-minded *Al Covo* is one of Venice's foodie havens, with a consistently high reputation, thanks in part to its use of only the very best local ingredients. Main courses are €25–30, and there's a glorious seven-course *menu degustazione* for €76 in the evening; at lunch there's a four-course menu at around €45. Mon, Tues & Fri–Sun 12.45–3pm & 7.30–11pm; closed mid-Dec to mid-Jan.

Al Garanghelo Via Garibaldi 1621 ☎041 520 4967, ⓦgaranghelo.com; map p.154. Run by brothers Lucio and Simone, this *osteria* is the best place to eat on Via Garibaldi. Lucio – who also runs the nearby *Giorgione* – often regales his guests with Venetian songs, so it's not the best place for a quiet evening, but the food is decent and not expensive, with mains in the region of €15. In good weather there are seats out in the street. Mon & Wed–Sun 11.30am–3.30pm & 5.30–10.30pm.

★ **Corte Sconta** Calle del Pestrin 3886 ☎041 522 7024; map p.154. Secreted in a lane to the east of San Giovanni in Brágora, with a lovely vine-covered courtyard, this restaurant is one of Venice's finest. You might find it difficult to resist ordering the day's specials, which could easily result in a bill not far short of €100 per person – and it would be just about the best meal you could get in Venice for that price. Main courses are generally in the region of €25–30, which is fair enough for cooking of this quality in Venice. Booking several days in advance is essential for most of the year. Tues–Sat 12.30–2pm & 7–10pm.

CoVino Calle del Pestrin 3829 ☎041 241 2705, ⓦcovinovenezia.com; map p.154. This fourteen-seat open-kitchen micro-restaurant, which opened in 2013, is regarded by some as one of the best restaurants to have opened in Venice for a long time, while others find it more than a little pretentious. But nobody would dispute that it's unlike anywhere else in the city, and is serious about its food. The menu is different every day, and you pay a fixed sum for your meal: €27 for one main course or €36 for two (with dessert and coffee in both cases), plus €16 or €21 for three glasses of wine. At dinner there's also a No credit cards. Booking essential, of course. Mon & Thurs–Sun 12.30–3pm & 7–10.30pm, Wed 7–10.30pm.

THE NORTHERN ISLANDS

★ **Al Gatto Nero** Fondamenta Giudecca 88, Burano ☎041 730 120, ⓦgattonero.com/it; map p.183. Founded way back in 1946, this is an outstanding trattoria, located just a minute's walk from the busy Via Galuppi, opposite the Pescheria. It's been run since the 1960s by the Bovo family, and what they don't know about the edible delicacies of the lagoon, and the wines of the region, isn't worth knowing. If you want one of the canalside tables,

book a week ahead. You'll be spending in the region of €50–60 each, excluding wine. Tues–Sat 12.30–3pm & 7.30–9pm, 12.30 noon–3pm; closed one week in July & most of Nov.

Acquastanca Fondamenta Manin 48, Murano ☎041 319 5125, ⓦacquastanca.it; map p.179. Run by Murano natives Giovanna Arcangeli (ex-*Harry's Bar*) and Caterina Nason, *Acquastanca* is a strikingly good-looking place (lots of bare wood, brick and stone) and the menu is small but classy, with the emphasis on fresh fish. Main courses are in the region of €20–25, and the front-of-house bar serves good *cicheti* and wines. Mon & Fri 9am–11pm, Tues–Thurs & Sat 9am–8pm.

Busa alla Torre Campo S. Stefano 3, Murano ☎041 739 662; map p.179. This place has long been regarded as the most dependable trattoria on Murano – unfortunately, though, the kitchen is open for lunch only (Tues–Sun noon–3pm). For the rest of the day it functions as a café-bar. Tues–Sun 9am–5pm.

Da Romano Via Galuppi 221, Burano ☎041 730 030, ⓦdaromano.it; map p.183. This huge and historic Burano restaurant has been in business for more than a century, and its refined fish and seafood dishes have no lack of local devotees – the fish-broth risotto is famous. The columned dining room is impressive too. You'll pay in the region of €60/person. Summer Mon & Wed–Sat noon–3pm & 6.30–9pm, Sun noon–3pm; winter open only for lunch.

La Perla ai Bisatei Campo San Bernardo 1e, Murano ☎041 739 528; map p.179. This is a basic but very good neighbourhood bar-trattoria, tucked into a corner of the island that very few tourists pass through. Pasta dishes, risotto and *frittura* form the core of the menu, and prices are amazingly low – many mains are under €10. The only downside is that it's not open in the evenings. No credit cards. Daily noon–2.30pm.

★ **Venissa** Fondamenta Santa Caterina 3, Mazzorbo ☎041 527 2281, ⓦvenissa.it; map p.183. As soon as it opened, in 2010, *Venissa* become one of Venice's foodie havens. The personnel have changed since then, but the philosophy hasn't – this restaurant uses the resources of the lagoon and the restaurant's garden and vineyard to create a menu that mixes the traditional and the innovative to sometimes brilliant effect. Main courses are €40–50, and there are three fabulous set menus: five courses for €110, seven for €150, and nine for €175 (all excluding wine). The dining room is stylishly modern and intimate (booking is essential), and there are tables outside in good weather. In the adjoining wine bar there's a simpler and less expensive menu on offer, with mains courses at €20–25. Restaurant April–Oct Mon & Wed–Sun noon–3pm & 7–11pm; wine bar May–Oct Mon, Tues & Thurs–Sun 11am–11pm; Nov–April Mon, Tues & Thurs–Sun noon–3pm & 7–11pm.

THE SOUTHERN ISLANDS

Al Storico da Crea Imbarcadero del Redentore 212, Giudecca ☎041 296 0373; map p.192. Occupying light and airy upper-floor premises in the farthest reaches of Giudecca's biggest boatyard, this is a good-value trattoria which has the added attraction of a fantastic view of the southern lagoon from the (few) outside tables, at the top of the steps. Main courses are around €20. Tues–Sun noon–3pm & 6.30–10pm.

Alla Palanca Fondamenta Ponte Piccolo 448, Giudecca ☎041 528 7719; map p.192. If you want a low-cost sit-down lunch, you couldn't do better than to pop over to this bar-trattoria – the food is plain but fine, and the view of the city from the outside tables is magnificent. Meals are served from midday to 2.30pm; before and after that, it's one of Giudecca's busiest bars. Mon–Sat 7am–8.30pm.

Da Sandro Calle Michelangelo 53c, Giudecca ☎041 520 0119; map p.192. Having relocated from its original site (now occupied by *Al Storico da Crea*), the *osteria* formerly known as *Mistrà* retains a canteen-like atmosphere and solid local following; the menu is of course strong on fish and seafood (mains around €20), but they do pizzas too, and the new location has a small garden. Mon–Wed noon–2.30pm & 6.30–11pm.

BARS AND SNACKS

One of the most appealing aspects of Venetian social life is encapsulated in the phrase *"andemo a ombra"*, which translates literally as an invitation to go into the shade, but is in fact an invitation for a drink – more specifically, a small glass of wine (an *ombra*), customarily downed in one. (The phrase is a vestige of the time when wines were unloaded on the Riva degli Schiavoni and then sold at a shaded kiosk at the base of the Campanile; the kiosk was shifted as the sun moved round, so as to stay in the shade.) Stand at a bar any time of the day and you won't have to wait long before

11

VENETIAN DRINKS

The Veneto has been very successful at developing **wines** with French and German grape varieties (notably Merlot, Cabernet, Pinot Bianco, Pinot Grigio, Müller-Thurgau, Riesling, Chardonnay and Gewürztraminer) and now produces more DOC (*Denominazione di origine controllata*) wine than any other region. In addition to the trio of famed Veronese wines – **Valpolicella** (red), **Bardolino** (red) and **Soave** (white) – **prosecco**, a light, Champagne-like wine from the area around Conegliano, is now widely sold abroad. Don't miss a chance to sample the delicious **Cartizze**, the finest type of prosecco – and don't turn your nose up at **prosecco spento** (without the fizz). Wines from neighbouring Friuli are well worth exploring too: the most common reds are Pinot Nero, Refosco, Raboso, Merlot and Cabernet, with Tocai, Pinot Bianco and Sauvignon the most common whites.

At the start of the evening you might indulge in a **spritz** (white wine and soda) or **spritz con bitter** (the same, plus Aperol or Campari or – the darkest, bitterest and most Venetian variety – Select); for an extra twist ask for a spritz made with prosecco. Other popular aperitifs include **fortified wines** such as Martini, Cinzano and Campari. For the real thing, order *un Campari bitter*; ask for a "Campari-soda" and you'll get a ready-mixed version from a little bottle. Crodino, easily recognizable by its lurid orange colour, is a non-alcoholic alternative. You might also try Cynar, an artichoke-based sherry-type liquid often drunk as an aperitif.

For a nightcap, there's a daunting selection of **liqueurs**. Amaro is a bitter after-dinner drink which is served by almost every Italian restaurant. The top brands, in rising order of bitterness, are Montenegro, Ramazotti, Averna and Fernet-Branca. Amaretto is a much sweeter concoction with a strong taste of marzipan. Sambuca is a sticky-sweet aniseed brew, often served with a coffee bean in it and set on fire. Strega is another drink you'll see in every bar – the yellow stuff in elongated bottles: it's as sweet as it looks but not unpleasant. Also popular, though considered slightly vulgar, is *limoncello*, a bitter-sweet lemon spirit that's becoming increasingly trendy abroad. The home-grown Italian firewater is **grappa**, which is made from the leftovers of the wine-making process (skins, stalks and the like). Originally from Bassano di Grappa in the Veneto, it's now produced just about everywhere.

Beer (*birra*) is nearly always a lager-type brew that comes in bottles or on tap (*alla spina*) – standard measures are a third of a litre (*piccola*) and two-thirds of a litre (*media*). Commonest and cheapest are the Italian brands Peroni, Moretti and Dreher; to order these, either state the brand name or ask for *birra nazionale* – otherwise you may be given a more expensive imported beer. You may also come across darker beers (*birra scura* or *birra rossa*), which have a sweeter, maltier taste and resemble stout or bitter.

a customer drops by for a reviving mouthful. Occasionally you'll come across a group doing a *giro di ombre*, the highly refined Venetian version of the pub-crawl; on a serious *giro* it's almost obligatory to stop at an *enoteca* – a bar where priority is given to the range and quality of the wines.

Most bars serve some kind of **food**, their counters usually bearing trays of characteristically Venetian fat little crustless sandwiches (*tramezzini*), which are stuffed with delicious fillings such as eggs and mushrooms, eggs and anchovies or Parma ham and artichokes. Some bars will have a selection of *cicheti* as well, and even a choice of two or three more substantial dishes each day.

SAN MARCO

Al Volto Calle Cavalli 4081 ☎041 522 8945, ⊚enotecaalvolto.com; map p.36. This dark little bar is an *enoteca* in the true sense of the word – 1300 wines from Italy and elsewhere, 100 of them served by the glass, some cheap, many not; good *cicheti*, too, plus more substantial fare. Daily 10am–3pm & 6–11pm.

Bácaro Jazz Salizzada Fondaco dei Tedeschi 5546 ☎041 528 5249, ⊚bacarojazz.com; map p.36. A jazz-themed bar-restaurant that's long been a big hit with young Venetians and tourists, mainly on account of its late hours; there's food, but the kitchen isn't the main attraction, unless you're hungry at midnight (they stop cooking at 1am). Some might raise an eyebrow at the bra-festooned ceiling. Daily noon–3am.

Devil's Forest Calle dei Stagneri 5185 ☎041 520 0623, ⊚devilsforest.com; map p.36. The busiest bar in the vicinity of Campo San Bartolomeo, this is a fairly convincing facsimile of a British pub, with a good range of beers and TV screens for the football. Daily 11am–1am.

★**I Rusteghi** Corte del Tintor 5513 ☎041 523 2205, ⊚airusteghi.com; map p.36. A small *osteria*, secreted away in a tiny courtyard close to Campo San Bartolomeo, with great (if expensive) *cicheti*, a superb selection of wines (some of them very special indeed) and a congenial host – plus a few outside tables. Daily 11.30am–3pm & 6.30pm–midnight.

DORSODURO

Ai Artisti Fondamenta della Toletta 1169a ☎041 523 8944, ⊚enotecaartisti.com; map p.82. This smart little *osteria-enoteca*, located a few metres south of San Barnabà, is a good choice for post-Accademia refreshment, whether you're in need of a light meal or just a glass and a snack. The wine cellar holds a good selection of vintages from all over Italy. It is very small, though, so you may have to wait for a table or a stool at the window counter. If you reserve a table, make sure you turn up on time – if you're more than 10min late, your table will be given to someone else. Tues–Sat 12.45–3pm & 7–11pm (sittings at 7pm & 9pm).

Bakarò do Draghi Calle della Chiesa 3665 ☎041 528 9731, ⊚bakaro.it; map p.82. Taking its name from the two dragons on the wall opposite, this is a tiny, friendly and always busy café-bar, off the north side of Campo Santa Margherita. Tasty *cicheti* and a good range of wines. The back room exhibits the work of local photographers and artists. Daily 10am–midnight.

Café Noir Crosera S. Pantalon 3805 ☎041 710 227; map p.82. A favourite student bar, often with live music on Tues. Open Mon–Fri 11am–2am, Sat & Sun 7pm–2am.

★**Cantina del Vino già Schiavi** Fondamenta Nani 992 ☎041 523 0034, ⊚cantinaschiavi.com; map p.82. Known to Venetians as the *Cantinone* or *Al Bottegon*, this is a great bar and wine shop opposite San Trovaso. Excellent *cicheti* and generously filled panini too. Mon–Sat 8.30am–8.30pm.

Da Còdroma Fondamenta Briati 2540 ☎041 524 6789; map p.82. Perennially popular with Venice's students and with folk of all ages from the surrounding parishes, this wood-panelled *osteria* has refectory-style tables for basic meals, but most of the punters are here for a glass, a snack and a chat. It hosts occasional poetry readings and live music as well. Tues–Sat 10am–4pm & 6–11pm (kitchen open noon–2.30pm & 7–10pm).

El Chioschetto Záttere al Ponte Lungo 1406a ☎348 396 8466; map p.82. This waterfront bar, as its name suggests, is a kiosk with outdoor tables. An excellent place to sit with your spritz and a sandwich and watch the sun set over Giudecca. Has a DJ (and sometimes live music) April–Sept Wed–Sun 6–9pm. Daily: June–Sept 9am–11pm; Oct–May 9am–9pm – unless the weather's bad, in which case it might not open at all.

Estro Calle Crosera 3778 ☎041 476 4914, ⊚estrovenezia.com; map p.82. This good-looking bar was set up by two brothers who really know their wine, and have a particular liking for organics. You can drop in for a glass (from around €3), or linger over a bottle and a selection of *cicheti* and sandwiches. There are tables at the back for full-blown meals (mains around €25 and set menus for €50-ish), but though the food can be good, it's the wine that's the main event here. Mon & Wed–Sun 10am–11pm.

Impronta Cafè Calle Crosera San Pantalon 3815 ☎041 275 0386, ⊚improntacafevenice.com; map p.82. A very welcome addition to the Venetian scene, *Impronta Cafè* is a distinctively bright, stylish and youthful bar-café-restaurant that's busy at all hours of the day. Drop in for a quick coffee or an evening spritz or a nightcap, or sit down for a meal – the menu is very small (often just a couple of main dishes, at €13–16), but it changes daily. Mon–Fri 7am–2am, Sat 8am–2am.

Margaret DuChamp Campo S. Margherita 3019 ☎041 528 6255; map p.82. Despite the challenge from the neighbouring *Orange*, *Margaret DuChamp* is still the first-choice Santa Margherita bar for the style-conscious. It has ranks of seats out on the campo for much of the year. Daily 9am–2am.

★ **Osteria alla Bifora** Campo S. Margherita 2930 ☎041 523 6119; map p.82. A candlelit wood-beamed and brick interior, friendly service, good wine, excellent *cicheti* and large plates of meat and cheese if you need more calories – the *Bifora* is the most atmospheric place for a pit stop on Campo Santa Margherita. Daily noon–2am.

Vinus Venezia Calle del Scaleter 3961 ☎041 715 004; map p.82. A bijou and very pleasant wine bar, near San Rocco; the stock of wines isn't huge, but it's been chosen with great care, and the panini are succulent. Mon–Fri 10am–3pm & 6–11.30pm, Sat 10am–11.30pm.

SAN POLO AND SANTA CROCE

★ **All'Arco** Calle del'Ochialer 436 ☎041 520 5666; map p.100. A great stand-up Rialto bar, tucked under the end of the sottoportego opposite San Giovanni Elemosinario, does superb *sarde in saor* and other snacks. Mon–Sat 8am–3pm.

★ **Al Mercà** Campo Cesare Battisti 213 ☎347 100 2583; map p.100. This minuscule stand-up Rialto bar is perfect for a quick little panino and glass of prosecco. Mon–Thurs 9am–2.30pm & 6–8pm, Fri & Sat closes 9.30pm.

Al Prosecco Campo S. Giacomo dell'Orio 1503 ☎041 524 0222, ⊕alprosecco.com; map p.100. As you'd expect, the Veneto's finest sparkling wines are something of a speciality at this high-class *osteria* – and the snacks are good as well. The outside tables, overlooking one of the nicest squares in the city, are another draw. Mon–Sat: summer 9am–9pm; winter 9am–8pm.

★ **Da Lele** Campo dei Tolentini 183; map p.100. As you can tell by the opening hours, this tiny and authentic stand-up bar attracts a lot of custom from workers en route to or from Piazzale Roma. Sandwiches and rolls made freshly to order, and wine by the glass for less than €1. Mon–Fri 6am–8pm, Sat 6am–2pm.

Do Mori Calle Do Mori 429 ☎041 522 5401; map p.100. Hidden just off Ruga Vecchia San Giovanni, this single narrow room, with no seating, is packed every evening with home-bound shopworkers, Rialto porters and ever-increasing numbers of tourists. It may have become too well-known for its own good, but the *cicheti* are decent, and it has a good range of low-cost wines. Mon–Sat 8am–8pm.

Do Spade Sottoportego delle Do Spade 860 ☎041 521 0574, ⊕cantinadospade.com; map p.100. *Do Spade* is the current occupant of a well-hidden building that's been used as an *osteria* since the fifteenth century. It's a smart little place, which offers a concise and good-quality restaurant menu and an excellent spread of *cicheti* at the bar. Mon & Wed–Sun 10am–3pm & 6–10pm, Tues 6–10pm.

★ **Il Mercante** Fondamenta dei Frari 2564 ☎041 524 1877; map p.100. For many years this place – directly opposite the front door of the Frari – was a pretty belle époque-styled bar-café. Given a thorough revamp and a moody new colour scheme in 2016, it's now possibly the best cocktail bar in Venice. The upstairs gallery is a great spot to spend a late-night hour or two. Tues–Sat 7pm–2am.

Osteria da Filo Calle del Tentor 1539 ☎041 524 6554; map p.100. Located close to Campo San Giacomo dell'Orio, this is a homely little bar, furnished with an ad hoc array of old chairs, tables and sofas, with miscellaneous table lamps strewn about the place. Bookcases provide material for browsing while you're snacking or sipping a spritz. It has live music once a week too. Mon–Fri 4–11pm, Sat & Sun 11am–11pm.

Ruga Rialto Ruga Vecchia S. Giovanni 692 ☎041 521 1243; map p.100. This perennially popular Rialto *bácaro* does serve basic meals in the back room and tiny courtyard, but is best for drinks and *cicheti* in the dark and narrow bar. Mon–Sat 11am–2.30pm & 6pm–1am, Sun 11am–2.30pm & 6–10pm.

CANNAREGIO

Al Cicheto Calle della Misericordia 367a ☎041 716 037; map p.120. Terrific neighbourhood *bácaro*, serving top-quality snacks and larger meals to a regular clientele: it's just yards from the train station, but almost completely off the tourist track. Mon–Fri 10.30am–3.30pm & 5.30–10.30pm, Sat 5.30–10.30pm.

★ **Al Parlamento** Fondamenta Savorgnan 511 ☎041 244 0214; map p.120. This spacious and very friendly bar is the area's smartest, with pale wood furnishings and lengths of rope slung in rows across the ceiling to impart a touch of maritime cool. Good snacks and cocktails, tables beside the Cannaregio canal, and live music too. Daily 7.30am–1.30am.

Al Timon Fondamenta degli Ormesini 2754 ☎041 524 6066; map p.120. With its attractively spartan neo-traditional decor, this *osteria* has been a big hit with Venice's students and twenty-somethings – most nights, the crowd spills out onto the canalside. The meals are OK (steaks are the big thing here), but this is really a place for a snack and a drink or two with your mates. Daily 6pm–1am.

Birreria Zanon Fondamenta dei Ormesini 2735 ☎041 476 2347; map p.120. A no-nonsense and perpetually busy canalside bar (with a few outdoor tables) that's notable for its unusually extensive beer list; also has good *cicheti* and excellent sandwiches. Daily 8.30am–midnight.

Cantina Vecia Carbonera Rio Terrà della Maddalena 2329 ☎041 710 376; map p.120. Old-style *bácaro* with a young, studenty clientele. Good wine, excellent snacks and – unlike many Venetian bars – plenty of space to sit down. Tues–Sun 10am–3pm & 5–11pm.

11

★ **Da Luca e Fred** Rio Terrà S. Leonardo 1518 ☎041 716 170; map p.120. Terrific old *cichetteria*, serving excellent snacks and simple meals to a regular clientele, a few of whom are usually to be found sitting outside, watching the world go by. Very few tables inside, so if you want to eat here in winter, be prepared to wait for a space. Mon & Wed–Sun 9am–9pm.

Il Santo Bevitore Fondamenta Diedo 2393a ☎041 717 560; map p.120. A very friendly neighbourhood bar, close to Santa Fosca. Attracting a young crowd, it makes a big thing of its huge choice of beers – it has the best range in Venice. Inevitably for an Italian "pub", it adds a faux-Irish touch, with a quotation from W.B. Yeats over the door. Satellite TV ensures a full house for big football games. Mon–Sat 4pm–2am, Sun noon–2am.

★ **La Cantina** Strada Nova 3689 ☎041 522 8258; map p.120. A long-established *enoteca* with a good range of wines, and substantial and excellent (but not inexpensive) snacks and light meals. Daily 11am–11pm.

MQ10 Fondamenta di Cannaregio 1020 ☎041 713 241; map p.120. The spartan interior of this cool and friendly Cannaregio bar is just slightly bigger than the ten square metres of the name, but most customers don't linger indoors – the canalside tables are the draw, along with the cocktails. Instead of the *cicheti*, it offers a nice array of salads, panini and cold plates. Daily 7.30am–1am.

Osteria ai Ormesini da Aldo Fondamenta degli Ormesini 2710 ☎041 715 834; map p.120. One of a number of gritty local bars beside this long canal, *da Aldo* is a pleasant spot for a lunchtime snack in the sun, and has a good selection of beers, like the neighbouring *Zanon*. Mon–Sat 11am–4pm & 6pm–1am.

Paradiso Perduto Fondamenta della Misericordia 2540 ☎041 720 581; map p.120. A fixture on the Venice scene since the 1980s, *Paradiso Perduto* is packed to the rafters most nights, with a predominantly young crowd. The restaurant section is like a boho refectory and the atmosphere at the tables is usually terrific, though there are better kitchens in the neighbourhood. Go for the drinks, the *cicheti* and the buzz. Frequent live music, with the emphasis on blues and jazz. Thurs–Mon 10am–midnight.

Taverna al Remer Campiello Remer 5701 ☎041 522 8789, ⊕alremer.it; map p.120. Slotted into the corner of a tiny square that opens out onto the Canal Grande, this timber-beamed bar-restaurant is a very atmospheric spot for a drink; the weekday buffet lunch, at €25, is excellent, and from 5.30 to 7pm there's a "happy hour" buffet to accompany the *aperitivi*. Daily noon–midnight (kitchen closes 10pm).

PICNICKING IN VENICE

The price of restaurants in Venice makes picnicking an attractive option, but you can't just spread your lunch wherever you like: bylaws forbid picnicking on the Piazza and other busy tourist spots, and it's illegal to sit down on a bridge. To be on the safe side always use a bench, not the pavement.

The best places to buy food – especially fruit and veg – are the markets that are held in various squares every day except Sunday: the biggest and best is of course the **Rialto**, but you'll also find a few stalls on **Campo Santa Maria Formosa** (Castello), **Campo Santa Margherita** (Dorsoduro) and between **Ponte delle Guglie** and **Campiello dell'Anconeta** in Cannaregio. Fresh produce is also sold from barges moored by **Campo San Barnaba** (Dorsoduro) and at the top end of **Via Garibaldi** (Castello). Virtually every parish has its **alimentari**; as you'd expect, the cheaper ones are those farthest from San Marco. Alternatively, you could get everything from one of Venice's **supermarkets**, which are becoming more numerous by the year, with the ever-rising number of tourists.The city has several branches of Coop: on Campo Santa Marina (Castello); on the corner of Salizzada San Lio and Calle Mondo Nuovo (Castello); by the Piazzale Roma vaporetto stop for services to Murano (Cannaregio); and on Campo San Giacomo dell'Orio (Santa Croce). Other supermarkets include: Punto Simply, beside the Rossini cinema in Salizzada del Teatro (San Marco) and tucked between houses 3019 and 3112 on Campo Santa Margherita (Dorsoduro); Conad, at Záttere Ponte Lungo 1491, by the San Basilio vaporetto stop (Dorsoduro), at Rio Terà Frari (San Polo) and at Strada Nova 3660, near San Felice (Cannaregio); and Prix, at Fondamenta San Giacomo 203a (Giudecca). Most are open daily 8.30am–8/8.30pm, though some of the smaller ones close for a couple of hours in the middle of the day, and on Sunday.

For **local wines**, Venice has branches of a wine merchant called La Nave d'Oro, at Campo S. Margherita 3664 (Dorsoduro), Calle del Mondo Novo 5786b (Castello) and Rio Terrà San Leonardo 1370 (Cannaregio); these shops sell not just bottles but also draught Veneto wine to take out, and are open Mon, Tues & Thurs–Sat 9am–1pm & 5–8pm, Wed 9am–1pm. In addition, many wine bars sell bottles to take away, as do most *alimentari*.

Un Mondo diVino Salizzada S. Canciano 5984a ☎ 041 521 1093; map p.120. Occupying a marble-fronted and wood-beamed old butcher's shop, this little *bácaro* has rapidly built up a great reputation, for its fantastic array of *cicheti* and its fine selection of wines. Prices are quite steep, but quality is high. Daily 10am–11pm.

CENTRAL CASTELLO

★ **Al Portego** Calle Malvasia 6015 ☎ 041 522 9038, ⓦ osteriaalportego.org; map p.136. In the middle of the day this superb *bácaro* is always crammed with customers eating *cicheti*; in the evening there's often a queue for a place at one of the tiny tables, where some well-prepared basics (pasta, risotto, *fegato alla veneziana* etc) are served. Daily 10.30am–2.30pm & 5.30–10.30pm.

Enoiteca Mascareta Calle Lunga Santa Maria Formosa 5183 ☎ 041 523 0744; map p.136. Perpetually busy wine bar with delicious *cicheti* and a small menu of more substantial food. The wine list is well chosen, and there's an unusually wide choice of gins too. Daily 7pm–2am.

Osteria da Baco Salizzada S. Provolo 4621 ☎ 041 523 0557; map p.136. The ever-busy *Osteria da Baco* is a genuine old-style *osteria* – the nearest one to the Piazza. A wide selection of sandwiches and *cicheti*. Daily 8.15am–midnight.

EASTERN CASTELLO

Alla Rampa Salizzada S. Antonin 3607; map p.154. Shabby and one hundred percent authentic bar, which has been in existence for half a century. Great for an inexpensive *ombra*. Mon–Sat 8am–8pm.

El Réfolo Via Garibaldi 1580; map p.154. There are several bars on and around Via Garibaldi, the social hub of eastern Venice, and this is the best of them; being quite remote, it's not overrun with tourists, but you won't be made to feel like an intruder either. The snacks are good, and when the weather is decent you can sit outside. Tues–Sun 10.30am–11pm, or later if the place is busy.

11

CAFÉS, PASTICCERIE AND GELATERIE

When **coffee** first appeared in Venice around 1640, imported by the Republic from the Levant, it was treated as a medicine – the first coffee outlet on the Piazza was called *Il Rimedio* (the Remedy). Today the city has many excellent cafés, ranging from the studenty places on Campo Santa Margherita to the historic coffee houses of the Piazza, whose prices will prompt you to dally just so you can feel you've had your money's worth.

As with bars, if you **sit in a café** you will be charged more, and if you **sit outside** the bill will be even higher. Nearly all **pasticcerie** also serve coffee and alcohol, but will have at most a few bar stools; they're all right for a swift caffeination before the next round of church-visiting, but not for a session of postcard writing or a longer recuperative stop. Elbow-room in the city's *pasticcerie* is especially restricted first thing in the morning, as the citizens pile in for a coffee and *cornetto* (croissant). You can also stop for a coffee at some of Venice's **gelaterie**, though several of the best *gelaterie* do nothing but *gelati*. Opening hours of *gelaterie* are notoriously unreliable, especially in winter – if trade is slack, many of them shut down earlier than advertised.

SAN MARCO

Florian Piazza S. Marco 56–59 ☎ 041 520 5641, ⓦ caffeflorian.com; map p.38. The most famous café in Venice began life in 1720, when Florian Francesconi's *Venezia Trionfante* (Venice Triumphant) opened for business here, and the place is still redolent of the eighteenth century, though the gorgeous interior – a frothy confection of mirrors, stucco and frescoes – is a nineteenth-century pastiche. Its prices match its pedigree: a simple cappuccino at an outside table will set you back €12, and you'll have to take out a mortgage for a cocktail; if the "orchestra" is playing, you'll be taxed another €6 (per person) for the privilege of hearing them. (*Quadri* and *Lavena* levy a similar surcharge.) Daily 9am–midnight (but often closes earlier in winter); closed Tues in winter.

Igloo Calle della Mandola 3651 ☎ 041 522 3003; map p.36. Luscious homemade ice cream – the summer fruit concoctions are especially delicious. Daily: May–Sept 11.30am–8.30pm; Oct, Nov & Feb–April 11.30am–7.30pm.

Lavena Piazza S. Marco 133–134 ☎ 041 522 4070, ⓦ lavena.it; map p.38. Wagner's favourite café (there's a commemorative plaque inside) is the second member of the Piazza's top-bracket and exorbitantly expensive trio. For privacy you can take a table in the narrow little gallery overlooking the bar. The coffee is no way inferior to *Florian* or *Quadri*, and you can keep down the price by drinking at the bar – you'll pay just a couple of euros there, as opposed to more than €10 if you sit outside. Daily 9.30am–midnight (but often closes earlier in winter); closed Tues in winter.

★ **Marchini Time** Campos S. Luca 4589 ☎ 041 241 3087; map p.36. Sample the succulent *Marchini* pastries with a cup of top-grade coffee at this sleek and ever-busy café. Daily 7.30am–8.30pm.

Paolin Campos S. Stefano 2962 ☎ 041 522 5576; map p.36. Campo Santo Stefano now has more cafés and restaurants than ever before, but the unpretentious *Paolin* has been here longer than any of them. In addition to drinks it serves decent ice cream, and the outside tables have a very nice setting. Daily 8am–11pm.

Quadri Piazza S. Marco 120–124 ☎ 041 522 2105; map p.38. *Quadri* can claim an even longer lineage than *Florian*, as coffee has been on sale here since the seventeenth century, and prices are in the same price league too, though you can save a lot by taking your cappuccino at the tiny bar. It's also the one Piazza café you're sure to find open late on a winter night. On the other hand, it's not as pretty as *Florian*, and its name doesn't have quite the same lustre, partly because Austrian officers patronized it during the occupation, while the natives stuck with *Florian*. There's a *Quadri* bistro next to the café and a restaurant upstairs; the bistro is good and the restaurant is excellent, but both are pricy – in the case of the restaurant, very pricy indeed. Daily 9am–midnight.

Rosa Salva Calle Fiubera ☎ 041951 521 0544; map p.38; & Merceria S. Salvador 5020 ☎ 041 522 7934, ⓦ rosasalva.it; map p.36. Founded way back in the 1870s, *Rosa Salva* serves what some would say is the best coffee in Venice, and very good pastries too. The ambience of these two branches can be rather brisk, though– the most characterful *Rosa Salva* is over by Santi Giovanni e Paolo. Mon–Sat 7.30am–8.30pm.

Venchi Calle dei Fabbri 998a ☎ 041 241 2314, ⓦ venchi. com; map p.38. Like *Rosa Salva*, *Venchi* started in the 1870s, but in this case the birthplace was Turin. They create terrific chocolates – the hazelnut *gianduja* is a speciality. For ice cream, however, there are better options. Mon–Sat 10am–10pm, Sun 10am–9pm.

DORSODURO

★ **Il Caffè** Campo S. Margherita 2963 ☎ 041 528 7998; map p.82. Known locally as *Caffè Rosso*, for its big red signboard, this small, atmospheric, old-fashioned café-bar is another student favourite. Good sandwiches, and lots of seats outside in the campo. Mon–Sat 7am–1am.

★ **Il Doge** Campo S. Margherita 3058 ☎ 041 523 4607; map p.82. Well-established, very friendly and extremely good hole-in-the-wall *gelateria*, which also does a superb *granita*, made in the traditional Sicilian way. Mon–Sat 9am–midnight, Sun 9am–9pm, but often closes earlier in off-season; closed Nov & Dec.

Nico Zàttere ai Gesuati 922 ☎ 041 522 5293; map p.82. This café-*gelateria*, which has occupied its prime location overlooking the Giudecca canal for the best part of ninety years, is celebrated for an artery-clogging creation called a *gianduiotto da passeggio* – a paper cup with a block of praline ice cream drowned in whipped cream. Mon–Wed & Fri–Sun 6.45am–10pm.

Tonolo Crosera S. Pantalon 3764 ☎ 041 523 7209; map p.82. Established back in the 1880s, this is one of the busiest cafés on one of the busiest streets of the student district; especially hectic on Sunday mornings, when the *Tonolo* cakes are in high demand. Tues–Sat 7.45am–8pm, Sun 7.45am–1pm.

SAN POLO AND SANTA CROCE

Alaska Calle Larga dei Bari 1159; map p.100. A somewhat eccentric organic *gelateria*, dishing out flavours such as artichoke, turmeric and asparagus amid the more traditional concoctions. It's not the smoothest ice cream in Italy, but definitely worth a try. Daily 11am–10pm.

★ **Caffè del Doge** Calle dei Cinque 609 ☎ 041 522 7787, ⓦ caffedeldoge.com; map p.100. Fantastically good coffee (the company supplies many of the city's bars and restaurants), served in a chic unfussy setup very close to the Rialto bridge. Daily 7am–7pm.

★ **Rizzardini** Calle della Madonetta 1415 ☎ 041 522 3835; map p.100. Founded in 1742, *Rizzardini* is one of the best outlets for the less florid varieties of Venetian pastries; good coffee too. Mon & Wed–Sun 7am–8pm, closed Aug.

CANNAREGIO

Gelateria Ca' d'Oro Strada Nova 4273 ☎ 041 522 8982; map p.120. A wide range of wonderfully smooth ice creams is served at Andrea Busolin's long-established shop. Daily 10am–midnight (10pm in winter).

Il Gelatone Rio Terà Maddalena 2063 ☎ 041 720 631; map p.120. Nearby *Grom* (a national chain) gets more of the tourist trade, but this place (or the *Ca' d'Oro*) would still win a local vote for the title Best Gelateria in Cannaregio. Daily: mid-Jan to April & Oct to mid-Dec 10am–9pm; May–Sept 10am–10.30pm.

Pasticceria Nobile Calle del Pistor 1818 ☎ 041 720 731, ⓦ pasticcerianobile.it; map p.120. Established in the 1930s, this is still the classiest café in Cannaregio, and is always thronged with locals at breakfast and after work; the pastries and biscuits are excellent. Tues–Sun 6.40am–8.30pm; closed July & two weeks in Feb.

Torrefazione Cannaregio Strada Nova 1337 ☎ 041 716 371, ⓦ torrefazionecannaregio.it; map p.120. Coffee is pretty well all they do at this tiny stand-up café (though you will get croissants in the morning), and they are extremely good at it, having been in business there since 1930. Mon–Sat 7am–7.30pm.

CENTRAL CASTELLO

Bonifacio Calle degli Albanesi 4237 ☎ 041 522 7507; map p.136. Compact and always busy café-bar-*pasticceria*, a few minutes' stroll east of the Piazza. Closed for renovation when we went to press, but should reopen soon, with much the same opening hours as before. Mon–Wed & Fri 6.30am–7pm, Sat & Sun 7.30am–7pm.

Didovich Campo Marina 5910 ☎ 041 523 0017; map p.136. A highly regarded *pasticceria* – some say with the city's best *tiramisù* and *pastine* (aubergine, pumpkin and other savoury tarts). Standing room only inside, but it has outdoor tables. Mon–Sat 7am–7.30pm, plus Sun 8am–2pm in winter.

★ **La Boutique del Gelato** Salizzada S. Lio 5727 ☎ 041 522 3283; map p.136. Top-grade ice creams – as good as any in Venice – are created at this tiny outlet. Daily mid-Feb to Nov 10.30am–8.30pm (sometimes later in high season).

Pasticceria Chiusso Salizzada dei Greci 3306 ☎ 041 523 1611; map p.136. An award-winning *pasticceria* (known locally as *Da Pierino*, after the owner), with terrific buttery home-made pastries and very nice coffee. It's always packed at the start of the day, as people drop in for a coffee and cornetto on their way to work. Mon, Tues & Thurs–Sun 7am–8pm.

Ponte delle Paste Ponte delle Paste 5991 ☎ 041 522 2889; map p.136. Excellent *pasticceria* with a small "tea room" – a good place to relax after visiting San Zanipolo. Daily 7am–8pm.

Rosa Salva Campo SS Giovanni e Paolo 6779 ☎ 041 522 7949; map p.136. With its marble-topped bar and outside tables within the shadow of Santi Giovanni e Paolo, this is the most characterful of the three *Rosa Salva* branches in the *centro storico*. The coffee and home-made ice cream are superb. Daily 8am–8pm.

11

Festivals, the arts and nightlife

Venice has a good number of late-opening bars, some of which have live music or DJs. Music in Venice, to all intents and purposes, means opera (at the world-famous Fenice) and classical music – though the Teatro Malibran has been known to stage concerts by Italian rock bands, major names rarely come nearer than Padua, and the biggest tend to favour Verona. That said, Venice's calendar of special events is pretty impressive, with the Carnevale, the Film Festival and the Biennale ranking among the continent's hottest dates. Carnevale attracts hordes of tourists (as was the intention when the modern version of the festival was created), but for a more authentically Venetian experience, come to the city for the Festa del Redentore, the city's most exuberant religious festival, or for the boat races that attend the Regata Storica.

FESTIVALS

Venice celebrates enthusiastically a number of special days either not observed elsewhere in Italy, or, like the Carnevale, generally celebrated to a lesser extent. Although they have gone through various degrees of decline and revival, most of them are still strongly traditional in form. These are the main events, arranged chronologically.

CARNEVALE (FEBRUARY/MARCH)

John Evelyn wrote of the 1646 **Carnevale**: "All the world was in Venice to see the folly and madness… the women, men and persons of all conditions disguising themselves in antique dresses, & extravagant Musique & a thousand gambols." Today's Carnevale is not quite so riotous, but it's nonetheless become the city's main tourist jamboree, and is dreaded by many Venetians for the influx of heavy-drinking foreigners it brings.

The origins of the Carnevale can be traced in the word itself: *carne vale*, a "farewell to meat" before the rigours of Lent. The medieval European carnival developed into a period of liberation from the constraints of social rank, and a means of quelling discontent by a ritualized relinquishing of power. Venice's Carnevale – which became so famous that the city's mask-makers had their own guild (the *mascarei*) – had its heyday in the eighteenth century, when it began on December 26 and lasted until Shrove Tuesday.

Today's Carnevale is officially limited to **the ten days leading up to Lent**, finishing on Shrove Tuesday with a masked ball for the glitterati, and dancing in the Piazza for the plebs. Having ceased with the collapse of the Republic, Carnevale was revived in 1979 by a group of non-Venetians, prompted by the Carnival-themed theatre performances at that year's Biennale. The city authorities, sensing a way of attracting tourists in the dead months of the year, soon gave their support, and nowadays the town hall organizes various pageants and performances during the festival, beginning with the "Flight of the Angel" (see page 60) on the first Sunday of Carnevale. (On the previous day, the twelve "Marys", from whom the next year's "Angel" will be chosen, are presented to a make-believe doge – see page 60 for more.) For Venetians, however, Carnevale kicks off a week earlier, with the Festa Veneziana, which takes place on the Saturday and is centred in Cannaregio; the Festa Veneziana is not aimed at tourists, but inevitably it has become a tourist draw – in 2018, more than 20,000 turned up to watch the parades down the Cannaregio canal. On the following day there's a spectacle called the Corteo Acqueo di Carnevale, a parade of boats down the Canal Grande, which sees all of the city's rowing clubs take part.

During the ten days of the official Carnevale you'll spot the most extravagant costumes on the Piazza in the evenings, when people who have spent thousands of euros on their costumes install themselves at the tables of *Florian*, but even at lunchtime you'll see businesspeople doing their shopping in the classic white mask, black cloak and tricorne hat, an ensemble known as a *baùta*. Masks are on sale throughout the year (though few of them are made in Venice), and during Carnevale there's a mask-making marquee on Campo San Maurizio. If you want to hire a full outfit, the places to try are Pietro Longhi (ⓦ pietrolonghi. com), Nicolao (ⓦ nicolao.com), Atelier Marega (ⓦ marega. it) and Flavia (ⓦ veniceatelier.com). You'll find an events calendar at ⓦ carnivalofvenice.com.

SU E ZO PER I PONTI (MARCH/APRIL)

Held on the **fourth Sunday of Lent**, Su e Zo Per I Ponti (Up and Down the Bridges; ⓦ suezo.it) is a privately organized fun day that was first held in 1975 and has since become a fixture of the Venetian calendar. In essence it's a non-competitive orienteering event in aid of charity, in which participants are given a map of the city on which key sights (including plenty of bars) have to be ticked off. The start line is in the Piazza, where you register on the morning of the jaunt.

FESTA DI SAN MARCO (APRIL)

April 25 – the feast day of **St Mark** – begins with a Mass in the Basilica, followed by a gondola race from Sant'Elena to the mouth of the Canal Grande. Some Venetian men continue the tradition of giving their wife or girlfriend a red rosebud (*boccolo*) on this day, hence the alternative name: Le Festa del Boccolo.

LA SENSA AND VOGALONGA (APRIL–JUNE)

The feast of **La Sensa** happens on the **Sunday after Ascension Day** – the latter being the day on which the doge enacted the wedding of Venice to the sea (see page 198). A feeble modern version of that ritual is followed by a gondola regatta, but far more spectacular is the **Vogalonga** or "long row", held a week later. Established in 1974, the Vogalonga is open to any crew in any class of rowing boat (there's always a good number of wacky vessels), and covers a 32-kilometre course from the Bacino di San Marco out to Burano and back, with the competitors setting off from in front of the Palazzo Ducale around 9am.

FESTA DI SAN PIETRO (JUNE/JULY)

Held in the week of June 29, the **Festa di San Pietro** is a small-scale festival of concerts, open-air shows and food stalls, held around the church of San Pietro di Castello. Entirely untouched by tourism, it's an authentic antithesis to Carnevale.

FESTA DEL REDENTORE (JULY)

For Venetians it's not Carnevale that's the city's quintessential festival – it's the **Festa del Redentore**,

12

which commemorates the end of the plague of 1576. Celebrated on the **third Sunday in July and the preceding Saturday**, the festa is centred on Palladio's church of the Redentore, which was built in thanksgiving for the city's deliverance from that terrible epidemic. On the Saturday the bishop of Venice marks the commencement of the festive weekend by leading a procession to the church, crossing the Giudecca canal on a pontoon bridge that's supported by dozens of boats strung across the waterway from the Záttere. By the evening the Bacino di San Marco is clogged with small vessels, as people row out for a picnic on the lagoon, then at around 11.30pm there's the mother of all firework displays, after which it's traditional to row to the Lido for the sunrise. In 2014 there were rumours that Venice's budget crisis would necessitate the cancellation of the Festa del Redentore and the Regata Storica. Both events went ahead, but their survival can't be taken for granted.

THE REGATA STORICA (SEPTEMBER)

Held on the **first Sunday in September**, the **Regata Storica** is the annual trial of strength and skill for the city's gondoliers and other expert rowers. It starts with a procession of historic craft along the Canal Grande course, their crews all decked out in period dress, followed by a series of races right up the canal. Re-enacting the return of Caterina Cornaro to her native city in 1489 (see page 304), the opening parade is a spectacular affair, and is followed by a race for young rowers in two-oared *pupparini*; the women come next (in boats called *mascarete*), followed by a race for canoe-like *caorline*; and then it's the men's race, in specialized two-man racing gondolas called *gondolini*.

The Regata Storica has been increasingly marketed as a touristic spectacle, but there's nothing artificial about the smaller *regate* that are held throughout the year: the **Regata di San Zanipolo** (late June); the **Regata di Murano** (early July); the **Regata di Malamocco** (mid-July); the **Regata del Redentore** (during the Festa del Redentore); the **Regata di Pellestrina** (early Aug); and the **Regata di Burano** (late Sept).

FESTA DELLA SALUTE (NOVEMBER)

Named after the church of the Salute, the **Festa della Salute** is a reminder of the plague of 1630–31, which killed one third of the city's population. The church was built after the outbreak, and every **November 21** people process to it over a pontoon bridge across the Canal Grande, to give thanks for good health, or pray for it.

CLASSICAL MUSIC AND OPERA

Classical concerts, with a very strong bias towards the eighteenth century (and Vivaldi in particular – barely a day goes by without a performance of the *Four Seasons*), are given at various venues, such as the **Palazzo Prigione Vecchie**, the **Scuola Grande di San Giovanni Evangelista**, the **Scuola di San Teodoro**, **Palazzo Albrizzi**, **the Teatrino Grassi** and the churches of **Santo Stefano**, the **Frari**, **San Stae**, **San Samuele**, **San Vidal**, **San Giacomo di Rialto**, the **Ospedaletto** and the **Pietà**. In addition, the Centre de musique romantique française (ⓦ bru-zane.com) often holds concerts of nineteenth- and twentieth-century French music in its HQ, the Palazzetto Bru Zane, Calle Zane 2368 (San Polo) – it's near the Scuola di San Giovanni Evangelista. Tickets for concerts at these venues are usually €15–30, with reductions for students and children. The two big venues are as follows.

La Fenice Campo San Fantin ☎041 786 511, ⓦ teatrolafenice.it. The third-ranking Italian opera house after Milan's La Scala and Naples' San Carlo, La Fenice has opera and ballet performances throughout the year; classical concerts are held in the Fenice's Sale Apollinee. Seats for the opera cost €40–200 on most nights, but you'll pay rather more for the opening night of a production; prices are a little lower in midweek than at the weekend. Tickets can be bought online, at the Fenice box office and at the Venezia Unica/Hellovenezia offices at Piazzale Roma and the train station.

Teatro Malibran Campiello del Teatro Malibran ⓦ teatrolafenice.it. The Malibran and Sale Apollinee share top billing as the city's prime venues for classical recitals; the Malibran also has occasional opera, jazz and rock shows. Tickets for the Malibran (around €25–70) can be bought from the same places as for the Fenice; its own box office sells tickets only on the night of the concert, from around 1hr before the start.

THEATRE

The Teatro San Gallo, near the Piazza, stages a trashy and expensive "The Story of Venice" event for the tourists every night, but the city has a few genuine theatres too, including a couple of risk-taking ventures.

Teatro a l'Avogaria Corte Zappa 1617, Dorsoduro ☎041 099 1967, ⓦ teatroavogaria.it. Founded in 1969 by director Giovanni Poli (a crucial figure in the revival of interest in *commedia dell'arte*), the Teatro a l'Avogaria specializes in experimental drama and offbeat productions of well-established repertoire; dance sometimes features too. Tickets cannot be bought on the door, and prices aren't fixed – instead, you're asked to make a donation.

Teatro Fondamenta Nuove Fondamenta Nuove 5013 ☎041 522 4498, ⓦ teatrofondamentanuove.it.

Occupying a building at the western end of Fondamente Nuove, this small and adventurous theatre offers a programme of drama interspersed with dance, music and performance art events.

Teatro Goldoni Calle Teatro ☎041 240 2014, ⓦteatrostabileveneto.it. Venice's main theatre, which operates in partnership with the Teatro Verdi in Padua and the Olimpico in Vicenza, has a reputation for high-class drama, with work by the eponymous dramatist regularly appearing on the bill. It also stages opera, concerts and ballet from time to time.

CINEMA

In addition to the cinemas listed below, from late July to late August an open-air cinema is installed on Campo San Polo, usually with half a dozen non-dubbed English-language films on the programme. Films start each night at around 9pm, and it's worth an evening of anyone's holiday, if only for the atmosphere.

Giorgione Rio Terrà dei Franceschi 4612a, Cannaregio ☎041 522 6298. A small two-screen cinema: Sala B is used for less mainstream films than those shown in Sala A, and non-dubbed English-language films are shown on Tuesdays from October to May.

La Casa del Cinema Salizzada S. Stae 1990, Santa Croce ☎041 524 1320. To watch films in this fifty-seat art-house cinematheque you need to pay for annual membership, which costs €35, or €25 for students.

Multisala Astra Via Corfu 12, Lido ☎041 526 5736. Another two-screener, running the same programmes as the Giorgione, but slightly out of sync.

Multisala Rossini Salizzada del Teatro 3997a, San Marco ☎041 241 7274. Occupying the vast old Teatro Rossini, the three-screen Multisala Rossini is Venice's chief outlet for mainstream films.

THE FILM FESTIVAL

The **Venice Film Festival** (Mostra Internazionale d'Arte Cinematografica), founded in 1932 as a propaganda showcase for Mussolini's "progressive" Italy, is the world's oldest and the most important in Europe after Cannes. Originally the festival had no competitive element, but with the creation of the Leon d'Oro (the Golden Lion) in 1949, the organizers created a focal point for the rivalries that beset this narcissistic business: almost every Festival is beset with vehement disputes over the programming and prizes. Despite this, the festival has been going from strength to strength in recent years, with an increasing number of big American productions choosing Venice for the premiere screening, in advance of autumn release back home.

The eleven-day Film Festival takes place on the Lido every year in late August and/or early September. Posters advertising the schedule appear weeks in advance, and

NIGHTLIFE

There's no getting around the fact – Venice is not a young city. The most buzzing area of the city is Dorsoduro, where various outposts of the university keep the bars busy. Bear in mind, however, that most of these venues are small and there are strict bylaws against late-night noise, so "live music" often entails nothing wilder than an aspiring singer-songwriter on acoustic guitar. Lack of funding seems to have put an end to the Venezia Suona festival, which used to stage **live music** in various campi for one day in June or July, but the Veneto jazz festival in July and August (ⓦvenetojazz.com) always stages a gig or two in Venice.

Some bars have occasional DJ nights, but there has not been a genuine club in Venice for many years. On the mainland, Mestre and Marghera have a few clubs, which are listed in the local press, but the real action is further away, out in the northern reaches of the lagoon at **Jesolo** – in summer, just stroll into town after 11pm on a Friday or Saturday night and you'll find the current hot spots. The problem is that though there are plenty of buses out to Jesolo, there's no night service back, so you have to take a taxi to the Punta Sabbioni vaporetto stop (for services to the Lido) or all the way to Venice, or get a lift with someone – and the Jesolo–Venice road is notorious for the accidents that occur when hundreds of inebriated young Italians go blasting back home.

Only one aspect of Venice's nightlife attracts customers from the mainland, and that's the **Casinò** (ⓦcasinovenezia.it), which occupies the magnificent Palazzo Vendramin-Calergi (Cannaregio) on the Canal Grande. It operates from 11am until 2.45am every day (the gaming tables are open from 4pm – before then, only the slots are in operation), the minimum age is 18, and the dress code is fairly relaxed – even jeans are acceptable in the rooms given over to slot machines, though jacket and tie are obligatory for the "French" games such as roulette and *chemin de fer*. The casino is owned by the city, but the mayor has plans to sell it off, a short-term cash-generating plan that has raised a great deal of local opposition.

the tourist offices will have the festival programme a fair time before the event. The main venue is the Palazzo del Cinemà, next to the *Excelsior* hotel on Lungomare G. Marconi; other screenings take place in the PalaBiennale marquee, in the four-screen Palazzo del Casinò, and in the Sala Giardino. Tickets are available to the general public on the day before the performance, at the Palazzo del Cinemà and PalaBiennale ticket offices, and at the Biennale HQ in Ca'Giustinian, a short distance west of the Piazza at Calle del Ridotto 1364. For online info, go to ⓦ labiennale.org.

ART AND PHOTOGRAPHY EXHIBITIONS

The **Venice Biennale**, Venice's premier cultural event, is covered on page 161. At any time of any year there will be a few **special exhibitions** in town, the chief venues being Ca' Pésaro, the Fondazione Cini, the Guggenheim, the Museo Correr, the Museo Fortuny, Palazzo Cavalli Franchetti, Palazzo Loredan, Palazzo Grassi, the Querini-Stampalia, the Scuola Grande di San Giovanni Evangelista, the Casa dei Tre Oci on Giudecca (ⓦ treoci.org) and the Officina delle Zattere, opposite San Trovaso (ⓦ officinadellezattere.it). In addition, the Fondazione Prada often stages substantial shows of contemporary art in its spectacular Venetian base, the Palazzo Corner della Regina (ⓦ fondazioneprada.org). On a more modest scale, the **Fondazione Bevilacqua La Masa** (ⓦ bevilacqualamasa.it) holds occasional exhibitions at its HQ, Piazza San Marco 71c. The commercial art galleries of Venice are generally timorous.

12

L'ISOLA

Shopping

Venice has always been a mercantile city, and today its shops rake in millions of euros every day from the visiting throngs. It's indicative of the dominance of the tourist industry that Venice's central post office building has now become an emporium for big-spending foreigners, while the city's one proper department store, *Coin*, was forced to close due to a massive rent increase. That said, some authentically Venetian outlets and workshops are still in operation: the manufacture of exquisite decorative papers is a distinctively Venetian skill; small craft studios continue to produce beautiful handmade bags and shoes; and of course there are lots of shops selling glass, lace and Carnevale masks. (With masks, lace and glass, much of the stuff on sale is low quality, mass-produced and imported – we've recommended only the outlets for genuine Venetian items.)

ANTIQUES

The antiques shops around **San Maurizio** and **Santa Maria Zobenigo** cater for the wealthiest collectors, so bargain hunters should head to the **antiques fairs** that crop up throughout the year in Campo San Maurizio, where the stalls groan under the weight of old books,

prints, silverware and bric-a-brac. The traders in the **San Barnaba** district are also slightly downmarket, running the kind of places where you could find a battered wooden cherub or an old bronze door-knocker.

ART MATERIALS

Arcobaleno Calle delle Botteghe 3457, San Marco ☎041 523 6818; map p.36. As the name implies, *Arcobaleno* (Rainbow) is the first stop for pigments, though they sell a variety of other artistic paraphernalia. Mon–Fri 9am–12.30pm & 4–7.30pm, Sat 9am–12.30pm.

Testolini Fondamenta Orseolo 1756 ⓦtestolini.it; map

p.36. Also Campiello Corner 5587, Cannaregio; map 120. The city's best-known stationers, with a vast range of paper, pens, briefcases and more. Fondamenta Orseolo, the bigger branch, has a good range of fine-art materials. Fondamenta Orseolo Mon–Sat 9.30am–1pm & 2.30–7pm; Campiello Corner Mon–Sat 8.45am–7.15pm.

BOOKS

Alberto Bertoni Calle de la Mandola 3637b, San Marco ☎041 522 9583; map p.36. For remaindered and secondhand books, including a lot of art-book bargains. Mon–Sat 9am–1pm & 3–7.30pm.

★ **Filippi Editore** Caselleria 5284, Castello ☎041 523 6916, map p.136. Also Calle del Paradiso 5763, Castello ☎041 523 5635, ⓦlibreriaeditricefilippi.com; map p.136. This family-run business – Venice's oldest surviving publisher – produces Venice-related facsimile editions, including Francesco Sansovino's sixteenth-century guide to the city (the first city guide ever published), and sells a huge array of books about Venice. Both branches Mon–Sat 9am–12.30pm & 3–7.30pm.

Goldoni Calle dei Fabbri 4742, San Marco ☎041 522 2384; map p.36. A good general bookshop; also keeps an array of maps and posters. Mon–Sat 9am–7.30pm, Sun 11am–1.30pm & 2.30–7pm.

★ **Libreria Acqua Alta** Calle Lunga S. Maria Formosa 5176b, Castello ☎041 296 0841; map p.136. Luigi Frizzo's labyrinthine bookshop is like no other, with thousands of books – nearly all secondhand, and nearly all Italian – stacked on every available surface, with some displayed in bathtubs and even in a gondola, to protect

them from high tides (the back door opens directly into the water). There's even a staircase built from water-damaged hardbacks. Daily 9am–8pm.

Libreria della Toletta Sacca della Toletta 1214, Dorsoduro ☎041 523 2034, ⓦlibreriatoletta.it; map p.82. Sells reduced-price books, mainly in Italian, but some dual-language and translations; keeps a good stock of Venice-related titles. Two adjacent branches sell art, architecture, design and photography titles, including bargains on Electa books. Mon–Sat 9am–7.30pm, Sun 3–7pm.

Libreria MarcoPolo Campo Santa Margherita 2899, Dorsoduro, ☎041 822 4843; map p.82; also Fondamenta Ponte Lungo 282, Giudecca ☎041 847 3867; ⓦlibreriamarcopolo.com; map p.192. Now relocated from its old home by San Giovanni Crisostomo, this fine independent bookshop, run by an expat New Yorker, now has two branches – on Campo Santa Margherita, which is mainly for new Italian titles, and over on Giudecca, which has a stock of secondhand and out-of-print books, some of them in English. Campo Santa Margherita Mon–Sat 10am–10pm, Sun 11am–8pm; Giudecca Mon–Sat 10am–8pm.

CLOTHES

As you'd expect, many of the top-flight Italian **designers and fashion houses** – such as Versace, Missoni, Gucci, Armani, Prada and Dolce e Gabbana (the only ones with a

Venetian connection) – are represented in Venice, with their outlets being clustered close to the Piazza, in the **Mercerie**, **Calle Vallaresso** and **Calle Larga XXII Marzo**. For more

VENEZIA AUTENTICA

Venetian artisans were once famed worldwide, but nowadays they are an endangered species. So **Venezia Autentica**, a venture set up to help small and authentically Venetian businesses – especially craftspeople – by bringing their work to the attention of tourists, is a very welcome initiative. At the moment, the scheme has around forty participants, ranging from milliners and shoemakers to leather workshops and jewellers (plus a few *osterie*). More details can be found at ⓦveneziaautentica.com, where you can buy a Venezia Autentica Friends pass, which for €10 gives you a ten percent discount whenever you spend €30 or more at one of the listed places.

13

moderately priced clothes, you'll find the likes of Benetton, Sisley and Stefanel in the Mercerie area.

Barena Calle Minelli 4260B, San Marco ☎ 041 523 8457, ⓦ barenavenezia.com; map p.36. If you're looking to add something 100-percent-Venetian to your wardrobe, this is the place to find it. Founded in 1961, and taking its name from the local word for mud flat, *Barena* specialises in designs that are inspired by traditional Venetian work clothes. The men's jackets and coats are particularly good – stylish and durable, they are made from top-quality wool cloth, a fabric that became a speciality in Venice as long ago as the thirteenth century. The prices are reasonable too – jackets start at under €400. Mon, Tues & Thurs–Sat 10am–1pm & 4–7.30pm, Wed 4–7.30pm.

Diesel Salizzada Pio X 5315, San Marco ☎ 041 241 1937, ⓦ diesel.com; map p.36. Like Benetton, the edgier *Diesel* was founded in the Veneto; their flagship two-storey store is on the San Marco side of the Rialto bridge. Mon–Sat 10.30am–7pm, Sun 11am–1.30pm & 2–7pm.

★ **Il Tabarro San Marco** Calle Scaleter 2235, San Polo ☎ 041 524 6242, ⓦ monicadaniele.com; map p.100. Stepping into this wonderfully overcrammed and cosy shop is like slipping back in time. A *tabarro* is an old-fashioned cloak, and Monica Daniele sells them here, but what makes this place amazing is its stock of hats – all conceivable types and colours, stacked in towers on every available surface. Mon–Sat 9am–6pm.

FOOD AND DRINK

Restaurants, bars and so on are covered in our Eating and Drinking chapter, as are tips on the best places to buy picnic supplies (see page 224). For something a bit more special, try these shops.

★ **Cioccolateria VizioVirtù** Calle del Forner 5988, Castello ☎ 041 275 0149, ⓦ viziovirtu.com; map p. 136. This shop, very near the church of San Lio, creates the most extraordinary chocolates – they're not cheap, but a single VizioVirtù truffle will give your taste buds an experience to remember. Daily 10am–7.30pm; closed Aug.

Dai do Cancari Calle delle Botteghe 3455, San Marco ☎ 041 241 0634, ⓦ daidocancari.it; map p.36. If you want to take home a top-quality bottle of wine, check out this shop, close to Santo Stefano – it has a superlative

selection of Italian vintages. Daily 10.45am–1.15pm & 2.30–8pm (in summer sometimes open as late as 11pm).

I Tre Mercanti Calle al Ponte de la Guerra 5364, Castello ☎ 041 522 2901, ⓦ itremercanti.it; map p.136. Located very close to the Piazza, this mouthwatering shop, run by three foodie entrepreneurs, has a well-selected stock of fine wine and food garnered from all over Italy. Also does excellent panini and luscious takeaway tiramisù. Daily 11am–7.30pm.

Vino e…Vini Salizzada del Pignater 3565–66, Castello ☎ 041 521 0184, ⓦ venditavino.venezia.it; map p.154. An excellent wine shop, with knowledgeable and helpful staff. Daily 10am–1pm & 4–9pm.

GLASS

For Venetian **glass** you should go to the main source of production, **Murano**. The Piazza and its environs are prowled by well-groomed young characters offering free boat trips to the island – on no account accept, as you'll be subjected to a relentless hard sell on arrival. You'll find the more tasteful work in the showrooms listed below – unless stated otherwise, they are located on Murano. Don't buy anything that doesn't have the "Vetro Artistico Murano" trademark – the shops are awash with fake Murano ware, much of it from China. Real Murano glass (see page 181) is expensive stuff: top-quality wine-glasses cost from around €60 each; small vases tend to cost upwards of €300; and for larger table-top items you'll be paying a hefty four-figure sum.

Atmosfera Veneziana Calle dei Fuseri 4340, San Marco ☎ 041 241 3256, ⓦ atmosferaveneziana.com; map p.36. Venice is awash with fake Murano glass, but Theresa Caponsacco's wonderful little shop sells only the genuine stuff; she has a range of portable items (and chandeliers), but is especially good for Murano beads, both antique and modern. Mon–Sat 10am–7.30pm.

Barovier & Toso Fondamenta Vetrai 27–29 ☎ 041 739 049, ⓦ barovier.com; map p.179. This is a family-run firm which can trace its roots back to 1295, which makes it one of the hundred oldest companies in the world. Predominantly traditional designs, but by no means stuffy. Mon–Thurs 9.15am–12.30pm & 1–5.30pm.

★ **Berengo** Fondamenta Vetrai 109a ☎ 041 527 6364; map p.179; also Calle Larga San Marco 412–13, San Marco ☎ 041 241 0763, ⓦ berengo.com; map p.38. This firm pioneered a new approach to Venetian glass manufacture, with foreign artists' designs being vitrified by Murano glass-blowers. Berengo glass tends to be large-scale, and extremely expensive, as you'd expect. Murano Mon–Sat 9am–6pm; San Marco daily 10am–8pm.

Davide Penso Riva Longa 48 ☎ 041 527 4634, ⓦ davidepenso.com; map p.179. The jewellery sold here is both manufactured and designed by Davide Penso's workshop, which specializes in giving a new slant to traditional Murano styles. You can watch pieces being made in the showroom. Daily 10am–6pm.

Elle&Elle Fondamenta Manin 52 ☎ 041 527 4866; map p.179. Outlet for the sleek small-scale glasswork of Nason & Moretti, a long-established Murano firm that consistently produces attractive modern items. Daily 10.30am–1pm & 2–6pm.

L'Isola Calle de le Botteghe 2970, San Marco ☎ 041 523 1973, ⓦ lisola.com; map p.36. A showcase for work by Carlo Moretti, the doyen of modernist Venetian glass artists. Daily 10.30am–7.30pm.

Rossana & Rossana Riva Longa 11 ☎ 041 527 4076, ⓦ ro-e-ro.com; map p.179. Beautiful and highly delicate goblets and vases, by master glass-maker Davide Fuin, are the main attraction here. Daily 10am–6pm.

Seguso Viro Fondamenta Manin 77 & Fondamenta Venier 29 ☎ 041 527 5353, ⓦ segusoviro.com; map p.179. The Seguso family has been active on Murano since the 1390s, but the modern-day company owes its existence to Archimede Seguso, one of the great figures in the story of Murano glass, who founded the firm of Seguso Vetri d'Arte in the 1930s. *Seguso Viro*, an offshoot established by one of Archimede's sons, produces slightly more unusual items than the original Seguso firm, but nothing too wacky. Both branches Mon–Fri 9am–6pm.

★ **Venini** Fondamenta Vetrai 47–48 ☎ 041 273 7204; map p.179; also Piazzetta dei Leoncini 314, San Marco ☎ 041 522 4045, ⓦ venini.com; map p.38. One of the great modern producers, *Venini* often employs designers from other fields of the applied arts. Both branches Mon–Sat 9.30am–5.30pm.

JEWELLERY

ABC Calle del Tentor 1839, Santa Croce ☎ 041 524 4001, ⓦ orafaabc.com; map p.100. The studio of master goldsmith Andrea d'Agostino produces some lovely rings, bracelets and other pieces, with some especially attractive items made using the Japanese layering technique known as *mokume*. Tues–Sat 9.30am–12.30pm & 3.30–7.30pm.

Perlamadre Calle delle Botteghe 3182, Dorsoduro ☎ 340 844 9112, ⓦ perlamadredesign.com; map p.82. Patrizia Iacovazzi makes wonderful pieces of bold glass jewellery in her tiny Dorsoduro workshop; her lustrous necklaces cost less than €200 – remarkably inexpensive, all things considered. Mon–Sat 10.30am–1pm & 3.30–6pm.

LACE, LINEN AND FABRICS

During its long commercial heyday, Venice was esteemed all over Europe for the quality of its textiles. The city's close connections with Byzantium were the original basis of the industry, which later benefited from Venice's trading networks in the Islamic world and the further reaches of Asia. Top-quality cotton and woollen fabrics were produced and sold here, along with silks and other luxurious weaves, and a handful of companies in Venice continue to manufacture these ornate and expensive cloths in small quantities. The same goes for the celebrated **lace of Burano** – though most of the stuff sold as Burano lace is no such thing (see page 182).

Bevilacqua Campo S. Maria del Giglio 2520, San Marco; map p.36; also Fondamenta della Canonica 337b, San Marco ☎ 041 241 0662, ⓦ luigi-bevilacqua.com; map p.38. Founded in 1875 and still owned by the Bevilacqua family, this is a venerable manufacturer of fabulous velvets and damasks, the most luxurious of which are produced in a factory over in the Santa Croce *sestiere*, on looms made three hundred years ago. Prices are eye popping: a single cushion can cost well over €500, and the finest fabrics go for €5000 (sic) per metre. Both branches Mon–Sat 10am–7pm, Sun 10am–5pm.

Fortuny Fondamenta S. Biagio 805, Giudecca ☎ 041 528 7697, ⓦ fortuny.com; map p.192. The retail office of the *Fortuny* factory sells astonishingly plush fabrics at astonishing prices: upward of €300/metre in some cases. Mon–Sat 10am–1pm & 2–6pm (Nov–March closed Sat).

Jesurum Calle del Sartor da Veste 2024 ☎ 041 523 8969, ⓦ jesurum.it; map p.36. Renowned for its exquisite lace, the long-established (but no longer Venetian-owned) *Jesurum* also produces bed linen, towels and other fabrics. Daily 10.30am–7.30pm.

★ **Kerer** Calle Canonica 4328a, Castello ☎ 041 523 5485, ⓦ kerer.it; map p.136. The vast *Kerer* showroom sells a wide range of lace, both affordable and exclusive; it's installed in the Palazzo Trevisan-Cappello, across the Ponte Cappello at the rear of the Basilica di San Marco. Mon–Sat 10am–6pm, Sun 10am–12.30pm.

Lidia Via Galuppi 215, Burano ☎ 041 730 052, ⓦ dallalidia.com; map p.183. The oldest lace shop on the island, *Lidia* sells new and vintage lacework – a handmade hankie can cost as much as €500, while a hand-embroidered bedsheet goes for more than €3000. The upstairs room is in effect a private museum of Burano lace. Daily 9.30am–6.30pm.

Martina Vidal Via San Mauro 307–11, Burano ☎ 041 073 5523, ⓦ martinavidal.com; map p.183. Most of the stuff sold in Burano's shops is machine-made, imported and shoddy; at Martina Vidal everything is of high quality, and there's some genuine handmade Burano work here too. It's very expensive (a single doily for over €1000), though not to a degree that's disproportionate to the hours and labour that go into making it. Daily 9.30am–6pm.

Venetia Studium Calle delle Ostreghe, San Marco 2428, ☎ 041 522 9281; map p.36; also Ponte del Lovo

13

4753, San Marco; map p.36; and Calle del Bastion 186, Dorsoduro; map p.82; ⊚ venetiastudium.com. If real Fortuny is out of your range, try *Venetia Studium*, which sells reasonably priced lamps, bags and scarves in Fortuny-style (and Fortuny-approved) pleated velour and crepe. All branches daily 11am–6pm.

MAGIC AND MODELS

★ **La Scialuppa** Calle Seconda Saoneri 2681, San Polo ☎ 041 719 372, ⊚ veniceboats.com; map p.100. Wonderfully detailed and well-priced models, model kits and plans for all types of Venetian boats are made and sold by Gilberto Penzo, at this shop very close to the Frari. Kits start at around €30. Mon–Sat 9.30am–12.30pm & 3–6pm.

Mistero e Magia Ruga Giuffa 4924–25, Castello ☎ 041 522 7797, ⊚ misteroemagia.eu; map p.136. Venice's first ever magic store, which Alberto De Curti and Daniele Malusa opened in 2015, on the south side of Campo Santa Maria Formosa. Alberto and Daniele speak English and French, will happily demonstrate tricks to the kids, and hold regular workshops too, with guest magicians. Mon–Fri 8am–7pm, Sat 8am–2pm.

MASKS

Many of the Venetian **masks** on sale today are derived from traditional Carnevale designs: the ones representing characters from the *commedia dell'arte* (Pierrot, Harlequin, Columbine) for example, and the classic white half-mask called a *volto*, which has a kind of beak over the mouth so the wearer could eat and drink. Most of the masks of this type are churned out by factories located outside of Italy, but the ones sold in the places listed below are hand-crafted, and are sold alongside pieces of more modern inspiration – including some highly imaginative creations.

★ **Ca' Macana** Calle delle Botteghe 3172, Dorsoduro ☎ 041 277 6142; map p.82; also Sacca della Toletta 1169, Dorsoduro, ⊚ camacana.com; map p.82. Huge mask workshop, with perhaps the biggest stock in the city; it has a smaller branch on the other side of Campo San Barnaba, at Sacca della Toletta 1169. And if the kids are getting bored, you can take them to the Calle delle Botteghe shop for a mask-painting session. Both branches daily: summer 10am–8pm; winter 10am–6.30pm.

Kartaruga Calle Paradiso 5756–58, Castello ☎ 041 241 0071, ⊚ kartaruga.com; map p.136. This is the main shop and studio of a business, whose robust and inventive masks are used by many film-makers, theatre companies and advertisers. They also run mask-making workshops, for which you can sign up on the website. There's a second outlet nearby at Calle delle Bande 5369-5370, and a third at Calle della Bissa 5467, near Campo San Bartolomeo. Mon–Fri 10am–7pm.

La Bottega dei Mascareri Calle dei Saoneri 2720, San Polo ☎ 041 524 2887; Ponte di Rialto 80, San Polo; ⊚ mascarer.com; both map p.100. Run for many years by the brothers Sergio and Massimo Boldrin, *La Bottega dei Mascareri* sells some wonderfully inventive masks, such as faces taken from Tiepolo paintings or Donald Sutherland in Fellini's *Casanova*. Both branches daily 9am–6pm.

La Pietra Filosofale Frezzaria 1735, San Marco ☎ 041 528 5885; map p.36. After a long career in theatre, Carlo Setti now devotes his time to masks, producing Carnevale classics, portraits and faces of his own invention. Though he does work with the traditional papier-mâché, it's his leather masks that are most distinctive. Daily 9.30am–7.30pm.

Tragicomica Calle dei Nomboli 2800, San Polo ☎ 041 721 102, ⊚ tragicomica.it; map p.100. A good range and some nice eighteenth-century styles, as you might expect from a shop that's opposite Goldoni's house. Daily 10am–7pm.

PRINTS, POSTCARDS, PAPER AND STATIONERY

★ **Ebrû-Alberto Valese** Campiello S. Stefano 3471, San Marco ☎ 041 523 8830, ⊚ albertovalese-ebru.it; map p.36. Valese not only produces some of the most gorgeous marbled papers in Venice, but also transfers the designs onto silk scarves and a variety of ornaments; the marbling technique he uses is a Turkish process called *ebrû* (meaning "cloudy") – hence the alternative name of his shop. Mon–Sat 10am–1.30pm & 2.30–7pm, Sun 11am–7pm.

Il Pavone Fondamenta Venier 721, Dorsoduro ☎ 041 523 4517, ⊚ ilpavonevenezia.com; map p.82. Nice wood-block-printed papers, folders and so on, plus an interesting line in personalized rubber stamps and *Ex Libris* bookplates. Daily 10am–5.30pm.

Legatoria Piazzesi Campiello della Feltrina 2511, San Marco ☎ 041 522 1202; map p.36. This paper-producer and bookbinder was founded way back in 1851 and claims to be the oldest such shop in Italy. Using the old wood-block method of printing, it makes stunning hand-printed papers and cards, and a nice line in pocket diaries, too. Mon–Sat 10am–1pm & 3–7pm.

Paolo Olbi Ponte Ca' Fóscari 3253, Dorsoduro ☎ 041 523 7655, ⊚ olbi.atspace.com; map p.82. The founder of this bookbindery and stationery shop was largely responsible for the revival of paper marbling in Venice; today Olbi sells a range of marbled notebooks, diaries and other paper goods from his workshop by the entrance to the main university building. Daily 10.30am–12.30pm & 3.30–7.30pm.

Polliero Campo dei Frari 2995, San Polo ☎041 528 5130; map p.100. A bookbinding workshop that sells patterned paper as well as heavy, leather-bound albums of handmade plain paper. Mon–Sat 10am–1pm & 3.30–7.30pm, Sun 10.30am–1.30pm.

SHOES, BAGS AND LEATHER

To the north and west of the Piazza, around the **Mercerie**, **Calle Vallaresso** and **Calle Larga XXII Marzo**, big names such as Vogini and Bottega Veneta uphold Venice's reputation as a market for expensive leather goods. What follows is a rundown of the city's more idiosyncratic outlets.

Daniela Ghezzo Segalin Calle dei Fuseri 4365, San Marco ☎041 522 2115, ⓦdanielaghezzo.it; map p.36. Established in 1932 by Antonio Segalin then run by his son Rolando until 2003, this workshop is now operated by Rolando's star pupil Daniela Ghezzo, who produces wonderful handmade shoes, from sturdy brogues to whimsical Carnival footwear. A pair of Ghezzos will set you back at least €700. Daily 10am–1pm & 3–7pm.

Francis Model Ruga Ravano 773a, San Polo ☎041 521 2889, ⓦfrancismodel.it; map p.100. In business since 1965, the Model father-and-son team sells high-quality handbags and briefcases from their tiny Rialto workshop. Prices start at around €200, rising to €1100. Mon–Sat 10am–7pm, Sun 10.30am–6pm.

Giovanna Zanella Calle Carminati 5641, Castello ☎041 523 5500, ⓦgiovannazanella.it; map p.136. Though she also sells bags and hats from her shop near the church of San Lio, inventive and occasionally wacky handmade shoes (with little windows above the toes, for example) are what have made Giovanna Zanella's reputation. You'll pay from around €400 for a pair. Mon–Sat 1–8pm.

★ **Il Grifone** Fondamenta del Gaffaro 3516, Dorsoduro ☎041 522 9452, ⓦilgrifonevenezia.it; map p.82. Toni Peressin's shop, near the Tolentini, sells his handmade briefcases, satchels, notebooks, purses and other sturdy leather pieces at decent prices. Tues & Fri 10am–6pm Wed, Thurs & Sat 10am–1pm & 4–7pm.

Mori & Bozzi Rio Terrà Maddalena 2367, Cannaregio ☎041 715 261; map p.120. Stylish women's footwear from a good range of small labels, plus a small selection of women's clothing. Daily 9.30am–7.30pm.

PRATO DELLA VALLE

Padua and the southern Veneto

Situated a little under forty kilometres west of Venice, the ancient university city of Padua is a half-an-hour train journey away from Venice. However, Padua has more than enough sights to fill a more protracted stay, notably the Cappella degli Scrovegni, with its astonishing fresco cycle by Giotto, the Basilica di Sant'Antonio, which contains some of the finest sculpture in the Veneto, and the vast Palazzo della Ragione, the frescoed medieval hall that overlooks Padua's twin market squares. To the south of Padua are the enticing small towns of Monsélice and Montagnana, whose medieval town walls have survived in almost pristine form. If you need a rest from urban pursuits, explore the green Colli Euganei (Euganean Hills) or visit one of the villas on the Brenta, to which the Venetian gentry used to withdraw to escape the summer heat.

The Brenta

The southernmost of the three main rivers that empty into the Venetian lagoon (the other two are the Sile and Piave), the **Brenta** caused no end of trouble to the earliest settlers on both the mainland and the islands: on the one hand, its frequent flooding made agriculture difficult, and on the other, the silt it dumped into the lagoon played havoc with Venice's water channels. Land reclamation schemes were carried out from the eleventh century, but it was in the fourteenth century that Venice began the large-scale canalization of the Brenta, an intervention which both reinforced the banks of the river and controlled the deposition of its contents in the lagoon. The largest of the artificial channels, La Cunetta, which runs from Strà to Chioggia, was finished as recently as 1896, but by the sixteenth century the management of the Brenta was sufficiently advanced for the land along its lower course, from Padua to the river-mouth at Fusina, to become a favoured building site for the Venetian aristocracy.

Some of these Venetian **villas** were built as a combination of summer residence and farmhouse – most, however, were intended solely for the former function. From the

14

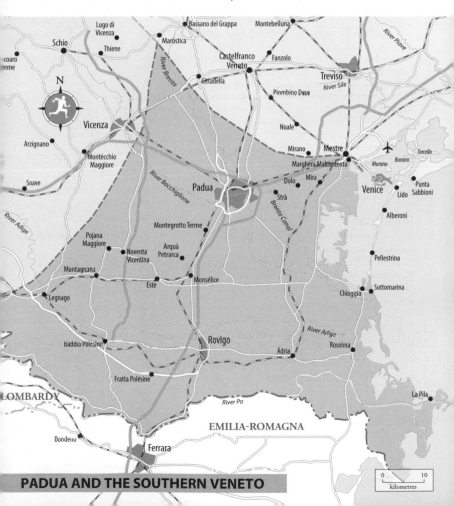

PADUA AND THE SOUTHERN VENETO

sixteenth century to the eighteenth, the period from mid-June to mid-November was the season of the *villeggiatura*, when the patrician families of Venice would load their best furniture onto barges and set off for the relative coolness of the Brenta. Around one hundred villas are left standing: some are derelict, a large number are still inhabited and a handful are open to the public. Of this last category, two are outstanding – the **Villa Fóscari** at Malcontenta and the **Villa Pisani** at Strà.

14 Villa Fóscari

Malcontenta di Mira • April–Oct Tues & Fri–Sun 9am–noon • €10 • ⓦ lamalcontenta.com

Sometimes known as the Villa Malcontenta, the **Villa Fóscari** was designed in 1559 for the brothers Alvise and Niccolò Fóscari by **Palladio**, and is the nearest of his villas to Venice. None of Palladio's villas more powerfully evokes the architecture of ancient Rome: the heavily rusticated exterior suggests the masonry of Roman public buildings; the massive Ionic portico alludes to classical temple fronts (which Palladio believed to be derived from domestic architecture); and the two-storey main hall was inspired by the bath complexes of imperial Rome, as was the three-sectioned arched window (a feature known as a thermal window, from the Roman *thermae*). Palladio was practical as well as erudite: to keep the living quarters well clear of the swampy land, he raised them on a high podium, and to keep costs down he used the cheapest materials that would do the job – look closely at the columns and you'll see that they're made out of hundreds of bricks in the shape of cake slices.

The main hall and the rooms leading off it (only some of which are open to the public) were frescoed as soon as the walls were up, by **Battista Franco** and **Giovanni Battista Zelotti**, a colleague of Veronese; their work includes what is said to be a portrait of a woman of the Fóscari family who was exiled to the house as punishment for an amorous escapade, and whose consequent misery, according to legend, was the source of the name *Malcontenta*. The reality is more prosaic – the area was known by that name long before the Fóscari arrived, either because of some local discontent over the development of the land or because of political *malcontenti* who used to hide out in the nearby salt marshes.

Villa Pisani

Strà • Tues–Sun: April–Sept 9am–8pm; Oct 9am–6pm; Nov–March 9am–5pm • €10 house and garden, €4.50 garden only (free on first Sun of month) • ⓦ villapisani.beniculturali.it

At **STRÀ**, virtually on the outskirts of Padua, stands the immense **Villa Pisani** or **Nazionale**. The branch of the Pisani family for whom this place was built was an astronomically wealthy dynasty of bankers, based in Venice in the similarly excessive Palazzo Pisani at Santo Stefano. When Alvise Pisani was elected doge of Venice in 1735, the family celebrated by commissioning the villa from the Paduan architect **Girolamo Frigimelica**; later on the work was taken over by **F.M. Preti** (see page 293). By 1760 it was finished – the biggest such residence to be built in Venetian territory during that century. It has appealed to megalomaniacs ever since: Napoleon bought it from the Pisani in 1807 and handed it over to Eugène Beauharnais, his stepson and Viceroy of Italy; and in 1934 it was the place chosen for the first meeting of Mussolini and Hitler.

The house has been stripped of nearly all its original furnishings, and the eighteenth-century frescoes of smiling nymphs and smirking satyrs that decorate some of the rooms aren't much more engaging than the almost blank walls you'll see elsewhere. The one pulse-quickening room is the **ballroom**, its ceiling covered with a dazzling fresco of *The Apotheosis of the Pisani Family*, the last major piece painted by **Giambattista Tiepolo** before his departure for Spain in 1762, at the age of 66. If you're trying to puzzle out what's going on: the Pisani family, accompanied by Venice, are being courted by the Arts, Sciences and Spirits of Peace, while Fame plays a fanfare in praise of the Pisani and the Madonna looks on with appropriate pride. The monochrome frescoes on Roman themes around the musicians' gallery are by Giambattista's son, Giandomenico.

In the **gardens**, the long fishpond ends at a stable-block which from a distance might be mistaken for another grand house. The most celebrated feature of the gardens is the perfectly tended maze (closed in winter and bad weather), which winds around a low stone tower.

ARRIVAL AND DEPARTURE   THE BRENTA VILLAS

By bus You can get to Malcontenta by bus from Piazzale Roma (€1.50). It takes twenty minutes, but make sure you catch the ACTV Padua-via-Malcontenta bus, which goes only once an hour. (Other Padua buses pass the other villas covered below, but not Malcontena.) On your way back from Malcontenta, if the first bus that comes along isn't going to Venice, take it as far as Corso del Popolo in Mestre, then cross the road for a #4 to Piazzale Roma – you can do it on the one ticket, which is valid for 75min. The bus journey from Venice to Strà, 25 minutes on from Malcontenta (€5 from Venice), gives you a good view of dozens of villas on the way. They are particularly thick on the ground from Oriago onwards (16km out of Venice), the most attractive stretch being centred on the elongated town of Mira, shortly after Oriago.

14

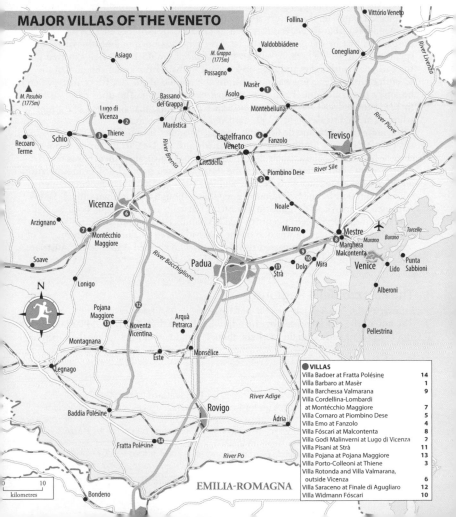

MAJOR VILLAS OF THE VENETO

● **VILLAS**

Villa Badoer at Fratta Polésine	14
Villa Barbaro at Masèr	1
Villa Barchessa Valmarana	9
Villa Cordellina-Lombardi at Montécchio Maggiore	7
Villa Cornaro at Piombino Dese	5
Villa Emo at Fanzolo	4
Villa Fóscari at Malcontenta	8
Villa Godi Malinverni at Lugo di Vicenza	2
Villa Pisani at Strà	11
Villa Pojana at Pojana Maggiore	13
Villa Porto-Colleoni at Thiene	3
Villa Rotonda and Villa Valmarana, outside Vicenza	6
Villa Saraceno at Finale di Agugliaro	12
Villa Widmann Fóscari	10

By Burchiello During the eighteenth century, the mode of transport the gentry used for the *villeggiatura* was a capacious vessel known as the *Burchiello*. The modern *Burchiello* is one of a small flotilla of pleasure craft that shuttles tourists along the Brenta, making a few brief stops at selected villas, pausing rather longer for lunch, and finally unloading them at Padua or Venice to catch the bus or train back to where they started. Day-trips on the *Burchiello* (ⓦ ilburchiello.it) cost around €100 (excluding meals).

14 Padua

Extensively reconstructed after the damage caused by World War II bombing, and hemmed in by the sprawl which has accompanied its development into the most important economic centre of the Veneto, **PADUA** (Padova) is not at first sight as alluring as many of the region's towns. It was, however, one of the most important cultural centres of northern Italy, and retains plentiful evidence of its impressive lineage in its churches, museums and frescoed interiors. In recent years, civic efforts to polish and pedestrianize the city centre – even to the extent of mapping out the medieval street plan in marble flagstones – have made it easier to conjure up the context of Padua's many historic buildings.

Legend has it that Padua was founded in 1185 BC by Antenor of Troy – a story propagated first by the Roman historian Livy, who was born in a nearby village and spent much of his life here. A Roman *municipium* from 45 BC, the city thrived until the barbarian onslaughts and the subsequent Lombard invasion at the start of the seventh century. Recovery was slow, but by the middle of the twelfth century, when it became a free commune, Padua was prosperous once again. The university was founded in 1221, and a decade later the city became a place of pilgrimage when **St Anthony**, who had arrived in Padua in 1230, died and was buried here.

The monstrous **Ezzelino da Romano** occupied Padua for two decades from 1237, and struggles against the **Scaligeri** of Verona lasted until the **Da Carrara** family established their hold in 1337. Under their domination Padua's cultural eminence was secured – Giotto, Dante and Petrarch were among those attracted here – but Carraresi territorial ambitions led to conflict with Venice, and in 1405 the city's independence ended with its conquest by the neighbouring republic. Though politically nullified, Padua remained an artistic and intellectual centre: Donatello and Mantegna both worked here, and in the seventeenth century Galileo conducted research at the university, where the medical faculty was one of the most advanced in Europe. With the fall of the Venetian Republic the city passed to Napoleon, who handed it over to the **Austrians**, after whose regime Padua was annexed to Italy in 1866.

The Palazzo della Ragione

Piazza delle Erbe • Feb–Oct Tues–Sun 9am–7pm; Nov–Jan Tues–Sun 9am–6pm • €6, or PadovaCard

The hub of the city is formed by the adjoining **Piazza della Frutta** and **Piazza delle Erbe**, still the sites of Padua's main markets, though nowadays clothes rather than fruit are

---

THE PADOVACARD

Costing €16 for 48 hours or €21 for 72 hours, the **PadovaCard** (ⓦ padovacard.it) allows one visit for one adult and one child under 14 to twelve sites in the city and environs, including the Musei Civici degli Eremitani, Cappella degli Scrovegni and Palazzo della Ragione. There are further discounts on the other main attractions, as well as free parking in the Piazza Rabin car park by Prato della Valle, free travel on the APS buses, free bicycle rental and discounts at some bed and breakfasts. It's available from the tourist offices and at the Eremitani museum, or can be bought online at ⓦ cappelladegliscrovegni.it. Note that advance booking is required for the Scrovegni Chapel, for which an extra €1 booking fee is payable.

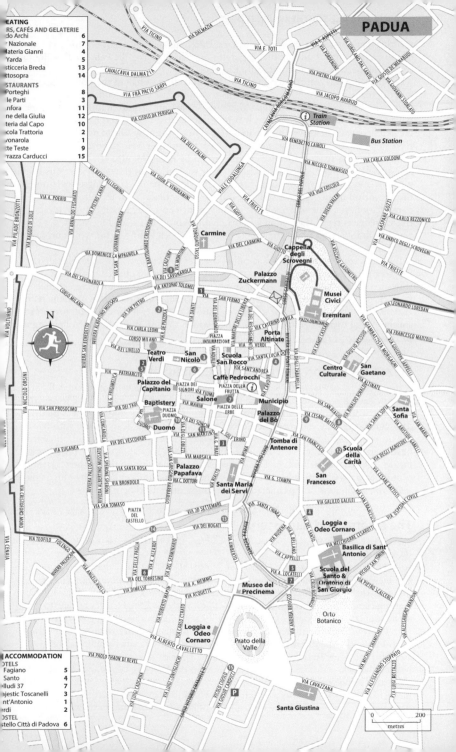

PADUA

Train Station

Bus Station

Carmine

Cappella degli Scrovegni

Palazzo Zuckermann

Musei Civici

Eremitani

Porta Altinate

Teatro Verdi

San Nicolò

Scuola San Rocco

Caffè Pedrocchi

Centro Culturale

San Gaetano

Santa Sofia

Palazzo del Capitano

Salone

Municipio

Baptistery

Palazzo del Bò

Tomba di Antenore

Scuola della Carità

Duomo

Palazzo Papafava

San Francesco

Santa Maria dei Servi

Loggia e Odeo Cornaro

Basilica di Sant' Antonio

Scuola del Santo & Oratorio di San Giorgio

Museo del Precinema

Orto Botanico

Loggia e Odeo Cornaro

Prato della Valle

Santa Giustina

N

0 200
metres

14

mostly what's on sale in the former square. Butchers' stalls and bars occupy the arcades of the extraordinary building that separates the two piazzas – the **Palazzo della Ragione** or the **Salone**, as it's more commonly known.

The building was constructed in the 1210s, and the vast hall of the upper storey was originally divided into three parts, to accommodate the law courts of justice – hence the appellation *della Ragione*, meaning "of reason". Its decoration would once have been as astounding as its size, but the frescoes that Giotto and his assistants created here were destroyed by fire in 1420, though some by **Giusto de' Menabuoi** have survived. It was after this fire that the partition walls were removed, creating a single enormous space, which was then painted by **Nicola Miretto** (1425–40), whose 333-panel astrological calendar covers all four walls. Each of the twelve sections begins with the apostle appropriate to that month (the larger panel) and progresses through the allegorical figures representing the month, the zodiacal sign, the planet and constellation, the type of work done in that month and the human figure representing the astrological type. The ceiling was originally painted as a deep blue starry sky but was rebuilt following a hurricane in 1756 and has been letting in the wind and rain ever since.

The black stone in the far corner, called the *pietra del vituperio* (stone of insults), played a part in the judicial system: insolvent Paduans were obliged to sit on it three times, repeating the words "I renounce my wordly goods", prior to being expelled from the city. The gigantic wooden horse at the other end is modelled on Donatello's *Gattamelata*, and was made for a joust in 1466. One other feature to look for: on the southern wall there's a golden sun, through which the sun shines at noon, lighting up the meridian line that's set into the floor.

Piazza dei Signori and the Corte Capitaniato

At the west end of **Piazza dei Signori**, which lies a little to the west of Piazza della Frutta, rises the early fifteenth-century **Torre dell'Orologio**; volunteers open up the tower to show the workings of the clock (Wed, Fri & Sat 10–11.30am; donations accepted). Through its archway you enter the **Corte Capitaniato**, a quiet, leafy square with two old university buildings: to your left is the **Palazzo del Capitanio**, the sixteenth-century headquarters of the city's Venetian military, and beyond it stands the university's arts faculty, the **Liviano**. Behind the Fascist-era facade of the Liviano there's the fourteenth-century **Sala dei Giganti**, where the frescoes include a portrait of Petrarch, which you can see if you attend one of the concerts that are sometimes held here.

The Duomo and Baptistery

Piazza Duomo • **Duomo** Mon–Sat 7.30am–noon & 3.30–7.30pm, Sun 8am–1pm & 3.30–8.45pm • Free • **Baptistery** Daily 10am–6pm • €3, or PadovaCard

Immediately southwest of the Piazza dei Signori stands Padua's **Duomo**; blank outside and barren within, it may be the only cathedral in Italy that contains nothing of interest. The adjacent Romanesque **Baptistery**, though, is a wonder. Built by the Da Carrara clan in the thirteenth century, it's lined with dazzling frescoes by **Giusto de' Menabuoi** (c.1376), a cycle of teeming scenes that makes a fascinating comparison with Giotto's more monumental work in the Cappella degli Scrovegni – the treeful of children watching Christ's entry into Jerusalem is a typically beguiling detail. Look for the figure in the red headdress on the left side of the panel showing Christ healing the sick – it's a portrait of Petrarch, who died shortly before the frescoes were painted. The polyptych **altarpiece**, also by Menabuoi, was stolen in 1972 but quickly recovered, minus some of its wooden framework; it's flanked by startling frescoes of the Apocalypse. Don't overlook the **mausoleum of Fina Buzzaccarini** (on the wall opposite

14

the altar), wife of Francesco I da Carrara, and one of the city's most assiduous artistic patrons; she's shown on the front being presented to the Virgin by John the Baptist..

The Cappella degli Scrovegni

Entry via the Musei Civici, Piazza Eremitani 8 • Daily 9am–7pm; you must book in advance to see the frescoes • ⓦ cappelladegliscrovegni.it

Padova's most celebrated works of art are the **Giotto frescoes** in the astounding **Cappella degli Scrovegni**, a cycle that constitutes one of the key works in the development of European art. They are also among the most fragile, because the walls on which they are painted are permeated with damp rising from the chapel's swampy foundations. Extraordinary measures have been taken to preserve the frescoes. Entrance to the chapel is through a sophisticated airlock: at the time printed on your ticket, the glass door to the waiting room slides open to allow the next set of 25 visitors in, and almost immediately shuts again. Once inside, a high-tech system lowers the humidity of the waiting room to that of the chapel, and filters away any stray spores and pollutants. Fifteen minutes later another door leading to the chapel itself opens and you have a quarter of an hour (or 20min at quiet periods) to take in the frescoes before being ejected.

The frescoes

The chapel was commissioned in 1303 by Enrico Scrovegni in atonement for his father's usury, which was so vicious that Dante allotted him a place in the *Inferno* – he died screaming "give me the keys to my strong box" and was denied a Christian burial. As soon as the walls were built, Giotto was commissioned to cover every inch of the interior with frescoed illustrations of the lives of Jesus, Mary and Joachim (Mary's father), and the story of the Passion; the finished cycle, arranged in three tightly knit tiers and painted against a backdrop of saturated blue, presents an artistic vision of the same order as that of the Sistine Chapel. Looking towards the altar, the tiers on the right depict (from top to bottom) *The History of Joachim*, *The Childhood of Christ* and *The Passion*; the tiers on the left comprise *The Life of the Virgin*, *Christ's Public Life* and *Christ's Death and Resurrection*.

The Scrovegni series is a marvellous demonstration of Giotto's unprecedented attention to the inner nature of the protagonists – the exchange of looks between the two shepherds in *The Arrival of Joachim* is particularly powerful, as are *The Embrace of Joachim and Anna at the Golden Gate* and *The Visit of Mary to Elizabeth*. On occasion even the buildings and landscape have been manipulated to add to the drama, for example in the *Deposition* (immediately right of the *Crucifixion*), where a strong diagonal leads the eye straight to the faces of Jesus and Mary.

Beneath the main pictures are shown the Vices and Virtues in human (usually female) form, while on the wall above the door is the *Last Judgement*, with two angels rolling back the painting to remind us that this is an imaginative scene and not an authoritative vision of eternity. An alleged self-portrait (fourth from the left at the bottom) places Giotto firmly among the redeemed, and directly above the door is a portrait of Scrovegni presenting the chapel; his tomb is at the far end, behind the altar with its statues by **Giovanni Pisano**.

Musei Civici

Piazza Eremitani 8 • Tues–Sun 9am–7pm • €10 with the Palazzo Zuckermann, or €13 including the Cappella Scrovegni too, or PadovaCard

The **Musei Civici Eremitani**, formerly the monastery of the Eremitani, is a superbly presented museum complex that contains the Museo Archeologico and the Museo d'Arte-Medioevale e Moderna. The archeological collection, on the ground floor, has a vast array of pre-Roman, Roman and paleo-Christian objects, with an absorbing section on the unique language spoken in the Veneto before the establishment of Roman hegemony. Upstairs, the vast Museo d'Arte houses extensive and varied collections of fourteenth- to nineteenth-century art from the Veneto and further afield, usually arranged in roughly chronological order. There are tracts of workaday stuff here, but names such as Titian, Tintoretto and Tiepolo leaven the mix, and spectacular highpoints are provided by the Giotto *Crucifixion* that was once in the Scrovegni chapel, and a fine *Portrait of a Young Senator* by Bellini. In the midst of the ranks of French, Flemish and miscellaneous Italian paintings you'll also happen upon a shockingly vivid sequence of pictures by Luca Giordano, featuring a repulsive depiction of Job and his boils. The Capodilista collection contains a rich seam of sixteenth-century works, including four mysterious landscape allegories by Titian and Giorgione.

Palazzo Zuckermann

Corso Garibaldi 33 • Tues–Sun 10am–7pm • €10 combined with Musei Civici, or €13 including the Cappella degli Scrovegni or PadovaCard

A third section of the Musei Civici lies across Corso Garibaldi in the **Palazzo Zuckermann**, which has been refurbished to house two minor museums. The first of these, the **Museo d'Arte, Arti Applicate e Decorative**, has jewellery, fabrics, pottery and furniture from the fourteenth century onwards. The second floor is devoted to the **Museo Bottacin**: featuring more than 50,000 coins, medals and seals, this is one of the largest numismatic museums in the world.

The Eremitani

Piazza Eremitani • Mon–Fri 7.30am–12.30pm & 3.30–7pm, Sat & Sun 9am–12.30pm & 4–7pm • Free

The nearby church of the **Eremitani**, built at the turn of the fourteenth century, was almost completely wrecked by an Allied bombing raid in 1944 and has been fastidiously rebuilt. The worst aspect of the bombardment was the near total destruction of **Mantegna**'s frescoes of the lives of St James and St Christopher – during World War II, only the destruction of the Camposanto in Pisa was a comparably severe blow to Italy's artistic heritage.

Produced between 1454 and 1457, when Mantegna was in his mid-twenties, the frescoes were remarkable for the thoroughness with which they exploited fixed-point perspective – a concept central to Renaissance humanism, with its emphasis on the primacy of individual perception. Furthermore, Mantegna's compositions had to take into account the low viewpoint of the person in the chapel. The extent to which he overcame these complex technical problems can now be assessed only from the fragments preserved in the last chapel to the right of the high altar. On the left wall is the St James cycle, put together from pieces found in the rubble; and on the right is the life of St Christopher – the well-preserved bottom panel, showing the giant's martyrdom, was removed from the wall before the war.

Of the church's other frescoes, the finest are those by the late fourteenth-century Paduan painter Guariento, in the chancel and the second and fourth chapels of the right aisle.

Porta Altinate and Santa Sofia

Santa Sofia: Via Santa Sofia 102 • Mon & Tues 9.30–11.30am & 4–7.30pm, Wed–Sat 7.30–11.30am & 4–7.30pm, Sun 9am–12.30pm & 6–8pm • Free

Straddling one end of Via Altinate, to the south of the Eremitani, the **Porta Altinate** was one of the gates of the medieval city, and bears a plaque recording its violent recapture from Ezzelino da Romano on June 20, 1256. At the eastern end of the street rises the bulging brick facade of **Santa Sofia**, the oldest church in Padua. It dates back to the sixth century, though most of today's beautiful structure dates from the twelfth and thirteenth centuries. The apse in particular shows Veneto-Byzantine influence, and is reminiscent of Santi Maria e Donato on Murano.

14

Palazzo del Bò

Via VIII Febbraio • Guided tours only, Mon–Fri 9.30am–5.30pm (in English 10.30am, 12.30pm, 4.30pm), Sat 9.30am–12.30pm (in English 10.30am & 12.30pm) • €7

A short distance south of the Porta Altinate stands the university's main block, the **Palazzo del Bò** – the name translates as "of the Ox", after an inn that used to stand here. Established in September 1221, the University of Padua is older than any other in Italy except that of Bologna, and the coats of arms that encrust the courtyard and Great Hall attest to the social and intellectual rank of its alumni. The first permanent **anatomy theatre** was built here in 1594, a facility that doubtless greatly helped William Harvey, who went on to develop the theory of blood circulation after taking his degree here in 1602. Galileo taught physics here from 1592 to 1610, declaiming from a lectern that is still on show. And in 1678 Elena Lucrezia Corner Piscopia became the first woman ever to collect a doctoral degree when she was awarded her doctorate in philosophy here – there's a statue of her in the courtyard.

Caffè Pedrocchi

Piazzetta Pedrocchi • Piano Nobile open Tues–Sun 9.30am–12.30pm & 3.30–6pm • €4, or PadovaCard • Ⓦ caffepedrocchi.it

The Bò's neighbour, the Neoclassical **Caffè Pedrocchi**, was designed by Giuseppe Japelli in 1831 for Antonio Pedrocchi, dubbed by Stendhal "the best caterer in Italy". Priding itself as the city's main intellectual salon (it was here that an abortive uprising against the Austrian occupation was launched on February 9, 1848), the *Pedrocchi* used to stay open night and day, hence its nickname, "the café without doors". The building now has a multiplicity of functions – the glossy and expensive café-restaurant occupies the ground floor, with a concert hall, conference centre and exhibition space upstairs.

A staircase on the Piazzetta Pedrocchi side of the building leads up to the **piano nobile**, where highly decorative rooms radiate off a central hall: pictures of ancient Rome by Ippolito Caffi adorn the Roman Room, painted mirrors gleam in the Moorish Chamber and stars shine in the ceiling of the vivid blue Egyptian Room. You'll also find the **Museo del Risorgimento e dell'Età Contemporane** here: covering local history from 1797 until 1948, the rooms of uniforms and guns are of limited interest, but the films and photos from World War II are worth a look.

Piazza Antenore and Via San Francesco

Piazza Antenore, south of the Bò, is the site of the **Tomba di Antenore**, alleged resting place of the city's legendary founder. From steps by the tomb you get a glimpse of one of the city's **Roman bridges** – the three-arched **Ponte Romano di San Lorenzo**. On **Via San Francesco**, which flows into Piazza Antenore, stands **Palazzo Zabarella**, which was founded in the twelfth century and owned by the Da Carrara family, then the Zabarella family, who resided here for more than four hundred years from 1405. A fine example of a Paduan aristocratic townhouse, it was thoroughly restored in the 1990s, and is now used for exhibitions.

Scuola della Carità

Via San Francesco 61 • Thurs & Sat 10am–noon & 4–6pm, Fri 4–6pm • Donations accepted

Heading down the picturesque arcades of Via San Francesco brings you to the **Scuola della Carità**, on the corner of Via Santa Sofia. The frescoed hall of this medieval hospital was decorated by Dario Varotari the Elder (1539–96), whose paintings illustrate the life of Mary – the cycle shows the death of Joseph, a rarely depicted event. It also has a fine wood-panelled ceiling that follows the curve of the building.

The Basilica di Sant'Antonio

Piazza del Santo • April–Oct daily 6.30am–7.45pm; Nov–March Mon–Sat 6.30am–6.45pm, Sun 6.30am–7.45pm • Free

Within eighteen months of his death in 1231, St Anthony of Padua had been canonized and his tomb was attracting so many pilgrims that it became necessary to rebuild the small church in which he had been buried. The end product of the rebuilding – the immense **Basilica di Sant'Antonio**, or **Il Santo** – was completed in 1301. The **exterior**, with its simple brick facade and a roofline of minaret-like belltowers and Byzantine domes, is a highly distinctive jumble, and the **interior** is similarly hybrid – the main part is like other large Italian mendicant churches, but the ambulatory, with its radiating chapels, resembles the French pilgrimage churches of the period.

Cappella del Santo

The focal point of the building, the **Cappella del Santo**, is in the left aisle, where the saint's tomb is encompassed by a sequence of nine beautiful **panels** showing scenes from St Anthony's life. Carved between 1505 and 1577, these constitute the most important series of relief sculpture created in sixteenth-century Italy. Reading from the left: St Anthony receives his Franciscan habit; a jealous husband stabs his wife, whom the saint later revived; St Anthony raises a man from the dead to prove the innocence of his father; he revives a drowned woman (panel by Sansovino); he revives a baby scalded to death in a cauldron (Sansovino and Minello); he directs

---

ST ANTHONY OF PADUA

Born in 1195 in Lisbon, **St Anthony** (christened Fernando) was a canon of the Augustinian order in Coimbra before he donned the Franciscan habit in 1220 and set off for Morocco, having been inspired to undertake his mission by five Franciscan friars who had been martyred by the Moroccan infidels. Soon taken ill in Africa, he sailed back to Portugal but was blown off course and landed in Sicily. From there Anthony headed north to Assisi, thence to a hermitage near Forlì, where his oratorical skills and profound knowledge of the scriptures were discovered when he was called upon to speak at a service for which no one had thought to prepare a sermon. After that he embarked on a career as a peripatetic preacher, addressing ever-increasing audiences in northern Italy and southern France, performing miracles and bringing unbelievers into the fold. The "hammer of heretics" was esteemed by both St Francis and Pope Gregory IX, the latter acclaiming him as "Doctor Optime" upon hearing of Anthony's death in 1231.

St Anthony's chaste life is symbolized by the lily that is his distinguishing feature in images of him. He is also often portrayed holding the infant Jesus, a reference to an incident when he was observed from afar cradling the Son of God. His popularity continued to grow after his death, and the abundance of letters, photographs and gifts around his shrine confirms the endurance of the belief in Anthony's wonder-working powers. He is the patron saint of Portugal, lost property, and the less-exalted animal species – the last honour comes from the legend that he preached to fishes when he could find no human audience.

mourners to find the heart of a miser in his coffer (Tullio Lombardo); he restores the severed foot of a boy (Tullio Lombardo); a heretic throws a glass which miraculously breaks the floor and remains intact; and a newborn baby tells of the innocence of its mother (Antonio Lombardo).

The rest of the church

Adjoining the chapel is the **Cappella della Madonna Mora** (named after its fourteenth-century French altar statue), which in turn lets onto the **Cappella del Beato Luca**, where St Anthony's body was first placed. Dedicated to Luca Belludi, St Anthony's closest companion, the latter chapel contains a fine fresco cycle by **Giusto de' Menabuoi**, including scenes from the lives of the Apostles Philip and James the Less, and *St Anthony Revealing to Luca Belludi that Padua will be Liberated from Ezzelino*, with an idealized version of the city, parts of it recognizable, as backdrop.

Back in the aisle, just before the Cappella del Santo, is Padua's finest work by **Pietro Lombardo**, the monument to Antonio Roselli (1467). More impressive still are the high altar's bronze sculptures and reliefs by **Donatello** (1444–45), the works that introduced Renaissance classicism to Padua. Unfortunately you can't get close enough to see them properly. The gloomy neo-Gothic frescoes of the apse, choir and presbytery were begun by **Achille Casanova** in 1903, and took about forty years.

Built onto the furthest point of the ambulatory, the **Cappella delle Reliquie** or **del Tesoro** was designed in the 1690s by Filippo Parodi, a pupil of Bernini. Its most important relics are a thorn from Christ's crown, and St Anthony's tongue, vocal chords and jaw, which are kept in reliquaries in the central of the three niches behind the balustrade. It's alleged that when the saint's remains were exhumed for reburial in the basilica in 1263 it was discovered that his flesh had turned to dust – except for the tongue, which glistened as if still alive. Also on show are scraps of the saint's tunic, and the coffin in which his bones lay until the 1980s.

In the **Cappella di San Giacomo**, off the right aisle, there's a glorious *Crucifixion*, frescoed in the 1370s by Altichiero da Zevio, who also painted the scenes from the life of St James. Other things to seek out are the **monuments to Cardinal Pietro Bembo and Alessandro Contarini**, which face each other on the nave's second pair of columns and were both designed by Sanmicheli in the 1550s, and the **tomb of Gattamelata**, in the first chapel on the right. The fresco on the interior wall of the facade is a more recent addition, *St Anthony Preaching from the Walnut Tree* by **Pietro Annigoni** (1985). The ghastly painting above the first altar on the left is also by him.

Museo Antoniano and Museo della Devozione Populare

Tues–Sun 9am–1pm & 2–6pm • €3, or €7 with Scuola del Santo & Oratorio di San Giorgio

Parts of the immense cloisters are occupied by the **Museo Antoniano** and the **Museo della Devozione Populare**. The former, on the first floor, is a collection of paintings (including a fresco of *Sts Anthony and Bernardine* by **Mantegna**, which once adorned the basilica's facade), ornate incense-holders, ceremonial robes and other paraphernalia

---

GATTAMELATA

Apart from the mighty basilica, the main sight on Piazza del Santo is Donatello's **monument to Gattamelata** ("The Honeyed Cat"), as the *condottiere* Erasmo da Narni was known. He died in 1443 and this monument was raised ten years later, the earliest large bronze sculpture of the Renaissance. It's a direct precursor to Verrocchio's equestrian monument to Colleoni in Venice (and Colleoni was under Gattamelata's command for a time), but could hardly be more different: Gattamelata was known for his honesty and dignity, and Donatello has created a figure who has the aura of a thoughtful tactician, quite unlike Verrocchio's image of almost thuggish power. The modelling of the horse makes a double allusion: to the equestrian statue of Marcus Aurelius in Rome, and to the horses of San Marco in Venice.

linked to the basilica; the latter, on the ground floor, is a history of votive gifts, with copious examples of the genre. The **Mostra Antoniana**, an audiovisual presentation (in Italian) of St Anthony and his work, is on perpetual show nearby.

Scuola del Santo

Piazza del Santo • Tues–Sun 9am–1pm & 2–6pm • €3, or €7 joint ticket with the Oratorio di San Giorgio & Museo Antoniano

The **Scuola del Santo**, on the southern side of the basilica, was a confraternity run on the same lines as the *scuole* of Venice, and was founded soon after Anthony's canonization, though this building dates only as far back as the early fifteenth century. The ground floor is still used for religious purposes, while upstairs is maintained pretty much as it would have looked in the sixteenth century, with its fine ceiling and paintings dating mainly from 1509–15. Four of the pictures are said to be by **Titian**: *The Jealous Husband Stabbing his Wife*, with an almost insignificant intervention by the saint in the background; *St Anthony Reattaching the Severed Foot of a Young Man*; *The Distribution of Blessed Bread*; and *The Newborn Infant Defends the Honour of its Mother*. If any of these are genuine, they would be the earliest known extant works by him. Some of the other paintings are charming oddities, such as *St Anthony Confronting Ezzelino da Romano* – a perilous diplomatic exercise which may or may not have happened. Next door, the **Museo al Santo** is used for one-off exhibitions, often drawing on the resources of the Musei Civici.

Oratorio di San Giorgio

Piazza del Santo • Tues–Sun 9am–1pm & 2–6pm • €3, or €7 joint ticket with the Scuola del Santo & Museo Antoniano

The **Oratorio di San Giorgio** was founded in 1377 as a mortuary chapel, and its frescoes by **Altichiero di Zevio** and **Jacopo Avanzi** were completed soon after. Recently restored, their work is an engaging and colourful narrative romp: the scenes from the life of St George on the left wall, for example, show not just the customary dragon-slaying, but also the saint being released by angels from a wheel of torture; and the opposite wall is adorned with a depiction of St Lucy remaining immoveable as her persecutors attempt to haul her off to a brothel with the help of a team of oxen.

Loggia e Odeo Cornaro

Via Cesarotti 37 • Feb–Oct Tues–Fri 10am–1pm, Sat & Sun 10am–1pm & 4–7pm • €3, or PadovaCard

Standing a short way east of the Basilica, the **Loggia e Odeo Cornaro** are the remains of a set of buildings constructed in 1524 for Alvise Cornaro, a prominent figure in the intellectual, scientific and artistic life of the city. The main attraction here is the Odeo, where Cornaro held concerts and literary gatherings; the vault of its octagonal chamber has Roman-style decorations with a series of grotesque figures, while the walls of the shell-hooded niches are painted with watery landscapes. You can admire the ceiling of adjoining Loggia, but the theatre above is closed.

Orto Botanico

Via dell'Orto Botanico • April & May daily 9am–7pm; June–Sept Tues–Sun 9am–7pm; Oct Tues–Sun 9am–6pm; Nov–March Tues–Sun 9am–5pm • €10, or €5 with PadovaCard • ⓦ www.ortobotanico.unipd.it

A good place to relax after a visit to the Basilica is Padua's **Orto Botanico**, the oldest botanic gardens in Europe. Planted in 1545 by the university's medical faculty as a collection of medicinal herbs, the gardens are laid out much as they were originally. Goethe came here in 1786 to see a palm tree that had been planted in 1585; the same tree still stands. There is, however, a spectacular new section to the Orto

14

Botanico: a 100-metre glasshouse that's divided into five sections, ranging from the tropical to the subarctic. The artificial climates are maintained by a self-sufficient system that utilises rainwater and solar energy to control the heating, ventilation, irrigation and electricity supply.

Prato della Valle

14

A little to the south of the Basilica sprawls the **Prato della Valle**, which is claimed to be the largest piazza in Italy but is not so much a piazza as a small park encircled by major roads. The greenery in the centre follows the oval plan of the extinct Roman amphitheatre; the two rings of statues commemorate 78 worthy Paduans, both native and honorary.

Santa Giustina

Summer: Mon–Fri 7.30am–noon & 3–8pm, Sat & Sun 6.30am–1pm & 3–8pm; winter: Mon–Sat 8am–noon & 3–8pm, Sun 8am–1pm & 3–8pm • Free

In the southeast corner of the Prato looms the sixteenth-century **Basilica di Santa Giustina**, which at 120m long is one of the world's largest churches. The exterior is a mighty box of raw brick and the interior is somewhat clinical, with little of interest except **Paolo Veronese**'s altarpiece of *The Martyrdom of St Justina*, some highly proficient carving on the choirstalls and a sarcophagus that reputedly once contained the relics of Luke the Evangelist (in the left transept).

In the right transept an arch opens onto the **Martyrs' Corridor**, named after the martyrs whose bones were found in the well that stands at the head of the corridor. Miscellaneous fifth- to twelfth-century architectural fragments line the way to the **Sacellum di Santa Maria e San Prosdocimo**, burial place of St Prosdocimus. He was the first bishop of Padua back in the fourth century, when the church was founded, and is depicted here on a fifth-century panel. You may want to pop into the shop by the well, to buy a bottle of its Olio del Benessere (Oil of Good Health), an allegedly versatile herbal medicine that Santa Giustina's monks have been concocting for the past thousand years.

Museo del Precinema

Prato della Valle 1 • Mon & Wed–Sun 10am–4pm • €5 • ⓦ minicizotti.it

On the top floor of the Palazzo Angeli you'll find one of the Veneto's most engaging private museums, the **Museo del Precinema – Collezione Minici Zotti**. Subtitled "un museo di magiche visioni", this wonderful collection of shadow puppets, magic lanterns and other optical instruments (plus a few mechanical musical instruments) was assembled by Laura Minici Zotti in the course of thirty years of research into the precursors of cinematography, and is now run by the founder's son. Gorgeous contraptions with names such as the Praxinoscope, Zogroscope, Megalethoscope and the Panoptic Polyorama fill the rooms under the roof, from one of which you can survey the streets through a camera obscura, similar to the device that Canaletto used in creating his panoramic scenes.

ARRIVAL AND GETTING AROUND

By train Trains arrive in the north of the city centre, just a few minutes' walk up Corso del Popolo from the old city walls.

Destinations Bassano (16 daily; 1hr 5min); Belluno (13 daily; 2hr–2hr 30min); Castelfranco (19 daily; 35min); Feltre (12 daily; 1hr 30min); Monsélice (every 30min; 25min); Venice (every 20min for most of the day; 25–50min); Verona (every 30min; 45min–1hr 15min); Vicenza (every 20min; 15–30min).

By bus and tram The main APS bus station is next to the train station at Piazzale della Stazione. Tickets cost €1.30, are valid for 75min and can be bought from any shop displaying the APS sign (tickets bought on-board cost €2). The tickets are also valid for the single-line tram system, which runs north–south through the city, via the station, the Musei Civici and Prato della Valle.

INFORMATION

Tourist offices There are tourist offices at the train station (Mon–Sat 9am–7pm, Sun 10am–4pm; ☎049 201 0080, ⓦturismopadova.it) and in the centre of the city at Galleria Pedrocchi 9 right next to *Caffè Pedrocchi* (same hours).

Listing publications Events are listed in the quarterly booklet *Padova Today*, which can be obtained from the tourist offices, and some bars and hotels. Of the local newspapers, the most comprehensive for listings is *Il Mattino*.

ACCOMMODATION

Padua makes an obvious base for exploring the Veneto, as it's a main rail hub and it has plenty of reasonably priced accommodation. In high season, however, you should still book ahead, as the town draws thousands of pilgrims.

Al Fagiano Via Locatelli 45 ☎049 875 0073, ⓦalfagiano.com; map p.245. This friendly two-star has forty rooms over four floors, with four different colour schemes (Red, Orange, Blue and White). The rooms are on the small side, but all have a/c, TV and hairdryers. **€90**

Al Santo Via del Santo 147 ☎049 875 2131, ⓦalsanto.it; map p.245. Located virtually next door to the Basilica, this three-star hotel is comfortable, if rather austere. Some rooms have views of the Basilica. **€90**

Belludi 37 Via Luca Belludi 37 ☎049 665 633, ⓦbelludi37.it; map p.245. This slickly renovated palazzo near the Basilica di Sant'Antonio has fifteen tasteful rooms decorated in neutral tones. All rooms are spacious, with high ceilings, luxurious bathrooms and DVD players, but it's worth paying the extra for views of the Basilica; the best is no. 107, with its own balcony. **€150**

Majestic Toscanelli Via dell'Arco 2 ☎049 663 244, ⓦtoscanelli.com; map p.245. The most appealing of the city's four-stars, with elegant, well-appointed rooms; it's located in the old Jewish quarter, just south of Piazza delle Erbe. **€180**

Ostello Città di Padova Via Aleardo Aleardi 30 ☎049 875 2219, ⓦostellopadova.it; map p.245. Padua's friendly HI hostel is in a quiet street in the south of the city, a short walk from Prato della Valle. Check-in 7–9.30am & 3.30–11pm; reception is closed between these times; 11.30pm curfew. Beds are in six-bed dorms, with some four-bed rooms for families. Dorms **€20**

Sant'Antonio Via S. Fermo 118 ☎049 875 1393, ⓦhotelsantantonio.it; map p.245. A plain, unfussy and inexpensive three-star. Rooms at the back have views over the Ponte Molino; the nicest are nos. 311 and 312, on two levels, with a small sitting area upstairs. **€70**

★ Verdi Via Dondi dall'Orologio 7 ☎049 836 4163, ⓦwww.albergoverdipadova.it; map p.245. A friendly boutique three-star, very near to Piazza Signori. The fourteen rooms are all a good size and have modern furnishings, and the tariffs are amazingly low. **€90**

EATING

As in any university city, there's plenty of choice when it comes to unpretentious **bars** and **restaurants**. Catering for the midday stampede of ravenous students, Padua's bars and cafés generally produce very good **snacks** too – there are dozens of places in and around Piazza delle Erbe, Piazza Duomo and Piazza dei Signori.

RESTAURANTS

Ai Porteghi Via Cesare Battisti 105 ☎049 660 746, ⓦaiporteghi.com; map p.245. Filippo Betteto's much-lauded *Ai Porteghi*, which has been in business since 1983, is a high-class neo-traditional restaurant, with a lovely rustic wood-panelled dining room. *Secondi* are mostly €20–25, which is reasonable, and there's a €35 set menu. Mon 6–11pm, Tues–Sat noon–3pm & 6–11pm, Sun noon–3pm.

Belle Parti Via Belle Parti 11 ☎049 875 1822, ⓦristorantebelleparti.it; map p.245. The very elegant *Belle Parti*, just off Via Verdi, has long been ranked as one of Padua's finest restaurants. With mains upward of €30, it is not cheap, but the quality is unerringly high and the service perfect. A highlight of the antipasto menu is the *gran crudità di mare* – a local raw fish speciality. Booking advisable. Mon–Sat 12.30–2.30pm & 7.30–10.30pm.

★ L'Anfora Via dei Soncin 13 ☎049 656 629; map p.245. The best-known old-style *osteria* in central Padova, with *secondi* around €15, and delicious snacks at the bar. Kitchen open Mon–Sat 12.30–3pm & 8–11pm; bar open 9am–11.30pm.

Nane della Giulia Via Santa Sofia 1 ☎049 660 742; map p.245. There has been an *osteria* in this former hospital since 1820. The present one is a trendy and unpretentious trattoria that serves reasonably priced Veneto specialities (*secondi* €10–15), using locally sourced and seasonal products. The summer garden is lovely too. Tues 7–11.30pm, Wed–Sun noon–2.30pm & 7–11.30pm.

★ Osteria dal Capo Via degli Obizzi 2 ☎049 663 105, ⓦwww.osteriadalcapo.it; map p.245. This small, refined and very friendly trattoria, located just off Piazza del Duomo, has been serving food since the 1950s and has become a secure Padua favourite, so booking is essential in the evenings. Main courses are €15 on average. Mon 7.30–11pm, Tues–Sat noon–2.30pm & 7.30–11pm.

Piccola Trattoria Via Rolando da Piazzola 21 ☎049 656 163, ⓦpiccolatrattoria.it; map p.245. The homely and very popular *Piccola Trattoria* has a distinctive menu that focuses on Sardinian specialities such as suckling pig, all

14

14

superbly presented. Its *secondi* are around €16. Tues–Sat noon–2.30pm & 8–11pm.

Savonarola Via Savonarola 38 ☎049 875 9128, ⓦsavonarola-pizzeria-trattoria.it; map p.245. If all you want is a pizza, head for this pizzeria-trattoria just outside the city walls; service can be somewhat frenetic, but the atmosphere is always buzzy. Tues–Fri 12.30–2.30pm & 7.30pm–midnight, Sat & Sun 7pm–midnight.

Sette Teste Via Cesare Battisti 44 38 ☎347 040 5158, ⓦosteriasetteteste.it; map p.245. A very smart and hospitable modern *osteria*, with an excellent selection of wines at the bar, and a nice Padovan-Venetian menu, at €12–20 for *secondi* – *baccalà* is always available, naturally, along with tripe and various beef dishes. Mon & Wed–Sun noon–11.45pm.

Terrazza Carducci Via Giosuè Carducci 2 ☎049 876 6183; map p.245. Old-style family-run trattoria, with a traditional and good-value menu – most *secondi* are in the €15–20 range. The rooftop terrace (summer only) gives an oblique view of the Prato della Valle, and is a pleasant place to pass an evening. Mon–Tues & Thurs–Sun noon–2.30pm & 7.30–10.30pm.

CAFÉS AND GELATERIE

Gelateria Gianni Via Calvi Pietro Fortunato 12; map p.245. This little *gelateria*, located just off Piazza Garibaldi, sells the best ice cream in Padua, without question. The menu of flavours is constantly changing, and often features mixtures you won't find anywhere else. Daily 10.30am–midnight.

Pasticceria Breda Via Umberto I 26 ⓦpasticceriabreda. it; map p.245. Founded in 1967, *Pasticceria Breda* is the creator of Padua's finest cakes, and the coffee is good too. Take a seat under the arcades and watch the passing traffic on one of Padua's smartest streets. Tues–Sun 7.30am–8pm.

Sottosopra Via XX Settembre 77 ⓦwww. sottosoprapadova.it; map p.245. The "Upside down" bar-bistrot is an intriguing Anglo-Mediterranean mix, with a list of fifty teas to complement its menu of wines, snacks and light meals. Run by a very friendly couple, it attracts an unusually varied clientele, from retired couples to students. It's in a quiet part of town and has outdoor tables in summer. Tues–Fri noon–3pm & 7pm–1am, Sat noon–3pm & 6pm–1am, Sun 6pm–midnight (opens 5pm Sun in winter).

DRINKING

Padua's nightlife tends to fluctuate in sync with term time; during the summer vacation things are rather somnolent.

Ai do Archi Via Nazario Sauro 23; map p.245. Small wine bar off Piazza Signori, with a very lively vibe. Good music (often reggae, loud) and a great atmosphere, with tasty bruschetta and *crostini* to accompany your drinks. Daily 6.30pm–2am.

★ **Bar Nazionale** Piazza delle Erbe 41; map p.245. Situated by the steps leading up to the Palazzo della Ragione, this bar is the ideal place to people-watch while

you nurse an aperitif; the food is good too. Daily 8am–9pm.

La Yarda Via Dondi dall'Orologio 1; map p.245. Situated on the same cobbled square as the Liviano, this bar is packed with students every term-time evening, when the music is played loud, but it can be very peaceful at other times, especially if you sit at one of the tables in the shade of the piazza's trees. Mon–Sat 10am–midnight, Sun 6–11pm.

Colli Euganei

A few kilometres to the southwest of Padua the **Colli Euganei** or Euganean Hills – which are now protected as a national park (ⓦparcocollieuganei.com) – rise abruptly out of the plains, their slopes patched with vineyards between scattered villages, villas and churches. Between Padua and the hills lie the spa towns of **ÁBANO TERME** and **MONTEGROTTO TERME**, which for much of the year are crowded with customers for the hot radioactive waters and mud baths. It's been like this for centuries, as the names of the towns indicate: *Ábano* comes from Aponeus, a Roman god of healing, while *Montegrotto* is said to derive from "mons aegratorum", meaning "mountain of the infirm". Packed with big and expensive modern hotels, these are far from the most enticing spots in the Veneto.

Arquà Petrarca

A car is necessary for exploring the hills, as buses are few and far between, even to the medieval village of **ARQUÀ PETRARCA**, the gem of the Colli Euganei.

Casa del Petrarca

Via Valesella 4 • Tues–Sun: March–Oct 9am–12.30pm & 3–7pm; Nov–Feb 9am–12.30pm & 2.30–5.30pm • €4, or PadovaCard

The Da Carrara family gave the poet **Francesco Petrarca** (Petrarch) a piece of land here on which to realize his dream of a "delightful house surrounded by an olive grove and a vineyard". He spent the last summers of his life (1369–74) in his idyllic home and this is where he died. Not only does the house, the **Casa del Petrarca** still stand, but his desk and chair are still intact too, as are various parts of the original fabric of the interior. Petrarch's sarcophagus is in the centre of the village, with one epitaph penned by him and another by his son-in-law, who placed it here.

14

Monsélice

In earlier times **MONSÉLICE** was perched on the pimple of volcanic rock – La Rocca – around the foot of which it now winds. Of the five concentric walls that then protected it, all that remains of them and their towers is a small section of the outer ring and a citadel right on the hill's crest – the rest was demolished for building stone in the nineteenth century. (It's a source of local pride that the *tracchite* stone that paves much of Venice came from the quarries of Monsélice.) The remnants make a powerful impression though, and the town possesses a fortress which is the equal of any in the Veneto.

Piazza Mazzini and around

From the train station, the route to the centre crosses the Canale Bisato, from whose bridge you can look back to the **Villa Pisani** (sometimes open for exhibitions), which was a stopover for the Pisani family as they travelled by water from Venice to their estates in Montagnana. The fragmentary town wall leads to the **Torre Civica**, built by Ezzelino da Romano in 1244 and repaired in 1504. Facing the Torre Civica across the central **Piazza Mazzini**, just beyond the wall, is the **Loggetta**, a seventeenth-century addition to the **Palazzo del Monte di Pietà**.

Museo San Paolo

Via 28 Aprile • April–Oct Fri 10am–noon & 3–6pm, Sat & Sun 10am–1pm & 2–7pm; Nov–March Sat & Sun 10am–6pm • €4

At the top of the square, the **Museo San Paolo** – the town's tiny archeological museum – occupies the restored ruins of a Romanesque church. Focusing on the Roman era, it consists chiefly of inscribed stones, but really isn't one of the Veneto's most enthralling collections.

Antiquarium Longobardo

Via del Santuario • April–Nov daily 10am–noon & 3–5pm • €2

Via del Santuario, the road up to the Castello, rises out of Piazza Mazzini. A short way along, the **Antiquarium Longobardo** displays the contents of Lombard tombs discovered on the hill above, including coins, weapons, some unusually complete sarcophagi and a beautiful gold cross.

Castello di Monsélice

Guided tours daily: March–Oct at 9am, 10am, 11am, 3pm, 4pm & 5pm; Nov–Feb 10am, 11am, 2pm & 3pm • €8 • ⓦ castellodimonselice.it

The mighty **Castello di Ezzelino**, more often known as **Ca' Marcello** or the **Castello di Monsélice**, dates back to the eleventh century and was expanded in the thirteenth century by Ezzelino, who added the square tower across the courtyard (the coat of arms was appended after the town came under Venetian rule in 1405). The interior was altered in the fourteenth century by the Da Carrara clan, then in the following century the two main sections were linked by an annexe that was built by the Marcello family;

a library (sixteenth-century) and family chapel (eighteenth-century) were the only later changes. The castle's immaculate appearance is down to **Count Vittorio Cini**, who inherited the derelict building after it had been in the tender care of the Italian army during World War I, and sank a fortune into restoring it and furnishing each section in the appropriate style, even down to the *marmorino* flooring, stained red with bull's blood in the traditional manner. The furniture assembled by Cini comprises one of Italy's finest collections of its kind, and the three-room **armoury**, in the ground floor of Ezzelino's tower, is similarly impressive.

La Rocca

Duomo Vecchio • Daily 9am–noon & 3–6pm • Free

Via del Santuario, the road up **La Rocca**, passes the featureless **Palazzo Nani** (so called because of the stone dwarves – *nani* – on the surrounding wall) before reaching the **Duomo Vecchio**, where fourteenth-century fresco fragments and a Romano-Gothic polyptych on the high altar are the principal attractions. Just beyond the duomo a gateway guarded by two Venetian lions gives onto the Via Sette Chiese, a private road leading up to the **Villa Duodo**. The seven churches of the road's name are the seven pilgrimage churches of Rome, represented as a line of six chapels leading to the church of **San Giorgio** at the top.

Sinners could earn pardon for their misdemeanours by praying their penitential way up the hill to San Giorgio, where figures of martyred saints are arranged in cabinets. The chapels, church, triumphal arch and the main part of the villa were all designed in the late sixteenth century by **Vincenzo Scamozzi**. Now a centre for the study of hydrology, the villa was commissioned by the son of Francesco Duodo, a hero of the Battle of Lépanto; the land was donated by the Venetian state in thanks for services rendered.

Mastio Federiciano

Group guided tours (minimum 10 people) April–Oct Tues–Sun 9am–noon; individual admission on Sun 2.30–6pm • €4

On the summit of La Rocca, on the site of the Lombard necropolis, stands the **Mastio Federiciano** (Frederick's Keep), which was constructed in the early thirteenth century by the Emperor Frederick II; the exterior and the views are the tower's principal attractions.

ARRIVAL AND INFORMATION

MONSÉLICE

Trains Monsélice is easily accessible by train from Venice (hourly; 50min), Padua (every 30min; 25min), Montagnana (11 daily; 25min) and Este (10 daily; 8min).

Tourist office Via del Santuario 6 (Tues–Sat 9.30am–12.30pm & 3–6pm, ☎0429 783 026, ⓦ monseliceturismo.it).

Este

The ceramics-producing town of **ESTE**, on the southern edge of the Colli Euganei, claims to be the Veneto's oldest town with a history that can be traced back to the tenth century BC. The Este family, famous as the rulers of Ferrara, first came to power here, before the town fell successively to Ezzelino da Romano III, the Scaligeri, the Carraresi and the Visconti, until finally becoming part of Venice's domain in 1405.

Piazza Maggiore

From the train station Via Principe Amadeo runs straight to the central **Piazza Maggiore**, passing the blank-faced **Basilica di Santa Maria delle Grazie** (with a fourteenth-century Byzantine *Madonna*) and the Romanesque church of **San Martino** with its scarily wonky tower. On the south side of the piazza, Via Matteotti passes under the **Porta Vecchia**, a clock tower built on the site of a much earlier defensive tower.

> **BYRON AND THE SHELLEYS IN ESTE**
>
> The privately owned **Villa de Kunkler**, round the back of the Castello, was **Byron**'s residence in 1817–18, a stay commemorated by a plaque on the villa's wall. The house actually played a greater part in Shelley's life than Byron's – his daughter Clara fell ill while staying here, and died as a result of being carried by her father on an overnight gallop to see a doctor in Venice. When the Shelleys returned here a few days later, Percy wrote his poem of mourning for past splendour, *Lines Written Among the Euganean Hills*.

14

The Castello and Museo Nazionale Atestino

Castello gardens April–Sept 9am–7pm; Oct–March 9am–5pm • Free • **Museo Atestino** Daily 8.30am–7.30pm • €5

Leave Piazza Maggiore on the north side and you'll immediately come to the ruins of the **Castello dei Carraresi**; founded by the Este dynasty and rebuilt by the Carraresi family in 1340, the fortress is now surrounded by attractive gardens. Adjacent to the gardens stands the **Museo Nazionale Atestino**, where an outstanding collection of pre-Roman artefacts is installed on the first floor, while much of the ground floor is given over to Roman remains. The room devoted to medieval and Renaissance pieces includes a fine *Madonna and Child* by **Cima da Conegliano**. There's also a display of local pottery, a craft for which Este has been famous for since before the Renaissance, and some curious tombstones from the fifth century BC which preserve the alphabet of the ancient language known as Venetico.

The Duomo

Daily 10am–noon & 4–6pm

On the west side of Piazza Maggiore, Via Cavour leads to the **Duomo**, also known as the Abbaziale di Santa Tecla, which was rebuilt between 1690 and 1708 after an earthquake. The oval plan of its Baroque interior anticipated the design of the Pietà in Venice by several decades. The only painting of note is **Giambattista Tiepolo**'s huge altarpiece of *St Thecla Calling on God for the Cessation of the Plague*.

ARRIVAL AND INFORMATION   ESTE

By train There are ten trains a day from Monsélice, the journey takes 8min.

Tourist office The chief tourist office of the Colli Euganei is at Via Guido Negri 9, by the entrance to the Castello gardens (April–Sept Tues–Sun 9.30am–4.30pm; Oct–March Mon–Sat 9am–4pm; ☎ 0429 600 462).

EATING

Le Strie Via Pescheria Vecchia 1 ☎ 0429 94 967, ⓦ ristorantelestrie.it. A marvellous restaurant on a road parallel to Via Matteoti. "The Witches" is run by a mother and daughter team who make inventive use of local produce – the ravioli with black truffle and mushrooms is delectable. Main courses are €12–15. Tues–Fri 9am–3pm & 7–11.30pm, Sat & Sun 10am–3.30pm & 6–11.30pm.

Montagnana and around

The pride of **MONTAGNANA**, fifteen minutes down the rail line from Este, is its medieval city walls, raised by the ubiquitous Ezzelino da Romano after he had flattened the town in 1242. The walls were later strengthened by the Carraresi family as Padua's first line of defence against the Scaligeri to the west. It was not until the War of the League of Cambrai in the early sixteenth century that the battlements were called upon to fulfil their function, and when the hour came they were found wanting – controlled by the Venetians at the start of hostilities, Montagnana changed hands no fewer than thirteen times in the course of the war. After that the walls were not used defensively

14

> **VILLA BADOER**
>
> A trip to **FRATTA POLÉSINE**, 35km southwest of Montagnana, will appeal to fans of **Palladio**'s buildings. The **Villa Badoer** (March–Oct Thurs–Sun 10am–noon & 3.30–6.30pm; Nov–Feb Sat–Thurs; €3), designed in the 1560s, is one of his most eloquent flights of architectural rhetoric, with its distinctive curving colonnades linking the porticoed house to the storage spaces at the side. None of the original furnishings are left, but restorers have uncovered the villa's late sixteenth-century grotesque frescoes by **Giallo**, a recherché Florentine; a small archeological museum now occupies part of the villa.

again. With a circumference of nearly 2km and 24 polygonal towers spaced at regular intervals, these are among the finest medieval fortifications in Italy, and the relatively sparse development around their perimeter makes them all the more impressive.

The Castello di San Zeno

Tues 3–6pm, Wed–Sat 9.30am–12.30pm & 4–7pm (3–6pm in winter), Sun 10am–1pm & 4–7pm (3–6pm in winter) • €2.50

Gates pierce the city walls at the cardinal points of the compass, the entrances to the east and west being further reinforced by fortresses. The **eastern** gate (Porta Padova) is protected by the **Castello di San Zeno**, built by Ezzelino in 1242, with a watchtower to survey the road to Padua; the Castello now houses the **Museo Civico e Archeologico**, which displays various rather dull objects uncovered around the town, from Neolithic arrowheads to medieval ceramics. The musical section shows off costumes and other memorabilia pertaining to Montagnana's favourite sons, the tenors Giovanni Martinelli and Aureliano Pertile.

The Rocca, Duomo and Villa Pisani

Duomo: daily 8am–2pm & 3–7pm • Free • Villa Pisani: closed to the public

On the **western** side of town, the **Rocca degli Alberi** was built by the Da Carrara family in 1362 to keep the roads from Mantua and Verona covered – today it houses one of the town's youth hostels. The centre of Montagnana is the Piazza Vittorio Emanuele, dominated by the late Gothic and rather gloomy **Duomo**. The most arresting feature of its exterior, the marble portal, was a later addition, possibly designed by Sansovino. **Veronese**'s altarpiece, a *Transfiguration*, is less engaging than the huge anonymous painting of the *Battle of Lépanto* on the left as you enter – it's said to represent accurately the position of the ships at one point in the battle.

Outside the walls, just beyond the Porta Padova, is Palladio's magnificent, if crumbling, **Villa Pisani**, built for a branch of the Pisani family of Venice as a summer residence and administrative centre for their mainland estates.

Villa Pojana

Via Castello 43 • April–Oct Wed, Sat & Sun 10am–1pm & 3–6pm • €5 • ⓦ villapoiana.it

On the southern edge of Pojana Maggiore, 6km north of Montagnana, stands the **Villa Pojana**, the finest of three villas built by the Pojana family in this area. Commissioned by Bonifazio Pojana – whose wife had provided the dowry for Palladio's wife – it was designed in the late 1540s, and is notable for the austere simplicity of its facade and the finesse of its frescoed decoration, which takes its inspiration from ancient Rome. A display of beautiful wooden models shows several of Palladio's villas as he designed them rather than as they were built; there are plans to convert the basement into another exhibition area.

Vicenza, Verona and around

Midway between Padua and Verona, affluent Vicenza tends to be overlooked by tourists, yet its streets form one of the most impressive urban landscapes in Italy, owing largely to Andrea Palladio – perhaps the most influential architect that Western Europe has ever produced. Buildings by Palladio and his acolytes are plentiful in the city and the countryside, and the Villa Rotonda and Villa Valmarana are among the area's highlights. In Verona, remnants of the more distant past are what make the place so attractive: though there are a number of Renaissance palazzi, the medieval period has left a stronger mark in the *centro storico*. Traces of ancient Rome are evident too, with the immense and prominent Arena – venue for the famous opera festival. And Verona's location, enclosed in a loop of the Adige River and encompassed by green hills, is the most alluring of any Veneto city.

Vicenza

The evolution of **VICENZA** follows a course familiar in this part of northern Italy: development under imperial Rome, destruction by Attila, Lombard occupation, attainment of a degree of independence followed by struggles with neighbouring towns, rule by the Scaligeri of Verona in the fourteenth century and then absorption into the Venetian empire in 1404, after which its fortunes shadowed those of the ruling city. The numerous surviving fifteenth-century palaces of Vicenza reflect its status as a Venetian satellite, with facades reminiscent of the Canal Grande, but in the latter half of the sixteenth century the city was transformed by the work of an architect who owed nothing to Venice but a lot to ancient Rome, and whose rigorous yet flexible style was to influence every succeeding generation – Andrea di Pietro della Gondola, alias **Palladio**.

Palladio's buildings – which have earned Vicenza a listing as a **UNESCO World Heritage Site** – attract a steady stream of architectural students and less specialized visitors, but it's business travellers who bring in most of the hotel revenue. (The city's calendar is strewn with commercial events, one of the biggest being the biennial trade fair for priestly vestments and other religious paraphernalia, an event that draws buyers from all over the world.) Though the economic malaise that has afflicted Italy in recent years has had an impact here (in 2015, for example, one of Italy's most famous brands, bike component manufacturer **Campagnolo**, announced plans to switch much of its production to Romania), Vicenza remains one of Italy's main wealth-generators, being Europe's largest centre for the production of textiles as well the focus of Italy's "Silicon Valley" and a major producer of steel, gold and jewellery.

15

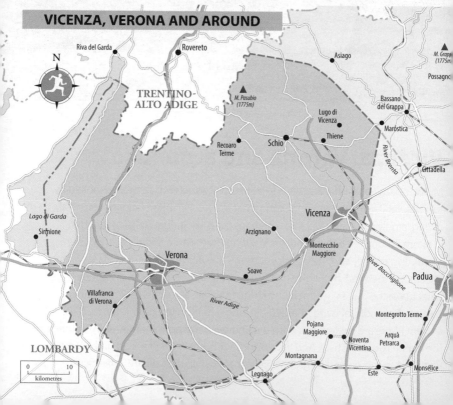

VICENZA, VERONA AND AROUND

Riva del Garda
Rovereto
Asiago
M. Grapp (1775m)
Possagno

TRENTINO-ALTO ADIGE

M. Pasubio (1775m)
Bassano del Grappa
Lugo di Vicenza
Maróstica
Recoaro Terme
Schio
Thiene
River Brenta
Cittadella

Lago di Garda
Sirmione
Vicenza
Arzignano
Montecchio Maggiore
River Bacchiglione
Padua

Verona
Soave
Villafranca di Verona
River Adige
Montegrotto Terme
Arquà Petrarca
Pojana Maggiore
Noventa Vicentina

LOMBARDY
Montagnana
Este
Monsélice
Legnago

0 — 10
kilometres

THE VICENZA CARD

The €15 **Vicenza Card** is valid for seven days and gives admission to the Teatro Olimpico, Palazzo Chiericati, Santa Corona, the Museo Naturalistico-Archeologico, the Museo Diocesano, the Gallerie di Palazzo Leoni Montanari, the Palladio Museum and the Museo del Risorgimento. The €18 family version of the card, for two adults and up to four children, is valid for three days. You can buy the Vicenza Card at all of the above museums except Palazzo Chiericati, Santa Corona and the Museo Naturalistico-Archeologico.

Within the girdle of industrial estates and factories, much of Vicenza's *centro storico* is an amalgam of Gothic and classical buildings that today looks much as it did when the last major phase of construction came to an end at the close of the eighteenth century. This historic core is compact enough to be explored in a day, but the city and its environs require a short stay to do them justice.

Corso Andrea Palladio

15

The main street of Vicenza, the **Corso Andrea Palladio**, is a vestige of the Roman street-plan and cuts right through the old centre from the Piazza Castello (overlooked by an eleventh-century tower, once part of the Scaligeri fort) down to the Piazza Matteotti. The first major building comes near the start of the Corso, on the far side of Piazza Castello – it's the fragmentary **Palazzo Porto-Breganze**, Palladio's last palace in Vicenza. None of Palladio's townhouses was completed to plan, but none of the others is as flagrantly unfinished as this one.

Particularly striking on the Corso itself are the following houses: no. 13, the Palazzo Thiene Bonin-Longhare (by Palladio's follower Scamozzi); no. 38–40, Palazzo Pagello (1780); no. 47, Palazzo Thiene (fifteenth-century); no. 67, Palazzo Brunello (fifteenth-century – have a look at the courtyard); no. 98, Palazzo Trissino (now the town hall; also by Scamozzi); no. 147, Palazzo da Schio (fifteenth-century, restored), which is known as the Ca' d'Oro as it once had gilded decoration and bears a slight resemblance to the Ca' d'Oro in Venice; and no. 163, the **Casa Cogollo**, known as the Casa del Palladio even though it's unlikely that he designed it (despite what the plaque says) and he certainly never lived there. None of the churches on the Corso is of any interest to non-parishioners.

Pinacoteca di Palazzo Chiericati

Piazza Matteotti 37–39 • Tues–Sun: July & Aug 10am–6pm; Sept–June 9am–5pm • €7, or Vicenza Card

The Corso Palladio ends at one of the architect's most imperious buildings, the Palazzo Chiericati. Begun in 1550 and completed about a hundred years later, this commission was a direct result of Palladio's success with the Basilica, being a house for one of the Basilica's supervisors, Girolamo Chiericati. It's now the home of the **Pinacoteca Palazzo Chiericati**, many of whose pieces were gathered in the 1810s to keep them out of the grasp of the marauding French.

The paintings are housed mainly on the second floor, where celebrated names such as Veronese, Memling, Tintoretto, Giambattista Tiepolo, Van Dyck, the Bassano family and Luca Giordano punctuate a picture collection that's given its backbone by Vicentine artists – notably Montagna, Buonconsiglio, Maffei and Carpioni. Though none of these local artists is likely to knock you flat, there are some intriguing pieces here: the tiny bronze plaquettes and rock-crystal carvings made by the once-famous Valerio Belli, for example, and Francesco del Cairo's orgasmic *Herodias with the Head of the Baptist*. The low-ceilinged attic rooms now house the bequest of Giuseppe Roi, a collection mostly of drawings and watercolours, which includes small works by Tiepolo, Manet and Morandi.

15

ANDREA PALLADIO

Born in Padua in 1508, **Andrea di Pietro della Gondola** came to Vicenza at the age of 16 to work as a stonecutter. At 30 he became the protégé of a local nobleman, Count Giangiorgio Trissino, who directed his architectural training, took him to Rome, gave him the classicized name **Palladio** and brought him into contact with the dominant class of Vicenza. Some of these men were landowners, recently enriched now that peace had returned to the mainland after the War of the League of Cambrai, many were wealthy soldiers, and a decent percentage were well educated. They turned to Palladio to design houses that would embody their financial and intellectual rank and their corporate superiority to their Venetian rulers.

Between 1540 and his death in 1580 Palladio created around a dozen palaces and public buildings in Vicenza and an even larger number of villas on the Vicentine and Venetian farming estates in the surrounding countryside, as well as the churches of the Redentore and San Giorgio Maggiore in Venice. But what made Palladio more influential than any other architect in Western history was the publication, in 1570, of his *Quattro Libri dell'Architettura*. Earlier architects had written works of theory, but Palladio's treatise was unique in its practical applicability, in that it combined a survey of Roman architecture and his own projects with a discussion of building methods – it was both a manual and a demonstration of the principles of harmony and proportion. And though Palladianism eventually came to be associated with bland orderliness, Palladio's own work is highly imaginative and undogmatic. Even if you've previously been inclined to agree with Herbert Read's opinion that "In the back of every dying civilization there sticks a bloody Doric column," you might well leave Vicenza converted to the Palladian cause.

Teatro Olimpico

Piazza Matteotti 11 • Tues–Sun: July & Aug 10am–6pm, Sept–June 9am–5pm • €11, or Vicenza Card • ⓦ teatrolimpicovicenza.it

The **Teatro Olimpico** – the oldest indoor theatre in Europe – is one of the Veneto's most stunning buildings. Approached in 1579 by the members of the humanist Accademia Olimpica to produce a design for a permanent theatre, Palladio devised a covered amphitheatre derived from his reading of Vitruvius (architect to Augustus) and his studies of Roman structures in Italy and France. In terms of the development of theatre design, the Teatro Olimpico was not a progressive enterprise – contemporaneous theatres in Florence, for example, were far closer to the modern proscenium-arch design – but it was the most comprehensive piece of classical reconstruction of its time, and the men responsible for it were suitably proud of their brainchild: the toga-clad figures above the stage are portraits of Palladio's clients.

Palladio died soon after work commenced, and the scheme was then overseen by Scamozzi, whose contribution to the design is its most startling feature. The theatre was to open with a lavish production of *Oedipus Rex*, so Scamozzi devised a backstage perspective of an idealized Thebes, creating the illusion of long urban vistas by tilting the wooden "streets" at an angle that demands chamois-like agility from the actors. *Oedipus Rex* inaugurated the theatre on March 3, 1585; the theatre was little used in the years that followed, and the original scenery was never removed. The Teatro Olimpico is still in use today, though fire regulations severely restrict audience numbers.

Piazza dei Signori

The hub of Vicenza is **Piazza dei Signori**, which has the city's main concentration of cafés and bars, and is regularly occupied by market stalls. What makes this space unforgettable is the Palazzo della Ragione, the most portentous of Palladio's creations.

The Basilica

Basilica ⓦ www.basilicapalladiana.vi.it **Museo del Gioiello** Tues–Fri 3–7pm, Sat & Sun 11am–7pm • €8 • ⓦ museodelgioiello.it

Palazzo della Ragione, widely known simply as the **Basilica** – which is how the architect referred to it – was designed in the late 1540s, but not finished until the second decade of the next century. It was Palladio's first public project and it secured his reputation. The architect himself had no doubt as to its merit: "This building can be compared to ancient ones and placed with the most beautiful of the major buildings that have been made by the ancients," he wrote. The monumental regularity of the Basilica disguises the fact that the Palladian building is effectively a stupendous piece of buttressing – the colonnades enclose the fifteenth-century brick meeting-hall of the city council, an unstable structure that had defied a number of attempts to prop it up before Palladio's solution was put into effect. The vast Gothic hall (which had to be rebuilt after bomb damage in World War II) is now used for exhibitions, while on the ground floor, in the midst of the jewellers' shops, there's a new **Museo del Gioiello**. Billed the first jewellery museum in Italy, it has nine rooms arranged by slightly tenuous themes (Symbol, Magic, Function, Beauty, etc), and has the ambience of a shop in which nothing is for sale.

The rest of the piazza

Facing the Basilica across the Piazza dei Signori is a late Palladio building, the unfinished **Loggia del Capitaniato**, which was built as accommodation for the Venetian military commander of the city (the *Capitano*). Completing the enclosure of this side of the piazza is the sixteenth-century **Monte di Pietà**, which brackets the seventeenth-century church of San Vincenzo. The slender **Torre di Piazza** reached its present altitude in 1444, having been started in the twelfth century and raised in 1311; its clock is claimed to have been the first such public timepiece in Italy, and to this day it still functions perfectly.

15

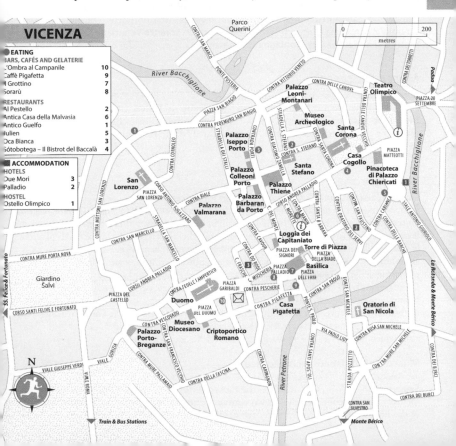

VICENZA

0   200
metres

Parco Querini

River Bacchiglione

Palazzo Leoni-Montanari
Teatro Olimpico
Museo Archeologico
Santa Corona
Palazzo Iseppo Porto
Casa Cogollo
Palazzo Colleoni Porto
Santa Stefano
Pinacoteca di Palazzo Chiericati
San Lorenzo
Palazzo Thiene
Palazzo Barbaran da Porto
Palazzo Valmarana
Loggia dei Capitaniato
Torre di Piazza
PIAZZA DEI SIGNORI
Basilica
Giardino Salvi
Duomo
Casa Pigafetta
Oratorio di San Nicola
Museo Diocesano
Palazzo Porto-Breganze
Criptoportico Romano

River Fretrone

N

▼ Train & Bus Stations

Monte Bérico

Piazza dell'Erbe and Casa Pigafetta

The city's old fruit and vegetable market square, **Piazza dell'Erbe**, is at the back of the Basilica, glowered over by medieval **Torre del Tormento**, which was once the prison tower. In nearby Contrà Pigafetta there's Vicenza's architectural oddity, the florid and Spanish-influenced **Casa Pigafetta**. Built in 1481, it was the birthplace of Antonio Pigafetta, who set out with Magellan on his voyage of 1519 and kept a record of the expedition. Unlike his leader, Pigafetta lived to see his home town again.

Oratorio di San Nicola

Piazzetta San Nicola • Check with the tourist office for opening hours • Free

From Casa Pigafetta it's a short walk to the **Oratorio di San Nicola**. If the Museo Civico's collection has given you a taste for **Francesco Maffei**'s work, you'll not want to miss this little building, which has a welter of paintings by him and his contemporary **Carpioni**, including Maffei's delirious altarpiece of *The Trinity*. The Oratorio stands by the Retrone River, at the far end of Vicenza's most picturesque bridge, the humpbacked **Ponte San Michele**, which was built in 1620.

15

Duomo

Piazza Duomo • Mon–Fri 10.30–noon & 3.30–5.30pm, Sat 10.30am–noon • Free

The vast and bland **Duomo**, founded before the eighth century but substantially rebuilt – chiefly from the fourteenth to the sixteenth centuries – was bombed to bits in 1944 and carefully reconstructed after the war. A polyptych by **Lorenzo Veneziano** (fifth chapel on right) and a *Madonna* by **Montagna** (fourth chapel on left) are the best of its paintings.

Museo Diocesano

Piazza Duomo 2 • Tues–Sun 10am–1pm & 2–6pm • €5, or Vicenza Card

Aside from the usual collection of church vestments and silverware, the **Museo Diocesano** has a well-presented display of stone fragments from Roman times onwards, including a fine fourth-century relief of the three Magi. There are no great masterpieces in the picture galleries, however.

Santa Corona

Contrà Santa Corona • Tues–Sun: July & Aug 9am–5pm, Sept–June 10am–6pm • €3, or Vicenza Card

Far more interesting and uplifting than the duomo is the Dominican church of **Santa Corona** on the other side of the Corso Palladio. Begun in 1261 to house a thorn from Christ's crown, it has what's said to be the oldest Gothic interior in the Veneto; the thorn itself is displayed in the church on Good Friday, but for the rest of the year is kept locked away. The church is an upliftingly bright building, and it has two magnificent paintings: an *Adoration of the Magi* painted in 1573 by **Paolo Veronese** (third chapel on the right), and a luminous *Baptism of Christ* (opposite), a late work by **Giovanni Bellini** which is encased in an elaborate frame that Bellini himself designed. Also take time to look at the late fifteenth-century inlaid **choirstalls**, the extraordinary seventeenth-century *pietra dura* **altarpiece**, the simple **Cappella Valmarana**, which was added to the crypt in 1576 by Palladio, and the anonymous *Madonna* in the left aisle, which includes a view of Vicenza around 1500, added by Fogolino.

Museo Naturalistico-Archeologico

Tues–Sun: July & Aug 10am–1.45pm; Sept–June 9am–12.30pm & 2–4.45pm • €3.50, or Vicenza Card

Santa Corona's cloisters now house the **Museo Naturalistico-Archeologico**, which includes various collections of skewered insects, stuffed birds and fossils; the highlight of the historical section is a fine fourth-century Roman mosaic.

Palazzo Leoni Montanari

Contrà Santa Corona 25 • Tues–Sun 10am–6pm • €5, or Vicenza Card • W gallerieditalia.com

Now owned by the Sanpaolo banking group, the opulent Baroque **Palazzo Leoni Montanari** has been restored as a showcase for selections from the three art collections that the bank has accumulated over the years. In the profusely decorated rooms of the *piano nobile*, paintings by Canaletto, Francesco Guardi and Tiepolo feature in a survey of eighteenth-century Veneto art that also includes a room of quirky scenes of everyday Venetian life created by Pietro Longhi and his followers. Another room on this floor houses some top-quality sixth- to third-century BC ceramics from the necropolis of Ruvo di Puglia. Also on this floor you'll see Agostino Fasolato's tumultuous *Fall of the Rebel Angels*, an extraordinary table-top sculpture which was carved around 1750 and was once regarded as one of Padua's major attractions. Upstairs there's a thematic display of more than one hundred Russian icons (about a quarter of the bank's hoard), a remarkable and well-presented array that spans the period from the thirteenth century to the twentieth. One-off exhibitions – usually excellent – are held on the ground floor.

15

Santo Stefano

Piazzetta Santo Stefano • Mon–Fri 8.30–9.45am & 4–6pm, Sat & Sun 9am–12.30pm

The church of **Santo Stefano** merits a call chiefly for **Palma il Vecchio**'s luscious *Madonna and Child with St George and St Lucy*, on the last altar on the left. Take a look too at the three small golden pictures on the front and sides of the high altar's tabernacle – *The Resurrection* is attributed to Giambattista Tiepolo, while *St Peter* and *St John the Baptist* are definitely by his son, Giandomenico.

Palazzo Thiene

Contrà San Gaetano Thiene 11 • Admission free, by booking at least a week ahead on ☎ 0444 339 989

The entrance to Santo Stefano faces the immense Palazzo Negri and its mighty Gothic neighbour, the Casa Fontana, but more intimidating than either is Palladio's rugged **Palazzo Thiene**, on the Corso side of them. Built in the 1540s, this palace was planned to occupy the entire block down to the Corso and across to Contrà Porti; in the end, work progressed no further than the addition of this wing to the block that had been built at the end of the fifteenth century. (The facade of the Gothic portion is on Contrà Porti.) Palladio was not simply the most inventive and knowledgeable architect in the Veneto, he was also cost-effective: his columns are nearly always made of brick covered with a skim of plaster, and, as an inspection of the Thiene residence will reveal, his rough-hewn stonework is just cunningly worked brick as well. Now a bank's HQ, the Palazzo Thiene is every bit as impressive inside as outside. Reflecting the highly cultured tastes of the Thiene family, the profuse decoration of the main living rooms is dominated by subjects from classical mythology, and much of the decor – notably the amazing stuccowork by Alessandro Vittoria – dates from the period of the palace's construction. Some of the paintings and sculptures were commissioned in the eighteenth century, but these are remarkably well integrated into the overall scheme, making this the finest domestic interior in the city.

Contrà Porti

There's no better example than **Contrà Porti** of the way in which the builders of Vicenza skilfully grafted new houses onto old without doing violence to the line of the street: the palaces here span two centuries, yet the overall impression is one of cohesion.

Palazzo Barbaran da Porto – Palladio Museum

Contrà Porti 11 • Tues–Sun 10am–6pm • €6, or Vicenza Card • W palladiomuseum.org

Palladio's **Palazzo Barbaran da Porto**, which was designed around 1570 and subsequently embellished by others, is now occupied by the Centro Internazionale di Studi di Architettura "A. Palladio", which organizes Vicenza's prestigious annual architecture conference and has turned the palazzo into the **Palladio Museum**, a place "in which thinking about architecture is fostered". The focus is of course largely on Palladio, and it's brilliantly done, with large-scale cutaway models of most of his major buildings, and a host of imaginative audiovisual displays – on the walls of every room, the projected images of various authorities on the architect deliver short but illuminating (and subtitled) talks on all aspects of Palladio's work and milieu. And the building is in itself impressive, especially the grand Salone di Cesare, where Palladio's patrons are represented in the guise of Roman emperors.

The other Contrà Porti palaces

On the west side of Contrà Porti stands a sweep of fine Gothic houses, the best being the fourteenth-century **Palazzo Colleoni Porto** (no. 19); next door is Palladio's **Palazzo Iseppo Porto**, designed a few years after the Thiene and a couple of decades before the Barbaran da Porto. Luigi da Porto, the author of the story on which Shakespeare based his *Romeo and Juliet*, died at no. 15 in 1529.

Corso Antonio Fogazzaro

Contrà Riale (itself not short of grand houses) connects Contrà Porti to **Corso Antonio Fogazzaro**, a busy road with a spread of architectural attractions. At the Corso Palladio end stands the **Palazzo Valmarana** (no. 16), where Palladio's use of overlapping planes makes the design of the facade legible in the narrow street and at the same time integrates the palace with the flanking buildings. The palazzo was planned to be three times bigger than what you see today.

San Lorenzo

Piazza San Lorenzo • Daily 7am–noon & 3.30–7pm • Free

Corso Antonio Fogazzaro opens out at the thirteenth-century Franciscan church of **San Lorenzo**, where the fourteenth-century marble portal is the best feature. The dimensions of the interior are impressive, but it's a rather austere space, with bare red-brick walls and plain white vaulting. **Montagna**'s fresco of the *Beheading of St Paul*, in the chapel on the left of the chancel, would once have been stunning, but has now faded away. The tranquil cloister can be entered from a door at the top of the left aisle.

Santi Felice e Fortunato

Corso Santi Felice e Fortunato • Daily 9am–noon & 3–6pm • Free

The basilica of **Santi Felice e Fortunato** – the oldest church in Vicenza – stands hidden behind shops and apartments about fifteen minutes' walk west of the centre, along the Corso of the same name. Dating back to immediately after the Edict of Constantine (313 AD), it was wrecked by Magyar invaders in 899 and then by earthquakes in 1117, and was largely reconstructed in the twelfth century – that's the date of the leaning campanile. Recent restorations have stripped away later accretions to reveal the form of the church at around that period. Remnants of the earliest building have survived – portions of fourth- and fifth-century mosaics have been uncovered in the nave and right aisle, and a door off the right aisle leads into a fourth-century martyrs' shrine. The museum alongside the church contains some ancient sarcophagi and architectural fragments.

The outskirts: Monte Bèrico and the villas

Rising behind the rail line, **Monte Bèrico** is seen by everyone who comes to Vicenza, but not actually visited by many, which is a pity as an expedition up the hill has a number of attractions: an amazing view (on a clear day the horizon is a switchback of mountain peaks), a clutch of excellent paintings and one of Europe's most influential buildings, the Villa Rotonda.

Buses for Monte Bèrico leave the bus station approximately every ninety minutes from Monday to Saturday; on Sunday there is a more frequent service from Viale Roma. If you decide to walk, the most direct route from the Basilica is to cross Ponte San Michele, carry on to Strada Pozzetto then along Contrà San Silvestro, which brings you to Viale Risorgimento; on the other side of this major road junction, Via Casanova leads to the **Portici**, an eighteenth-century arcade built to shelter the pilgrims on their way up to the church. The walk will take about half an hour from the centre.

Basilica di Monte Bèrico

Viale X Giugno • Summer Mon–Sat 6am–12.30pm & 2.30–7.30pm, Sun 6am–7pm; winter Mon–Sat 6am–12.30pm & 2.30–6pm, Sun 6am–7pm • Free

In 1426–28 Vicenza was struck by an outbreak of bubonic plague, in the course of which the Virgin appeared twice at the summit of Monte Bèrico to announce the city's deliverance. A chapel was raised on the spot that the Virgin had obligingly marked out for its construction, and it duly became a place of pilgrimage. It was enlarged later in the century, altered again in the sixteenth century and then, at the end of the seventeenth, replaced by the present **Basilica di Monte Bèrico**. The church was extended so that the nave of the fifteenth-century version became the transepts of the new church, leaving the Gothic facade stuck onto the Basilica's right side. Pilgrims regularly arrive here by the busload, and the glossy interior of the church, all gilding and fake marble, is immaculately maintained to receive them.

The church's best painting, **Montagna**'s *Pietà* (1500), hangs in the chapel on the right side of the apse, while *The Supper of St Gregory the Great* (1572) by **Veronese** is to be seen in the old refectory of the adjoining monastery, which it shares with the fossil collection amassed by the resident Franciscans. The Veronese painting, the prototype of *The Feast in the House of Levi* in Venice's Accademia, was badly damaged in June 1848, in the final phase of the battle of Vicenza, the major military engagement of the anti-Austrian uprising that swept across much of the Veneto in 1848. The battle reached its climax on Monte Bèrico, and on the last day of fighting one of the Austrian generals, Prince Liechtenstein, was killed inside the church. Enraged by his death, Croat troops of the Austrian army slashed the Veronese painting with their bayonets: a small reproduction on the adjoining wall shows what a thorough mess they made of it, and what a good job the restorers did.

Museo del Risorgimento e della Resistenza

Viale X Giugno 87 • Tues–Sun: July & Aug 10am–2pm, Sept–June 9am–1pm & 2.15–5pm • Free

The **Piazzale della Vittoria**, in front of the Basilica, was built to commemorate the dead of World War I; today it's a car park and a belvedere for the best view across the city. Carry on towards the summit of the hill for ten minutes and you'll come to the **Museo del Risorgimento e della Resistenza**. The museum is an impressively thorough display, paying particular attention to Vicenza's resistance to the Austrians in the mid-nineteenth century and to the efforts of the anti-Fascist Alpine fighters a century later, and has good English information sheets in each room.

Villa Valmarana

Stradella dei Nani 87 • March–Oct daily 10am–6pm • €10 • ⓦ villavalmarana.com

Ten minutes' walk from the Basilica (from the angle of the Portici, take Via d'Azeglio then Via Bastian) stands the **Villa Valmarana ai Nani** – meaning "of the dwarves", after the figures on the garden wall. Still owned by the family for which it was built, it's an undistinguished eighteenth-century house made extraordinary by its gorgeous decoration, a cycle of frescoes created in 1757 by **Giambattista and Giandomenico Tiepolo**.

There are two parts to the house. The main block, the **Palazzina**, was frescoed by Giambattista, drawing his imagery from the epic poems of Virgil, Tasso and Ariosto –

you're handed a brief guide to the paintings at the entrance. Giambattista also painted one wall of the **Foresteria**, the guest wing, but here the bulk of the work was done by his son. Giandomenico's scope was somewhat narrower than his father's (carnivals and bucolic pleasures were his favourite themes), and he doesn't quite have the senior Tiepolo's apparently effortless virtuosity, but a similar air of wistful melancholy pervades his scenes, and his fluency is always impressive.

La Rotonda

Via della Rotonda 45 • March 10–Nov 10 10am–noon & 3–6pm; rest of year 10am–noon & 2.30–5pm villa Wed & Sat, grounds Tues–Sun • €10 for both villa and grounds, €5 for grounds only • ⓦ villalarotonda.it

From the Villa Valmarana, the narrow Stradella Valmarana descends to **La Rotonda**, a building unique among Palladio's villas in that it was designed not as the main building of a farming estate but as a pavilion for entertainments and the enjoyment of the landscape. Begun in 1566, it was commissioned by Vicenza-born Paolo Almerico as his retirement home, after years in Rome in the service of the papacy, but was not finished until about 1620, by which time it had passed into the hands of the Capra family. (The Capra whose name appears on the main pediment of the villa finished the development of the site in the 1640s, when he commissioned the chapel that stands by the entrance gate.) Almerico chose a hill-top site "surrounded by other most pleasant hills, which present the appearance of a vast theatre", and Palladio's design certainly makes the most of its centre-stage setting. The combination of the pure forms of the circle and square was a fundamental concern of many Renaissance architects (Leonardo, Bramante and Michelangelo all worked at it), and the elegance of Palladio's solution led to innumerable imitations – for example Thomas Jefferson's rejected plan for the official residence of the US president was a near facsimile of the Rotonda.

Only a walk round the lavishly decorated rooms will fully reveal the subtleties of the Rotonda's design, which gives a strong impression of being as symmetrical as a square while in fact having a definite main axis. The garden can be given a miss, as it's not much more than a narrow belt of grass and gravel.

ARRIVAL AND INFORMATION
VICENZA

By train The train station is a 10min walk southwest of the historic centre – just go straight ahead when you come out of the station.

Destinations Castelfranco Veneto (16 daily; 30–40min); Cittadella (15 daily; 25min); Padua (every 20min; 15–30min); Thiene (20 daily; 25min); Treviso (13 daily; 45min–1hr 15min); Venice (every 30min; 45min–1hr 20min);

Verona (every 30min; 25–60min).

Information The main tourist office is by the entrance to the Teatro Olimpico, at Piazza Matteotti 12 (daily 9am–5.30pm; ☎ 0444 320 854). For listings, pick up a copy of the local papers – *Il Gazzettino* or *Il Giornale di Vicenza*, or check out ⓦ vicenza.com or ⓦ vicenzae.org.

ACCOMMODATION

Vicenza has no central one-star **hotels**, and most of the hotels in the upper categories are rather soulless places, aimed at businesspeople and attendees at the city's frequent conferences and trade fairs. But the business traffic keeps demand high, so if you want to stay in Vicenza, always reserve a room in advance.

★ **Due Mori** Contrà Do Rode 26 ☎ 0444 321 886, ⓦ hotelduemori.com; map p.265. Friendly old-fashioned two-star hotel by the Piazza dei Signori. Its rooms are mostly capacious, and are plainly but comfortably furnished; there's wi-fi throughout, but no TV. **€90**

Ostello Olimpico Viale Antonio Giuriolo 9 ☎ 0444 540 222, ⓦ ostellovicenza.com; map p.265. Vicenza's

HI hostel occupies a three-storey Art Nouveau building very near the Teatro Olimpico. It's a spartan place, and it overlooks a busy road junction, but the staff are friendly and the location is central. Reception 7–10am & 3–11pm; check-in 3–11pm. Dorms from **€22**

★ **Palladio** Contrà Oratorio dei Servi 27 ☎ 0444 325 347, ⓦ www.hotel-palladio.it; map p.265. Once a budget hotel, the *Palladio* has been totally transformed into a sleek four-star, and is now the plushest hotel in the city centre. Its 23 rooms have minimalist modern furnishings, including comfortable Japanese mattresses and wall radiators that look like abstract paintings. Room 302 at the top has the largest balcony. **€160**

EATING

In contrast to Verona and Padua, good restaurants are not numerous in Vicenza's *centro storico* – which means it's sensible to book a table in high season. Popular specialities include *baccalà alla Vicentina* (made by marinating dried cod in milk and oil) and *sopressa*, a kind of salami from the Pasubio and Recoaro valleys, generally eaten with a slice of grilled polenta.

RESTAURANTS

★ **Al Pestello** Contrà S. Stefano 3 ☎ 0444 323 721, ⦿ ristorantealpestello.it; map p.265. Homely, well-priced (*secondi* around €17) and long-established *ristorante* by San Stefano. One of the best places in town for sampling *baccalà alla Vicentina* and other local specialities. The dining room is quite small, but in summer there are a few more tables in the street. Mon, Thurs & Fri 7.30–11pm, Sat & Sun 12.30–2.30pm & 7.30–11pm.

Antica Casa della Malvasia Contrà delle Morette 5 ☎ 0444 543 704, ⦿ anticacasadellamalvasia.it; map p.265. This bustling restaurant, just off Piazza dei Signori, offers a good range of well-prepared local standards, at around €15 for *secondi*. The dining rooms are handsome and spacious (the colour scheme is a nice mix of pistacchio and bare brick), and in good weather there are seats in the alleyway outside. Tues–Sat 11.30am–3pm & 7–11.30pm.

Antico Guelfo Contrà Pedemuro S. Biagio 92 ☎ 0444 547 897, ⦿ anticoguelfo.it; map p.265. Run by young Padova-born chef Luca Menegon, the chic *Antico Guelfa* offers a small menu of imaginative dishes (typically three or four fish/meat, plus a vegetarian option), prepared with top-quality local ingredients. Main courses are around €20. The bare-brick dining room is one of the nicest in the city, too. Mon & Wed–Sun noon–3pm & 7–11pm.

Julien Contrà Jacopo Cabianca 13 ☎ 0444 326 168; map p.265. The menu at this cool modern restaurant-bar has interesting combinations such as black ravioli with fish and ginger, and the clientele ranges from cool young *aperitivi*-sippers to families having a meal with their children. Expect to pay around €16 for your main course. Mon–Sat noon–2.30pm & 6–11.30pm, Sun 6–11.30pm.

Oca Bianca Contrà Porti 20a ☎ 0444 542 193, ⦿ trattoriaocabianca.com; map p.265. A small, congenial and dependable no-frills trattoria a few minutes' walk from Piazza dei Signori. The menu always features *baccalà* but is otherwise often exclusively meaty; main courses are €10–15. Mon noon–2.30pm, Tues–Fri noon–2.30pm & 7.30–10.30pm, Sat 7.30–10.30pm.

★ **Sótobotega – Il Bistrot del Baccalà** Corso Palladio, 196 ☎ 0444 544 414; map p.265. The best place in town for lunch – the dining area consists of a single line of tables in the wine cellar of Il Ceppo, Vicenza's finest delicatessen, and the emphasis is placed, unsurprisingly, on *baccalà* – there's even a *baccalà* tasting menu, at around €25. But if salt cod isn't your thing, there are other high-quality light dishes on offer. The wines are excellent too. Tues–Sun 11.30am–3.30pm.

CAFÉS AND GELATERIE

★ **Caffè Pigafetta** Contrà Pescaria 12; map p.265. For many Vicentines, this is where the city's best coffee is served – it's certainly where you'll get the biggest choice of brews. The teas and pastries are excellent too. Mon–Sat 8am–8pm.

Sorarù Piazzetta Andrea Palladio 17; map p.265. Attractive old-world *pasticceria*-café in the shadow of the Basilica. You can have a coffee and cake inside at the bar or at its outdoor tables, next to the statue of Palladio. Mon, Tues, Thurs & Fri 7.30am–1.30pm & 3.30–7.30pm, Sat & Sun 7.30am–7.30pm.

DRINKING

L'Ombra al Campanile Contrà Fontana 2; map p.265. There are plenty of bars in the zone between the Duomo and the Basilica, and this traditional and atmospheric *enoteca* – which occupies a locale that's been a bar for three hundred years and has been run by the same family for three generations – is the best of them. It has an excellent selection of wines, and nice sandwiches too. Daily 9am–

2pm & 5–9pm.

Il Grottino Piazza dell'Erbe 2; map p.265. The bars within the arcades of the Basilica tend to attract more of the passing traffic, but the dimly lit *Il Grottino*, which occupies a cellar bar beneath the building, is more atmospheric than any of them, and has tables out in the open air too. Mon–Fri 5pm–2am, Sat & Sun noon–2am.

> ## VICENZA'S CULTURAL CALENDAR
>
> Culturally the busiest time of the year is from May, when the big-name **Vicenza Jazz Festival** (⦿ vicenzajazz.org) takes place, through to August. There's a glut of concerts, opera productions and plays during this season, with many of the best performances being shown in the Teatro Olimpico.

15

Around Vicenza

The countryside around Vicenza is dotted with hundreds of **villas**, many of them created in and after the mid-sixteenth century, as Venice's upper classes diverted their money into agriculture as a way of protecting the economy against the increasing uncertainties of seaborne trade. The tourist office in Vicenza hands out a booklet and a map plotting the location of many of them, but several are in the middle of nowhere, others are falling to bits and many of the better-kept specimens are closed to the public. But a few of the accessible villas of wider interest lie within the orbit of Vicenza's public transport network (in addition to the Villa Valmarana and Villa Rotonda – see page 269), and these are covered below. Other villas of the Veneto are dealt with in the appropriate sections of this guide –for example, the entries on the **Brenta** (see page 241), **Masèr** (see page 305), **Montagnana** (see page 259) and **Castelfranco Veneto** (see page 294).

15

Villa Cordellina-Lombardi

Via Lovara 36, Montecchio Maggiore • April–Oct Tues & Fri 9am–1pm, Wed, Thurs & Sat–Sun 9am–1pm & 3–6pm; Nov–March Mon–Fri • €3 • A few buses from Vicenza go through Montecchio Maggiore, but many more pass through nearby Alte Ceccato, which is about a 15min walk away

A must for admirers of Giambattista Tiepolo, the eighteenth-century **Villa Cordellina-Lombardi** stands on the northern outskirts of the small town of **MONTECCHIO MAGGIORE**, 13km to the southwest of Vicenza. His frescoes in the entrance hall – *The Clemency of Scipio, The Clemency of Alexander* and, on the ceiling, *The Light of Reason Driving out the Fog of Ignorance* – are a touch less exuberant than the later ones at the Villa Valmarana, but they are gorgeous creations.

Villa Porto-Colleoni

Corso Garibaldi 2, Thiene • Guided tours mid-March to early Nov Tues–Fri & Sun 3, 4 & 5pm, Sat 10am & 11am • €10 • ⓦ www.castellodithiene.com • To get to Thiene from Vicenza, take the Schio train; it leaves virtually every hour and takes around 25min

It was only with the ending of the War of the League of Cambrai in 1516 that the landowners of the Veneto were able to disregard defensive considerations when building homes out of the urban centres – prior to that, the great houses of the terra firma were a sort of cross-breed between a castle and a palace. The most imposing example of this genre still standing is the **Villa Porto-Colleoni** (aka Il Castello di Thiene), built in the 1470s at **THIENE**, a bland textile town 20km north of Vicenza.

The crenellated corner towers, large central block and the encircling protective wall are all features that would have been common in this area in the fifteenth century, although this house, with its facade decorations and ornate Gothic windows, was probably more precious than most. The mandatory tour of the interior makes the most of the workaday sixteenth-century frescoes; the plethora of equine portraits is explained by the fact that the Colleoni had a tradition of service in the Venetian cavalry.

Villa Godi Malinverni

Via Palladio 44 • May–Sept Tues 3–7pm, Sat 9am–2pm & Sun 10am–7pm; March, April, Oct & Nov Tues, Sat & Sun 2–6pm • €6 • ⓦ villagodi.com • An infrequent bus runs from Thiene to Lugo, on its way to Calvene – there's a stop by the Porto-Colleoni

Palladio's first villa, the **Villa Godi Malinverni**, was built in 1537–42 some 8km to the north of Thiene, on the edge of **LUGO DI VICENZA**. The plan that isn't much different from that of old fortified villas like the Porto-Colleoni, but it's clearly more of a country house than a castle. It's a plain but handsome structure: in marked contrast to Palladio's later work, it doesn't have a single feature that refers to the architecture of ancient Rome.

Professor Remo Malinverni restored the house in the early 1960s, and installed his collection of nineteenth-century Italian paintings in some of the rooms; elsewhere in the building you'll find a fossil museum – but neither display can really compete with the sixteenth-century frescoes, some of which show Giambattista Zelotti (he of the Villa Fóscari at Malcontenta) on top form.

Verona

With its Roman sites and streets of pink-hued medieval buildings, the irresistible city of **VERONA** has more in the way of historic attractions than any other place in the Veneto except Venice itself. Unlike Venice, though, it's not a city overwhelmed by the tourist industry, important though that is to the local economy. Verona is the largest city of the mainland Veneto, and its success is largely due to its position at the crossing of the major routes from Germany and Austria to central Italy and from the west to Venice and Trieste.

Set within the low amphitheatre that the wide River Adige has carved out of the hills, Verona conveys a sense of ease that you don't find in the region's other cities. As you walk past the great Roman arena or along the embankments or over the bridges that span the broad curves of the Adige, you'll be struck by the spaciousness of the city. With cars and buses barred from many of the squares and narrow medieval lanes of the historic centre, this is a city that invites dawdling.

15

Brief history

Verona's initial development as a **Roman** settlement was due to its straddling the main east–west and north–south lines of communication. A period of decline in the wake of the disintegration of the Roman Empire was followed by revival under the Ostrogoths, who in turn were succeeded by the Franks – Charlemagne's son, Pepin, ruled his kingdom from here. By the twelfth century Verona had become a city-state, and in the following century, after three decades under the rule of the murderous Ezzelino da Romano, it flourished under the della Scala family, otherwise called the **Scaligeri**. Ruthless in the exercise of power – they once employed Werner von Urslingen, self-styled "enemy of God and of compassion" – the Scaligeri were at the same time energetic patrons of the arts, and many of Verona's finest buildings date from the century of their rule. Both Giotto and Dante were guests of the family, the latter dedicating his *Paradiso* to Can Francesco della Scala, head of the family at the time. Under Can Francesco – more widely known as **Cangrande** – Verona became the chief supporter of the Ghibelline cause in northern Italy and reached the zenith of its independent existence, taking control of Vicenza in 1314, of Padua in 1318 and of Treviso in 1329, just days before Cangrande's death.

The reign of the Scaligeri ended at midnight on October 19, 1387, when Antonio della Scala fled the city, surrendering it to Gian Galeazzo Visconti of Milan. Absorption into the **Venetian empire** followed in 1405, and Venice continued to govern Verona

---

THE VERONA CARD

A **biglietto unico**, costing €6, allows one visit to San Zeno, the Duomo, Sant'Anastasia and San Fermo. It can be bought at any of these churches, which individually charge €2.50 for admission. The **Verona Card** (Ⓦveronacard.it) gives access to all of these churches, plus Galleria d'Arte Moderna, Arche Scaligeri, the Arena, the Torre dei Lamberti (but you have to pay an extra €1 there), the Museo Lapidario, Castelvecchio, the Casa di Giulietta, the Tomba di Giulietta, and the Teatro Romano, as well as unlimited travel on city buses. The 24hr version of the card costs €18, the 72hr €22. It's available at *tabacchi* displaying the Verona Card sign (there's one at the station), at participating museums, and at the tourist office; the period of validity begins when you first use it (not when you buy it).

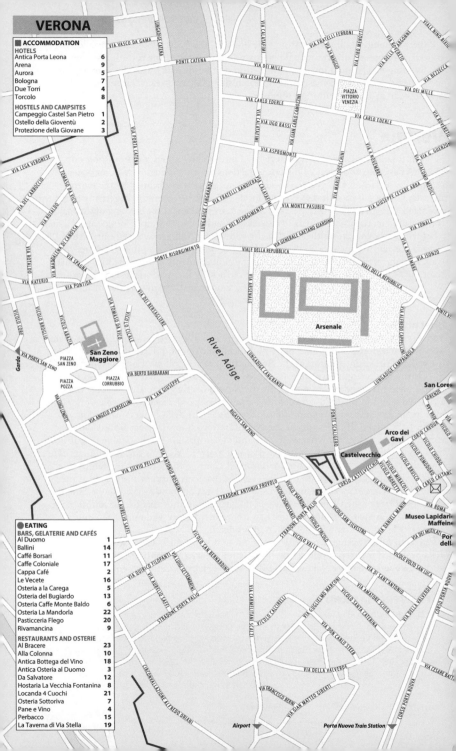

VERONA

PIAZZA VITTORIO VENEZIA

Arsenale

River Adige

San Zeno Maggiore

PIAZZA SAN ZENO

PIAZZA POZZA

PIAZZA CORRUBBIO

Garda

San Lore

Arco dei Gavi

Castelvecchio

Museo Lapidari Maffeine

Por dell

Airport   Porta Nuova Train Station

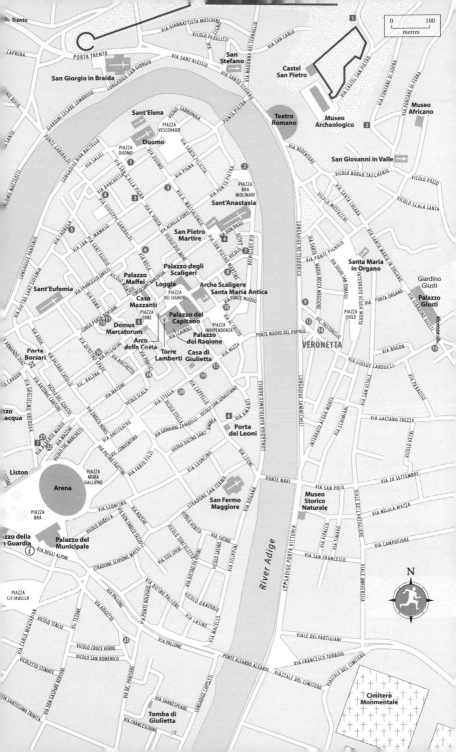

down to the arrival of Napoleon. Verona's history then shadowed that of Venice: a prolonged interlude of Austrian rule, brought to an end by the unification of Italy.

From the Porta Nuova to Piazza Brà

Coming from the train station, you pass Verona's south gate, the **Porta Nuova**, built in the sixteenth century by Michele Sanmicheli, then messed about by the Austrians in the nineteenth. From the wide Corso Porta Nuova, which begins here, the red roofs and towers of the city stand out on a clear day against the backdrop of the Torricelle and Lessini mountains. At the other end of the Corso, the battlemented arches of the **Portoni della Brà** (1389), formerly part of the city walls, mark the entrance to the historic centre. Built by the Visconti family, the Portoni once carried a covered walk from the Castelvecchio to their residence, of which only the **Torre Pentagona** remains, behind the **Palazzo della Gran Guardia** (1610) on the right.

Through the arches of the Portoni, the broad expanse of **Piazza Brà** opens up. (*Brà*, by the way, is the Veronese dialect version of *braida*, meaning "meadow".) It's bordered on the south side by the huge and under-used Gran Guardia (formerly a sort of military school, now an exhibition space), on the east by the nineteenth-century **Palazzo del Municipale**, on the west by the arcades and cafés of the **Liston**, and at the far end by the mightiest of Verona's Roman monuments, the **Arena**.

The Arena

Piazza Brà • Mon 1.30–7.30pm, Tues–Sun 8.30am–7.30pm, but closes 3.30pm during the opera season (see page 286) • €10, or Verona Card; €1 on first Sun of month Oct–May • ⓦ arena.it

Originally measuring 152m by 123m overall, the **Arena** was the third largest of all Roman amphitheatres, after the Colosseum and the amphitheatre at Capua. Dating from the first century AD, it has survived in remarkable condition, despite the twelfth-century earthquake that destroyed all but four of the arches of the outer wall. The interior was scarcely damaged by the tremor, and nowadays audiences pack the 44 stone tiers to watch gargantuan opera productions where once crowds of around twenty thousand gathered for gladiatorial contests, mock naval battles and the like.

Museo Lapidario Maffeiano

Piazza Brà 28 • Tues–Sun 8.30am–2pm • €4.50, or Verona Card, or €11 joint ticket with the Arena, or €7 joint ticket with Castelvecchio; €1 on first Sun of month Oct–May

On the southern side of Piazza Brà, next to the Portoni della Brà, is one of Verona's more obscure museums, the **Museo Lapidario Maffeiano**; the large courtyard and two upstairs rooms contain miscellaneous Greek, Etruscan and Roman statues and inscriptions, none of which is likely to grip the non-specialist.

Piazza delle Erbe

Via Mazzini – the main route of Verona's *passeggiata* – leads north from the Arena, past expensive clothes and jewellery shops, to **Piazza delle Erbe**, a lively and handsome square tightly enclosed by medieval and Renaissance palazzi. Originally a major Roman crossroads and the site of the forum, the piazza is still the heart of the city. As the name suggests, the market used to sell mainly vegetables, but nowadays most of the stalls sell an assortment of clothes, souvenirs and fast food.

Lined along the square's central axis, and camouflaged by the stalls, are the **Colonna Antica** (a fifteenth-century lantern on a marble pillar), the **Capitello** (a fourteenth-century pavilion where public servants were invested with their office), the fountain of **Madonna Verona** (commissioned in 1368 by Cansignorio della Scala) and finally the column of the Lion of St Mark, demonstrating Verona's links with Venice – this

15

specimen is a copy of one destroyed during the Pasqua Veronese (Veronese Easter), as the city's 1797 uprising against the French is known.

On the left as you look from the Via Cappello end, past the tall houses of the old Jewish ghetto, stands the **Domus Mercatorum**, which was founded in 1301 as a merchants' warehouse and exchange and is now a bank and chamber of commerce. At the far end, the Baroque **Palazzo Maffei** has been taken over by shops, apartments and an expensive restaurant; to the left of Palazzo Maffei rises the fourteenth-century **Torre del Gardello**, while to the right stands the **Casa Mazzanti**, which is covered with sixteenth-century murals. On the eastern side of the piazza, to your right, Verona's highest tower, the twelfth-century **Torre dei Lamberti** soars over the **Palazzo del Ragione**, from which springs the **Arco della Costa** (Arch of the Rib), hanging over the route through to the Piazza dei Signori. Cynical folklore has it that the whale's rib suspended under the arch will fall if an adult virgin passes underneath.

The Palazzo della Ragione

Galleria d'Arte Moderna Achille Forti Tues–Fri 10am–6pm, Sat & Sun 11am–7pm • €4, or €8 with Torre dei Lamberti, or Verona Card
Torre dei Lamberti daily 8.30am–7.30pm • €6, or €8 with Galleria d'Arte Moderna, or Verona Card, plus €1 for the lift

A right turn after the Arco della Costa leads into the courtyard known as the **Corte Mercato Vecchio**, which is dominated by a beautiful fifteenth-century staircase. The steps lead to the first floor of the **Palazzo della Ragione**, formerly the law courts and now home to the **Galleria d'Arte Moderna Achille Forti**. Artists who were born or worked in Verona make up the core of this modest but well-presented collection, which also features a small number of works by some of the bigger names of twentieth-century Italian art, such as Boccioni, Balla, Morandi and Martini. The most frequently reproduced image, however, is Francesco Hayez's *Meditazione*, painted in 1851 as an allegory of Italian disappointment at the failure of the 1848 uprisings; it's not altogether clear why disappointment should have loosened the young woman's clothing so revealingly.

For a dizzying view of the city, ascend the 84m **Torre dei Lamberti**, Verona's highest tower. The lift takes you up to the first level, and then it's 125 steps to the top.

Piazza dei Signori

Piazza dei Signori, sometimes known as Piazza Dante after the grimly pensive statue of the poet in the centre, is the site of the **Palazzo degli Scaligeri**, the old residence of the great ruling family. Extending from it at a right angle are the graceful arches of Verona's outstanding early Renaissance building, the late fifteenth-century **Loggia del Consiglio**, former assembly hall of the city council. The rank of Roman notables along the roof includes Verona's most illustrious native poet, Catullus. Opposite stands Sanmicheli's splendid gateway to the **Palazzo del Capitano**, which is separated from the Palazzo del Ragione by a stretch of excavated Roman street. For a closer look at the subterranean remains, visit the Centro Internazionale di Fotografia, in the **Scavi Scaligero** (under the Cortile dei Tribunale of the Palazzo del Capitano), where photography exhibitions are held amid Roman and medieval tombs, mosaics, paving stones and sewers.

The Arche Scaligere

June–Sept daily 10am–1pm & 3–6pm • €1, or Verona Card

Passing under the arch linking the Palazzo degli Scaligeri to the Palazzo del Capitano, you come to the little twelfth-century church of **Santa Maria Antica**, in front of which, within a railed compound, are ranged the **Arche Scaligere**, which are among the finest funerary monuments in Italy.

Over the side entrance to the church, an equestrian statue of Cangrande I (d.1329) grins on the summit of his tomb's pyramidal roof; the statue is a copy, the original

15

being displayed in the Castelvecchio. In 2004 the mummified body of Cangrande – whose name means "Big Dog" – was removed from its sarcophagus and subjected to an examination which established that he'd died from a huge dose of digitalis (a drug derived from foxglove). It's known that one of Cangrande's physicians was executed by his successor, Mastino II; it's thus probable that the ambitious Mastino (meaning "mastiff"), having had his uncle murdered by the doctor, quickly covered his tracks by eliminating his henchman. The tombs (*arche*) of the rest of the della Scala clan are enclosed within a wrought-iron palisade decorated with ladder motifs, the family emblem – *Scaligeri* is the adjective derived from *Scala*, which means ladder or step. Mastino I (d.1277), founder of the dynasty, is buried in the simple tomb against the wall of the church; Mastino II (d.1351) is to the left of the entrance, opposite the most florid of the tombs, that of Cansignorio ("Top Dog"; d.1375), which has been comprehensively restored in recent years. The unassuming tombs of the two who didn't take canine names, Giovanni (d.1359) and Bartolomeo (d.1304), are between Mastino II and Cansignorio.

15

Sant'Anastasia

Piazza Sant'Anastasia • March–Oct Mon–Sat 9am–6pm; Sun 1–6pm; Nov–Feb Mon–Sat 10am–1pm & 1.30–5pm, Sun 1–5pm • €2.50, or *biglietto unico*, or Verona Card

A short distance north of the Arche Scaligere rises **Sant'Anastasia**, the city's largest church. Started in 1290 and completed in 1481, it's mainly Gothic, with undertones of the Romanesque. The early fourteenth-century carvings of New Testament scenes around the doors are the most arresting feature of its bare exterior; the highlight of the spacious and richly decorated interior is **Pisanello**'s delicate fresco of *St George and the Princess* (above the chapel to the right of the altar), a work in which the normally martial saint appears as something of a dandy. A touch screen allows you to zoom in on details that are hard to make out from ground level. Also well worth a look are the fresco by Altichiero on the right wall of the adjacent **Cappella Cavalli**, and the nearby altarpiece of *The Madonna, St Francis and St Augustine*, by Verona-born **Girolamo dai Libri**.

San Pietro Martire

Piazza Sant'Anastasia • Sat & Sun 2–6pm • Free

To the left of Sant'Anastasia's facade is an eye-catching tomb, the freestanding monument to Guglielmo di Castelbarco (1320) by Enrico di Rigino. To its left, on one side of the little piazza fronting Sant'Anastasia, stands the lovely but deconsecrated church of **San Pietro Martire**, or San Giorgetto. Ransacked by Napoleon's troops, it retains numerous little patches of fresco which make for an atmospheric interior, though the highlight is the vast lunette fresco on the east wall. Easily the strangest picture in Verona, it is thought to be an allegorical account of the Virgin's Assumption, though the bizarre collection of animals appears to have little connection with the bemused-looking Madonna. Painted in the early sixteenth century by Giovanni Falconetti, it is thought to be a copy of a Swiss tapestry, and was commissioned by two knights in Emperor Maximilian's army, who can be seen kneeling on either side of the fresco, against a background depicting an idealized Verona.

Duomo

Piazza Duomo • March–Oct Mon–Sat 10am–5.30pm, Sun 1.30–5.30pm; Nov–Feb Mon–Sat 10am–1pm & 1.30–5pm, Sun 1.30–5pm • €2.50, or *biglietto unico*, or Verona Card

Verona's **Duomo** lies a short distance from the Roman **Ponte Pietra**, which was destroyed in 1945 by the retreating Germans, but rebuilt using mostly the original stones and bricks. Consecrated in 1187, the Duomo has been worked on almost constantly over the centuries and the campanile's bell-chamber wasn't added until 1927. As a whole it's

Romanesque in its lower parts, developing into Gothic as it goes up; the two doorways are twelfth-century – look for the story of Jonah and a dragon-like whale on the south porch, and the figures of Roland and Oliver, two of Charlemagne's paladins, flanking the superb west portal. The interior has a splendid organ, and fascinating architectural details around each chapel and on the columns – particularly fine is the **Cappella Mazzanti** (last on the right). In the first chapel on the left, an *Assumption* by **Titian** occupies an architectural frame by Sansovino, who also designed the choir.

The door at the end of the left aisle gives access to the churches of **San Giovanni in Fonte** and, straight ahead, **Sant'Elena**, in front of which lie the remnants of the presbytery of a fourth-century basilica, whose form Sant'Elena roughly follows. Mosaics from the second half of the fourth century can be seen in Sant'Elena itself, while the adjacent San Giovanni in Fonte contains a masterpiece of Romanesque sculpture: a large baptismal font covered with biblical scenes. The gated alley immediately to the left of the Duomo's facade leads to the cloister, where you can see the foundations and mosaics of a larger, fifth-century basilica which was built nearby when the earlier one was partly destroyed.

15

Casa di Giulietta

Via Cappello 23 • Mon 1.30–7.30pm, Tues–Sun 8.30am–7.30pm • €6, or €7 joint ticket with the Tomba di Giulietta, or Verona Card; €1 on first Sun of the month Oct–May

South of Piazza delle Erbe runs Via Cappello, where, at no. 23, you'll find the **Casa di Giulietta** – the busiest attraction in Verona, and the least substantial. Although the "Capulets" (Capuleti) and the "Montagues" (Montecchi) did exist, Romeo and Juliet were entirely fictional creations; and though bloody feuds were commonplace in medieval Verona (the head of one family invited his enemy to a truce-making meal, and informed him afterwards that he'd just eaten the liver of his son), there's no record of these two clans being at loggerheads. The association of this house with Juliet is based on nothing more than its picturesque balcony, but notwithstanding the facts a bronze Juliet has been shoved into a corner of the courtyard, and her right breast has been polished bright by the groping hands of school-age pilgrims hoping for luck in love. The house itself, constructed at the start of the fourteenth century, is in a fine state of preservation, but the rooms are largely empty and the displays reek of desperation: the bed from Zeffirelli's film of *Romeo and Juliet* is displayed as if it were an item of significance, for example.

San Fermo

Stradone San Fermo • March–Oct Mon–Sat 10am–6pm, Sun 1–6pm; Nov–Feb Mon–Sat 10am–1pm & 1.30–5pm, Sun 1–5pm • €2.50, or *biglietto unico*, or Verona Card

Via Cappello leads into Via Leoni with its Roman gate, the **Porta Romana dei Leoni**, and segment of excavated Roman street, exposed 3m below today's street level. At the end of Via Leoni and across the road stands the red-brick church of **San Fermo Maggiore**, whose exterior betrays the fact that it consists of two churches combined. The

---

"ROMEO'S HOUSE" AND "JULIET'S TOMB"

The Casa di Giulietta is the foremost of Verona's spurious **Romeo and Juliet** attractions, but the city has a couple of other shrines to the ill-fated couple: **"Romeo's house"**, a private dwelling at Via Arche Scaligere 4; and the **Tomba di Giulietta**, in the southeast of the city, in the cloister of the deconsecrated San Francesco al Corso (Mon 1.30–7.30pm, Tues–Sun 8.30am–7.30pm; €4.50, free on first Sun of month Oct–May, or €7 joint ticket with the Casa di Giulietta, or Verona Card), which also has a collection of frescoes that have been removed from various Veronese houses and churches, the oldest of them dating from 996.

Benedictines built the original one in the eighth century, then rebuilt it in the eleventh to honour the relics of St Fermo and St Roch (the former was supposedly martyred on this site); very soon after, flooding forced them to superimpose another church for day-to-day use, a structure greatly altered in the early fourteenth century by the Minorites. The Gothic upper church has numerous fourteenth-century frescoes and a fine wooden keel-vault – constructed in 1314, the ceiling is the oldest such vault in the Veneto, and is adorned with the faces of 416 saints. The Romanesque lower church, entered from the right transept, has some well-preserved twelfth-century frescoes on its columns, and the foundations of a fifth-century paleo-Christian church have been uncovered too.

Porta Borsari

After the Arena and the Teatro Romano, Verona's most impressive Roman remnant is the **Porta Borsari**, a structure that was as great an influence on the city's Renaissance architects as the amphitheatre. Now reduced to a monumental screen bestriding the road at the junction of Via Armando Diaz and Corso Porta Borsari (west of Piazza delle Erbe), it was Verona's largest Roman gate; the inscription dates it at 265 AD, but it's almost certainly older than that.

Corso Cavour

Busy **Corso Cavour**, which stretches away from the Porta Borsari, is lined with bulky Renaissance palazzi, including two by **Michele Sanmicheli** (1484–1559) – the handsome **Palazzo Canossa**, at no. 48, and the **Palazzo Bevilacqua**, at no. 19. The two could hardly be more different: the former a handsome, restrainedly classical design with a shallow facade, the latter an ornately carved Mannerist effort. Sanmicheli, Verona's most illustrious native architect, left his mark elsewhere in the city too, most obviously in the shape of the great fortified gateways of the Porta Nuova and the Porta Palio (both near the train station), and in the Palazzo Pompei, now the home of the Museo Storico Naturale.

San Lorenzo
Corso Cavour 28 • Mon–Sat 9am–noon & 3–5pm, Sun 3–6pm • Free

Opposite the Palazzo Bevilacqua stands the Romanesque **San Lorenzo**, in the courtyard of which you'll see fragments dating back to the eighth century, the period of the church's foundation. The narrow, plain interior, which dates from the mid-twelfth century, is mostly notable for the women's galleries and for a miscellany of columns – atop the columns in the transept are two capitals that date back to Charlemagne, displaying his imperial eagle.

Arco dei Gavi and the Ponte Scaligero

A short distance beyond the Palazzo Canossa, set back from the road on the right, stands the **Arco dei Gavi**, a first-century Roman triumphal arch; originally raised in the middle of what is now the Corso, it was demolished by Napoleon's troops then rebuilt here in 1932. This is the best vantage point from which to admire the **Ponte Scaligero**; built by Cangrande II between 1355 and 1375, the bridge was blown up by the Germans in 1945 – the salvaged material was used for the reconstruction.

Museo di Castelvecchio
Corso Castelvecchio 2 • Mon 1.30–7.30pm, Tues–Sun 8.30am–7.30pm • €6, or €7 joint ticket with Museo Maffeiano, or Verona Card; €1 on first Sun of month Oct–May

The fortress from which the Ponte Scaligero springs, the **Castelvecchio**, was commissioned by Cangrande II at around the same time, and became the stronghold for Verona's subsequent rulers, all of whom altered it in some way – the last major addition, the small

THE CASTELVECCHIO RAID

In November 2015 the Castelvecchio suffered perhaps the biggest art heist ever to be carried out in Italy, when Pisanello's *Madonna of the Quails*, **Mantegna**'s *Holy Family* and more than a dozen other paintings were stolen from the museum. The fact that the thieves had struck just after the museum had closed for the day, but before the alarm system had been switched on for the night, led investigators to suspect an inside job. And so it proved. In May 2016 the paintings were recovered on an island in the Dniester river, close to the border with Moldova. Pasquale Silvestri Riccardi, a guard at the Castelvecchio, was convicted of the robbery, along with five others, including his Moldovan girlfriend.

fort in the inner courtyard, was built by Napoleon. Opened as the city museum in 1925, it was damaged by bombing in World War II, but reopened in 1964 after restoration by **Carlo Scarpa**. Scarpa's conversion of the Castelvecchio is one of his most impressive projects, leading the visitor through a labyrinth of chambers, courtyards and open-air walkways – a route fascinating to explore in itself, thanks largely to Scarpa's subtle use of materials and textures. Halfway through the itinerary, you'll come face to face with the equestrian figure of **Cangrande I**, removed from his tomb and strikingly displayed on an outdoor pedestal – a perfect demonstration of Scarpa's extraordinary ability to maximize the visual impact both of the objects in the museum and of the building itself.

The museum contains lots of fine medieval sculpture, an array of weapons and other artefacts, and a large collection of paintings, all of it perfectly displayed. Many of the pictures are unremarkable, but there are some outstanding pieces too – look out for the exquisite *Madonna of the Quails* by **Pisanello**, **Mantegna**'s *Holy Family*, the bizarre *Madonna of the Passion* by Crivelli, a *Madonna* by **Giovanni Bellini**, and **Veronese**'s *Descent from the Cross*. Some lesser-known local artists also feature strongly, such as Francesco Morone, Giovanni Francesco Caroto, and the sculptor Giovanni Zebellana, whose *Madonna, Christ and St Anne*, carved in the late fifteenth century, is one of the Castelvecchio's most touching works of art.

Basilica di San Zeno Maggiore

Piazza San Zeno • March–Oct Mon–Sat 8.30am–6pm, Sun 12.30–5pm; Nov–Feb Mon–Sat 10am 1pm & 1.30–5pm, Sun noon–5pm • €2.50, or *biglietto unico*, or Verona Card

A little over a kilometre northwest of the Castelvecchio stands the **Basilica di San Zeno Maggiore**, one of the most significant Romanesque churches in northern Italy. A church was founded here, above the tomb of the city's patron saint, as early as the fifth century (Zeno was the bishop of Verona in the 360s), but the present building and its campanile were raised in the first half of the twelfth century, with additions continuing up to the end of the fourteenth. Its **rose window**, representing the Wheel of Fortune, dates from around 1200, as does the magnificent **portal**, whose lintels bear relief sculptures representing the months and the miracles of Zeno, while the tympanum shows Zeno trampling the Devil. The reliefs to the side of the portal, also from this period, show scenes from the Old and New Testaments and various allegorical scenes – notably *The Hunt of Theodoric*, in which the Ostrogoth king of Italy chases a stag down into Hell. (Theodoric, who ruled the peninsula from 493 to 526, based his court in Ravenna but so close was his attachment to Verona that for centuries the city was known in his native Germany as "Theodoric's city".) Extraordinary bronze panels on the **doors** depict scenes from the Bible and more miracles of Zeno, in a style influenced by Byzantine and Ottoman art; most of those on the left date from around 1100, most of the right-hand panels from a century later. Wooden doors protect the panels from the elements, but they can be examined from inside the church.

Areas of the lofty and simple **interior** are covered with frescoes, dating from the twelfth to the sixteenth centuries. Diverting though these are, the most compelling painting is the high altar's luminous *Madonna and Saints* by **Mantegna**. In the apse of the left aisle is a disarmingly cheerful fourteenth-century painted marble figure of St Zeno, typically represented as dark-skinned (it's believed he came from Africa) and with a fish on his crook (legend has it that when called upon to exorcize Emperor Gallienus' daughter, Zeno was found fishing); the saint's tomb is in the beautifully colonnaded crypt beneath the raised choir.

Don't leave without a wander round the elegant, twin-columned arcades of the cloisters; a *Last Judgement* can be made out amid the fragmentary frescoes on the eastern wall, to which the tomb of an illegitimate Scaliger is also attached.

San Giorgio in Braida

Lungadige San Giorgio 6 • Thurs–Sat 10am–5.30pm, Sun 1–7pm • Free

On the far side of the river, opposite the Duomo, stands **San Giorgio in Braida**, which in terms of its artworks is the richest of Verona's churches. A *Baptism* by **Jacopo Tintoretto** hangs over the door, while the main altar, designed by **Sanmicheli**, incorporates a marvellous *Martyrdom of St George* by **Paolo Veronese**.

Santo Stefano

Via Scaletta Santo Stefano 2 • Thurs–Sat 9.30am–5.30pm, Sun 12.30–5.30pm • Free

It's a short walk along the embankment from San Giorgio to the delightful Romanesque **Santo Stefano**. One of the city's oldest churches, it was founded in the fifth century but gained its present shape in the twelfth; later additions include sixteenth-century frescoes and incongruous Baroque chapels.

Teatro Romano and Museo Archeologico

Regaste Redentore 2 • Mon 1.30–7.30pm, Tues–Sun 8.30am–7.30pm • €4.50, or Verona Card; €1 on first Sun of month Oct–May

On the south side of Ponte Pietra stands the first-century BC **Teatro Romano**; much restored, the theatre is now used for concerts and plays (the entrance is 150m south of the Ponte Pietra). When the restorers set to work clearing later buildings away from the theatre, the only one allowed to remain was the tiny church of Santi Siro e Libera – built in the tenth century but altered in the fourteenth.

Above the Teatro Romano, the **Museo Archeologico** occupies the buildings of an old convent; its well-arranged collection features a number of Greek, Roman and Etruscan finds. Steps to the side of the theatre lead to the ugly **Castel San Pietro**, built by the Austrians on the site of a Visconti castle which had been destroyed by Napoleon.

Santa Maria in Organo

Piazzetta Santa Maria in Organo 1 • Thurs & Fri 10.30am–5.30pm, Sat 10am–4.30pm, Sun 11am–5.30pm • Free

In the heart of the **Veronetta** district stands the church of **Santa Maria in Organo**, which possesses what Vasari praised as the finest choirstalls in Italy. Dating from the 1490s, the marquetry was the work of one Fra Giovanni, a Benedictine monk called in when his monastic order decided to transform the church they had been given in 1444. Astonishing in their precision and use of perspective, they are replete with fascinating details: look out for a skull with a mouth shaped like a gondola – a dig at Verona's all-powerful neighbour. More of Fra Giovanni's handiwork can be seen in the sacristy, and the church's sixth-century crypt (entered via the sacristy) is also worth a look, for its reused Roman columns.

Giardino Giusti

Via Giardino Giusti 2 • Daily: April–Sept 9am–8pm; Oct–March 9am–sunset • €7

Close to Santa Maria in Organo you'll find one of the finest formal gardens in the country, the **Giardino Giusti**. Created in the 1570s by Count Agostino Giusti, the garden has faced an uncertain future for the past few years, since ownership passed to no fewer than twenty different members of the Giusti family, following the death of the diplomat Justo Giusti. After feuding between some of the heirs, the whole estate – the grounds plus the splendid Palazzo Giusti (which is not open to the public) – has been put up for sale, but for the time being the garden's fountains and shaded corners continue to provide the city's most pleasant refuge from the streets, as it has done for centuries. Goethe and Mozart both paid a visit, and were much impressed.

ARRIVAL AND INFORMATION

VERONA

By plane If you're flying into Verona's Valerio Catullo airport, 12km from the city centre, you can take an ATV bus (every 20min 6.30am–11.30pm; €6) to the Porta Nuova train station; the journey takes 15min.

By train From Verona Porta Nuova station it's a 20min walk to Piazza Brà: as you come out of the station veer right, across the bus station, then head straight along Corso Porta Nuova. It's not a lovely walk, so it may be best to buy a Verona Card then hop on a bus.

Destinations Milan (every 30min; 1hr 20min–2hr); Padua (every 30min; 45min–1hr 20min); Venice (every 30min; 1hr 10min–2hr 20min); Vicenza (every 30min; 25–60min).

By local bus Buses leave from outside Verona's train station. Tickets can be bought for €1.30 from inside the train station, or from machines by the bus ranks, or for €2 on board; alternatively, you can get ten rides for €11.70 or a day pass for €4. Tickets are valid for 90min.

By car There are car parks signed off the Corso Porta Nuova just before Piazza Brà, or there is free parking across the river, beyond Santo Stefano.

Information The tourist office is on the south side of Piazza Brà, tucked into the old town walls at Via degli Alpini 9 (summer Mon–Sat 9am–7pm, Sun 9am–6pm; winter Mon–Sat 10am–6pm, Sun 10am–4pm; ☎ 045 806 8680, ☯ tourism.verona.it & ☯ veronatouristoffice.it). As well as providing information, it organizes walking tours, runs a hotel-booking service and can book tickets for the Arena. Another good source of info on local events is ☯ verona.net.

ACCOMMODATION

Verona's **hotel prices** rise sharply during peak periods, which include the opera season and the numerous trade fairs in the autumn. Whatever time of year you're coming to Verona, reserve your room well in advance.

Antica Porta Leona Via Corticella Leoni 3 ☎ 045 595 499, ☯ anticaportaleona.com; map p.274. A very elegant four-star with 23 spacious rooms and a fitness centre in the basement, which has a small pool. All rooms have steam showers, while the five "opera suites" (their names and decor pay tribute to Verdi's masterpieces) are equipped with whirlpool baths. **€280**

Arena Stradone Porta Palio 2 ☎ 045 803 2440, ☯ albergoarena.it; map p.274. There are hardly any one-star hotels in central Verona – this one, next to Castelvecchio, has been refurnished quite recently, and is the best of the bunch. Rooms without private bathroom are €30 cheaper than en-suite rooms. **€100**

Aurora Piazza delle Erbe ☎ 045 594 717, ☯ hotelaurora. biz; map p.274. This three-star is one of the most attractive mid-range places in the city. Many rooms have a view of the Piazza delle Erbe, and the staff are welcoming and knowledgeable. Excellent buffet breakfast on the terrace overlooking the square. **€190**

Bologna Piazzetta Scalette Rubiani 3 ☎ 045 800 6830, ☯ hotelbologna.vr.it; map p.274. This three-star hotel, just off Piazza Brà, has been rejuvenated quite recently, with new furnishings throughout and flashy new bathrooms.

Seven of the rooms give you a glimpse of the Arena – the top-floor suite with a roof terrace and outdoor jacuzzi is the place to be if you want to splash out. **€170**

Due Torri Piazza Sant'Anastasia 4 ☎ 045 595 044, ☯ hotelduetorri.duetorrihotels.com; map p.274. Located right next door to the church of Sant'Anastasia, the *Due Torri* began life as an inn on the Milan–Venice route, but for some time has been Verona's best-known five-star hotel. The 89 supremely comfortable rooms are decorated in nineteenth-century Imperial style, with lavish use of pink Veronese marble in the bathrooms. If you're pushing the boat out, this is the place to stay. **€270**

★**Torcolo** Vicolo Listone 3 ☎ 045 800 7512, ☯ hoteltorcolo.it; map p.274. Extremely welcoming two-star hotel within 100m of the Arena, just off Piazza Brà. It's run by two sisters who have been in the business for more than thirty years, and is a favourite with the opera crowds, so book ahead. Breakfast is an extra €10. **€150**

HOSTELS AND CAMPSITES

Campeggio Castel San Pietro Via Castel S. Pietro 2 ☎ 045 592 037, ☯ campingcastelsanpietro.com; map p.274. This pleasant site, out by the old city walls, is the only place to camp near the centre of Verona. To get to the site take a bus to Via Marsala and then it's a steep walk up the hill. April–Sept. Per person from **€10**, per tent **€10**

15

Ostello della Gioventù Salita Fontana del Ferro 15 ☎045 590 360, ⓦostelloverona.it; map p.274. The official HI hostel is in Villa Francescatti, a beautiful sixteenth-century villa behind the Teatro Romano; as it's quite a walk from the centre, it's best to take a bus to Piazza Isolo (#73 and #91 both go there from the station), then walk the last 300m up the hill. With nearly 250 beds (some in family rooms), it's very rarely booked out. The midnight curfew is extended during the opera season. Price includes breakfast, and dinner is available for €8, if ordered in advance. Dorms €18

Protezione della Giovane Via Pigna 7 ☎045 596 880, ⓦprotezionedellagiovane.it; map p.274. Spartan but friendly convent-run hostel for women, with an 11pm curfew, although there is some flexibility for guests with opera tickets. Dorms €22, doubles €54; July & Aug doubles €60

EATING

Your money goes a lot further in Verona than it does in Venice: numerous **trattorie** offer full meals for less than €30, and Verona's cuisine – which is much meatier and richer than Venice's, with horsemeat being a speciality – can also be sampled in many of the city's unpretentious *osterie*. All *osterie* serve both drinks (with snacks) and full meals; we've listed under "Restaurants" the ones in which the emphasis is on eating more than drinking.

RESTAURANTS AND OSTERIE

Al Bracere Via Adigetto 6a ☎045 597 249, ⓦalbracere. com; map p.274. Occupying a building that was once a church, then a barn, then a warehouse, this spacious and busy pizzeria-restaurant has an extensive list of good-sized pizzas, which are baked in a wood-fired oven. The rest of the menu is OK, if not outstanding. Daily noon–3pm & 6.30pm–midnight.

Alla Colonna Largo Pescheria Vecchia 4 ☎045 596 718; map p.274. In business for more than thirty years now, this is perhaps the best no-frills trattoria in the city centre, and it's packed most evenings, so booking is advisable. It's renowned for its *cotoletta* (veal cutlet), which comes in three sizes, the biggest of which is vast. Main courses begin at less than €10, and there's also a €15 set lunch. Mon–Sat noon–2.30pm & 7pm–11.30pm.

Antica Bottega del Vino Vicolo Scudo di Francia 3a ☎045 800 4535, ⓦbottegavini.it; map p.274. In business since 1890 (albeit with a brief interruption in 2010), this is one of the most celebrated establishments in Verona, chiefly on account of its fantastic selection of wines. (It's a wine bar too, so you can just pop in for a glass and snack.) The dining room is hugely characterful, and the food is reliably good but not inexpensive, with mains around €20–25. Daily 11am–midnight.

★ **Antica Osteria al Duomo** Via Duomo 7a ☎045 800 4505; map p.274. There has been an *osteria* here for at least a century, and it still serves old Veronese favourites such as *pastissada* (horse stew) and *bigoli* with *sugo d'asino* (donkey sauce). Prices are low (most *secondi* around €10), the decor is quirky (with a miscellany of musical instruments hanging on the walls), and the hosts are terrific. Mon–Sat 11.30am–2.30pm & 7pm–midnight.

Da Salvatore Piazza S. Tomaso 6 ☎045 803 0366, ⓦpizzeriadasalvatorevr.com; map p.274. Tucked under the arcades of a riverside road junction, this is the most stylish and the busiest pizzeria in Verona. Tues–Sat 12.30–2.30pm & 7–11pm, Sun 7–11pm.

Hostaria La Vecchia Fontanina Piazzetta Chiavica 5 ☎045 591 159, ⓦristorantevecchiafontanina.com; map p.274. Good-value (most *secondi* around €10 and there's a €12 set lunch)and centrally located restaurant, with tables on the tiny piazza. It's not haute cuisine, but the food is honest and the staff are friendly. Mon–Sat 11am–3pm & 7pm–midnight.

★ **Locanda 4 Cuochi** Via Alberto Mario 12 ☎045 803 0311, ⓦlocanda4cuochi.it; map p.274. Run by four young chefs, this stylish open-kitchen restaurant has a more inventive menu than many in Verona, though the emphasis is still very much on meat. The atmosphere – buzzy, cool and friendly – is distinctive, and prices are lower than you might expect – *secondi* are around €15. Tues 7.30–10.30pm, Wed–Sun 12.30–2.30pm & 7.30–10.30pm.

Osteria Sottoriva Via Sottoriva 9 ☎045 801 4323; map p.274. Medieval Via Sottoriva is one of the most atmospheric streets in the city, and has several decent places to eat. None of its *osterie* is more convivial than this one, which serves Verona specialities at reasonable prices (mains all under €15), and in hefty portions. Tripe is something of a speciality, and horsemeat is always on the menu. In summer you can eat at the tables outside, under the arches. Mon,

---

VINITALY

As the Veneto produces more DOC **wine** than any other region in Italy, with the region's most productive vineyards – Soave, Valpolicella and Bardolino – lying within the hinterland of Verona, it's not surprising that Italy's main wine fair, **Vinitaly** (ⓦvinitaly.com), is held in Verona; lasting for four days at the end of March or beginning of April, it offers infinite sampling opportunities. Day-tickets cost about €50.

Tues & Thurs–Sun 11am–3pm & 6–10.30pm.

Pane e Vino Via Garibaldi 16a ☎045 800 8261, ⊕trattoriapanevino.it; map p.274. A classy old-school trattoria near the Duomo. Main courses on the meat-centric menu are around €18, and there's a very satisfying €50 *menu degustazione* of recipes that make full use of the local Amarone wine. The house Amarone is a cut above most house wines too. Mon & Thurs–Sun 12.30–2.15pm & 7.30–10.15pm, Tues 12.30–2.15pm.

★ **Perbacco** Via Carducci 48a ☎045 594 193, ⊕trattoriaperbacco.com; map p.274. Located a short way out of the centre, near the Giusti gardens, this simple neighbourhood trattoria offers a small menu of traditional Veronese cooking at remarkably low prices – main courses are all under €10. In good weather, tables in the vine-covered garden augment the small and intimate dining room. Mon, Tues & Thurs–Sat 12.30–2pm & 7.30–10pm.

La Taverna di Via Stella Via Stella 5c ☎045 800 8008, wtavernadiviastella.com; map p.274. An excellent city-centre trattoria, with very professional service, generous portions of unpretentious local dishes, and modest prices, with main courses all under €20. Popular with locals and tourists alike, so reservations are sensible in summer. Mon 7.15–11pm, Tues & Thurs–Sun 12.15–2.15pm & 7.15–11pm.

BARS, GELATERIE AND CAFÉS

Al Duomo Vicolo Duomo 1 ☎045 800 4060; map p.274. The shaded courtyard of this smart *caffè-pasticceria*, just a few yards from the cathedral, is a very pleasant and quiet spot for a coffee and cake. Daily 7.15am–8pm.

★ **Ballini** Via S. Maria Rocca Maggiore 4a ⊕gelateriaballini.it; map p.274. Andrea Ballini has built up a big following since opening his *gelateria* at the far end of the Ponte Nuovo in 2011. Flavours such as fig and almond are used in season, and his pear cooked in Valpolicella is delectable. The best ice cream in town. Mon–Fri 1–11pm, Sat & Sun noon–1.30pm & 3–11pm.

Caffè Borsari Via Porta Borsari 15/D; map p.274. Still known to many Veronese by its original name – *Caffè Tubino* – this homely little cave of a place serves what might be the finest coffee in Verona, and amazing hot chocolate too. Daily 7.30am–8pm.

Caffè Coloniale Piazzetta Viviani 14c ☎045 801 2647; map p.274. Excellent coffee and hot chocolate, plus cakes and light meals (the cakes are better than the meals); the outdoor terrace is another attraction. Daily 7.30am–midnight.

Cappa Café Piazzetta Brà Molinari 1a ☎045 800 4516; map p.274. Lying just down from the Roman bridge, this smart bar has been popular since it opened way back in 1966; it can get very crowded at weekends, but you can always take your drink to one of the nearby benches,

or lean on the parapet and gaze over the river. Mon–Sat 9am–2am, Sun 9am–midnight.

Le Vecete Via Pelliciai 32; map p.274. Big and atmospheric city-centre *osteria* with a delicious selection of the savoury tartlets known as *bocconcini*. The menu includes pasta dishes, risottos and other plain dishes. The wine list is excellent, ranging from swiggable to the very expensive. Daily noon–4pm & 6.30–11.30pm.

Osteria a la Carega Via Cadrega 8 ☎045 806 9248, ⊕osterialacarega.com; map p.274. Friendly, small and studenty *osteria* with a few outside tables in the side yard. A fine selection of inexpensive wines, plus excellent sandwiches and simple meals. Has jazz and other live music on Thursdays. If you're wondering about the sign above the door – *carega* is Veronese dialect for "chair". Daily noon–2.30pm & 7–11pm.

Osteria del Bugiardo Corso Porta Borsari 17a ☎045 591 869 ⊕buglioni.it/osteria; map p.274. This long-standing *osteria* is always thronged with locals grabbing a quick snack and a glass – the wine list is outstanding. There's a small meal menu too, but unless you enjoy eating elbow-to-elbow with strangers, it's maybe best to stick to the drinks and antipasti. Sun–Thurs 11am–midnight, Fri & Sat 11am–1am.

Osteria Caffè Monte Baldo Via Rosa 12 ☎045 803 0579, ⊕osteriamontebaldo.com; map p.274. A very attractive and popular *osteria* near Piazza delle Erbe, with excellent antipasti and more substantial dishes (€12–20), and a wide range of wines available by the glass. The bottle-lined lower room opens out onto the street, which makes it particularly nice in summer, and there's another dining room upstairs. Unusually, the kitchen is in operation continuously from noon. Mon–Thurs 10am–11pm, Fri 10am–midnight, Sat 11am–midnight, Sun 11am–11pm.

★ **Osteria La Mandorla** Via Alberto Mario 23 ☎045 597 053; map p.274. This tiny, old-fashioned and hundred percent authentic bar is just a minute's stroll from the Arena; the atmosphere is great, and the wines and snacks are very good. Mon 5pm–2am, Tues–Sun 11am–2pm & 5pm–2am.

Pasticceria Flego Via Stella 13a ☎045 803 2471; map p.274. In the opinion of many Veronese, *Pasticceria Flego* is the best *pasticceria* in town. For elegance it can't be beaten, and in addition to superb cakes and coffee, it has a long list of teas. There's a second branch at Porta Borsari 9. Both branches Tues–Sun 7.30am–7.30pm.

Rivamancina Vicolo Quadrelli 1 ☎045 803 3585, ⊕rivamancina.it; map p.274. Located near the Ponte Nuovo, on the far side of the Adige, this is the best-known cocktail bar in Verona. The vibe is friendly, and it often has live music. Tues–Thurs & Sun 6pm–2am, Fri & Sat 6pm–3am.

15

CARNEVALE IN VERONA

One of the most enjoyable days in the calendar is Verona's **Carnevale**, held on the Friday before Shrove Tuesday. In contrast to its rather self-conscious and commercialized Venetian counterpart, this is a purely local event, centred on a huge and loud procession that winds through the centre from Piazza Brà, with hundreds of people larking about in fancy dress and chucking confetti all over the place. The parade is led by a character called the Papa del Gnocco – most of the city's restaurants serve gnocchi in his honour for the day.

MUSIC AND THE ARTS

The *Spettacoli* section of the local paper, *L'Arena*, is the best source of up-to-date information about what's on.

Opera The city's opera festival, held in the Arena from mid-June to early September, has been a major draw since 1913. The focus is primarily on the warhorses of the nineteenth-century Italian repertoire, with a lavish production of *Aïda* invariably on the programme. Tickets range from around €25 for a perch high up on the terraces to €200 for central stalls seats, and can be bought from the ticket office at Via Dietro Anfiteatro, or at the tourist office, or by phone or online (☎ 045 800 5151, ⊕ arena.it). For the rest of the year Verona's opera moves to the Teatro Filarmonico in Via Roma, off Piazza Brà (same website).

Classical music, theatre and dance A season of ballet and of Shakespeare and other dramatists in Italian is the principal summer fare at the Teatro Romano. Some events here are free; for the rest, if you don't mind inferior acoustics park yourself on the steps going up the hill alongside the theatre. The city has two other major old venues: the Teatro Nuovo (⊕ teatronuovoverona.it), at Piazza Viviani 10, which has plays and classical music; and the Teatro Ristori (⊕ teatroristori.org), at Via Teatro Ristori 7, which presents music and dance.

Rock and jazz June's Verona Jazz festival at the Teatro Romano attracts international names, and big rock events crop up on the Arena's calendar.

15

BASSANO DEL GRAPPA

The northern Veneto

Lacking a city of Verona's or Padua's appeal, the area extending from Venice
to the southern edge of the Dolomites is the least-visited part of the Veneto
– most of the tourists who pass through it are hurrying on to the ski-slopes
of Cortina d'Ampezzo and the other winter resorts of the Dolomites. But if
this region's attractions are generally more modest than those of the area to
the west, they offer some excellent day-trips from Venice, the most obvious
of which is the prosperous and lively city of Treviso, just 30km north of the
lagoon. Some of the Veneto's finest medieval buildings and frescoes are to
be seen here, and Treviso's position at the centre of the rail network makes it
a good base from which to investigate the crannies of the region.

To the west of Treviso, the beautiful little walled town of **Castelfranco Veneto** – birthplace of Giorgione and home of one of his greatest paintings – also sits in the middle of a web of rail lines that connects Venice to the regional centres of Padua, Vicenza, Treviso and Belluno. A hop westward from Castelfranco brings you to another ancient walled town, **Cittadella**, while to the north lies **Bassano del Grappa**, the ultimate source of the fiery grappa spirit and site of one of Italy's most distinctive bridges. Two other remarkable old towns lie within a short radius of Bassano: **Maróstica**, famous for its ceremonial chess game played with human "pieces"; and **Ásolo**, historically a rural retreat for the Venetian aristocracy, and just a few kilometres from the finest country house in all of Italy – the **Villa Barbaro** at **Masèr**. A short way to the north of Masèr, lodged on a ridge overlooking the valley of the Piave, **Feltre** boasts another historic centre that's been little changed by the last four centuries.

Due north of Treviso, the rail line into the far north of the Veneto runs through **Conegliano**, a town where life revolves round the production of wine, and of the sparkling prosecco in particular. From there a service continues up through **Vittorio Veneto**, with its remarkably preserved Renaissance streets, and on to **Belluno**, in effect the mountains' border post.

Treviso

TREVISO is a smart and self-sufficient commercial centre and the capital of a province that extends to the north almost as far as Belluno, but to most tourists it's known merely as the place that the cheap flights go to. It deserves far more visitors than it gets – it's a lively place, and has some fine works of art, and the townscape within the sixteenth-century walls is often appealing too. A lack of local dressing stone led in the thirteenth century to the use of frescoes to decorate the houses, and these painted facades, along with the lengthy porticoes that shelter the pavements and the fast-running canals that cut through the centre (complete with water wheels), give many of the streets an appearance quite distinct from that of other towns in the region.

As with every settlement in the area, it used to be under Venetian control, but it was an important town long before its assimilation by Venice in 1389. As early as the eighth century it was minting its own coinage, and by the end of the thirteenth century, when it was ruled by the Da Camino family, Treviso was renowned as a refuge for artists and poets and as a model of good government. (Dante, in the *Purgatorio*, praises Gherardo da Camino as a man "left from a vanished race in reproof to these unruly times".) Plenty of evidence of the town's early stature survives in the form of Gothic churches, public buildings and, most dramatically of all, the paintings of **Tomaso da Modena** (1325–79), the dominant artist in northern Italy in the years immediately after Giotto's death.

Calmaggiore

Some of the best of Treviso's arcades and frescoes are in the main street of the historic centre, **Calmaggiore**, where modern commerce – epitomized by the locally based Benetton, the town's major employer – has reached the sort of compromise with the

---

THE CITY WALLS

Treviso's longest unbroken stretch of the **city walls** runs along the northern edge of the centre, between the Porta dei Santi Quaranta and Porta San Tomaso. The fortification of Treviso was undertaken in 1509, at the start of the War of the League of Cambrai, and the work was finished around 1517, with the construction of these two monumental gates.

past that the Italians seem to arrange better than anyone else. Modern construction techniques have played a larger part than you might think in shaping that compromise: Treviso was pounded during both world wars, and on Good Friday 1944 around half its buildings were destroyed in a single bombing raid.

The early thirteenth-century **Palazzo dei Trecento**, at the side of the **Piazza dei Signori**, was one casualty of 1944 – a line of indented brick round the exterior shows the level at which the rebuilding began, and you can also see the extent of the damage in photos

THE NORTHERN VENETO

AUSTRIA

0   10
kilometres

TRENTINO-
ALTO ADIGE

Bolzano

Ortisei

Sella
(3151m)

Moena

Cavalese

San Martino
di Castrozza

Croda Rossa
(3139m)

Cristallo
(3221m)

Tofane
(3243m)

Tre Cime di
Lavaredo
(2999m)

Misurina

Cortina d'Ampezzo

Marmolada

Pelmo
(3168m)

Antelao
(3263m)

Calalzo di
Cadore

M. Civetta
(3218m)

FRIULI-
VENEZIA-
GIULIA

Pale di
San Martino

River Piave

DOLOMITES

Ponte nelle Alpi

Cima d'Asta
(2847m)

Belluno

N

ALPAGO

NEVEGAL

CANSIGLIO

M. Ortigara
(2105m)

Feltre

Revine

Vittorio Veneto

Follina

Udine

M. Grappa
(1775m)

Asiago

Valdobbiádene

Conegliano

Possagno

River Livenza

M. Pasubio
(1775m)

Lugo di
Vicenza

Bassano
del Grappa

Masèr

Asolo

Montebelluna

River Piave

Thiene

Maróstica

Ecoaro
Terme

Schio

Castelfranco
Veneto

Fanzolo

Cittadella

Treviso

River Sile

Vicenza

Piombino Dese

Arzignano

Montécchio
Maggiore

Noale

Mirano

Mestre

Burano

Torcello

Soave

River
Bacchiglione

River Brenta

Strà

Dolo

Mira

Marghera Malcontenta

Murano

Venice

Lido

Cavallino

Punta Sabbioni

Padua

displayed under the neighbouring arcades. The adjoining **Palazzo del Podestà**, with its high tower, is a late nineteenth-century structure, concocted in the appropriate style. Piazza dei Signori is the main meeting place in town, and the scene of the daily *passeggiata*.

San Vito and Santa Lucia

Piazza San Vito • Mon–Fri 8am–noon, Sat & Sun 8am–noon & 3.30–6.30pm • Free

Incorporated into the back of the Palazzo del Podestà are the conjoined medieval churches of **San Vito** and **Santa Lucia**, tucked behind the Monte di Pietà (municipal pawnshop) on the edge of Piazza San Vito. The latter is the more interesting – it's a tiny chapel with extensive frescoes by **Tomaso da Modena** and his followers. San Vito has even earlier paintings (twelfth- and thirteenth-century) in the alcove through which you enter from Santa Lucia.

The Loggia dei Cavalieri

Via Martiri della Libertà

The patricians' meeting place known as the **Loggia dei Cavalieri** stands close to the Palazzo dei Trecento on Via Martiri della Libertà. Built in the early thirteenth century and pieced back together after the 1944 air raid, it was decorated first with a brick pattern and grotesque figures, and then with romanticized scenes from the Trojan wars, scraps of which are still visible. Recently restored, it's remarkable more for the fact of its survival than for its appearance, but it warrants a look if you're strolling that way towards the Santa Caterina side of town.

The Duomo

Piazza del Duomo • Daily 7.30am–noon & 3.30–6.30pm • Free

The **Duomo** of Treviso, **San Pietro**, stands at the end of Calmaggiore. Founded in the twelfth century, as were the **campanile** and perpetually closed **baptistery**, San Pietro was much altered between the fifteenth and nineteenth centuries (when the huge portico was added), and then rebuilt to rectify the damage of 1944. The oldest clearly distinguishable feature of the exterior is the pair of eroded Romanesque lions at the base of the portico; fragments of Romanesque wall are embedded in the side walls too.

The interior is chiefly notable for the **crypt** – a thicket of twelfth-century columns with scraps of fourteenth- and fifteenth-century frescoes (if it's locked, ask the sacristan) – and the **Malchiostro Chapel** (to the right of the chancel), with frescoes by **Pordenone** and a much-restored *Annunciation* by **Titian**. Although Pordenone and Titian were the bitterest of rivals, their pictures were commissioned as part of a unified scheme, representing the conception and birth of Christ; the 1944 bombs annihilated the crowning piece of the ensemble – a fresco by Pordenone on the chapel dome, representing *God the Father*. Paintings by **Paris Bordone**, the most famous Trevisan artist, hang in the vestibule of the chapel and in the sacristy. Other things to search out are the monument to Bishop Zanetti by **Pietro Lombardo**, on the left wall of the chancel, the tomb of Bishop Nicolò Franco by **Lorenzo and Giambattista Bregno**, in the chapel to the left of the chancel, and **Lorenzo Bregno**'s figure of *St Sebastian*, on the first pillar of the left aisle.

The Pescheria and Casa dei Carraresi

To the east of Piazza dei Signori, the old fish market – the **Pescheria** – occupies an island in the middle of Treviso's broadest canal, a location determined by health regulations. Nowadays fruit and vegetables are sold here too; the stalls do most of their trade in the mornings. On the approach to the Pescheria, on Via Palestra, you'll find

16

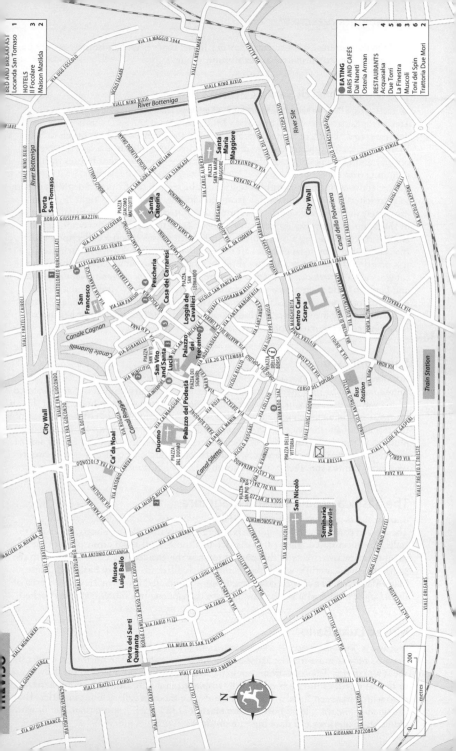

the **Casa dei Carraresi**, a fourteenth-century hostel that's been handsomely restored and turned into Treviso's principal art-exhibition venue.

The Musei Civici di Santa Caterina

Piazzetta Mario Botter • Tues–Sun 9am–12.30pm & 2.30–6pm • €6, or €10 with Museo Bailo • ⓦ museicivicitreviso.it

Treviso's great fresco cycle – Tomaso da Modena's *Life of St Ursula* – is in the deconsecrated church of **Santa Caterina**. Painted for the now-extinct church of Santa Margherita sul Sile, the frescoes were detached from the walls in the late nineteenth century and now take pride of place in the impressive complex that houses the city's main museum collections.

More frescoes by Tomaso and his school can be seen in the Cappella degli Innocenti, to your left as you enter the church from the cloister, while to your right there's an exquisitely delicate fresco of the Madonna, attributed to Gentile da Fabriano. The rest of the complex comprises an extensive archeological section, with the emphasis on Roman relics (including a fine fourth-century bath mosaic), and a collection of pictures that's typical of provincial galleries all over Italy – acres of hackwork interrupted by a few paintings for which any gallery director would give a year's salary. In this second category are a *Crucifixion* by **Jacopo Bassano**, the *Portrait of Sperone Speroni* by **Titian** and **Lorenzo Lotto**'s intense *Portrait of a Dominican*. Elsewhere you'll find a lot of Paris Bordone, pictures by Giandomenico Tiepolo and Francesco Guardi, and a trio of pastels by Rosalba Carriera, including one that might be a portrait of her more illustrious contemporary, Antoine Watteau.

San Francesco

Via San Francesco • Daily 8am–noon & 3–6pm • Free

To the north of Santa Caterina stands the thirteenth-century church of **San Francesco**, which was restored early in the twentieth century after years as a military depot. It's an immense hall of a church with a high ship's-keel ceiling and patches of fresco, including the top half of another vast *St Christopher* and a *Madonna and Saints* by **Tomaso da Modena** in the chapel to the left of the chancel. Close to the door on the right side of the church is the tomb of Francesca, **daughter of Petrarch**, who died in 1384, twenty years after **Dante's son**, Pietro, whose tomb is in the left transept.

The Basilica di Santa Maria Maggiore

Piazza Santa Maria Maggiore • Daily 8–11.45am & 3–6pm • Free

The eastern part of the *centro storico* is where the city's small workshops and market stalls are concentrated, giving this district an almost small-town atmosphere. One of the most attractive streets in this part of town is the arcaded Via Carlo Alberto, to the south of Santa Caterina, which passes the largely fifteenth-century **Basilica di Santa Maria Maggiore**. The church contains the most venerated image in Treviso, a fresco of the *Madonna*, originally painted by Tomaso da Modena but subsequently retouched.

Museo Luigi Bailo

Borgo Cavour 24 • Tues–Sun 10am–6pm • €6, or €10 with Santa Caterina museum • ⓦ museicivicitreviso.it

Treviso's newest museum, the **Museo Luigi Bailo**, is located in the northwest corner of the *centro storico*. The collection – an extensive array of art produced in the Treviso area in the twentieth century – is beautifully displayed in a sixteenth-century monastery onto which has been fused a sleek and handsome modern gallery, built in 2015. The dominant presence is local-born **Arturo Martini** (1889–1947), more than 100 of whose paintings, sculptures and drawings are on show.

16

San Nicolò

Via San Nicolò • Mon–Fri 8am–noon & 3.30–6pm • Free

The severe Dominican church of **San Nicolò**, dominating the southwest corner of the *centro storico* just over the River Sile from the train station, upstages the Duomo in almost every department. Wrapped round several of its massive pillars are delicate frescoes by **Tomaso da Modena** and his school, of which the freshest are the *Sts Jerome, Romuald, Agnes and John* by Tomaso himself, on the first column on your right as you enter. The towering *St Christopher* on the wall of the right aisle, with feet the size of sleeping bags, was painted around 1410, probably by **Antonio da Treviso**. Equally striking is the composite tomb of Agostino d'Onigo on the left wall of the chancel, created in 1500 by **Antonio Rizzo** (who did the sculpture) and **Lorenzo Lotto** (who painted the attendant pages). The *Madonna and Saints* in the chancel is a collaboration between Savoldo and the little-known Marco Pensaben, painted twenty years after the Onigo tomb, while a third joint work, an *Incredulity of St Thomas*, stands on the altar of the Monigo chapel, on the right of the chancel – **Sebastiano del Piombo** is attributed with the upper section and **Lotto** with the lower gallery of portraits. The frescoes on the chapel's side walls are by fourteenth-century Sienese and Riminese artists.

Seminario Vescovile

Piazzetta Benedetto XI 2 • Mon–Fri: summer 8am–6pm; winter 8am–12.30pm & 3–5.30pm • Free

The figures of Saints Agnes and Jerome in San Nicolò are an excellent introduction to the art of Tomaso da Modena, but for a fuller demonstration of his talent you should visit the neighbouring **Seminario**, where the **chapter house** (*sala del capitolo*) is decorated with forty portraits of members of the Dominican order, executed by the artist in 1352. Although these are not portraits in the modern sense of the term, in that they don't attempt to reproduce the appearance of the men whose names they bear, the paintings are astonishing in their observation of idiosyncratic reality. Each shows a friar at study in his cell, but there is never a hint of the formulaic: one man is shown sharpening a quill, another checks a text through a magnifier, a third blows the surplus ink from his nib, a fourth scowls as if you've interrupted his work.

16

ARRIVAL AND INFORMATION   TREVISO

By train The train station is on the south side of the centre, 100m outside the walls.
Destinations Castelfranco Veneto (15 daily; 25min); Cittadella (13 daily; 35min); Conegliano (every 30min; 15–25min); Venice (every 30min; 35min); Vicenza (13 daily; 45min–1hr 10min).

By bus There are half-hourly buses to Padua and Venice (hourly at weekends) from the bus station in Lungosile Antonio Mattei, up the road from the train station.
Information The tourist office is at Via Fiumicelli 30 (Mon 10am–1pm, Tues–Sat 10am–5pm, Sun 10am–4pm; ☎ 042 254 7632, ⦻ visittreviso.it).

ACCOMMODATION

The vast majority of Treviso's **hotels** are characterless Eurobusiness places and most are outside the old centre, though there are two large four-stars, the *Carlton* and the *Continental*, near the station if you are desperate.

Il Focolare Piazza Ancilotto 4 ☎ 0422 56 601, ⦻ albergoilfocolare.net; map p.291. This agreeable and very central three-star, which for many years was known as the *Campeol*, has recently been thoroughly freshened up: the rooms, formerly dowdy, are now light and simply furnished. Some are quite confined – an extra €20 or so will get you one of the larger ones. Only the reception is on the ground floor, and there is no lift. €110

★ **Locanda San Tomaso** Viale Burchiellati 5 ☎ 0422

541 550 or ☎ 346 951 3652, ⦻ locandasantomaso. it; map p.291. The six rooms of this charming, family-run B&B have been decorated with painstaking attention to detail. All are spacious, and are nicely adorned with antiques, paintings and bric-a-brac. €95

★ **Maison Matilda** Via Jacopo Riccati 44 ☎ 0422 582 212, ⦻ maisonmatilda.com; map p.291. Treviso's first boutique hotel, located near the Duomo, adds a much-needed touch of style to the city's hotels: just five double rooms plus one suite, all furnished in an individual and unshowy sumptuous style, with roll-top baths, antique furnishings and floor-sweeping curtains. €180

EATING

Treviso's **restaurants** offer rather more choice than its hotels. Radicchio is the most famous local ingredient, and tiramisù – which many think is a traditional dessert – was invented here in the late 1960s.

RESTAURANTS AND CAFÉS

Acquasalsa Vicolo Pescheria 41 ☎0422 544 982, ⓦacquasalsa.com; map p.291. Occupying a prime location under the arches on the outer side of the Pescheria, *Aquasalsa* is a buzzy modern *osteria* that offers a wide selection of meals and snacks. Grilled fish dishes are around €15, while small plates of anchovy and *baccalà* are just €3 – a perfect accompaniment to a glass or two, sipped at one of the outside tables. Daily 11.30am–2pm & 7–11pm.

★ **Due Torri** Via Palestro 8 ☎0422 541 243, ⓦristoranteduetorri.it; map p.291. The *Antica Contrada delle Due Torri*, to give it its full name, offers a sophisticated take on local fish and meat specialities, and offers exceptional value – most main courses are in the region of €16. The brick-lined interior is inviting, and the well-informed staff are attentive. Mon & Wed–Sun 12.30–2.30pm & 7.30–11pm.

La Finestra Via Armando Diaz 24 ☎0422 411292, ⓦpizzerialafinestra.it; map p.291. *La Finestra* serves possibly the best pizzas in Treviso, plus a small menu that usually features some excellent seafood and a vegetarian option. The look of the place is smartly minimalist, and in summer there are outside tables at the back of the restaurant. Mon & Wed–Sun noon–3pm & 7–11pm.

Muscoli Via Pescheria 23; map p.291. The punters spill out onto the fish market island from the ever-popular *Muscoli*. Try the delicious fig and blue cheese sandwiches at the bar or go further inside for a more substantial meal – from just €10. Mon–Tues & Thurs–Sat 8am–2pm & 5pm–midnight, Sun 8am–2pm.

Toni del Spin Via Inferiore 7 ☎0422 543 829, ⓦristorantetonidelspin.com; map p.291. This convivial trattoria has been winning plaudits for many years. The risottos are excellent, as is the pasta *con ragù d'anatra*, and the *secondi* menu is packed with meaty Trevisan classics, such as *bocconcini di vitello al radicchio* and *coniglio alle olive*. Good value too, with most main courses under €15. Mon 7.30–10.30pm, Tues–Sun 12.30–2.30pm & 7.30–10.30pm.

Trattoria Due Mori Via Bailo 9 ☎0422 540 383, ⓦtrattoria2mori.com; map p.291. You can get good Trevisan cooking at moderate prices at this large, bright and friendly restaurant, which occupies a site on which there's been a hostelry for more than six hundred years. Expect to find *baccalà* and other fish dishes on the menu, along with goose, guinea fowl and eel. Most main courses are less than €15. Mon, Tues & Thurs–Sun 11.30am–2.30pm & 6.30–11pm, Wed 11.30am–2.30pm.

DRINKING

For **bars**, Piazza Signori is the centre of the action, especially during the *passeggiata*; the surrounding streets and squares are full of small places where locals gather.

★ **Dai Naneti** Vicolo Broli 2; map p.291. Standing at the mouth of the alley alongside the large Benetton store next to the Palazzo dei Trecento, this busy, rough-edged bar offers wines and superb panini and other snacks – but no coffee, and no seats. Mon–Sat 9am–2.30pm & 5.30–9pm.

Osteria Arman Via Manzoni 27 ☎0422 547 747, ⓦosteriaarman.it; map p.291. Founded a century and a half ago, this family-run establishment sells wine from its own vineyard to accompany generous helpings of local staples, at around €10–15 for *secondi*. Or you can just have a drink and a snack at the front-of-house bar. Mon–Sat 9am–4pm & 6pm–midnight.

Castelfranco Veneto

In the twelfth century **CASTELFRANCO VENETO** stood on the western edge of Treviso's territory, and from the outside the old town looks much as it must have done when the Trevisans had finished fortifying the place against the Paduans. The battlemented and moated brick walls, raised in 1199, run almost right round the centre, and five of their towers still stand, the largest being the clock tower-cum-gate known as the **Torrione**. Of all the walled towns of the Veneto, only Cittadella and Montagnana bear comparison with Castelfranco, and the place has one other outstanding attraction: it was the birthplace of Giorgio da Castelfranco – **Giorgione** – and its Duomo possesses a painting which on its own is enough to vindicate Vasari's judgement that Giorgione's place in Venetian art is equivalent to Leonardo da Vinci's in that of Florence.

The **Castello** – as the walled part of Castelfranco is known – is so small that you can walk in through one gate and out through the opposite one in three minutes flat.

Within the walls you'll find the **Casa Giorgione** (which is almost empty except for a frieze that's hopefully attributed to the great man) and the eighteenth-century **Teatro Accademico** in Via Garibaldi (open during occasional exhibitions), but nothing can hold a candle to the Castelfranco *Madonna*.

The Duomo

Piazza San Liberale • Daily 8am–noon & 3–6pm • Free

Known simply as the **Castelfranco Madonna**, Giorgione's *Madonna and Child with St Francis and St Liberale* hangs in the eighteenth-century **Duomo**. This is one of only six surviving paintings that can indisputably be attributed to **Giorgione**, the most elusive of all the great figures of the Renaissance. So little is known for certain about his life that legends have proliferated to fill the gaps – for instance, the story that his premature death in 1510, aged 34 at most (his birthdate is unknown), was caused by bubonic plague, caught from a lover. The paintings themselves have compounded the enigma and none is more mysterious than this one, in which a boldly geometrical composition is combined with an extraordinary fidelity to physical texture and the effects of light, while the demeanour of the figures suggests a sort of melancholy preoccupation.

At first sight the scenes appears naturalistic, but look more closely and you'll see that strange laws are in operation here. For one thing, the perspective isn't consistent – the Madonna's throne has one vanishing point, the chequered foreground another. And while the sun is rising or setting on the distant horizon, the shadow cast by the armoured saint suggests a quite different source of light, and the shadows of St Francis and the throne imply a third. Even the identity of the armoured figure is far from clear: most favour Liberale, the local patron saint and co-dedicatee of the Duomo, but he might be St George or St Theodore (the first patron saint of Venice).

However, some facts are known about the picture's origin. It was commissioned by Tuzio Costanzo, probably in 1505, to honour his son, Matteo, who had been killed in battle the previous year. The church for which the piece was painted was demolished long ago, but the present arrangement of this chapel (dating from 1935) re-creates that devised by Giorgione's patron, with the painting placed so that the three figures look down at Matteo's tomb.

16

The rest of the church

After perusing the Giorgione, you might want to spend a minute admiring the huge adjacent altarpiece, which was sculpted by Torretto, the master of Canova; Torretto's young apprentice is said to have carved the little castle at the feet of St Liberale. The only other paintings in the Duomo likely to hold your attention are in the **sacristy**: fragments of the first fresco cycle painted by Paolo Veronese, they were removed from the Villa Soranza by Napoleon's troops, who demolished the entire building and carted the pictures off to Paris, whence they were later repatriated. The interior of the Duomo itself was designed by the local architect **Francesco Maria Preti**, whose ashes are interred in the nave, underneath the dome (Preti's major contribution to the landscape of the Veneto is the Villa Pisani at Strà); the facade is a late nineteenth-century hack job.

ARRIVAL AND DEPARTURE   **CASTELFRANCO VENETO**

By train Castelfranco is a major crossroads of the Veneto rail network.

Destinations Belluno (12 daily; 1hr 20min–1hr 40min); Feltre (12 daily; 50min–1hr); Padua (19 daily; 35min); Treviso (10 daily; 25min); Venice (20 daily; 55min); Vicenza (16 daily; 40min).

Information The tourist office is at Via F.M. Preti 66 (Wed & Thurs 9.30am–12.30pm, Fri & Sat 9.30am–12.30pm & 3–6pm; ☎ 042 349 1416).

EATING

★**Alle Mura** Via Francesco Maria Preti 69 ☎ 042 349 8098. Seafood – especially fish – are the speciality here, and the quality of the cooking has made this place indisputably Castelfranco's top restaurant. It's not a cheap place to eat in the evening (expect to pay around €50/ person), but the set menu at lunchtime is excellent value. In good weather an outdoor marquee supplements the cosy dining room, which has pictures on every vertical surface, and Polynesian rugs and bags hanging from the rafters. Mon–Wed & Fri–Sun 12.30–2.30pm & 7–11pm.

Around Castelfranco

The major attraction within a short radius of Castelfranco is the wonderfully preserved town of **Cittadella**, which can easily be reached by train, as it's a station on the Treviso–Vicenza line. Buses and the Venice–Castelfranco *locale* trains stop at the village of **Piombino Dese**, where you can see one of Palladio's most influential villas. Palladio's **Villa Emo** is also reachable by bus, but the gaps in the bus timetable make a visit much more feasible by car.

Cittadella

When Treviso turned Castelfranco into a garrison, the Paduans promptly retaliated by reinforcing the defences of **CITTADELLA**, 15km to the west. The **fortified walls** of Cittadella were built in the first quarter of the thirteenth century, and are even more impressive than those of its neighbour, forming an almost unbroken oval round the town. You enter the town through one of four rugged brick gateways, built on the cardinal points of the compass; if you're coming from the train station it'll be the **Porta Padova**, the most daunting of the four, flanked as it is by the Torre di Malta. The tower was built as a prison and torture chamber by **Ezzelino da Romano III**, known to those he terrorized in this region in the mid-thirteenth century as the "Son of Satan". Basing his claim to power not on any dynastic or legalistic argument, but solely on the exercise of unrestrained military might, Ezzelino was the prototype of the despotic rulers of Renaissance Italy, and his atrocities earned him a place in the seventh circle of Dante's *Inferno*, where he's condemned to boil eternally in a river of blood.

Villa Emo

Via Stazione 5, Fanzolo • Daily: April–Sept 10am–6pm; Oct–March 10am–5.30pm • €10 • Ⓦ villaemo.org • Buses from Castelfranco 6 times daily, Mon–Sat

Just 8km northeast of Castelfranco, in **FANZOLO**, stands one of the best-maintained and most sumptuous of Palladio's houses, the **Villa Emo**, now familiar to a wider audience as the home of John Malkovich in the film *Ripley's Game*. In 1556 the Venetian government set up a department called the Board of Uncultivated Properties, to promote agricultural development on the terra firma and distribute subsidies to landowners. One of the first to take advantage of this initiative was Leonardo Emo, who commissioned the villa from Palladio around 1564, when he switched his financial interests to farming. With its central accommodation and administration block and its arcaded wings for storage, stables, dovecotes and so on, the building belongs to the same type as the earlier Villa Barbaro at Masèr (see page 305), and as at Masèr the main living rooms are richly frescoed, though nobody would claim that **Giambattista Zelotti**'s scenes and rubber-necked grotesques are in the same league as Veronese's work in the Barbaro house.

Villa Cornaro

Via Roma 104, Piombino Dese • May–Sept Sat 3.30–6pm • €7

Palladio's villas fall into two broad types: the first was designed as the focus of a large, cohesive farm, and takes the form of a low central block with attached lateral buildings; the second was usually designed as the living quarters of a more scattered estate, and takes the form of a tall house with a freestanding pedimented porch. The Villa Barbaro belongs to the first category, while to the second category belong the Villa Pisani at Montagnana, the Villa Fóscari at Malcontenta and the **Villa Cornaro**, built in the 1550s at **PIOMBINO DESE**, 9km southeast of Castelfranco. The majestic double-decker portico is the most striking element of the exterior, and when Palladian style was imported into colonial America, this became one of his most frequently copied devices. Unfortunately, the villa's decoration – by the obscure eighteenth-century artist Mattia Bortoloni – isn't anything to get excited about, and opening hours are very restricted, as this fabulous house is privately owned.

Bassano del Grappa

Situated on the River Brenta where it widens on its emergence from the hills, **BASSANO DEL GRAPPA** has expanded rapidly this century, though its historic centre remains largely unspoilt by twentieth-century mistakes. It's better known for its manufacturing and produce, and for the events of the two world wars than for any outstanding architecture or monuments, but its situation in the lee of the imposing Monte Grappa (1775m), with the Dolomites beyond, is impressive enough. For centuries a major producer of ceramics and wrought iron, Bassano is also renowned for its **grappa** distilleries and delicacies such as *porcini* (dried mushrooms), white asparagus and honey.

Almost all of Bassano's sights lie between the Brenta and the train station; go much further in either direction and you'll quickly come to recently developed suburbs. Walking away from the station, the orbital Viale delle Fosse stands between you and the town centre, following the line of the fourteenth-century outer walls. Cross the road, turn right, then left to get to Via Da Ponte, which forms a main axis through the centre; the statue is of **Jacopo Da Ponte**, the pre-eminent member of the dynasty of Renaissance painters more commonly known simply as the Bassano family.

Piazza Garibaldi

Piazza Garibaldi, one of the centre's two main squares, is overlooked by the 42m **Torre Civica**, once a lookout tower for the twelfth-century inner walls, now a clock tower with spurious nineteenth-century battlements and windows. On the other side of the piazza, the fourteenth-century church of **San Francesco** carries a plaque in honour of the Resistance fighters of World War II; a few fresco fragments remain inside, including an *Annunciation* in the porch.

The Museo Civico

Piazza Garibaldi 34 • Mon & Wed–Sun 10am–7pm • €7 • Ⓦ museibassano.it

The cloister of San Francesco now houses the **Museo Civico** where the downstairs rooms are devoted to Roman and other archeological finds. Upstairs is a collection of sixteenth- to eighteenth-century works, including paintings by the da Ponte family, better known by the name **Bassano**. Elsewhere in the museum are some huge frescoes detached from a palace in Piazzetta Montevecchio, two luminous pictures by Bartolomeo Vivarini and a number of plaster works by **Canova**, two thousand of whose drawings are owned by the museum. There's also a room devoted to the great baritone **Tito Gobbi**, who was born in Bassano.

Piazza Libertà

Adjacent to Piazza Garibaldi lies **Piazza Libertà**, with its seventeenth-century sculpture of San Bassiano, the patron saint of Bassano, and the all-too-familiar winged lion of Venice. Dominating the left-hand side of the piazza, the church of **San Giovanni** was founded in 1308 but is now overbearingly Baroque. Under the arches of the fifteenth-century **Loggia** on the other side are the frescoed coats of arms of the various Venetian governors of Bassano. On Thursday mornings both the central squares host a huge weekly market.

Ponte degli Alpini

From Piazza Libertà's far right-hand corner, Piazzetta Montevecchio, the original core of the town, leads to a little jumble of streets and stairways running down to the river and the **Ponte degli Alpini**, which takes its name from the Alpine soldiers who last rebuilt the bridge in 1948. The river was first bridged at this point in the late twelfth century, and replacements or repairs have been needed at regular intervals ever since, mostly because of flooding. The present structure was designed by **Palladio** in 1568, and built in wood to make the bridge as flexible as possible – torrential meltwater would demolish an unyielding stone version. Badly damaged by the retreating German army in World War II, the bridge was restored in accordance with Palladio's design, as has been the case with every repair since the day of its completion.

Museo degli Alpini

Via Angarano 2 • Tues–Sun 9am–8pm • Free

On the west side of the bridge you'll find the **Taverna al Ponte**, home of the **Museo degli Alpini**. The Alpine soldiers, who crossed it many times during World War I on their way to Monte Grappa and Asiago, saw the bridge as a symbol of their tenacity, and so adopted it as their emblem. They still have strong associations with Bassano, and take part in parades here, looking as though they've just stepped out of some nineteenth-century

---

MUSIC IN BASSANO

Bassano has a lively arts calendar, with an **opera festival** in July and August, as well as jazz, dance and classical music events over the summer months (Ⓦ operaestate.it).

THE WAR MEMORIALS OF BASSANO

The two world wars took a particularly heavy toll on the Bassano area, and the town and its environs are strewn with memorials to the dead of those conflicts. The **Viale dei Martiri**, near the Duomo, is named after the Resistance fighters who were rounded up in the hills and hanged from trees along this street in September 1944. At one end is the **Piazzale Generale Giardino**, with its Fascist-style memorial to the general, who died in 1935; a World War I monument in similar vein stands below in the **Parco Ragazzi del'99**, named after the "Lads of '99", who as teenagers were slaughtered in the last phase of World War I. Five thousand of them are entombed in the vast **Tempio Ossario**, just outside the walls, on the south side of town.

The area's major **war memorial**, however, is 35km away on the summit of **Monte Grappa**. Built in 1935 on the spot where Italian troops repulsed the Austrian army's offensive in 1917, it's the burial place of some 12,000 Italian and 10,000 Austro-Hungarian dead, and the design of the monument – a vast tiered edifice with a "Via Eroica" running along the mountain ridge – is typical of the bombastic classicism of Fascist war memorials. From the summit (1775m) the strategic importance of the peak is obvious: on a clear day you can see as far as Venice.

---

adventure yarn. The museum is small but gives a fascinating insight into the fighting on the Italian front, which at times was every bit as grim as the more notorious Somme.

Palazzo Sturm

Via Schiavonetti 7 • Mon & Wed–Sat 9am–1pm & 3–6pm • €5 • @ museibassano.it

On the town side of the bridge, if you follow Via Ferracina downstream for a couple of minutes you'll come to the eighteenth-century **Palazzo Sturm**, which houses two museums. On the ground floor the Museo Remondini gives a well-illustrated account of the history of printing, with pride of place given to the Remondini printing works, which was founded in Bassano in the seventeenth century; upstairs is an extensive collection of the town's famed majolica ware.

The castle and Duomo

North of the Ponti degli Alpini, Via Gamba takes you up to the remnants of the **castle**; the huge and precarious-looking tower was built in the twelfth century by the Ezzelini. The campanile of the **Santa Maria in Colle Duomo**, within the castle walls, is a conversion of another tower, while the church itself dates from around 1000; it contains two paintings by Leandro Bassano.

ARRIVAL AND INFORMATION	BASSANO DEL GRAPPA

By train Trains run from Venice fifteen times daily; the journey takes 1hr 15min–1hr 40min.

By bus Bus services all run from in front of the train station, and connect with Ásolo (6 daily), Masèr (4 daily), Possagno (6 daily), Maróstica and Vicenza (hourly); services are much less frequent on Sundays.

Information Head to the Museo Civico, Piazza Garibaldi 34 (Mon & Wed–Sun 10am–7pm, Tues 3–7pm; @ 0424 519 917, @ bassano.eu).

ACCOMMODATION

Al Castello Piazza Terraglio 19 @ 042 422 8665, @ hotelalcastello.it; map p.297. Situated right by the castle at the top of the town, this is the only hotel in the old centre. It's a pleasant three-star with eleven rooms – best of all is no. 10, which has a small balcony overlooking the square. €120

Brennero Via Torino 7 @ 042 422 8538, @ hotel brennero.com; map p.297. Friendly and plain modern three-star hotel just outside the city walls – the rooms facing north have magnificent views of the mountains. €80

Ostello Don Cremona Via Chini 6 @ 042 421 9137, @ ostellobassanodelgrappa.it; map p.297. The town's hostel, 300m south of the old walls, has doubles with bathrooms and small dorms with shared bathrooms. Reception open 2–9pm. Dorms from €18, doubles €48

16

> ## GRAPPA
>
> There's nowhere better to sample the local firewater than *Nardini*, a grappa distillery founded in 1779 at the foot of the Ponte degli Alpini; these days the distilling process takes place elsewhere, but the original shop and bar are still functioning here (daily 8.30am–8.30pm; ⊛nardini.it). You can also taste and buy the stuff in the **Museo della Grappa** at nearby Via Gamba 6 (daily 9am–7.30pm; free; ⊛grappa.com), which is in effect a showcase for the Poli distillery.

EATING

Al Caneseo Via Vendramini 20 ☎042 422 8524; map p.297. A rustic family-run restaurant with a small menu of Abruzzo and Veneto specialities. Most main courses are less than €10. Tues–Sun 12.30–3pm & 7.30–10.30pm.

★ **Alla Caneva** Via Matteotti 34 ☎335 542 3560; map p.297. A cosy *osteria* that does delicious snacks as well as more substantial dishes, including a range of grilled meats. You can eat well here for €30/head. Mon 9.30am–3pm,

Wed–Sun 9.30am–3pm & 5.30pm–midnight.

Osteria Terraglio Piazzale Terraglio 28 ☎042 452 6158, ⊛osteriaterraglio.it; map p.297. A very smart bar-restaurant with an interestingly non-traditional menu, artfully presented. Main courses cost around €16. The outdoor tables, facing the *Castello* hotel across the square, are Bassano's nicest spot for fresh-air eating or a late-night drink. Mon 6pm–2am, Tues–Sun 10am–2am.

Maróstica

Seven kilometres to the west of Bassano, the walled town of **MARÓSTICA** was yet another stronghold of Ezzelino da Romano, whose fortress glowers down on the old centre from the crest of the hill of Pausolino. The fortress, the lower castle and the almost intact ramparts that connect them make a dramatic scene, but Maróstica's main claim to fame is the **Partita a Scacchi** – a chess game played every other September with human "pieces" on the chessboard-patterned **Piazza Castello**, the central square of the town.

Castello Inferiore

Piazza Castello • Daily 9am–noon & 3–6.30pm • €5

Maróstica was run by the Ezzelini for quite a time, the monstrous Ezzelino III having been preceded by Ezzelino the Stutterer and Ezzelino the Monk (he retired to a monastery). However, it was a less hideous dynasty of despots, the Scaligeri of Verona, who constructed the **town walls** and the **Castello Inferiore** – the latter was built by Cangrande della Scala, and his successor, Cansignorio, raised the walls in the 1370s. You get a great view of the town from the castle ramparts, and costumes for the Partita a Scacchi are usually on show inside.

Castello Superiore

A path round to the left of the forgettable Baroque church of the Carmine winds up through an olive grove to the **Castello Superiore**, which was built by the Ezzelini and later expanded by the Scaligeri. Only the walls remain but within them a restaurant has been built, which has a marvellous view. It's only when you're at the top that you realize there's a road up, much less steep than the path, but longer; if you take this route back down, look out for the cyclists who train on the hill.

ARRIVAL AND INFORMATION MARÓSTICA

By bus A bus service runs between Maróstica and Bassano every 30min, and takes 20min; the stop is outside the lower castle.

Information The tourist office is in the lower castle (Mon–Sat 10am–noon & 3–6pm, Sun 3.30–6pm).

ACCOMMODATION AND EATING

★ **Due Mori** Corso Mazzini 73 ☎042 447 1777, ⓦduemori.it. Maróstica has one superb hotel in the walled centre, the boutique *Due Mori*, which occupies a stylishly modernized seventeenth-century building just above the piazza. Prices rise sharply on Partita weekends, of course. **€110**

★ **Osteria Madonnetta** Via Vajenti 21 ☎042 475 859, ⓦosteriamadonnetta.it. Close to the lower end of the main piazza, this welcoming place is perhaps the most genuine *osteria* in the Veneto – it is still run by the family who founded it in 1904. Locally raised duck, goose and rabbit usually feature on the meat-heavy menu, and puddings are wonderful. *Secondi* are all under €15. Mon–Wed & Fri–Sun 10am–3pm & 6pm–midnight.

Possagno

As you approach **POSSAGNO**, a small town lodged at the base of Monte Grappa, one of the strangest sights in the Veneto hits you: a huge temple that rises above the houses like a displaced chunk of ancient Rome. It was built by **Antonio Canova**, one of the dominant figures of Neoclassicism, who was born here in 1757. The family home now houses a magnificent museum of his work, and just as you can't come to grips with Tintoretto until you've been to Venice, an excursion to Possagno is essential to understanding Canova.

Gypsotheca e Museo Antonio Canova

Via Canova 74 • Tues–Sat 9.30am–6pm, Sun 9.30–7pm • €10 • ⓦ museocanova.it

Shortly after Canova's death in 1822, all the working models that had accumulated in his studio in Rome were transported to Possagno, and here, from 1831 to 1836, an annexe was built onto the Canova house for the display of the bulk of the collection. A second addition was built by Carlo Scarpa in 1957, and the **Gypsotheca e Museo Antonio Canova** is now one of only two complete displays of an artist's working models in Europe – the other being Copenhagen's collection of pieces by Thorvaldsen.

The process by which Canova worked towards the final form of his sculptures was a painstaking one, involving the creation of a series of rough clay models (*bozzetti*) in which the general shape would be refined, then a full-scale figure in gypsum plaster (*gesso*), and finally the replication of the plaster figure in marble, using small nails to map the proportions and contours from the plaster model to the marble statue. Preparatory works from all stages of Canova's career are shown in the Gypsotheca, and even if you're repelled by the polish of the finished pieces, you'll probably be won over by the energy and spontaneity of the first drafts – such as the tiny terracotta model for the tomb of Pope Clement XIV or the miniature group of Adam and Eve weeping over the body of Abel.

Canova's range was remarkable: among the works collected in the vast main hall you'll find portraits, images of classical heroes, the funerary monument for Maria Christina of

---

MARÓSTICA'S CHESS GAME

The **Partita a Scacchi** originated with an everyday story of rival suitors, the only unusual aspect being that the matter was decided with chess pieces rather than swords. In 1454 two men, Vieri da Vallonara and Rinaldo d'Angarano, both petitioned the *podestà* of Maróstica, Taddeo Parisio, for the hand of his daughter, Lionora. Parisio decreed that the matter should be decided by a chess match, with the winner marrying Lionora and the loser being consoled with the prize of her younger sister, Oldrada. The game – which was won by Vieri, Lionora's secret favourite – was played with live pieces here in the square. This is re-enacted with great pomp with five hundred people in the costume of the time, with music, dancing and fireworks.

The game takes place four times in the second week of September in even-numbered years – once on Friday and Saturday, and twice on Sunday. Tickets for a seat in the specially erected grandstands, which hold around 3500 people, cost from €15 to €80, and can be bought from ⓦmarosticascacchi.it.

Austria (which was adapted by Canova's pupils for his own tomb in Venice's Frari) and a large *Deposition*, a bronze version of which is to be found in the Tempio. Notions of Canova as a bloodless pedant are dispelled by *Hercules and Lichas* and *Theseus and the Centaur*, two overpowering tableaux of violence that are each over 3m high, while the adjoining room displays a more intimate and even erotic side, including a *Sleeping Nymph* and the famous *Graces*. More models are kept in the adjoining house (the Casa Canova), alongside Canova's dreadful paintings of winsome Venuses and frolicking nymphs – they will not dispose you to disagree with the artist's own low opinion of his pictorial talents.

The Tempio

Stradone del Tempio • Tues–Sun: April–Oct 9am–noon & 3–6pm; Nov–March 9am–noon & 2–5pm • Free

Donated to the town to serve as its new parish church, the **Tempio** was designed by Canova with assistance from **Giannantonio Selva** (architect of La Fenice in Venice) and constructed from 1819 to 1832. Both Roman and Greek classical sources were plundered for its composition – the body of the building is derived from the Pantheon, but its portico comes from the Parthenon. The cool precision of the interior is disrupted by a sequence of ghastly paintings of the *Apostles*, and an appalling altarpiece for which Canova himself was the culprit. To the right is the bronze version of the *Deposition* in the Gypsotheca (cast posthumously in 1829), and opposite is the **tomb of Canova** and his half-brother Monsignor G.B. Sartori, with a self-portrait bust to the right. Designed by Canova for a different occupant, this tomb is not the Veneto's only memorial to the sculptor – the other one, infinitely more interesting, is in the Frari in Venice. In good weather the sacristan opens the stairs to the top of the dome (€2) – the view of the Asolean hills and the plain of the Piave is marvellous.

ARRIVAL AND DEPARTURE POSSAGNO

You can reach Possagno most easily by **bus** from Bassano (6 daily; 1hr) or Ásolo (7 daily; 40min).

Ásolo and around

Known as "la città dei cento orizzonti" (the city of the hundred horizons), the medieval walled town of **ÁSOLO** presides over a tightly grouped range of 27 gentle peaks in the foothills of the Dolomites. Fruit trees and pastures cover the lower slopes of the Asolean hills, and a feature of life in the town itself is the festivals that take place at the various harvest times.

Paleolithic settlements have been found in the region, but the earliest documented settlement here was the Roman town called Acelum, which thrived from the second century BC until its destruction by Attila. Following resettlement, a succession of feudal lords ruled Ásolo, culminating with the vile **Ezzelino da Romano**, whose parents were born in the town. Ezzelino wrested Ásolo from the bishop of Treviso in 1234, and a network of castles over much of the Veneto shows the extent of his conquests in the years that followed. On his death in 1259 the townspeople of Ásolo ensured that the dynasty died with him by butchering the rest of his family.

The end of the fifteenth century was marked by the arrival of **Caterina Cornaro** (see page 304). Her celebrated court was attended by the likes of Cardinal Bembo, one of the most eminent literary figures of his day, who coined the verb *asolare* to describe the experience of spending one's time in pleasurable aimlessness. Later writers and artists found the atmosphere equally convivial: Gabriele d'Annunzio wrote about the town, Robert Browning's last published work – *Asolando* – was written in Ásolo, and the explorer Freya Stark spent the last twenty years of her life here.

Piazza Maggiore

The main road into town from Bassano enters the southern Porta Loreggia, by the Villa Freya, where Freya Stark lived until her death in 1993, aged 100. From here, Via Browning continues up the hill; no. 151, formerly the house of Pen Browning, bears a plaque recording his father's stay in 1889. At the top is the hub of the town, **Piazza Maggiore** (otherwise known as Piazza Garibaldi), where a big antiques fair is held on the second weekend of each month (except July & Aug). To the south stands the **Duomo**, which has a couple of good pictures by Jacopo Bassano and Lorenzo Lotto.

The Museo Civico

Via Regina Cornaro 74 • Sat & Sun 9.30am–12.30pm & 3–6pm • €5

The fifteenth-century Loggia del Capitano now contains the **Museo Civico**, where you'll find a pair of dubiously attributed Bellinis, a portrait of Ezzelino painted a good couple of centuries after his death and a brace of large sculptures by Canova. More diverting are the memorabilia of Ásolo's residents, especially the portraits, photos and personal effects of the actress **Eleonora Duse**. The lover of d'Annunzio and many others, Duse was almost as well known for her tempestuous relationships as for her roles in the plays of Shakespeare, Hugo and Ibsen, and she came to Ásolo to seek refuge from public gossip. Although she died in Pittsburgh while on tour in 1924, her wish was to be buried in Ásolo, and so her body was transported back here, to the church of Sant'Anna. The town's theatre is of course named after her – it occupies part of the **Castello Pretorio**, up the road from the museum. Once the home of Caterina Cornaro, the castle also has a bar and a children's play area, and there are great views from its walls.

The Rocca

Sat & Sun 10am–6pm • €2

16

CATERINA CORNARO

From 1489 to 1509 the Castello of Ásolo was the home of **Caterina Cornaro**, one of the very few women to have played a decisive part in Venetian history. Born into one of Venice's most powerful families, Caterina was betrothed at the age of 14 to the philandering Jacques II, king of the strategically vital island of Cyprus. The prospective groom then prevaricated, until Venetian promises of help against the belligerent Turks finally pushed him into marriage. Within a year Jacques was dead, in all likelihood poisoned by Marco Venier, the Venetian governor of Famagusta harbour. A few weeks later Caterina gave birth to a son, after whose christening the Venetian fleet set sail for home. No sooner had the detested Venetians left than the city was taken over by men of the Royal Council, Caterina jailed and her son handed over to her detested mother-in-law, Marietta. (Marietta's hatred of Caterina was to an extent due to resentment of the latter's beauty: when Marietta was the mistress of Jacques' father she'd lost a chunk of her nose in a fight with his wife, who'd caught her in bed with the king.)

News of the **insurrection** reached the Venetian galleys, who promptly returned and overpowered the city. Their reappearance was a mixed blessing. The death of Caterina's son at the age of one was taken by Venier as a cue to propose marriage; spurned, he plotted to kill her instead, but was discovered and hanged. For nine years Caterina resisted Venice's political pressure until at last, in 1489, she was forced to **abdicate** in order to gain much-needed weapons and ships against a new Turkish attack. Brought back to Venice to sign a deed "freely giving" Cyprus to the Republic, she was given the region of Ásolo as a sign of Venice's indebtedness, and a joust was held on the frozen Canal Grande in her honour. In Ásolo her court was constantly under the eye of the Council of Ten, who dispatched any man rumoured to be her lover for fear that a new dynasty should be started. Eventually Ásolo, too, was taken away from her by the Emperor Maximilian, and she returned to seek asylum in Venice, where she died soon after, in 1510.

Ásolo's ruined medieval fortress, the **Rocca**, is reached by taking Via Collegio up the hill from the back of Piazza Brugnoli (the car park next to Piazza Garibaldi) and going through the Porta Colmarian. Built on Roman foundations, the Rocca stands 350m above sea level, and the views are worth the effort of the climb.

The Tomba Brion

San Vito d'Altivole • Daily 8am–sunset • #4 CTM bus from Ásolo to San Vito (Mon–Sat 6 daily; 15min) passes close to the cemetery

Five kilometres south of Ásolo, adjoining the municipal cemetery of the village of San Vito d'Altivole, stands the extraordinary **Tomba Brion**, the masterpiece to which the great Venetian architect **Carlo Scarpa** (1906–78) devoted much of the last nine years of his life. Though commissioned by the Brion family (owners of a local electronics company) as their mausoleum, this is much more than a commemoration of one particular group of individuals. Constructed as an L-shaped enclosure of some 2200 square metres, Scarpa's necropolis is an architectural complex in miniature, in which the various elements – tomb, temple, pools, grass – are deployed in a way that creates a highly evocative "formal poetry", to use the architect's own phrase. The Tomba Brion exemplifies Scarpa's renowned attention to the relationship of forms in space and to the properties of well-crafted materials: wood, mosaic, concrete and metal are combined exquisitely in a work that is both massive and delicate, and is distinctively a Scarpa design while simultaneously raising a multitude of references – to the Viennese Secession, to Frank Lloyd Wright, to Japanese traditional architecture and even to Mayan ruins. Scarpa, as he wished, is himself buried here, beneath a marble plinth in a shady corner.

16

Villa Barbaro

Via Cornuda 7, Masèr • April–Oct Tues–Sat 10am–6pm, Sun 11am–6pm; Nov–mid-Dec & mid-Feb–March Sat & Sun 11am–5pm • €9 • Ⓥ villadimaser.it • Bus from Bassano or Treviso

The **Villa Barbaro** at **MASÈR**, 7km east of Ásolo, has a claim to be the most beautiful house in Italy, because the careers of two of the central figures of Italian civilization in the sixteenth century – **Palladio** and **Paolo Veronese** – crossed here and nowhere else.

The villa was built in 1557–58 for **Daniele and Marcantonio Barbaro**, men whose diverse cultural interests set them apart from most of the other wealthy Venetians who were then beginning to farm the Veneto. Both were prominent figures in Venice. Marcantonio served as the Republic's ambassador to Constantinople and became one of the procurators of San Marco, a position that enabled him to promote Palladio's scheme for the church of the Redentore (see page 193). Daniele, the more scholarly of the pair, edited the writings of Vitruvius, wrote on mathematics and perspective and founded the botanical gardens in Padua; he was also Venice's representative in London and was later elected patriarch of Acquileia, as well as becoming the official historian of Venice. The association between Palladio and the brothers was very close by the time the villa was begun – in 1554 Daniele and Palladio had visited Rome, and they'd worked together on Barbaro's edition of Vitruvius – and the process of designing the house was far more of a collaborative venture than were most of Palladio's projects.

The interior

The Villa Barbaro was a working farm in which was embodied a classical vision – derived from writers such as Livy – of the harmony of architectural form and the well-ordered pastoral life. Farm functions dominated the ground floor – dovecotes in the end pavilions, stables and storage space under the arcades, administrative offices on the lower floor of the central block. It's in the living quarters of the *piano nobile* that the more rarefied aspect of the brothers' world is expressed, in a breathtaking series of **frescoes** by Veronese (1566–68) that has no equal anywhere in northern Italy. You need to be a student of Renaissance iconography to decode unassisted the allegorical figures in the amazing trompe l'oeil ceiling of the **Hall of Olympus** – the scheme was devised by Daniele Barbaro and centres on the figure of Eternal Wisdom – but most of the other paintings require no footnotes. The walls of the Villa Barbaro are the most resourceful display of visual trickery you'll ever see – servants peer round painted doors, a dog sniffs along the base of a fictional balustrade in front of a landscape of ruins, illusory statues throw counterfeit shadows, flagstaffs lean in alcoves that aren't there. At the end of an avenue of doorways, a huntsman (probably Veronese himself) steps into the house through an entrance that's a solid wall – inevitably it's been speculated that the woman facing the hunter at the other end of the house was Veronese's mistress. On top of all this, there's some remarkable architectural sculpture by **Alessandro Vittoria**: chimneypieces in the living rooms, figures in the tympanum of the main block and the ornate **nymphaeum** in the garden at the back. The last incorporates a pond that used to be the house's fish-tank, and whose waters were channelled through the kitchens and out into the orchards.

The Tempietto

In the grounds in front of the villa (now separated by a road) stands Palladio's **Tempietto**, the only church by him outside Venice and one of his last projects – commissioned by Marcantonio a decade after his brother's death, it was built in 1580, the year Palladio himself died. From the outside it's clear that the circular domed temple is based on the Pantheon, but the interior reveals a different form, the tiny side chapels creating a modified Greek-cross plan – thus combining the mathematically pure form of the circle with the liturgically perfect form of the cross. Another surprise is the richness of the stucco decoration, much of which is again by Vittoria.

16

ARRIVAL AND INFORMATION   ÁSOLO

Arrival There are regular buses to Ásolo from Bassano. If you want to get there from Venice, the quickest route is to take a train to Treviso, where you won't have to wait more than an hour for a bus to Ásolo (some change at Montebelluna), though it can be longer on Sundays – in addition to the direct services, all buses to Bassano go through Ásolo and Masèr. The bus drops you at the foot of the hill, whence a connecting minibus will take you up into the town.

Information The tourist office is at Piazza Garibaldi 73 (Thurs–Sun 9.30am–12.30pm & 3–6pm; ☎ 042 352 9046, ⊛ asolo.it).

ACCOMMODATION

Ásolo is an expensive little town, with two of the Veneto's flashiest hotels, the *Villa Cipriani* and *Al Sole*, but there are alternatives for those on more sensible budgets. Note that all accommodation is booked solid on the second Sunday of every month, when the antiques fair takes over the centre of town.

★ **Agriturismo Sant'Andrea** Via Cornuda 72, Masèr ☎ 042 356 5358, ⊛ agrsantandrea.it. This friendly wine-making *agriturismo*, down the road from the Villa Barbaro, makes the perfect base for exploring the region. There are eleven plain but comfortable rooms, three of which have cooking facilities. There's an ample buffet breakfast, too. €75

Duse Via Browning 190 ☎ 042 355 241, ⊛ hotelduse. com. The only inexpensive hotel in the centre, this three-star has 14 rooms, most of them spacious. €120

EATING AND DRINKING

Antica Osteria Al Bacaro Via Browning 165 ☎ 042 355 150. Atmospheric and welcoming rustic *osteria* with a very local feel. The food is unpretentious and well prepared (the menu changes daily), and prices are reasonable – expect to pay €10–15 for *secondi*. Mon–Tues & Thurs–Sun noon–3pm & 6–10pm.

★ **Locanda Baggio** Via Bassane 1, Casonetto ☎ 042 352 9648, ⊛ locandabaggio.it. Located 1km northeast of the town in the hamlet of Casonetto, the Baggio family's restaurant offers superb and inventive cooking. The tasting menu (€65 per person, excluding wine) is a real treat. They also have an excellent wine list, from vineyards all over Italy, plus some foreign vintages, including wines from Slovenia and Lebanon. Tues–Sat noon–3pm & 7.30–10.30pm, Sun noon–3pm.

Feltre

The historic centre of **FELTRE**, spread along a narrow ridge about 20km north of Masèr, owes its beguiling appearance to a disaster. At the outbreak of the War of the

League of Cambrai, Feltre declared its allegiance to Venice – and so, when the army of Emperor Maximilian I swept into town in 1509, it was decided to punish Feltre by wiping its buildings and a hefty number of its inhabitants from the face of the planet. The Venetians took care of the reconstruction, and within a few decades the streets had been rebuilt. They still look pretty much as they did when the scaffolding came down. You're not going to find the town crawling with students making notes on the architecture of the Renaissance, and neither will you want to stay over, but you'll have to travel a long way to get a better idea of how an ordinary town looked in sixteenth-century Italy. And on top of that, there's the beauty of Feltre's position – the Dolomites in one direction, the valley of the Piave in the other. The last stretch of the train journey from the south, along the Piave from Valdobbiádene, is terrific too.

The lower town

From the train station, down in the modern part of town, the shortest route to the old quarter is to cross straight over into Viale del Piave, over Via Garibaldi and along Via Castaldi, which brings you to the **Duomo** and **Baptistery**, at the foot of the ridge. The oldest section of the much-altered duomo is the fifteenth-century apse; its main objects of interest are a tomb by Tullio Lombardo (on the right wall of the chancel) and the *Pala della Misericordia* (second altar of right aisle), by local sixteenth-century painter Pietro de Marascalchi, who also painted the *John the Baptist* on the fourth altar of the right aisle, and possibly the altarpiece in the chapel to the right of the chancel. At the top of the steps going past the side of the porticoed baptistery, on the other side of the road, is the discreet south gate (1494), from where a long covered flight of steps rises into the heart of the old town.

16

The old town

The steps from the lower town emerge by the sixteenth-century **Municipio**, which has a portico by Palladio. Goldoni's earliest plays, first performed in 1729 in the old Palazzo Pretorio (the building at a right angle to the Municipio), were soon afterwards staged in the Municipio's own theatre, the exquisite little **Teatro della Sena**, which was redesigned at the start of the nineteenth century and fully merits its nickname of "La piccola Fenice".

Under the gaze of the inescapable Venetian lion, two Feltrian luminaries face each other across the stage-like **Piazza Maggiore: Panfilo Castaldi** and Vittorino de' Rambaldoni, usually known as **Vittorino da Feltre**. The former was instrumental in the development of printing in Italy, and according to some it was Castaldi rather than Gutenberg who was the first European to develop moveable type – the inscription on the plinth categorically declares him to be its inventor. Vittorino's fame rests on the school he ran in Mantua in the first half of the fifteenth century, under the financial patronage of the Gonzaga family, which took in pupils from aristocratic families and unprivileged backgrounds alike, and put them through a regimen in which, for the first time, a broad liberal education was combined with a programme of physical training.

Behind Piazza Maggiore rises the keep of the medieval castello, just below which stands the church of **San Rocco** – go round the back where there is a good view of the mountains. The carved wall between the steps going up to the church is a fountain by Tullio Lombardo.

Via Mezzaterra

Most of the houses on the main street of old Feltre, **Via Mezzaterra**, date from the sixteenth century, and several are decorated with external frescoes by **Lorenzo Luzzo** (1467–1512) and his pupils. Feltre's most important artistic figure, Luzzo is more widely known as **Il Morto da Feltre** (The Dead Man of Feltre), a nickname prompted perhaps by the pallor of his complexion, or by his morose demeanour. Having begun with spells in Rome and Florence, Il Morto's career received something of a boost when he was called in to help Giorgione on the Fondaco dei Tedeschi in Venice.

The Museo Civico and Museo Rizzarda

Museo Civico Via L. Luzzo • Fri, Sat & Sun: mid-June to mid-Sept 9.30am–6pm; rest of year 10.30am–12.30pm & 3–6pm **Museo Rizzarda** Via del Paradiso 8 • Same hours as Museo Civico • €4 each, or €5 joint ticket

The **Museo Civico**, at the end of Via L. Luzzo, the equally decorous continuation of Via Mezzaterra on the other side of the piazza, contains Il Morto's *Madonna with St Vitus and St Modestus* and other pieces by him, plus paintings by Cima and Gentile Bellini, and a display of Roman and Etruscan finds. Il Morto's finest work is generally held to be the fresco of the *Transfiguration* in the **Ognissanti** church; this building is rarely open, but if you want to try your luck, go out of the Porta Oria (right by the Museo), down the hill and then along Borgo Ruga for a couple of hundred metres.

The **Museo Rizzarda,** close to the Museo Civico, doubles as the town's collection of modern art and an exhibition of wrought-iron work, most of it by **Carlo Rizzarda** (1883–1931), the former owner of the house and the collector of many of the paitings here. It might not sound appetizing, but the finesse of Rizzarda's pieces is remarkable.

ARRIVAL AND DEPARTURE   FELTRE

By train There are no direct trains to Feltre from Venice, but Feltre is a stop on the Padua–Belluno line (12 daily) – you can intercept these trains at Castelfranco. The journey from Padua to Feltre takes 1hr 30min, and it's a further 30min to Belluno.

16

Conegliano

Travelling north from Treviso, it's at the amiable town of **CONEGLIANO** that the landscape ceases to be boringly flat, as the terrain starts to rise towards the Dolomites. It markets itself to tourists as *La Città Murata* (Walled City), on the strength of fortifications that bear witness to its medieval history, most notably the six decades of occupation by the Da Carrara and Della Scala (Scaliger) warlords, prior to annexation by Venice in 1389. But to the untrained eye the vestigial walls of Conegliano aren't especially remarkable, and in truth what this town is really about is **wine**, particularly prosecco – the surrounding hills are patched with vineyards, and the production of wine is central to the economy of the district. Italy's first wine-growers' college was set up in Conegliano in 1876, and today there are a couple of well-established **wine routes**: the **Strada del Vino Rosso**, which follows a looping 68km course southeast to Oderzo, and the more rewarding **Strada del Prosecco**, a straighter 42km journey west to Valdobbiádene. The former takes you through Merlot, Cabernet and Raboso country; the latter passes the Bianco dei Colli, Prosecco and Cartizze producers – the last, a more refined version of prosecco, could be mistaken for champagne with a small effort of will.

Via XX Settembre

The old centre of Conegliano, adhering to the slope of the Colle di Giano and presided over by the castello on its summit, is right in front of you as you come out of the train station. After crossing the principal street of the modern town (Corso V. Emanuele–Corso G. Mazzini) you pass through a portico and into the original high street – **Via XX Settembre**. Lined with fifteenth- to eighteenth-century houses, this is an attractive street on any day, but to see it at its best you should turn up on a Friday morning, when the weekly **market** sets up camp.

The Duomo

Via XX Settembre • Daily 8am–noon & 3–7pm • Free

The most decorative feature of Via XX Settembre is the unusual facade of the **Duomo**, a fourteenth-century portico, frescoed at the end of the sixteenth century by **Ludovico Pozzoserrato**, which joins seamlessly the buildings on either side. The interior of the church has been rebuilt, but retains fragments of fifteenth-century frescoes; the major adornment of the church, though, is the magnificent altarpiece of *The Madonna and Child with Saints and Angels*, painted in 1493 by **Giambattista Cima**, the most famous native of Conegliano.

The Sala dei Battuti

July Sat & Sun 10am–noon & 4–6pm; Aug Sat & Sun 10am–noon • Free

Alongside the duomo, at the top of the steps facing the door off the right-hand aisle of the church, is the **Sala dei Battuti** or Hall of the Flagellants, the frescoed meeting place of a local confraternity. The pictures are mostly sixteenth-century and depict scenes from the *Creation* to the *Last Judgement*, incorporating the weirdest *Ascension* you'll ever see, with the ascendant Christ half out of the frame and a pair of footprints left behind at the point of lift-off.

The Casa Museo di G.B. Cima

Via G.B. Cima 24 • Sat & Sun 4–7pm • Free

Cima's birthplace, at the rear of the duomo, has been restored and converted into the **Casa Museo di G.B. Cima**. Formally unadventurous, Cima exemplifies the conservative strand in Venetian painting of the early sixteenth century, but at their best his paintings have something of the elegiac tone of Giovanni Bellini's later works. The museum has some high-class reproductions, but not a single real painting by Cima.

16

The Museo Civico

Piazza San Leonardo • Tues–Sun 10am–12.30pm & 2.30–6.30pm • €2.50

The **Museo Civico**, which is housed in the tallest surviving tower of the reconstructed tenth-century castello on top of the hill, is reached most quickly by the steep and cobbled Calle Madonna della Neve, which begins at the end of Via Accademia, the street beside the palatial Accademia cinema, and follows the town's most impressive stretch of ancient wall. (The Scaligeri raised the wall in the 1330s, and half a century later the Carraresi made it higher.) The museum has some damaged frescoes by Pordenone and a small bronze horse by Giambologna, but most of the paintings are "Workshop of…" or "School of…", and the displays of coins, maps, archeological finds, armour and so forth are no more fascinating than you'd expect. To pad things out there's a section devoted to famous people with local connections, complete with terracotta busts of Arturo Toscanini, who got married in Conegliano, and Mozart's great librettist Lorenzo da Ponte, who was born in nearby Cèneda. But it's a lovingly maintained museum, and the climb through the floors culminates on the tower's roof, from where you get a fine view across the vine-clad landscape.

CONEGLIANO'S FESTIVALS

Conegliano has a major wine festival in September, as well as other smaller artistic celebrations that month. The biggest folkloric event in the calendar is the **Dama Castellana**, a gigantic draughts game played on Piazza Cima with human pieces in early June (Ⓦdamacastellana.it). Initiated in 1241 to mark a victory over the troops of Treviso, the game is nowadays preceded by a costumed procession and flag-twirling, and followed by a gruelling ritual in which the losers have to shove the winners up the hill to the castle in a cart. In traditional style, fireworks bring the fun to a close.

The castello shares the summit with the heavily restored **Santa Orsola**, the minuscule remnant of the ancient church of San Leonardo, which was Conegliano's main church from its foundation in the twelfth century until the demolition of everything but the apse and a single chapel in the middle of the eighteenth.

ARRIVAL AND INFORMATION CONEGLIANO

By train Getting to Conegliano on public transport from Venice is easy – nearly all the half-hourly Venice to Udine trains stop here; the journey from Venice takes 50–70min.
Tourist office Via XX Settembre 61, on the corner of Piazza

G.B. Cima (Tues & Wed 9am–1pm, Thurs–Sun 9am–1pm & 2–6pm; ☎0438 21 230). Well stocked with information, including the latest list of recommended prosecco outlets, plus details of the wine routes.

ACCOMMODATION AND EATING

Canon d'Oro Via XX Settembre 131 ☎0438 34 246, ⓦhotelcanondoro.it. The first-choice hotel in town, this Best Western four-star is housed in one of the street's fine frescoed palazzi. It has a terraced garden to the rear, and whirlpool baths in the more expensive rooms. **€110**
Città di Venezia Via XX Settembre 77–79 ☎0438 23 186, ⓦtrattoriacittadivenezia.it. An unfussily stylish *osteria*, specializing in fish and seafood. The menu is small but the quality is always good, as is the price,

with *secondi* averaging €15. In summer the front terrace is a very nice place to eat. Tues–Sun noon–2.30pm & 7–10.30pm.
★ **Trattoria Stella** Via Accademia 3 ☎0438 22 178. An old-fashioned and immensely welcoming little trattoria in the heart of the old town, offering simple and honest home cooking, with decent house wine too. Mon–Wed & Fri–Sat noon–2.30pm & 7–10pm, Thurs noon–2.30pm.

Vittorio Veneto

The name **VITTORIO VENETO** first appeared on the map in 1866 when, to mark the unification of Italy and honour Vittorio Emanuele II, the first king of the new country, the neighbouring towns of Cèneda and Serravalle were knotted together and rechristened. A new town hall was built midway along the avenue connecting the two, and the train station constructed opposite, in the hope that the towns would grow closer together. To an extent they have, but the visitor emerging from the station still steps straight into a sort of no-man's-land.

The old quarter of Serravalle is very alluring, as are the environs. From the centre of town there are paths leading up into the encircling wooded hills, with the most rewarding area for walkers lying to the northeast in the **Bosco del Cansiglio**, a plateau forested with beech and pine which was once husbanded by the Venetian state as a source of timber for oars.

Cèneda

Cèneda, overlooked by the seventh-century Lombard castle of San Martino (now the bishop's residence), is the less appealing of the town's halves – having a more open situation than Serravalle, it has inevitably developed as the commercial centre of Vittorio Veneto. It is, nonetheless, worth a visit for the **Museo della Battaglia**.

The Museo della Battaglia

Piazza Giovanni Paolo I • Tues–Fri 9.30am–12.30pm, Sat–Sun 10am–1pm & 3–6pm • €5 • ⓦmuseobattaglia.it

The **Museo della Battaglia**, which is housed in the sixteenth-century Loggia Cenedese, is reached by turning right out of the station and walking until you come to the road junction of Piazza San Francesco di Assisi, where you turn right – a good twenty-minute walk in total. The battle of Vittorio Veneto, which lasted from October 24 to November 3, 1918, was the triumphant final engagement of World War I for the Italian army (which is why most towns in Italy have a Via Vittorio Veneto) and this well-designed museum is dedicated to the climactic engagement. Upstairs, in the impressive Aula Civica Cenedese, crucial episodes in the history of Cèneda are depicted in nineteenth-century frescoes. The nondescript duomo, on the same piazza, has nothing of interest inside.

Santa Maria Annunziata del Meschio
Via Pontavai

Cèneda's only interesting church is **Santa Maria Annunziata del Meschio**, where on the main altar you'll find a luscious *Annunciation* by Andrea Previtali (c.1470–1528), a pupil of Giovanni Bellini. If you turn left off the Cèneda–Serravalle road down Via Armando Diaz, instead of going right for the cathedral square, you'll quickly come across it.

Serravalle

Serravalle, wedged in the neck of the gorge between the Col Visentin and the Cansiglio (the name means "Valley Lock"), is an entirely different proposition from its partner. Once through its southern gate – to the left of which the ruined walls disappear into the trees on the valley side – you are into a town that has scarcely seen a demolition since the sixteenth century.

The Museo del Cenedese
Piazza Marc'Antonio Flaminio 1 • Summer Sat & Sun 10am–noon & 3–6pm; winter Sat & Sun 10am–noon & 3–5pm • €3 • Ⓦ museocenedese.it

Most of the buildings along Via Martiri della Libertà, Via Roma and Via Mazzini, and around the stage-like Piazza Marcantonio Flaminio, date from the fifteenth and sixteenth centuries – the handsomest being the finely painted and shield-encrusted Loggia Serravallese (rebuilt c.1460). This is now the home of the **Museo del Cenedese**, a small jumble of a museum, featuring some fine furniture and a delicate *Madonna and Child* by Jacopo Sansovino.

16

The churches of Serravalle

Time is more profitably spent in the churches of Serravalle than in its museum. One of the best-preserved fresco cycles in the Veneto covers the interior of **San Lorenzo dei Battuti** (same ticket & hours as museum), immediately inside the south gate. Painted around 1450, the frescoes were damaged when Napoleon's troops used the chapel as a kitchen, but restoration subsequent to the uncovering of the cycle in 1953 has rectified the situation.

The **Duomo**, across the swift-flowing River Meschio on the far side of the Piazza Flaminio from the Museo, is a dull eighteenth-century building with a medieval campanile; an altarpiece of *The Virgin with St Peter and St Andrew*, produced in 1547 by **Titian** and his workshop, is the sole reason to go inside.

Follow the road past the duomo and you'll immediately come to a flight of steps. This leads to a path that winds through the woods to the **Santuario di Santa Augusta** – go for the walk, not for the building. (If you're in town on August 21, the festival of St Augusta's martyrdom, you'll be treated to a huge fireworks display and all-night party.) Carry on up Via Roma instead of veering across Piazza Flaminio and you'll pass the remnant of the castello and, eventually (outside the walls), the partly frescoed church of **San Giovanni Battista**, which has beautiful cloisters (ask the sacristan for admission, as the cloisters belong to the adjacent Carmelite monastery). Further out still, and a few yards over the river stands **Santa Giustina**. It was founded in 1226 by the Camino clan, who for around three hundred years were the rulers of Treviso province. It contains a superb funerary monument, the **tomb** erected in 1336 by Verde della Scala (Scaliger) for her husband, Rizzardo VI da Camino, who had been killed in battle. The four praying warriors that support the Gothic sarcophagus were probably purloined from an older pulpit or other such structure.

By train To get to Vittorio Veneto from Venice you need to change at Conegliano, from where there are ten northward connections a day (20min). These trains take a further 40min to reach Belluno.

By bus The bus station is across the main road from the train station, behind the post office. Bus #1 shuttles

between Cèneda and Serravalle every 30min.

Destinations Belluno (1 daily; 1hr); Conegliano (11 daily; 45min).

Tourist office Near the train station at Viale della Vittoria 110 (Mon 9.30am–12.30pm, Tues–Sun 9.30am–12.30pm & 3–6pm; ☎ 0438 57 243).

Belluno

The most northerly of the major towns of the Veneto, **BELLUNO** stands at the point where the tiny River Ardo flows into the Piave, in the shadow of the eastern Dolomites. Once a strategically important ally of Venice, which took the town under its wing in 1404, it is today a provincial capital and attached more firmly to the mountainous region to the north than to the urban centres to the south: the network of the Dolomiti Bus company radiates out from Belluno, trains run fairly regularly to the terminus at Calalzo, and the tourist office's handouts are geared mostly to hikers and skiers. Many visitors to the town use the place simply for its access to the mountains, and miss out on its attractions – of which there are quite a few, besides its breathtaking position.

Belluno has two distinct but adjacent centres, reached by walking straight ahead from the train station. The hub of the modern town, the spot where you'll find its most popular bars and cafés, is the wide **Piazza dei Martiri** (named after a group of partisans executed in the square by the Nazis in 1944). Off the south side, a road leads to the **Piazza del Duomo**, the kernel of the old town.

Piazza del Duomo

The sixteenth-century **Duomo** or Basilica di San Martino (daily 7am–6pm), a Gothic-classical amalgam built in the pale yellow stone that's a distinctive feature of Belluno, has had to be completely reconstructed twice after earthquake damage, in 1873 and 1939. **Tullio Lombardo** was the architect of most of it, but the stately campanile was designed in 1743 by **Filippo Juvarra**, best known for his rebuilding of central Turin. The elegant interior – a long barrel-vault ending in a single dome, with flanking aisles – has a good painting by Jacopo Bassano and another by Palma il Giovane.

Occupying one complete side of the piazza, at a right angle to the duomo, is the residence of the Venetian administrators of the town, the **Palazzo dei Rettori**, a late fifteenth-century building with Baroque trimmings. A relic of more independent times stands on the right – the twelfth-century **Torre Civica**, all that's left of Belluno's medieval castle.

Palazzo Fulcis

Via Roma 28 • Tues, Wed & Fri 9.30am–12.30pm & 3.30–6.30pm, Thurs 9.30am–12.30pm, Sat & Sun 10am–6pm • €8

The huge **Palazzo Fulcis** – Belluno's most significant eighteenth-century building – has recently been refurbished to house the collections that used to be held by the Museo Civico. A substantial quantity of fine porcelain is on show here, but of wider appeal is the work of Belluno's three best-known artists, all of whom were born here between 1659 and 1676: the painters Sebastiano and Marco Ricci, and the virtuoso sculptor-woodcarver Andrea Brustolon (who features prominently in Venice's Ca' Rezzonico). All three are to be found in the top-floor galleries, where there's also an engaging series of artless *ex voto* paintings. Among the earlier art displayed on the floor below, the placid Paduan artist Bartolomeo Montagna stands out.

Piazza del Mercato and Via Mezzaterra

Via Duomo ends at the **Piazza del Mercato**, a tiny square hemmed in by porticoed Renaissance buildings; until the Venetians shifted the administrative offices to the Piazza del Duomo, this was the nerve centre of Belluno, and even after the Venetian alterations it remained the commercial core. Its fountain dates from 1410 and the **Monte di Pietà** (no. 26) from 1501, making it one of the oldest pawnshops in Italy. One of the prime claimants to the honour of being the originator of pawnshops is Martino Tomitani (later St Bernardine of Feltre), a Franciscan friar from the village of Tomo, in the vicinity of nearby Feltre. The principal street of the old town, **Via Mezzaterra**, goes down from the Piazza del Mercato to the fourteenth-century Porta Rugo (veer left along the cobbled Via S. Croce where Mezzaterra becomes Via 1 Novembre), where you get a fine view along the mountain-backed valley of the Piave.

San Pietro

Vicolo San Pietro • Jan–June & Sept–Dec Sun 7am–noon; July & Aug Sun 7am–noon & 3–6pm

The church of **San Pietro**, just off Via Mezzaterra, is more interesting than its unprepossessing exterior may suggest. It was founded in the fourteenth century and rebuilt in 1750; the chapel to the right of the main altar contains parts of the original Gothic church, and a pair of old cloisters also survive, one of them with fifteenth-century frescoes that were uncovered in 1989. The main altarpiece is by **Sebastiano Ricci**, paintings by **Andrea Schiavone** are to be seen over the door and to the sides of the high altar, and **Brustolon** carved the angels over the baldachin and retables of the second altars on both sides, which were brought here from a demolished Jesuit church – which is why they don't fit perfectly.

16

Santo Stefano

Via Roma • Daily 8am–noon & 3–6pm

If you follow Via Roma from Piazza dei Martiri you'll soon come to the church of **Santo Stefano**. A bright Gothic building (1486) with banded arches and alternating brown and white columns, it has yet more carvings by **Brustolon**: a crucifix in the left aisle and a pair of pale wooden angels near the high altar.

ARRIVAL AND INFORMATION | BELLUNO

By train No trains run straight from Venice to Belluno – you need to change at Conegliano or Castelfranco Veneto. You can also get to Belluno from Padua (directly or via Castelfranco) – there are twelve trains a day, taking 2hr–2hr 30min.

Tourist office Piazza del Duomo 1 (Mon–Sat 9.30am–12.30pm & 2.30–6pm, Sun 10am–noon; ☎ 0437 940 083, ⊛ infodolomiti.it). Has a good source of leaflets on Belluno and its province.

ACCOMMODATION AND EATING

Al Borgo Via Anconetta 8 ☎ 0437 926 755, ⊛ alborgo. to. This restaurant is a couple of kilometres from the centre (it's across the river, in the direction of Feltre), but is well worth the excursion – it's a family-run place, offering superb food (including home-produced salami and sausages) in a delightful setting. Expect to pay around €40 each, excluding wine. It also offers B&B, with three double bedrooms costing up to €150/night in high season. Mon 12.30–2pm & Wed–Sun 12.30–2pm & 7.30–9pm.

Cappello e Cadore Via Ricci 8 ☎ 0437 940 246, ⊛ albergocappello.com. The long-established three-star hotel, tucked away off the main square, is the best place to stay in the centre of Belluno. Its 32 rooms are plain but comfortable and quiet, and some have whirlpool baths. **€90**

Terracotta Borgo Garibaldi 66 ☎ 0437 291 692, ⊛ ristoranteterracotta.it. The friendly and elegant *Terracotta* is the best restaurant in central Belluno. Ingredients gathered from the mountains are the basis of the small but well-composed menu, which therefore changes with the seasons, but you can expect to find some excellent fish dishes at any time of year, at around €20 for a main course. The set lunch menu, at €20 including a glass of wine and coffee, is a bargain. In summer, tables are set out in the lovely garden. Mon & Thurs–Sun noon–2pm & 7.30–9.30pm, Wed 7.30–9.30pm.

SAN PIETRO IN CASTELLO

Contexts

History

In the midst of the waters, free, indigent, laborious, and inaccessible, they gradually coalesced into a Republic.
Edward Gibbon

Beginnings

Though the Venetian lagoon supported small groups of fishermen and hunters at the start of the Christian era, it was only with the barbarian invasions of the fifth century and after, that sizeable communities began to settle on the mudbanks. The first mass migration was provoked by the arrival in the Veneto of **Attila the Hun**'s hordes in **453**, but a large number of the refugees struck camp and returned to dry land once the danger seemed to be past. Permanent settlement was accelerated a century later, when, in **568**, the Germanic **Lombards** (or Longobards), led by **Alboin**, swept into northern Italy.

A loose conglomeration of island communes arose, each cluster of islands drawing its population from one or two clearly defined areas of the Veneto: the fugitives from Padua went to **Malamocco** and **Chioggia**; the inhabitants of **Grado** mainly came from Aquileia; and Altino supplied many of the pioneers of **Torcello**, **Burano** and **Murano**. Distinct economic, ecclesiastical and administrative centres quickly evolved: Torcello was the focal point of trading activity; Grado, the new home of the bishop of Aquileia, was the Church's base; and Heraclea (now extinct) was the seat of government. The lagoon confederation was not autonomous, though – it owed **political allegiance to Byzantium**, and until the end of the seventh century its senior officials were the **maritime tribunes**, who were effectively controlled by the imperial hierarchy of Ravenna.

The refugee population of the islands increased steeply as the Lombard grip on the Veneto strengthened under the leadership of **Grimoald** (667–71), and shortly after this influx the confederation took a big step towards independence. This is one of the many points at which Venetian folklore has acquired the status of fact; tradition has it that a conference was convened at Heraclea in 697 by the patriarch of Grado, and from this meeting sprang the election of the **first doge**, to unify the islands in the face of the Lombard threat. In fact, it was not until **726** that the lagoon settlers chose their first leader, when a wave of dissent against Emperor Leo III throughout the Byzantine Empire spurred them to elect **Orso Ipato** as the head of their provincial council.

After a period during which the old system of government was briefly reinstituted, Orso Ipato's son **Teodato** became the second doge in 742. Yet the lagoon administration – which was now moved from Heraclea to **Malamocco** – was still not autonomous: like his father, Teodato took orders from the capital, and the **fall of Ravenna** to the Lombards in 751 did not alter the constitutional relationship between Byzantium and the confederation.

At the close of the eighth century, the Lombards were overrun by the Frankish army of **Charlemagne**, and in **810** the emperor's son **Pepin** sailed into action against the proto-Venetians. Malamocco was quickly taken, but Pepin's fleet failed in its attempt to pursue the settlers when they withdrew to the better-protected islands of **Rivoalto**, and retreated with heavy losses. Now the seat of government in the lagoon was shifted for

453	726
First settlements in the Venetian lagoon, as people flee from Attila the Hun	The proto-Venetians elect their first leader, Orso Ipato

THE DOGES OF VENICE

Paoluccio Anafesto 697–717
Marcello Tegalliano 717–726
Orso Ipato 726–737
interregnum 737–742
Teodato Ipato 742–755
Galla Gaulo 755–756
Domenico Monegario 756–764
Maurizio Galbaio 764–787
Giovanni Galbaio 787–804
Obelario degli Antenori 804–811
Agnello Participazio 811–827
Giustiniano Participazio 827–829
Giovanni Participazio I 829–836
Pietro Tradonico 836–864
Orso Participazio I 864–881
Giovanni Participazio II 881–887
Pietro Candiano I 887
Pietro Tribuno 888–912
Orso Participazio II 912–932
Pietro Candiano II 932–939
Pietro Participazio 939–942
Pietro Candiano III 942–959
Pietro Candiano IV 959–976
Pietro Orseolo I 976–978
Vitale Candiano 978–979
Tribuno Memmo 979–991
Pietro Orseolo II 991–1008
Otto Orseolo 1008–1026
Pietro Centranico 1026–1032
Domenico Flabanico 1032–1043
Domenico Contarini 1043–1071

Domenico Selvo 1071–1084
Vitale Falier 1084–1096
Vitale Michiel I 1096–1102
Ordelafo Falier 1102–1118
Domenico Michiel 1118–1130
Pietro Polani 1130–1148
Domenico Morosini 1148–1156
Vitale Michiel II 1156–1172
Sebastiano Ziani 1172–1178
Orio Mastropiero 1178–1192
Enrico Dandolo 1192–1205
Pietro Ziani 1205–1229
Giacomo Tiepolo 1229–1249
Marin Morosini 1249–1253
Ranier Zeno 1253–1268
Lorenzo Tiepolo 1268–1275
Jacopo Contarini 1275–1280
Giovanni Dandolo 1280–1289
Pietro Gradenigo 1289–1311
Marino Zorzi 1311–1312
Giovanni Soranzo 1312–1328
Francesco Dandolo 1329–1339
Bartolomeo Gradenigo 1339–1342
Andrea Dandolo 1343–1354
Marin Falier 1354–1355
Giovanni Gradenigo 1355–1356
Giovanni Dolfin 1356–1361
Lorenzo Celsi 1361–1365
Marco Corner 1365–1368
Andrea Contarini 1368–1382
Michele Morosini 1382

the last time, to Rivoalto, the name by which the central cluster of islands was known until the late twelfth century, when it became generally known as **Venice**. The **Rialto** district, in the core of the city, perpetuates the old name.

From independence to empire

In the **Treaty of Aix-la-Chapelle**, signed by Charlemagne and the Byzantine emperor shortly after Pepin's defeat, Venice was declared to be a dukedom within the Eastern Empire, despite the fact that by now the control of Byzantium was little more than nominal. The traders and boatmen of the lagoon were less and less inclined to acknowledge the precedence of the emperor, and they signalled their recalcitrance through one great symbolic act – **the theft of the body of St Mark** from Alexandria in 828. St Mark, whose posthumous arrival in Venice was held to be divinely ordained

810

828

Pepin's invasion; the islands of Rivoalto (later Rialto) become the centre of the lagoon settlement

The body of St Mark is brought to Venice, to be enshrined in the new Basilica

Antonio Venier 1382–1400
Michele Steno 1400–1413
Tommaso Mocenigo 1414–1423
Francesco Fóscari 1423–1457
Pasquale Malipiero 1457–1462
Cristoforo Moro 1462–1471
Nicolò Tron 1471–1473
Nicolò Marcello 1473–1474
Pietro Mocenigo 1474–1476
Andrea Vendramin 1476–1478
Giovanni Mocenigo 1478–1485
Marco Barbarigo 1485–1486
Agostino Barbarigo 1486–1501
Leonardo Loredan 1501–1521
Antonio Grimani 1521–1523
Andrea Gritti 1523–1538
Pietro Lando 1538–1545
Francesco Donà 1545–1553
Marcantonio Trevisan 1553–1554
Francesco Venier 1554–1556
Lorenzo Priuli 1556–1559
Girolamo Priuli 1559–1567
Pietro Loredan 1567–1570
Alvise Mocenigo I 1570–1577
Sebastiano Venier 1577–1578
Nicolò da Ponte 1578–1585
Pasquale Cicogna 1585–1595
Marino Grimani 1595–1605
Leonardo Donà 1606–1612
Marcantonio Memmo 1612–1615
Giovanni Bembo 1615–1618

Nicolò Donà 1618
Antonio Priuli 1618–1623
Francesco Contarini 1623–1624
Giovanni Corner I 1625–1629
Nicolò Contarini 1630–1631
Francesco Erizzo 1631–1646
Francesco Molin 1646–1655
Carlo Contarini 1655–1656
Francesco Corner 1656
Bertucci Valier 1656–1658
Giovanni Pésaro 1658–1659
Domenico Contarini 1659–1675
Nicolò Sagredo 1675–1676
Alvise Contarini 1676–1684
Marcantonio Giustinian 1684–1688
Francesco Morosini 1688–1694
Silvestro Valier 1694–1700
Alvise Mocenigo II 1700–1709
Giovanni Corner II 1709–1722
Alvise Mocenigo III 1722–1732
Carlo Ruzzini 1732–1735
Alvise Pisani 1735–1741
Pietro Grimani 1741–1752
Francesco Loredan 1752–1762
Marco Foscarini 1762–1763
Alvise Mocenigo IV 1763–1778
Paolo Renier 1779–1789
Lodovico Manin 1789–1797

(see page 39), was made the patron saint of the city in place of the Byzantine patron, St Theodore, and a basilica was built alongside the doge's castle to accommodate the holy relics. These two buildings – the **Basilica di San Marco** and the **Palazzo Ducale** – were to remain the emblems of the Venetian state and the repository of power within the city for almost one thousand years.

By the end of the ninth century the population of the islands of central Venice was increasing steadily. The city was comprehensively protected against attack, with chains slung across the entrance to the major channels and fortified walls shielding the waterfront between the Palazzo Ducale and the area in which the church of Santa Maria Zobenigo now stands. Before the close of the following century, the Venetian **trading networks** were well established – military assistance given to their former masters in Byzantium had earned concessions in the markets of the East, and the Venetian economy was prospering from the distribution of eastern goods along the waterways of northern Italy.

1082

The Byzantine emperor formalizes preferential treatment for Venetian traders

1095

The First Crusade, which Venice takes as an opportunity to extend its presence in the Aegean and Middle East

Slav pirates, operating from the shelter of the Dalmatian coast, were the greatest hindrance to Venetian trade in the northern Adriatic, and in the year **1000** a fleet set out under the command of **Doge Pietro Orseolo II** to subjugate the troublemakers. The successful expedition was commemorated each subsequent year in the ceremony of the **Marriage of Venice to the Sea**, in which the city's lordship of the Adriatic was ritually confirmed (see page 35). However, although the Doge of Venice could now legitimately claim the title "Duke of Dalmatia", there remained the problem of the **Normans** of southern Italy, whose navy threatened to confine the Venetians to the upper part of the Adriatic. The breakthrough came in **1081**, when the Byzantine Emperor Alexius Comnenus, himself endangered by Norman expansion, appealed to Venice for aid. The resulting naval battles left Venice as the protector of the Eastern Empire's seaboard and earned invaluable commercial rights for its traders. In a charter of 1082, known as the Crisobolo (Golden Bull), the emperor declared Venetian merchants to be exempt from all tolls and taxes within his lands. In the words of one historian – "On that day Venetian world trade began."

Venice and the Crusades

In 1095 Pope Urban II called for a Christian army to wrest the Holy Land from the Muslims, and within four years Jerusalem had been retaken by the **First Crusade**. Decades of chaos ensued, which the Venetians, typically, managed to turn to their commercial advantage. Offering to transport armies and supplies to the East in return for grants of property and financial bonuses, Venice extended its foothold in the Aegean, the Black Sea and Syria, battling all the time (sometimes literally) against its two chief maritime rivals in Italy – Pisa and Genoa. While it was consolidating its overseas bases, Venice was also embroiled in the political manoeuvrings between the papacy, the Western emperor and the cities of northern Italy, the conclusion of which was one of Venice's greatest diplomatic successes: **the reconciliation of Emperor Frederick Barbarossa and Pope Alexander III** in 1177, in Venice.

Now a major European power, Venice was about to acquire an empire. In November 1199 Count Tibald of Champagne proposed a **Fourth Crusade** to regain Jerusalem, which twelve years earlier had fallen to Saladin. Venice was commissioned, for a huge fee, to provide the ships for the army. In 1202 the forces gathered in Venice, only to find that they couldn't raise the agreed sum. In the negotiations that followed, the doge obtained a promise from the French commanders that the Crusade would stop off to reconquer the colony of Zara, recently captured from Venice by the King of Hungary. No sooner was that accomplished than the expedition was diverted, after Venetian persuasion, to Constantinople, where the succession to the imperial throne was causing problems and, furthermore, Venetian merchants were losing ground to merchants from Pisa and Genoa.

The upshot was the **Sack of Constantinople in 1204**, one of the most disgusting episodes in European history. Thousands were slaughtered by the Christian soldiers and virtually every precious object that could be lifted was stolen from the city, mainly by the Venetians, who were led in person by the blind octogenarian doge, Enrico Dandolo. So vast was the scale of the destruction that a contemporary historian regretted that the city had not fallen instead to the infidel. Ultimately the consequences were disastrous – not only did no help reach the forces in the Holy Land, but the

1204	1297	1310
In the wake of the Fourth Crusade, Venice gains control of "one quarter and half a quarter" of the former Roman Empire	The Serrata del Maggior Consiglio defines the families allowed to participate in the government of Venice	The revolt of Bajamonte Tiepolo

Eastern Empire was fatally divided between the native Greeks and the barbaric westerners. The Ottoman conquest of Constantinople in 1453, and the consequent peril of western Europe, were distant but direct results of the Fourth Crusade. Venice got what it wanted, though – "one quarter and half a quarter" of the Roman Empire was now under its sway, with an almost uninterrupted chain of ports stretching from the lagoon to the Black Sea.

The Genoese Wars

The enmities created within the Eastern Empire by the Fourth Crusade were soon to rebound on Venice. The Genoese were now the main opposition in the eastern markets, maintaining a rivalry so violent that some Venetian historians refer to their succession of conflicts as the **Five Genoese Wars**. Genoa's hatred of Venice led to an alliance with the dethroned Byzantine dynasty, whose loathing of the Venetians was no less intense; within months of the Pact of Ninfeo (1261), **Michael Palaeologus VIII** was installed as emperor in Constantinople. Venice now faced a struggle to hold onto its commercial interests against the favoured Genoese.

For the rest of the century, and almost all the fourteenth century, the defeat of Genoa was the primary aim of Venice's rulers. Both sides suffered terrible setbacks: at the Battle of **Curzola** (1298) 65 ships out of a Venetian fleet of 95 were lost, and 5000 Venetians taken captive; at the Sardinian port of **Alghero** (1353) the Genoese navy lost a similar proportion of its vessels. The climax came with the Fourth War of Genoa, better known as the **War of Chioggia**. Following a victory over the Venetians at Zara in 1379, the Genoese fleet sailed on to Venice, supported by the Paduans and the Austrians, and quickly took Chioggia. This was the zenith of Genoa's power – in August **1380** the invaders were driven off, and although the treaty signed between the two cities seemed inconclusive, within a few decades it was clear that Venice had at last won the battle for economic and political supremacy.

Political upheaval

It was during the Genoese campaigns that the **constitution** of Venice arrived at a state that was to endure until the fall of the Republic, the most significant step in this evolution being the **Serrata del Maggior Consiglio of 1297**, a measure which basically allowed a role in the government of the city only to those families already involved in it. Not surprisingly, many of those disenfranchised by the Serrata resented its instigator, **Doge Pietro Gradenigo**, and when Venice lost its tussle with the papacy for possession of Ferrara in 1309, it seemed that Gradenigo had scarcely a single supporter in the city. Yet the insurrection that came the following year was a revolt of a patrician clique, not an uprising of the people; its leader – **Bajamonte Tiepolo** – had personal reasons for opposing the doge and appears to have wanted to replace the new system with a despotic regime headed by himself. Tiepolo's private army was routed in the centre of the city, but his rebellion had a permanent effect upon the history of Venice, in that it led to the creation in 1310 of the **Council of Ten**, a committee empowered to supervise matters of internal security. Though the Council was intended to be an emergency measure, its tenure was repeatedly extended until, in 1334, it was made a permanent institution.

1348–49	1355	1380
The Black Death	Doge Marin Faller executed for treason	Defeat of Genoa in the War of Chioggia; Venice is now Italy's supreme maritime trading nation

The most celebrated attempt to subvert the Venetian government followed a few years later, in **1355**, and this time the malefactor was the doge himself – **Marin Falier**, who ironically had played a large part in the sentencing of Bajamonte Tiepolo. Falier's plot to overthrow the councils of Venice and install himself as absolute ruler seems to have been prompted by his fury at the lenient treatment given to a young nobleman who had insulted him. Exploiting the grievances felt against certain noble families by, among others, the director of the Arsenale, Falier gathered together a group of conspirators, many of whom were drawn from the working class, a section of Venetian society that was particularly affected by the economic demands of the rivalry with Genoa. (War had recently broken out again after a long period of truce, and to make the situation worse, the **Black Death of 1348–49** had killed around sixty percent of the city's population.) Details of the planned coup leaked out; Falier was arrested and on April 17, eight months after becoming doge, he was beheaded on the steps of the Palazzo Ducale.

Terra firma expansion

The sea lanes of the eastern Mediterranean were the foundation of Venice's wealth, but its dominance as a trading centre clearly depended on free access to the rivers and mountain passes of northern Italy. Thus, although Venetian foreign policy was predominantly eastward-looking from the start, a degree of intervention on the mainland was inevitable, especially with the rise in the fourteenth century of dynasties such as the **Scaligeri** in Verona and the **Visconti** in Milan.

The unsuccessful battle for Ferrara was Venice's first territorial campaign; the first victory came thirty years later, in 1339, when the combined forces of Venice, Florence and a league of Lombard cities defeated the Scaligeri, allowing Venice to incorporate **Castelfranco**, **Conegliano**, **Sacile**, **Oderzo** and, most importantly, **Treviso** into the domain of the Republic. Having thus made safe the roads to Germany, the Venetians set about securing the territory to the west. The political and military machinations of northern Italy in this period are extremely complicated, with alliances regularly made and betrayed, and cities changing hands with bewildering frequency. The bare outline of the story is that by **1405** Venice had eradicated the most powerful neighbouring dynasty, the **Carrara** family of Padua, and had a firm hold on **Bassano**, **Belluno**, **Feltre**, **Vicenza**, **Verona** and **Padua** itself. The annexation in **1420** of **the Friuli** and **Udine** virtually doubled the area of the terra firma under Venetian control, and brought the border of the empire right up to the Alps.

Many Venetians thought that any further expansion would be foolish. Certainly this was the view of **Doge Tommaso Mocenigo**, who on his deathbed urged his compatriots to "refrain…from taking what belongs to others or making unjust wars". Specifically, he warned them against the ambitions of **Francesco Fóscari** – "If he becomes doge, you will be constantly at war…you will become the slaves of your masters-at-arms and their captains." Within a fortnight of Mocenigo's funeral in 1423, Fóscari was elected as his successor, and Venice was soon on the offensive against the mightiest prince of northern Italy – **Filippo Maria Visconti** of Milan. In the first phase of the campaign nothing except a tenuous ownership of Bergamo and Brescia was gained, a failure for which the Venetian mercenary captain, **Carmagnola**, served as the scapegoat. He was executed in 1432 for treason, and his place taken by Erasmo da Narni, better known as

1420	1453
Annexation of the Friuli extends Venice's mainland empire to the Alps	The Turks take Constantinople; beginning of the decline of Venice's influence in the Middle East

Il Gattamelata. The **Treaty of Cremona** (1441) confirmed Venetian control of **Peschiera**, **Brescia**, **Bergamo** and part of the territory of **Cremona**, and by now **Ravenna** was also officially part of the Venetian dominion, but still the fighting did not stop. Peace on the mainland finally came in **1454**, with the signing of a treaty between Venice and the new ruler of Milan, **Francesco Sforza**, Venice's erstwhile ally against the Visconti. Ravenna didn't stay Venetian for long; the rest of its mainland empire, though, remained intact until the coming of Napoleon.

The Turkish threat

The other Italian states might have taken concerted action against Venice had it not been for the fact that the entire peninsula now faced the common threat of the Ottoman Turks, as was acknowledged in the pact drawn up at **Lodi** later in 1454 between Venice, Milan, Naples, Florence and the Papal States. Open conflict between Venice and the Turks had broken out early in the century – the Republic winning the naval battle of Gallipoli in 1416 – but the policy of terra firma expansion kept the majority of Venice's warships on the rivers of the north, so reliance had to be placed on diplomatic measures to contain the Turkish advance. They were ineffective. Reports of a Turkish military build-up under the command of **Sultan Mehmed II** were not treated with the necessary urgency, and the consequence was that Western troops sent to defend **Constantinople** against the sultan's army were insufficient to prevent the fall of the city in **1453**.

The trade agreement which the Venetians managed to negotiate with the sultan could not arrest the erosion of its commercial empire in the East. The Turkish fleets penetrated into the northern Aegean and many times in the last years of the century the Turkish cavalry came so close to Venice that the fires from the villages it destroyed could be seen from the Campanile of San Marco. In **1479** Venice was forced to sign away the vital port of **Negroponte** and a batch of other Aegean islands; the defeat of the Venetian navy at **Sapienza** in **1499** led to the loss of the main fortresses of the **Morea** (Peloponnese), which meant that the Turks now controlled the so-called "door to the Adriatic". Virtually the only bright spot in all the gloom came about through the marriage of the Venetian **Caterina Cornaro** to the King of **Cyprus** in 1468. In 1473 the king died, and the ensuing political pressure on the widow paid off in **1489**, when Caterina handed over the island to the government of Venice.

The sixteenth century

In **1494** Italy was invaded by **Louis XII of France**, an intervention which Venice lost no time in exploiting. By playing the various territorial contenders off against each other (mainly France and the Habsburgs), Venice succeeded in adding bits and pieces to the terra firma empire, and in 1503 signed a disadvantageous treaty with the Turks so as to be able to concentrate its resources on the mainland. Given the accumulated hostility to Venice, it was a dangerous game, and when the Republic began to encroach on the papal domain in Romagna, it at last provoked a unified response from its opponents. The **League of Cambrai**, formed in **1508** with Pope Julius II, Louis XII, Emperor Maximilian and the king of Spain at its head, pitted almost every power in Europe

1489

Caterina Cornaro surrenders Cyprus to Venice

1499

Vasco da Gama opens up the sea route to India, weakening Venice's trade networks against the Venetians, in a pact that explicitly declared its intention of destroying Venice's empire as a prelude to conquering the Turks.

The ensuing war began calamitously for Venice – its army was crushed by the French at **Agnadello**, city after city defected to the League, and Venice prepared for a siege. The siege never came, and in the end the conflicting interests of the League enabled the Venetians, through subtle diplomacy, to repossess nearly everything they had held at the start of the war. Nonetheless, when the fighting finished in **1516** many of the cities of the Veneto had been sacked, much of the countryside ruined and the Venetian treasury bled almost dry.

Worse was to come. Clearly **the discovery of the New World** was going to have significant repercussions for Venice, but the most catastrophic of the voyages of discovery from Venice's point of view was that of **Vasco da Gama**. In September **1499**, da Gama arrived back in Lisbon having reached India via the Cape of Good Hope. The slow and expensive land routes across Asia to the markets and docks of Venice could now be bypassed by the merchants of northern Europe; from the moment of da Gama's return, the economic balance of Europe began to tilt in favour of the Portuguese, the English and the Dutch.

The Habsburgs and the Ottomans

In **1519**, with the accession of the 19-year-old **Charles V**, the Habsburg Empire absorbed the massive territories of the Spanish kingdom, and after the **sack of Rome in 1527** the whole Italian peninsula, with the sole exception of Venice, was under the young emperor's domination. Meanwhile, the **Turks** were on the move again – **Syria** and **Egypt** had been taken in **1517**; **Rhodes** had fallen to **Suleiman the Magnificent** in **1522**; and by **1529** the Ottoman Empire had spread right along the southern Mediterranean to Morocco. To survive, Venice had to steer a path between these two empires and France, the other superpower of the period. It did survive, but at a cost. When a combined Christian fleet took on the Turks at **Prevesa** in **1538**, the supreme commander, acting under Charles V's instructions, was so concerned to prevent the Venetians profiting from an allied victory that his tactics ensured a Turkish victory; the Venetians were obliged to accept a punitive treaty shortly afterwards. Even the great allied success at **Lépanto** in **1571** didn't work to Venice's advantage, as the Habsburg commander of the fleet, Don John of Austria, refused to consolidate the Venetian position by sailing east after the victory. In the subsequent negotiations, Venice was forced to surrender **Cyprus**, whose brutal capture by the Turks had been the reason for the allied offensive in the first place.

The seventeenth century

Relations between Rome and Venice were always fractious. Venice's expansion on the mainland was a source of irritation, especially when it turned its attention to areas over which the Vatican claimed sovereignty, but papal animosity was also caused by the restrictions imposed on the pope's authority within the Republic's boundaries. The pope was Venice's spiritual overlord, the Venetians agreed, but the doge and his officers were the masters in temporal affairs. The problem for the papacy was that the doge's notion of what constituted temporal affairs was far too broad, and at the start of the seventeenth century **Pope Paul V** and the Republic came to a head-on clash.

1508–16	**1571**
War of the League of Cambrai, pitting Venice against the major powers of Europe	Venice participates in the defeat of the Turks at the Battle of Lépanto, but nonetheless loses Cyprus

Two incidents provoked the row: Venice's insistence that the pope should routinely approve its candidate for the office of patriarch; and its determination not to hand over to papal jurisdiction two clerics it had decided to prosecute. Matters came to a head with the **papal interdict of 1606** and the excommunication of the whole city. Venice's resistance, orchestrated by the scholar-priest **Paolo Sarpi**, was fierce – the Jesuits were expelled, priests within Venetian territory ordered to continue in their duties and pamphlets printed putting the Venetian case. One year later the interdict was lifted, damaging the prestige of the papacy throughout Europe.

No sooner was the interdict out of the way than the Spanish and Austrian **Habsburgs** entered the fray again. The Austrian branch was the first to cause trouble, by encouraging the piratical raids of the **Uskoks**, a loosely defined and regularly obstreperous community living along the Dalmatian coast. Venice took retaliatory action, Archduke Ferdinand objected and a half-hearted war dragged on until **1617**, when, under the peace terms, the Uskoks were removed from their seaports.

The Spanish Habsburgs were more devious, attempting, in **1618**, to subvert the Venetian state with a wild scheme that has always been known as **the Spanish Conspiracy**. Masterminded by the Spanish viceroy of Naples and the Spanish ambassador to Venice, the plot involved smuggling a Spanish army into the city in disguised groups of two or three, and then inciting a mutiny among a contingent of Dutch mercenaries already lodged there. Just how convoluted the conspiracy was can be gathered from the fact that its betrayal resulted in the execution of around three hundred people.

And then, after half a century of ceasefire, the **Turks** renewed their harassment of the Venetian colonies, concentrating their attention on the one remaining stronghold in the eastern Mediterranean, **Crete**. The campaign lasted for 25 years, ending in **1669** with the inevitable fall of the island. Even then the war with the Turks was not over; in **1699**, under the command of **Doge Francesco Morosini**, the Venetians embarked on a retaliatory action in the **Morea**, and succeeded in retaking the region. By 1715, however, all his gains had been turned to losses once more, and in the **Treaty of Passarowitz** in **1718** Venice was forced to accept a definition of its Mediterranean territories drawn up by the Austrians and the Turks. It was left with just the Ionian islands and the Dalmatian coast, and its power in these colonies was little more than hypothetical.

The plague of 1630 and its aftermath

Meanwhile, at home, a significant change in the social structure of the city had been happening. The population of the Venetian upper class had been declining since the middle of the sixteenth century, a situation that was exacerbated in 1630 by a terrible outbreak of plague. By the time the plague had receded, there were around 1600 patrician adult males left, approximately one thousand fewer than a hundred years earlier. Needing to fill scores of government posts, and being short of cash, the city's rulers decided to **"unlock" the Maggior Consiglio** by admitting new families to the ranks of the nobility in return for hefty payments. By 1720 more than 120 families had paid their way into the ruling elite, mostly Venetian merchants and businessmen, though a sizeable minority came from mainland cities such as Padua and Verona. They were regarded by many of the old guard as vulgar *arrivistes*, but among their number were some clans who were to become extremely influential, such as the Rezzonico family, owners of one of the last great palaces on the Canal Grande.

1606	**1618**
Conflict with Rome results in a papal interdict, excommunicating the people of Venice	The so-called Spanish Conspiracy attempts to overthrow the Venetian Republic

The end of the Venetian Republic

Venice in the eighteenth century became a political nonentity, pursuing a foreign policy of unarmed neutrality of which one historian wrote, "She sacrifices everything with the single object of giving no offence to other states." When the **Treaty of Aix-la-Chapelle** in **1748** confirmed Austrian control of the neighbouring areas of the mainland, the Venetians felt compelled to send ambassadors to the Austrian court in a humiliating attempt to wheedle guarantees of their possessions on the terra firma. At home, the division between the upper stratum of the aristocracy and the ever-increasing poorer section was widening, and all attempts to dampen discontent within the city by democratizing its government were stifled by the conservative elite.

Politically trivial and constitutionally ossified, Venice was now renowned not as one of the great powers of Europe, but rather as its playground. Hester Thrale observed in 1789 that no other place was "so subservient to the purposes of pleasure", and William Beckford recorded the effects of a life spent between the ballroom and casino: "Their nerves unstrung by disease and the consequence of early debaucheries, allow no natural flow of lively spirits…they pass their lives in one perpetual doze."

The conflict between Austria and post-Revolutionary France quickly brought about the end of the Venetian Republic. In May 1796 **Napoleon Bonaparte** entered Milan at the head of the French army; in February of the following year Mantua, the last Austrian stronghold in Italy, fell to the French. Yet the Venetians rebuffed Napoleon's repeated invitations to join an anti-Austrian alliance, and French troops in the Veneto were subjected to numerous acts of violent resistance, with Verona proving notably recalcitrant. On April 17, 1797 Napoleon temporarily mollified the Austrians by handing over the Veneto to them (even though the Venetian Republic was still a neutral state), then waited for a pretext to polish off the Republic. Just three days later the Venetians duly provided him with one, by attacking a French naval patrol off the Lido. "I will have no more Inquisitors. I will have no more Senate; I shall be an Attila to the state of Venice," Bonaparte proclaimed; war was declared on Venice, and on May 9 an ultimatum was sent to the city's government, demanding the dissolution of its constitution.

On Friday, **May 12, 1797** the Maggior Consiglio met for the last time. By 512 votes to twenty, with five abstentions, the Council voted to accede to Napoleon's demands; the last doge of Venice, **Lodovico Manin**, handed to his valet the linen cap worn beneath the ducal crown, saying – "Take it, I shall not be needing it again." The Venetian Republic was dead.

The nineteenth century

Within days a provisional democratic council had been formed and there were French troops in the city, many of them occupied with stripping the place of its art treasures and shipping them off to Paris. On this occasion, the French didn't stay long, because in the **Treaty of Campo Formio**, signed in October, Napoleon relinquished Venice to the Austrians. The French were soon back, though – in **1805** Napoleon joined the city to his Kingdom of Italy, and it stayed under French domination until the aftermath of Waterloo, ten years later. It then passed back to the Austrians again, and remained a Habsburg province for the next half-century, the only break in Austrian rule coming with the **revolt of March 1848**, when the city was reinstituted as a republic under the leadership of **Daniele**

1630	1669	1718
Another outbreak of plague hits Venice	Crete, formerly a Venetian possession, falls to the Turks	The Treaty of Passarowitz reduces Venice's Mediterranean territories to the Ionian islands and the Dalmatian coast

Manin. The rebellion, which ignited uprisings all over the Veneto, lasted until **August 1849**, when a combination of starvation, disease and bombardment forced the Venetians to surrender. Liberation finally arrived in the wake of Prussia's defeat of the Austrians at Sadowa in **1866**. Soon afterwards, Venice was absorbed into the Kingdom of United Italy.

In many respects the Austrians were better for Venice than the French had been. Although the French initiated modernization schemes such as the creation of public gardens and the cemetery of San Michele, not all of the fifty or so religious buildings and forty palaces that they demolished were destroyed for good reason; in addition to which, they also wrecked the shipyards and confiscated hundreds of works of art. The Austrians' urban improvements were more benign; they filled in some of the more unhygienic canals (the origin of the *rio terrà*), built a rail link with the mainland and undertook two major, albeit controversial, restoration projects – the Fondaco dei Turchi and the church of Santi Maria e Donato on Murano.

Venice went through most of the nineteenth century in a state of destitution. There were no more government jobs to provide a source of income, and Trieste was the Austrians' preferred port on the Adriatic. By 1820 about one quarter of its population had been reduced to begging. Families that had once been among the city's wealthiest were obliged to sell their most treasured possessions; the Barbarigo family sold seventeen paintings by Titian to the tsar, for example. Later in the century, even the churches were selling their property to pay for their upkeep. It's been calculated that of the moveable works of art that were to be found in Venice at the fall of the Republic, only four percent remains.

Manufacturing activity within the city revived towards the end of the nineteenth century; there were flour mills on Giudecca, glass factories on Murano, lace workshops on Burano. The opening of the Suez Canal in 1869 brought a muted revival to the Arsenale docks. Already, though, **tourism** had emerged as the main area of economic expansion, with the development of the **Lido** as Europe's most fashionable resort. It was the need for a more substantial economic base than bathing huts, hotels and a few pockets of industrial production that led, in the wake of World War I, to the development of the industrial complex on the marshland across the lagoon from Venice, at **Porto Marghera**.

The growth of Mestre-Marghera

As recently as 1913 the Baedeker guide could describe Venice as a "shipbuilding, cotton spinning and iron working centre", but by the end of World War I Venice was finished as a maritime centre. Battleships had been built in the Arsenale, but the proximity of enemy forces persuaded the navy to dismantle the docks in 1917 and switch its yards to Genoa and Naples. The new port of **Marghera** was not a shipyard but a processing and refining centre to which raw materials would be brought by sea. In 1933 a **road link** was built to carry the workforce between Venice and the steadily expanding port, whose progress was of special concern to Mussolini's government. (Venice was the second city in Italy in which organized Fascism appeared; as early as 1919 the local newspaper published an appeal for the formation of Fascist squads.) After World War II (from which Venice emerged undamaged) Marghera's growth accelerated even more rapidly. The consequences were not those that had been predicted.

1797	1815	1848–49
Napoleon takes Venice; the Venetian Republic ceases to exist	After Napoleon's defeat at Waterloo, Venice comes under Austrian rule	Led by Daniele Manin, Venice rebels against the Austrians, who reassert control the following year

What happened was that the factory workers of Marghera, instead of commuting each day from Venice, simply decamped to the mainland. Housing in Marghera's neighbour, **Mestre**, is drier, roomier and cheaper to maintain than the apartments in Venice, and as a result the population of **Mestre-Marghera** (which is part of the *comune* of Venice) is today more than three times that of the historic centre of Venice, which is now less than 30,000, or just under 55,000 if you count Murano, Burano, the Lido and the other lagoon islands. And the population is falling rapidly; from 1994 to 2004 it shrank annually by an average of 800, but with the death rate now more than double the birth rate, the decline is accelerating. Apart from polluting the environment of the lagoon, Mestre has siphoned so many people of working age from the islands that the average age of Venice's population is now the highest of any major European city, with around 40 percent of its inhabitants over 65. Moreover, the percentage of native Venetians in the city is declining rapidly. When a flat is sold in Venice, it's much likelier that the buyer will be a non-Venetian than a native. And if a Venetian does buy the property, it's probable that it's with a view to renting it out to tourists.

Venice today

Each year Venice has around 30 million tourist "presences" – a figure representing the total number of days that its 7 million visitors spend in the city. (In other words, if you're in Venice for 3 days, you clock up 3 presences.) Around half these people don't even stay for one night, and thus contribute almost nothing to the city's economy. It's hardly surprising that many think it's just a matter of time before the town hall charges some sort of admission fee – in 2018 turnstiles were installed for a while near the train station to regulate the flow of pedestrians into the city, an action that some think will prove to be a harbinger of things to come. With much of the central government subsidy being diverted directly into the flood barrier, something has to be done to pay for the maintenance of the city.

While the city is certainly feeling the effects of tourism, the city is dependent on its tourists: tourism generates more than seventy percent of the city's income, through the innumerable restaurants and hotels (the number of hotel beds is increasing by about 2000 per year), and the 500-plus souvenir shops (whereas only half a dozen plumbers are registered in Venice). Every year proposals are put forward to break this dependency. A science park, a national library, a marine technology centre – all have been suggested as projects that could give Venice a more active role in twenty-first-century Italy, and all have come to nothing.

Venice in crisis

Some have proposed that efforts should be concentrated on furthering the city's reputation for crafts and restoration work – a good idea, but one that received a setback when the European Centre for the Training of Craftspeople was not permitted to extend its occupancy of the island of San Servolo. Others see the internet and global information technologies as offering an opportunity for Venice to remake itself. One person who has championed this notion is **Massimo Cacciari**, professor of philosophy at the University of Venice and mayor of the city from 1993 to 2000 and 2005 to 2010. As Cacciari sees it, Venice's best hope lies in its being classified as an area of special

1866	1895	1917	1933
Venice is absorbed into the Kingdom of Italy	The first Venice Biennale is held	The navy dismantles its dockyards in the Arsenale	A road link is built between Venice and Mestre, on the mainland; Mestre's population quickly expands, as Venice's falls

economic need by the European Union, which would give it access to funds for major infrastructure repairs and improvements, such as the laying of fibre-optic cables in tandem with the dredging of canals.

In an attempt to tackle the problem of depopulation, Cacciari tried to get the municipality and conservation groups to apply themselves to the restoration of old houses rather than old churches and other such monuments, so that the historic centre could provide housing at prices comparable with those in Mestre. In the last fifteen years or so there has been a notable increase in the number of new housing projects in the historic centre – a stroll around La Giudecca, for example, will reveal numerous signs of regeneration. But there's little sign of the city creating new economic foundations for itself: whenever a major property is sold in Venice it's nearly always destined to become a hotel.

Furthermore, in recent years the town hall has launched a spate of ill-considered and hideously expensive infrastructure projects, such as a new marina at San Nicolò, which has seen eight million euros squandered on legal preliminaries. More than 200 million euros have been spent on a tramline to Mestre that has proved to be unreliable and doesn't meet any obvious need. Worst of all, there's the scandal of the flood barrier (see page 343).

Some opponents of the barrier alleged from the start that the scheme would be a gigantic palm-greasing exercise, and their fears seemed justified when, in the summer of 2014, officers of the financial police raided 140 offices in various parts of the country, having spent three years investigating the alleged rigging of contracts for the project. Among those arrested were Giovanni Mazzacurati, formerly the head of Consorzio Venezia Nuova (the consortium in charge of the construction), and Giorgio Orsoni, the incumbent mayor of Venice. Of the €5.6 billion funnelled into the barrier, it has been estimated that as much as one billion has gone astray in a labyrinth of corruption.

In early 2015 it was disclosed that the town hall had a shortfall of €56 million in its annual operating budget, and debts totalling more than 400 million. Cuts in various services have reduced the yearly shortfall to about €30 million, but it's not apparent to anyone how that gap might be filled. Although tourists spend a lot of money on food and accommodation (it's estimated that during the ten days of Carnevale alone, some €40 million are spent in Venice), not enough of that money filters through to the city's administrators via taxes, and even if taxes were paid scrupulously, it still wouldn't be anything like enough to maintain this fragile and extraordinary city. The current mayor, Luigi Brugnaro (the first mayor of Venice to have been born on the mainland), is a vocal champion of the huge cruise ships that are now so controversial in Venice (see page 191), and has done little to persuade the residents of the *centro storico* that he sees any future for the city other than as a high-culture resort.

1988	2012	2014	2018
Construction of the flood barrier begins	Population of the Venetian lagoon islands falls below 60,000; in 1945 it had been 170,000	Venice's mayor is arrested in connection with financial corruption and the flood barrier project	Population of Venice's *centro storico* falls below 55,000

Venetian painting and sculpture

After just a day in Venice you notice that the light is softer than that on the mainland and changes more during the course of a day. Reflecting off the water and the white stone facades, it gives shifting impressions of places that would otherwise be shadowed, and adds shimmering highlights to solid brickwork. In view of the specific qualities of Venetian light, it's scarcely surprising that the city's painters emphasized colour and texture rather than structure and perspective. The political and social peculiarities of Venice were equally influential on the development of its art, as will become apparent in the following thumbnail account.

Byzantine Venice

The close political and commercial ties between the early Venetian state and the Byzantine Empire (see the "History" section) led to a steady exchange of works of art between the two, and to the creation of the most important work of art from that period – the **Pala d'Oro** on the high altar of the Basilica di San Marco. Begun as a collaboration between Venetian and Byzantine craftsmen, it epitomizes the Venetian taste for elaborate decoration and creates the impression of a complex content unified by a dazzlingly rich surface. The *Pala* was later expanded with panels stolen from Constantinople during the sack of 1204, a wholesale plundering which provided Venice with a hoard of artefacts that was to nourish its craftsmen and artists for centuries.

It is notable that the earliest Venetian painter of renown, **Paolo Veneziano** (working from the 1330s to at least 1358), shows far stronger affinities with Byzantine work than with the frescoes created by Giotto at the start of the century in nearby Padua. He generally employs a flat, gold background and symmetrical arrangements of symbolic figures, rather than attempting a more emotional representation of individuals. Two paintings in the Accademia show these characteristics: a *Madonna and Child Enthroned* and a polyptych that achieves the same overall effect as that of the Pala d'Oro – and indeed it was he who was commissioned to paint the **cover of the Pala d'Oro**, now in San Marco's museum. A work believed to be by Paolo Veneziano has recently been revealed during restoration of an altarpiece in the church of San Zaccaria.

The first room of the Accademia is full of work displaying this indebtedness to Byzantine art, and Byzantium remained a living influence in the city up to the seventeenth and eighteenth centuries, sustained in part by the influx of refugees following the **fall of Constantinople** in 1453. The neo-Byzantine *Madoneri* (the main school of the Greek community) are represented in the **Museo Dipinti Sacri Bizantini**, where the paintings show a complete indifference to the post-Renaissance cult of the artist and to notions of aesthetic novelty. The young Cretan **El Greco** (1545–1614) worked with the *Madoneri* for a while, before setting out for fame and fortune in Spain.

Gothic painting and sculpture

Deemed to be relics of a barbaric age, a huge number of Gothic paintings and sculptures were destroyed in the seventeenth and eighteenth centuries. The reinstatement of the Gothic is in large part due to the determination of John Ruskin, whose preoccupation was the Gothic architecture and sculpture of Venice. His meticulous work on **Santi Giovanni e Paolo**, mapping the change from Gothic to Renaissance through a study of the **funerary sculpture**, is still a useful analysis.

Santi Giovanni e Paolo's main apse contains the **tomb of Doge Michele Morosini** (d.1382), described by Ruskin as "the richest monument of the Gothic period in Venice", although its figures (apart from those at the head and foot of the doge) have an awkward, un-Gothic stiffness. More interesting sculpturally is the **tomb of Doge Marco Corner** (d.1368) opposite, which was carved in the workshop of the non-Venetian **Nino Pisano**. Slightly later is San Marco's **rood screen**, by the two brothers **Pietro Paolo and Jacobello Dalle Masegne**, who made a study of the work of Pisano and northern European Gothic sculpture. The other high points of Gothic sculpture in Venice are also architecturally related – the **Palazzo Ducale's capitals**, **corner sculptures** and **Porta della Carta** (though the main figures on the Porta are nineteenth-century replicas of fifteenth-century originals).

Paolo Veneziano's unrelated namesake, **Lorenzo Veneziano** (working 1356–72), marries a distinctly Gothic element to the Byzantine elements in Venetian painting. The large polyptych in the Accademia is a fine example of his work, showing a roundedness in the face and hands and in the fall of the drapery, and a sinuousness of pose in the figures that suggests the influence of Gothic painters such as Simone Martini of Siena.

Around 1409 **Gentile de Fabriano**, the exemplar of the style known as **International Gothic**, frescoed parts of the Palazzo Ducale with the help of his pupil **Pisanello**. These frescoes are all now destroyed, and the nearest example of Pisanello's work is his *St George* (1438–42) in Verona's church of Sant'Anastasia. Even in this one piece it's possible to see what the Venetians would have found congenial in his art: chiefly an all-over patterning that ties the content of the painting to the picture plane and eschews the illusion of receding space.

The work of Gentile and Pisanello was most closely studied in Venice by **Michele Giambono** (working 1420–62), represented in the Accademia by a *Coronation of the Madonna in Paradise* (1447) and in the church of San Trovaso by *St Chrysogonus* (c.1450). These claustrophobic paintings are of the same date as Padua's frescoes by Mantegna and sculptures by Donatello – Giambono and others in Venice were happily working in a sophisticated High Gothic style at a time when the Renaissance was elsewhere into its maturity.

Early Renaissance painting

Petrarch, who lived in Venice in the 1360s, described the Republic as "a world apart", and nothing illustrates this insularity better than the reception of Renaissance ideas in the city. Venetians were chary of overemphasizing the individual, a tendency implicit in the one-point perspective of Renaissance painting; in addition, the use of abstract mathematical formulas in the depiction of form was alien to the pragmatic Venetian temperament. When the principles of the Florentine Renaissance did belatedly filter into the art of Venice, they were transformed into a way of seeing that was uniquely Venetian.

The Vivarini family

Key figures in this period of absorption were the **Vivarini** family – **Antonio** (c.1419–80), his brother **Bartolomeo** (c.1430–91) and son **Alvise** (c.1445–1505). Antonio's work, though still part of the Gothic tradition, marks a shift away from it, with his more angular line and construction of pictorial spaces consistent with the rules of one-point perspective – as in the *Madonna and Child* triptych in the Accademia, painted in collaboration with Giovanni d'Alemagna. A more humanistic temperament is embodied in the paintings of **Alvise**, manifested less through his depiction of space than through his representation of people. He individualizes his figures, giving an emotional charge to narratives which had to that point functioned symbolically. The *St Clare* in the Accademia is an excellent example of his work, establishing an unprecedentedly intimate contact between the saint and the viewer.

The Bellini family and Carpaccio

The pre-eminent artistic dynasty of this transitional period was that of **Jacopo Bellini** (c.1400–70), once a pupil of Gentile da Fabriano, and his sons **Gentile** (c.1429–1507) and **Giovanni** (c.1430–1516). Jacopo suffered from the anti-Gothic zealotry of later years, and his two major cycles of paintings – at the Scuola di San Marco and the Scuola di San Giovanni Evangelista – were destroyed. From descriptions of these works, it would appear that the two *Madonna*s in the Accademia are rather restrained in their decoration; other pieces by him can be seen in the Museo Correr.

Giovanni is the one whom people mean when they refer simply to "Bellini". In the Accademia he's represented by a number of *Madonna*s, a series of allegorical panels and a couple of large altarpieces. Other works around Venice include altarpieces in San Zaccaria, San Pietro (Murano), the Frari and Santi Giovanni e Paolo. In the majority of these paintings the attention is concentrated on the foreground, where the arrangement of the figures or a device such as a screen or throne turns the background into another plane parallel to the surface, rather than a receding landscape. That this was a conscious choice which had nothing to do with his perspectival skills is demonstrated by the **San Giobbe altarpiece** (in the Accademia), in which a meticulously worked-out illusionistic space would have suggested the presence of an extra chapel. A fundamental humanism pervades much of Giovanni's output – although his *Madonna*s show an idealized version of motherhood, each possesses an immediacy which suggests to the viewer that this ideal could be attainable.

Meanwhile, **Gentile** was pursuing a form of painting that was also a specifically Venetian Renaissance phenomenon – the *istoria* or narrative painting cycle. At least ten of these were commissioned by public bodies between around 1475 and 1525; the three remaining cycles in Venice are the *Miracles of the Relic of the True Cross* (Accademia), by five artists including Gentile and **Carpaccio**, and the *St Ursula* cycle (Accademia) and the *St George and St Jerome* cycle (Scuola di San Giorgio degli Schiavoni), which are both by Carpaccio. To the modern observer the story line of the *Relic* and *St Ursula* cycles in particular can seem to be naive pretexts for precise renditions of the pageant of Venetian social life and a wealth of domestic minutiae. The details of the paintings were not mere incidentals to the narrative, however – a person hanging out washing or mending a roof would have been perceived as an enhancement of the physical reality of the miracle, and not as a distraction from the central event.

High Renaissance painting

While these narrative cycles were being produced Giovanni Bellini was beginning to experiment with oil paint, which was soon to displace tempera (pigment in egg yolk) as the preferred medium. Whereas tempera had to be applied in layers, the long drying time of oil allowed colours to be mixed and softened, while its thick consistency enabled artists to simulate the texture of the objects depicted. Close examination of later paintings by Bellini shows he used his fingers to merge colours and soften light, and two of his young assistants at the time – **Giorgione** and **Titian** – were to explore even further the potential of the new medium, developing a specifically Venetian High Renaissance style.

Giorgione

Giorgione (1475–1510) seems custom-built for myth: little is known about him other than that he was tall and handsome and he died young (possibly of plague). The handful of enigmatic works he created were innovative in their imaginative self-sufficiency – for instance, the Venetian collector Michiel, writing in 1530, was unable to say precisely what was the subject of *The Tempest* (Accademia), perhaps Giorgione's most famous image. His only altarpiece, still in the cathedral at Castelfranco (his home town), isolates the Madonna and the two saints from each other by enthroning the Madonna against a landscape while the attendant saints stand against a man-made background. Despite the serenity of the individual figures, the painting instils in the viewer a disquieting sense of elusiveness.

Titian

Given his long life and huge output, **Titian** (c.1485–1576) is very badly represented in his home town: a *Presentation in the Temple*, a *Pietà* left unfinished at his death and a couple of minor works in the Accademia; a handful in the Salute; the *Assumption* and *Pésaro Altarpiece* in the Frari – and that's more or less it. (Napoleon made off with a good crop of Titians, including a *Venus* which he hung in his tent; the Louvre now has a fine collection.)

Titian, like Giorgione, used the qualities of oils to evoke a diffuse light and soften contours – in contrast with the contemporaneous art of Rome, the city of Michelangelo, where the emphasis was on the solidity and sculptural aspects of the objects depicted. Artists in Florence were answerable to an imperious ruling family; in Rome they had to comply with the wishes of successive popes; but Titian's success was so great that he could virtually pick and choose from a host of clients from all over the continent, and the diversity of works he produced – portraits, allegories, devotional paintings, mythologies – remains unsurpassed in Western art. His technical range is as impressive as the range of subject matter; the earliest works are highly polished and precisely drawn, but in the later pieces he tested the possibilities of oil paint to their limit, using his bare hands to scrape the canvas and add great gobbets of paint (see the Accademia *Pietà*).

Del Piombo, Palma il Vecchio and Lotto

Giorgionesque is an adjective used to describe a number of early sixteenth-century Venetian painters, in reference to the enrichment of colour popular at the time and to the increasingly oblique and suggestive approach to content. **Sebastiano del Piombo**, who studied under Giovanni Bellini with Titian and Giorgione, before moving to Rome in 1611, is one of the artists to whom the term is applied; his altarpiece of **San Giovanni Crisostomo** in the eponymous church is best work still in Venice. Another is **Palma il Vecchio** (1480–1528); although he was sometimes frivolous in a way that Giorgione and Titian rarely were, his strongest work in Venice is a redoubtable *St Barbara* in Santa Maria Formosa. The most interesting painter of this period and type is **Lorenzo Lotto** (c.1480–1556), represented in the Accademia by the psychologically acute *Portrait of a Young Man*. The rivalries of other painters eventually drove Lotto from Venice, and it's not too fanciful to see a reflection of the artist's anxieties in his restless, wistful paintings.

Tintoretto

Born three years after Bellini's death and nine years after that of Giorgione, **Tintoretto** (1519–94) grew up during the period in which the ascendancy of Titian became established. Princes were sending agents to Venice to buy the latest Titian, no matter what the subject, and every visiting dignitary would want to be painted by him. Titian's exploratory attitude to paint and the increasing Venetian receptivity to individual style were both exploited by the energetic and competitive younger artist. The painting that made his reputation, the *Miracle of the Slave* (Accademia; 1548), shows how he learned from Titian's experiments and distanced himself from them. Tintoretto's palette is as rich as Titian's, but is aggressively vivid rather than sensuous, and uses far stronger lighting. And while Titian is concerned with the inner drama of an event, Tintoretto's attention is given to the drama of gesture.

Tintoretto's dynamic style was not universally acclaimed. Pietro Aretino, Titian's close friend and most vociferous champion, disparaged the speed and relative carelessness of Tintoretto's technique, and one member of the Scuola di San Rocco said he would give his money towards the decoration of the *scuola*'s building as long as Tintoretto was not commissioned. He didn't get his way, and the San Rocco cycle is the most comprehensive collection of paintings by the artist. Dramatic perspectival effects, bizarre juxtapositions of images and extraordinarily fluid brushwork here make the substantial world seem otherworldly – the converse of the earlier *istorie* cycles.

Veronese

In contrast, the art of **Paolo Veronese** (1528–88), who moved to Venice from Verona in his twenties, conveys worldly harmony rather than spiritual turbulence. This is particularly evident in his work for architectural settings (San Sebastiano in Venice and the Villa Barbaro at Masèr), where he constructed logical spaces that complement the form of the buildings. More urbane than Tintoretto, he nonetheless attracted controversy; in his *Christ in the House of Levi* (Accademia) the naturalistic representation of German soldiers was interpreted as a gesture of support for Protestantism. Veronese's response to his accusers revealed a lot about the changing attitude towards the status of the artist; claiming licence to depict what he wanted, he simply changed the title of the work from *The Last Supper* to the title by which it's now known.

Renaissance sculpture

Venetian **sculpture** in the Renaissance was conditioned by the society's ingrained aversion to the over-glorification of the individual and by the specific restrictions of the city's landscape. Freestanding monumental work of the sort that was being commissioned all over Italy is conspicuous by its absence. The exception to prove the rule, the **monument to Colleoni**, was made by the Florentine artist **Verrocchio**. Venetian sculptors worked mainly to decorate tombs or the walls of churches, and up to the late Renaissance no clear distinction was made between sculptors, masons and architects. Beyond the Renaissance, sculpture was generally commissioned as part of an architectural project, and it's usually futile to try to disentangle the sculpture from its architectural function.

Pietro Lombardo (c.1438–1515) was born in Cremona and went to Rome before arriving in Venice around 1460. His development can be charted in the church of Santi Giovanni e Paolo; his first major monument, the **tomb of Doge Pasquale Malipiero**, is pictorially flat and smothered with carved decoration, but the **monument to Doge Pietro Mocenigo**, with its classicized architectural elements and figures, is a fully Renaissance piece. In true Venetian style the latter glorifies the State through the man, rather than stressing his individual salvation – the image of Christ is easily overlooked. Pietro's sons **Antonio** (c.1458–1516) and **Tullio** (c.1460–1532) were also sculptors and assisted him on the Mocenigo monument. Tullio's independent work is less pictorial; his **monument to Doge Andrea Vendramin** (also in Santi Giovanni e Paolo) is a complex architectural evocation of a Roman triumphal arch, though again the whole is encrusted with decorative figures.

Jacopo Sansovino, who went on to become the Republic's principal architect, was known as a sculptor when he arrived in Venice from Rome in 1527. More of a classicist than his predecessors, he nonetheless produced work remarkably in tune with Venetian sensibilities – his figures on the logetta of the Campanile, for example, animate the surface of the building rather than draw attention to themselves. **Alessandro Vittoria** was the major sculptor of the middle and later part of the century; originally a member of Sansovino's workshop, Vittoria developed a more rhetorical style, well demonstrated in the figures of St Jerome in the Frari and Santi Giovanni e Paolo.

The Baroque period

The High Baroque style in painting and sculpture was largely a Roman phenomenon and the Venetians, whose distrust of Rome led in 1606 to a papal interdict, remained largely untouched by it. Suitably enough, the only Venetian interior that relates to Roman Baroque is the Jesuit church, the **Gesuiti**.

After the hyper-productive **Palma il Giovane**, who seems to have contributed something to the majority of the city's church interiors, it was up to foreign painters – **Johann Lys**, for instance – to keep painting alive in the city. Much the same is true of sculpture; the Venetian **Baldassare Longhena** early in his career turned from sculpture to architecture, leaving the field to the Bolognese **Giuseppe Mazza** (bronze reliefs in Santi Giovanni e Paolo) and the Flemish **Juste Le Court** (high altar of the Salute), although Le Court's Venetian pupil **Orazio Marinelli** (portrait busts in the Querini-Stampalia) did achieve a measure of celebrity. A particularly successful artist towards the end of the seventeenth century was **Andrea Brustolon** of Belluno, best known for his sculptural furniture (Ca' Rezzonico).

The eighteenth century

The last efflorescence of Venetian art began around the start of the eighteenth century, as Venice was degenerating into the playground of Europe. The highly illusionistic decorative paintings of **Giambattista Piazzetta** (1682–1752) mark the first step and foreshadow the work of **Giambattista Tiepolo** (1696–1777), whose ever-lightening colours and elegant, slightly disdainful Madonnas typified the sensuous but melancholy climate of the declining Republic. There's a similarity of mood to most of Tiepolo's work – from the dizzying trompe l'oeil ceiling painted in the Ca' Rezzonico to celebrate a marriage, to the airy *Virgin in Glory* painted for the Carmini.

Another major figure of the period was **Rosalba Carriera** (1675–1758), the first artist to use pastel as a medium in its own right. She was known chiefly as a portraitist, and the Ca' Rezzonico and the Accademia both contain a fine selection of her work – the latter featuring a *Self-Portrait in Old Age* which expresses a melancholy temperament usually suppressed from her pictures. (Incidentally, Carriera was not Venice's only woman artist: Marietta Robusti, Tintoretto's daughter, was known as a fine portraitist, and Carriera's contemporary Giulia Lama has a *Judith and Holofernes* on display in the Accademia.)

By this time, Venetian art was being siphoned out of the city in large quantities, with people such as the English consul Joseph Smith sending pictures home by the crateful. Aristocrats on the Grand Tour were particularly interested in topographical work – kind of upmarket postcards – and in this area the pre-eminent artist was **Canaletto** (1695–1768), whose work was copied and engraved to make further saleable items. Don't be misled into believing he showed the "real" Venice – he idealized the city, changing spatial arrangements in order to suit a harmonious composition and sometimes even altering individual buildings. Canaletto's work in Venice is as sparse as Titian's – there's only one painting by him in the Accademia and a couple in Ca' Rezzonico.

More sombre is the work of **Francesco Guardi** (1712–93), whose images of the lagoon and imaginary architectural scenes are frequently swathed in atmospheric mist and dotted with a few prophetic ruins. Genre painters were also popular at this time, none more so than **Pietro Longhi** (1708–85), whose wonderful illustrations of Venetian life (painted with a technique that is at best adequate) can also be seen in the Accademia and the Ca' Rezzonico. Longhi's production line was as busy as Canaletto's, as his workshop churned out copies of his most popular paintings to meet demand.

The last word on the painting of the Venetian Republic should be devoted to **Giandomenico Tiepolo** (1727–1804), seen at his best in the cycle of frescoes painted for his home and now installed in the Ca' Rezzonico. Freed from the whims of clients, he produced here a series of images that can with hindsight be seen as symbolic of the end of an era, with Sunday crowds gawping at a peepshow and clowns frittering away their time flirting and playing.

To the present day

After the fall of the Republic, art in Venice became the domain of outsiders. **Turner**, who visited the city three times, was its supreme painter in the nineteenth century, but as Ruskin said, you'd only have to stay in Venice for a few days to learn about it what Turner had learnt. **Whistler**, **Monet** and **Sargent** were among other visitors. The only Venetian nineteenth-century artist of note is **Frederico Zandomeneghi** (1841–1917), and he decamped for Paris in 1874 to join the Impressionists' circle.

The story of art in Venice since then is no more cheerful. The internationally known artists who stayed as guests of **Peggy Guggenheim** between 1949 and 1979 came and left without making an impact on its cultural life. Every two years the **Biennale** brings in the hotshots of the international art world, but does little to help young Venetian artists. The few Italian artists who have worked here have not exactly galvanized the city; the painter **Lucio Fontana** lived in Venice in the 1950s, and **Emilio Vedova** – a founder member of the avant-garde groups *Fronte Nuovo* and *Gruppo degli Otto* – taught at the Accademia until his death in the mid-1980s.

Venetian architecture

This is just a brief chronology of Venetian architectural styles, intended simply as a means of giving some sense of order to the city's jumble of buildings. For more detailed accounts, refer to the "Books" section.

Byzantine Venice

Although settlement of the lagoon began as far back as the fifth century, no building has survived intact from earlier than the start of the eleventh century. The very first houses raised on the mud flats were "built like birds' nests, half on sea and half on land…the solidity of the earth…secured only by wattle-work", according to a letter written in 523 by a Roman official named Cassiodorus. Many of the earliest shelters were only temporary, constructed as refuges from the barbarian hordes of the mainland and abandoned as soon as the threat had receded, but with the Lombard invasions of the second half of the sixth century, communities uprooted from northern Italy began to construct more durable buildings on the islands. Some of the materials for these buildings were scavenged from Roman temples and dwellings, and a few of these fragments – used over and over again in succeeding centuries – can still be seen embedded in the walls of some of Venice's oldest structures. The great majority of the lagoon's buildings were still made of wood, however, and of these nothing is left.

Public buildings

From the twelfth century onwards the houses of the richest families were made from brick and stone, raised on foundations that rested on wooden piles hammered deep into the impacted clay and sand of the islands (a technique that has remained basically unchanged ever since). Prior to this period, such materials were reserved for the most important public buildings, and so it is that the **oldest structure in the lagoon** is a church – the **cathedral at Torcello**. Founded in 639 but altered in 864 and again, comprehensively, in **1008**, it takes its form from such early Christian basilicas as Sant'Apollinare in Ravenna. The prototypes of the Western Empire influenced other lagoon churches either founded or rebuilt in the eleventh and twelfth centuries – for example **Sant'Eufemia** on Giudecca, **Santi Maria e Donato** on Murano and **San Giovanni Decollato** and **San Nicolò dei Mendicoli** in central Venice – but the predominant cultural influence on the emergent city was **Byzantium**, on which the lagoon confederation was originally dependent.

Santa Fosca on Torcello and **San Giovanni di Rialto**, traditionally the oldest church in Venice, are Byzantine in their adherence to a Greek-cross plan, but the building in which the Byzantine ancestry of Venice is most completely displayed is the **Basilica di San Marco**. Like the cathedral of Torcello, San Marco was extensively rebuilt in the eleventh century, but the basic layout – an elongated version of the five-domed Greek-cross design of Constantinople's Church of the Apostles – didn't change much between the consecration of the first basilica in 832 and the completion of the final version in 1094. As much as its architectural form, the mosaic decoration of San Marco betrays the young city's Eastern affiliations – and it was in fact begun, as soon as the shell of the church was completed, by artists from Constantinople.

Domestic architecture

Byzantium has also left its mark on the **domestic architecture** of Venice, even though the oldest specimens still standing date from the late twelfth century or early thirteenth, by which time the political ties between the two cities had been severed. The high and rounded Byzantine arch can be seen in a number of Canal Grande palaces – the **Ca' da Mosto**, the **Donà** houses, the neighbouring **Palazzo Loredan** and **Palazzo Farsetti** and the **Fondaco dei Turchi**. All of these buildings have been altered greatly over the years, but paradoxically it's the one that's been most drastically reconstructed – the Fondaco dei Turchi – which bears the closest resemblance to the earliest merchants' houses. Descended from the Roman villas of the mainland, they had an arcade at water level to permit the unloading of cargo, a long gallery on the upper storey and lower towers at each end of the facade. Frequently they were embellished with relief panels (*paterae*) and insets of multicoloured marble – another Byzantine inheritance, and one that was to last, in modified form, for hundreds of years (for example in the predilection for heraldic devices on the fronts of houses).

Gothic Venice

Building land is scarce in Venice, and the consequent density of housing imposed certain restrictions on architectural inventiveness – ground plans had to make the fullest possible use of the available space (hence the rarity of internal courtyards and the uniformly flat facades) and elevations had to maximize the window areas, to make the most of the often limited natural light. Thus architectural evolution in the domestic buildings of Venice is to be observed not so much in the development of overall forms but rather in the mutations of surface detail, and in particular in the arches of the main facades. Nearly all the rich families of Venice derived their wealth from trade, and the predominant shipping lanes from Venice ran to the East – so it was inevitable that **Islamic features** would show through in Venetian architecture. As the thirteenth century progressed, the pure curve of the Byzantine arch first developed an upper peak and then grew into a type of ogival arch – as at the **Palazzo Falier** near Santi Apostoli, and the **Porta dei Fiori** on the north side of the Basilica. This Islamicized Byzantine shape was in turn influenced in the fourteenth century by contact with the Gothic style of the mainland, so producing a repertoire that was uniquely Venetian.

The masterpiece of Venetian Gothic is also the city's greatest civic structure – the **Palazzo Ducale**. Begun in 1340, possibly to designs by **Filippo Calendario**, the present building was extended in a second phase of work from 1423 onwards, culminating in the construction of the most elaborate Gothic edifice in Venice – the **Porta della Carta**, by **Giovanni and Bartolomeo Bon**.

Imitations and variations of the Palazzo Ducale's complex tracery can be seen all over the city, most strikingly in the **Ca' d'Oro**, begun by Giovanni Bon at much the same time as work began on the extension of the Palazzo Ducale. The Ca' d'Oro represents the apex of Gothic refinement in Venice's domestic architecture; for monumental grandeur, on the other hand, none can match the adjoining Gothic palaces on the Volta del Canal – the **Palazzi Giustinian** and the **Ca' Fóscari**.

Gothic churches

Ecclesiastical architecture in fourteenth- and fifteenth-century Venice is not as idiosyncratic as its secular counterpart – the religious communities who built the churches, affiliated to orders on the mainland, tended to follow the architectural conventions that had been established by those orders. In some of Venice's Gothic churches the old basilical plan prevailed over the cruciform (eg at **Madonna dell'Orto**), but the two most important churches of the period, the immense **Santi Giovanni e Paolo** (Dominican) and the **Frari** (Franciscan), display many of the basic features of contemporaneous churches in the Veneto: the Latin-cross plan, the pointed arches, the high nave with flanking aisles and the chapels leading off from the transepts. Yet even these churches have distinctively Venetian characteristics, such as the use of tie beams and the substitution of lath and plaster vaulting for vaults of stone – both necessary measures in a place with no bedrock for its foundations to rest on. In a few Gothic churches the builders capitalized on the availability of skilled naval carpenters to produce elegant and lightweight ceilings in the shape of an inverted **ship's keel** – for example at **Santo Stefano** and **San Giacomo dell'Orio**.

Early Renaissance

The complicated hybrid of Venetian Gothic remained the city's preferred style well into the second half of the fifteenth century, long after the classical precepts of Renaissance architecture had gained currency elsewhere in Italy. The late work of **Bartolomeo Bon** contains classical elements mixed with Gothic features (for example, the portal of **Santi Giovanni e Paolo** and the incomplete **Ca' del Duca**, both from c.1460), but the first architect in Venice to produce something that could be called a classical design was **Antonio Gambello**, with his land gate for the **Arsenale** (1460). Gambello was not a committed proponent of the new ideas, however, and had work on his church of **San Zaccaria** not been interrupted by his death in 1481, it would have resembled a northern European Gothic church more closely than any other in Venice.

In the 1470s another dynasty of stonemason-architects succeeded the Bon family as the leading builders in Venice – **Pietro Solari** and his sons **Antonio and Tullio**, otherwise known as the **Lombardi**. Having worked with followers of Donatello in Padua in the 1460s, Pietro Lombardo was familiar with the latest principles of Tuscan architecture, but the chief characteristics of his own work – the elaborately carved pilasters and friezes, and the inlaid marble panels of various shapes and sizes – are not so much architectonic as decorative. The chancel of **San Giobbe**, the courtyard screen of the **Scuola di San Giovanni Evangelista**, the tiny church of **Santa Maria dei Miracoli** and the facade of the **Scuola di San Marco** represent the best of the Lombardis' architecture. Over-ornate though many of their building projects were, their style was closely imitated by numerous Venetian architects; nobody is certain, for example, whether the **Palazzo Dario** (on the Canal Grande) was designed by Pietro Lombardo or one of his "Lombardesque" acolytes.

Antonio Rizzo, a contemporary of Pietro Lombardo, was similarly esteemed as both a sculptor and architect. After the fire of 1483, Rizzo was put in charge of the rebuilding of the entire **east wing of the Palazzo Ducale**, and it was he who designed the **Scala dei Giganti**, a work which displays a typically Venetian delight in heavy ornamentation.

Codussi and his successors

The most rigorous and inventive Venetian architect of the early Renaissance was the man who took over the design and supervision of San Zaccaria after the death of Gambello – **Mauro Codussi** (sometimes spelled Coducci). His first commission in the city, the church of **San Michele in Isola** (1469), is not purely classical – the huge lunette and inset roundels are Venetian idiosyncracies – but its proportions and clarity, and the use of classical detail to emphasize the structure of the building, entitle it to be known as the **first Renaissance church in Venice**. Codussi reintroduced the traditional Greek-cross plan in his other church designs (**Santa Maria Formosa** and **San Giovanni Crisostomo**), his impetus coming in part from a scholarly revival of interest in the culture of Byzantium and in part from the work of Renaissance theorists such as Alberti, whose *De Re Aedificatoria* proclaimed the superiority of centrally planned temples. In his secular buildings the influence of Alberti is even more pronounced, especially in his **Palazzo Vendramin-Calergi**, which is strongly reminiscent of Alberti's Palazzo Rucellai in Florence. Codussi was employed by the Venetian nobility, the *scuole* (he designed staircases for both the **Scuola di San Giovanni Evangelista** and the **Scuola di San Marco**) and the religious foundations, yet despite his pre-eminence it was only after archival research in the nineteenth century that he was identified as the author of all these buildings – a fact indicative of the difference between the status of the architect in Renaissance Florence and in Venice.

The economic effects of the War of the League of Cambrai limited the amount of building work in Venice at the start of the sixteenth century, but it was nonetheless a period of rapid transformation in the centre of the city; the **Campanile** of San Marco was completed, and the **Torre dell'Orologio** and **Procuratie Vecchie** were built – the last two being commenced to designs by Codussi. In the aftermath of serious fires, major projects were undertaken in the Rialto district as well – notably the **Fabbriche Vecchie** and the **Fondaco dei Tedeschi** – but the architects of the generation after Codussi (who died in 1504) were generally undistinguished. **Guglielmo dei Grigi** designed the **Palazzo dei Camerlenghi** at the foot of the Ponte di Rialto and went on to add the **Cappella Emiliana** to Codussi's San Michele in Isola. **Bartolomeo Bon the Younger** took over the supervision of the Procuratie Vecchie after Codussi's death, and began the **Scuola di San Rocco** in 1515 – a project that was completed by **Scarpagnino** (Antonio Abbondi), the man in charge of the rebuilding of the Rialto markets after the fire of 1514. **Giorgio Spavento**, described by the diarist Marin Sanudo as "a man of great genius", was the most talented architect of this period, and with **San Salvatore** he produced its best church design.

High Renaissance

The definitive classical authority for the architectural theorists of Renaissance Italy was **Vitruvius**, architect to the Emperor Augustus, and it was in Venice in 1511 that the first printed edition of his *De Architectura* was produced. However, the consistent application of classical models was not seen in Venice until after the sack of Rome by the imperial army in 1527. A large number of Roman artists then sought refuge in Venice, and it was with this influx that the advances of such figures as Raphael, Michelangelo and Bramante were absorbed into the practice of Venice's architects.

Sansovino and Sanmicheli

Of all the exiles, the one who made the greatest impact was **Jacopo Sansovino**. Despite his limited architectural experience – he was known mainly as a sculptor when he arrived in Venice – Sansovino was appointed Proto of San Marco on the death of Bartolomeo Bon in 1529, a position that made him the most powerful architect in the city, and which he was to hold for the next forty years. From 1537 onwards a group of buildings by Sansovino went up around the Piazzetta, completely changing the appearance of the area; the **Zecca** (Mint) was the first, then the **Loggetta** at the base of the Campanile and then the most celebrated of all his designs – the **Libreria Sansoviniana**. Showing a familiarity with the architecture of ancient Rome that was unprecedented in Venice, the Libreria is still unmistakeably Venetian in its wealth of surface detail, and the rest of Sansovino's buildings similarly effect a compromise between classical precision and Venetian convention. Thus his palace designs – the **Palazzo Dolfin-Manin** (1538) and **Palazzo Corner della Ca' Grande** (1545) – are clearly related to the houses of the Roman Renaissance, but perpetuate the traditional Venetian division of the facade into a central bay with symmetrically flanking windows. Though principally a secular architect, Sansovino did also design churches; the religious buildings by him that still stand are **San Francesco della Vigna**, **San Martino di Castello**, **San Giuliano** and the apse of **San Fantin**.

Of Sansovino's contemporaries, the only one of comparable stature was **Michele Sanmicheli**. More proficient as an engineer than Sansovino, he was employed early in his career by Pope Clement VII to improve the military defences of Parma and Piacenza, and in 1535 was taken on as Venice's military architect. The **Fortezza di Sant'Angelo** (1543), protecting the Lido entrance to the lagoon, was his largest public project, and in addition to this he built two of the most grandiose palaces in the city – the **Palazzo Corner Mocenigo** in San Polo (1545) and the **Palazzo Grimani** (c.1559) on the Canal Grande.

Palladio and Scamozzi

Andrea Palladio, Italy's most influential architect in the second half of the sixteenth century (indeed, one of the most influential architects of any epoch), was based in nearby Vicenza yet found it difficult to break into Venice's circle of patronage. In the 1550s his application for the position of Proto to the Salt Office (supervisor of public buildings) was turned down, and his project for the Palazzo Ducale's Scala d'Oro rejected; later schemes for the Ponte di Rialto and the rebuilding of the entire Palazzo Ducale were no more successful. He was never asked to undertake a private commission in the city. The facade of **San Pietro in Castello** was his first contract (eventually built in a much altered form), and it was the religious foundations that were to provide him with virtually all his subsequent work in Venice. Palladio's churches of **San Giorgio Maggiore** (1565) and the **Redentore** (1576) are the summit of Renaissance classicism in Venice; the scale on which they were composed, the restraint of their decoration, the stylistic unity of exterior and interior, the subtlety with which the successive spaces were combined, and the correctness of their quotations from the architecture of imperial Rome – all these factors distinguished them from all previous designs and established them as reference points for later churches.

Once Palladio's churches had been finished, the islands of San Giorgio Maggiore and Giudecca presented much the same face to the main part of the city as they do today. The work of his closest follower, **Vincenzo Scamozzi**, brought the landscape of the Piazza very close to its present-day state – it was Scamozzi who completed the Campanile end of the Libreria Sansoviniana and began the construction of the **Procuratie Nuove** in 1582. Another Venetian landmark, the **Ponte di Rialto**, was built at this time; its creator, **Antonio da Ponte**, was also in charge of the repair and redesign of the Palazzo Ducale after the fire of 1577, and designed the new **prisons** on the opposite bank of the Rio di Palazzo. The bridge connecting the prisons to the Palazzo Ducale – the **Ponte dei Sospiri** (Bridge of Sighs) – was the work of **Antonio Contino** (1600).

Baroque architecture

Although there are a few sixteenth-century Venetian buildings that could be described as proto-Baroque – **Alessandro Vittoria**'s **Palazzo Balbi** (1582), with its encrusted decoration and broken pediments, is one example – the classical idiom remained entrenched for some time as the stylistic orthodoxy in Venice, as is demonstrated by the appointment of the unadventurous **Bartolomeo Monopola** to complete the final stages of the **Palazzo Ducale** in the first decades of the seventeenth century. The colossal **Palazzo Pisani** at Santo Stefano, possibly by Monopola, is further evidence of the city's aesthetic conservatism.

It was not until the maturity of Venice's finest native architect, **Baldassare Longhena**, that the innovations of the Baroque made themselves fully felt. Longhena's early work – for example the **Palazzo Giustinian-Lolin** and the **Duomo** at **Chioggia** (both 1624) – continues the Palladianism of the previous century, but with his design for the votive church of **Santa Maria della Salute** (1631) he gave the city its first Baroque masterpiece. In its plan the Salute is indebted to Palladio's Redentore, but in its use of multiple vistas, and devices such as the huge volutes round the base of the dome, it introduces a dynamism that was completely alien to Palladio's architecture. In 1640 Longhena became the Proto of San Marco, and between then and his death in 1682 he occupied a position in Venetian architectural circles as commanding as Sansovino's had been. Among his major projects were the completion of the **Procuratie Nuove**, the addition of a grand staircase and library to the monastic complex of **San Giorgio Maggiore** and the design of two of the Canal Grande's most spectacular palaces – the **Ca' Pésaro** and the **Ca' Rezzonico**.

When compared to much of the work being produced in other parts of Italy at this time, Longhena's brand of Baroque was quite sober. Yet it was the chief exception in his output – the grotesque facade of the **Ospedaletto** – which proved in the short term to be especially influential. Its most direct descendant was **Alessandro Tremignon**'s facade for the church of **San Moisè** (1668), which is choked with sculpture by Heinrich

Meyring. **Giuseppe Sardi**'s church of **Santa Maria del Giglio** (1680) can also be traced back to the Ospedaletto, but on the other hand Sardi's work is equally redolent of the architecture of the sixteenth century – his facade for Scamozzi's **San Lazzaro dei Mendicanti** could be seen as a deliberate rejection of the excesses of the Baroque. His other prominent designs are the **Scuola di San Teodoro** and the facades of **San Salvatore** and **Santa Maria di Nazareth** (the Scalzi), all of them rather routine efforts.

The eighteenth century

The concerted reaction against Baroque began with the work of Sardi's nephew, **Domenico Rossi**. Rossi's facade for the church of **San Stae** (1709) is essentially a neo-Palladian design enlivened by the addition of some exuberant pieces of sculpture, and his rebuilding of the **Palazzo Corner della Regina** is closer to the palace projects of Sansovino than to such works as Longhena's nearby Ca' Pésaro. **Andrea Tirali**, Rossi's exact contemporary (1657–1737), was an even more faithful adherent to the principles of the sixteenth century – the portico he added to the church of **San Nicolò da Tolentino** is strictly classical, and his facade for **San Vitale** is a straight plagiarism of San Giorgio Maggiore. Another church of this period – **San Simeone Piccolo** – is one of the most conspicuous in Venice, standing as it does right opposite the train station. Designed in 1718 by **Giovanni Scalfarotto** (Rossi's son-in-law), its facade and plan are derived from the Pantheon, but the vertical exaggeration of its dome makes it closer in spirit to Longhena's Salute.

The most significant architect of the period was **Giorgio Massari** (1687–1766), whose church of the **Gesuati**, begun in 1726, combines Palladian forms (for example the facade and the arrangement of the interior bays) with understated Rococo details (the ceiling frames). His later church of the **Pietà**, based on Sansovino's destroyed Incurabili church, is more sober in its use of decoration, and his design for the last of the great palaces of the Canal Grande, the **Palazzo Grassi** (1748), is the severest of all his buildings.

The Palladian creed was kept alive in late eighteenth-century Venice through innumerable academic and polemical publications. Two of the leading figures in this movement were **Antonio Visentini** (1688–1782) and Scalfarotto's nephew, **Tommaso Temanza** (1705–89), both of whom taught architecture at the Accademia. Temanza was the more important architect, and his **Santa Maria Maddalena** was the first uncompromisingly Neoclassical building in Venice.

The nineteenth century

With the work of **Giannantonio Selva**, a pupil of Visentini and Temanza, Neoclassicism entered its most spare and fastidious phase. His first large scheme was **La Fenice** opera house (1790), where exterior adornment was reduced to the minimum necessary to signify the building's function and importance. Selva's career was undisturbed by the subsequent collapse of the Venetian Republic, and his other main works – the churches of **San Maurizio** (1806) and **Nome del Gesù** (1815) – were created under French rule.

During the second period of French occupation (1806–15) a large number of buildings were demolished to facilitate urban improvement schemes. Four churches were knocked down to make space for the **Giardini Pubblici**, for instance, and by the time the French were ejected by the Austrians a total of nearly fifty religious buildings had been demolished. The most celebrated loss was that of Sansovino's **San Geminiano**, pulled down in 1807 to make room for the construction of the **Ala Napoleonica**, a ballroom wing added to the Procuratie Nuove, which was then serving as a royal palace. In the 1830s the designer of the ballroom, **Lorenzo Santi**, went on to build the **Palazzetto Bucintoro** coffee house at the west end of the Giardinetti Reali (now the main tourist office), and the **Palazzo Patriarcale** alongside the Basilica.

Alterations to Venice's network of canals and streets, which had been started by the French with schemes such as the creation of **Via Garibaldi**, were accelerated under Austrian rule. Most of Venice's *rii terrà* (infilled canals) originated in the period of Austrian occupation, and a number of new bridges were constructed at this time too – including the ones at the **Accademia** and **Scalzi**, the first bridges to be put across the Canal Grande since the Ponte di Rialto. It was the Austrians who connected Venice by rail with the mainland (1846), and in 1860 they expanded the train station, demolishing Palladio's church of **Santa Lucia** in the process. And the first major **restoration projects** were carried out under Austrian supervision – at the **Fondaco dei Turchi**, at **Santi Maria e Donato** on **Murano** and on the north facade of **San Marco**.

Major town-planning schemes continued after Venice joined the Unified Kingdom of Italy. In the 1870s two wide thoroughfares were completed – the **Strada Nova** in Cannaregio and **Calle Larga XXII Marzo** between San Moisè and Santa Maria Zobenigo – and **Campo Manin** was opened up in 1871. The brief industrialization of central Venice in the late nineteenth century has left behind one prominent hulk – the **Mulino Stucky**, built on Giudecca in 1895. The hotels and middle-class housing developments of the **Lido** – which became a fashionable resort in this period – have outlived the city's industrial sites.

To the present

In 1933 Venice was joined by road to the mainland, and five years later the Rio Nuovo was cut from the recently created Piazzale Roma towards the Canal Grande. The chief buildings of the Fascist era are the **fire station** on the Rio di Ca' Fóscari (which continues the Rio Nuovo), and the **Palazzo del Casinò** and **Palazzo del Cinema** on the Lido. Few buildings worth a mention have been put up in Venice since then – the least objectionable are, perhaps, the **train station** (1954) and the **Cassa di Risparmio di Venezia** in Campo Manin, designed in 1964 by **Pier Luigi Nervi** and **Angelo Scattolin**. The density and antiquity of most of Venice's urban fabric makes intervention particularly problematic for the modern architect. Understandable Venetian resistance to new developments, hardened by such insensitive twentieth-century efforts as the extension to the **Hotel Bauer-Grünwald**, adds further difficulties, and accounts for the fact that two of the most interesting modern schemes, **Frank Lloyd Wright**'s Ca' Masieri and **Le Corbusier**'s plan for a civic hospital in Cannaregio, never left the drawing board. Though small items are occasionally added to the assortment box of architectural styles that is the **Biennale** site, major new schemes will always be rare; of the two big building contracts awarded in the late 1990s, one was for the reconstruction of a destroyed structure (**La Fenice**), and the other is for a site that will have no living occupants – David Chipperfield's extension to the **San Michele cemetery**. In the twenty-first century there has been just one major addition to the cityscape of central Venice – Santiago Calatrava's ill-starred **Ponte della Costituzione**, spanning the Canal Grande from the edge of Piazzale Roma (see page 164).

Conservation and restoration

In 1818 Byron published the fourth section of *Childe Harold's Pilgrimage*, in which is encapsulated the Romantic notion that if Venice isn't actually sinking, then it ought to be:

Venice, lost and won,
Her thirteen hundred years of freedom done
Sinks, like a sea-weed into whence she rose!

Ever since, it's been a commonplace that Venice is doomed to aquatic extinction. The city is threatened by water, by salt, by air pollution and by local subsidence, and faces massive problems of conservation and restoration. Over the past quarter-century the Italian government has set aside colossal amounts of money, under the terms of the so-called Special Laws for Venice, to underwrite projects ranging from schemes to restore single paintings through to grandiose plans to control the encroachments of the Adriatic. In addition to the intrinsic difficulties of each project, the major interventions prompt interminable arguments about the very purpose of restoration – should Venice be turned into even more of a museum piece, its buildings preserved in the aspic of contemporary restoration techniques, or should parts of the city be rebuilt, reintroducing industry and modern housing? On the one hand, Venice desperately needs the income from tourism, and on the other its population has plummeted since World War II and its houses are in such a state that around ninety percent of bathrooms still empty directly into the canals.

Flooding

On **November 4, 1966**, the waters of the Adriatic, already dangerously high after two successive high tides had been prevented from receding by gale-force southeasterly winds, were disturbed by an earth tremor. The resulting tidal wave breached Venice's *Murazzi* (the sea walls), and for the next 48 hours the sea level remained an average of almost 2m above the mean lagoon level – in other words, more than 1m above the pavement of the Piazza, the lowest point of the city. Venice was left with no power or telephone lines, and buildings were awash with filthy water, mud and oil from broken storage tanks.

Outside Venice, the flooding did not immediately provoke extreme concern, partly because floods in Venice were nothing new, and partly because attention was focused on the same-day disaster in Florence, where a flash flood killed several people and caused massive damage to numerous works of art. Nobody was hurt in the Venice flood and no artefacts were lost, but the photographs of water swirling through the doors of San Marco and around the courtyard of the Palazzo Ducale did highlight the perilous condition of the city. When floods almost as bad occurred in the following year, the international campaign to save Venice was already gathering strength, and similarly severe floods in 1979 and 1986 kept the situation in the public eye.

The causes of the flooding

Called the **acqua alta** (high water), the winter flooding of the city is caused by a combination of seasonal tides, fluctuations in atmospheric pressure in the Adriatic and persistent southeasterly winds, and has always been a feature of Venetian life. With a surface area of some 550 square kilometres, the Venetian lagoon is the largest in Italy, and with an average depth of just 1.2m this large body of water is very sensitive to the vagaries of the climate. In recent years, however, its sensitivity has increased markedly: the frequency of flooding increased markedly in the latter half of the last century, and between 2000 and 2013 there were eight highest-category floods (ie, at least 140cm above the mean), which is more than in the preceding fifty years. Though most of the dozens of *acque alte* that happen every year are less than one metre above the mean level, and less than 10 percent of the city is submerged during a one-metre flood, the statistics are nonetheless indicative of a relentless trend.

A rise in sea level has played a part in this, but the rise so far has been too small to account for the increase in the frequency and severity of flooding. The worsening situation would seem to be largely a local phenomenon related to recent changes in the balance of the lagoon.

Certainly the workings of the lagoon have been interfered with in an unprecedented way during the past century. The extraction of water and natural gas has caused some distortion of the underlying strata, and large areas of land have been reclaimed, for the airport and industrial sites on the periphery of the lagoon, and in central Venice itself – notably around the docks and the Tronchetto car parks. These reclamation schemes, combined with alterations to the lagoon's inlets and water channels to allow ships to reach the refineries of Marghera, have reduced the extent of the lagoon's mud flats and salt marshes by more than 60 percent since 1900. As a result, around 20 percent of the lagoon's plant species and 50 percent of its bird species have been lost during the past century. Leaving aside their function as a wildlife habitat, the marshes and mud flats play a crucial role in dissipating the energy of the incoming water, so the effect of their reduction has been to increase the destructiveness of the tides.

The barrier

That said, few would argue against the proposition that shifts in global weather conditions are making more of an impact with each passing year, and it's clear that global warming will be a significant factor in Venice's predicament in the coming decades. Most experts predict that the mean sea level will rise and the climate become more turbulent in this part of the Mediterranean, and it's this likelihood that led to the idea of installing a **tidal barrier** across the three entrances to the lagoon. This concept began to take shape in 1982, but it wasn't until November 1988 that the first component of the prototype was towed into place close to the Porto di Lido. Known locally as MOSE (an acronym for "Modulo Sperimentale Elettromecanico", the prototype's full title), and immediately nicknamed **Moisè** (Moses), after the Old Testament's great divider of the waters, it was assembled by the Consorzio Venezia Nuova, a consortium of engineering companies. Many years later, after input from the creators of London's Thames Barrier, MOSE reached its definitive form. It was to comprise 79 huge steel flaps, which would lie on the floor of the lagoon, forming a submerged barrage some 2km long in total; when the water rose to a dangerous level, air would be pumped into the flaps and the barrier would then float upright to protect the city.

The construction of the barrier

The original deadline for the completion of MOSE was 1995; come the deadline, there was little more to show than a forlorn segment of the barrier anchored off the Arsenale. At the end of 2000 the stabilization of the lagoon became a more urgent problem than ever. On **November 6**, as freakish rainfall continued over much of western Europe and whole regions of Italy were classified as disaster areas, Venice was inundated by the worst *acqua alta* since 1966. Two weeks later the *acqua alta* surged again to more than 120cm above the mean high-tide level – the fifth time the tide had passed the 110cm mark that winter. The Italian parliament duly took notice. In **April 2003**, more than twenty years after the first plan for MOSE was submitted to the government, Silvio Berlusconi attended a ceremony in Venice to mark the **start of work on the construction of the barrier**.

However, no sooner had Berlusconi been defeated in the **2006 general election** than the incoming centre-left government of Romano Prodi conducted an audit of every major infrastructure project in the country, and found that MOSE had massive budget deficit. Nonetheless, the Prodi government agreed that abandoning MOSE would be tantamount to signing the city's death warrant, and in **November 2006** it re-approved the project. Progress since then has been excruciatingly slow, in part because of the financial chicanery that was exposed in 2014 (see page 327), and partly because of a succession of technical fiascos.

In 2014 the *Nuova Venezia* newspaper published photographs that showed that the barrier's steel gates had become badly corroded by salt water and were encrusted with barnacles and mussels. It was not altogether clear why these issues had not been anticipated by the Consorzio, who had originally predicted that maintenance of the water gates would cost between 30 and 40 million euros every five years; after the photos appeared, it was suggested that this figure would turn out to be the annual expenditure. (It has been suggested that the Consorzio, having secured perpetual rights to maintain the barrier, would not be too bothered by its apparent accounting error.) There was more: for example, a lock constructed at Malomocco to allow ships to enter the lagoon whenever the gates are raised was found to be too tight for the biggest tankers – a miscalculation that will cost €20 million to correct. And, with terrible irony, it seems that the submerged gates have changed the flow of water into the lagoon, leading to a worsening of the *acqua alta*. Not only that: the concrete caissons that hold the gates in place are sinking into the seabed more quickly than any part of Venice itself. The barrier is now due to become operational in 2021; few Venetians believe it will ever work.

Pollution

A major objection to the barrier has been that it will further inhibit the cleansing effects of the tides, already diminished in parts of the lagoon by land reclamation. Twice-daily tidal movements and the activity of waste-digesting marine life were

OBJECTIONS TO THE BARRIER – AND ALTERNATIVE SCHEMES

As you see from graffiti in various parts of Venice, support for the barrier is by no means complete. Some objectors argue that in the event of a sudden tidal surge the barrier will simply not be strong enough to resist the push of the water. Italia Nostra – Italy's national heritage group – have insisted that the alteration of the lagoon's shipping channels and the cessation of land reclamation would be cheaper and more effective responses to the worsening floods. Proponents of the barrier, on the other hand, have argued that these non-mechanical interventions wouldn't offer protection against the effects of global warming. That may be true, but some projections show a rise in the level of the Mediterranean by as much as 30cm within the next century – if that figure turns out to be correct, sooner or later it will be necessary to keep the barrier closed permanently. This would, of course, drastically change the ecology of the lagoon, and require massive investment in water management and purification systems – a project of much greater complexity, and expense, than the barrier itself.

While arguments over the barrier have raged, a host of less extravagant projects have made progress all over the lagoon. Embankments and pavements are being rebuilt and raised at numerous flood-prone points (most conspicuously around the Palazzo Ducale), the jetties at the Lido, Malamocco and Chioggia inlets have been strengthened, and tracts of land reclaimed for industrial use have been allowed to flood again. The largest of these schemes involves the reinforcement of the 60km of the lagoon's outer coastline; the beaches at Jesolo, Cavallino, the Lido, Pellestrina, Sottomarina and Isola Verde have been extended within a grid of stone groynes and artifical reefs, thereby dissipating the energy of the waves, while the sand dunes at Cavallino have been planted with marram grass, which binds the sand and thus makes the dunes a more effective windbreak.

AID GROUPS AND RESTORATION

Restoration in Venice is principally a collaborative venture between UNESCO and the city's Superintendencies of Art and of Monuments. The former coordinates the fundraising and restoration proposals from the multitude of aid groups set up in various countries after the 1966 floods; the latter pair oversee the restoration centres in Venice, the cataloguing of endangered buildings and objects and the deployment of restoration teams.

The first top-to-toe makeover for a Venetian building was that of Madonna dell'Orto, undertaken by the British Italian Art and Archives Rescue Fund, which in 1971 became **Venice in Peril**. The city authorities were criticized at the time for their tardiness in commissioning restoration work on Venice's crumbling stonework. Their cautiousness was to an extent vindicated when it became apparent that the restoration of Sansovino's Loggetta – initially hailed as an unqualified success – had done as much damage as it had repaired. A major restoration of the Miracoli church turned out to be similarly ill-advised: salt was soon eating at the walls from inside and excreting white crusts onto the marble cladding. The cleaning and strengthening of the Porta della Carta was undertaken with far greater circumspection, and so far it seems that all is well; the lessons learnt on that project are being employed on the continuous restoration of the Basilica di San Marco and the Palazzo Ducale.

More than thirty groups worldwide are now devoted to the rescue of Venice, all of them open to offers of financial help. If you want to make a donation to ViP, contact them at Venice in Peril, Hurlingham Studios, Ranelagh Gardens, London SW6 3PA (☎020 7736 6891, ⓦveniceinperil.org). In the US, the main aid organization is **Save Venice Inc**, 133 East 58th Street, Suite 501, New York, NY 10022 (☎212 737 3141, ⓦsavevenice.org).

---

enough until fairly recently to keep the water relatively fresh – fresh enough, until the 1980s, for Venetians to swim in it.

Much of the **pollution** is the fault of the industrial complexes of Mestre-Marghera, which, though now being wound down, have dumped thousands of tons of zinc, copper, iron, lead and chrome into the lagoon, creating a toxic sludge so dangerous that nobody has devised a safe way of dredging the stuff out. Chemical fertilizers seeping into the water from the mainland add to the accumulation of phosphates in the water, a situation that used to be exacerbated by the use of phosphate-rich detergents in Venetian homes. Plants, fishes and other forms of marine life are being suffocated by algae that thrive on these phosphates, forming a foul-smelling scum that is thickened by the rotting animal and vegetable matter.

The town hall has now banned the sale of phosphate-enriched detergents, and steps have been taken to restore the equilibrium of the lagoon's ecosystem: salt marshes and fish farms are being reconstructed at various places in the lagoon; wetlands are being created on the periphery; and waste disposal sites are being consolidated. But local action such as this will not be enough. Venice's lagoon is threatened by the grossly polluted water of the whole upper Adriatic, into which the Po and numerous other waterways disgorge their effluents. In the 1950s and 1960s Lake Erie was threatened with the same sort of marine disaster as now faces the Venice region; regulations imposed in the 1970s seem to have rescued the lake. As yet, no comparable action has been taken to cleanse the Po.

The other environmental problem facing Venice is that of **air pollution**, which worsened in phase with the industrialization of Mestre-Marghera. Sulphur dioxide combines with the salty and humid air of the lagoon to make a particularly vicious corrosive which eats at brick, stone and bronze alike. The conversion of domestic heating systems from oil to gas has helped to cut down the sulphur dioxide in the atmosphere, and expenditure on industrial filtration has had an effect too, but Marghera's factories still pump tens of thousands of tonnes of the gas into the atmosphere each year. The prevailing winds carry the fumes from the Marghera stacks inland, but even though the bulk of the emissions are someone else's problem, the ambient air of Venice was one of the factors the Italian trades union congress had in mind when they christened the city Italy's "capital of pollution".

Subsidence and erosion

The industries at Marghera used to threaten Venice from below as well as from above. Drawing millions of gallons of water directly from the ground, they caused a dramatic fall in the water table and threatened to cause the subsidence of the entire city. Calamity was averted in 1973, when the national government built two aqueducts to pipe water from inland rivers to the refineries and factories of Marghera and the houses of Venice. In 1975 the artesian wells at Marghera were sealed, and by the end of the century there was evidence that this measure had resulted in a rise of 2cm in the land level of some parts of the historic centre.

Local subsidence will continue to be a problem, though. The majority of buildings in Venice are built on wooden pilings driven deep into the mudbanks. Interference with the lagoon's equilibrium has resulted in an increase in the number of extremely low tides as well as the number of floods, and occasionally the water level falls so far that air gets at the pilings, causing them to decay. The water also moves more quickly through the canals than it used to, which increases the erosion. Furthermore, those people who were unable to afford proper wood-piled foundations have used a mixture of rubbish and rubble instead, which slowly compressed over time.

Another crucial factor is the erosive effect of motorized boats. A study in the 1990s showed that the foundations of sixty percent of the buildings on the Canal Grande had been damaged by the wash from the vaporetti, and the situation has become a lot worse in the meantime: in the past two decades, the volume of motor-powered traffic has doubled, and the tankers and giant cruise ships (see page 191) that pass close to the *centro storico* create eddies that last long after the ship has passed by. The net result is that material is being washed out from underneath the building and pavements, while high-tide water is breaking through the stone dampcourses and seeping up through the porous brickwork. All over the city, walls are in effect dissolving. In the narthex of San Marco, the damp has now risen to a height of more than six metres, causing damage to the ancient mosaics.

Books

A comprehensive Venetian reading list would run on for dozens of pages, and would include a vast number of out-of-print titles. Most of our recommendations are in print, and those that aren't shouldn't be too difficult to track down through online booksellers such as ⓦabebooks.co.uk. Books marked with ★ are particularly recommended.

FICTION

★**Italo Calvino** *Invisible Cities.* Characteristically subtle variations on the idea of the City, presented in the form of tales told by Marco Polo to Kublai Khan. No explicit reference to Venice until well past halfway, when Polo remarks – "Every time I describe a city I am saying something about Venice."

Michael Dibdin *Dead Lagoon.* Superior detective story starring Venice-born Aurelio Zen, a cop entangled in the political maze of 1990s Italy. Zen is the protagonist of many fine books by Dibdin; in this one, he leaves Rome for Venice to trace a wealthy businessman who has disappeared.

E.T.A. Hoffmann *Doge and Dogaressa.* Fanciful reconstruction of events surrounding the treason of Marin Falier, by one of the pivotal figures of German Romanticism. Lots of passion and pathos, narrated at headlong pace. It's included in *Tales of Hoffmann,* published by Penguin.

★**Henry James** *The Aspern Papers* and *The Wings of the Dove.* The first, a hundred-page tale about a biographer's manipulative attempts to get at the personal papers of a deceased writer, is one of James's most tautly constructed longer stories. The latter, one of the three vast and circumspect late novels, is a magnificent book but is perhaps best approached after acclimatizing yourself with the earlier stuff.

Donna Leon *Acqua Alta.* Liberally laced with an insider's observations on daily life in Venice, this is perhaps the most atmospheric of Leon's long sequence of highly competent Venice-set detective novels.

★**Thomas Mann** *Death in Venice.* Profound study of the demands of art and the claims of the flesh, with the city itself thematically significant rather than posing as a mere exotic backdrop. Richer than most stories five times its length and infinitely more complex than Visconti's sentimentalizing film.

★**Marcel Proust** *Albertine Disparue.* The Venetian interlude, occurring in the penultimate novel of Proust's massive novel sequence, can be sampled in isolation for its acute dissection of the sensory experience of the city – but to get the most from it, you've really got to knuckle down and commit yourself to the preceding ten volumes of *À la Recherche.*

Frederick Rolfe (Baron Corvo) *The Desire and Pursuit of the Whole.* A transparent exercise in self-justification, much of it taken up with venomous ridicule of the English community in Venice, among whom Rolfe moved while writing the book in 1909. (Its libellous streak kept it unpublished for 25 years.) Snobbish and incoherent, redeemed by hilarious character assassinations and gorgeous descriptive passages.

Arthur Schnitzler *Casanova's Return to Venice.* Something of a Schnitzler revival followed the release of Kubrick's *Eyes Wide Shut,* which was adapted from a novella by this contemporary and compatriot of Freud. This similarly short and intense book also explores the dynamics of desire, but from the perspective of a desperate man who is rapidly approaching the end of his life.

ART AND ARCHITECTURE

★**James S. Ackerman** *Palladio.* Concise introduction to the life, works and cultural background of the Veneto's greatest architect. Especially useful if you're visiting Vicenza or any of the villas.

★**Svetlana Alpers and Michael Baxandall** *Tiepolo and the Pictorial Intelligence.* This brilliant book analyses with exhilarating precision the way in which Tiepolo perceived and re-created the world in his paintings, and demolishes the notion that Tiepolo was merely a "decorative" artist. Though they devote most space to the frescoes at Würzburg, Alpers and Baxandall discuss many of the Tiepolo paintings in Venice and the Veneto, and their revelatory readings will really enrich any encounter with his art. The reproductions

maintain Yale's customary high standards.

Patricia Fortini Brown *Venetian Narrative Painting in the Age of Carpaccio.* Rigorously researched study of a subject central to Venetian culture yet often overlooked in more general accounts. Fresh reactions to the works discussed are combined with a penetrating analysis of the ways they reflect the ideals of the Republic at the time. Worth every penny.

★**Richard Goy** *Venice: The City and its Architecture.* Published in 1997, this superb book instantly became the benchmark. Eschewing the linear narrative adopted by previous writers on the city's architecture, Goy goes for a multi-angled approach, devoting one part to the growth of the city and its evolving technologies, another to its "nuclei" (the Piazza, Arsenale, Ghetto and Rialto), and the last to its building types (palazzi, churches, etc). The result is a book that does full justice to the richness and density of the Venetian cityscape – and the design and choice of pictures are exemplary.

Deborah Howard *The Architectural History of Venice; Jacopo Sansovino: Architecture and Patronage in Renaissance Venice; Venice and the East.* The first of these books is a classic introduction to the subject (and has been elegantly repackaged by Yale), while the latter's analysis of the world within which Sansovino operated is of wider interest than you might think. Howard's latest book, *Venice and the East*, is a fascinating and characteristically rigorous examination of the ways in which the fabric of the city was conditioned by the close contact between Venice's merchants and the Islamic world in the period 1100–1500. It's a truism that San Marco and the Palazzo Ducale are hybrids of Western and Islamic styles, but this splendidly illustrated study not only has illuminating things to say about those two great monuments – it makes you look afresh at the texture of the whole city.

★ **Peter Humfrey** *Painting in Renaissance Venice.* Spanning the period from the middle of the fifteenth century to the end of the sixteenth (Jacopo Bellini to Tintoretto, in other words), this is the best concise overview of the subject – lay readers should start here before going on to David Rosand's more exhaustive book.

Michael Levey *Painting in Eighteenth-Century Venice.* On its appearance in 1959 this book was the first detailed discussion of its subject. Now in its third edition, it's still the most thorough exposition of the art of Venice's last golden age, though it shows its age in its concentration on heroic personalities – Giambattista Tiepolo in particular.

David Rosand *Painting in Sixteenth-Century Venice.* Covers the century of Giorgione, Titian, Tintoretto and Veronese as thoroughly as most readers will want; especially good on the social networks and artistic conventions within which the painters created their work.

★ **John Ruskin** *The Stones of Venice.* Enchanting, enlightening and infuriating in about equal measure, this is still the most stimulating book written about Venice by a non-Venetian. If half a million words of Ruskin is too much for you, go for the abridged one-volume version published by Da Capo.

John Steer *Venetian Painting: A Concise History.* Whistle-stop tour of Venetian art from the fourteenth to the eighteenth century. Skimpy and undemanding, but a useful aid to sorting out your thoughts after the visual deluge of Venice's churches and museums, and the plentiful pictures come in handy when your memory needs a prod.

HISTORY AND SOCIETY

Patricia Fortini Brown *Venice and Antiquity.* This fascinating book explores a subject that strangely no one has tackled in depth before – the ways in which an imperialist city with no pre-Christian past went about classicizing its pedigree. Drawing on a vast range of cultural artefacts, from the great monuments to private manuscripts and medals, Brown adds a new dimension to the history of Venice between the thirteenth and the sixteenth centuries, the city's Golden Age. It's not easy going but the effort is worthwhile, and superlative pictures go some way to leaven the text.

Christopher Hibbert *Venice: The Biography of a City.* The usual highly proficient Hibbert synthesis of a vast range of secondary material. Very good on Venice's changing social fabric, with more on twentieth-century Venice than most others. Excellent illustrations too – but, bafflingly, it's currently out of print on both sides of the Atlantic.

Jonathan Keates *The Siege of Venice.* The depth of Keates's research is evident on every page of this study of the Venetian uprising of 1848–49; the book is a thoroughgoing piece of historical reconstruction and a thrilling and emotionally engaging narrative, which will have you sharing the author's manifest admiration for its protagonists.

Frederic C. Lane *Venice: A Maritime Republic.* The most authoritative one-volume socio-economic history of the city in English, based on decades of research. Excellent on the infrastructure of the city, and on the changing texture of everyday life, though it's a rather more arduous read than John Julius Norwich's populist history.

★ **John Julius Norwich** *A History of Venice.* Although it's far more reliant on secondary sources than Lane, and nowhere near as compendious (you won't learn much, for example, about Venice's finances, which is a major omission in a history of the quintessential mercantile city), this book is unbeatable for its grand narrative sweep.

★ **Margaret Plant** *Venice: Fragile City.* Most histories of Venice tend to give the impression that there's little to say about the two hundred years since the fall of the Republic. This survey, concentrating on post-1797 Venice, comprehensively fills the void, encompassing not just the changes in the city's appearance during that time, but also its economic, political and cultural life, and the responses of the legion of writers, artists and film-makers who have been inspired (or in some instances, repelled) by the place.

Mark Thompson *The White War.* Italy's role in World War I – when its armies pushed out of the Veneto into what is now the northeastern corner of the country – is just a sideshow in many non-Italian histories of the conflict, and is often badly misrepresented within Italy. Thompson's book is more than a magisterial account of the catastrophes and triumphs of the campaigns – it's a brilliant explication of the part the war has played in the formation of the nation's self-identity.

A VENETIAN MISCELLANY

★ **Paolo Barbaro** *Venice Revealed*. The title is exactly right – if any book can be said to reveal the reality of present-day Venice, this is it. Written by a native Venetian, following his return after an absence of two decades, it's an evocative portrait of an ailing but endlessly stimulating city, written from deep affection. An essential corrective to the gauzy mythologizing that blights too many books on the city.

★ **Giacomo Casanova** *History of My Life*. For pace, candour and wit, the insatiable seducer's autobiography ranks with the journals of James Boswell, a contemporary of similar sexual and literary stamina. The twelve-volume sequence (here handsomely repackaged into six paperbacks) takes him right across Europe, from Madrid to Moscow. His Venetian escapades are covered in volumes two and three of Willard Trask's magnificent translation.

Polly Coles *The Politics of Washing: Real Life in Venice*. Coles' account of her year living in Venice with her Italian husband and their children is a refreshingly honest and unsentimental portrait of the contemporary city, as experienced by someone who is more than a tourist but less than a Venetian.

Robert C. Davis and Garry R. Marvin *Venice, the Tourist Maze: A Cultural Critique of the World's Most Touristed City*. A well-researched, well-written and ultimately – inevitably – somewhat depressing history and analysis of the impact of tourism on Venice.

Régis Debray *Against Venice*. The modern-day cult of Venice is an easy target, so it's to be expected that Régis Debray – sometime comrade of Che Guevara and adviser to François Mitterrand – should score a few hits in the course of this seventy-page polemic. It's a provocative, if self-satisfied, counterblast to the verbiage of so much writing on Venice.

Milton Grundy *Venice: An Anthology Guide*. A series of itineraries of the city fleshed out with appropriate excerpts from a huge range of travellers and scholars. Doesn't cover every major sight in Venice, but the choice of quotations couldn't be bettered.

Henry James *Italian Hours*. Urbane travel pieces from the young Henry James, including five essays on Venice. Perceptive observations on the paintings and architecture of the city, but mainly of interest in its evocation of the tone of Venice in the 1860s and 1870s.

★ **Giulio Lorenzetti** *Venice and its Lagoon*. The most thorough cultural guide ever written to any European city – Lorenzetti seems to have researched the history of every building, canvas and alley. Though unmanageable as a workaday guidebook (it gives more than fifty pages to the Palazzo Ducale, for example, and even has an index of

indexes), it's indispensable for all those besotted with the place. Hard to find outside Venice, but every bookshop in the city sells it.

Michelle Lovric *Venice: Tales of the City*. There have been many miscellanies of writings on the subject of Venice, but Lovric has unearthed some fascinating pieces that have eluded other anthologists.

★ **Predrag Matvejevic** *The Other Venice*. While barely mentioning any of the major sights, Matvejevic illuminates the city from a variety of unusual angles, in a sequence of elegant little essays on such topics as the flora and fauna of the lagoon, the trades of Venice and the idiosyncrasies of its language.

Mary McCarthy *Venice Observed*. Originally written for the *New Yorker*, McCarthy's clear-eyed and brisk report is a refreshing antidote to the gushing enthusiasm of most first-hand accounts from foreigners in Venice. The Penguin edition combines it with her equally entertaining *The Stones of Florence*.

James Morris *Venice*. Some people acclaim this as the most brilliant book ever written about Venice; to others it's much too fey and self-regarding. But if you can't stomach the style, Morris's knowledge of Venice's folklore provides ample compensation.

Jane da Mosto *The Science of Saving Venice* and *The Venice Report*. Though a little out of date (they were published in 2004 and 2009), these two books, produced by Venice in Peril, give an expert analysis of the environmental and social problems facing the city.

John Pemble *Venice Rediscovered*. This is one of the most engrossing academic studies of the city to have appeared in recent years, concentrating on the ever-changing perceptions of Venice as a cultural icon since it ceased to exist as a political power. An eloquent writer, totally uninfected by the preciousness that overcomes so many writers on Venice, Pemble unearths stories missing from all other histories.

Salvatore Settis *If Venice Dies*. A closely argued polemic against the destruction of Venice (and other historic cities) by the homogenising forces of free-market capitalism. It's not entirely clear, though, how Settis imagines that the citizens of Venice might reclaim their city's autonomy.

Stefan Zweig *Casanova: A Study in Self-Portraiture*. A fascinating study of Casanova's life and autobiography, offering a persuasive analysis that differs strikingly from the clichéd image of Casanova as a real-life Don Juan – in fact, Zweig presents him as the very antithesis of Don Juan the misogynistic seducer. Though brief, this is the best book on its subject.

Italian

Although it's not uncommon for the staff of Venetian hotels and restaurants to speak some English, you'll make a lot more friends by attempting the vernacular. Outside the city, you might be able to get by in English at tourist offices, but in the depths of the Veneto you shouldn't expect to encounter fluency in English.

You'd do well to master at least a little **Italian**, a task made more enjoyable by the fact that your halting efforts will often be rewarded by smiles and genuine surprise that an English-speaker should make an attempt to learn Italian. When **speaking** to strangers, the third person is the polite form (ie Lei instead of Tu for "you"); using the second person is a mark of disrespect or stupidity. Also remember that Italians don't use "please" and "thank you" half as much as we do; it's all implied in the tone, though if you're in any doubt, err on the polite side.

The **Venetian dialect** virtually qualifies as a separate language, with its own rules of spelling and grammar, and distinctive pronunciation. However, you'll probably encounter it only in the form of street signs, dialect proper names (see page 10) or the occasional shop or restaurant name.

Pronunciation

Italian is spoken exactly as it's written, and usually enunciated with open-mouthed clarity. The only difficulties you're likely to encounter are the few **consonants** that are different from English:

c before e or i is pronounced as in **ch**urch, while **ch** before the same vowels is hard, as in **c**at.

sci or **sce** are pronounced as in **sh**eet and **sh**elter respectively.

g is soft before **e** and **i**, as in **g**eranium; hard when followed by **h**, as in **g**arlic.

gn has the ni sound of English onion.

gli in Italian is softened to something like li in English, as in stallion.

h is not aspirated, as in honour.

The great majority of Italian words are **stressed** on the penultimate syllable; an **accent** (´ or `) sometimes denotes non-penultimate stresses, but these accents are often omitted in written Italian. Note that the ending -ia or -ie counts as two syllables, hence trattoria is stressed on the **i**. We've put accents on names throughout the text wherever it isn't immediately obvious how a word should be pronounced: for example, in Fóscari, the accent is on the first **o**; similarly the stress in Pésaro is not on the **a**, where you'd expect it, but on the **e**. We've omitted accents on some of the more common exceptions (like Isola, stressed on the I), some names (Domenico), and words that are stressed similarly in English, such as archeologico and Repubblica.

Phrasebooks and dictionaries

The best phrasebook is *Italian: Rough Guide Phrasebook*, which has a huge but accessible vocabulary in dictionary format, a grammar section, a detailed menu reader and useful scenarios. These scenarios can also be downloaded free as audio files from ⓦroughguides.com. As for dictionaries, Collins and OUP both publish a comprehensive range.

WORDS AND PHRASES

BASICS

Good morning Buongiorno
Good afternoon/evening Buonasera
Good night Buonanotte
Goodbye Arrivederci
Hello/goodbye Ciao (informal; to strangers use phrases above)
Yes Si
No No
Please Per favore
Thank you (very much) Grázie (molte/mille grazie)
You're welcome Prego
Alright/that's OK Va bene
How are you? Come stai/sta? (informal/formal)
I'm fine Bene
Do you speak English? Parla inglese?
I don't understand Non ho capito
I don't know Non lo so
Excuse me Mi scusi
Excuse me (in a crowd) Permesso
I'm sorry Mi dispiace
I'm here on holiday Sono qui in vacanza
I'm English/Scottish/American/Irish/Welsh/Australian Sono inglese/scozzese/americano/irlandese/gallese/australiano
I live in… Abito a…
Today Oggi
Tomorrow Domani
Day after tomorrow Dopodomani
Yesterday Ieri
Now Adesso
Later Più tardi
Wait a minute! Aspetta!
In the morning Di mattina
In the afternoon Nel pomeriggio
In the evening Di sera
Here/there Qui/là
Good/bad Buono/cattivo
Big/small Grande/píccolo
Cheap/expensive Economico/caro
Early/late Presto/tardi
Hot/cold Caldo/freddo
Near/far Vicino/lontano
Vacant/occupied Libero/occupato
Quickly/slowly Velocemente/lentamente
Slowly/quietly Piano
With/without Con/senza
More/less Più/meno
Enough, no more Basta
Bill/check Il conto
Mr… Signor…
Mrs… Signora…
Miss… Signorina…(il Signor, la Signora, la Signorina when speaking about someone else)

NUMBERS

1 uno
2 due
3 tre
4 quattro
5 cinque
6 sei
7 sette
8 otto
9 nove
10 dieci
11 undici
12 dodici
13 tredici
14 quattordici
15 quindici
16 sedici
17 diciassette
18 diciotto
19 diciannove
20 venti
21 ventuno
22 ventidue
30 trenta
40 quaranta
50 cinquanta
60 sessanta
70 settanta
80 ottanta
90 novanta
100 cento
101 centuno
110 centodieci
200 duecento
500 cinquecento
1000 mille
5000 cinquemila
10,000 diecimila
50,000 cinquantamila

SOME SIGNS

Entrance/Exit Entrata/Uscita
Free entrance Ingresso libero
Gentlemen/Ladies Signori/Signore
WC/Bathroom Gabinetto/Bagno
Vacant/Engaged Libero/Occupato
Open/Closed Aperto/Chiuso
Arrivals/Departures Arrivi/Partenze
Closed for restoration Chiuso per restauro

Closed for holidays Chiuso per ferie
Pull/Push Tirare/Spingere
Out of order Guasto
Drinking water Acqua potabile
To let Affítasi
Platform Binario
Cash desk Cassa
Go/Walk Avanti
Stop/Halt Alt
Customs Dogana
Do not touch Non toccare
Danger Perícolo
Beware Attenzione
First aid Pronto soccorso
Ring the bell Suonare il campanello
No smoking Vietato fumare

DRIVING

Left/Right Sinistro/Destro
Go straight ahead Sempre diritto
Turn to the right/left Gira a destra/sinistra
Parking Parcheggio
No parking Divieto di sosta/Sosta vietata
One-way street Senso único
No entry Senso vietato
Slow down Rallentare
Road closed/up Strada chiusa/guasta
No through road Vietato il transito
No overtaking Vietato il sorpasso
Crossroads Incrocio
Speed limit Limite di velocità

TRANSPORT

Aeroplane Aeroplano
Bus Autobus/pullman
Train Treno
Car Macchina
Taxi Taxi
Bicycle Bicicletta
Ferry Traghetto
Ship Nave
Hydrofoil Aliscafo
Hitch-hiking Autostop
On foot A piedi
Bus station Autostazione
Train station Stazione ferroviaria
Ferry terminal Stazione maríttima
Port Porto
A ticket to… Un biglietto a…
One-way/return Solo andata/andata e ritorno
Can I book a seat? Posso prenotare un posto?
What time does it leave? A che ora parte?
When is the next bus/train/ferry to…? Quando parte
   il prossimo pullman/treno/traghetto per…?

Do I have to change? Devo cambiare?
Where does it leave from? Da dove parte?
What platform does it leave from? Da quale binario
   parte?
How many kilometres Quanti chilometriis it? sono?
How long does it take? Quanto ci vuole?
What number bus is it to…? Che numero di autobus
   per…?
Where's the road to…? Dovè la strada per…?
Next stop please La prossima fermata,per favore

QUESTIONS AND DIRECTIONS

Where? Dove?
(where is/are…?) (Dov'è/Dove sono)
When? Quando?
What? Cosa?
(What is it?) (Cos'è?)
How much/many? Quanto/Quanti?
Why? Perché?
It is/there is È/C'è
(Is it/is there…?) (È/C'è…?)
What time is it? Che ore sono?
How do I get to…? Per arrivare a…?
How far is it to…? Quant'è lontano a…?
Can you give me a lift to…? Mi può dare un passaggio
   a…?
Can you tell me when to get off? Mi può dire dove
   scendere alla fermata giusta?
What time does it open? A che ora apre?
What time does it close? A che ora chiude?
How much does it cost (… do they cost?) Quanto
   costa? (Quanto costano?)
What's it called in Italian? Come si chiama in Italiano?

ACCOMMODATION

Hotel Albergo
Is there a hotel nearby? C'è un albergo qui vicino?
Do you have a room… Ha una cámera…
for one/two/three people per una/due/tre
   person(a/e)
for one/two/three nights per una/due/tre notte/ i
for one/two weeks per una/due setti-man(a/e)
with a double bed con un letto matrimoniale
with a shower/bath con una doccia/un bagno
with a balcony con balcone
Hot/cold water acqua calda/fredda
How much is it? Quanto costa?
It's expensive È caro
Is breakfast included? È compresa la prima colazione?
Do you have anything cheaper? Ha qualcosa che costa
   di meno?
Full/half board Pensione completa/ mezza pensione
Can I see the room? Posso vedere la camera?
I'll take it La prendo

I'd like to book a room Vorrei prenotare una camera
I have a booking Ho una prenotazione
Can we camp here? Possiamo campeg- giare qui?
Is there a campsite nearby? C'è un camping qui vicino?
Tent Tenda
Cabin Cabina
Youth hostel Ostello per la gioventù

I'd like to book a table for two people at eight o'clock Vorrei prenotare una tavola per due alle otto
We need a knife Abbiamo bisogno di uncoltello
A fork Una forchetta
A spoon Un cucchiaio
A glass Un bicchiere
What do you recommend? Che cosa mi consiglia lei?
Waiter/waitress Cameriere/a
Bill/check Il conto
Is service included? È incluso il servizio?
I'm a vegetarian Sono vegetariano/a

IN THE RESTAURANT
A table Una tavola

MENU GLOSSARY

This glossary should allow you to decode most menus; it concludes with a summary of Venetian specialities (see page 213).

BASICS AND SNACKS
Aceto Vinegar
Aglio Garlic
Biscotti Biscuits
Burro Butter
Caramelle Sweets
Cioccolato Chocolate
Focaccia Oven-baked snack
Formaggio Cheese
Frittata Omelette
Gelato Ice cream
Grissini Bread sticks
Marmellata Jam
Olio Oil
Olive Olives
Pane Bread
Pane integrale Wholemeal bread
Panino Bread roll
Patatine Crisps
Patatine fritte Chips
Pepe Pepper
Pizzetta Small cheese and tomato pizza
Riso Rice
Sale Salt
Tramezzini Sandwich
Uova Eggs
Yogurt Yoghurt
Zucchero Sugar
Zuppa Soup

STARTERS (ANTIPASTI)
Antipasto misto Mixed cold meats and cheese (and a selection of other things in this list)
Caponata Mixed aubergine, olives, tomatoes and celery
Caprese Tomato and mozzarella salad
Insalata di mare Seafood salad

Insalata di riso Rice salad
Melanzane in parmigiana Fried aubergine in tomato and parmesan cheese
Mortadella Salami-type cured meat
Pancetta Bacon
Peperonata Grilled green, red or yellow peppers stewed in olive oil
Pomodori ripieni Stuffed tomatoes
Prosciutto Ham
Salame Salami

PIZZAS
Biancaneve "Black and white": mozzarella and oregano
Calzone Folded pizza with cheese, ham and tomato
Capricciosa Literally "capricious": topped with whatever they've got in the kitchen, usually including baby artichoke, ham and egg
Diavolo Spicy, with hot salami or Italian sausage
Funghi Mushroom; tinned, sliced button mushrooms unless it specifies fresh mushrooms, either funghi freschi or porcini
Frutti di mare Seafood, usually mussels, prawns, squid and clams
Margherita Cheese and tomato
Marinara Tomato and garlic
Napoli/Napoletana Tomato, anchovy and olive oil (and sometimes mozzarella)
Quattro formaggi "Four cheeses", usually including mozzarella, fontina, gorgonzola and qruyère
Quattro stagioni "Four seasons": the toppings split into four sections, usually including ham, peppers, onion, mushrooms, artichokes, olives and egg
Romana Anchovy and olives

THE FIRST COURSE (IL PRIMO)

SOUPS
Brodo Clear broth
Minestrina Any light soup
Minestrone Thick vegetable soup

Pasta e fagioli Pasta soup with beans
Pastina in brodo Pasta pieces in clear broth
Stracciatella Broth with egg

PASTA

Cannelloni Large tubes of pasta, stuffed
Farfalle Literally "bow"-shaped pasta; the word also means "butterflies"
Fettuccine Narrow pasta ribbons
Gnocchi Small potato and dough dumplings
Lasagne Lasagne
Maccheroni Tubular spaghetti
Pasta al forno Pasta baked with minced meat, eggs, tomato and cheese
Penne Smaller version of rigatoni
Ravioli Small packets of stuffed pasta
Rigatoni Large, grooved tubular pasta
Risotto Cooked rice dish, with sauce
Spaghetti Spaghetti
Spaghettini Thin spaghetti
Tagliatelle Pasta ribbons, another word for fettucine
Tortellini Small rings of pasta, stuffed with meat or cheese
Vermicelli Very thin spaghetti (literally "little worms")

PASTA SAUCES

Aglio e olio (e peperoncino) Tossed in garlic and olive oil (and hot chillies)
Arrabbiata Spicy tomato sauce
Bolognese Meat sauce
Burro e salvia Butter and sage
Carbonara Cream, ham and beaten egg
Frutta di mare Seafood
Funghi Mushroom
Matriciana Cubed pork and tomato sauce
Panna Cream
Parmigiano Parmesan cheese
Pesto Ground basil, pine nut, garlic and pecorino sauce
Pomodoro Tomato sauce
Ragù Meat sauce
Vongole Clam and tomato sauce

THE SECOND COURSE (IL SECONDO)

MEAT (CARNE)
Agnello Lamb
Bistecca Steak
Cervello Brains
Cinghiale Wild boar
Coniglio Rabbit
Costolette Chops
Cotolette Cutlets

Fegatini Chicken livers
Fegato Liver
Involtini Steak slices, rolled and stuffed
Lingua Tongue
Maiale Pork
Manzo Beef
Ossobuco Shin of veal
Pollo Chicken
Polpette Meatballs (or minced balls of anything)
Rognoni Kidneys
Salsiccia Sausage
Saltimbocca Veal with ham
Spezzatino Stew
Tacchino Turkey
Trippa Tripe
Vitello Veal

FISH (PESCE) AND SHELLFISH (CROSTACEI)
Acciughe Anchovies
Anguilla Eel
Aragosta Lobster
Baccalà Dried salted cod
Bisato Eel
Branzino Sea bass
Calamari Squid
Caparossoli Type of clam
Cape lungue Razor clams
Cape sante Scallops
Cicala di mare/Cannocchia/Canoche Mantis shrimp
Coda di rospo Monkfish
Cozze Mussels
Dentice Dentex (like sea bass)
Gamberetti Shrimps
Gamberi Prawns
Granchio Crab
Granzeola Spider crab
Merluzzo Cod
Moleche/moeche Soft-shelled crabs
Nasello Hake
Orata Bream
Ostriche Oysters
Pescespada Swordfish
Pólipo Octopus
Ricci di mare Sea urchins
Rombo Turbot
San Pietro John Dory
Sarde Sardines
Schie Shrimps
Seppie Cuttlefish
Sogliola Sole
Tonno Tuna
Triglie Red mullet
Trota Trout
Vongole Clams

VEGETABLES (CONTORNI) AND SALAD (INSALATA)

Asparagi Asparagus
Basílico Basil
Bróccoli Broccoli
Cápperi Capers
Carciofi Artichokes
Carciofini Artichoke hearts
Carotte Carrots
Cavolfiori Cauliflower
Cavolo Cabbage
Ceci Chickpeas
Cetriolo Cucumber
Cipolla Onion
Fagioli Beans
Fagiolini Green beans
Finocchio Fennel
Funghi Mushrooms
Insalata verde/insalata mista Green salad/mixed salad
Melanzana Aubergine/eggplant
Orígano Oregano
Patate Potatoes
Peperoni Peppers
Piselli Peas
Pomodori Tomatoes
Radicchio Chicory
Rucola Rocket
Spinaci Spinach
Zucca Pumpkin
Zucchini Courgettes

DESSERTS, CHEESES, FRUIT AND NUTS

DESSERTS (DOLCI)

Amaretti Macaroons
Cassata Ice-cream cake with candied fruit
Gelato Ice cream
Macedonia Fruit salad
Torta Cake, tart
Zabaglione Dessert made with eggs, sugar and Marsala wine
Zuppa inglese Trifle

CHEESE (FORMAGGI)

Caciocavallo A type of dried, mature mozzarella cheese
Fontina Northern Italian cheese used in cooking
Gorgonzola Soft blue-veined cheese
Mozzarella Bland soft white cheese used on pizzas
Parmigiano Parmesan cheese
Pecorino Strong-tasting hard sheep's cheese
Provolone Hard strong cheese
Ricotta Soft white cheese made from ewe's milk, used in sweet or savoury dishes

FRUIT (FRUTTA) AND NUTS (NOCE)

Ananas Pineapple
Anguria/Coccómero Watermelon
Arance Oranges
Banane Bananas
Ciliegie Cherries
Fichi Figs
Fichi d'India Prickly pears
Frágole Strawberries
Limone Lemon
Mándorle Almonds
Mele Apples
Melone Melon
Pere Pears
Pesche Peaches
Pignoli Pine nuts
Pistacchio Pistachio nut
Uva Grapes

COOKING TERMS

Affumicato Smoked
Al dente Firm, not overcooked
Al ferro Grilled without oil
Al forno Baked
Al Marsala Cooked with Marsala wine
Al vapore Steamed
Alla brace Barbecued
Alla griglia Grilled
Allo spiedo On the spit
Arrosto Roasted
Ben cotto Well done
Bollito Boiled
Brasato Cooked in wine
Cotto Cooked (not raw)
Crudo Raw
Fritto Fried
Grattugiato Grated
In úmido Stewed
Lesso Boiled
Milanese Fried in egg and breadcrumbs
Pizzaiola Cooked with tomato sauce
Ripieno Stuffed
Sangue Rare
Surgelato Frozen

DRINKS

Acqua minerale Mineral water
Aranciata Orangeade
Bicchiere Glass
Birra Beer
Bottiglia Bottle
Caffè Coffee
Cioccolata calda Hot chocolate
Ghlaccio Ice

Granita Iced coffee or fruit drink
Latte Milk
Limonata Lemonade
Selz Soda water
Spremuta Fresh fruit juice
Spumante Sparkling wine
Succo Concentrated fruit juicewith sugar
Tè Tea
Tónico Tonic water
Vino Wine
Rosso Red
Bianco White
Rosato Rosé
Secco Dry
Dolce Sweet
Litro Litre
Mezzo Half
Quarto Quarter
Salute! Cheers!

VENETIAN SPECIALITIES

ANTIPASTI E PRIMI

Acciughe marinate Marinated anchovies with onions
Bigoli in salsa Spaghetti with butter, onions and
   sardines
Brodetto Mixed fish soup, often with tomatoes and
   garlic
Castraura Artichoke hearts

Granseola alla Veneziana Crab cooked with oil, parsley
   and lemon
Pasta e fasioi Pasta and beans
Prosciutto San Daniele The best-quality prosciutto
Risotto alla sbirraglia Risotto with chicken, vegetables
   and ham
Risotto alla trevigiana Risotto with butter, onions and
   chicory
Risotto di cape Risotto with clams and shellfish
Risotto di mare Mixed seafood risotto
Sopa de peoci Mussel soup with garlic and parsley

SECONDI

Anguilla alla Veneziana Eel cooked with lemon and
   tuna
Baccalà mantecato Salt cod simmered in milk
Fegato veneziana Sliced calf liver cooked in olive oil
   with onion
Peoci salati Mussels with parsley and garlic
Risi e bisi Rice and peas, with parmesan and ham
Sarde in saor Marinated sardines
Seppie in nero Squid cooked in its ink
Seppioline nere Baby cuttlefish cooked in its ink

DOLCI

Frittole alla Veneziana Rum- and anise-flavoured
   fritters filled with pine nuts, raisins and candied fruit
Tiramisù Dessert of layered chocolate and cream,
   flavoured with rum and coffee

Small print and index

A ROUGH GUIDE TO ROUGH GUIDES

Published in 1982, the first Rough Guide – to Greece – was a student scheme that became a publishing phenomenon. Mark Ellingham, a recent graduate in English from Bristol University, had been travelling in Greece the previous summer and couldn't find the right guidebook. With a small group of friends he wrote his own guide, combining a contemporary, journalistic style with a thoroughly practical approach to travellers' needs.

The immediate success of the book spawned a series that rapidly covered dozens of destinations. And, in addition to impecunious backpackers, Rough Guides soon acquired a much broader readership that relished the guides' wit and inquisitiveness as much as their enthusiastic, critical approach and value-for-money ethos. These days, Rough Guides include recommendations from budget to luxury and cover more than 120 destinations around the globe, from Amsterdam to Zanzibar, all regularly updated by our team of roaming writers.

Browse all our latest guides, read inspirational features and book your trip at **roughguides.com**.

Rough Guide credits

Editor: Aimee White
Cartography: Katie Bennett
Managing editor: Rachel Lawrence
Picture editor: Aude Vauconsant

Cover photo research: Tom Smyth
Senior DTP coordinator: Dan May
Head of DTP and Pre-Press: Rebeka Davies

Publishing information

Eleventh edition 2019

Distribution

UK, Ireland and Europe
Apa Publications (UK) Ltd; sales@roughguides.com
United States and Canada
Ingram Publisher Services; ips@ingramcontent.com
Australia and New Zealand
Woodslane; info@woodslane.com.au
Southeast Asia
Apa Publications (SN) Pte; sales@roughguides.com
Worldwide
Apa Publications (UK) Ltd; sales@roughguides.com
Special Sales, Content Licensing and CoPublishing
Rough Guides can be purchased in bulk quantities
at discounted prices. We can create special editions,
personalised jackets and corporate imprints tailored to
your needs. sales@roughguides.com.
roughguides.com

Printed in China by CTPS
The publishers and authors have done their best to
ensure the accuracy and currency of all the information
in **The Rough Guide to Venice & the Veneto**, however,
they can accept no responsibility for any loss, injury, or
inconvenience sustained by any traveller as a result of
information or advice contained in the guide.

Help us update

We've gone to a lot of effort to ensure that this eleventh
edition of **The Rough Guide to Venice & the Veneto** is
accurate and up-to-date. However, things change – places
get "discovered", opening hours are notoriously fickle,
restaurants and rooms raise prices or lower standards. If
you feel we've got it wrong or left something out, we'd like
to know, and if you can remember the address, the price,
the hours, the phone number, so much the better.

Please send your comments with the subject line
"**Rough Guide Venice & the Veneto Update**" to mail@
uk.roughguides.com. We'll credit all contributions and
send a copy of the next edition (or any other Rough Guide
if you prefer) for the very best emails.

Reader's updates

Thanks to all the readers who have taken the time to write in with comments and suggestions (and apologies if we've
inadvertently omitted or misspelt anyone's name):

Joseph Boughey, Kate Adams, Professor Bernt Brendemoen, Nick Molyneux, Pat & Ken Pike.

ABOUT THE AUTHOR

Jonathan Buckley has written and contributed to several Rough Guides on Italy and music.
He has also published ten novels, and was shortlisted for the 2015 BBC National Short Story
award. He lives in Brighton.

Photo credits

(Key: T-top; C-centre; B-bottom; L-left; R-right)

Index

Map symbols

The symbols below are used on maps throughout the book

✈	Airport	⊙	Statue	– – – –	Waterbus route	▪	Building
✗	Airstrip	♦	Place of interest	●●••●	Traghetto	✝ ➡	Church
P	Parking	⊠	Gate	═════	Road		Park
★	Bus station	⛯	Lighthouse	▬▬▬▬	Motorway		Beach
✉	Post office	⌅	Mountain range	══▬══	Railway		Marsh
ⓘ	Tourist office	▲	Mountain peak	────	Tram route		Christian cemetery
⊞	Hospital	⚓	Waterbus stop	━━━━	Wall		Jewish cemetery

Listings key

■ Accommodation

● Eating/drinking

● Shopping

City plan

The **city plan** on the pages that follow is divided as shown:

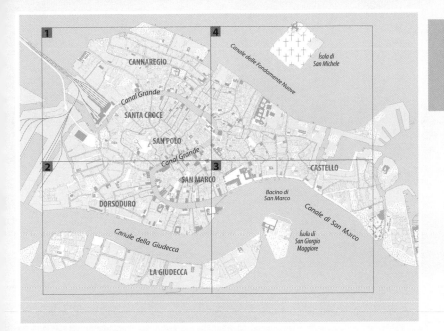

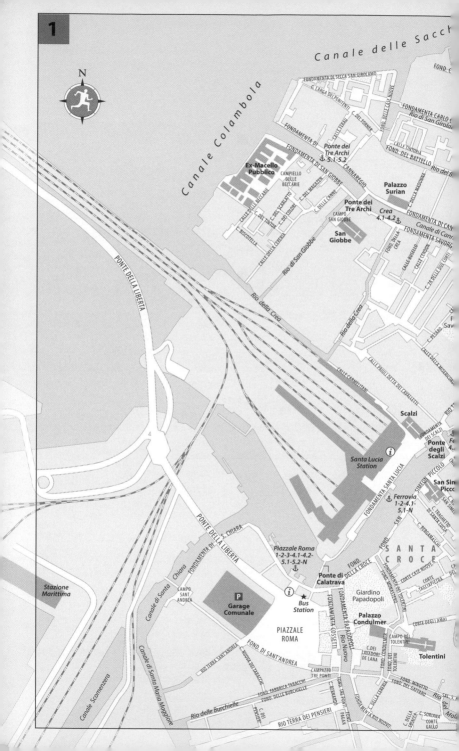

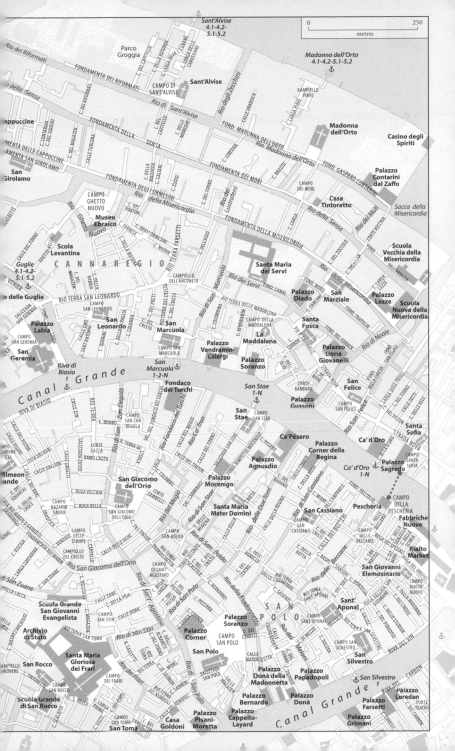

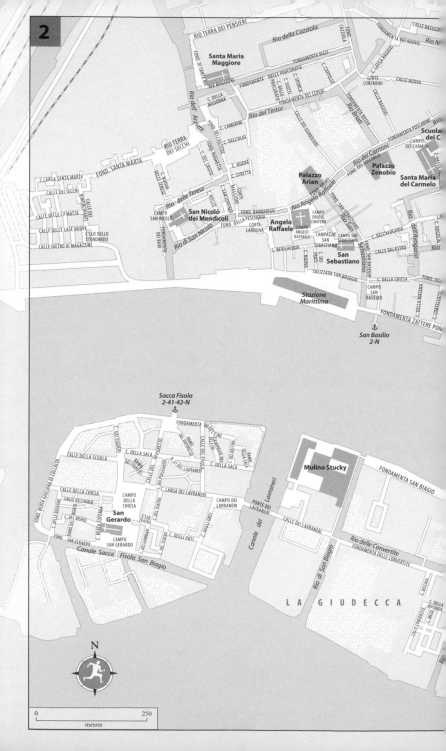

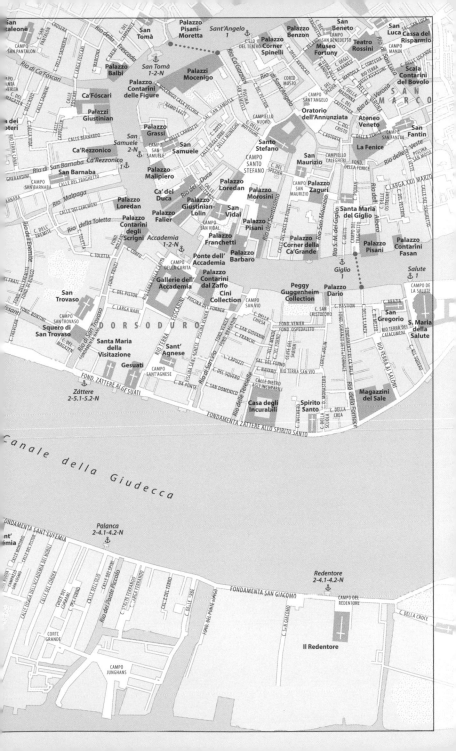

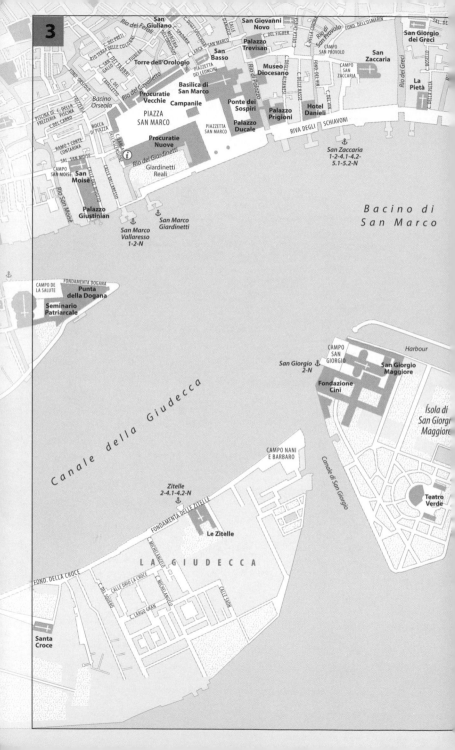

3

Rio dei Fuseri
San Giuliano
Rio Terrà delle Colonne
C. DEGLI SPECCHIERI
C. DEI PRETI
C. DELL'ANGELO
San Giovanni Novo
C. DEL FIGHER
FOND. DELL'OSMARIN
SAL. DE

C. DEI FABBRI
SAN MARCO
LARGA
Palazzo Trevisan
CAMPO SAN PROVOLO
Rio di San Provolo
San Giorgio dei Greci

Torre dell'Orologio
PIAZZETTA DEI LEONCINI
San Basso
Museo Diocesano
CAMPO SAN ZACCARIA
San Zaccaria

Rio dei Cavalletto
Procuratie Vecchie
Basilica di San Marco
Ponte dei Sospiri
Rio di Palazzo
C. DELLE RASSE
CALLE DELL'OVO

Bacino Orseolo
Campanile
Palazzo Prigioni
Hotel Danieli
La Pietà

PIAZZA SAN MARCO
PIAZZETTA SAN MARCO
Palazzo Ducale
RIVA DEGLI SCHIAVONI
Rio dei Greci

Procuratie Nuove
⚓ San Zaccaria
1-2-4.1-4.2-
5.1-5.2-N

Rio dei Giardinetti
Giardinetti Reali

CAMPO SAN MOISÈ
San Moisè

Palazzo Giustinian

⚓ San Marco Vallaresso 1-2-N
⚓ San Marco Giardinetti

Bacino di San Marco

CAMPO DE LA SALUTE
FONDAMENTA DOGANA
Punta della Dogana

Seminario Patriarcale

Harbour

CAMPO SAN GIORGIO
San Giorgio ⚓ 2-N
San Giorgio Maggiore

Fondazione Cini

Isola di San Giorgio Maggiore

Canale della Giudecca

Canale di San Giorgio

CAMPO NANI E BARBARO

Teatro Verde

Zitelle 2-4.1-4.2-N ⚓
FONDAMENTA DELLE ZITELLE
Le Zitelle

FOND. DELLA CROCE
CALLE DRIO LA CROCE
C. DEL SQUERO
CALLE SAON

LA GIUDECCA

Santa Croce

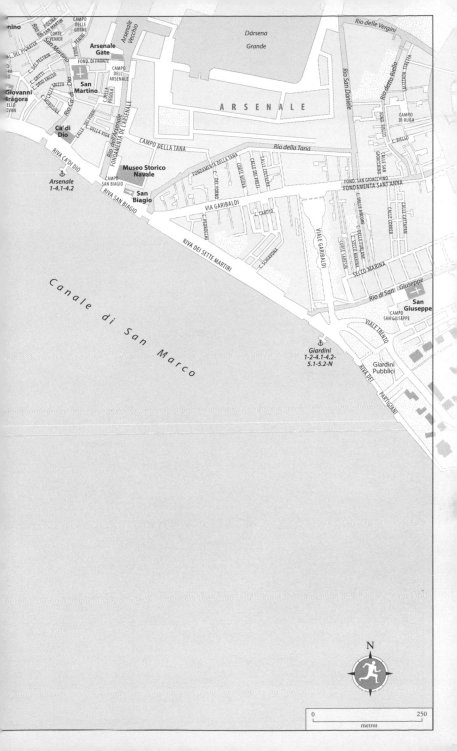

Cimit
4.1–4

Casino degli
Spiriti

Cimitero

Canale delle Fondamente Nuove

Sacca della
Miscericordia

Santa
Maria della
Misericordia

Santa
Caterina

Gesuiti

Palazzo
Dona della
Rosa

Fondamente Nuove
4.1-4.2-5.1-5.2-12-13

Oratorio dei
Crociferi

Palazzo Zen

Palazzo
Albrizzi

Palazzo
Seriman

Palazzo
Mangilli

Santi Apostoli

San Lazzaro
dei Mendicanti

Ospedale Civi
4.1-4.2-5.1-5.

Santa Maria
del Pinto

Ca' da
Mosto

Palazzo
Falier

San
Canciano

Ospedale
Civile

Rialto
Mercato
1

San Giovanni
Crisostomo

Santa Maria
dei Miracoli

Palazzo
Soranzo-
van-Axel

Scuola Grande
di San Marco

Santi Giovanni
e Paolo

Fabbriche
Vecchie

Teatro
Malibran

Colleoni Monument

Ospedaletto

Palazzo dei
Camerlenghi

Fondaco
dei Tedeschi

Palazzo
Pisani

BARBARIA DELLE TOLE

San
Giacomo
di Rialto

Ponte
di Rialto

Rialto
1-2-N

San
Bartolomeo

Palazzo
Ruzzini

Palazzo
Cappello

Palazzo
Dolfin-Manin

San Lio

San Lorenzo

Scuola di
San Teodoro

Santa Maria
della Fava

CAMPO DI
SANTA MARIA
FORMOSA

Palazzo
Grimani

Scuola di
San Giorgio
degli Schiavoni

San
Salvador

Santa
Maria
Formosa

Palazzo
Querini
Stampalia

Palazzo
Zorzi

San
Giuliano

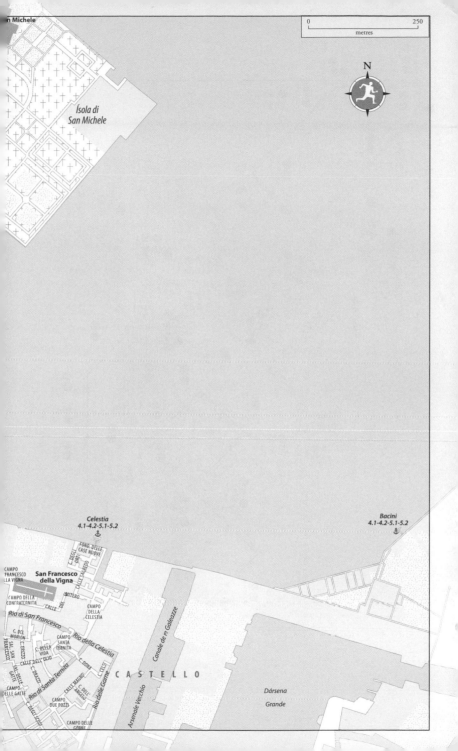

n Michele

0   250
                        metres

N

Ísola di
San Michele

Celestia   Bacini
4.1-4.2-5.1-5.2   4.1-4.2-5.1-5.2

FOND. DELLE
CASE NUOVE

CAMPO
FRANCESCO   San Francesco
LA VIGNA   della Vigna

CAMPO DELLA
CONTRAFTERNITA   CIMITERO
                                        CAMPO
Rio di San Francesco   DELLA
                                        CELESTIA

C. DEL
MORION   CAMPO   Rio della Celestia
           SANTA
C. DELLA   TERNITA
VIDA   Canale de rª Galeazze
DELL'OLIO   C. DORE

CAMPO   C. DEL
DELLE GATTE   ANGELO

Rio di Santa Ternita   C A S T E L L O

CAMPO
DUE POZZI   Dársena

CAMPO DELLE   Grande
GORNE

Arsenale Vecchio

MAIN WATER BUS SERVICES

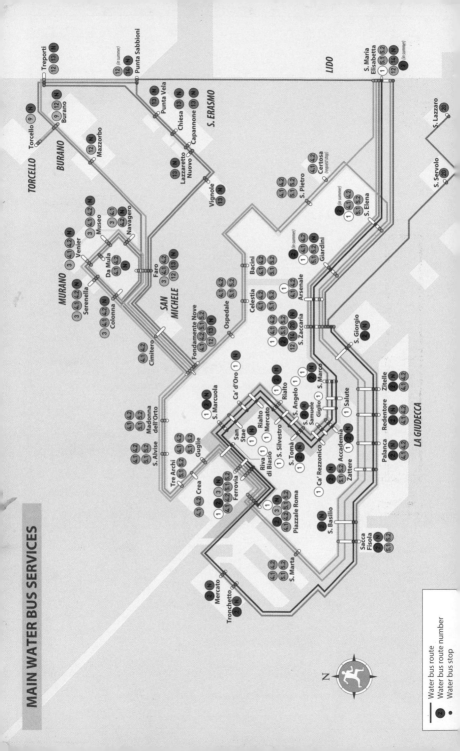

TORCELLO

Torcello 9 N

BURANO

Burano 9 N 12 N

Treporti 12 13 N

Punta Sabbioni 12 (in summer) 13

Mazzorbo 12 N

Punta Vela 13 N

Chiesa 13 N

Capannone 13 N

S. ERASMO

Lazzaretto Nuovo 13 N

Vignole 13 N

MURANO

Venier 3 4.1 4.2 N

Museo 3 4.1 N

Da Mula 4.1 4.2 N

Navagero 4.1 4.2 N

Serenella 3 4.1 4.2 N

Colonna 3 4.1 4.2 N

Cimitero 4.1 4.2 N

SAN MICHELE

Faro 12 13 N

Fondamente Nove 4.1 4.2 5.1 5.2 12 13 N

Ospedale 4.1 4.2

Celestia 4.1 4.2 5.1 5.2

Bacini 4.1 4.2 5.1 5.2

S. Pietro 4.1 4.2 5.1 5.2

Certosa (report stop) 4.1 4.2 5.1 5.2

S. Elena 1 (in summer) 4.1 4.2 5.1 5.2

S. Maria Elisabetta 1 5.1 5.2 N 2 (in summer) 12 14 N

LIDO

S. Lazzaro 20

S. Servolo 20

Giardini 1 (in summer) 4.1 4.2 N 20

Arsenale 1 4.1 4.2

S. Zaccaria 1 4.1 4.2 5.1 5.2 12 14 20 N

S. Giorgio 2 N

Tre Archi 4.1 4.2 5.1 5.2

S. Alvise 4.1 4.2 5.1 5.2

Madonna dell'Orto 4.1 4.2

Crea 4.1 4.2 N

Guglie 4.1 4.2 5.1 5.2

Ferrovia 1 2 3 N 4.1 4.2 5.1 5.2

Piazzale Roma 1 2 3 N 4.1 4.2 5.1 5.2

Riva di Biasio 1

San Marcuola 1 2 N

Ca' d'Oro 1

San Stae 1

Rialto Mercato 1

S. Silvestro 1

Rialto 1 2 N

S. Tomà 1

S. Angelo 1

S. Samuele 1

Giglio 1

S. Marco 1

Salute 1

Ca' Rezzonico 1

Accademia 1 N

Zattere 2 N 5.1 5.2 6 N

S. Basilio N

Sacca Fisola N 5.1 5.2

S. Marta 4.1 4.2 5.1 5.2

Mercato N

Tronchetto N

LA GIUDECCA

Palanca 4.1 4.2

Redentore 4.1 4.2

Zitelle 4.1 4.2 N

N

── Water bus route
1 2 Water bus route number
● Water bus stop